Obelisk

A History of Jack Kahane
and the Obelisk Press

Jack Kahane

Obelisk

A History of Jack Kahane and the Obelisk Press

NEIL PEARSON

LIVERPOOL UNIVERSITY PRESS

First published 2007 by
Liverpool University Press
4 Cambridge Street
Liverpool L69 7ZU

British Library Cataloguing-in-Publication data
A British Library CIP record is available

ISBN 978-1-84631-101-7 *cased*

Typeset by Koinonia in Golden Cockerel
Printed and bound in the European Union by
Bell and Bain Ltd, Glasgow

For Natalie

As good almost kill a Man as kill a good Book;
who kills a Man kills a reasonable creature, God's Image;
but hee who destroyes a good Booke, kills reason it selfe,
kills the Image of God, as it were in the eye.

John Milton, *Areopagitica*

We should not only be able to defend to the death
other people's right to say things with which we disagree,
we must also allow them to do it in abominable prose.

John Mortimer, introduction to *Books in the Dock*
by C. H. Rolph

Contents

Acknowledgements

I would like to thank the following institutions for making me so welcome when I visited, and for offering such valuable assistance to me in the writing of this book: Harry Ransom Humanities Research Center, University of Texas; Special Collections Research Center, Syracuse University; Berg Collection, New York Public Library; Division of Rare and Manuscript Collections, Cornell University; Bibliothèque Nationale de France; National Library of Scotland; Bodleian Library, Oxford University; Cambridge University Library; Special Collections, Leeds University Library; British Newspaper Library, Colindale; National Portrait Gallery archives, London; British Publisher Archives, Reading University; Reading Room, Victoria and Albert Museum; Special Collections, Sussex University Library; and the British Library, the best place to think in London, and my office while this book was being written.

Staff at the following institutions gave me invaluable long distance help, responding to my enquiries with unfailing courtesy and efficiency: Beinecke Rare Book and Manuscript Library, Yale University; Widener Library, Harvard University; University of North Carolina Library; Princeton University Library; James Ford Bell Library, University of Minnesota; Southern Illinois University Library; University of Iowa Library; and the Dartmouth College Library, New Hampshire.

My agent Jamie Crawford, and Anthony Cond and Helen Tookey at Liverpool University Press, have gone out of their way to offer me help and support. Brian Bugler and Sylvia Brownrigg both found time to talk to me about their respective grandparents, Eric Benfield and Gawen Brownrigg; Patrick Wright talked to me about Benfield's career as a sculptor; Caroline Theakstone at Getty Images found me pictures of some of the more obscure Obelisk writers; Aine Gibbons, librarian at Queen's University, Belfast, located a thesis for me that had defeated the British Library; Chris Casson let me consult

ACKNOWLEDGEMENTS

his extensive and impressive collection of books by and about the
Paris expatriates; and Tom Goldwasser, of Goldwasser Books, San
Francisco, kindly showed me letters from Henry Miller to Richard
Thoma acquired by his shop.

Peter Mendes cast his eye over the bibliography, made some
extremely useful suggestions, and provided me with information
about the two Obelisk books originally published by the Fortune
Press which would otherwise have passed me by. Paul Mortimer
loaned me his unpublished thesis on the Mancunian playwright
Stanley Houghton, a rich resource for the section of this book's introduction dealing with Kahane's early years, and was also good enough
to read the finished section (and spot a mistake). Margaret Harmsworth, daughter of the publisher Desmond Harmsworth, invited
me to her home in Paris and showed me letters which James Joyce
and his daughter Lucia had written to her father; these unpublished
documents provided me not only with invaluable information but
also a powerful visceral thrill, and I am grateful to Margaret for sharing
them with me. John Baxter, who lives in the rue de l'Odéon apartment building which was once home to Sylvia Beach and Adrienne
Monnier, was good enough to let me sit in his library for a couple of
days and fillet it of bibliographical information relating to the Obelisk
Press; his buy-everything-in-any-edition approach to collecting made
his library especially useful to me, and both his location and his
hospitality are unimprovable. Susanna Gross provided much-needed
support during the early stages of this project, and later read sections
of the manuscript: she knows how important her good opinion is
to me. And I am grateful to Rick Gekoski, of Gekoski Rare Books,
London: his amused interest, helpful suggestions and constant
encouragement have done more than he knows to keep this project
moving forward.

Three people remain to be thanked. Paul Kahane, the nephew of
Jack Kahane, was generous with his time and hospitality, and trusted
me with precious family documents and photographs. I am especially
glad for him that this book is finished at last. James Armstrong was
the first Obelisk bibliographer. His checklist of Obelisk Press books,
first published in the Spring 2002 edition of *The Book Collector*, provided
me with the map I needed when I first started on this project, and his
generosity in sharing with me the books and papers he had amassed
during his own research made my job much easier than it would

ACKNOWLEDGEMENTS

otherwise have been. I am immensely grateful to him. Finally, Natalie Galustian has put up with more talk of second impressions, cancel title-pages and variant bindings than anyone could reasonably be expected to endure. The mistakes in this book are all mine; the reason it's finished is her.

Key to Reference Works

The following list is a key to the reference works and collections cited in this bibliography:

Armstrong: James Armstrong, 'The Obelisk Press Imprint 1931–1950', *The Book Collector*, Vol. 51, No. 1, Spring 2002. Also used to refer to books in Mr Armstrong's private collection

Baxter: Private collection of John Baxter

BL: British Library

BNF: Bibliothèque Nationale de France

Bodleian: Bodleian Library, University of Oxford

Casson: Private collection of Chris Casson

CUL: Cambridge University Library

d'Arch Smith: Timothy d'Arch Smith, *R. A. Caton and the Fortune Press: A Memoir and a Hand-List* (Asphodel Editions, 2004)

Ford: Hugh Ford, *Published in Paris: American and British Writers, Printers, and Publishers, 1920–1939* (Garnstone Press, 1975)

Gertzman: Jay Gertzman, *A Descriptive Bibliography of Lady Chatterley's Lover* (Greenwood, 1989)

Gibbs: Linnea Gibbs, *James Hanley: A Bibliography* (William Hoffer, 1980)

Gostock: Private collection of Chris Gostock

HRC: Harry Ransom Humanities Research Center, University of Texas

NLS: National Library of Scotland

NYPL: New York Public Library

Roberts and Poplawski: Warren Roberts and Paul Poplawski, *A Bibliography of D. H. Lawrence* (Cambridge University Press, 2001)

Shifreen and Jackson: Lawrence J. Shifreen and Roger Jackson, *Henry Miller: A Bibliography of Primary Sources* (Alyscamps Press, 1993)

SIU: Southern Illinois University

Slocum and Cahoon: John J. Slocum and Herbert Cahoon, *A Bibliography of James Joyce 1882–1941* (Yale University Press, 1953)

Woolf: Cecil Woolf, *A Bibliography of Norman Douglas* (Rupert Hart-Davis, 1954)

A Very British Pornographer:
The Life of Jack Kahane

Eighty years on, anyone who spent more than twenty minutes on the Paris literary scene between the two world wars seems to have had a book written about them. Books about James Joyce and Ernest Hemingway and Henry Miller and Ezra Pound were inevitable, Gertrude Stein wrote her own until biographers took the hint, and lesser literary lights – Robert McAlmon, Harry and Caresse Crosby, Nancy Cunard, Natalie Barney – all wrote memoirs which added to the mystique surrounding both themselves and the world in which they moved. Biographies duly followed. Then came books by or about the period's bit-part players, those who contributed more to the life of the Left Bank than to its legacy: Kiki of Montparnasse, John Glassco, Aleister Crowley, Bravig Imbs, Jimmie the Barman, Henri Broca and Flossie Martin, Ralph Cheever Dunning and Wambly Bald, and armies of White Russians and black Americans, crooks and contessas, junkies and jazzmen and hopheads and whores without number or name.

This blanket coverage of the period is what makes the neglect of Jack Kahane (pronounced Ker-hayne) so strange. The founder of the Obelisk Press and publisher of Henry Miller, Lawrence Durrell and Anaïs Nin, Kahane was born in Manchester in 1887. He was badly wounded during the Great War, and spent the rest of his life in France. He was a novelist and short story writer during the 1920s, became a publisher in Paris in 1929, and in 1934 introduced Henry Miller to the world when the Obelisk Press published the first edition of *Tropic of Cancer*. As well as four other books by Miller – *Aller Retour New York*, *Black Spring*, *Max and the White Phagocytes* and *Tropic of Capricorn* – Kahane also published Richard Aldington's incendiary anti-war novel *Death of a Hero*, and early work by Lawrence Durrell and Anaïs Nin. He defied the prim censoriousness of the time by publishing Norah C. James's *Sleeveless Errand*, James Hanley's *Boy*, Radclyffe Hall's *The Well of Loneliness* and D. H. Lawrence's *Lady Chatterley's Lover*, all of which had been banned in England, and he reaffirmed for 1930s' Paris the role it had established for itself during the twenties, that of proud defender of 'difficult' literature in the face of prudish and litigious government. Kahane was inspired in his calling by the saintly Sylvia Beach, who in 1922 and with no previous experience had published the first edition of James Joyce's *Ulysses* from her tiny bookshop on the rue de l'Odéon, and his work was continued in the 1950s by his son, Maurice Girodias: Girodias founded the Olympia Press, which, like Obelisk before it, issued important works of literature which no other publisher would touch, among them J. P. Donleavy's *The Ginger Men*, Terry Southern and Mason Hoffenberg's *Candy*, and, crowningly, Vladimir Nabokov's *Lolita*.

So why, when every artist's model and cocktail mixer from the era has been scrutinised and discussed, has Jack Kahane been so comprehensively forgotten? It's true that Kahane was a comparatively late arrival in expatriate Paris, and that the Obelisk Press operated during a period that served as an aftershock to the literary earthquake generated by the previous decade. But he was in Paris, publishing, by 1928, and plays a walk-on role in many books on the period devoted to more illustrious names than his. The problem isn't his timing. A partial explanation is that the achievements of Kahane the publisher seem to have been overlooked because of the comparative ordinariness of Kahane the man. Harry and Caresse Crosby, Natalie Barney and Nancy Cunard were all perfect casting for the Jazz Age: as well as being variously outrageous they were languid and striking and memorable. Kahane was socially unexceptional, plain and gangly, and spoke French with a Manchester accent. Consumption killed Ernest Walsh and Emanuel Carnevali while they were still young, beautiful and infinitely promising; Kahane wheezed his way through an adulthood that was often little more than premature dotage, and frequently spent months confined to bed. Defying convention, the Crosbys' marriage was thrillingly open; obeying convention, Kahane's was ploddingly adulterous.

And then – crucially – there was the question of money. Almost without exception, the men and women behind the literary presses of Paris were rich; they had made their 'profits', whether by inheritance or marriage, before a single page had been printed. Nancy Cunard's great-grandfather had founded the shipping line in 1840, and when her father, Sir Bache, married her mother, Maud Alice Burke, another couple of million dollars was added to the family coffers. Cunard's Hours Press, which she ran from 1928 to 1931, was never likely to fold for lack of funds. Harry Crosby was from a vastly wealthy Bostonian family; after serving as an ambulance driver in the First World War, he and his wife Caresse settled in Paris and reinvented themselves as artists and patrons. Their imprint, the Black Sun Press, produced sumptuous volumes in limited editions that were expensive to produce, expensive to buy, and as much works of art in themselves as they were vehicles for the artistry of others. When book sales were sluggish and money for parties, drugs and racehorses ran low, Harry simply wired home for more. Daddy would heed the call, and the party would continue. The life of Harry Crosby is the quintessentially Montparnassian biography. He was mad, bad, and dangerous to know. He was wealthy and handsome and sex-crazed and drug-stuffed. He died romantically, by his own hand, and left a pretty corpse. (Actually, *two* pretty corpses: Crosby and his lover, Josephine Bigelow, shot themselves in a suicide pact.) If your art wasn't up to the job, then this was exactly the sort of life to lead to ensure you left a mark: noisy, scandalous and eye-catching. In the complacent, self-regarding world of literary Paris between the wars, quiet heroism and diligent, unshowy achievement would always struggle to be noticed.

Robert McAlmon – Hemingway referred to him as 'McAlimony' – used the money he had come into on marrying the heiress Winifred Ellerman (who wrote under the pseudonym Bryher) to bankroll a Paris imprint called Contact Editions. Without his wife's money the small print runs and even smaller sales of Contact's unbendingly highbrow list – combined with McAlmon's innate lassitude and lack of business sense – would have seen the enterprise fail almost before it began. Bookseller Edward Titus was married to the cosmetics tycoon Helena Rubenstein. She provided her husband with the endless subsidy he needed to keep his sepulchral bookshop in the rue Delambre afloat. More museum than commercial enterprise, At the Sign of the Black Manikin had a few books for sale, but nothing as interesting as its collection of rare manuscripts and first editions, which Titus had put together using his wife's chequebook. The list of books issued by Titus was impossibly rarefied: although his Black Manikin Press published an early edition of *Lady Chatterley's Lover* in 1929, and had a modest success with Ludwig Lewisohn's *The Case of Mr Crump* in 1926, most of its titles were unlikely ever to trouble the bestseller lists. Work by Ralph Cheever Dunning, Kenneth McNeil Wells and William van Wyck, slim volumes of even slimmer verse published in editions of between one and five hundred copies, created as little stir then as they do now: *The Legend of Ermengarde*, for example, by the troubadour Uc Saine and translated into modern verse by Homer Rignaut from the fourteenth-century Provençal, still obstinately refuses to sell. But a lack of subscribers didn't bother Titus in the slightest: instead, slow sales provided him with gratifying evidence that he was out of the mainstream, above the fray, and ahead of his time.

Even if he'd wanted to, Jack Kahane couldn't afford to adopt such a position: for him, publishing had to pay. Almost alone among the independent publishers, Kahane had no independent means, and he was also one of the few who wasn't homosexual, infertile, or otherwise childless. He had a wife and children to support: keen as he was to find the next Joyce or Eliot, Kahane was even keener to feed his family. His business experience as a textile salesman in Manchester before the Great War had given him an eye for a market, as well as an understanding that his own taste would not always be shared by those whose custom he was looking to attract. Compromises would be necessary. If publishing a piece of worthless rubbish was likely to produce profits that could underwrite the publication of a book of high literary worth but limited commercial prospects, he would publish and be damned. He had ideals, but he also had a business to run. He wanted to make his name, but first he had to make his living. The result of this level-headed view of a publisher's obligations, rare among the proprietors of the period, was a list for which the word eclectic seems scarcely adequate.

Kahane's business plan was forged by necessity. Taking its name from the suitably phallic monument in the Place de la Concorde, Kahane founded the Obelisk Press in 1929. In order to subsidise the books that the Obelisk Press had come into existence to promote – slow-selling works of genuine literary merit – Kahane built up a sideline in what were known at the time as 'd.b's: dirty books. Most of these 'd.b's, many written pseudonymously by Kahane himself, were no such thing. Mildly titillating in an end-of-the-pier kind of way, and encased in lurid, eye-catching covers (often designed by members of Kahane's immediate family at no extra cost), most of them promised much more than they delivered – and were certainly no match for Henry Miller's visceral and unblinking approach to sex in *Tropic of*

Cancer, which Kahane published in 1934. But while they did their job at the time, selling steadily and keeping the Obelisk Press afloat, the 'dirty books' seem to have scuppered Kahane's reputation, then and now.

The books issued by presses such as Contact Editions and the Three Mountains Press were written by the high command of the Modernist avant-garde, published in editions of one or two hundred copies, and sold at a high price to a discerning few. Although this approach did nothing to ensure a lasting literary reputation for the presses' authors (no one originally published by Titus at Black Manikin, for example, is still read today) it does seem to have vouch-safed an enduring critical respect for the publishers themselves. The Obelisk Press, on the other hand, published anything it thought would sell, in relatively large editions of a thousand or so copies; it spent little on their presentation and sold them as cheaply as the economic climate would allow. In the ten years of its existence the Obelisk Press published some quite unspeakable rubbish, and it's perhaps under-standable that no scholarly eye has yet been drawn to the imprint that bequeathed the world such deathless classics as *Half O'Clock in Mayfair*, *Mad About Women* or my personal eye-watering favourite, the timeless triumph that is Gladys Sheila Donisthorpe's *Loveliest of Friends!*. Under-standable, but mistaken: with the sole exception of Sylvia Beach's Shakespeare and Company (which only published three books, two by and one about James Joyce) no expatriate literary publisher of the period achieved a higher or more enduring literary strike rate than Jack Kahane at the Obelisk Press. A bibliography of the press, and an appraisal of its proprietor, is long overdue.

1920s' PARIS AND THE 'EXPATRIATES', TALENTED AND OTHERWISE

Most of the foreigners in Paris during the 1920s, artists and hangers-on alike, had come to the city not just to arrive but to escape. Fleeing suffocating social and family expectation, they set up home in Montparnasse or the Boulevard St Michel, thrilled to be in Paris, certainly, but absolutely ecstatic to be no longer in Boston or New York or London. Gone was the need to conform; gone also was the need to deny one's vocation or one's nature. The family business was left far behind (although the family money usually made the trip), and life, real life, could begin. These incomers are habitually referred to in histories of the period as expatriates, but while it's true that there was a large and permanent non-French community in Paris throughout the 1920s, it was made up almost entirely of a constantly changing, transient population. The arrivals were mostly American – figures vary, but 25,000 is a conservative estimate – and most were simply tourists on an extended stay, sightseers who flocked to the bars and cafés of Montparnasse not because they were typically French, but because they were full of people who spoke English, people who looked, dressed and sounded like themselves. Contact with the natives was in most cases restricted to ordering drinks and asking for room keys, and the whole area bore as much resemblance to the real France as today's Costa del Sol does to the real Spain. To the American abroad, the Boulevard du Montparnasse was romantic and charming, sleazy and sinful, carefree and gay – but it wasn't French, and almost everyone who crowded into the Dingo and La Coupole and La Rotonde during the 1920s sooner or later found their way back home, as they had always intended to do.

For most of those who arrived in Paris with artistic aspirations the experience was a salutary one. In the world of the arts aspiration and ability are often strangers, and thousands of would-be Joyces and Picassos quickly discovered that merely throwing in one's job at the bank, getting on a boat to Europe and starting to drink absinthe were not enough in themselves to establish oneself as a significant cultural force. Bewitched by the endless opportunities for fun afforded them by their new surroundings even the genuinely talented often forgot the need to temper freedom with self-discipline. One such was the American writer Robert McAlmon. As Paris-based publisher of Contact Editions during the 1920s, McAlmon acted as midwife to a new generation of writers, among them William Carlos Williams and Ernest Hemingway. That McAlmon himself is so little known today can be explained not by a lack of talent – he was a good, if not a great writer – but by the destructive potential of 'freedom'. Born in South Dakota, McAlmon was bookish, brilliant and homosexual, characteristics he rightly thought would be better appreciated in Paris. Bryher's marriage to McAlmon had enabled her to break free from her family and pursue her relationship with the poet Hilda Doolittle; it also enabled McAlmon to stop worrying about money, to live in Paris, and to find himself. Tragically for him, what he found was a talented but deeply flawed dilettante, a writer resentful of and intimidated by the achievements of others, a drunkard who preferred to dazzle the clientele of the Montparnasse cafés with his verbal pyrotechnics rather than stay at home and commit them to paper. In the early 1920s Robert McAlmon was the coming man; by the end of the decade, he'd gone.

The McAlmon trajectory was followed by many who made the pilgrimage to Paris after the First World War. Paris offered tolerance, freedom of expression, like minds. The exchange rate was fantastically generous to foreigners arriving with dollars or pounds, and accommodation was plentiful, spacious and cheap. Alcohol fuelled the social life of Paris, and new arrivals – especially Americans fleeing Prohibition – were absolutely determined to have too much of a good thing. Hordes of foreigners would gather in the four renowned bars of Montparnasse – Le Dôme, La Coupole, La Rotonde and Le Select – hoping for a glimpse of someone famous, but happy to settle for getting drunk. Crowds would spill across the *terrasses* and onto the pavements, facing each other like rival armies across the Boulevard Montparnasse. Cocaine was widely available, and hashish, and opium. Brothels were everywhere. The city offered so many disincentives to work to those who could afford them that it's perhaps understandable that the writers who achieved most while in Paris tended to be those with the least money.

The constant stream of tourists and dilettantes and drop-outs and dopeheads passing through the revolving door of French customs control was a permanent feature of the 1920s. But Paris never turned anyone into a genius. Thousands arrived wide-eyed, found themselves, were disappointed by the discovery, drank and fucked and smoked to forget, and when the money ran out went home to the regular, sensible job that was always going to claim them in the end – leaving the true expatriates behind.

JACK KAHANE: A TRUE EXPATRIATE

Unlike most of the cultural refugees who arrived in the French capital in the 1920s and 1930s, Jack Kahane's love affair was not just with Paris, but with the whole of France. The future publisher of *Tropic of Cancer* and proprietor of the Obelisk Press had fallen in love with the country as a young man in Manchester, and had long been a champion of its culture. Born in 1887, Kahane claimed to have read all of Balzac by the time he left school, and in 1912 led a campaign for more French music to be played by Manchester's orchestra, the Hallé, which he felt had become staid and over-fond of the Teutonic under the influence of its principal conductor, the German maestro Hans Richter. When war broke out in 1914, the gangly and tubercular Kahane immediately enlisted, determined to defend not so much England as his adopted homeland of France. He fought with distinction, was badly wounded in the process, and after the war was nursed through a long convales-cence by the wife he'd married in 1917, a Frenchwoman from a wealthy and self-made family, Marcelle Girodias. By the early 1920s the family had settled in Rozoy-en-Multien, forty miles from Paris. Their son Maurice had already been born: three more children were to follow. By the time Jack Kahane established himself as a publisher in 1929, he saw himself as thoroughly French. But he was a comparative latecomer to literary Paris, despite his early arrival in France. In the 1920s, while Joyce and Hemingway and Stein and Pound were building their reputations, Kahane was forty miles away, trying to earn enough as a hack writer to feed his family. Throughout one of the most seismic decades in literary history Kahane remained, geographically and artistically, outside Paris.

But he was getting closer. Jonas Kahane had been born in Manchester on 20 July 1887 to Selig and Susy Kahane, Roumanian Jews who had moved to England around 1870.[1] Known as Jack or Jackie almost from birth, Kahane was the seventh of eight children, five of them girls. Amelia, the eldest, was already nineteen when Jackie was born. Sally, too, was grown up; both girls had been born in Romania before their parents' emigration. A seven-year gap before the birth of the Kahanes' next child, Louis, in 1875 suggests a period of adjustment to their new country, and the transition was a successful one: well-educated, indus-trious and determined to do well, Selig became a prosperous shipper of cotton goods, installed his family in an imposing home in Broughton, an affluent suburb of Manchester, and set about proclaiming his wealth by expanding his family. After Louis came Fanny, then Evalyne, then Jeannie. Jeannie was a year old when Jackie was born, and Jackie was a year older than the last arrival, Fred.

Selig Kahane had become a naturalised Briton in 1881, and his flourishing career typified that of the hard-working immigrant made good. He pushed himself, and grabbed every opportunity his adoptive boomtown offered him. Manchester in the late nineteenth century was a city which not only generated industry but rewarded it too, and Selig became a wealthy man: he employed live-in domestic staff to help run his increasingly unwieldy household, and as successive daughters married and moved out more staff were moved in, further increasing the home comforts of those left behind. Selig Kahane's family was growing accustomed to a life of plenty, but it was a life that wouldn't last.

In 1893 Selig made two disastrous business decisions. First he formed a company with his son-in-law, Amelia's husband Arthur Lobel; then Selig's son Louis declared his intention to go into business with a friend. The fact that Louis was still a teenager did not give Selig pause. Instead, he saw it as evidence of his son's precocity, and became the new company's guarantor. But Louis was a boy, and Lobel a waster. Both companies failed, and ruin loomed. That winter, early one Saturday morning, Selig Kahane went to work as usual. Arriving at his office in Chepstow Buildings in Oxford Street, he collected the keys from the janitor and smoked his usual cigarette while he chatted with his fellow early-birds. His cigarette finished, he went off by himself to the part of the building that housed his office, locked the door, sat down behind his desk and ripped his throat open with a pattern knife. At the inquest it was decided that Selig Kahane had committed suicide while insane.[2]

Since his death in 1939, anyone wanting to know anything about Jack Kahane has had to rely almost exclusively on two volumes of memoirs. One, *Memoirs of a Booklegger*, was written by Kahane himself and published in the year of his death; the other, *The Frog Prince*, was written by Kahane's son Maurice Girodias, later to become a publisher himself and the founder of the Olympia Press. (Girodias took his mother's maiden name as a fledgling publisher in Nazi-occupied Paris, having realised that a Jewish surname was unlikely to advance his career.) Memoirs are more forgetful than biographies, and *Memoirs of a Booklegger* is discursive, selective and unreliable: it provides detail where you could do with less, and none where you would be grateful for any. Kahane's amnesia is nowhere more acute than on the subject of his childhood. His father's suicide took place in 1893, when Jackie was six years old. Three years later he was orphaned when his mother Susy went to Harrogate to take the waters, developed a clot in her leg which was misdiagnosed, and died at the age of 46. The bald noting of his parents' deaths, stripped of all detail, takes up less than two lines of *Memoirs of a Booklegger*.[3] For all his later immersion in France and all things French, and for all his loathing of the starched and stifling rectitude of his homeland, Kahane's emotional make-up remained stoically, ineradicably British. To Kahane pain was not for sharing, but something to be borne, silently, like a man. The idea (an idea very popular among the less gifted expatriates, and among the less gifted generally) that suffering is the compost which enables creativity to flourish, that trauma can and should be recycled into art, remained Britishly unattractive to Kahane throughout his life.

One of the few childhood memories, good or bad, that Kahane divulges in *Memoirs of a Booklegger* is of a kickaround in the street with his beloved younger brother Fred, using a bustle belonging to one of his sisters as a makeshift ball. The incident is used not to evoke a happy childhood scene but rather to illustrate the era into which Kahane felt he'd been born, a stifling Victorianism from which he was determined to escape at the earliest opportunity. In his memoir Kahane characterises his childhood as one of suffocation under the propriety of an upstanding and respectable Victorian household. His older sisters, who raised him, were born squarely into the Victorian era, and did everything they could to instil in him a belief in the value of abstinence: abstinence from smoking, from drinking, from women. As a boy Kahane dutifully obeyed his sisters, but he never shared their vision of what constituted a life well lived, and in *Memoirs of a Booklegger* his childhood is skimmed, a time too dreary and oppressive – and painful – to be dwelt on. Instead, the reader is quickly transported to the time in Kahane's life when he first feels free from the influence of his family and comes alive to himself: the conquest, with friends, of Manchester's cultural institutions in his late adolescence.

Growing up, Jack Kahane had known both affluence and hardship, and by adolescence he'd decided which state he preferred: 'My family seemed to be in a state of chronic impecuniosity, and poverty comes the harder when one has known another state. Moreover, few people can adapt themselves to poverty who have not been born to it. My family was no exception, and probably made the worst of such resources as they still possessed.'[4] One resource still available to them in the wake of their parents' deaths was Jackie's brain. According to

Maurice Girodias, before the death of his parents Jackie's family was one 'where money and religion had been cheerfully transmuted into music and letters. He was expected to become a scholar or an artist.'[5] When the money dried up 'little was left of former glory – all that endured was devotion to the life of the mind. Systematically Jackie devoured not only the English classics but also Balzac and the Symbolists. He studied Chinese and knew Keats by heart.'[6] Kahane studied Chinese in his late teens while hoping for a posting to Shanghai with the shipping company for which he was working; everything else he read for fun. Between 1900 and 1903 he attended Manchester Grammar School on a Foundation Scholarship, mixing with boys who were as bright as he was and as rich as he used to be. His love of literature and music had already been awakened at home but his schooling helped cement the arts as central to his life. It also fed his francophilia. Kahane claimed to have read all forty-odd volumes of Balzac's *Comédie Humaine*, in the original French, while still at school.[7] If true, this could go some way to explaining a school record which was rarely distinguished. Educated alongside the very brightest boys of Manchester, Jackie Kahane attained mid-table respectability in most subjects, doing slightly better in Classics and English, and coming stone last with impressive regularity in Drawing. His results in French were variable, but probably explained by varying degrees of application: in his finals he came equal second.[8]

Kahane was a stringy, gangly boy, and his self-consciousness about his appearance made him shy. He seems not to have enjoyed his schooldays, and on at least one occasion later in life blamed the ethos at schools such as his for turning out just the sort of repressed, sex-starved Englishmen who thirty years later ensured Obelisk's more lubricious titles sold so well. But although most of Manchester Grammar School's extracurricular activities failed to interest Kahane, he seems rarely to have missed a meeting of the school's Debating Society.[9] Whatever the motion – the competence of the government, the benefits of boarding schools, the abolition of corporal punishment, the existence of ghosts – the schoolboy Kahane had both a ready opinion and a flair for delivering it. Kahane's facility with language led eventually to a career in letters, but its first benefit was to ease him through what might otherwise have been a difficult adolescence.

In his late teens and newly confident, Kahane began to strike out on his own, quickly moving as far away from his sisters' idea of propriety as his various dalliances would carry him. The process was accelerated by his increasing financial independence: Kahane discovered he'd inherited his father's flair for business, and quickly established himself in Manchester's cotton and velvet trades. But his knack for making money was matched by a knack for spending it: an increasingly flamboyant Kahane was doing his best to live like a Regency buck, and the accessories of a Regency buck were expensive. Neither Kahane nor his friend and workmate, Harold Brighouse, saw their futures in commerce. Art was the way forward: they would first make their fortunes, then their names. Kahane bet Brighouse that he, Kahane, would be the first to be mentioned in print in the *Manchester Guardian*.[10] Brighouse accepted, but although Kahane won the bet it would be Brighouse, the author of *Hobson's Choice*, who would later claim for himself the renown that would always elude his friend.

Kahane won his bet with Brighouse as a result of the intransigence of Hans Richter, then principal conductor of Manchester's Hallé Orchestra. The Hallé's repertoire at the time was rigidly Teutonic: lots of Wagner, lots of Beethoven, and nothing at all of the new wave of French music – Debussy, Ravel, Duparc, Fauré, Dukas – then being heard in London. In *Memoirs of a Booklegger* Kahane grudgingly acknowledges Richter's genius, but sees no reason why that should require him to like him as a man: 'A big, snuffy, bearded, fat German, Richter was a god, a German god, but a god. About him had collected a thick and even impenetrable bunch of sycophantic worshippers, Germans and others, who would allow no word of criticism against their cigar-smoking, beer-drinking, potato-salad-devouring darling'.[11] This less than dispassionate portrait of one of the finest conductors of the twentieth century leaves the reader in no doubt that, in Kahane's eyes, Richter's nationality would have been enough to damn him on its own; that he was a German who was also dismissive of French music put him absolutely beyond the pale. Richter, the man who 'ruled music in Manchester with a baton of toughened steel',[12] had either to change or be forced from his post, and Kahane resolved to be the cause of either outcome. He led a deputation which met with Richter to plead for more French and English music to be included in the orchestra's repertoire. They were shown the door. Undeterred, Kahane founded the Manchester Musical Society. Enthusiasm outstripped musical accomplishment, but the concert programmes, stuffed full of new French and English music, succeeded in attracting the city's more adventurous music-lovers. When the Hallé drifted into deficit Kahane saw his chance both to move against Richter and to collect on his bet with Harold Brighouse.

Writing in his now official capacity as the Honorary Secretary of the Manchester Musical Society, Kahane composed a letter to the *Manchester Guardian.* (It was published on 20 January 1911, and was Kahane's first appearance in print.) He argued that the programming policy of the Hallé had become retrogressive and stale, and demanded that the people of Manchester be given the opportunity to hear the music of new composers such as Reger, Delius and Mahler. Worried that the strident tone of his letter would kill the debate before it had begun, Kahane took the precaution of writing a pseudonymous letter taking the first to task, and then wrote a third in his own name which triumphantly demolished the arguments of the second. All three were published, and the debate caught fire: 'Letters poured into the *Guardian* from everywhere, heaping contumely on me, backing me up, quoting what their great-grandfather had said in 1770. Here was a full-dress newspaper controversy that aroused the attention of the whole musical world'.[13] Whether the controversy in the letters page of the *Manchester Guardian* was the sole or even partial cause of Richter's resignation is debatable, but the timing of the maestro's departure – just after the letters' publication – allowed Kahane to claim a glorious victory, and confirmed him in his view of himself as the person best qualified to set Manchester's new cultural course.

But he wasn't the only man in the city who wanted the job. Much as he would have preferred to be the lone hero, keeping the flag of the avant-garde flying in the face of stolid middle-class conservatism, Kahane instead found himself part of a movement. In what was to become a recurring phenomenon of the twentieth century, a vibrant Mancunian counterculture was emerging, a counterculture keen to challenge not only the stuffy conformism of its own city but also the artistic primacy of London. The movement came to encompass art, literature and drama as well as music, and its headquarters would be established in two of Manchester's most forward-thinking artistic institutions: the Gaiety Theatre, and the Swan Club.

THE SALONS OF MANCHESTER

Hallé's arrival in Manchester from Paris in 1857 had ensured that for the rest of the century the city would have a seat at musical England's top table. But although high standards of musicianship had been maintained the tenure of Hans Richter as musical director, supported by audiences drawn mainly from the prosperous and mostly German-Jewish merchant class of Manchester, had resulted in an unadventurous and repetitive repertoire and a consequent diminution of the orchestra's national standing. No such thing was ever likely to happen to Manchester's theatrical life.

In 1900 Manchester was home to sixteen professional theatres, providing high drama, low comedy, grand opera, music hall, Shakespeare, melodrama and burlesque for an audience that was huge, loyal and proud of its city's theatrical history. There had been a theatre in Manchester since 1753; Henry Irving had served his apprenticeship in the city, establishing a reputation on Manchester's stages before London had ever heard of him; private members' clubs had been founded to circumvent the objections of prosecutors and prigs and to bring Ibsen's plays to Manchester, where they were 'listened to intelligently while the West End die-hards were still calling them "an open drain... morbid, unhealthy, disgusting".[14] This crusading spirit wasn't confined to the professional ranks: Ibsen's most controversial play, *Ghosts*, received its British premiere at a Manchester amateur theatre, the Athenaeum, and the profusion of amateur dramatic societies across the region not only encouraged theatre-going but also provided young local writers with an outlet for their work. Among the beneficiaries of this hot-housing were many of Kahane's friends.

Manchester's theatrical life seemed to be full to bursting point, but in 1907 Annie Horniman and Ben Iden Payne spotted a gap in the market. Miss Horniman (as she was always known) was a woman with a vision; equally importantly, she was a woman with a legacy. While travelling in Germany she'd been impressed by the country's systemic approach to the provision of theatre. The subsidised repertory system was one she was keen to import to Britain, and Manchester, with its large audiences and adventurous tastes, was the obvious location for the venture.

Despite the profusion of theatre in Manchester at the turn of the century there had been very little space on its stages, among the

Shakespeare revivals and undemanding melodramas, for the production of 'good new plays'[15] that were 'sincere works of art'.[16] With the advent of Miss Horniman's company it was suddenly possible for local dramatists to see their work produced on the professional stage and in their home town, work that would be reviewed and talked about. Kahane craved recognition but lacked any practical ability in his first love, music, and it was this pragmatic reason, rather than any vocational one, that was about to push him towards the stage.

Now twenty years old, Jack Kahane had little idea of what he wanted to do with his life; all he had was a clear idea of the sort of life it should be. After the suicide of their father, Kahane's sisters and their families had struggled to adapt to their newly impoverished circumstances. Jack was determined to ensure that he would never have to. In his post-adolescent years in Manchester, the years between leaving school and the outbreak of the First World War, money came easily to Kahane – although not the ability to keep it. He worked hard at his velvet business when he worked at all, but usually restricted his exertions to an hour or two each day, and quickly spent the proceeds on his ongoing project of self-invention. He overcame his insecurity about his appearance by changing it completely. He became a dandy: monocles, canes and expensive tailors were all deployed to convince Manchester – or at least that part of Manchester which spent its time star-gazing in the American Bar of the Midland Hotel – that Jack Kahane was the coming man. His new and striking outward appearance attracted attention, and his gift of the gab ensured that he kept it.

Between 1908 and 1912 Kahane joined almost every society, association and supper club in Manchester, and where they didn't exist, he created them. As well as founding the Manchester Musical Society in order to fight Richter, he was also a noisy recruit to the Manchester Playgoers' Club. For many years before Kahane's arrival, the Club had been content to trundle along uncontentiously, organising social gatherings, lectures, and cut-price theatre trips for its members. Suspiciously soon after Kahane's enrolment a meeting was called at the Midland Hotel to discuss the future policy and direction of the Club: the first speaker from the floor was a Mr. J. Kahane.[17] Citing the example set by the Manchester Musical Society (founder: J. Kahane) he exhorted the Club to do more to find and foster local theatrical talent. He proposed the founding of an amateur dramatic society to present new and controversial work, a society to rival the reputation of the Stockport Garrick; he condemned the frittering away of the Club's time and money on useless social functions; and he risked losing the support of the meeting by berating his fellow theatre-lovers for benefitting from cut-price theatre tickets which could only hurt the finances of the theatres they claimed to be supporting. But when he called for the committee to stop inviting actors to address the Club's meetings, on the unassailable grounds that actors were far too stupid as a species to have anything interesting to say on any subject, the members realised that they had amongst them a man who could lead them out of the wilderness. Shortly afterwards they made him Club Secretary.

Kahane liked the sound of his own voice, but he wasn't alone. Everyone who knew him in Manchester agreed that he was an accomplished orator and a brilliant conversationalist – the most brilliant, according to Harold Brighouse, that he'd ever heard.[18] Fortunately, Manchester had a club for this, too: the Brasenose Club. Based at 94 Mosley Street, the Brasenose Club was a supper club attended by the finest talkers, and worst listeners, in Manchester. Kahane attended regularly. Celebrities were entertained at the club after the opening of their plays or the delivery of their lectures, and although membership was skewed towards the theatre, the Brasenose was a meeting-place for artists in all disciplines, from all generations, and from all over the country. It was a *salon* with a sit-down dinner thrown in. Kahane loved clubs like this. Part of his love for them arose out of a genuine passion for the arts, and an evangelical zeal to bring them to as many people as possible, but his motives weren't completely altruistic. Clubs like the Brasenose provided him with the opportunity not only to talk himself, but also to talk to those he admired, those whose books he'd read, whose concerts he'd attended, whose plays he'd seen. Association of this kind was enormously important to Kahane. He had a lifelong infatuation with celebrity – or reputation, as it was called in 1910. He longed to be at the centre of things, to be admired and talked about, and was fascinated by people who were, so much so that, in his early twenties and having yet to create anything of his own to excite the interest of the cultured classes, it made him happy simply to stand next to people like Arnold Bennett or Frank Harris, to drink with them, share jokes with them, to feel himself one of their kind if not yet one of their number. But shoulder-rubbing only provided Kahane with a short-term shot of self-validation. Soon he was planning the opening of a new club, one conceived along the lines of the Brasenose but more finely attuned to his own personal requirements. Chief among these was the requirement that Kahane himself should be more centre-stage in the club's activities. The Brasenose was long-established, run by people who'd lived longer and achieved more than Kahane and his friends. Since a takeover was unrealistic and the playing of a supporting role unacceptable, it was clear that a new club was needed, one which would embrace the new, the challenging, and the untried, one which would establish the direction the arts would take for the coming generation, one which would allow young under-achievers to get drunk and talk too much without having to suffer the beady disdain of the already great. The Swan Club was born. Proprietor: J. Kahane.

THE SWAN CLUB AND THE MANCHESTER SCHOOL

Described some years later by the *Manchester Guardian* as 'a boyish experiment in Bohemianism',[19] the Swan Club began life in what Kahane described as 'a lugubrious upstairs room of a third-rate restaurant'[20] attached to the Swan Inn, near Market Street. There were four founder members: Kahane, Harold Brighouse, Walter Mudie and C. F. Kenyon, who wrote under the pseudonym of Gerald Cumberland. Walter Mudie was a descendant of Charles Mudie, whose subscription library had exercised such a stranglehold on the Victorian publishing industry that he'd been able to browbeat publishers into introducing the three-volume novel, a huge boon to his business since it enabled him to rent the same book to three customers simultaneously. Walter Mudie was working in Mudie's Manchester branch when he first met Kahane, but had no intention of spending the rest of his life in the family business. Growing municipal provision of public libraries was hitting Mudie's hard, and in any case Walter had already decided on a career in music. It was this shared passion, discovered while Kahane was teaching Mudie French, which had led to the two becoming friends. Cumberland and Kahane had already known each other for some years, and were to remain close until Cumberland's death in 1927.

According to Kahane, each of the Swan Club's founders was differently indispensable to the venture:

Each one of us had definite artistic ambitions that made a convenient link: Brighouse sternly intent upon dramatic laurels: Mudie's head ringing with musical compositions: Kenyon [Cumberland] already with some reputation as a book critic, a poet and a biographer: I with play-writing as my intellectual stand-by, but perhaps merely delighted to bask in the friendship of the others, who, because they had obviously nothing to fear from me, spoiled me.

... We were not a social enterprise, but a school of thought. We were out to smite the Philistines... We were each to produce works of art according to our genius, and when they were introduced to the public they were to bear our sign, the Swan. We were going to leave our mark on our generation and show the world that what Manchester writes to-day London will flock to see (if we were playwrights) or to buy (if we were poets, novelists etc.) to-morrow.[21]

The first task facing the Swan Club's executive was to expand the membership. Kahane recruited members of Miss Horniman's theatrical company, among them Basil Dean and Esmé Percy, and Cumberland brought W. P. Price-Heywood, 'chartered accountant, leader writer, vegetarian, social reformer: one of the strangest mixtures of a man you could meet.'[22] Brighouse swelled the ranks with the recruitment of Ernest Marriott, a local librarian and talented artist who drew caricatures of Swan Club recruits for display on the walls of its meeting-room, and who designed the Swan Club device found on the title-pages of many of its members' publications. Brighouse also introduced his long-time friend and fellow playwright, Stanley Houghton.

Houghton had had his one-act play *The Dear Departed* staged by the Horniman Company in 1908. Popular with audiences at the turn of the century, these one-act plays, short *divertimenti*, were used by theatres as pre-show fillers. They were the live equivalent of B-movies, their casts were usually drawn from a company's understudies and stage management, and they were an unknown playwright's best chance of reaching an audience. *The Dear Departed*, a barbed comedy about a group of greedy relatives who gather at the house of a patriarch they mistakenly believe to be dead, had been an instant success at the Gaiety, and had transferred to London the following year to the Coronet Theatre in Notting Hill, where it played as a curtain-raiser to Shaw's *Widowers' Houses*, and where it was a success all over again. Shaw praised it, Ellen Terry praised it, critics praised it. Audiences started coming for the curtain-raiser as much as the Shaw, and the *Manchester*

Weekly Chronicle proudly trumpeted the local boy's conquering of the capital: 'no more striking enthusiasm has been seen in London for some time.'[23] *The Dear Departed* went on to appear regularly in the Manchester repertory, and between 1909 and 1912 it was joined at the Gaiety by five more of Houghton's plays: one-acters, four-acters, comedies and dramas.

Houghton's success made life difficult for the Swan Club's core membership. Now settled at around fifteen, the club was holding its regular lunchtime meetings in rooms opposite the Theatre Royal – right next door to the Gaiety. The location gave members plenty of opportunity to see for themselves just how well Houghton was doing, and the result was a vague resentment which threatened to curdle into outright envy. The Club's aims had always been hazy, but Houghton's fast-growing reputation now forced the question.

Kahane and his fellow founder members of the Swan Club had always known what they were against: censorship, cultural unadventurousness, reverence for the past and fear of the new were crimes against Art to be opposed at every turn. What they were *for* they found harder to articulate. A new movement? Certainly. A new movement led by themselves? Naturally. A new movement committed to...? So far, that meeting hadn't taken place. According to Basil Dean, at the Swan Club 'there were no rules, no subscriptions, and no credentials beyond an ability to speak one's own mind and to be ready for instant contradiction.'[24] This 'instant contradiction' would usually come from Kahane, remembered by Brighouse as 'the flaming romantic of the Swan Club table'.[25] But for all Kahane's oratory his lack of vision, combined with the directionless oppositionism of the Club itself, was always going to find itself badly exposed as soon as it was confronted by real talent and real achievement. Houghton had both, and he quickly became what Kahane and his cohorts had spent so much time and energy trying to become themselves: the leader of a movement.

The defining characteristics of the Manchester School of dramatists are crystallised in the work of Stanley Houghton. His success was built on solid foundations. He'd long been involved as both writer and actor in Manchester's vibrant amateur dramatic societies, and had made a study of the great dramatists of the present and recent past – particularly Ibsen, from whom he'd learned both structure and an unblinking approach to subject matter. He'd worked as an unpaid theatre critic on the *Manchester City News*, reviewing everything from amateur dramatics to music hall, and later wrote book and theatre reviews for the *Manchester Guardian*. Houghton and Ben Iden Payne had been contemporaries at Manchester Grammar School, and when Payne was made the first director of Miss Horniman's new company at the Gaiety Theatre Houghton was well placed, and well prepared, to benefit.

From the outset, Horniman and Iden Payne had been determined to use their new theatre to discover and promote local talent, and although Houghton's *The Dear Departed* had borrowed both its story and its structure from a Maupassant short story called *En Famille*, its voice was original, and the *accent* of the voice was unmistakable: Lancastrian. For the first time Manchester's theatregoers saw people who dressed and sounded like themselves presented on a Manchester stage: drawing rooms were replaced by parlours, aristocrats and farmhands by factory owners and mill workers, tiaras and ballgowns by cloth caps and hobnailed boots. Audiences saw a world they recognised, a world they moved in, reflected back at them from the stage – and crucially, it was a world as likely to be hopeful and happy as malign. The lazy critical assumption that proletarian literature is by nature pessimistic has lumbered the playwrights of the Manchester School with a reputation for dourness and gloom that is inaccurate and unfair. Houghton and the other Manchester dramatists would often present the privations of working-class life, but their work – especially that of Houghton and Brighouse – is leavened both by humour and by a palpable affection for their characters and the lives they lead. (The charge of terminal bleakness is far more easily pinned onto an author Kahane would publish more than twenty years later: D. H. Lawrence, whose plays are contemporaneous with and thematically similar to those of the Manchester School, but with the added ingredients of hopelessness, corpse-washing, crippling poverty, and black lung.)

At the time of the Swan Club's inception, then, of the fifteen members Stanley Houghton was by far the best known, a fact which led those members whose genius remained publicly unacknowledged to grow disdainful of the idea that success could be anything but a corrupting influence on an artist. Houghton, by nature a quiet and reserved man, began to find himself the target of banter which bordered on spite. Basil Dean recalled that 'it was part of the intellectual snobbery of the Club to profess contempt for commercial success. Houghton, a gentle, kindly creature with curly hair, heavily-lidded eyes, a prominent nose and a permanent look of faint anxiety, managed good-naturedly to smile away chaff that contained more than a tinge of envy.'[26] Dean's recollection is endorsed by that of Gerald Cumberland: 'In this little coterie Houghton was a veritable whale among the minnows... In conversation he could be ready, and his repartee was frequently brilliant... But I must confess that I rarely saw him in company in which there were not two or three who were hostile to him.'[27] Kahane, whose Wildean wit was as yet unmatched by a Wildean career, was almost certainly one of Houghton's chief tormentors. His own torment would come later, destined as he was to spend so much of his life – first as a playwright, then novelist, and finally as a publisher – coveting the very success that as a young man he purported to despise.

Kahane's hold on his position as the Swan Club's ringmaster began to loosen as Houghton's success and consequent fame began to impinge upon the group. According to Gerald Cumberland, Harold Brighouse was the first to break ranks: 'Brighouse worshipped success, so he worshipped Houghton. The rest of us, if we worshipped anything at all, worshipped genius, and as Kahane was the only one among us who had a touch of that divine quality, we rather tended to worship him... [He] played and played hard. He talked; he ragged; he listened to music and saw plays; he fell in love; he indulged harmless vices.'[28] For the twenty-four-year-old Kahane the desk seems to have been an insufficiently adulatory audience: anything was preferable to work. The explanation may have been simply a youthful inability to focus, it may have been a reluctance to jeopardise a so far untested reputation for brilliance, it may have been that his father's suicide had led to a mistrust of the notion that hard work is its own reward. But whatever the explanation for his indolence, Kahane's aspirations were put at a severe disadvantage when set against the tireless diligence of both Houghton and Brighouse.

Harold Brighouse served his dramatic apprenticeship as diligently as Stanley Houghton had served his. In 1902, while working as a cloth salesman, Brighouse had been posted to London. The charms of the capital were lost on Kahane, as they are on most Mancunians – 'that hollow Mecca',[29] he called it – but for Brighouse the move south was a revelation. Knowing no one, and by disposition feeling no need to cultivate new friends, he spent every spare moment at the theatre. Holiday leave was especially welcome, not because it enabled him to return to Manchester but because it meant he could add a midweek matinée to his theatre-going schedule and see eight shows a week instead of only seven. This two-year immersion left him besotted with theatre as an art form, but outspokenly contemptuous of most of its output. ('Better than booing is silence,' he wrote in a memoir. 'It is lethal but, calling for restraint, rare.'[30]) His conviction that he could write better plays than the ones he was paying to watch was soon vindicated.

Newly married and back in Manchester once more, Brighouse first began to write more from necessity than from vocation. When the business he worked for faltered he was faced with unemployment, and although he avoided redundancy, the threat of it – combined with an aspiration made keener by Houghton's growing reputation – ignited his career. In 1909 he sent three one-act plays to Ben Iden Payne at the Gaiety, one of which was a witty little playlet called *Lonesome-Like*, which, although it would later become a fixture in theatre repertoires all over the country, would now have to wait another two years for its first performance. Instead of presenting *Lonesome-Like*, Iden Payne chose to introduce Brighouse to Manchester's theatregoers with another play from the three, an inferior squib called *The Doorway*. It premiered at the Gaiety in April 1909 to no great acclaim, and although Brighouse was kept busy by theatres in Glasgow and London over the next two years, his work wasn't seen again in Manchester until 1911.

One of the few parts of Manchester which *did* know about Brighouse's growing reputation around the country was the Swan Club. With both Houghton and Brighouse in the ascendant, Kahane now found himself in an uncomfortable position. The good news was that he was finally where he'd always wanted to be, at the centre of an artistic movement that was beginning to change the country's cultural landscape. The bad news was that he'd had nothing to do with its inception, had contributed nothing to its growth, and had produced nothing that would be establishing his reputation any time soon. It was time to shut up, sit down, and write.

In 1912 a company in Manchester called Sherratt and Hughes was persuaded to publish a small edition of *Two Plays*, by Jack Kahane. The plays were *The Master*, a one-acter, and *Black Magic*, 'A Modern Tragedy in Three Acts'. Sherratt and Hughes' usual line of business was the publication of textbooks, and the sales figures of *Two Plays* did nothing to convince them that there might be more money to be made in drama. The small and flimsy paperbound volume carries a woodcut by the Swan Club's in-house artist, Ernest Marriott, on its front panel. The woodcut is of an ancient warrior, possibly Roman, and if it has any connection at all with the contents of the book I've missed it. But poor production values, microscopic sales figures and baffling ornamentation were all minor cavils. The book was finished, it existed. Kahane the dramatist was published, if as yet unperformed.

Throughout his life Kahane had the unfortunate knack of being in almost the right place at almost the right time, and his short career as a playwright is a case in point. By 1912 the Manchester School was no longer a secret to the rest of the country. Transfers of Gaiety productions to theatres all over England and Scotland not only had the effect of turning a local movement into a national phenomenon, they also encouraged the provinces to challenge London's view of itself as the seat of national culture, thereby fostering regional movements of their own. The benefits of this diaspora were felt most keenly by the artists themselves, whose thriving careers increasingly carried them away from their home town. Manchester School dramatist Harold Chapin became the director of the Glasgow Repertory Theatre: as well as staging the first British production of a Chekhov play (*The Seagull*, in 1909) the theatre presented three early works by its director's old friend Harold Brighouse. Basil Dean decided that acting was no job for an adult, and left Miss Horniman's company to become the first Controller of the Liverpool Repertory Theatre, now the Liverpool Playhouse. Ben Iden Payne left Britain altogether, first running the Empire Theatre in Syracuse, New York, and then in 1916, at the Princess Theatre on Broadway, presenting the world premiere of Brighouse's most famous and enduring play, *Hobson's Choice*.

Stanley Houghton achieved his greatest success nearer home. *Hindle Wakes* was first performed under licence by the Lord Chamberlain at the Aldwych Theatre, London, in 1912, and later that year was presented in Manchester with its original cast. It played without a curtain-raiser, was an instant hit, and ran for two uninterrupted weeks at a theatre accustomed to changing its programme daily. The fact that so many dignitaries, organisations and editorials found its subject matter disgusting only added to its success. Then as now, scandal was box office.

Hindle Wakes is the story of a mill girl's seduction by the mill owner's son: when his dishonourable conduct is exposed, he does the honourable thing and proposes. It's a plot which held no surprises for Edwardian audiences, who would often have seen it played out between a louche drawing-room cad and a scullery maid. 'Problem plays' had always been presentable on stage provided the playwright's resolution of the problem was morally unambiguous, but in *Hindle Wakes* Houghton rejected social and theatrical convention in favour of psychological truth, as Ibsen had done before him, and so forced English drama to grow up, to acknowledge the world as it was. In *Hindle Wakes* the mill girl Fanny Hawthorn hears out Alan Jeffcote's proposal of marriage – and rejects it. He's a nice enough man, she tells him, but she was only after a little fun – just as he was – and if she *does* ever marry it will be to a far better man than him. Alan is at first hurt, but then delighted. In a great leap forward for British theatre, the couple decide not to do the right thing, as a result of which everyone lives happily ever after.

Houghton's masterstroke was to serve up this revolutionary plot twist not in a sombre drama whose characters are tortured by guilt and regret, but in a cheerful comedy populated by characters determined to be happy, whose preferred guiding star is not social conformism but plain speaking and common sense. Plain-speaking, commonsensical Manchester *loved* it. After its opening two-week run in October, *Hindle Wakes* was revived in December, and five separate touring productions took to the road. A bowdlerised version flopped in the United States, but wherever the play was performed as Houghton wrote it, it was a huge success. *Hindle Wakes* became Houghton's monument and, with Brighouse's *Hobson's Choice*, the most famous and enduring product of the Manchester School.

All of which meant that by the time Kahane's play *The Master* was given its premiere at the Gaiety on 27 November 1913, both the play and its author had a lot to live up to. Like Houghton, Kahane had read, seen, and been heavily influenced by Ibsen. But where Houghton had been liberated, Kahane was enslaved. *Hindle Wakes* shows Houghton's absorption of Ibsen to have been complete, an absorption which enabled Houghton to synthesise Ibsen's influence and turn it into a world-view uniquely his own. In the last act of Ibsen's *A Doll's House* Nora Helmer at last walks out on her infantile husband and their airless marriage: refusing to be unhappy simply because society requires her to be she defies the world, leaving nothing behind her but the resounding echo of a slammed door. The influence that *A Doll's House* exerted on Houghton's writing of *Hindle Wakes* is clear. But in *Hindle Wakes* the world has moved on: the sexes have begun to understand each other, and although sadness and regret remain, tragedy is no longer inevitable. The play shows Houghton to have digested all his reading and theatregoing, and to be speaking with a voice of his own.

Kahane's absorption, on the other hand, was far from complete. Self-regarding romantic that he was, his reading of Ibsen led to an infatuation, even an identification, with Eilert Løvborg, the writer in *Hedda Gabler* whose addiction to an unachievable idealism dooms him to failure. Løvborg appears almost completely undisguised in *The Master*, a one-act play set 'in the living-room of a cottage in a fishing-village'.[31] (The lesson of writing about what is familiar to you was lost on Kahane.) Ann, a fisherman's wife, is jealous of her husband's love of his master, the sea. On a stormy morning she and her father try to persuade him to stay at home, but his determination to earn enough money to buy his own boat and be his own man leads him to put pride before both reason and love. James Gillon arrives from 'the hills' – Ann's lost home. As Løvborg does for Hedda, so Gillon represents the life, and possibly the man, Ann turned away from when she married her husband. As they talk, the ardour they feel rises in counterpoint to the gathering storm outside. When Ann's husband returns home, she tells him of her intention to leave, but he trumps her with the news that his boat, and therefore all hope, has been shattered on the rocks. Ann turns to Gillon: 'The sea masters everyone. It's mastered him and it's mastered me. It's mastered you. Good-bye, James Gillon. [Curtain]'.[32]

The Master is as overheated and under-developed as the above synopsis makes it sound: it was respectfully received, and quickly forgotten. Presented as a curtain-raiser for H. M. Richardson's *The Awakening Woman*, and running, it seems, for precisely one performance, Kahane could hardly have expected much critical attention. But people rallied round: the 'A. N. M.' who reviewed the play for the *Manchester Guardian* was almost certainly the Manchester playwright Allan Monkhouse, and he did his best for his friend: 'Mr. Kahane seizes sometimes on gaudy trifles, but his piece has tragic quality, and imagination keeps always the better of sentiment. His diction, in the earlier passages, has a fine bleakness, but it can be surprising, too.'[33] In his review Monkhouse is careful to lay the blame for any shortcomings in the performance on people he doesn't know: 'Mr Keogh had not sufficient faith in his author's lines, and the first part of the play did not go as well as it should have done. Mr [Esmé] Percy, as the lover from the hills, brought off the difficult ecstasies very well'.[34]

But a bad night out is not always the actor's fault, and having read *The Master* my sympathy is with Mr Keogh: whatever else he would prove to be, Kahane was not a playwright. Worse, his continuing status as a complete unknown – despite having now been published, performed, *tested* – must have been made agonisingly clear to him when he took his seat at the Gaiety on 27 November 1913 for what would prove to be the only home-town performance his play would ever receive. A copy of that evening's theatre programme survives in an archive held at Manchester City Library. It identifies the author of *The Master* as 'J. Cahane'.[35]

THE END OF THE MANCHESTER SCHOOL

By the time *The Master* opened and closed in the winter of 1913, the Swan Club had ceased to exist and the glory days of the Manchester School were over – if 'glory days' is not too roseate a phrase to describe a movement which looked set to deliver profound change to the British theatrical landscape, but which ultimately failed to mature into a defining cultural force. James Agate was later dismissive of the idea that the Manchester School had achieved enough to be classified as a movement at all: 'Houghton's *Hindle Wakes* was a bright flash in what turned out to be a very small pan, and Harold Brighouse never followed up *Hobson's Choice*. The only first-class work...was Allan Monkhouse's *Mary Broome*'.[36] The last-named play is now forgotten, and the first two are the only ones the movement produced which are still regularly performed today, less than a hundred years after they were written. Agate has a case, but it's not watertight. He believed that a fundamental lack of talent, of artistic staying power, lay behind the movement's loss of momentum, but extenuating circumstances played a leading role in killing off the Manchester School – in many cases, literally – and in reducing the size of its legacy to British theatrical life. In December 1913, less than a month after Jack Kahane's stage debut in Manchester, Stanley Houghton was taken ill in Venice and brought home to Manchester, where he died of meningitis at the age of 32. Although prolific in what turned out to be the short time available to him – so prolific that when Miss Horniman brought down the curtain on her involvement with the Gaiety in 1921, she was able to mark the occasion by staging an entire season of his plays – Houghton's early death deprived the Manchester School of both its prime achiever and its sense of self. Worse was to follow.

By 1913, most of the Swan Club's alumni were no longer living or working in Manchester, and by travelling further afield had begun to garner for themselves some of the fame that as a collective they had brought to their home town. Chapin and Dean were running theatres in Glasgow and Liverpool respectively; Iden Payne would shortly leave England for the United States; Esmé Percy's highly successful acting career was taking in many other venues besides Manchester; and Brighouse had taken up residence in the 'hollow Mecca' of London. Houghton's death and the diaspora of Manchester's theatrical talent were heavy body-blows to the standing of the Manchester School. Another, delivered later, would be the passing from theatrical fashion of the 'curtain-raiser'; much of the best work of the Manchester dramatists is to be found in these taut, witty and quintessentially Lancastrian one-act plays, and when opportunities to see them began to disappear, the reputations of their authors suffered accordingly. But, inevitably, the *coup de grâce* was delivered by the cataclysm of the First World War.

The Swan Club membership comprised idealistic young men of fighting age: it was inevitable that the war would take a heavy toll. Of the fifteen or so regular members, Houghton died of natural causes shortly before the war began; others, Walter Burgess among them, were killed in action; and Ernest Marriott, a conscientious objector, also died, in 1918. Of those who survived the war, Charles Abercrombie died shortly afterwards, having been awarded the CMG and the DSO whilst commanding a battalion, and Gerald Cumberland died in 1927. The rest were almost all non-writers: Ben Iden Payne went on to become director of the Shakespeare Memorial Theatre at Stratford-upon-Avon between 1935 and 1942, and Basil Dean moved from theatre to film, where a successful career as a producer saw him continuing to champion the Lancastrian cause by promoting the screen career of Gracie Fields. But of the Swan Club writers, only Harold Brighouse seems to have survived into old age. Unfit for active war service, he joined the Royal Air Force Intelligence Staff, based at the War Ministry. His later work never came close to matching the success either of his early one-act plays or of *Hobson's Choice*. According to Kahane, this was because he 'began to dramatize the inhabitants of the *salons* of Mayfair, or as near as made no matter. What a calamity! as if a great *genre* painter should turn to fashionable portraiture.'[37] In Brighouse's defence, his efforts to find new subject matter were born of necessity: the First World War had not only killed a large part of Manchester's pre-war artistic community, it had also destroyed the world, lifestyles and attitudes with which its members' writing had concerned itself. The pre-1914 cultural landscape in which these writers had worked was utterly obliterated. The future was delivered not to Manchester, but to Modernism.

THE FIGHT FOR FRANCE

Before the war, Kahane's direct contact with France was limited to two or three trips to Paris, for two or three days at a time. He'd visited the Louvre, the Luxembourg Gardens and the Tuileries, he'd browsed the *bouquinistes* and dined at the Americain. He'd been a tourist. But the francophilia he'd cultivated since his schooldays, and which had fuelled his opposition to Richter's dogmatic leadership of the Hallé, was now so radicalised by the German invasion of France and Belgium that his first impulse was to enlist not for his home country but his adopted one. He went to the French Consulate and asked to join the Foreign Legion.

Kahane tells the story of this abortive mission in *Memoirs of a Booklegger*:[38] the dubious decision to wear a Savile Row suit and monocle whilst attempting to enlist in one of the world's most Spartan military units, and the bemused reaction of the wizened little Frenchman who interviews him – and who suggests that Kahane's request might be more easily expedited in, well, France. In *Memoirs of a Booklegger* this tone, self-deprecating and played for laughs, is used by Kahane to recount his entire war history – or rather, that part of his war history he is willing to share.

There's much about Kahane that is easy to dislike. As a young man he was vain, affected, and drearily evangelical about his own genius. He mistook appearance for content, noise for action, and oppositionism for achievement. Neither age nor experience did much to make him more likeable, and when he settled in France after the war he merely exchanged all his old shortcomings for new ones. But, as we shall see, during the war itself his actions were heroic, and his health, fragile even before hostilities began, was completely destroyed as a result of the injuries he sustained and the conditions in which he lived. His convalescence features strongly in *Memoirs of a Booklegger* – given that it covered ten years of his life it could hardly be overlooked – but on the reasons for the convalescence, he is silent. Just like his unhappy childhood, Kahane's war record can be pieced together. That it has to be is a mark of the man.

Kahane's determination to enlist wasn't undermined by his abortive visit to the French Consulate. He threw in his job (an action made more satisfying by the fact that his employer was German) and took the train to London on 5 August 1914, the day after Britain declared war on Germany. Myopic, stick-thin and still wearing his monocle, his approach to the Grenadier Guards met with as little success as his attempt to join the French Foreign Legion, and he was referred instead to the 2nd (City of London) Royal Fusiliers. On realising that the battalion was unlikely to see front-line action, he applied to the War Office to work as an interpreter alongside the regular troops. He passed an examination in German and French, submitted to a medical 'conducted by supercilious R. A. M. C. officers who passed me not without reluctance and crushing condescension',[39] and was made a cavalry second-lieutenant.

Kahane's determination to seek out front-line action as soon as possible was characteristic of callow new recruits. In 1918 the eighteen-year-old Ernest Hemingway enlisted to serve with the American Red Cross. Looking back in 1942 he was amazed and amused by his naivety: 'I was an awful dope when I went to the last war. I can remember just thinking we were the home team and the Austrians were the visiting team'.[40] He wasn't the only one: volunteering for service as drivers, either with an international ambulance corps or with a French unit providing military transport, was a popular option among young and idealistic Americans with no experience of soldiering. Given the nature of the work action was almost inevitable, and for those with a physical disability who were determined to enlist it was often the only option. Hemingway's poor eyesight made passing an army medical impossible, and John Dos Passos was so short-sighted it was all he could do to *locate* the eye-chart, never mind read from it. But for reasons known only to the military, near blindness wasn't seen as an obstacle to a career as an ambulance driver: Dos Passos was signed up, taught to drive, and then dispatched to Italy. There were many others: e. e. cummings, Harry Crosby, Louis Bromfield, Malcolm Cowley, Larry Barretto, Sidney Howard, Charles Nordhoff (whose book was the basis for the 1935 film *Mutiny on the Bounty*), Dashiell Hammett (enlisted, but struck down with tuberculosis before leaving for Europe), John Howard Lawson (communist, playwright, future Hollywood screenwriter and the most ideologically committed of the Hollywood Ten), Robert Hillyer, William Seabrook – many writers who would later play leading roles in the literary life of Paris during the 1920s spent the Great War defending what would become their adoptive country.

Artists already settled in Paris were also heavily involved in the war effort. Gertrude Stein had been a resident since 1903, and had lived with Alice B. Toklas since 1909. Stein was five foot one and dumpy, Toklas was four foot eleven and built like a sparrow: together they spent the war driving supply trucks for French hospitals. Edith Wharton had lived in Paris since 1907: she wrote articles about her visits to the front lines, worked for the Red Cross, and was awarded the Légion d'Honneur for her work with Belgian refugees. The incorrigibly grand *grande dame* Natalie Barney was never going to find taking orders easy, and her contribution became defiance: Barney stayed in Paris throughout the war, and continued to welcome guests to her *salon*. (Obelisk author Cyril Connolly was to make much the same proudly obstinate stand in 1939 when, just as the Second World War began, he launched the avowedly highbrow arts periodical *Horizon*.) Barney's *salon* was a romantic hot-house as much as an artistic one, and in August 1914 she issued her own idiosyncratic battle cry: 'Let's go to love the way they go to war'[41] – thereby beating the hippies to their slogan by more than half a century.

After enlisting in August, Kahane spent the next few months in full cavalry uniform, clanking around London with his spurs on upside-down. Orders to sail eventually came through, and by Christmas he was in Marseilles attached to Railway Supply, trying to memorise a book of French and English military terms he'd never heard of in either language. Geographically he was further away from the fighting than he'd been in England, but after trading places with an officer attached to the Royal Horse Artillery Kahane moved a step closer to the action. He was charged with overseeing the landing of the Jodpore Lancers, and then sent north with the Horse Artillery by rail to Lillers, finally within measurable distance of the front. He applied for an attachment to an infantry battalion, and joined the 5th Cavalry Brigade as a requisition officer: 'My duties turned out to be to buy a few pounds of potatoes every now and then and an odd bundle of hay. I have never in my life come across a more supererogatory job'.[42]

Most Great War literature condemns the betrayal of the ordinary ranks, and attacks the complacency and incompetence of officers and politicians – Kahane would later publish one of the most coruscating examples, Richard Aldington's *Death of a Hero* – and on active service he was quickly converted to the lions-led-by-donkeys point of view. He watched preparations for the Battle of Loos ('Everybody was on his toes, including the Kaiser and the High Command, who certainly knew as much about it as we did'[43]), and noticed that officers, most of whom had more titles than ability, 'spent part of the time in heavy contempt of the new troops who were to win the war for them'.[44] But although critical of the prosecution of the war, Kahane's desire to take a more active part in it remained undiminished.

He would soon get what he wished for, but before seeing the action which all but killed him he found himself involved in a minor incident involving lost money, the investigation of which generated enough paperwork to bring a less officious institution than the army to its knees. According to Kahane, he was sent ahead during final preparations for the Battle of Loos to find a suitably luxurious billet for his brigadier. When the press of troops made further progress impossible, he left his car at a crossroads to ask for advice from one of the officials directing traffic. Returning to his car, he found that a small bag containing more than four thousand francs, money relating to his duties as requisitions officer, had disappeared. Whatever the truth about the missing money, the repercussions for Kahane would be protracted and expensive. They would also have to wait. The Battle of Loos had begun.

The Battle of Loos was part of a major Allied offensive conducted on the Western Front in 1915. Badly thought out, badly prepared for, badly prosecuted, and ending in failure and carnage, it's a representative example of the murderous chaos habitually visited on troops by their officers during the Great War, a failure of leadership which has exercised poets, novelists and historians ever since. The battle was the brainchild of the French Commander-in Chief, Joseph Joffre. Haig had serious misgivings but politics prevailed, and against his better judgement he committed six divisions to 'The Big Push'. His fears proved well-founded: there were insufficient shells for the preliminary artillery offensive to be fully effective; the terrain was difficult, and was made more difficult still by the thunderstorms predicted well in advance by every weather report; the front line troops were suffering from fatigue even before the battle began, while the reserves were both out of position and new to battle. Worse still, poison gas – chlorine – was deployed for the first time, and Allied strategists made the surely predictable discovery that its effectiveness was dependent on which way the wind was blowing. More than two and a half thousand British troops became casualties of their own side's gas attack.

The Battle of Loos lasted four days and cost fifty thousand British casualties (among them Rudyard Kipling's son John, whose body was never found). If Kahane's account of his near-participation in the battle is accurate, the failure was *so* abject that it probably saved his life: neither the artillery bombardment nor the subsequent infantry push subdued the German lines sufficiently to enable the cavalry unit to which he was attached to advance. According to the version of events Kahane gives in *Memoirs of a Booklegger*, this resulted in his getting no closer to the front line than his brigade's stables. But a different story emerged later.

Having sacrificed fifty thousand British troops so as not to be rude to an ageing French general, the military top brass now immersed themselves in a meticulous examination of the circumstances surrounding the disappearance of Requisition Officer Kahane's petty cash. A court of enquiry was convened, and the evidence sifted. Kahane's testimony in his defence is less than convincing. He issued a receipt for monies received from the Field Cashier 'but did not count the money when he received it'; he was 'under the impression' that he had paid bills due to local suppliers; and '[the] omission to include the sums of francs 600 and francs 1665 received from the Cashier he attributes to forgetfulness'.[45] Further pleadings of inexperience, understaffing and overwork do little to bolster his case. Most suspicious of all is item nine in Kahane's mitigating testimony: 'That on one occasion his coat containing many papers was stolen from a car'.[46] This statement, made by Kahane under oath at a military court of enquiry, directly refutes his memoir, in which he maintains that the money is what went missing from the car, not papers. Another piece of evidence casts doubt on Kahane's contention that he spent his time at Loos on standby for battle with his cavlary unit: at the court of inquiry Kahane looked to impress upon his accusers the understandable reasons for his poor bookkeeping by reminding them that 'during the Loos attack he had no clerk and he was detached from his brigade for about 10 days to look after a coal depot at Wardrecques'.[47]

The investigation into Kahane lasted three months, and in February 1916 a report was sent by the investigating officer to the War Office in London: 'I am of opinion that the loss was due to carelessness and ignorance on the part of this officer, and I do not consider that it is desirable to bring him to trial by court martial'.[48] Instead, Kahane was ordered to pay back the money out of his own pocket. Whether it was lost as a result of bad luck, incompetence or downright criminality can now never be known. But the available evidence doesn't do Kahane any favours, and financial reliability was not to prove one of his strong points as a publisher.

Kahane had still not seen front-line action, and with the suspicion of embezzlement now surrounding him he was additionally motivated to seek yet another transfer. His next attachment, to the 1st Battalion of the Royal Fusiliers, found him a place in the trenches for the first time, trenches guaranteed to bring him the action he'd craved for so long: the trenches surrounding the Belgian city of Ypres.

It wasn't until twenty years after the end of the Great War (and only a few months before war broke out again) that Jack Kahane wrote anything about his wartime experiences, a delay which contrasts him with almost every writer who served in the conflict and survived. While others sought to understand, describe and exorcise the cataclysm through which they'd lived, Kahane spent the following two decades keeping his counsel, preferring instead to write novels in which his young and foolish characters chase each other through a prelapsarian world of champagne and chocolates and nightclubs and fun. Many possible reasons for this present themselves. One – that Kahane, not a writer of the magnitude of Hemingway or Aldington or Graves, was intimidated by the scale of the subject – explains only why Kahane never wrote a great war novel, not why he never wrote about the war at all. It's also true that Kahane, not just British but

an emotionally buttoned northerner as well, was never dispositionally suited to any kind of authorial self-disclosure. But his complete
silence on the subject is probably best explained by the fact that for
the rest of his life he lived with the war's effects on a daily basis. A
crisis is not anatomised until the crisis has passed, and while other
writers emerged from the war either physically unscathed or with
injuries from which they recovered, Kahane's health was permanently
damaged. He was never afforded a tranquility from which to recollect
his experience, and seems to have preferred to write himself out of
his own life, and into a happier, less painful world.

Kahane devotes more than a third of *Memoirs of a Booklegger* to his
wartime experiences, but only two pages to his time in the trenches.
His court case was settled by February 1916; his transfer to the Royal
Fusiliers would have placed him at Ypres shortly after. The Second
Battle of Ypres took place in the spring of 1915, the Third – Passchendaele – in the second half of 1917: the two battles respectively inflicted
sixty thousand and a quarter of a million British casualties. Although
Kahane's time in the sector fell between these two apocalyptic confla-
grations there was never a good time for a soldier to be posted to
Ypres, and when Kahane arrived in 1916 not only was there constant
skirmishing, but German forces had begun to experiment with two
new weapons: chlorine gas, and 'liquid fire' – flame-throwers.

Kahane's new posting was hell. He tells the story in his memoir,
but briefly, and sketchily. It's the wording of Kahane's preamble to
the story which tells us most about the man: 'Life in the trenches
has been described so often and so well that I shall not attempt to
emulate better writers than I. Moreover I hate the idea of describing
it. It is like exposing one's sores. It was altogether detestable from
beginning to end.' [49]

Self-deprecating, understated, emotionally reserved: Kahane was
in love with France, but he was made in Britain. This tone, dispassionate and slightly gruff, is maintained throughout his account of
the incident – the double incident – which permanently wrecked
his health, and which almost took his life. This is as much as he was
prepared to tell about what happened to him in trench H19, just off
the Menin Road:

> I sat there with a second-lieutenant who was beginning trench fever, a
> pessimistic sergeant, and about thirty men. We were bombarded with the
> utmost intensity for four hours. A shell burst almost at my feet and I had

the distinct impression of going up in the air. To my surprise I found that I was still alive. I crawled along to where the trenches branched off almost at right angles, and where a detachment of another battalion should have been. There was nobody and indeed practically no trench. I crawled back to the other flank. The same state of affairs; nobody and no trench to speak of. The adjacent landscape battered out of recognition. We were isolated and I attempted to telephone the jolly news to the rear. But the telephone wires had been blown out of existence. A nice state of affairs.[50]

A Lewis gunner keeps German troops at bay; finding continued resistance, they resume shelling:

and one drops plump in the trench and explodes. When I come to myself I find the casualties are one man hit in the tail by a sand-bag, nothing to talk about, and every tooth in my head loosened by the concussion. Two or three came out where I sat. I was trembling uncontrollably, but otherwise quite cheerful. The strafe ended. Nobody could go to a casualty station because we couldn't get there. In the evening they came up from headquarters and were quite surprised to find us all alive and trembling. We went out of the line.[51]

Kahane's deliberate filleting of any explicit emotion from his account of the shelling has a curious and moving result on his writing. The detached, journalistic tone; the short sentences; the adjectival understatement; the 'anti-climactic' climax which is all the more moving for being uninflected: for the only time in his life, Kahane sounds like Hemingway. By substituting reserve for artistry, Kahane accidentally achieves a trademark Hemingway effect: a visceral response in the reader triggered not by what is included but by what is left out.

We can be sure there was more to tell because in 1977 Kahane's son, Maurice Girodias, told it. Girodias followed his father into publishing, taking his mother's maiden name to avoid persecution during the German occupation of Paris in the Second World War. In the 1950s he founded the Olympia Press which, like Obelisk before it, published a mixture of smut and art, thereby ensuring the imprint made money as well as reputations. Olympia published Burroughs' *Naked Lunch*, Donleavy's *The Ginger Man* and Nabokov's *Lolita* in their first editions, as well as providing a living to young writers such as Alexander Trocchi and Christopher Logue, recruited by Girodias to write pseudonymous pornography. In 1977 Girodias published the first volume of his memoirs, *The Frog Prince*, in which he provides the reader with information about Ypres that Kahane had withheld:

At Ypres Jackie met at last with fear, which he had dismissed up to then as unworthy of a proud man. Fear was everywhere in that universal horror, in that blind struggle in blood and mud. First gassed, then blown up by an exploding shell, he wound up in the hospital in a pitiful state; but he was still more or less in one piece, and at least now he would be saved from front-line duty.[52]

According to Kahane he spent two months in a dental hospital in Boulogne undergoing many painful operations on his mouth and jawbone, but feeling vaguely embarrassed that he was not actually *wounded*. He doesn't mention being gassed – and at no point in *Memoirs of a Booklegger* does he refer to the tuberculosis which had troubled him since childhood and which must now have been exacerbated not just by the gas but by the freezing and sodden conditions in the trenches. Furthermore, the trembling that had started in the trenches continued, a legacy of shell-shock, or gas, or both. He would have been in a far better condition if he'd merely been wounded; as it was, his health was shattered and would never return.

Kahane was declared unfit for further service at the front. This was no hardship: his experience of combat had cured him of any desire for more, and in any case he now had a very good reason to live. After leaving the hospital at Boulogne Kahane continued to convalesce, and during that time married the girl he'd been courting for two years, a Frenchwoman called Marcelle Girodias. Marcelle had been born in Spain, and had spent most of her life outside France. She was pretty, so her brothers had to find something else to tease her with: since she was short and a little plump, they nicknamed her Trois-Pommes. Her father Léon was a prominent and wealthy engineer who'd been supervising the construction of a railway near Almeria when Marcelle was born, and his work building rail networks all over North Africa, Portugal and Argentina had kept the family constantly on the move throughout her childhood. Marcelle's high-born mother Marcelline, known as Mamita, was Spanish, but her love for France and all things French – and especially all things Parisian – was all-consuming. So, while Léon continued to work in Argentina, the children were sent back to France to be educated, dumpy little Marcelle was sent to a convent school, and by the time she graduated she had turned into a slender and elegant young woman. When Léon returned from South America he settled his family in Paris, buying a large apartment near the Champs Elysées. Marcelle had spent her childhood riding horses bareback across the Argentine pampas, and never outgrew the feelings of awkwardness and confinement which *la vie parisienne* induced in her. She was consequently delighted when, on the outbreak of war, her father moved the family once more, this time to a large villa near Marseilles.

Marcelle had met Jack in a sandy cove just outside Marseilles near the port of Cassis, shortly after Kahane's arrival in France. Both had been in the company of friends who, seeing the signs, had kept each other occupied while Jack and Marcelle walked apart. Marcelle spoke no English; Kahane, smitten and tongue-tied, found he could speak neither English nor French. A pocket dictionary had seen them through this unpromising beginning, and now, in 1917, the two were married. Kahane was a little short on prospects, especially when compared to his over-achieving father-in-law, but war was rendering prospects irrelevant. Kahane was in uniform, a volunteer defending the country that both he and the Girodias family loved, and consequently, they loved him. For the moment, shared francophilia was enough; other less compatible traits would emerge later, but were for now consigned to the background.

Although the marriage would last a lifetime, the honeymoon was short. As soon as Jack was well enough to resume duties he was made a Transportation Staff Officer attached to the Cavalry Corps Headquarters. Work was light and combat non-existent, and Kahane was able to discharge his duties fully and competently even when faintness and fatigue overtook him, which was often. Attached to the Fourth Army, he coordinated railway supply lines to the sector of the front east of Dunkirk, and while stationed there often socialised with the French and American airmen attached to the Lafayette and other squadrons. (It's probable that it was here that Kahane met the American pilot Harold Buckley, whose war memoir, *Squadron 98*, he was to publish in 1933.) From Dunkirk he was sent as part of a British and French expeditionary force to Italy, where he spent most of the rest of the war supervising the movement of troops around the entire Italian rail network. (He was briefly recalled to France in March 1918, and was in Doullens when Marshall Foch assumed command of the Allied forces on the Western front.) Kahane spent the last months of the war near the front at Piave, the sector where the eighteen-year-old Ernest Hemingway was wounded while working for the American Red Cross. Kahane took his job seriously, and the fervour with which he worked (at least, it looked fervent to his less than committed Italian counterparts) earned him the soubriquet *il pazzo capitano*, 'the Mad Captain'. His commanding officer was more respectful of his efforts: Kahane was recommended for the DSO, since '[w]ithout this officer's untiring efforts the successful concentration of the British troops on the Italian front would not have been possible'.[53] He was also mentioned in dispatches.

The armistice brought Kahane relief and joy, but not demobilisation. When peace was declared he was in the Adige valley. From there he drove to Trento, through a contraflow of defeated and starving Austrian soldiers selling their medals for scraps of food, and from Trento on to Innsbruck, where celebrations were necessarily muted since there was nothing there to celebrate *with*. On the journey north Kahane saw dog flesh being sold by the roadside at extortionate prices, and in Innsbruck itself nothing of value, nutritional or otherwise, had survived the rapacity of the retreating German army.

The logistical problems posed by the armistice meant that Kahane was now even busier than he'd been during the last phase of the war. Allied troops would shortly need transport home, and since it was Kahane's job to ensure that the Italian railway system ran on time, he was unlikely to find peacetime peaceful for a few months at least. The presence of a British battalion in an Adriatic coastal town made it necessary for Kahane to visit the region in order to assess the preparedness of the local railway network for the task that lay ahead. As a result, Kahane found himself embroiled in one of the most farcical incidents of the First World War, an episode straight out of *opera buffa* in which the leading roles were taken, fittingly, by Italy, and by one of that country's most lunatic sons.

FIUME

Thirty miles from today's north-eastern border of Italy, the Croatian name for the town, then and now, is Rijeka; the Italians called it Fiume. Part of the Habsburg Empire during the eighteenth and nineteenth centuries, Fiume was under Hungarian control before the First World War, was briefly occupied by the Italians after it, and then counter-occupied by an alliance of French, British and American troops in November 1918 to prevent Italy from laying claim to the town before its fate was decided by the Paris Peace Conference of 1919. The population of Rijeka/Fiume was mostly Croatian until the end of the nineteenth century, when Budapest started to encourage Italian immigration in order to dilute a nascent Slavic nationalism: now there were a few more Italians than Croats. Officialdom was still controlled by Hungary – although the French local command was keen to use the town as a supply depot for their eastern army, and were citing the threat posed by the Italian troops as an excuse to take control. The port itself had little room for local fishermen as it was currently providing mooring for ships from the fleets of Britain, France, Italy, and Austria. Why the Austrians were there, nobody knew.

Given the circumstances, the fact that Fiume was in need of a visit from a logistics officer was hardly surprising, and Kahane was as keen to get there as the Italians were to keep him away. The boat from Venice on which he was due to sail left deliberately early, and only lavish bribery induced the owner of a motor dinghy to speed him out to the departing steamer. When he arrived in Fiume he reported to the commanding officer of the York and Lancaster regiment, but only after a long search for the non-existent HQ. (The colonel was eventually found lodging on a commandeered liner moored in the harbour.)

Fiume was in chaos, and the chances of improving the situation were slim. Although nominally under British command, the town was being run – and overrun – by the Italians. The British troops, monoglots to a man, were unable to establish any sort of control over people with whom they couldn't communicate, and were also unable to pacify the outraged Slav community for the same reason. Since armed force against an ally was out of the question, there was no way of effectively challenging the Italian commanders' assertion that Fiume was now part of Italy. (In fact, the evidence on which the Italians based this claim – that Fiume had been promised to Italy under the terms of the London Pact, signed by the allies in 1915 – was wrong. Territories *had* been promised to Italy in return for its wartime allegiance, but while Trento, Trieste and the Dodecanese were among them, the town of Fiume was not.)

Kahane spoke French and atrocious Italian, which was enough to see him appointed Fiume's unofficial Kofi Annan:

> I was made British member of various international commissions which seemed to exist chiefly to put a brake on Italian greed. On one such commission the American member had no use for commissions, the

Frenchman, a young captain, was too bored by the business to appear and, besides, he had a very absorbing mistress, so he gave me his proxy, and the Croat was on my side; thus I had an overwhelming majority for everything I wanted to carry out.[54]

In effect, Kahane had a block vote. But while this helped to solve problems unrelated to the Italians – Kahane was able to organise the shipping of aid to starving Serbs in the north, for example – the crisis caused by the Italian garrison's claim on the town remained intractable.

It was about to get worse. Details of the London Pact – including the omission of Fiume from the list of promised territories – had been published in Russia by *Izsvestia* following the October Revolution in 1917, and when the Peace Conference got under way in Versailles in January 1919, the truth became impossible to ignore. Nationalist sentiment was not minded to admit that it had made a mistake, and instead rounded on the country's leaders for negotiating such a bad bargain. When Woodrow Wilson made a bad situation worse by retrospectively renegotiating the Pact at Versailles, removing the Dalmatian territories from the agreement, Italian nationalists looked around for someone to restore their honour and to claim for them what was rightfully (and in the case of Fiume, wrongfully) theirs.

The man they got was Gabriele d'Annunzio. A self-styled warrior-poet, d'Annunzio was born in Pescara, on the Adriatic coast, in 1863. He was extremely short, comically spindly and prematurely bald. He was also – wouldn't you know it – a disciple of Nietzsche. His first book of verse was published while he was still in his teens, and as he got older his love poetry gave way to work with a more martial twang, work which extolled the virtues of valour, conquest and love of one's country. He was hugely successful with women (it must have been the poetry) and among his many lovers were the actress Eleonora Duse, in her day second in fame only to Sarah Bernhardt, and the painter Romaine Brooks, the psychologically disturbed and mainly lesbian partner of Natalie Barney. Probably psychotic and certainly fascist, d'Annunzio stood for parliament on the Socialist ticket in 1900, before finding his natural home in the emerging Nationalist Party. At party rallies d'Annunzio's poetic flair and mesmeric oratory were powerfully combustive, and the stock of both the party and of d'Annunzio himself rose in tandem. It fell again after a disastrous war with Libya in 1911 (a war opposed by the young Benito Mussolini, at the time the editor of a socialist newspaper), and d'Annunzio, fleeing ridicule and debt, settled in Paris. He was persuaded to return to Italy in 1914: the government had signed the Pact of London, and in so doing had committed themselves to declaring war on Germany. This would be a tough sell to the Italian people, for whom the Libyan disaster was a recent and painful memory, but d'Annunzio's elephantine conceit couldn't resist his government's invitation to issue the country's call to arms. At a ceremony held near Genoa to unveil a statue to Italy's founding father, Garibaldi, d'Annunzio's messianic speech catapulted Italy into war, and this time Mussolini approved. Neutrals were quickly silenced: the leader of the Italian parliament was denounced by Mussolini as 'the foulest man ever born to the shame of Italy. I would like to put five bullets from a revolver into his stomach.' (In 1914, Italian libel laws lacked teeth.) D'Annunzio's electrifying speechmaking rallied the country around the flag, dissent was suppressed, and in May 1915 Italy entered the war.

D'Annunzio first enlisted as a cavalry officer before later switching to the air force, where as a pilot he led raids on Austrian seaports. By the end of the war he was a national hero, the recipient of more commendations and medals than his undersized tunic could carry. He was ideally placed politically to rage against Woodrow Wilson's disregard of pre-war treaties: he wrote articles for Mussolini's newspapers and spoke from balconies all over Rome, agitating for action.

When it was confirmed that under the terms of the Paris Conference Fiume would form part of the new country of Yugoslavia, Rightist agitation reached crisis point. The Italian garrison had been ordered out of the town by the Allies in September 1919 after encouraging the Italian population to riot and then standing by while shops were looted and fighting broke out. In retaliation for their expulsion Mussolini, who in March had founded the Fascist Party, visited the town and sent a very public telegram to d'Annunzio back in Rome: '[All] the great family of the Italian people supports you with impetuous faith, unending admiration and undying sympathy.'[55] Striving manfully to match Mussolini for fatuous self-importance, d'Annunzio replied: 'My thanks to you and your companions. I am ready. We are ready. All are ready.'[56]

He was ready.

Until the Italian garrison started to incite the local population, life in Fiume was relatively comfortable for Jack Kahane. There was a limit to what he could get done, but supplies and money were plentiful and Kahane's official position ensured he had plenty of both. Occasionally British troops were confined to barracks by commanding officers keen to avoid a politically embarrassing punch-up between allies, but Fiume was mostly good for Kahane. His health was fragile, he tired quickly and would often struggle to catch his breath, but both the climate and the undemanding workload were helpful in stabilising his condition. He also had a personal reason to be happy. His wife Marcelle (whom he always called Mars) had been mortally ill with Spanish influenza while Kahane was in Venice. Her two sisters had died in the same outbreak, but Marcelle pulled through, and in April 1919 she gave birth to their first child, who was named Maurice in honour of Marcelle's brother who had been killed in action on the eastern front in 1915.

In September 1919 d'Annunzio marched on Fiume. He had to march, because the trucks which were supposed to be waiting for him and his fellow mutineers at the town of Ronchi never turned up. D'Annunzio capitalised on this chaos by capitalising it, and the Ronchi March became a heroic staging post on the road to Fiume's liberation, a nifty piece of repackaging which concealed the comical cock-up that it actually was. Transport was eventually picked up in Palanovam, and D'Annunzio arrived in Fiume in an open Fiat, made straight for the Military Governor's office, and informed him that he was claiming the town for Italy. Italy begged to differ. The government denounced d'Annunzio's insurgency, Mussolini's newspapers denounced the government, and d'Annunzio let them get on with it while he dug himself in.

The allies would eventually leave it to Italy to solve the Fiume crisis on its own. But before English, French and American troops were ordered back to their respective warships, still moored in Fiume's harbour, Kahane had the opportunity to witness at first hand fascism in action. Some of the accoutrements of d'Annunzio's administration in Fiume were just so much lunatic frippery: the renaming of majors and captains as 'centurions' and 'pro-Consuls'; the daily morning speech delivered from a balcony to a crowd specially rounded up for the purpose (Mussolini was watching and learning); the attempt to govern the town using the medieval system of craftsmen's guilds. But other innovations were less easy to laugh at: the death penalty was introduced and much used, votes were rigged as a matter of course, and a personality cult was encouraged to grow around d'Annunzio who, long before the title was conferred on Mussolini, came to be known as *Il Duce*. (D'Annunzio also established one of the immutables of fascist chic by dressing his followers in black shirts.)

Kahane's love of France was long-standing and inviolate but it was intensified by his wartime experience, which confirmed him in his long-held suspicions of her European neighbours. He was disgusted by the Allied withdrawal from Fiume:

> To this day I do not understand the attitude of the British Government. It was then that began our, to me, inexplicable policy of spineless surrender to the exigencies of every country in the world except the only worth-while allies and friends we had, the French. If we had stood by the French with a fraction of the loyalty we showed to the greatest of our enemies, not the French, as our Government continuously and cravenly feared, but we ourselves should have had the hegemony of Europe, and we should have been able to dictate to the world and given it peace, as well as prosperity, for a century.
>
> Well, these are dreams, idle dreams, and, as I write this [in early 1939], we have once again bitten the dust before the Germans, having repeatedly done so to the Italians. The winged ironmonger Chamberlain is dictating to us a policy of surrender all along the line, which will not avert war, and which is swiftly paving the way to the destruction of the British Empire. I hope I am wrong.[57]

Dictating to the world and preserving the Empire are questionable aspirations, but taken all in all he wasn't wrong enough.

D'Annunzio was finally thrown out of Fiume in January 1921. Under the terms of the Treaty of Rapallo, signed the previous November, Italy and Yugoslavia had declared Fiume/Rijeka an independent state. In response, D'Annunzio demonstrated how comprehensively he had lost touch with reality by declaring war on his own country; an Italian blockade of the harbour and a few shells lobbed in the general direction of his villa were enough to bring the illegal occupation to an end. By then, Kahane and the rest of the Allied troops had long gone. He'd been withdrawn from Fiume in 1919: he'd had enough of war, enough of the army, and nowhere near enough of his pregnant wife. Determined to get himself demobilised, he secured himself a few days' leave and headed for Paris.

THE INVALID, AND THE NOVELIST

Once in Paris Kahane found that, thanks to a rather exalted old boys' network, getting himself out of the army was the work of an afternoon. The press officer for the British delegation at the Peace Conference was G. H. Mair, a former journalist at the *Manchester Guardian* and a friend of Kahane's from his Swan Club days. Mair's headquarters at the Astoria Hotel on the Champs-Elysées had a direct telephone line to the office of the Attorney General in London, and the Attorney General was Gordon Hewart, an alumnus of Manchester Grammar School. Coaxed by Mair, Kahane made the call and timorously explained his position to Hewart's private secretary. The secretary called the War Office, and when Kahane returned to Italy he found his demobilisation papers waiting for him, together with instructions from the War Office that he should be released immediately. The instructions were unignorable, personally signed as they were by the Secretary for War, Winston Churchill. (Kahane's association with Churchill was slight, but real. In 1906 Churchill stood for parliament in the constituency of Manchester North West and won; Kahane had been a voluntary helper during the campaign. Churchill lost the seat two years later to the Conservative candidate William Joynson-Hicks, who later played a perversely useful role in Kahane's life: as Home Secretary, 'Jix' became the most virulent and enthusiastic censor of the written word that Britain ever produced, and was responsible for the prosecution of many of the books, first published in England, which later found a home at the Obelisk Press.)

Kahane left the army on 15 June 1919 and never considered returning to England. On the rare occasions he thought of Manchester, it was as 'a smoky cloud hovering over my youth, that made the brightness of my present life seem still brighter'.[58] He'd married a Frenchwoman; he had a son, Maurice, now two months old and born in France; he had parents-in-law who had lost three of their four children during the war and who were understandably keen to keep their only surviving child close by. He considered his options, but the decision was an easy one: accepting the invitation of his in-laws, Kahane moved his family in to Léon and Mamita's apartment on the Avenue du Bois de Boulogne (now the Avenue Foch) in the sixteenth arrondissement of Paris.

The Avenue du Bois was (and is) one of the most expensive residential streets in the French capital. More than a hundred metres across and lined with wide tree-lined boulevards, the Avenue runs between the Arc de Triomphe and the Bois de Boulogne on the western edge of the city. Home in 1919 to aristocrats, millionaires and an invigorating sprinkling of *demi-mondaines*, its 'apartments' are not the one-bedroom boxes the word usually describes, but the kind of palatial single-storey spreads to be found on London's Park Lane or Manhattan's Fifth Avenue. The address bears witness to Léon's wealth and standing, and the dandyism Kahane had cultivated in Manchester to make himself stand out was now deployed in the Avenue du Bois to make sure he fitted in.

Kahane had married for love, but the fact that he had at the same time married into a family of wealth and reputation had escaped the attention of nobody. In 1915, no one in uniform and about to see action at the front could seriously claim to have prospects, but Kahane had nonetheless managed to charm Léon into approving of the marriage to his daughter. Now that he'd survived Kahane knew there was an unspoken bargain to be kept, and he set about keeping it. The first opportunity to come his way after leaving the army must have reassured Léon that his confidence in his son-in-law had not been misplaced.

The future of Fiume had been all but decided at the Peace Conference: it would form part of the new country of Yugoslavia. But although d'Annunzio continued to be an embarrassment to the Italian government nationalist opinion at home was hardening, and Italy's leaders were under pressure to secure a settlement in Paris which saw Fiume recognised as Italian territory. Since this was unlikely to come about as a result of direct negotiation, pro-Italian agencies were keen to find someone, known and trusted by all parties, who could broker a back-door deal. As a result, Kahane's breakfast was interrupted one morning by a pro-Italian Slav called Ossionach.

Whoever had the idea for the scheme Ossionach proposed had almost certainly overestimated the influence Kahane could exert, but the approach did much to improve his standing in the eyes of his father-in-law, especially when the details of the proposal were made clear. Italy, said Ossionach, proposed to 'buy' Fiume from the new Yugoslav government. Kahane's job would be to convey this fact to the Serbian delegation at the Peace Conference, and let it be known that in return for Fiume Italy would not only relinquish its claim on Spalato (now Split), but would also finance the building of a new port for the city. Kahane's reward for brokering the deal would be the concession for the port's construction. The idea was ridiculous and doomed to fail, but Kahane realised that other people's over-estimation of his status was playing well with his father-in-law, and so he spent the next two months attempting to wield an influence he didn't have at a succession of meetings set up for him by Mair, his contact at the Peace Conference. Inevitably, the project came to nothing, but private appointments (albeit fruitless ones) with statesmen of the magnitude of Lloyd George and Woodrow Wilson at least served to consolidate Kahane's standing in his own house-hold. His father-in-law was also impressed by his business expertise, which after many years Kahane now redeployed to take advantage of the huge trade in surplus goods that came to be centred around Paris immediately after the war – especially the trade in coal, British stocks of which Kahane sold to the coal-strapped French through a company he set up with two other newly demobilised officers which they ran from an office on the Avenue de l'Opéra.

Newly married and now a father, Kahane's energetic attempts to establish himself as a man of means are understandable, but it was inevitable that such exertions would soon expose the fragility of his health. He complained of feeling constantly tired, and Marcelle insisted he should see a specialist. Tuberculosis was diagnosed in his one remaining lung; fresh air and complete rest were prescribed. Paris, he was told, would kill him. After only a few months of living in the city he'd loved from a distance all his life, Jack and Marcelle left Maurice in the care of his grandparents, and travelled to the Auvergne in search of a cure for a disease that would not be curable in Kahane's lifetime.

Kahane's stay at the Durtol sanatorium, in the Auvergne, stretched to five months, and Marcelle remained with him throughout his treat-ment. By December 1920 his condition had been stabilised, and he was discharged on the understanding that his future well-being would depend on the length and quality of his convalescence at home.

The length of Kahane's confinement at Durtol had impressed upon the family the severity of his illness, and it was clear that Paris would provide neither the air nor the peace that a recovering tuber-cular would need. A move away from the capital was essential, but it would also be necessary to stay within a commutable distance so that Jack could restart his Paris business interests when his health allowed. Seriously ill and unable to earn a living, Kahane once again found himself dependent on his father-in-law's money.

Chateau du Fond des Fôrets is a twenty-room mansion set in thirty acres of wooded and landscaped grounds, forty miles from the centre of Paris, and situated less than a mile outside Acy-en-Multien, 'a village ten centuries old, which comprised a hundred or so gray stone houses and a few farms scattered along a street of worn cobble-stones. In the twelfth century, Thomas a Becket built the church that still stands there and made the town notorious.'[59] A period of calm, quiet stability began. Set back from the road and surrounded by woods, the estate perfectly suited the needs of the young couple – and Jack's needs in particular. He took a back room for his study, and chaises longues were placed strategically through the house , and outside too when the weather permitted, so that he could read or rest whenever and wherever he chose. Maurice, two years old when the family moved in, found himself the sole proprietor of twenty acres of jungly playground, and Marcelle, as well as having her parents on hand, had staff to tend to the day-to-day upkeep of the house, leaving her with time to indulge her love of painting and to tend to her husband. A maid was employed indoors, a gardener tended the grounds, and an odd-job man was employed to run errands and carry out repairs.

Money wasn't a problem, time passed slowly and without incident, and Kahane gradually regained some of his health – although his outlook was slower to improve. Infirm and reliant on the kindness of others, his situation offended against his view of himself both as family breadwinner and as man about town, and although he had never been short of money-making ideas, his current circumstances limited his options. Early in 1920 Kahane had signed with the literary agent Eric Pinker, based in England, to whom Kahane had sent a few short stories in the hope that Pinker could place them with one of the many light fiction magazines so popular at the time: *Pan, Woman, Passing Show, The Wheatsheaf, Hutchinson's Magazine.* None of his submissions had been published, but in 1922 Kahane wondered again if he might be able to make some sort of living from his pen – although he worried about his literary as well as his physical stamina: 'To write a whole long novel seemed to me a task impossible of achievement, but as there was nothing in the world of a more active nature that I was allowed to attempt I at last decided to begin. Much to my surprise the task turned out to be easier of physical accomplishment than I could have imagined.'[60]

At the sanatorium, Kahane had passed his days by reading light – very light – French novels, one after the other, and had developed something of an addiction to them. The books' plots were virtually interchangeable: all of them featured beautiful girls, fearsome mothers, and handsome but disreputable young men looking to woo the former while avoiding the latter. Kahane loved the genre, its characters and milieux, but what particularly attracted him to the books was their uniquely French flavour.

The nearest contemporary English equivalent was the work of P. G. Wodehouse. Set in an identical social stratum to their French counterparts, Wodehouse's novels feature the same would-be wooers of elegant debs, not overly blessed with brains but socially presentable, who will be independently wealthy just as soon as mama sees sense about the trust fund. In the world according to Wodehouse, men chase women in order to please themselves, to please relatives, to secure their place in society, or to escape the nagging of a termagant aunt, and the complications caused by the courtship – drunken disorderliness in flower beds, the hurling of flowerpots in the middle of the night, the close proximity of pigs – are legion and hilarious. But while the sex war provides the fuel for most of Wodehouse's plots, sex itself never, ever, raises its head. Wodehouse's books are as irremediably virginal as Bertie's Aunt Agatha. In their French counterparts, however, the sexual attraction between the characters is overt, and although the books aren't explicit in their depiction of sex they freely acknowledge its existence, including its existence outside marriage. Young unmarried characters are left at the bedroom door at the end of a chapter, but at the beginning of the next they're found still together, happily sharing breakfast in bed. No tragedy befalls them, no one commits suicide, a happy ending is assured. Stuffy, repressed old England had no equivalent, and it was a gap in the market which Kahane resolved to address. In May 1922 he sketched out the plot of a novel, a novel in the French style. Light, risqué and humorous, it concerned itself with the French attitude to courtship and love, and sex and fidelity, but seen through the eyes of an English protagonist. Kahane felt there was a good chance that an English readership would fall in love with this sort of novel just as he had done. All he had to do was a) write one, and b) find an English company willing to take the risk of publishing it.

He lay on his chaise longue and worked all summer on his manuscript, giving it the provisional title of *Mado VIII* ('Mado' is the French diminutive for Madeleine). Using for his plot a lightly fiction-alised version of his own business dealings immediately after the war, Kahane created as his hero (named, oddly enough, Hemingway) a callow, slightly Woosterish young man about town, a would-be businessman looking to make enough money to establish his independence from his overbearing mother and the trust fund she administers, the contents of which only become his when he marries. The heroine, Joan Remington, is a girl from Manchester whom Hemingway meets on the train back to France following an abortive business trip to England. He's an English man about town living in Paris, she's a wide-eyed ingénue looking to broaden her horizons while retaining her virginity, and as the couple eat, drink, and dance their way around the fleshpots of Paris, Hemingway becomes increas-ingly besotted with the Lancastrian beauty whose mind is so open but whose legs remain closed. In return for the thrilling introduc-tion to Paris he gives her, Joan helps Hemingway in his latest business venture, hitherto doomed to failure. As a result of her intervention it succeeds handsomely, love blooms, and matters, you will be unsur-prised to learn, end blissfully for all parties.

It's not *Ulysses* (published that year, forty miles away in Paris), but it wasn't supposed to be. Confounding his own expectations, Kahane had succeeded in getting down on paper by September exactly the sort of book he'd envisaged writing in May: a fast, bubbly, slightly sexy love story featuring rascals and temptresses, dowagers and million-aires, innocents and rogues, the whole set in the most romantic city on earth, and seen through the eyes of an Englishman abroad. The book's style aspires to the dry, linguistically inventive hilarity of Wodehouse; that it doesn't scale those heights is no disgrace. The prose is funny, fluent and pacey, the characterisation is vivid, and the whole book is suffused with a sensuousness that makes both Paris and the lovers irresistible: no business meeting takes place without the shucking of oysters and the slurping of Pouilly, frantic dancing is topped and tailed by the opening of champagne, pretty girls answer their doors in peignoirs and their telephones in nothing at all, and everyone dresses for dinner and lives in hotels. Whether as a result of the focused concentration or the sexual frustration that prolonged infirmity brings, Kahane's first attempt at writing a saucy French novel had turned out rather well.

The search for a publisher turned out well, too. The only one with whom Kahane had ever had any contact was Grant Richards: the two men had once been introduced by Gerald Cumberland, whose memoir *Set Down In Malice* had been published by Richards in 1919 to great success. Richards was also the publisher of Kahane's old friend, Harold Brighouse. In early September Kahane sent *Mado VIII* to Brighouse, who was sufficiently impressed to recommend the manuscript to Richards. Richards wrote to Kahane in October offering to publish the book, and Kahane wrote back immediately to accept. Publication was scheduled for early the following year.

Kahane couldn't believe his luck, and he became puppyishly keen to please his new publisher. Told that the title *Mado VIII* was unlikely to sell many books he offered up endless alternatives – all of which were so hopeless that Richards eventually had to impose a title of his own, *Laugh and Grow Rich*. Kahane agreed to cuts to his manuscript so as not to offend the supposedly delicate sensibilities of the British reading public. He sent examples of his wife's artwork to Richards in the hope of landing her the contract for the dustwrapper design. (Richards declined.) Short stories began arriving at Richards' office, accompanied by notes from Kahane wondering if a collection of them might be worth publishing alongside the novel; Richards, having read them, advised Kahane to give his novel a clear run.

By the beginning of 1923 Kahane's health had improved as dramatically as his prospects. Publication of *Laugh and Grow Rich* was scheduled for March. At the time Kahane was travelling with his wife and in-laws in Spain, where Léon was to be awarded the the Grand Cross of the Order of Isabella the Catholic, the highest decoration available to non-Spaniards, for his work on a recently completed scheme to irrigate the Alicante valley. The family spent weeks being ushered from banquet to banquet, fêted by business moguls, cabinet ministers and royalty at every turn. Kahane the social climber relished the treatment lavished on them by the Spanish government; Kahane the underachiever knew that the fuss being made was not in his honour, and that the modest triumph of having his first book published was being comprehensively upstaged by a father-in-law who had never fully accepted him into the family.

Kahane's relationship with his French family was always marked by a sense of dislocation. Later, when he was running the Obelisk Press and spending most of his time alone in Paris, the dislocation would be of his own making, but he felt an outsider at home long before he willingly assumed the role. He felt the estrangement from his son Maurice most keenly. Kahane had been confined to Durtol sanatorium when Maurice was still a babe in arms, and even after his return he was almost always too ill to play with his young son. As Maurice grew, the child continued to prefer either his own company, exploring the grounds around the house, or the company of his more active, doting grandparents. His father's inert presence he found disconcerting:

> Coming back from my peregrinations, I sometimes come across the recumbent form of my father, like a horizon of gray hillocks... In the sharp autumn wind, buried under a mound of blankets, he dozes. In spring or summer, I see him propped up on pillows, reading. He must be extremely feeble. Sometimes our glances cross, but it's difficult to talk to him, for some reason that escapes us both.[61]

Kahane's feeling of apartness from his family extended to its adult members, too. His renunciation of his birthplace in favour of his life in France was near-total, but one intractable legacy of his Lancastrianism was his down-to-earth attitude to matters of the head, heart and soul, an attitude which ensured that he was constantly at odds with the Girodias family's susceptibility to vaguely alternative lifestyles. Spiritualism, vegetarianism, the writings of Madame Blavatsky: at one time or another Kahane found himself diverted from his evening meal of meat and two veg to inveigh against them all, a lone voice ranged against his entire family. Honour satisfied by these occasional supper-table rows, an uneasy peace would settle once more. But the Girodias mystical streak was at its most divisive when directed at baby Maurice, about whose name there was a deeper, if unspoken, froideur.

Maurice had been so named in honour of Marcelle's brother, killed at the front in 1915. A veteran of the war himself and a man who subsequently showed himself always prepared to assist a living old soldier or to honour a dead one, Kahane was more than happy to commemorate his dead brother-in-law in the christening of his first child. But for Marcelle's parents, who had seen their tally of children dwindle from four to one in the space of three years, the naming of little Maurice had a deeper significance: 'Mamita had no doubt that

[Maurice's] birth was the spirits' answer to her entreaties: Her son had been given back to her in the form of a grandson.'[62] This belief was held with varying degrees of conviction by the Girodias family members: for Mamita, it was a literal truth; for Léon, a fancy in which he was prepared to indulge his wife; Marcelle was prepared to admit the possibility in order to deaden the pain of the loss not only of Maurice but of her sisters as well.

Mindful of Kahane's implacable hostility to the idea, this corrosive piece of family lore was rarely mentioned, but it was faithfully adhered to, and the silence of the conspiracy made Kahane feel it all the more keenly. Maurice's preference for his grandfather's more active and playful company over the faltering attempts to engage the child made by his prone, wheezing, and frightening-looking father compounded Kahane's feelings of alienation from his son. Maurice, Kahane always felt, had been successfully recruited into the ranks of the credulous enemy.

In the 1920s, Grant Richards regularly took paid space in the *Times Literary Supplement* to publicise his list. The column was a light-hearted mix of shop talk, score-settling with critics and fellow publishers, and plugs for Richards' forthcoming publications. Richards recouped his outlay on the column from his authors, who had the cost of advertising their books in it deducted from their royalties. Kahane's first mention came in the edition of 8 March 1923, a week before the publication of *Laugh and Grow Rich*. The puff cost him eight shillings, and ran, in its entirety:

> Next week we hope to publish three books differing in character about as widely as is possible: Rachel Annand Taylor's 'Aspects of the Italian Renaissance' (12s. 6d.), with an introduction by Professor Gilbert Murray; a first novel, 'Laugh and Grow Rich' (7s. 6d.) by Jack Kahane; and 'Horse Racing for Beginners', by Geoffrey Gilbey (9d.).[63]

The following week, the day of publication, Richards was more effusive:

> Special interest is always taken in first novels, and I confess to building confidently on the future of the first novel that I am publishing today – Jack Kahane's 'Laugh and Grow Rich' (7s. 6d.). A well known bookseller, whom I have quoted on more than one occasion, writes: 'You have a winner in "Laugh and Grow Rich". It's the most piquant, startling, and amusing novel I've read for a long time.'[64]

Bigger mention, bigger bill: Kahane was charged £1 17s 6d for that one. But nothing could dampen Kahane's excitement at receiving his six copies of his first novel: not the number of misprints, nor the dustwrapper design (which he detested), nor the advertising costs, which meant that he was currently losing money on his book rather than making it. He was thrilled regardless:

> [The] book was there, it existed, my name was on the dust-jacket, on the cover, on the title-page. No, there's no doubt about it, of all the pleasures the forgiving godhead has granted undeserving mortals, the first book is surely amongst the purest and most exquisite.
>
> I was a writer, I was a novelist. I looked at myself in a mirror to see if my aspect had not somehow changed. I even caressed my pipe that had now become one of the appurtenances of 'a literary man'. And I sat down to await the 'criticisms' that would soon be flocking in.[65]

They didn't flock, but at least they trickled. In the same edition of the *Times Literary Supplement* that announced the book's publication, Kahane received his first review. The highbrow readership of the *TLS* was not Kahane's target audience, and the anonymous reviewer gives the impression of being a little insulted at having had something so lightweight placed before him. The review, while not completely damning, found Kahane's hero insipid: '[In] spite of the airs he gives himself, as a stylist in the art of love, over the merely sensual man, [he] does not by his actions or his conversation very sharply distinguish himself from the ordinary adventurer.'[66] Kahane's confidence took another blow when *Laugh and Grow Rich* went unmentioned in Richards' *TLS* column the following week. He wrote to his publisher to ask him if he should read anything into the omission, and wrote on the notepaper of the Chatham Bar and Grill-Room in Paris, a choice of stationery that may have been meant to suggest an air of offhand, leisured inquiry. But the desperation that lay behind the letter's composition was clear. Kahane had done the rounds of the English-language bookshops in Paris, and couldn't find himself anywhere. Why, Kahane asked, had Smith's and Brentano's not been supplied with copies of the book?

His correspondence at this time shows that all of Kahane's worries – the absence of reviews and the negativity of the first one; the lack of gushing phone calls and telegrams from his publisher; the apparent indifference of both the book trade and the reading public to the work Kahane had set before them – were the worries of the novice.

Kahane was unused to the workings of the publishing world. He wanted success and adulation, and he wanted it now. In his answering letters, the length and reassuring tone of which must have done much to calm Kahane's fears, Richards emphasised to his client that his confidence in the book remained high, that reviews always take a little time to appear (especially for first books) and that his column in the *TLS* would of course be plugging *Laugh and Grow Rich* in the future, when 'there is a special peg to hang things on... Reviews have hardly begun to come in yet; they always provide pegs... You say that you do hope that I have not backed a loser. Do not let any idea of that kind come into your head. It is not likely to be necessary. It is not worth while being nervous in that way. Especially nowadays it takes a book by a new writer a little while to get known, unless there is in it some special "news" interest which commands immediate attention in the papers.'[67]

In fact, such 'news' was to be found further on in Richards' letter. Kahane read that the Association of Circulating Libraries – among them the two most important non-retail outlets for new books, Boot's and W. H. Smith – had banned *Laugh and Grow Rich* as unsuitable for their readers. The news struck Kahane as calamitous, and what appalled him still more was his publisher's apparent equanimity in the face of it. Kahane had yet to learn the lesson that would later be the making of his own publishing career: that the publicly expressed outrage of prudes when confronted by 'immorality' is the best publicity a book can hope for. Richards had learned the lesson a long time before, and from now on whenever he plugged *Laugh and Grow Rich* in his *TLS* column he was always careful to mention its banned status. Richards hoped to fashion a scandalous reputation for the novel by exploiting both the publicity that had been given it by the Boot's and Smith's ban, and the laudatory notices that were beginning to appear in the press:

> 'For a first novel,' the *Sunday Times* says, 'it must be ranked high. It is very daring and very amusing. There are moments when you fear that a slight lapse of taste is about to be shown, but Mr Kahane slides very neatly over the thinnest of ice... The writing is good.' The *Glasgow Evening News* calls it 'a vivacious comedy on the French model. It is frank and free, indeed...Mr Kahane's writing sparkles like champagne.'[68]

Kahane had left France for Spain with the discouraging words of the *TLS* review – the only review the novel had received – ringing in his ears. He returned to discover that *Laugh and Grow Rich* had turned into a public and critical success, that a second English edition was being prepared together with a first American edition, and that his publisher was keen to receive the manuscript of his second novel as soon as possible so that he could capitalise on the publicity generated by the first. Revived, Kahane set to work.

When the manuscript for *Love's Wild Geese* arrived at Grant Richards' office in October 1923 the relationship between Richards and Kahane was thriving. Kahane himself was happy, in comparatively good health and optimistic about the future: in August Marcelle had given birth to their first daughter, Nicole. In the same month *Laugh and Grow Rich* had gone into a second printing in England, an American edition had been published by Brentano's, and Kahane had received his first royalty cheque. It was a very small royalty cheque, but Kahane was undeterred: 'Never mind, I was a writer, a literary man, about whom already clung a faint flavour, a faintly Byronic flavour, of immorality'.[69]

A couple of minor problems persisted. Kahane's hopelessness with titles had led Richards himself to christen *Laugh and Grow Rich*, and his client's attempts for the new book were no better: offerings such as *There and Back*, *The Ills We Have* and *Sweeter Unpossessed* were understandably rejected as 'treacly'.[70] Eventually, unable to stomach any more of Kahane's suggestions, Richards called a halt to the correspondence and informed his author that his new book would be called *Love's Wild Geese*. As well as terrible titles, Kahane was also bombarding Richards with designs for the book's dustwrapper drawn by his wife, Marcelle: they met with an equally unfavourable response. But for Richards these were minor irritations caused him by a new and enthusiastic writer whose first novel had created a small but encouraging stir among readers on both sides of the Atlantic, and who had now delivered a second which came with a ringing endorsement from Kahane's friend Gerald Cumberland, who had urged Richards to send it to the printer at once, sight unseen. At the end of October Richards took the proofs with him to the United States, intending to read them for his own pleasure during the boat trip and then to pass them on to an expectant Brentano's on his arrival.

But neither Richards nor Brentano's was enthusiastic: 'Grant Richards wrote to me that it was a pity I hadn't pursued the vein of my first book, and the American publisher accused me of trying to get away with an old manuscript that I had fished out from the back of my desk'.[71] *Love's Wild Geese* is the leaden story of two lovers from contrasting backgrounds, one infused with the carefree cosmopolitanism of Paris, the other with the dourly practical outlook of Manchester, in which Kahane casts himself in the lead role, that of the successful Manchester playwright he never managed to become in real life. As a piece of autobiographical revisionism it's fitfully interesting (at least, to me...), but as a novel it's relentless, oppressive and dull – everything *Laugh and Grow Rich* wasn't. In his memoir Kahane says that he had 'attempted to write a serious comedy with even a tragic undertone'.[72] I have no idea what one of those is, and neither did Brentano's who, like all other American publishers approached by Richards, turned the book down. The critical response was negligible, and although the book seems to have limped into a second impression, it was on every level a comprehensive failure.

It would take a change of name to resurrect Kahane's literary career, and that wouldn't come until 1928. For the next four years he tried to win back the readership he had started to build with *Laugh and Grow Rich*, and which he had lost so comprehensively with *Love's Wild Geese*, but it was a readership unwilling to give him a second chance. In January 1925 Grant Richards published Kahane's third novel, *The Gay Intrigue*. It was a return to the style of *Laugh and Grow Rich*, and on the day of its publication Richards talked up the book in his regular column in the *Times Literary Supplement*:

> Do my readers remember that spirited and intriguing novel 'Laugh and Grow Rich' by Jack Kahane (7s 6d)? Jack Kahane was a discovery, 'a master of laughter', the *Sketch* said. It was right. 'Laugh and Grow Rich' has amused hundreds of thousands in England, in America and Australia. Well, Jack Kahane has written another book in the same vein, 'The Gay Intrigue' (7s 6d), which is destined, unless I am much mistaken, to repeat the success of its predecessor.[73]

He was much mistaken: by the end of 1925, only 840 copies of *The Gay Intrigue* had been sold in the UK, at 7/6 each, and the sales figure for the whole of 1926 was eight. Richards managed to sell most of the remaining copies in the colonies, but two years after publication some 800 copies remained unsold, and a second printing was never needed. The wrapper was designed by Marcelle Kahane. The four guineas Richards paid her for her work upped the Kahane household's total revenue from *The Gay Intrigue* to just under £87.

In 1925, in circumstances entirely unrelated to Kahane's sales figures, Grant Richards went bust, and Kahane's agent Eric Pinker (who, given Kahane's literary stock at the time, must have been a very fine agent indeed) managed to secure for his client a three-book deal with Constable. Unfortunately, Kahane's first submission to them was enough to convince Constable that one would be ample. Kahane finished *The Vain Serenade* in March 1925. He was proud of the book and the new, more sober direction his writing had taken, and Brighouse had been full of praise when shown the early chapters, set in Salford. After the failure of *The Gay Intrigue* Kahane was keen to secure publication as soon as possible : 'I venture to say that [*The Vain Serenade*] will be an immense advance on the others. I have really no hesitation in asserting that it is a "sitter".'[74] Fourteen years later Kahane had no hesitation in asserting that *The Vain Serenade* (which he manages to avoid mentioning by name) 'turned out so serious that it was my dullest to date'.[75] The manuscript was delivered in May 1925; Constable's reader at the time was the novelist and bibliographer Michael Sadleir. His opinion of *The Vain Serenade* in 1925 was the opinion which Kahane arrived at in 1939, and publication was delayed while Constable suggested changes, and Kahane resisted them. A date of January 1926 was eventually agreed, but Kahane was unhappy with the delay (occasioned as much by a strike in the book industry as by Constable's foot-dragging). He was also frustrated by his publisher's understandable reluctance to publish anything and everything he threw at them: 'It doesn't look as though [Constable] will be willing to publish more than one of my novels a year. My production is greater than this. What about publishing under a pseudonym? I have a plan for a novel that I would as soon publish in this manner.'[76] The planned book was *Suzy Falls Off*, and would become the first of his 'Cecil Barr' novels.

The General Strike delayed publication still further, but *The Vain Serenade* finally appeared in February 1926 – and flopped horribly. Kahane had been paid an advance of £150 by Constable, but by June the book had managed to recoup only a third of it.

By now Kahane's largest readership was that of the light fiction magazines he had been supplying with short stories since 1924. The work wasn't regular (only ten of Kahane's stories seem ever to have been published, and those over a four-year period) but the money was crucial, as royalties from Kahane's novels were now almost non-existent. His next novel, *The Pure in Heart*, was completed in 1926, but publication again was held up while agent and author quibbled over changes. (The book eventually limped into print, published by Brentano's, in 1928. Nobody noticed.) Kahane had lost interest in *The Pure in Heart* as soon as it was completed (if not sooner), and had no desire to return to it. By the time Pinker wrote to him in June 1926 to tell him that *The Pure in Heart* was so bad as to be unpublishable, Kahane had moved on to *Suzy Falls Off*, the book that would not only revive his career as a novelist, but would also later kickstart his career as a publisher.

PARIS, AND PUBLISHING

As its title suggests, *Suzy Falls Off* returns to the landscape Kahane created so effectively in his first novel, *Laugh and Grow Rich*. It had taken him five years to admit to himself that the only thing he could write that anyone wanted to read was inconsequential froth, and it was a truth which hurt him for the rest of his life – although the money such writing brought in eased the pain for a while.

Kahane had originally planned to publish *Suzy Falls Off* pseudonymously so that he could push out more than the one book a year Constable were prepared to publish. It may also have been in the back of his mind that *The Gay Intrigue*, a book in the same light vein as *Laugh and Grow Rich* and *Suzy Falls Off*, had sunk like a stone three years earlier, probably because it was by the same writer who had only recently foisted on the world the turgid *Love's Wild Geese*. A 'new' author was needed. By 1928 both Kahane's health and prospects had improved sufficiently to allow him to be spending much of his time in Paris on business, where one of his favourite meeting places was the bar of the Cecil hotel. Later that year the English publisher John Long published *Suzy Falls Off*, by Cecil Barr, a sub-*Candide* romp in which Suzy, an innocent broad abroad, ends up with the right man in the end despite the best efforts of every other character in the book. It's silly, mildly saucy and instantly forgettable, but it quickly sold both to a British readership and an American publisher, as a result of which Kahane resolved to write nothing *but* silly, mildly saucy and instantly forgettable books in future.

This resolution was shored up later that year by a chance meeting between Kahane and a man called Henri Babou, a short, well-groomed Frenchman with a goatee beard and a thick Southern accent. Babou was a publisher of *éditions de luxe*, coffee-table art books much in vogue at the time. Kahane spent the luncheon party at which the two men met nodding politely as he pretended to listen to Babou's explanation of the *pochoir* method of colour reproduction, all the while wondering how he could get Babou down to Fond des Fôrets and persuade him to publish Marcelle's latest art project, an illustrated edition of the *Song of Solomon*. Although the meeting did take place, nothing came of the idea – but a new one presented itself. At the time, Babou was three books into a series entitled *Les Artistes du Livre* which celebrated the work of French book illustrators. The text was in French, but Kahane suggested that, translated into English, the books were as likely to sell to English and American coffee-table owners as French ones. Babou agreed, and so did Lowell Brentano, who was then running the publishing wing of the New York-based bookstore, but neither was prepared to sink money into the venture. Kahane considered his options. Tired of writing novels that no one wanted to read, and by now the father of four children (Sylvie and Eric had been born in 1924 and 1926, respectively), Kahane needed to make some money, something he was likelier to do as a businessman than a novelist. He offered to buy into Babou's business and supervise the production of the English-language version of the series, providing the translations himself. Babou was willing, but his price was high: three hundred thousand francs (ninety thousand pounds today). It was beyond the means of Kahane – but not of his father-in-law, who had witnessed Kahane's business dealings immediately after the war, and who had been sufficiently impressed then to come to his son-in-law's aid now. The deal was struck, and Kahane became a publisher.

Kahane the *littérateur* arrived in Paris in 1929, a comparative latecomer. But although the 1920s marked the zenith of expatriate productivity, the role of Paris as crucible for emerging social, artistic and literary movements in the twentieth century extended well before and after that decade. Gertrude Stein was one of the earliest colonists, arriving from the United States in 1902 with her brother Leo, who bought his first Cézanne the following year. Picasso moved to Paris in 1904, and in 1905 the Steins bought their first painting from him, as well as their first Matisse. The Steins and the Matisses and Picasso began to socialise, the artists brought their artist friends to meet their new patrons, and in an attempt to reclaim their home from the painters and sculptors and hangers-on who were by now to be found in it at all hours of the day and night, the Steins declared open house every Saturday evening, and every Saturday evening *only*. Alice Toklas moved in with Gertrude in 1907, Leo moved out, and this odd and touchingly devoted couple maintained the Saturday night *salon* at their home, 27 rue de Fleurus, for the next 31 years. The *salon* provided a meeting place mostly for painters (Picasso, Matisse, Gris) before the war, and mostly for writers (Hemingway, Sherwood Anderson, Scott Fitzgerald) after it, and became one of the most important cultural hot-houses of the twentieth century.

Another early arrival, also American, was Natalie Barney. Already in her twenties at the beginning of the century, Barney had been making full and frequent use of the romantic possibilities of Paris for some time when, in 1915, she met and fell in love with the painter Romaine Brooks. Their relationship was less than conventionally conducted and more than conventionally successful. Rich as Croesus, evangelically lesbian and unfamiliar with the concept of monogamy, Barney published the occasional book of epigrams, verse, or memoirs over the years, but knew that her real talent lay in her ability to make things happen for others: an introduction here, an encouragement (financial or otherwise) there. She founded a *salon* at her home at 20, rue Jacob in October, 1909. Predictably it was sapphically skewed, though it did admit men in numbers small enough to ensure they didn't dominate proceedings. The *salon* convened every Friday from four in the afternoon to eight in the evening, and provided lesbian writers and artists with a meeting place where their lifestyle was accepted and their work encouraged. Radclyffe Hall and her lover Una, Lady Troubridge were close friends and regular visitors, and Barney would later appear as Valerie Seymour, the doyenne of Parisian lesbian life, in *The Well of Loneliness*, Hall's relentlessly gloomy and primly sexless account of the persecution suffered by 'inverts', a novel that Kahane would later publish in Paris following its suppression in England.

The novelist Djuna Barnes always objected to being described as homosexual – 'I was never a lesbian', she would protest, 'I only loved Thelma Wood'[77] – but was in attendance at the rue Jacob often enough to enable her to publish *Ladies Almanack* in 1928, a bawdy satire in which all the regular guests at Barney's *salon* make barely disguised appearances. Barney herself appears as Dame Evangeline Musset, the indomitable and insatiable hostess; Janet Flanner, who under the pen-name Genêt wrote a regular letter from Paris for *The New Yorker* from 1925, and her lover, the novelist Solita Solano, appear as two journalists, Nip and Tuck; Radclyffe Hall was Tilly Tweed-in-Blood; Romaine Brooks was rechristened Cynic Sal, and given a whip to brandish; and a long-term lover of Natalie's, the ineffably aristocratic Elisabeth de Gramont, Duchesse de Clermont-Tonnere, had to get used to being called the Duchesse Clitoressa de Natescourt when her back was turned (and sometimes when it wasn't).

By the 1920s Barney's *salon* was a firm fixture in the cultural, social and sexual life of expatriate literary Paris: every Friday afternoon at 20, rue Jacob, writers met publishers and translators, artists met patrons, lovers met each other. And despite Natalie's almost ideological adultery, her relationship with the love of her life, Romaine Brooks, endured. Brooks had suffered an apocalyptic childhood: absent father, dead sister, mad brother, madder mother and a generous smattering of family suicides had all but destroyed in her any capacity for trust or happiness. The unsurprising result was an adult incapable of functioning socially, content only in solitude or the company of Natalie alone. Natalie's weekly gatherings of friends, lovers and hangers-on without number gave her ample cause both for anxiety and jealousy. The *soirées* were purgatory for Romaine, who avoided them whenever she could and was a stormy, unpredictable presence when she couldn't. But the two women were still a couple when Romaine Brooks died in 1970, at the age of 96, and the last convening of Natalie's *salon* took place on Friday, 3 February 1972. It met beside her grave. She had died two days before; she too was 96.

But the *salon* responsible for the most significant contribution to literary history wasn't really a *salon* at all. It was a bookshop. Sylvia Beach had arrived in Paris in 1916. A small, unassuming, birdlike woman, Beach had no literary talent herself but was determined to be of use to those who did. In 1919 she opened an English-language bookshop, Shakespeare and Company, on the rue Dupuytren, a trickle of a street set back from the Boulevard Saint-Michel. (The shop later moved round the corner to its more famous final address, 12, rue de l'Odéon). Beach soon realised that the thirst for books of many of her potential customers outstripped their ability to pay for them, and so, craving the company of writers almost as much as their custom, she started a lending library which operated out of the shop. It was one of the reasons 12, rue de l'Odéon became a magnet for novelists and poets,

French and foreign, *ancien régime* and *nouvelle vague*. Another reason was Beach's involvement in the publication of *Ulysses*, by James Joyce.

In 1922, after much hardship and heartache and with no prior experience of publishing, Sylvia Beach published the first edition of the greatest book of the twentieth century, a book which, but for her superhuman effort, would not have been published anywhere until many years later. Since 1920 Joyce had been a regular visitor to Shakespeare and Company, bombarding Beach with instructions and requests, using her shop as a boardroom, and endlessly revising and rewriting proofs, which not only delayed *Ulysses'* publication but threatened to bankrupt its tyro publisher. Joyce's regular visits to the shop caused even well-established authors, not just starstruck nobodies such as the young Ernest Hemingway, to hang around like lovesick schoolboys, hoping for a glimpse of him. Beach's association with Joyce was terrible for her peace of mind, but very good for business.

Sylvia Beach knew Gertrude Stein and Alice Toklas well. She attended their *salon*, they went to the theatre together, and Gertrude and Alice were members of Shakespeare and Company's lending library. But as Beach's relationship with Joyce deepened, so her relationship with Stein cooled. Stein was a jealous patron, and after the publication of *Ulysses* and the lionising of its author, Beach was gradually dropped from the rue de Fleurus circle. (She wasn't the only one: Stein's petulant factionalism eventually led to a diminution of her influence, while Beach's stock remained high.)

Beach was only an occasional visitor to the *salon* of Natalie Barney. Though lesbian she was not flamboyantly so; contentedly settled in a long-term relationship with her fellow bookseller Adrienne Monnier, she had no need of the sexual opportunities afforded by Barney's weekly gatherings, and although passionately interested in literature she was shy and self-conscious about her status as a mere reader, oddly unsure of herself in the company of creative people when encountered off her home patch.

(It's interesting to note that while many of the heterosexual expatriates in Paris took the opportunity to step outside the monogamous norms expected in their home countries, almost all of the lesbian expatriate community went to Paris in order to live in a way that the rest of society took for granted; they coupled up and settled down in a manner which, apart from the absence of a man, was conformity itself. Djuna Barnes and Thelma Wood, Stein and Toklas, Janet

Flanner and Solita Solano, Sylvia Beach and Adrienne Monnier: all conventional couples, barring the chromosome count. The proudly promiscuous Natalie Barney apart, the lesbian community of literary Paris was about as socially radical as a whist drive in Guildford.)

The *salons* of Sylvia Beach, Gertrude Stein and Natalie Barney provided a network of contacts and cultural cross-fertilisation for almost every artist passing through or living in Paris in the ten years following the Great War. Kahane missed it all. Instead, he arrived just in time for the Wall Street Crash.

There have been more propitious years to go into business than 1929, a year which would have been bad enough for Kahane without the disaster of an abyssal economic downturn. The Wall Street Crash affected him in three ways. Expatriates reliant on money sent from the States suddenly found themselves much poorer than they used to be and, this facet of bohemianism never having exerted much of a pull, they packed up and went home, drastically reducing the size of the market for English-language books in Paris. Those who stayed now found everything (including books) much more expensive, and so spent as little as they could. And the Crash also had a catastrophic effect on Léon's investment portfolio: no money would be available for bail-outs, which meant that Kahane's new scheme would have to succeed at the first attempt.

Other problems crowded in. Having safely cashed Kahane's cheque, it quickly became clear that Henri Babou intended to ensure that his new co-publisher remained 'the most somnolent of sleeping partners',[78] as a result of which Kahane found himself with almost nothing to do in his new business, apart from the agreed translation work on the *Artists du Livre* series. Also, his health was fragile once again. He was storing up trouble for himself, but he continued to work, and worked hard, delivering to Babou the translations for the English-language versions of *Hémard* and *Laboureur*, as well as working on the translation into English of French bestsellers for publication in Britain and the United States. He also secured the rights to *Sleeveless Errand*, by Norah C. James.

Norah James had finished *Sleeveless Errand* in the summer of 1928. She was working as a proofreader at the time, and since she now needed a publisher her employer, Cape, was the obvious first choice. She submitted the manuscript to Cape's chief literary adviser, the writer Edward Garnett. Alas, chief literary advisers to large publishing houses are perceptive critics. Garnett couldn't possibly have thought *Sleeveless Errand* was any good: his recommendation that Cape accept the book for publication must have been made because he saw commercial potential both in its 'daring' subject matter, and in the fact that its author was a woman. But Garnett was overruled by Jonathan Cape himself, who expressed concern that publishing an employee's first effort might lead to accusations of favouritism. This was almost certainly a pretext. Cape had been prosecuted the previous year for publishing Radclyffe Hall's *The Well of Loneliness*, and he subsequently took care not to publish any book likely to provoke the Home Secretary of the time, the notorious Grundyite William Joynson-Hicks. An approach to the Hogarth Press elicited polite praise from Leonard Woolf but no contract, and *Sleeveless Errand* was eventually placed with Eric Partridge at Scholartis Press. James was given a £25 advance, and proofs were sent to her for correction that winter.

Garnett's hunch that the book's faint whiff of scandal would boost sales proved correct, but so did Cape's hunch that such success would lead to trouble. By February 1929 the book was ready for publication. Eric Partridge reported that 1500 copies had been ordered by subscribers and booksellers: since the print run of the first edition was only five hundred copies, a second edition had to be printed before the first was even issued. Partridge had James sign 50 special copies, to retail at one guinea – three times the usual price of a novel – and was looking forward to a big payday. Then the police moved in.

Sleeveless Errand was to be published on 21 February. On the evening before, Partridge was visited at home by two plain-clothes policemen who insisted he take them to the Scholartis offices. There they removed every copy of the book they could find, and noted the names of all the booksellers who had placed orders for it. The following day every bookseller on the list was visited by the police. Partridge estimated that 'barring a few review copies and perhaps ten others (some of which were second edition, for the book had been subscribing well) all in Great Britian were reclaimed by "the Force"; about thirty copies got through to America, and among these were three or four of the signed edition'.[79]

In her memoir *I Lived in a Democracy* Norah James wrote that she only found out about the suppression of *Sleeveless Errand* when she passed a news placard on the day it was supposed to be published: 'apparently, it was an obscene book – simply because of the words used in it. I would have cut them out willingly if I'd been told it was necessary. But I'd never been told that. It never occured to me that it would be considered obscene to let the characters in it use the language they used in real life'.[80]

In March, Partridge was summoned to Bow Street Magistrates' Court to show reason why the book should not be destroyed. The prosecution complained that the book contained 'conversations by persons entirely devoid of decency and morality... Blasphemy is freely indulged in by all the characters, and filthy language and indecent situations appear to be the keynote'.[81] Partridge's defence was hamstrung both by lack of funds and by the farcical nature of the hearing, at which he was required to demonstrate his innocence rather than have the prosecution prove his guilt. Desmond MacCarthy noted 'that the book is moral was not denied in the lawcourts, but ignored'.[82]

The prosecution of *Sleeveless Errand* was baffling and bizarre. The book was vilified by the Crown for its obscenity and praised by its supporters for its high literary merit. Both sides were wrong. Even by the standards of 1929 the language of *Sleeveless Errand* is not extreme. Despite her declaration to the contrary, James had *not* let the characters speak in their natural demotic: 'bloody hell', 'balls', 'homos', 'whores', 'for Christ's sake', 'like Hell' and 'bitch' is as 'obscene' as the language gets, and while 'bloody' gets a good airing, most of the other epithets appear no more than a couple of times each in a book more than two hundred pages long. Perhaps James' sex counted against her; perhaps it was the book's casual acceptance of the lifestyle of its characters; or perhaps James' callow prose made her characters' disreputable nature too difficult to overlook. (Evelyn Waugh's *Decline and Fall* had appeared the previous year, and *Vile Bodies* would be published in the next: neither attracted judicial attention. Waugh's stylistic brilliance – combined, possibly, with his burgeoning literary reputation – seems to have indemnified him against any legal objections to the murky private lives of his characters.) Kahane had another theory: 'I have heard that a lady of great political importance had considered herself to be maligned in the book and had used her subterranean influence to have it banned'.[83] Partridge also suspected high-level skullduggery: 'Somebody in a certain newspaper (for "diplomatic", not moral reasons) sent a marked copy to the Home Office on the morning of the 19th February'.[84]

Whatever the reason for the prosecution, and despite disingenuous testaments to *Sleeveless Errand*'s literary merit from Edward Garnett, from Arnold Bennett in the *Evening Standard* and from Rebecca West in *Time and Tide*, the book was found guilty of obscenity and ordered to be destroyed. Accordingly, 785 of the 799 copies seized by the police were sent to the cutting machines in the Printers' Department of the Receiver's Office. The remainder were distributed to institutional libraries (including the British Library, the Bodleian, and Cambridge University Library), to the DPP, and to the Home Office. The Metropolitan Police retained one copy, 'for reference'.[85]

In Paris, Jack Kahane had read of the seizure of *Sleeveless Errand* in the *Continental Daily Mail*, and had followed the case closely. In 1929 he was still in partnership with Henri Babou, but his purchase and publication of Norah James' book would provide him with the template for the business that would occupy him for the next ten years: the Obelisk Press.

Kahane had managed to get hold of a copy of *Sleeveless Errand*, and on reading it saw not so much a good novel as a tremendous business opportunity. He was sure that the subject matter which had so scandalised the British establishment wouldn't raise an eyebrow in France, and that the book would be safe from prosecution if published in Paris. Kahane realised that this principle would hold good not just for *Sleeveless Errand*, but for many other books besides. It would be possible to run a notorious but entirely legal Paris-based business which made its money by exploiting the difference between what the British and the French thought was acceptable to print. *Sleeveless Errand* was the ideal title for such a venture: an innocuous book with a scandalous reputation, guaranteeing healthy sales. Kahane realised that if he published books which had already gained a reputation for obscenity in England he would be able to benefit from the free publicity given to him by an outraged and censorious British press. Tourists and businessmen would read about a 'filthy' book in London, and hunt it down when they were next in Paris. Kahane further realised that once a British publisher had fallen foul of the British courts, he would be able to buy the rights to the book cheaply from a company desperate to cut its losses – and what is more, a book in a well advanced pre-publication state.

In March 1929 Kahane made a deal with Eric Partridge for the English-language French publication rights to *Sleeveless Errand*, and in early April he paid Edward Garnett five hundred francs for an introduction to the new edition. By the end of the month *Sleeveless Errand*, published by Henri Babou and Jack Kahane, was available in the bookshops of Paris at a price of one hundred francs a copy. When it hit the steets Kahane took advertising space in the London press, announcing that 'in the event of other books of literary merit being banned in England, [he was] prepared to publish them in Paris within a month.'[86]

Kahane had set out his stall. Through the 1920s he'd watched with interest as small expatriate presses in Paris had taken advantage of French *laissez faire*. He'd watched as Sylvia Beach wrestled *Ulysses* away from Joyce, past the objections of moral guardians, and onto the printed page. But by 1929 Shakespeare and Company, the Three Mountains Press and Contact Editions were all defunct, and the way was clear for a newcomer. Kahane made a decision: financed by what he saw as inevitable profits from potboilers such as *Sleeveless Errand*, he would publish the next generation of unpublishable geniuses.

THE FREEDOM TO PUBLISH

The story of the founding of the Obelisk Press begins with Kahane's split from Babou, a traumatic event in Kahane's life, but one eased by a piece of good fortune.

In 1930 Kahane and Babou published Joyce's *Haveth Childers Everywhere* (see p. 83), soon after which Kahane's health collapsed completely. An intestinal operation was necessary, and the recovery from it confined him to bed for eight months. Babou took advantage of his partner's enforced absence to blow the company's money on a series of ill-advised and financially ruinous projects, and when Kahane was well enough to return to work he discovered there was almost nothing left to return *to*: his initial investment had gone, and so had the profits from sales of *Sleeveless Errand*, a total of nearly four hundred thousand francs. With Léon's money lost in the Wall Street Crash drastic economies had to be made at once, and in April 1931 Kahane moved the family from the palatial spread of Fond des Forêts to six rooms in the Auteuil district of Paris. When that address proved too expensive still they moved again, this time to a flat in an apartment block in Neuilly, a suburb to the west of Paris, and then once more to a still smaller ground floor flat in the same area.

Kahane needed to extricate himself from his partnership with Babou, but didn't know how; the answer, when it came, came out of nowhere. In 1931 the film studio RKO was poised to release a film called *Laugh and Get Rich*, starring Edna May Oliver and Hugh Herbert. The film was entirely unrelated to Kahane's novel, but Lowell Brentano saw a money-making opportunity. He cabled Kahane for permission to take action against the studio, and undertook to share any proceeds fifty-fifty. Kahane agreed, and expecting to hear nothing more was stunned when, a few days later, Bentano cabled him again with the news that RKO had settled for two thousand dollars. Pausing only briefly to wince at the realisation that Brentano had just made himself a thousand dollars simply by calling his lawyer, Kahane now found himself with the capital he needed to buy his freedom and set up in business on his own.

Kahane's involvement with *Sleeveless Errand* had crystallised a business plan in his mind:

> I would start a publishing business that would exist for the convenience of those English writers, English and American, who had something to say they could not conveniently say in their own countries. The next Lawrence or Joyce who came along would find the natural solution of his difficulties in Paris. And, of course, if any book that had reached publication (like *Sleeveless Errand*) met with disaster, my publishing house would automatically publish it in France... I worked out details, and examined the project on all sides to see if there were any flaws in it. But it seemed to me an impeccably logical conception.[87]

Notoriety is not the same thing as greatness, and by no stretch of the imagination could Norah C. James be regarded as 'the next Lawrence or Joyce'. But Kahane had seen his edition of *Sleeveless Errand* sell quickly to English tourists aware of the book's reputation, and was keen to repeat the trick as often as he could. Masterpieces unpublishable elsewhere were Kahane's prime objective, but masterpieces are difficult to find; in their absence, the scandalous would do.

As well as rescuing good, bad and indifferent books from English courtrooms, Kahane also decided he would bolster his list with the sort of saucy light erotica with which he'd passed the time in the sanatorium in Durtol. A few years earlier, the British government had pressed the French authorities to prosecute Frank Harris, then resident in Nice, when copies of his pornographic memoir *My Life and Loves* began to find their way into Britain, having been published in English on the continent. The French had declined to act against Harris, partly because the French courts had made themselves look ridiculous fifty years earlier when prosecutions had been launched against Flaubert and Baudelaire, partly because it would be impossible for a French jury to judge whether a book published in a foreign language was obscene, but mostly because they could find no law on the French statute books that either Harris or his printers had broken. If a book as explicit as *My Life and Loves* could be published in France without legal repercussions, then Kahane could surely publish mildly titillating, instantly forgettable trash 'for the Anglo-Saxon tourist visiting the continent, spicy enough to attract those timid souls, and yet not too much so as to avoid trouble with the French authorities'.[88] While convalescing from his operation, Kahane had written just such a novel: *Daffodil*. Armed with the stock he'd salvaged from his split with Babou, and with his own novels *Daffodil* and *Suzy Falls Off* – but as yet no masterpiece – Kahane looked around for a printer.

Sleeveless Errand had been printed by an Englishman called Herbert Clarke, owner of the Imprimerie Vendôme. His printing works were located in the Rue St-Honoré on the Right Bank of Paris, a hundred metres from the Place Vendôme, where the city's most exclusive jewellers, couturiers and banking houses were (and still are) concentrated. Clarke liked Kahane's business idea, Kahane liked Clarke, and *Daffodil* by 'Cecil Barr' went to press. The book was an instant success, and later became one of Obelisk's biggest sellers. The two men were on the verge of formalising their collaboration when Clarke died suddenly, leaving Kahane in an uneasy association with Clarke's foreman at the printing works, Marcel Servant: 'As no papers had been signed, my novel *Daffodil* was in a very equivocal position. In the end I saw that the simplest solution was to accept the new man's offer and go into business with him...though the conditions were lamentably different... However, I would have agreed to worse conditions, to get the new business going'.[89]

According to Girodias, it was financial necessity that forced his father's hand:

[M]y father found himself gradually forced into signing a partnership contract with the man, but at terms such that he was really working as a badly paid editor rather than as a partner; the printer also had the right to veto any book that he would consider too literary to be easily saleable, and my father was supposed to supply two books a year without royalties, as a contribution to the partnership. This was all extremely frustrating, but his financial situation was such that he had no choice left.[90]

The antagonism between Kahane and Servant persisted throughout their six-year partnership, but although Kahane disliked Servant intensely, the printer was at least hard-working and honest, and as such was a marked improvement on Henri Babou as a business partner. Despite their antipathy, the books of the Obelisk Press got published.

Obelisk took its name from the monument in the Place de la Concorde; given the nature of the company's projected output, its phallic appearance was not seen as an obstacle. Kahane's wife Marcelle designed the company's logo, an obelisk plinthed on a book (both she and Maurice were frequently recruited during Obelisk's existence to provide artwork for the company free of charge). Kahane's first publications in his new incarnation, however, appeared under the imprint of the Boulevard Library of Lighter Modern Fiction: only three titles were ever published, including Kahane's own *Suzy Falls Off*. The first book to appear bearing the Obelisk imprint was *Gold and Silver* by 'Henry Bridges' – almost certainly another pseudonym of Kahane himself.

The story of the Obelisk Press is told in this book's bibliographical notes on each title, and in the biographical profiles of their authors; the story of Jack Kahane himself during the Obelisk years is one of decline and disappointment. The success of the 'Cecil Barr' books, six in all, depressed him. They were all he could write that anyone wanted to read and, given the heavyweight literary company he kept, were often a source of deep embarrassment. The brilliant and ambitious founder of the Swan Club had never delivered, and Kahane felt his failure acutely. His poor health and constant financial worries also militated against his view of himself, a view which more closely resembled the hero of one of his own, detested, books: the carefree beau, monied, popular, constantly involved in romantic intrigue. But the antics of mildly erotic light fiction do not transfer well to the life of a frail and unprepossessing middle-aged man. According to Maurice Girodias, Marcelle learned to acclimatise to Jack's constant inconstancy: 'She was dedicated by nature to construction and continuity, just as he was to his own frivolous quests; they had

understood their differences and accepted each other with gratitude.'[91] But Kahane seems to have accepted himself less easily, and his
enthusiastic embracing of the role of French husband, with a wife
in the suburbs and mistresses all over the city, curdled in later years
into another reason for self-hatred. In the last Cecil Barr book, *Lady,
Take Heed!*, published in 1937, the atmosphere has soured: bright young
things shucking oysters and dancing until dawn have been replaced
by unhappy young women fleeing abusive step-fathers and falling into
the hands of Parisian brothel-keepers. 'Cecil Barr' dedicates the book
to Jack Kahane: 'without whose deep knowledge and wide experience of the subject this book could never have been written.'[92]

The darkening international situation did nothing for his peace
of mind. The Francophile – and Jewish – Kahane had long been
outraged by the Allies' willingness to allow Germany to rebuild
and re-arm after the Great War, and took no pleasure from having
correctly predicted the consequences. In 1937, by which time both his
health and his newspaper would have been telling him that the future
of the Obelisk Press was bleak, Kahane severed his links with Marcel
Servant and moved his office from the dingy cubicle he'd occupied in
the Vendôme printing works for the last six years to number 16, Place
Vendôme, in premises recently vacated by the literary agents Curtis
Brown. His office faced the Ministry of Justice and the Ritz Hotel;
trading neighbours included Cartier, the couturiers Coco Chanel
and Elsa Schiaparelli, and Renaissance art dealer Joseph Duveen, who
once made three quarters of a million dollars in commission from
one visit by the American banker (and Harry Crosby's uncle) J. P.
Morgan. The repositioning of Kahane's modest, ailing little business
on to one of the most expensive squares in Paris made no commercial sense: the office had no frontage – and even if it had it would
have been of little use. Shoppers came to the Place Vendôme to buy
evening dresses, diamonds and paintings, not books. The move was
a last gesture of self-validation, a nod in the direction of the life and
career Kahane had planned for himself in the arts clubs and hotel
bars of pre-war Manchester, a life and career which never came to
be. In the last lines of *Memoirs of a Booklegger*, he does what he can to
accept himself:

> Lascelles Abercrombie, the fine poet who has died so early, wrote to me
> a year or two ago: '...In my present situation, I am chiefly conscious of the
> complete failure of all my ambitions, having set out as a poet and ended as

a professor.' I am more resigned: I enjoy publishing other people's books, although that was not my ambition at the outset. I wonder how many of the people who have dreamed dreams see them fulfilled? [93]

In his own memoir, Maurice Girodias was more forthright. His father, he says, experienced great difficulty in writing *Memoirs of a Booklegger*, being reluctant to look too closely at a life he had wanted to live very differently, and reluctant also to acknowledge in public the effect of his life on those closest to him (the ellipses are Girodias's):

> A life that had misfired ... A fire spent in vain ... Great loves for persons unknown... Money had played a central role in all of that, as a hard symbol for the waste of all true values; indeed, an entire life spent in the search of that thing he disliked and distrusted so deeply: *money* ... The chaos and humiliation of it ... The four well-dressed children to whom he found himself unable to speak, either as a father or even as a friendly adult ... His perfect French wife, and her moral rectitude so overpowering that, liberated as they both were, he still couldn't look at her without feeling guilty ... Guilt, always guilt, a degrading, impoverishing sensation that he was made to feel for being a failed writer, a fickle lover, a frivolous publisher, a turncoat Jew. And he was supposed to write a jolly, dashing, entertaining book about all of that! [94]

Jack Kahane died of heart failure in his Neuilly apartment on 3 September 1939 – one of the Second World War's first casualties. His son Maurice Kahane continued to work as a publisher in Nazi-occupied Paris, but was able to do so only by abandoning his father's Jewish surname, and adopting the maiden name of his mother. As Maurice Girodias, in the 1950s he founded the Olympia Press, a Paris-based publishing company whose list was a mix of titillating, sometimes frankly pornographic pulp, and work of genuine literary merit unpublishable anywhere else. The first editions of Nabokov's *Lolita*, William Burroughs' *Naked Lunch*, and J. P. Donleavy's *The Ginger Man* were all published by Girodias, as were Terry Southern and Mason Hoffenberg's *Candy*, and the first English-language edition of *The Story of O*. Father and son were never close. The two publishers, on the other hand, understood each other perfectly.

NOTES

1 Family information taken from census records and birth, death and naturalisation papers held at The National Archives, Kew, London. Additional information supplied by Paul Kahane, Jack Kahane's nephew, in conversation with the author.

2 'Extraordinary Suicide of a Manchester Shipping Merchant', *Manchester Evening News*, 4 December 1893.

3 Jack Kahane, *Memoirs of a Booklegger* (Michael Joseph, 1939), p. 10.

4 Kahane, *Memoirs*, pp. 9–10.

5 Maurice Girodias, *The Frog Prince* (Crown, 1980), p. 9.

6 Girodias, *Frog Prince*, p. 11.

7 Kahane, *Memoirs*, p. 22.

8 Academic archives of Manchester Grammar School.

9 *Ulula*, magazine of Manchester Grammar School, various issues, 1900–1903.

10 Kahane, *Memoirs*, p. 9.

11 Kahane, *Memoirs*, p. 9.

12 Kahane, *Memoirs*, p. 16.

13 Kahane, *Memoirs*, p. 21.

14 A. Bendle and J. Knowlson, 'Curtain Call: Personal Reminiscences and Historical Detail on the Subject of the Manchester Theatres' (unpublished manuscript, written in 1977, held in Manchester Central Reference Library, Theatre Collection, ref. Th. 792.094273 Be 1). Cited in Paul Mortimer, 'The Life and Literary Career of Stanley Houghton', unpublished thesis (1984), kindly shown to me by the author.

15 B. Iden Payne, letter to the *Manchester Guardian*, 9 July 1907. The letter was published in the newspaper on 11 July.

16 Iden Payne, letter, 9 July 1907.

17 'Playgoers' Club: A Discussion on Policy', *Manchester Guardian*, 18 January 1912.

18 Harold Brighouse, *What I Have Had* (Harrap, 1953), p. 41.

19 *Manchester Guardian*, 17 May 1920.

20 Kahane, *Memoirs*, p. 24.

21 Kahane, *Memoirs*, p. 24.

22 Kahane, *Memoirs*, p. 25.

23 *Manchester Weekly Chronicle*, 2 July 1909.

24 Basil Dean, *Seven Ages: An Autobiography 1888–1927* (Hutchinson, 1970), pp. 66–67.

25 Brighouse, *What I Have Had*, p. 45.

26 Dean, *Seven Ages*, p. 66.

27 Gerald Cumberland, *Set Down in Malice* (Grant Richards, 1919), pp. 57–59.

28 Cumberland, *Set Down in Malice*, p. 57.

29 Kahane, *Memoirs*, p. 35.

30 Brighouse, *What I Have Had*, p. 33.

31 Jack Kahane, *Two Plays* (Sherratt and Hughes, 1912), p. 11.

32 Kahane, *Two Plays*, p. 32.

33 *Manchester Guardian*, 29 November 1913.

34 *Manchester Guardian*, 29 November 1913.

35 Gaiety Theatre programme, week commencing 24 November 1913, Manchester Library collection.

36 James Agate, cited in Bendle and Knowlson (see note 14).

37 Kahane, *Memoirs*, p. 35.

38 Kahane, *Memoirs*, p. 65.

39 Kahane, *Memoirs*, p. 70.

40 Ernest Hemingway, cited in Carlos Baker, *Ernest Hemingway: A Life* (Literary Guild, 1969), p. 61.

41 Jean Chalon, *Portrait of a Seductress* (Blond and Briggs, 1979), p. 122.

42 Kahane, *Memoirs*, p. 90.

43 Kahane, *Memoirs*, p. 92.

44 Kahane, *Memoirs*, p. 93.

45 Minuted testimony from the investigation, held in Kahane's service record, The National Archives, Kew, London.

46 Investigation testimony.

47 Investigation testimony.

48 Final report, held in Kahane's service record, The National Archives, Kew, London.

49 Kahane, *Memoirs*, p. 98.

50 Kahane, *Memoirs*, p. 99.

51 Kahane, *Memoirs*, pp. 99–100.

52 Girodias, *Frog Prince*, p. 24.

53 Kahane's service record, The National Archives, Kew, London.

54 Kahane, *Memoirs*, pp. 133–34.

55 Anthony Rhodes, *The Poet as Superman: D'Annunzio* (Weidenfeld and Nicolson, 1959), p. 172.

56 Rhodes, *The Poet as Superman*, pp. 172–73.

57 Kahane, *Memoirs*, p. 138.

58 Kahane, *Memoirs*, p. 146.

59 Girodias, *Frog Prince*, p. 34.

60 Kahane, *Memoirs*, p. 186.

61 Girodias, *Frog Prince*, p. 29.

62 Girodias, *Frog Prince*, p. 26.

63 *Times Literary Supplement*, 8 March 1923.

64 *Times Literary Supplement*, 15 March 1923.

65 Kahane, *Memoirs*, p. 188.

66 *Times Literary Supplement*, 15 March 1923.

67 Grant Richards to Jack Kahane, 25 March 1923. Letter in Grant Richards archive, British Library, London.

68 *Times Literary Supplement*, 5 April 1923.

69 Kahane, *Memoirs*, p. 191.
70 Grant Richards to Jack Kahane, 27 December 1923. Letter in Grant Richards archive, British Library, London.
71 Kahane, *Memoirs*, p. 202.
72 Kahane, *Memoirs*, p. 202.
73 *Times Literary Supplement*, 29 January 1925.
74 Jack Kahane to Eric Pinker, 13 January 1925. Letter in Pinker archive, Berg collection, New York Public Library.
75 Kahane, *Memoirs*, p. 203.
76 Jack Kahane to Eric Pinker, 25 July 1925. Letter in Pinker archive, Berg collection, New York Public Library.
77 Quoted in Diana Souhami, *Wild Girls* (Weidenfeld and Nicolson, 2004), p. 167.
78 Kahane, *Memoirs*, p. 217.
79 Eric Partridge, *The First Three Years: An Account and a Bibliography of the Scholartis Press* (Scholartis Press, 1930), p. 25.
80 Norah C. James, *I Lived in a Democracy* (Longmans, Green & Co., 1939), p. 230.
81 Trial transcript, Bow Street Magistrates' Court, 3 March 1929.
82 Partridge, *The First Three Years*, p. 25.
83 Kahane, *Memoirs*, p. 223.
84 Partridge, *The First Three Years*, p. 25.
85 Alan Travis, *Bound and Gagged: A Secret History of Obscenity in Britain* (Profile Books, 2000), p. 90.
86 Kahane, *Memoirs*, p. 224.
87 Kahane, *Memoirs*, pp. 227–28.
88 Girodias, *Frog Prince*, p. 88.
89 Kahane, *Memoirs*, p. 232.
90 Girodias, *Frog Prince*, p. 88.
91 Girodias, *Frog Prince*, p. 91.
92 Dedication page, *Lady, Take Heed!* (Obelisk Press, 1937).
93 Kahane, *Memoirs*, p. 278.
94 Girodias, *Frog Prince*, p. 242.

A Items

Books Published by
Jack Kahane and
the Obelisk Press

Including Important Later Foreign Editions
of Obelisk Titles

A–1 SLEEVELESS ERRAND

by NORAH C(ORDNER) JAMES

Title page
SLEEVELESS | ERRAND | A NOVEL | BY | NORAH C. JAMES | PREFACE
BY | EDWARD GARNETT | HENRY BABOU AND JACK KAHANE |
1, RUE VERNIQUET, PARIS | 1929

Collation
8vo. [x] 1–217 + [v]. 22 × 14.5 cm. All edges trimmed.

Pagination
[i–ii] blank; [iii] half-title; [iv] edition statement; [v] title-page; [vi]
blank; [vii] dictionary quotation; [viii] blank; [ix] disclaimer; [x] blank;
[1–3] preface; [4] blank; [5–217] text; [218–219] blank; [220] imprimerie:
PRINTED IN PARIS | BY THE | IMPRIMERIE VENDOME, 338 RUE
SAINT-HONORE; [221–222] blank.

Binding
Boards, ³/₄ rumpled paper effect, white grained cloth spine, in a
pictorial dustwrapper.

Front panel: Blank.

Spine: White. SLEEVELESS | ERRAND | BY | NORAH C. JAMES | H.
BABOU | & | J. KAHANE | PARIS [black]

Rear panel: Blank.

Wrapper
Front panel: Seated woman, half-empty glass in front of her. Stylised
sunlight in yellow. Signed 'M. Kahane'.

Spine: White.

SLEEVELESS | ERRAND | [drawing of decanter and glass] | NORAH
C. JAMES | PREFACE BY | EDWARD GARNETT | 100 Fr. Net [black] |
HENRY BABOU | AND | JACK KAHANE | PARIS [black on yellow]

Rear panel: White. Blank.

Front flap: White. Title, author, preface credit. Quotation from
Arnold Bennett's review in the *Evening Standard*.

Rear flap: White. Blank.

Blue-green wraparound band.
SEIZED BY THE LONDON POLICE | THE COMPLETE | AND

UNEXPURGATED TEXT | PREFACE BY EDWARD GARNETT

Publication
April 1929

Notes
Since the Scholartis edition was seized on the eve of publication and suppressed following a successful prosecution, strictly speaking it was never published. But the edition was printed up, and a few copies of the book managed to find their way into the hands of copyright libraries and collectors. Those few surviving copies must therefore be regarded as the first edition, and this Babou and Kahane edition as the second.

The dustwrapper is designed by Marcelle Kahane, Jack Kahane's wife.

According to Norah James' autobiography *I Lived in a Democracy*, a stage version of *Sleeveless Errand* was written but never published. Encouraged by Kahane's friend from Manchester, the theatrical producer Basil Dean, James had meetings with both Noël Coward and Tallulah Bankhead. When neither expressed interest, the project was dropped.

(b) SLEEVELESS ERRAND

Second issue.

Title page
As A–1.

Collation
As A–1.

Pagination
As A–1.

Binding
As A–1.

Wrapper
Front panel: As A–1.
Spine: White. SLEEVELESS | ERRAND | [drawing of decanter and glass] | NORAH C. JAMES | PREFACE BY | EDWARD GARNETT | 50

FRANCS [black] | THE OBELISK PRESS | PARIS [black on yellow]
Rear panel: White. Four titles, with blurbs, at Frs. 50 each.
Front flap: White. Title, author, preface credit. Quotation from Arnold
Bennett's review in the *Evening Standard*, with notice of unexpurgated
text beneath.
Rear flap: White. Blank.

Publication

1933

Notes

The dustwrapper is the only difference between A–1 and A–1(b).
Kahane, tyro publisher that he was, overestimated demand for the
book in 1929 and found himself with piles of unsold copies. These
were sold during the 1930s in the second-issue dustwrapper, the
revised wording of which claimed the book for the Obelisk Press.

The second-issue dustwrapper retains the same design as the first,
but the price on the spine is 50 FRANCS, the publisher has become
the Obelisk Press, and the rear panel carries advertisements for four
Obelisk titles, the latest of which – THE WELL OF LONELINESS –
indicates that the wrapper dates from no earlier than May 1933. The
Bennett review quoted on the front flap has been reset, and beneath
it now appears: Entirely unexpurgated edition of the | novel that was
SEIZED BY THE LONDON | POLICE.

A–2 JOSEPH HEMARD

by MARCEL VALOTAIRE

Title page
FRENCH BOOK ILLUSTRATORS | JOSEPH | HEMARD | A SHORT
AUTOBIOGRAPHY, WITH A CRITICAL STUDY BY | MARCEL
VALOTAIRE | AND A PORTRAIT OF HEMARD BY | JOSEPH
HEMARD | B [seated female nude] K | HENRY BABOU AND JACK
KAHANE | 1, RUE VERNIQUET, PARIS | IN CONJUNCTION WITH
| BRENTANO'S | NEW YORK 1929 LONDON

Collation
4to. [viii] 7–43 + [vii]. Illustration tipped in between [iv] and [v].
Thirteen illustrations tipped in between [40] and [41]. 26.5 × 20.5 cm.
Top edge trimmed.

Pagination
[i–ii] blank; [iii] half-title; [iv] limitation; [v] blank; [vi] pen and ink self-portrait of Hémard; [vii] title-page; [viii] copyright; [7–40] text; [41–43] bibliography; [44] blank; [45] imprimerie; [46–50] blank. Illustrations, printed on rectos only: [between [40] and [41]: [1] from *Scènes de la Vie de Bohème*; [2] from *La Malade Imaginaire*; [3] from *L'Homme aux Quarante Ecus*; [4] from *Monsieur de Pourceaugnac*; [5] from *Micromégas*; [6] from *La Vieulx par Chemins*; [7] from *Code Civil*; [8] from *Formulaire Magistrale*; [9] from *Le Capitaine Fracasse*; [10] from *Satyre Contre les Femmes*; [11] from *Cyrano de Bergerac*; [12] from *La Grammaire Française*; [13] from *La Guerre des Boutons*.

Binding
Boards. White grained cloth spine and fore-edges, rumpled paper effect of A–1 running down centre of front and rear boards. Spine lettered vertically in silver at foot: HEMARD. Motif of three wavy lines in silver at head.

Issued without dustwrapper.

Publication
August 1929

Notes
Second edition. 700 copies. The first edition was published in French by Henri Babou in 1928, as JOSEPH HEMARD: AUTOBIOGRAPHIE PAR LUI-MEME, number three in Babou's *Les Artistes du Livre* series.

The limitation page reads: THIS VOLUME IS THE FIRST NUMBER OF A SERIES THE GENERAL TITLE OF WHICH IS *FRENCH BOOK ILLUSTRATORS*. THE EDITION IS LIMITED TO SEVEN HUNDRED COPIES OF WHICH FIFTY ON IMPERIAL JAPANESE VELLUM CONTAINING A REPRODUCTION OF AN ORIGINAL WATER-COLOUR BY JOSEPH HEMARD: NOS. 1–50; AND SIX HUNDRED AND FIFTY COPIES ON WHITE VELLUM MOULD-MADE JOHANNOT: NOS. 51–700.

Kahane's collaboration with Valotaire on this title probably resulted in the publication of A–4 [see note to A–4].

A–3 HAVETH CHILDERS EVERYWHERE
by JAMES JOYCE

Title page
HAVETH CHILDERS | EVERYWHERE | FRAGMENT FROM | WORK
IN PROGRESS | by | JAMES JOYCE | HENRY BABOU AND JACK
KAHANE | PARIS | THE FOUNTAIN PRESS. – NEW YORK | 1930

Collation
4to. [vi] 7–73 + [iii]. 28.5 × 19.3 cm. Edges untrimmed.

Pagination
[i–ii] blank; [iii] half-title; [iv] limitation; [v] title-page; [vi] copyright;
[7–73] text; [74] colophon; [75–76] blank.

Binding
White heavy paper wrappers.

Front panel: HAVETH CHILDERS | EVERYWHERE [green] | BY |
JAMES JOYCE [black]

Spine: JAMES JOYCE – HAVETH CHILDERS EVERYWHERE [black]

Rear panel: Blank.

Issued in glassine wrapper and a green slipcase, edged in gold.

Publication
May 1930

Notes
First edition thus.

Limitation page reads: THIS VOLUME CONSTITUTING THE ONLY
| COMPLETE ORIGINAL EDITION OF A | FRAGMENT OF *WORK IN
PROGRESS*, | COMPOSED BY HAND IN FRESHLY CAST | ELZEVIR
CORPS 16, COMPRISES: 100 | COPIES ON IMPERIAL HAND-MADE
IRIDES- | CENT JAPAN, SIGNED BY THE WRITER | Nos 1 TO 100;
500 COPIES ON HAND- | MADE PURE LINEN VIDALON ROYAL
| (SPECIALLY MANUFACTURED FOR THIS | EDITION) Nos 101
TO 600; HALF OF | EACH CATEGORY BEING FOR THE UNITED
| STATES OF AMERICA. THERE HAVE ALSO | BEEN PRINTED:
10 COPIES CALLED | WRITER'S COPIES ON IMPERIAL HAND- |
MADE IRIDESCENT JAPAN, Nos I TO X; | 75 COPIES CALLED
WRITER'S COPIES ON PURE LINEN HAND-MADE | VIDALON

ROYAL, Nos XI TO LXXXV.

Slocum and Cahoon notes: 'The 100 copies on imperial handmade iridescent Japan paper were signed by Joyce in pencil under the limitation notice... Some copies were enclosed in a three-panel wrapper of stiff cardboard covered with gilt paper, within the slipcase.'

Although not called for in the limitation statement, all writer's copies examined are also signed in pencil by Joyce.

A–4 CLEANTE AND BELISE

by ANNE BELLINZANI FERRAND (LA PRESIDENTE FERRAND)

VELLUM COPIES

Title page
Cleante | and | Belise | Their loves and their letters | [illustration of naked woman and her lover] | Translated by Eric Sutton | Embellishments by Jean Dulac | Paris | Henry Babou | and | Jack Kahane | 1 Rue Verniquet

Collation
8vo. [xii] 7–240 + [vi]. Illustrations tipped in between [x] and [xi], [28] and [29], [66] and [67], [104] and [105], [240] and [241]. Twenty-two illustrations laid in between [242] and [243]. There is also an illustration tipped in after [200] but accounted for in the pagination. 19.6 × 13.5 cm. Edges trimmed but signatures irregularly folded, giving an untrimmed feel to the fore-edge.

Pagination
[i] marbled ffep.; [ii–vi] blank; [vii] half-title; [viii] limitation; [ix–x] blank; [xi] title-page; [xii] blank; [7–11] preface; [12] blank; [13] note to the reader; [14] blank; [15–240] text; [241] imprimerie: HAND SET IN COCHIN | AND PRINTED BY | DUCROS ET COLAS, | MASTER-PRINTERS, | PARIS; [242–245] blank; [246] marbled rear ep. Illustrations: Between [x] and [xi]: the lovers seated, kissing by candlelight; between [28] and [29]: Bélise at her balcony; between [66] and [67]: Bélise reclining as she talks to her lover and a servant looks on; between [104] and [105]: the lovers kissing at the riverside; [201]: Bélise, naked and spreadeagled on her bed; between [240] and [241]: Bélise, naked, reading a letter on her bed; between [242] and [243]: 1: duplicate title-page; 2: near duplicate of that between [x] and [xi], lacking

a chair upholstered in a floral design, and a domino; 3: duplicate of that between [x] and [xi]; 4: near duplicate of that between [66] and [67], with variant shading and lacking the border; 5: the lovers arriving at the masked ball; 6: near duplicate of that between [104] and [105], minus some fallen leaves; 7: Bélise writing a letter by moonlight; 8: duplicate of [201] minus the strategically placed rose, and lacking the border; 9: near duplicate of that between [240] and [241], slightly larger and lacking the border; 10: Bélise on her bed with a discarded letter, a maidservant in attendance; 11: duplicate of that between [28] and [29]; 12: Bélise at the convent; 13: duplicate of that between [66] and [67]; 14: near duplicate of [5], with variant shading and a border; 15: duplicate of that between [104] and [105]; 16: near duplicate of [7] with variant shading and fainter design on furniture, and with an additional vignette (see below); 17: duplicate of [201] except for slightly different shading of the vase; 18: near duplicate of that between [240] and [241], with variant shading; 19: duplicate of title-page illustration, minus the text; 20: near duplicate of [10], with variant shading and lacking both the border and the elaborate design at the foot of the bed; 21: near duplicate of that between [28] and [29], with variant shading and lacking the border; 22: duplicate of [12], lacking the border.

The illustrations that appear within the body of the text are hand-coloured, as are the smaller illustrations that appear as section headings, which are paginated and do not appear on the above list. The suite of illustrations bound together at the back of the book are not coloured, but do have small vignettes drawn beneath them that are not present on the illustrations carried in the text. This suite of illustrations is bound in to the vellum copies only.

Binding
Brown full morocco, lettered in gilt on spine: ERIC SUTTON | CLEANTE | & | BELISE | KAHANE
Front and rear panels blank.

Publication
October 1930

Notes
First edition in English. 320 copies: 20 on Imperial Japanese vellum, 300 on hand-made Montval paper.

First published as *Histoire nouvelle des amours de la jeune Bélise et de*

Cléante, par Mr D*** [Mme. A. Ferrand] in Paris in 1689. The letters which comprise the final section of the novel were added to the second edition (1691).

Limitation page reads: THIS EDITION IS LIMITED TO | 20 COPIES ON IMPERIAL | JAPANESE VELLUM, N^{OS} 1–20. | 300 COPIES ON HAND | MADE MONTVAL, N^{OS} 21–320. | N^{O} [stamped number] | PRINTED IN FRANCE

Signed by both Sutton and Dulac beneath the stamped number.

Maroon endpapers of a vaguely floral design.

Vellum copies were priced at Frs. 1300, or 10 guineas (more than £400 at 2005 prices).

Armstrong states that this title was issued in a box [not seen].

PAPER COPIES, 'SPECIALLY BOUND' [see notes]

Title page
As above.

Collation
8vo. [xii] 7–240 + [viii]. Illustrations tipped in between [x] and [xi], [28] and [29], [66] and [67], [104] and [105], [240] and [241]. There is also an illustration tipped in after [200] but accounted for in the pagination. 19.3 × 13 cm. Top edge gilt, others rough trimmed.

Pagination
[i] marbled ffep.; [ii–viii] blank; [ix] half-title; [x] blank; [xi] title-page; [xii] blank; [7–11] preface; [12] blank; [13] note to the reader; [14] blank; [15–240] text; [241] limitation and imprimerie: THIS EDITION, PRINTED | BY DUCROS ET COLAS, | MASTER-PRINTERS, PARIS, IS | LIMITED TO | 20 COPIES ON IMPERIAL | JAPANESE VELLUM, N^{OS} 1–20. | 300 COPIES ON HAND | MADE MONTVAL, N^{OS} 21–320. | N^{O} [stamped number] | *PRINTED IN FRANCE.*; [242–247] blank; [248] marbled rear ep. Illustrations: Between [x] and [xi]: the lovers seated, kissing by candlelight; between [28] and [29]: Bélise at her balcony; between [66] and [67]: Bélise reclining as she talks to her lover and a servant looks on; between [104] and [105]: the lovers kissing at the riverside; [201]: Bélise, naked and spreadeagled on her bed; between [240] and [241]: Bélise, naked, reading a letter on her bed.

Binding
Brown half morocco, with tan leather inserts containing two gilt squares at leading edges of front and rear panels. Lettered in gilt on spine: CLEANTE | AND | BELISE

Publication
October 1930

Notes
Marbled copper-and-gold endpapers.

The illustration bound in between [240] and [241] has a tissue guard not present in either the vellum or paper copies.

This issue, which sold for Frs. 390 or 3 guineas, has a reset half-title: the imprimerie and limitation that appears on the verso of the half-title in the vellum and paper issues appears in this issue on a leaf of its own, bound in after the text. Despite Obelisk Press publicity material issued at the time of publication suggesting that these specially bound copies were merely rebound paper issue copies, no specially rebound copy of the paper issue that conforms exactly to the collation and pagination of the paper copies has been located.

Armstrong states that this title was issued in a box [not seen].

PAPER COPIES

Title page
As above.

Collation
8vo. [viii] 7–240 + [ii]. 19.6 × 12.8 cm. Top edge rough trimmed, other edges untrimmed.

Pagination
[i–ii] blank; [iii] half-title; [iv] limitation; [v–vi] blank; [vii] title-page; [viii] blank; 7–11 preface; [12] blank; [13] note to the reader; [14] blank; [15–240] text; [241] imprimerie (as above); [242] blank. Illustrations tipped in between [vi] and [vii], [28] and [29], [66] and [67], [104] and [105], [240] and [241]. There is also an illustration tipped in after [200] but accounted for in the pagination. These illustrations are the same as those in the vellum copies, but are not coloured.

Binding
White heavy paper wrappers, folded over envelope-style on three sides.

Wrapper

Front panel: CLEANTE AND BELISE | ANNE FERAND

Spine: ANNE | FERRAND | CLEANTE | AND | BELISE

Rear panel: Blank.

Publication
October 1930

Notes

Copies issued in paper wrappers were priced at 160 francs, and were unsigned. According to Obelisk Press publicity material issued at the time of publication, subscribers could have their paper copies bound in half morocco [but see notes above].

Unlike the two issues above, Armstrong does not call for a box for this issue. However, the copy in the author's collection *is* housed in a marbled blue card box, which appears to be original.

A–5 LABOUREUR
by MARCEL VALOTAIRE

Title page
FRENCH BOOK ILLUSTRATORS [black] | LABOUREUR [brown] | A CRITICAL STUDY BY | MARCEL VALOTAIRE | *AND A PORTRAIT BY* | DUNOYER DE SEGONZAC | [woodcut device of a crab with the initials H and B in each of its pincers] [brown and white] | HENRY BABOU AND JACK KAHANE | 1, RUE VERNIQUET, PARIS [black] | 1929 [brown]

Collation
4to. [vii] 7–44 + [vi]. Top edge trimmed, other edges rough trimmed.

Pagination
[i–ii] blank; [iii] half-title; [iv] limitation; [v] blank; [vi] frontispiece illustration; [vii] title-page; [viii] copyright; 7–44 text; [45–46] bibliography; [47] illustration from *Hélène et Touglas* and imprimerie: *This volume dealing with the works of J. E. Laboureur was | hand set in Naudin, printed, and made in France | by Ducros and Colas, master-printers, Paris, 1929.*; [48–50] blank. Illustrations, printed on rectos only: between [48] and [49]: [1] from *Physiologie du Goût*; [2] from *L'Envers du Music-Hall*; [3] from

The Devil in Love; [4] from *Dans les Flandres Britanniques*; [5] from *Dans les Flandres Britanniques* (second illustration); [6] from *Petits et Grands Verres*; [7] from *Tableaus des Grands Magasins*; [8] from *Suzanne et le Pacifique*; [9] from *Trois Contes Cruels*; [10] from *Contes de Perrault*; [11] from *Le Portrait de Dorian Gray*; [12] from *Le Songe d'une Femme*; [13] from *Images de L'Arrière*.

Binding
Boards. White grained cloth spine and fore-edges, rumpled paper effect running down centre of front and rear boards [as on A–1]. Spine lettered vertically in silver at foot: LABOUREUR. Motif of three wavy lines in silver at head.

Issued without dustwrapper.

Publication
1930

Notes
First edition in English. 700 copies. The first edition was published in French by Henri Babou in 1929 also in an edition of 700 copies. It was number four in Babou's series, *Les Artistes du Livre*. Like A–2, this edition was translated by Jack Kahane.

The second (and far scarcer) of the two *Les Artistes du Livre* series to be issued by Babou and Kahane. It was also the last: Babou and Kahane's business partnership was dissolved shortly after publication.

The limitation page reads: THIS VOLUME IS THE SECOND NUMBER OF | A SERIES THE GENERAL TITLE OF WHICH | IS *FRENCH BOOK ILLUSTRATORS*. THE | EDITION IS LIMITED TO SEVEN HUNDRED | COPIES OF WHICH FIFTY ON IMPERIAL | JAPANESE VELLUM CONTAINING AN | ORIGINAL ENGRAVING BY LABOUREUR | NOS. 1 TO 50, AND SIX HUNDRED AND FIFTY | COPIES ON WHITE VELLUM MOULD-MADE | JOHANNOT: NOS. 51–700. | COPY No [number of copy stamped in]

The crab device on the title-page is an odd foreshadowing of the wrapper design for *Tropic of Cancer* [see A–32], and may have been the source of Maurice Kahane's inspiration.

A–6 DEATH OF A HERO (2 vols.)
by RICHARD ALDINGTON
SIGNED COPIES
Volume I

Title page
DEATH OF A HERO | A NOVEL | BY | RICHARD ALDINGTON | VOLUME I | HENRI BABOU AND JACK KAHANE | 1, RUE VERNIQUET, PARIS | 1930

Collation
Large 8vo. [xii] 3–194 + [ii]. 26.3 × 20.3 cm. Edges rough trimmed.

Pagination
[i–ii] blank; [iii] half-title ; [iv] limitation; [v] title-page; [vi] imprimerie: PRINTED IN FRANCE; [vii] Walpole quotation; [viii] blank; [ix] section heading; [x] blank; [xi–xii] dedicatory note to Halcott Glover; 3–194 text; [195–196] blank.

Binding
Plain stiff tan card wrappers covered in glassine.

Front wrapper: DEATH OF A HERO | RICHARD ALDINGTON | HENRY BABOU AND JACK KAHANE | 1, RUE VERNIQUET, PARIS [black]

Spine: DEATH | OF | A HERO | RICHARD | ALDINGTON | I | HENRY BABOU | AND | JACK KAHANE [black]

Rear wrapper: Blank.

Volume II

Title page
DEATH OF A HERO | A NOVEL | BY | RICHARD ALDINGTON | VOLUME II | HENRI BABOU AND JACK KAHANE | 1, RUE VERNIQUET, PARIS | 1930

Collation
Large 8vo. [vi] 5–213 + [iii]. 26.3 × 20.3 cm. Edges rough trimmed.

Pagination
[i–ii] blank; [iii] half-title; [iv] blank; [v] title-page; [vi] imprimerie: PRINTED IN FRANCE; 5–213 text; [214] second imprimerie: PRINTED

BY | HERBERT CLARKE, THE VENDOME PRESS | 338, RUE SAINT-HONORÉ, PARIS | SEPTEMBER 1930; [215–216] blank.

Binding
Plain stiff tan card wrappers covered in glassine.

Front wrapper: DEATH OF A HERO | RICHARD ALDINGTON | HENRY BABOU AND JACK KAHANE | 1, RUE VERNIQUET, PARIS [black]

Spine: DEATH | OF | A HERO | RICHARD | ALDINGTON | II | HENRY BABOU | AND | JACK KAHANE [black]

Rear wrapper: Blank.

Both volumes housed in a blue-green marbled chemise and slipcase. The chemise is lettered in gilt on the spine: DEATH OF A HERO | RICHARD ALDINGTON | 2 VOLS.

Notes
There are differences between the signed and unsigned issues. See notes to unsigned copies below.

UNSIGNED COPIES
Volume I

Title page
As A–6 Vol. I.

Collation
Large 8vo. [xiv] 3–194 + [iv]. 26.3 × 20.3 cm. Edges untrimmed.

Pagination
[i–iv]blank;[v]half-title;[vi]limitation;[vii]title-page;[viii]imprimerie: PRINTED IN FRANCE; [ix] Walpole quotation; [x] blank; [xi–xii] dedicatory note to Halcott Glover; [xiii] section heading; [xiv] blank; 3–194 text; [195–196] blank.

Binding
Plain stiff tan card wrappers covered in glassine. Endpapers retained by wrappers (not counted in pagination).

Front wrapper: DEATH OF A HERO | RICHARD ALDINGTON | HENRY BABOU AND JACK KAHANE | 1, RUE VERNIQUET, PARIS [black]

Spine: DEATH | OF | A HERO | RICHARD | ALDINGTON | I | HENRY BABOU | AND | JACK KAHANE [black]

Rear wrapper: Blank.

Volume II

Title page
As A–6 Vol. II.

Collation
Large 8vo. [viii] 5–213 + [iii]. 26.3 × 20.5 cm. Edges untrimmed.

Pagination
[i–iv] blank; [v] half-title; [vi] blank; [vii] title-page; [viii] imprimerie: PRINTED IN FRANCE; 5–213 text; [214] second imprimerie: PRINTED BY | HERBERT CLARKE, THE VENDOME PRESS | 338, RUE SAINT-HONORÉ, PARIS | SEPTEMBER 1930; [215–216] blank.

Binding
Plain stiff tan card wrappers covered in glassine. Endpapers retained by wrappers (not counted in pagination).

Front wrapper: DEATH OF A HERO | RICHARD ALDINGTON | HENRY BABOU AND JACK KAHANE | 1, RUE VERNIQUET, PARIS [black]

Spine: DEATH | OF | A HERO | RICHARD | ALDINGTON | II | HENRY BABOU | AND | JACK KAHANE [black]

Rear wrapper: Blank.

Both volumes housed in a blue-green marbled slipcase.

Publication
Autumn 1930

Notes
Third edition. First 'unexpurgated' edition [see below]. 300 copies, of which 100 are signed by the author.

The signed issue is printed on Japon paper and comes with a chemise as well as a slipcase, and is consequently slightly wider than the unsigned issue.

Both volumes of the signed issue have one fewer front free endpapers than the unsigned issue.

The page bearing the prologue section heading in Volume I is bound in in a different position in the signed and unsigned issues. The result is that in the signed issue the page containing the Walpole quotation is mispaginated.

Copies were sold for Frs. 1,300 or 10 guineas for the signed issue, and Frs. 390 or 3 guineas for unsigned copies.

Babou's forename is given as 'Henry' on the spine of both volumes but as 'Henri' on both title pages.

Death of a Hero was first published simultaneously, and in expurgated form, by Chatto and Windus in England, and by Covici, Friede in the United States, in 1929. While the Babou and Kahane edition restored all the material removed from its two predecessors, it is not, despite its claim, 'unexpurgated': as in the English edition, the word 'fuck' and its derivatives are softened to 'muck', 'mucker', 'mucking', etc. (The word 'cunt' is printed in full.) The first full-text edition was the Consul edition, published in England in 1965.

Despite the Babou and Kahane edition having been printed in September 1930, it had still not been published by 21 October, when Kahane mentioned in a letter to the Richards Press that the book would be 'ready very shortly'.

A–7 JAM TO-DAY
by MARJORIE FIRMINGER

Title page
JAM TO-DAY | A NOVEL | BY | MARJORIE FIRMINGER | [jampot] | THE VENDOME PRESS | 338, RUE SAINT-HONORÉ, PARIS | 1931

Collation
8vo. [viii] 9–284 + [iv]. [Dimensions unknown: BNF copy is cropped.]

Pagination
[i–ii] blank; [iii] title-page; [iv] blank; [v] section heading; [vi] blank; [vii] Carroll quotation; [viii] disclaimer; 9–284 text; [285] completion date; [286–288] blank.

Binding
White stiff paper wrappers.

Front panel: Rows of jampots, top and bottom, underlined in black.
JAM TO-DAY [red] | A NOVEL [triangular device] [black] | MARJORIE
FIRMINGER [red]

Spine: Not seen.

Rear panel: Blank.

Publication
December 1930

Notes
First edition.

The publication date is indicated in a letter from Firminger to
Wyndham Lewis dated 26 December 1930 [Wyndham Lewis Collection, Cornell].

Published by Herbert Clarke at the Vendome Press. Clarke died
suddenly shortly after publication, and rights to this title – and to
Firminger's next two books (never published) – passed to Kahane
when he bought Clarke's interest in the company, and renamed it the
Obelisk Press.

A shipment of this title was seized by British customs officers.
According to a Firminger letter Clarke was delighted, as it enabled
him to attach a label to unsold copies in France declaring the book
BANNED IN BRITAIN [sic]. A copy of this title in the author's collec-
tion carries such a sticker: a white disc with the words BANNED | IN
| ENGLAND printed in red.

Two different title-pages are to be found on this title [see below] and
precedence has not been established. It's possible that the legal problems that had so delighted Clarke made his successor nervous, and
that Kahane reissued the book without his company's imprint on the
title-page, hoping thereby to avoid prosecution while continuing to
make money.

(b) JAM TO-DAY

Title page
JAM TO-DAY | A NOVEL | BY | MARJORIE FIRMINGER | [jampot] |
PARIS | 1931

Collation
8vo. [viii] 9–284 + [iv]. 19.3 × 14.4 cm. Edges untrimmed.

Pagination
As A–7.

Binding
White stiff paper wrappers.

Front panel: As A–7.

Spine: JAM | TO-DAY [red] | MARJORIE | FIRMINGER | [jampot] [black] | PARIS [enclosed in two black lines] [black]

Rear panel: Blank.

Publication
1931

Notes
First edition, variant title-page [see notes to A–7].

According to Firminger, a 'cheap edition' was issued some months after initial publication. Since the only difference between this edition and A–7 is the title-page, it's difficult to see how this one could have sold for less. It is, however, the only variant located.

A–8 DAFFODIL

by CECIL BARR (JACK KAHANE)

Title page
DAFFODIL | OR | *ACCIDENTS WILL HAPPEN* | BY | CECIL BARR | AUTHOR OF | *SUZY FALLS OFF, etc.* | [Herbert Clarke woodcut] | THE VENDOME PRESS | 338, RUE SAINT-HONORÉ, PARIS

Collation
8vo. [vi] 7–301 + [iii]. 18 × 13.5 cm. [Edges cropped on BNF copy, original state unknown.]

Pagination
[i–ii] blank; [iii] dedication; [iv] blank; [v] title-page; [vi] copyright and publication: Published June 1931 | Reprinted June 1931 | " July 1931; 7–301 text; [302–304] blank.

Binding
Heavy paper wrappers.

Front panel: Yellow. Line drawing of sculptress fashioning lower half of nude figure. Daffodil in bottom right corner [black]. Daffodil | CECIL BARR | Author of "Suzy falls off" [black].

Spine: Unseen. [BNF copy rebound.]

Rear panel: White. Blank.

Publication
July 1931

Notes
First edition. ['3rd impression.']

No copy earlier than this, the so-called third impression, has been located. Kahane regarded *Daffodil* as the first Obelisk title: failure would have been unthinkable. He almost certainly exaggerated the number of times the book went to press in order to give the appearance of healthy sales, and so stimulate demand. Lending weight to this theory is the sign-off which appears at the end of the text on [301]: Paris, May, 1931. It seems unlikely that the book would have been set, proof-read and published in less than a month, and unlikelier still that it would have been reprinted twice by July. Wrappers of later Obelisk titles give more reasons for caution: they proclaim *Daffodil* to have reached its seventh, eighth, tenth and fourteenth impressions: none of these has been located, and they are presumed not to exist. Publisher's hyperbole notwithstanding, *Daffodil* was a success; only three titles on the Obelisk list needed more than two printings in Kahane's lifetime, and *Daffodil* was one of them. In his memoir Maurice Girodias says that *Daffodil* ran to six impressions. Although when it came to reliability Girodias was very much his father's son, six seems a more likely number than any given on *Daffodil*'s publication pages.

The book is dedicated 'TO "DAFFODIL"'. Who 'Daffodil' was – or whether, like 'Cecil Barr', she was a fiction – is unknown.

(b) DAFFODIL

Title page
As A–8.

Collation
[vi] 7–301 + [iii]. Top edge rough trimmed, others untrimmed.

Pagination
As A–8, except [vi] copyright and publication: Published June 1931 |
Reprinted June 1931 | " July 1931 | " July 1931 | " August 1931.

Binding
BNF copy rebound with original heavy paper wrappers bound in.
[?Front and rear flaps removed.]

Front panel: As A–8.

Spine: Not seen.

Rear panel. Yellow. Blank.

Publication
August 1931

Notes
First edition, second impression. ['5th IMPRESSION'.]

A fourth impression has not been located, and was probably never
printed [see notes, A–8].

[v] bears a woodcut logo and the initials H. C. (Herbert Clarke), and
the imprimerie on [v] credits publication to The Vendôme Press; no
Obelisk Press markings appear anywhere in or on the book.

(c) DAFFODIL

Title page
DAFFODIL | OR | *ACCIDENTS WILL HAPPEN* | BY | CECIL BARR |
AUTHOR OF | *SUZY FALLS OFF*, etc. | [logo] | OBELISK PRESS | 338,
RUE SAINT-HONORÉ, PARIS

Collation
8vo. [vi] 7–301 + [i] [see notes]. 19 × 14 cm. Edges untrimmed.

Pagination
[i–ii] blank; [iii] dedication; [iv] blank; [v] title-page; [vi] copyright and publication: Published June 1931 | Reprinted June 1931 | " July 1931 | " July 1931 | " August 1931 | " February 1932 | " June 1932 | " December 1932 | " May 1933; 7–301 text; [302] blank [see notes].

Binding
Heavy paper wrappers.

Front panel: As A–8.

Spine: Daffodil | CECIL BARR | [daffodil] | [logo] | Obelisk Press | 338 Rue St-Honoré | PARIS

Rear panel: Blank.

Publication
May 1933

Notes
First edition, third impression. ['9th IMPRESSION'.]

Sixth, seventh and eight impressions have not been located, and are presumed not to exist. [See notes, A–8.]

Only one copy located [author's collection] which may be lacking a rear endpaper.

(d) DAFFODIL

Title page
DAFFODIL | OR | *ACCIDENTS WILL HAPPEN* | BY | CECIL BARR | AUTHOR OF | *BRIGHT PINK YOUTH* , etc. | [logo] | THE OBELISK PRESS | 338, RUE SAINT-HONORÉ, PARIS

Collation
8vo. [vi] 7–301 + [iii]. 19.4 × 14.3 cm. Edges untrimmed.

Pagination
[i–ii] blank; [iii] dedication; [iv] list of previous works, with blurbs and reviews; [v] title-page; [vi] copyright and publication: Published June 1931 | Reprinted June 1931 | " July 1931 | " August 1931 | " February 1932 | " June 1932 | " December 1932 | " May 1933 | **Tenth large reprinting March 1935** | Reprinted July 1936; 7–301 text; [302–304] blank.

Binding
Yellow heavy paper wrappers with fold-over flaps.

Front panel: Line drawing of sculptress fashioning lower half of nude figure. Daffodil in bottom right corner [black]. 11th IMPRESSION [red] | Daffodil | CECIL BARR | THE OBELISK PRESS – PARIS [black]

Spine: Daffodil | CECIL BARR | [daffodil] [black] | 11th | IMPRESSION [red] | [logo] | Obelisk Press | 338 Rue St-Honoré | PARIS [black]

Rear panel: Blank.

Front flap: Novels by Cecil Barr, with blurbs and reviews, at Frs. 50 each.

Rear flap: Thirteen titles, with blurbs, at Frs. 50 each: 1. The Rock Pool; 2. Bessie Cotter; 3. Star Against Star; 4. The Gentle Men; 5. Tropic of Cancer; 6. Boy; 7. Daffodil (eleventh impression); 8. The Well of Loneliness; 9. My Life and Loves; 10. Storm; 11. The Lamb; 12. Sleeveless Errand; 13. Lady Chatterley's Lover.

Publication
July 1936

Notes
First edition, fourth impression. ['11th IMPRESSION'.]

No tenth impression has been located, and is presumed not to exist. [See notes, A–8.]

A blurb on [iv] announces that *Suzy Falls Off* has been translated 'into half a dozen languages', and that *Amour French For Love* has reached its seventh impression. If true, this bibliography is incomplete. [iv] also mentions A–8(f), describing it as 'one of the chief successes of the Paris season.'

One copy located [Casson collection].

(e) DAFFODIL

Title page
As A–8(d).

Collation
8vo. [vi] 7–301 + [iii]. 19.4 × 14.3 cm. Edges untrimmed.

Pagination
[i–ii] blank; [iii] dedication; [iv] list of previous works, with blurbs and reviews; [v] title-page; [vi] copyright and publication: Published June 1931 | Reprinted June 1931 | "July 1931 | "August 1931 | "February 1932 | "June 1932 | "December 1932 | "May 1933 | **Tenth large reprinting March 1935** | Reprinted July 1936 | "November 1936; 7–301 text; [302–304] blank.

Binding
Yellow heavy paper wrappers with fold-over flaps.

Front panel: Line drawing of sculptress fashioning lower half of nude figure. Daffodil in bottom right corner [black]. 12th IMPRESSION [red] | Daffodil | CECIL BARR | THE OBELISK PRESS – PARIS [black]

Spine: Daffodil | CECIL BARR | [daffodil] [black] | 12th | IMPRESSION [red] | [logo] | Obelisk Press | 338 Rue St-Honoré | PARIS [black]

Rear panel: Blank.

Front flap: Novels by Cecil Barr, with blurbs and reviews, at Frs. 50 each.

Rear flap: Thirteen titles, with blurbs, at Frs. 50 each: 1. The Rock Pool; 2. Bessie Cotter; 3. Star Against Star; 4. The Gentle Men; 5. Tropic of Cancer; 6. Boy; 7. Daffodil (twelfth impression); 8. The Well of Loneliness; 9. My Life and Loves; 10. Storm; 11. The Lamb; 12. Sleeveless Errand; 13. Lady Chatterley's Lover.

Publication
November 1936

Notes
First edition, fifth impression. ['12th IMPRESSION'.]

In this impression, the blurb on [iv] announces that A–8(f) is 'one of the chief successes of the Paris season'.

(f) DAFFODIL

Title page
Not seen.

Collation
8vo. Not seen.

Pagination
Not seen.

Binding
Blue cloth boards in a pictorial dustwrapper.

Wrapper
Front panel: Head of a blonde woman on a blue background. Daffodil [white, tooled in red, on blue] | CECIL BARR [white on blue]

Spine: White. Daffodil | CECIL BARR | [female nude in artistic pose] | [publisher's logo] | GREENBERG [blue]

Rear panel: White. Advertisement for eleven new fiction titles from the publisher's list [brown].

Front flap: White. Price [$2.00], title, author and blurb, with publisher's name and address at foot [brown].

Rear flap: White. Name and address slip for readers wanting details of future Greenberg titles [brown].

Publication
September 1934

Notes
Second edition. First US edition.

The SIU copy is inscribed by Kahane on the front free endpaper: 'To E. M. Grice | with the author's | good wishes. | "Cecil Barr" | Neuilly. 3 – X – 34.' The recipient appears to have been an American professor of Oriental Studies, though his relation to Kahane is unknown.

(g) COUCOU

Title page
CECIL BARR | COUCOU | OU | UN ACCIDENT | EST BIEN VITE ARRIVÉ | "Daffodil" | *ROMAN* | TRADUIT DE L'ANGLAIS PAR LOUIS MELETTA | PARIS | SOCIÉTÉ FRANÇAISE DE LIBRAIRIE | ET D'ÉDITIONS | 151 *bis*, RUE SAINT-JACQUES

Collation
[iv] 5–254 + [?ii]. 17.7 × 11.5 cm. Edges trimmed [BNF copy, rebound and possibly cropped.]

Pagination
[i] half-title; [ii] blank; [iii] title-page; [iv] copyright; 5–254 text; [255] imprimerie: 822 – 11 – 34. — RÉGIE IMP. CRÉTÉ — CORBEIL.; [256] blank.

Binding
Card wrappers.

Front panel: Peerlessly bad illustration in blue and black of an artist's model, topless, nippleless, and apparently blind, posing in front of a window overlooking something blue and murky which may or may not be Paris. CÉCIL | BARR | COUCOU | TRADUIT DE L'ANGLAIS | PAR | L. MELETTA

Spine: Not seen.

Rear panel: Not seen.

Publication
November 1934

Notes
Third edition. First edition in French.

Rare: one copy located [BNF].

The translation is by Louis Meletta. In *Memoirs of a Booklegger*, Kahane thanks Meletta, 'who has introduced me to many of the delights of the Paris it is so hard for a foreigner to know'. Meletta is the dedicatee of *Bright Pink Youth* [see A–31], where Kahane thanks him for 'cloth[ing] *Daffodil* in such bright French attire'.

(h) DAFFODIL

Title page
DAFFODIL | OR | *ACCIDENTS WILL HAPPEN* | BY | CECIL BARR | [logo] | THE OBELISK PRESS | 16, PLACE VENDOME, PARIS

Collation
8vo. [vi] 7–243 + [i]. 19.6 × 14 cm. Edges untrimmed.

Pagination
[i–ii] blank; [iii] dedication; [iv] copyright and publication: Published June 1931 | Reprinted June 1931 | " July 1931 | " August 1931 | " February 1932 | " June 1932 | " December 1932 | " May 1933 | **Tenth large reprinting March**

1935 | Reprinted July 1936 | " November 1936 | " January 1937 | " March 1937 | Reset October 1937 | (18th thousand); [v] title-page; [vi] blank; 7–243 text; [244] blank.

Binding
Yellow heavy paper wrappers with fold-over flaps.

Front panel: Line drawing of sculptress fashioning lower half of nude figure. Daffodil in bottom right corner [black]. 18th IMPRESSION [red] | Daffodil | CECIL BARR | THE OBELISK PRESS – PARIS [black]

Spine: Daffodil | CECIL BARR | [daffodil] | 18th | IMPRESSION | [logo] | Obelisk Press | 16 Place Vendôme | PARIS [black]

Rear panel: [logo] [black].

Front flap: Two titles by Cecil Barr, with blurbs and reviews, at Frs. 60 each.

Rear flap: Twelve titles, with blurbs, at Frs. 60 each: 1. Dark Refuge; 2. To Beg I Am Ashamed; 3. Half O'Clock in Mayfair; 4. Lady, Take Heed!; 5. The Rock Pool (2nd edition); 6. Boy; 7. Star Against Star (2nd impression); 8. Tropic of Cancer; 9. My Life and Loves; 10. Easter Sun (2nd large edition); 11. Storm (4th edition); 12. Sleeveless Errand

Publication
October 1938

Notes
Fourth edition. Second Obelisk edition. ['18th IMPRESSION'.]

Entirely reset, though retaining the livery of previous Obelisk impressions of this title. All misprints from previous Obelisk impressions are corrected, except for p. 166, l. 3: 'when' for 'where' [cf. p. 204, l. 4 in preceding Obelisk impressions]. The front flap states that *Lady, Take Heed!* has reached its '3rd Big Impression'.

(i) DAFFODIL

Title page
CECIL BARR | DAFFODIL | OR | *ACCIDENTS WILL HAPPEN* | THE OBELISK PRESS | PARIS

Collation
8vo. [vi] 7–271 + [i]. 17.5 × 11.4 cm. Edges trimmed.

Pagination
[i–ii] blank; [iii] half-title; [iv] blank; [v] title-page; [vi] copyright and dedication; 7–271 text; [272] imprimerie: IMPRIMÉ EN FRANCE | PAR BRODARD ET TAUPIN | IMPRIMEUR – RELIEUR | COULOM-MIERS – PARIS | IMPRIMEUR No 1170 | 49067 – 5 – 1955

Binding
Stiff paper wrappers.

Front panel: Yellow and white vertical stripes, title printed on a background of black brushstrokes. Daffodil [white] | *by* | *CECIL BARR* | OBELISK PRESS [black]

Spine: White. *CECIL | BARR* | DAFFODIL | OBELISK | PRESS [black]

Rear panel: White. MUST NOT BE IMPORTED INTO ENGLAND OR USA | Prix: 500 Frs. (b. c. + 1.l.) [black]

Publication
May 1955

Notes
Fifth edition. Third Obelisk edition.

Kahane's son, Maurice Girodias, had founded the Olympia Press in 1954, but occasionally reverted to the Obelisk imprint when he thought its reputation would help boost sales [see A–32(f), A–39(d), A–64 etc.]. Although no markings in the book confirm it, it seems highly likely that this edition was issued by him.

(j) FRENCH MODEL ('DAFFODIL')

Title page
FRENCH | MODEL | CECIL | BARR | this is a BEACON BOOK

Collation
Small 8vo. [vi] 7–188 + [iv]. 18 × 10.5 cm. Edges trimmed.

Pagination
[i] 'teaser' extract; [ii] blank; [iii] title-page; [iv] copyright; [v] half-title; [vi] blank; 7–188 text; [189–192] publisher's advertisements.

Binding
Illustrated stiff paper wrappers.

Front panel: Lurid colour illustration of an artist's model and her suitor.

TO GIRLS LIKE HER, SEX WAS A WAY OF LIFE. [yellow] | FRENCH | MODEL [red] | 35c | B 133 [blue, towards top right] | by Cecil Barr | THE RISQUE ESCAPADES | OF A PASSIONATE PLAYGIRL. [yellow]

Spine: FRENCH MODEL [red] TO GIRLS LIKE HER, SEX WAS A WAY OF LIFE. B 133 [black] [the whole printed horizontally, top to bottom]

Rear panel: Blue, with two women silhouetted in white. NAUGHTY | ... BUT OH, SO NICE! | [lurid blurb] [black]

Publication
1957

Notes
Sixth edition. Second US edition.
Beacon Books was an imprint of the publishers Greenberg, who issued the first American edition of this title in 1934 [see A–8(f)], and who in 1957 still held the copyright .

A–9 SUZY FALLS OFF
by CECIL BARR (JACK KAHANE)

Title page
SUZY FALLS OFF | BY | CECIL BARR | Author of | DAFFODIL | [logo] | 338, RUE SAINT-HONORÉ | PARIS

Collation
16mo. [viii] 9–241 + [iii]. 16.8 × 11.2 cm. Edges trimmed.

Pagination
[i] publisher's half-title; [ii] blank; [iii] title-page; [iv] copyright and publication: FIRST PUBLISHED IN: | ENGLAND 1928. | U. S. A. 1929. | GERMANY 1931. | BOULEVARD LIBRARY 1931.; [v] dedication; [vi] blank; [vii] contents; [viii] blank; 9–241 text; [242] imprimerie: Imprimerie Vendôme | 338. Rue Saint-Honoré | Paris; [243–244] blank.

Binding
Heavy paper wrappers with fold-over flaps.

Front panel: White, with blue bands at top and bottom.

[circle] THE BOULEVARD LIBRARY [white] | SUZY | FALLS OFF | BY | CECIL BARR | Author of | DAFFODIL [blue] | [logo] | Not to be taken into the British Empire and U. S. A. [white]

Spine: Not seen.

Rear panel: Not seen.

Front flap: White. Blurb [blue].

Rear flap: White. Two titles, with blurbs, at Frs. 50 each: 1. Jam To-Day; 2. Daffodil [blue].

Publication
November 1931

Notes
Third edition.

Rare: one copy located [BNF].

The first edition was published in England by John Long in 1928 [see C–8] and the second in the United States by Albert and Charles Boni in 1929 [see C–8(b)].

The circle on the front panel of the wrapper of the BNF copy is obscured by a shelfmark, but it almost certainly contains the price [12 Fr 50], as on the other two Boulevard Library titles [see A–10, A–13].

No. 1 (of 3) in the Boulevard Library of Lighter Modern Fiction [see A–10 and A–13]. It was probably issued with a wraparound band [see A–13].

(b) SUZY FALLS OFF

Title page
SUZY FALLS OFF | BY | CECIL BARR | (*Author of Daffodil*) | THE OBELISK PRESS | 16, PLACE VENDÔME, PARIS | 1944

Collation
8vo. [viii] 9–241 + [vii]. 17.7 × 11 cm. All edges trimmed.

Pagination
[i–ii] blank; [iii] title-page; [iv] copyright; [v] dedication; [vi] blank; [vii] contents; [viii] blank; 9–241 text; [242] imprimerie: IMP. KAPP | VANVES (SEINE) | C. O. L. 31.0915; [243–248] blank.

Binding
Paper wrappers.

Front panel: White, with vertical blue-grey bands left and right. SUZY | *FALLS OFF* | BY | CECIL BARR | THE OBELISK PRESS [black]

Spine: White. SUZY | *FALLS* | *OFF* | BY | CECIL | BARR | THE | OBELISK | PRESS [black]

Rear panel: White. * 65 fr. [black]

Publication
1944

Notes
Second Obelisk edition.

A–10 LOVELIEST OF FRIENDS!

By G(LADYS) SHEILA DONISTHORPE

Title page
LOVELIEST OF FRIENDS! | By | G. SHEILA DONISTHORPE | [logo] | 338, RUE SAINT-HONORÉ | PARIS

Collation
16mo. [x] 11–263 + [i]. 17 × 11.3 cm. Edges trimmed.

Pagination
[i–ii] blank; [iii] publisher's half-title; [iv] blank; [v] title-page; [vi] copyright; [vii] dedication; [viii] blank; [ix] Pope quotation; [x] blank; 11–263 text; [264] imprimerie: Imprimerie Vendôme | 338, Rue Saint-Honoré | Paris

Binding
White stiff paper wrappers with fold-over flaps.

Front panel: Blue bands top and bottom. 12 Fr 50 [blue in white circle] THE BOULEVARD LIBRARY [white on blue] | LOVELIEST | OF | FRIENDS! | BY | G. SHEILA DONISTHORPE [blue on white] | [logo] | Not to be taken into the British Empire and U. S. A. [white on blue]

Spine: White, blue banding. G. SHEILA | DONISTHORPE | LOVE-LIEST | OF | FRIENDS! | [logo] | Price: | Frs. 12. 50

Rear panel: Blue bands top and bottom. THE BOULEVARD LIBRARY [white on blue] | [Three titles, with blurbs: 1. Suzy Falls Off; 2. Loveliest of Friends!; 3. Possession] [blue on white] | THE BOULEVARD LIBRARY [white on blue]

Front flap: Blurb and review quotation.

Rear flap: Blurb for *Suzy Falls Off*, with review quotation.

Publication
January 1932

Notes
Third edition.

First published by Old Royalty Book Publishers in London in 1931, and by Claude Kendall in New York later the same year. Kahane paid Frs. 2,000 for the English-language continental rights to the book in November 1931, and published it in Paris two months later as the second title in The Boulevard Library of Modern Fiction series. In September 1932 Kahane wrote to Donisthorpe's agent William Bradley that '150 have been definitely sold and there are 900 on depot at Hachette's who inform us that perhaps 1/3, certainly not more, are sold.' By December, sales had reached 700 copies.

No. 2 (of 3) in the Boulevard Library of Lighter Modern Fiction [see A–9 and A–13]. It was probably issued with a wraparound band [see A–13, Binding].

A–11 GOLD AND SILVER
by HENRY BRIDGES (JACK KAHANE)

Title page
GOLD AND SILVER | A NOVEL | BY | HENRY BRIDGES | [logo] | THE OBELISK PRESS | 338 RUE SAINT-HONORÉ | PARIS

Collation
8vo. [vi] 7–324. [?Rear endpaper missing.]

Pagination
[i–ii] blank; [iii] title-page; [iv] copyright; [v] disclaimer; [vi] blank; 7–324 text. Imprimerie at foot of 324: Imprimerie Vendôme 338 rue Saint-Honoré – Paris.

Binding
Heavy paper wrappers.

Wrapper
Front wrapper: Silver, drawing of two louche women (one couchant, one rampant) in black. GOLD & SILVER | by | Henry Bridges [black].

Spine: Silver. GOLD | AND | SILVER [see notes] | [drawing of a smoking, monocled lesbian] | [logo] | 338 Rue Saint-Honoré | Paris [black].

Rear wrapper: Silver. [drawing of lesbian] [black] [see notes].

Publication
January 1932

Notes
First edition.

Three copies located, all rebound.

No publication date appears in the book. The BNF copy is date-stamped 29 January 1932, and Armstrong notes a review in the New York Herald three days later.

The BNF copy has a shelfmark obscuring a section of the spine which probably carries the author's name, and a barcode on the rear cover, possibly obscuring the price.

No copy examined has fold-over flaps. Either they were removed from all three copies examined during rebinding, or, since this title was the first to be published in what was to become the standard Obelisk Press livery, it may be that flaps were a refinement added to books published later.

The wrapper illustrations are by Marcelle Kahane, Kahane's wife, who also designed wrappers for some of the novels he published under his own name during the 1920s [e.g. C–7].

'Henry Bridges' was almost certainly Jack Kahane – when you've read a dozen of his novels a thirteenth is not difficult to identify. There is also good circumstantial evidence pointing to Kahane's authorship.

'Gold and silver' was 'the charming expression for the double-sexed'– 1920s' slang for bisexuality. The novel is set in the camp world of London's theatreland, and its summer vacation spots on the Côte d'Azur. Homo- and bisexual characters of both sexes provide the cast, recreational use of 'coco' (cocaine) is plentiful, and although opium is never mentioned by name the central character does a lot of drifting off after sucking on a pipe. The novel's milieu is a step or two further down the road to ruin than the characters in the novels of Cecil Barr are ever allowed to stray, and it seems likely that Kahane thought it prudent to invent a second pseudonym for the author of *Gold and Silver* so as not to alienate the faithful Barr readership – a readership which had come to expect healthy heterosexual naughtiness but which might have drawn the line at drugged-up gay promiscuity. In addition, *Daffodil* and *Suzy Falls Off* had both been published in 1931. *Gold and Silver* would have been the third Cecil Barr offering in less than a year, with Gladys Donisthorpe's *Loveliest of Friends!* as the only alternative. Such a thin list would not reflect well on the fledgling publishing house; inventing Henry would at least lengthen it to three.

Two other clues also point to Kahane's authorship. Firstly, one of the three copies located [author's collection] has a pencil annotation on the front free endpaper which reads: 'Who Henry Bridges! EK', suggesting the copy may be ex libris Eric Kahane (Jack's son). And secondly, if 'Henry Bridges' is a pseudonym it's precisely the sort of pseudonym Kahane would choose. His first was 'Cecil Barr', chosen because Kahane used to drink in a bar called the Cecil. For the second, why not draw inspiration from a bridge across the Seine just a short walk from Kahane's office in rue St-Honoré: the Pont Henri IV?

A–12 HERE'S LOOKING AT YOU
by GEORGE HOUGHTON

Title page
CELEBRITIES IN CARICATURE No. 1 | [device] | Here's Looking at You ~ | by HOUGHTON | with a Foreword by | HEROL EGAN | *CONTENTS* | Sisley Huddleston. | "Sparrow" Robertson. | Gilbert White. | Harry McElhone. | Patrick McCabe. | Jeff Dickson. | Sam Hellman. | Carl E. Freybe. | Col. Charles Sweeney. | Harry Ackerman. | Herol Egan. | Jack Dunhill. | Frank Meier. | Sid Horner. | Fred Payne.

Collation
4to. [iv] 15 caricatures + [iii]. 31 × 23.5 cm. Edges trimmed.

Pagination
[i] title-page; [ii] publication: FIRST PUBLISHED IN FEBRUARY MCMXXXII | BY THE OBELISK PRESS | 338, RUE SAINT-HONORÉ, PARIS, FRANCE; imprimerie: PRINTED BY THE VENDOME

PRINTING WORKS; and copyright; [iii] foreword; [iv] blank; 15 caricatures, unpaginated and printed on rectos only, in the order in which they appear on [i]; [30] blank; [31] artist's copyright; [32] blank.

Binding
White, unprinted stiff paper covers (not included in pagination) sewn in to orange paper wrappers with fold-over flaps.

Wrapper
Front panel: *CELEBRITIES IN CARICATURE No. 1* | HERE'S LOOKING AT YOU = | Houghton [facsimile signature] [black]
Rear panel: Blank.
Front flap: Price [THIRTY FRANCS]
Rear flap: Blank.

Publication
February 1932

Notes
First edition.

[31] reads in full: Although the artist retains full | Copyright on all drawings, the | originals are purchaseable by | arrangement. | Signed artist's proofs in full | colour suitable for framing can be | obtained from the Obelisk Press, | 338, Rue Saint-Honoré, Paris.

Herol Egan, one of the subjects of the book, writes a foreword on p. ii. In it, he identifies 'my good friend George William Houghton, who, in his spare time from doing drawings for the "Continental Daily Mail", has snatched odd hours to compile this folio.' Later, he writes: 'If somebody should pick up this book of sketches 30 years from now, probably not a single character could be recognised – with the exception of a well-known painter and a novelist of parts. The rest will fade out with the coming of a new generation... The infinite variety of the characters shows against what background Houghton has penned his drawings. He had a wide field of choice, for Paris is rich in material. He could have chosen the diplomats, the businessmen, the artists, or the writers. Happily he chose to take a cross section of them all, and has thus produced a book which will long be kept as an agreeable souvenir of a Paris which is passing.'

Rare: two copies located [BNF; HRC].

A–13 POSSESSION

by RAYMONDE MACHARD

Title page
POSSESSION | By | RAYMONDE MACHARD | COMPLETE | UNEXPURGATED ENGLISH VERSION | OF THE NOVEL THAT HAS SOLD | 290,000 COPIES (CERTIFIED) | IN FRANCE | [logo] | 338, RUE SAINT-HONORÉ | PARIS

Collation
16mo. [vi] 7–291 + [i]. 16.3 × 11.3 cm. Edges trimmed.

Pagination
[i] publisher's half-title; [ii] blank; [iii] title-page; [iv] copyright; [v] export embargo; [vi] blank; 7–291 text; [292] imprimerie: IMPRIMERIE VENDOME | MARCEL SERVANT | 338, RUE SAINT-HONORÉ | PARIS

Binding
Red and white stiff card wrappers, with tan wraparound band.

Front panel: Red bands, top and bottom. 12 Fr 50 [red in white circle] THE BOULEVARD LIBRARY [white on red] | POSSESSION | BY | RAYMONDE MACHARD [red on white] | ONLY ENGLISH VERSION OF THE FRENCH | NOVEL THAT SOLD 290,000 COPIES (CERTIFIED). | ENTIRELY UNEXPURGATED [red on white, boxed in red] | [logo] Not to be taken into the British Empire and U.S.A. [white on red]

Spine: BOULEVARD | LIBRARY | No. 3 | RAYMONDE | MACHARD [red on white] | POSSESSION [printed vertically] | [logo] | Price: | Fr. 12.50 [red on white]

Rear panel: Red bands, top and bottom. THE BOULEVARD LIBRARY [white on red] | THE BOULEVARD LIBRARY | OF LIGHTER MODERN FICTION | The first three volumes: [red on white] | [Three titles, with blurbs: 1. Suzy Falls Off; 2. Loveliest of Friends! ; 3. Possession] [red on white] | THE BOULEVARD LIBRARY [white on red]

Front flap: Blurb and review quotation for *Loveliest of Friends!*

Rear flap: Review quotation for *Suzy Falls Off.*

Wraparound band: Boulevard Library books | have that Continental | flavour you want when | you come to France. [black]

Publication
April 1932

Notes
Second edition. First edition in English.

First published as *La Possession: Roman de l'amour* by Flammarion, Paris, in 1927. Second and third impressions followed in 1928 and 1930.

Littered with misprints – p. 93, l. 18: 'a bouther' for 'about her'; p. 231, l. 24: 'her' for 'hers'; p. 254, l. 13: 'slighted' for 'alighted', among many others. These would have become issue points had the title ever run to a second impression, but this English-language version failed to emulate the inexplicable success of its French counterpart.

No translator is credited, but it was almost certainly Kahane: in *Memoirs of a Booklegger*, Kahane writes of 'a very mediocre novel that I had inherited from Clarke; it had been written by a friend of his, and I had no alternative but to publish it. I tried to polish it up, but I was not proud of it.'[1]

No. 3 (of 3) in the Boulevard Library of Lighter Modern Fiction [see A–9 and A–10].

A–14 POEMS
by LAURENCE DAKIN

Title page
POEMS | BY | LAURENCE DAKIN | [logo] | 338, RUE ST-HONORÉ – PARIS

Collation
8vo. [viii] 11–55 + [iii]. 19.5 × 14.5 cm. Top edge trimmed, other edges untrimmed.

Pagination
[i] half-title; [ii] blank; [iii] title-page; [iv] copyright; [v] dedicatory verse; [vi] blank; [vii] contents; [viii] blank; 11–55 text; [56] blank; [57] imprimerie: IMPRIMERIE VENDOME | MARCEL SERVANT | 338 Rue Saint-Honoré | Paris

Binding
White coarse-grain boards.

1 Kahane, *Memoirs*, p. 232.

Front panel: Blank.

Spine: Printed vertically, top to bottom: POEMS LAURENCE DAKIN [tan]

Rear panel: Blank.

Publication
July 1932

Notes
First edition.

Kahane published four books by Dakin: all are perfunctorily designed and bound, and only three manage to spell the author's name correctly [see A–58]. It seems likely that Dakin paid for his books to be published, and that Kahane did the bare minimum in keeping his side of the bargain.

A–15 THE LAMB

by PHILIPPE HERIAT

Cloth boards issue

Title page
PRIX THÉOPHRASTE – RENAUDOT | THE LAMB | (*L'INNOCENT*) | BY | PHILIPPE HÉRIAT | UNEXPURGATED TRANSLATION FROM THE FRENCH | BY | JACK KAHANE | [logo] | THE OBELISK PRESS | 338 Rue Saint-Honoré | PARIS

Collation
8vo. [xii] 13–436 + [ii]. 19 × 13.5 cm. Edges trimmed.

Pagination
[i–ii] blank; [iii] half-title; [iv] blank; [v] title-page; [vi] copyright and publication: *The French original, entitled "L'Innocent",* | *first published in 1931.* | *First published in English 1932.*; [vii] dedication; [viii] blank; [ix] Pascal quotation; [x] blank; [xi] section heading; [xii] blank; 13–436 text; [437–438] blank.

Binding
Black cloth boards stamped in gilt on spine, with a yellow printed dustwrapper and white wraparound band.

Spine of book: THE | LAMB | BY | PHILIPPE | HÉRIAT | OBELISK PRESS

Wrapper
Front panel: Ink drawing, signed M. Kahane, of a young and troubled couple.

A brilliant study of the strange relationship between | a young tennis-champion of distinguished | family and his sister. Entirely unexpurgated.[red on yellow]|The Lamb|by|Philippe Hériat [black on yellow] | ANDRÉ | MAUROIS | in the NEW YORK | TIMES: | "…endowed with | remarkable life… | In its description of | scenes of sensuality | this novel is extremely | audacious. Unques- | tionably its author | has a gift for painting | life… There is, from | the very beginning of | this book, a truthful- | ness of dialogue that | sometimes recalls | Tolstoy." [red on yellow]

Spine: THE LAMB|BY|PHILIPPE HÉRIAT|9/-|[logo]|THE OBELISK PRESS | PARIS [black on yellow]

Rear panel: [logo] [black on yellow]

Front flap: Blank.

Rear flap: Blank.

Wraparound band: [logo at left] READ THIS FINE NOVEL | unanimously awarded the | French Journalists' Prize [red on white]

Publication
July 1932

Notes
Second edition. First edition in English.

First published as L'Innocent by Denoël et Steele in Paris in 1931.

The book's continental English-language rights were offered to Kahane by William Bradley on 22 December 1931. Bradley's cover letter noted that the book had been banned in Britain already, 'which ought to be a good point for your edition'. Kahane spent the first three months of 1932 translating the book.

The wrapper illustration is by Marcelle Kahane, Jack Kahane's wife.

(b) THE LAMB

Paper bound issue

Title page
As A–15.

Collation
8vo. [xiv] 13–436 + [ii]. 19.3 × 13.6 cm. Top and bottom edges untrimmed, leading edge trimmed.

Pagination
[i–iv] blank; [v] half-title; [vi] blank; [vii] title-page; [viii] copyright and publication: *The French original, entitled "L'Innocent",* | *first published in 1931.* | *First published in English 1932.*; [ix] dedication; [x] blank; [xi] Pascal quotation; [xii] blank; [xiii] section heading; [xiv] blank;13–436 text; [437–438] blank.

Binding
Yellow heavy paper wrappers with no fold-over flaps.

Front panel: As A–15.

Spine: THE LAMB | BY | PHILIPPE HÉRIAT | [logo] | THE OBELISK PRESS | PARIS [black on yellow]

Rear panel: [logo] | IMPRIMERIE VENDOME | MARCEL SERVANT | 338, RUE SAINT-HONORÉ | PARIS

Publication
August 1932

Notes
Rare: only one copy located [Cornell]. Presumably issued simultaneously with the cloth-bound issue, at a lower price (no price appears on the book). Alternatively, it could be a pre-publication review copy.

(c) THE LAMB

Paper-bound issue, second impression

Title page
As A–15.

Collation
8vo. [xiv] 13–436 + [ii]. 19.3 × 13.6 cm. Edges untrimmed.

Pagination
[i–iv] blank; [v] half-title; [vi] blank; [vii] title-page; [viii] copyright and publication: *The French original, entitled "L'Innocent", | first published in 1931. | First published in English 1932.* | Reprinted August 1932.; [ix] dedication; [x] blank; [xi] Pascal quotation; [xii] blank; [xiii] section heading; [xiv] blank;13–436 text; [437] blank; [438] imprimerie: IMPRIMERIE VENDOME | MARCEL SERVANT | 338 Rue Saint-Honoré | Paris.

Binding
Yellow heavy paper wrappers with no fold-over flaps.

Front panel: As A–15.

Spine: THE LAMB | BY | PHILIPPE HÉRIAT | [logo] | THE OBELISK PRESS | PARIS [black on yellow]

Rear panel: As A–15

Publication
August 1932

Notes
Rare: only one copy located [Casson collection]. Differs in only two respects from A–15(b): the publication information on [viii] has been revised, and the imprimerie has been moved from the rear panel of the wrapper to [438].

A–16 STORM
by PETER NEAGOE

Title page
STORM | BY | PETER NEAGOE | [logo] | THE OBELISK PRESS | 338, RUE SAINT-HONORÉ | PARIS

Collation
8vo. [x] 11–304 + [iv]. 18.5 × 13.5 cm. Edges trimmed.

Pagination
[i–iv] blank; [v] half-title; [vi] blank; [vii] title-page; [viii] copyright; [ix] dedication; [x] blank; 11–304 text; [305] contents; [306] imprimerie: IMPRIMERIE VENDOME | MARCEL SERVANT | 338 Rue Saint-Honoré | Paris; [307–308] blank.

Binding
Heavy paper wrappers with fold-over flaps.

Wrapper
Front panel: Black and green. STORM [green on black] | AND MUCH
OTHER ASTOUNDING MATERIAL BY A GREAT NEW WRITER
| PETER NEAGOE | [logo] | 338, RUE SAINT-HONORÉ [black on
green]

Spine: Green. STORM | BY | PETER | NEAGOE | [logo] | The | Obelisk
Press | PARIS

Rear panel: Green. *BANNED IN AMERICA* | **What the critics think of
STORM:** | [seven blurbs] | Price: 50 Frs.

Front flap: Puff for *The Lamb*, with approving quote from André
Maurois.

Rear flap: Two titles, with blurbs, at Frs. 50 each: 1. Gold and Silver
(second impression before publication); 2. Daffodil (seventh impression).

Publication
22 August 1932

Notes
Second edition.

First published in Paris in February 1932 by New Review Editions, the
imprint of the periodical Neagoe co-edited with Samuel Putnam. For
the Obelisk edition, Kahane bulked up the rather slim first edition
by adding another five of Neagoe's stories to the collection: 'Gavrila's
Confession', 'Winning a Wife', 'The Last Call', 'The Holy Remedy' and
'Suzan and the Three Old Men'. (He dropped one: 'Dreams').

For the Obelisk edition Kahane dropped the introduction by Eugene
Jolas which had appeared in the New Review edition. This, and
Kahane's sensationalist approach to publicising the Obelisk edition
[see B–1], caused Jolas to end his friendship with Neagoe.

Banned in the United States, Storm sold well to Americans passing
through Paris, and Kahane saw it as a quintessential Obelisk title :

> Although a volume of short stories, and short stories, even by the greatest
> writers, are commonly considered unsaleable, thanks to the intrinsic
> merit of *Storm*, added to the halo that banning inevitably creates, plus, I
> feel justified in adding, terribly hard organizing work on my part, *Storm*

was a considerable success, made this author's name widely known, and did a great deal to consolidate the Obelisk Press.[2]

The American ban was lifted in 1934, and the book was published in the United States in 1935 under the title *Winning a Wife*.

Despite the claims made by the book's rear flap, neither a second impression of *Gold and Silver* nor a seventh impression of *Daffodil* has been located.

(b) STORM

Title page
As A–16.

Collation
As A–16.

Pagination
As A–16.

Binding
Heavy paper wrappers with fold-over flaps.

Wrapper
Front panel: Black and green. STORM [green on black] | 3rd. EDITION OF THIS REMARKABLE WORK, BANNED IN AMERICA. | PETER NEAGOE | [logo] | 338, RUE SAINT-HONORÉ [black on green]

Spine: As A–16.

Rear panel: As A–16.

Front flap: As A–16.

Rear flap: As A–16.

Publication
November 1932

Notes
First Obelisk edition, second impression ['3rd edition'].

With the exception of the rewording on the front wrapper, the collation is identical to A–16. Kahane's use of the term '3rd edition'

2 Kahane, *Memoirs*, p. 242.

is ambiguous. It is unlikely that he would have been so bibliographically fastidious as to include the New Review edition in his tally; if
he meant to imply that this was the third time Obelisk had issued the
book, the second impression has not been located, and is presumed
not to exist [see note to A–8, and note to A–18(c)].

(c) STORM

First Obelisk edition, third impression. ['Fourth impression'].

Title page
As A–16.

Collation
As A–16, except: 19.5 × 14.5 cm. Edges untrimmed.

Pagination
As A–16, except: [vi] publication: First published ... August 1932 | 2nd
Impression Sept. 1932 | 3rd " Nov. 1932 | 4th " Sept. 1936

Binding
Heavy paper wrappers with fold-over flaps.

Wrapper
Front panel: Black and green. STORM [green on black] | 4th
IMPRESSION OF THIS REMARKABLE WORK, BANNED IN
AMERICA | PETER NEAGOE | [logo] | 338 RUE SAINT-HONORÉ ,
PARIS

Spine: Green. STORM | BY | PETER | NEAGOE | 4th | IMPRESSION |
[logo] | The | Obelisk Press | PARIS [black]

Rear panel: Green. Blank.

Front flap: Title, author, the seven blurbs that appear on the rear panel
of A–16, and the price [Frs. 50].

Rear flap: Fourteen titles, with blurbs, at Frs. 50 each: 1. The Rock Pool;
2. Black Spring; 3. Bessie Cotter; 4. Star Against Star; 5. The Gentle
Men; 6. Tropic of Cancer; 7. Boy; 8. Daffodil (twelfth impression); 9.
The Well of Loneliness; 10. My Life and Loves; 11. Storm; 12. The Lamb;
13. Sleeveless Errand; 14. Lady Chatterley's Lover.

Publication
September 1936

Notes
The first version of this title to carry a publication history, on [vi].
According to this information, the second impression was issued in
September 1932. If it exists, this impression has not been located.

A–17 POMES PENYEACH
by JAMES JOYCE

Title page
Pomes Penyeach | by | James Joyce | Initial letters designed and Illumi-
nated by | Lucia Joyce | The Obelisk Press | Paris | Desmond Harmsworth
Ltd | London | 1932 [in facsimile of Joyce's hand] [ornament designed
by Lucia Joyce in bottom right-hand corner]

Collation
Rectangular 4to. [vi] 7–31 + [v]. Tissue guards laid in over each page of
text. 25.5 × 33 cm. Edges untrimmed.

Pagination
[i–iii] blank; [iv] copy number, author's signature; [v] title-page; [vi]
blank; 7–31 text [rectos only]; [32] blank; [33] limitation; [34] imprimerie:
IMPRIMERIE VENDOME | MARCEL SERVANT | 338 Rue Saint-
Honoré | Paris; [35–36] blank.

Binding
Unbound signatures housed in folder.

Folder: Boards covered in green silk with inner flaps and green silk
ties at leading edge.

Front panel: Pomes Penyeach | by James Joyce [gold, in facsimile of
Joyce's hand]

Spine and rear panel: Blank.

Text
A single poem to each recto, reproduced in facsimile manuscript
form. A printed version [green] of each poem appears on each tissue
guard, positioned to enable the reading of either when the guard is
in place. The first letter of each poem is designed and illuminated by
Joyce's daughter, Lucia.

Publication
September 1932

Notes

Fourth edition. First English edition (printed in France).

Co-published by the Obelisk Press and Desmond Harmsworth Ltd., in London, printed on Japan nacre paper in a de luxe edition of 25 copies, and 6 *hors de commerce* copies priced at Frs. 1,000.

The first edition of *Pomes Penyeach* was published by Sylvia Beach at Shakespeare and Company in 1927. (Slocum and Cahoon notes that there were two trial printings prior to the first edition. Although copies of these printings still exist, they were never intended for publication and do not, therefore, constitute an 'edition'.) The second edition, published by the Princeton University Press in an edition of 50 copies to secure American copyright, appeared in May 1931, and a pirated edition of 103 copies was issued in Cleveland later that year.

Slocum and Cahoon states that the number of *hors de commerce* copies is unknown. However, in a letter to a would-be reviewer in the United States, Kahane wrote: 'I regret that it is not materially possible to send you a review-copy of my edition of James Joyce's Poems [sic], as only twenty-five of these were produced, plus six copies not for sale, inscribed by Mr. Joyce with the name of the recipient.'[3]

The current known whereabouts of the Obelisk/Harmsworth edition is as follows:

No. 4: Yale University [ex libris John Slocum, Joyce's co-bibliographer]

No. 5: Yale University, bequest of Cole Porter

No. 9: Bibliothèque Nationale de France [donated by Joyce, March 1933]

No. 10: Private collection, London

No. 14: Laura Barnes collection [Harriet Weaver's copy, given to her by Joyce to replace the copy damaged in a fire at her home in May 1934 [see No. 18]. Additionally inscribed to her by the author]

No. 15: University College, Dublin

No. 16: James R. and Mary M. Patton collection

No. 17: Harmsworth family, England

No. 18: McFarlin Library, University of Tulsa [ex libris Harriet Weaver and signed by her. Fire-damaged [see No. 14]]

3 Kahane to Milton A. Abernethy, 19 April 1933, HRC.

No. 19: HRC

No. 21: Huntingdon Library, San Marino, California

No. 25: British Library

Hors de commerce copies:

1. Author's collection. Inscribed: 'Hors commerce for John [sic] Kahane James Joyce'.

2. New York State University, Buffalo, New York. Sylvia Beach's copy.

3. HRC. Inscribed: 'Hors commerce for Hubert Foss [Director of the Oxford University Press], James Joyce'. From the Hanley collection.

Kahane was still advertising the book for sale as late as 1936: on [3] of *The Obelisk: Notes and News No. 3* [see B–6] he writes that two copies are still unsold.

The year following the book's publication Kahane's friend, the composer Herbert Hughes, edited *The Joyce Book* [Sylvan Press and Humphrey Milford, OUP, 1933, 500 copies], musical settings of the poems in *Pomes Penyeach* by (among others) John Ireland, Arthur Bliss, Herbert Howells, George Antheil, Arnold Bax and Hughes himself.

[According to Armstrong, Obelisk published an edition of John Gay's *The Beggar's Opera* late in 1932, with illustrations by the Austrian artist Mariette Lydis. No copy of this book has been located, and it is assumed not to exist. Kahane did place advertisements for such a book, in the continental edition of the *Daily Mail* and the *New York Herald* (both published on 3 October 1932), and Armstrong even cites a review of the book published in the *Chicago Daily Tribune* on 26 September. It seems likely that the book was prepared for publication by Obelisk, and Lydis's work seen by the *Tribune*'s reviewer, but that the project was then cancelled late in its preparation. But Lydis's work was not wasted: an edition of *The Beggar's Opera*, carrying her illustrations, was published in Paris in 1937 by G. Govone for the Limited Editions Club, and reprinted by Heritage Press in New York later the same year.]

A–18 AMOUR FRENCH FOR LOVE

by CECIL BARR (JACK KAHANE)

Title page
AMOUR | FRENCH FOR LOVE | BY | CECIL BARR | AUTHOR OF |
DAFFODIL, SUZY FALLS OFF, etc. | [logo] | THE OBELISK PRESS | 338,
RUE SAINT-HONORÉ, PARIS

Collation
8vo. [viii] 9–384 + [ii]. 19 × 14.2 cm. All edges trimmed.

Pagination
[i–ii] blank; [iii] half-title; [iv] blank; [v] title-page; [vi] copyright and
publication: First published November 1932; [vii] dedication; [viii]
disclaimer; [9–11] contents; [12] blank; [13] chapter heading; [14] blank;
[15–384] text; [385] blank; [386] imprimerie: IMPRIMERIE VENDOME
| MARCEL SERVANT | 338 Rue Saint-Honoré | Paris

Binding
Heavy paper wrappers with fold-over flaps. Wraparound band.

Wrapper
Front panel: White, with red band at head running around spine
and across rear panel. Woman's line portrait in red, signed ?Dani.
amour | french for love [white on red] | BY | CECIL BARR | author of |
DAFFODIL | (8th IMPRESSION) [red on white]

Spine: amour | french | for | love | BY | CECIL BARR [white on red] |
[logo] | THE | OBELISK PRESS | PARIS [red on white]

Rear panel: Price 50 fr. [red on white]

Front flap: Title, author, blurb, with an advertisement for *Daffodil* (8th
impression) beneath.

Rear flap: Two titles, with blurbs: 1. Storm (3rd edition); 2. The Lamb.

Wraparound band: Reiterates the blurb on the front flap, and adds:
CANNOT BE BOUGHT in ENGLAND or U. S. A. 2ND IMPRES-
SION [see notes]

Publication
November 1932

Notes
First edition.

Dedicated to Kahane's friend Stuart Gilbert, critic, scholar and early champion of James Joyce. The dedication copy [Stuart Gilbert collection, HRC] is inscribed by the author on the title-page: 'To the high – and broad – browed Stuart Gilbert this copy no. oo (hors concours) of a futile study of futility from the perfectly browless Cecil Barr, Paris (Seine) November 1932.' Additionally inscribed: 'To the lofty and broad browed Gilbert from the perfectly browless Barr.'

The wraparound band described above is laid in to the Gilbert copy and is the only example located. The Gilbert copy of this book is a first edition, suggesting that the wraparound band's announcement of the second impression is another example of Kahane's tendency to anticipate healthy sales rather than wait for them to happen.

(b) AMOUR FRENCH FOR LOVE

Title page
As A–18.

Collation
As A–18.

Pagination
[i–ii] blank; [iii] half-title; [iv] blank; [v] title-page; [vi] copyright and publication: First published November 1932 | Reprinted November 1932 | " December 1932 | " December 1932; [vii] dedication; [viii] disclaimer; [9–11] contents; [12] blank; [13] chapter heading; [14] blank; [15–384] text; [385] blank; [386] imprimerie.

Binding
As A–18.

Wrapper
As A–18.

Publication
December 1932

Notes
First edition, second impression ['Fourth impression']. No copies of the November 1932 reprint or the first reprint of December 1932 have been located. Four reprints in two months seems unlikely, and they are presumed not to exist.

(c) AMOUR FRENCH FOR LOVE

Title page
As A–18.

Collation
As A–18.

Pagination
As A–18 except [vi], where the publication history reads: First published November 1932 | Reprinted November 1932 | " December 1932 | " December 1932 | " January 1933

Binding
As A–18.

Wrapper
As A–18.

Publication
January 1933

Notes
First edition, third impression ['Fifth impression']. Only one copy located [NLS], rebound in maroon boards with original wrappers laid in at rear.

(d) AMOUR FRENCH FOR LOVE

Title page
AMOUR = | FRENCH FOR LOVE | BY | CECIL BARR | LIVERIGHT PUBLISHING CORPORATION | NEW YORK 1934

Collation
8vo. [ffep. +xii] 13–317 + [v]. 19.2 × 13 cm. Edges trimmed.

Pagination
[ffep.] blank: [i] half-title; [ii] blank; [iii] title-page; [iv] copyright; [v] dedication; [vi] disclaimer; [vii–x] contents; [xi] second half-title; [xii] blank; 13–317 text; [318–322] blank.

Binding
Green boards.

Front panel: amour | french for love [black]

Spine: AMOUR | french | for | love | CECIL BARR | LIVERIGHT

Rear panel: Blank.

Wrapper
Not seen.

Publication
1934

Notes
First American edition.

A-19 HUMAN INSIGHTS
by ROBERT DAVIS

Title page
HUMAN INSIGHTS | BY | ROBERT DAVIS | [logo] | THE OBELISK
PRESS | 1933

Collation
8vo. [viii] 9–90 + [ii]. 18.3 × 13.2 cm. Edges trimmed.

Pagination
[i–ii] blank; [iii] half-title; [iv] blank; [v] title-page; [vi] copyright; [vii]
contents; [viii] dedication; 9–90 text; [91] blank; [92] imprimerie:
IMPRIMERIE VENDOME | MARCEL SERVANT | 338, Rue Saint-
Honoré | Paris

Binding
Brown stiff paper wrappers.
Front panel: Top and bottom partitioned by two horizontal lines, one
thick, one thin [black]. HUMAN INSIGHTS | [logo] | ROBERT DAVIS
[black]

Spine: ROBERT | DAVIS | HUMAN INSIGHTS [printed vertically] |
OBELISK | PRESS | PARIS [black]

Rear panel: Price : 12 frs. [black]

Publication
December 1932

Notes

First edition. Rare: three copies located [BNF; University of Wisconsin; University of Iowa].

A collection of hokey essays, some of which were previously published in the Paris edition of *The New York Herald*.

Dedicated 'To K...'

Copyright on [vi] reads: *All rights of reproduction, translation and | adaptation reserved for all countries including | Russia, Mandchukuo and the Island of Guam.* A Mandchukuoan piracy of this title has not been located.

A–20 THE QUEEN'S REVERIE
by ALBERT H. WHITIN

Title page
THE QUEEN'S REVERIE [red] | ALBERT H. WHITIN | THE OBELISK PRESS | PARIS | 1932

Collation
Large 8vo. [xiv] 7–35 + [ix]. 25.5 × 18.8 cm. Edges trimmed.

Pagination
[i] blank pink ffep.; [ii–vi] blank; [vii] half-title; [viii] blank; [ix] title-page; [x] blank; [7] foreword; [8] blank; 9–35 text; [36] blank; [37] imprimerie: IMPRIMERIE VENDOME | MARCEL SERVANT | 338, RUE SAINT-HONORÉ | PARIS; [38–43] blank; [44] blank pink rear ep. Plates tipped in between [viii] and [ix], [x] and [7], and then between every page of text up to [26] and [27]. No plates between [28] and [33]. Final plate between [34] and [35]. Text printed on rectos only. Headings on [7], [9], [35], and first letter on all pages of text printed in red.

Binding
Blue brushed cloth boards, stamped in gilt.

Front panel: Four fleurs de lys, one in each corner. THE QUEEN'S REVERIE | [crown] | [monogram 'M', between two thistles]

Spine: Blank.

Rear panel: Blank.

Publication
December 1932

Notes
First edition.

Tipped in to the front free endpaper of the NLS copy is an ALS from the author to Sir Francis James Grant, Lord Lyon, King of Arms, 'In token of appreciation of your gracious and helpful response to my wish for information of the correct design of the crown of Mary Queen of Scots...'.

Expensive to produce and of extremely limited appeal, this title was almost certainly a vanity project, published by Kahane at the author's expense.

A–21 SQUADRON 95

by HAROLD BUCKLEY

Title page
SQUADRON 95 | BY | HAROLD BUCKLEY | WITH FIVE DRAWINGS | BY | L. C. HOLDEN | AND MANY OTHER ILLUSTRATIONS | *An intimate history of the* | *95th Squadron, first American* | *Flying Squadron to go to the* | *front in the war of 1914–1918.* | [logo] | THE OBELISK PRESS | 338 RUE SAINT-HONORÉ | PARIS | 1933

Collation
8vo. [xiv] 17–227 + [iii]. 22.5 × 17 cm. All edges trimmed.

Pagination
[i–ii] blank; [iii] half-title; [iv] blank; [v] title-page; [vi] copyright; [vii] in memoriam; [viii] blank; [ix] author's foreword; [x] blank; [xi] *"Foreword by Captain Ernst Udet, leading German ace at the end of the war.";* [xii] blank; [xiii] second foreword; [xiv] blank; 17–227 text; [228] imprimerie: IMPRIMERIE VENDOME | MARCEL SERVANT | 338, RUE SAINT-HONORÉ | PARIS; [229–230] blank. Twenty-four photographic plates between: [iv] and [v]; [xii] and [xiii]; [xiv] and [17]; [32] and [33]; [48] and [49]; [52] and [53]; [60] and [61]; [64] and [65]; [68] and [69]; [76] and [77]; [84] and [85]; [92] and [93]; [96] and [97]; [100] and [101]; [108] and [109]; [112] and [113]; [116] and [117]; [124] and [125]; [128] and [129]; [132] and [133]; [140] and [141]; [144] and [145]; [148] and [149]; [156] and [157].

Binding
Blue cloth boards, stamped in gilt.

Front panel: Bucking mule, the squadron's logo.
Spine: SQUADRON | 95 | HAROLD | BUCKLEY | THE | OBELISK PRESS
Rear panel: Blank.

Publication
1933

Notes
First edition.

As well as the photographs, the book is illustrated with five draw-ings by Buckley's flying colleague, Lt. Lancing Colton 'Denny' Holden DSC, an ace credited with the downing of seven enemy aircraft in the last six weeks of the war.

The foreword is written by Ernst Udet. Udet was a Squadron Commander in the Pursuit Group led by Manfred Freiherr von Rich-thofen, the Red Baron. Udet served on the same section of the front as that patrolled by the 95th Squadron, and was the most successful German air ace to survive the war, with 62 enemy aircraft to his name. (This figure was beaten only by Richthofen himself, who accounted for 80 before being shot down and killed in April 1918.) Udet went on to serve in the Luftwaffe in the Second World War.

Although Kahane felt a strong affinity with fellow war veterans, it's probable that the cost of publishing this title was borne by the author: the book's drab livery is of the kind Kahane often used for vanity proj-ects, and it's unlikely that he would have countenanced the inclusion of expensive photographic plates unless someone else was picking up the bill.

In the NYPL copy, the words 'Hun' and 'Boche' have been blacked out by hand wherever they appear in the text. Not bibliographically significant, but interesting.

A–22 MAD ABOUT WOMEN
by N. REYNOLDS PACKARD

Title page
MAD ABOUT WOMEN | BY | N. REYNOLDS PACKARD | *Author of* | *SERPENTINING BOARDWALK* | [logo] | THE OBELISK PRESS | 338 Rue Saint-Honoré | Paris

Collation
8vo. [xii] 13–339 + [iv]. 19 × 13.8 cm. Edges trimmed.

Pagination
[i–iv] blank; [v] half-title ; [vi] blank; [vii] title-page ; [viii] copyright
and publication: FIRST PUBLISHED MARCH 1933.; [ix] dedication;
[x] blank; [xi] second half-title; [xii] blank; 13–339 text; [340] advertisement for *Amour French For Love* (4th impression) with blurb and
review quotations; [341–342] advertisement for *Storm*, with a recap
of its turbulent publishing history and review quotations; [343–344]
blank.

Binding
Heavy paper wrappers with fold-over flaps.

Front panel: Green and black art deco design, signed 'Turo', featuring
head shots of a rakish couple either side of a reclining nude woman
picked out in white and green. N. REYNOLDS PACKARD | MAD |
ABOUT | WOMEN [black]

Spine: N. REYNOLDS | PACKARD [black] | MAD ABOUT WOMEN
[printed vertically] | [logo] [green] | OBELISK PRESS | 338 Rue Saint-
Honoré | Paris [black]

Rear panel: Logo [green] housed in four concentric rectangles [green
– black – green – black]

Front flap: Title, author, blurb and price [50 frs.]

Rear flap: Three titles, with blurbs and (for the third) a review quotation, at Frs. 50 each: 1. Amour French For Love (4th impression, by
CECIL BARR, Author of "Daffodil" (8th impression)); 2. Storm (in its
third large edition); 3. The Lamb (2nd large printing).

Publication
March 1933

Notes
First edition.

The two promised volumes of memoirs advertised on [344] were
never published by the Obelisk Press.

The dedication on [ix] reads: TO PIBE | *Whose Delightful Distractions* |
Made The Completion | Of This Book Almost | Impossible. Pibe – her real name
was Eleanor, neé Cryan – was Packard's wife. Both were war reporters,

atheists and enthusiastic practitioners of free love. Packard's book *Rome Was My Beat* (1975) bears the dedication: TO MY WIFE'S LOVERS | *with appreciation and friendship.*

(b) MAD ABOUT WOMEN

Title page
As A–22.

Collation
8vo. [xii] 13–339 + [iv]. 19 × 13.8 cm. Edges trimmed.

Pagination
[i–iv] blank; [v] half-title ; [vi] blank; [vii] title-page ; [viii] copyright and publication: FIRST PUBLISHED MARCH 1933 | REPRINTED MARCH 1933; [ix] dedication; [x] blank; [xi] second half-title; [xii] blank; 13–339 text; [340] advertisement for *Amour French For Love* (4th impression) with blurb and review quotations; [341–342] advertisement for *Storm*, with a recap of its turbulent publishing history and review quotations; [343] advertisement for *The Lamb* with blurb and review quotations; [344] advertisement, with blurbs, for forthcoming publications: *The Young and Evil, Princess Galitzine* and *Reggie de Veulle.*

Binding
Heavy paper wrappers with fold-over flaps.

Front panel: As A–22.

Spine: As A–22.

Rear panel: As A–22.

Front flap: As A–22.

Rear flap: As A–22.

Publication
March 1933

Notes
First edition, second impression.

(c) MAD ABOUT WOMEN

Title page
As A–22.

Collation
As A–22.

Pagination
[i–iv] blank; [v] half-title; [vi] blank; [vii] title-page; [viii] copyright and publication: FIRST PUBLISHED MARCH 1933.|REPRINTED MARCH 1933.|REPRINTED MARCH 1933.; [ix] dedication; [x] blank; [xi] second half-title; [xii] blank; 13–339 text; [340] advertisement for *Amour French For Love* (4th impression) with blurb and review quotations; [341–342] advertisement for *Storm*, with a recap of its turbulent publishing history and review quotations; [343] advertisement for *The Lamb* [2nd large edition] with blurb and review quotations; [344] advertisement, with blurbs, for forthcoming publications: The *Young and Evil, Princess Galitzine* and *Reggie de Veulle.* Imprimerie: IMPRIMERIE VENDOME, MARCEL SERVANT, 338, RUE SAINT-HONORÉ – PARIS

Binding
Heavy paper wrappers with no fold-over flaps [see notes].

Front panel: As A–22.

Spine: Not seen [see notes].

Rear panel: As A–22.

Publication
March 1933

Notes
First edition, third impression.

One copy located [author's collection]. The copy is rebound preserving the wrappers. The spine of this impression has not been seen, and if it ever had fold-over flaps (and it probably did) they were cropped when the book was rebound.

A–23 THE WELL OF LONELINESS
by RADCLYFFE HALL

Title page
THE WELL OF LONELINESS | By | RADCLYFFE HALL | "... ... nothing extenuate, | Nor set down aught in malice." | with a commentary by | HAVELOCK ELLIS | [logo] | THE OBELISK PRESS | 338 RUE SAINT-HONORÉ | PARIS

Collation
8vo. [x] 13–512. 21.7 × 15 cm. Leading edge untrimmed.

Pagination
[i] half-title; [ii] blank; [iii] title-page; [iv] copyright; [v] dedication; [vi] blank; [vii] commentary; [viii] author's note; [ix] second half-title; [x] blank; 13–512 text.

Binding
Pale green heavy paper wrappers with fold-over flaps.

Wrapper
Front panel: Black border enclosing all text. THE | WELL OF LONELINESS | A Novel | by | Radclyffe Hall | Author of 'Adam's Breed' | * | With an Appreciation by | HAVELOCK ELLIS | This edition cannot be bought in | England or U. S. A.

Spine: THE | WELL OF | LONELINESS | by | Radclyffe Hall | * | 50 Frs. | [logo] | THE | OBELISK PRESS | PARIS

Rear panel: [logo]

Front flap: Blurb and five review quotations.

Rear flap: Fourteen titles, with blurbs, at Frs. 50 each: 1. The Rock Pool; 2. Black Spring; 3. Tropic of Cancer; 4. The Well of Loneliness; 5. Sleeveless Errand; 6. Lady Chatterley's Lover; 7. Bessie Cotter; 8. The Gentle Men; 9. Star Against Star; 10. Daffodil (eleventh impression); 11. My Life and Loves; 12. Boy; 13. Storm; 14. The Lamb.

Publication
1933

Notes
Besides the Cape first edition and its reincarnation as the Pegasus edition in Paris, the Obelisk edition of this title was also preceded

by the American (Covici, Friede) edition of 1929, one French and one German translation, and a number of piracies and cheap reprints.

A–24 LYCIDAS
by JOHN MILTON

Title page
LYCIDAS [red] | *A Lament for a friend drowned in his passage from* | *Chester on the Irish Seas,* 1637 | by | JOHN MILTON | PARIS | JACK KAHANE | At the Obelisk Press | 1933

Collation
Large 8vo. [vi] 1–10 + [iv]. 26 ×17 cm. Front and rear eps. inserted under folding flaps of covers. Edges untrimmed.

Pagination
[i–ii] blank; [iii] half-title; [iv] limitation and dedication; [v] title-page; [vi] blank; 1–10 text; [11] blank; [12] imprimerie: PRINTED UNDER THE DIRECTION OF | JACK KAHANE AND MADE IN FRANCE BY | IMPRIMERIE VENDÔME MARCEL SERVANT, | 338, RUE ST.-HONORÉ, PARIS.; [13–14] blank. First letter of poem and all headers printed in red.

Binding
White heavy paper wrappers with blank fold-over flaps. Sewn signature loosely laid in. Marbled chemise.

Front panel: LYCIDAS [red] | JOHN MILTON | JACK KAHANE | AT THE OBELISK PRESS | PARIS [black]

Rear panel: Blank.

Chemise spine: LYCIDAS [printed vertically, top to bottom] [gilt]

Publication
1933

Notes
Published in an edition of 25 copies, privately distributed and not for sale. Copies exist with the words 'HORS DE COMMERCE' printed on the dedication page. Whether these copies are part of the declared print run of 25, and Kahane simply ran out of dedicatees, or whether there were 25 personally dedicated copies as well as an additional

number of *hors de commerce* copies, is unknown.

Lycidas is mentioned in an Obelisk Press advertisement in *The New York Herald*, 12 June 1933.

The limitation on [iv] reads: THIS EDITION, COMPOSED IN 12 POINT | ELZEVIR AND PRINTED ON HAND-MADE | MONTVAL, CONSISTS OF TWENTY-FIVE | COPIES ONLY, EACH INSCRIBED WITH | THE NAME OF THE RECIPIENT. The name of each dedicatee is printed beneath the limitation: FOR | [DEDICATEE]

Copies located are as follows:

Bodleian Library: 'FOR HAROLD BRIGHOUSE'

Author's collection: 'FOR MICHEL BOUGOUSLAVSKI'

Sonoma State University Library: 'FOR AURIOL LEE'

University of California Library: 'FOR VIRGINIA VERNON'

Princeton University Library: 'FOR SYLVIA BEACH'

Dartmouth College Library: 'FOR CARESSE CROSBY'

British Library: out of series

Bibliothèque Nationale: out of series

Author's collection: 'HORS DE COMMERCE'

The Dartmouth College copy has a signed presentation card from the publisher laid in, which reads: 'Please accept this little edition of one of the finest pieces of English, done to please myself. Jack Kahane.' The copy was a gift to Dartmouth College from N. F. Page. A Norman F. Page was a graduate of the college, class of 1928.

A–25 THE YOUNG AND EVIL

by CHARLES FORD AND PARKER TYLER

Title page
THE YOUNG AND EVIL | by | CHARLES FORD | and | PARKER TYLER | [logo] | THE OBELISK PRESS | 338, RUE SAINT-HONORÉ, PARIS

Collation
8vo., ffep. inserted under folding flap of front cover, [x] 11–215 + [i], rear ep. inserted under folding flap of rear cover. 19.5 × 14.5 cm. Edges untrimmed.

Pagination
[ffep.] blank: [i–ii] blank: [iii] half-title; [iv] blank; [v] title-page; [vi] copyright, limitation; [vii] dedication; [viii] blank; [ix] contents; [x] blank; 11–215 text; [216] blank; [rear ep.] imprimerie on recto: IMPRIMERIE VENDOME | 338 Rue Saint-Honoré | Paris; verso blank.

Binding
Tan heavy paper covers with fold-over flaps.

Wrapper
Front panel: The | Young | And Evil | By | Charles Ford | and | Parker Tyler [red]

Spine: The | Young | And | Evil | By | Charles | Ford | And | Parker | Tyler | [logo] | The | Obelisk | Press | Paris [red]

Rear panel: [logo] [red]

Front flap: Title, authors, price [200 Frs.], blurb [red]

Rear flap: Seven titles, with blurbs, at Frs. 50 each: 1. Storm; 2. The Lamb; 3. Mad About Women; 4. Daffodil (9th impression); 5. Amour French For Love (fifth large impression); 6. The Well of Loneliness; 7. Sleeveless Errand. Plus: "Two volumes of **memoirs** in preparation, by Princess Aimée (Crocker) Galitzine and Reggie de Veulle. Price not yet fixed." [red]

Wraparound band carrying a puff from Gertrude Stein. Not seen, but according to Ford it reproduced Stein's pronouncement: '*The Young and Evil* creates this generation as *This Side of Paradise* by Fitzgerald created his generation.'

Publication
11 August 1933

Notes
First edition. 50 copies.

Limitation page reads: FIRST PRINTED 1933. | A special edition of 50 numbered | copies on pure linen Lafuna, signed by the authors, constitutes | the original edition.

Despite this wording, none of the special edition copies examined is numbered. This edition is signed by both authors below the statement of limitation.

The dedication reads: FROM C.F. TO K.T.Y | AND | FROM P.T. TO THE MOST INTIMATE GUEST.

K.T.Y. is the poet Kathleen Tankersley Young, a contributor to Ford's *Blues* magazine and the woman who introduced Ford to Tyler.

Originally entitled *Jump Back*.

(b) THE YOUNG AND EVIL

First edition, trade issue.

As A–25, except for the price (50 frs. or $2.00 for the trade issue) and the limitation page, which is unsigned.

Ford states that the trade issue 'may have numbered 2500 copies', and that 500 of these were burned by British customs.

A–26 FOR THE DURATION OR...?

by VIVIAN F. DELBOS

Title page
FOR THE DURATION OR ... ? | by | VIVIAN F. DELBOS | [logo] | THE OBELISK PRESS | 338, RUE SAINT-HONORÉ | PARIS

Collation
8vo. [x] 11–194 + [ii]. 17.8 × 13 cm. [BNF copy cropped. See notes.]

Pagination
[i–iv] blank; [v] half-title; [vi] blank; [vii] title-page; [viii] copyright and publication: FIRST PUBLISHED 1933; [ix–x] blank; 11–194 text; [195] imprimerie: MARCEL SERVANT | 338, Rue Saint-Honoré | Paris; [196] blank.

Binding
Paper wrappers.

Front panel: Pink and blue geometrical design.

V. F. DELBOS [pink on blue] | FOR | THE DURATION | OR ... ? | THE OBELISK PRESS [blue on pink]

Spine: Not seen.

Rear panel: Pink. Price 3/6 or 15 Frs. [blue]

Publication
August 1933

Notes
First edition.

Rare: only one copy located [BNF, rebound].

A–27 THE DREAM OF ABARIS AND OTHER POEMS
by LAURENCE DAKIN

Title page
THE DREAM OF ABARIS | AND OTHER POEMS | BY | LAURENCE DAKIN | [logo] | PARIS | 1933

Collation
8vo. [x] 13–78 + [iv]. 19.5 × 14.7 cm. Top edge trimmed, others untrimmed.

Pagination
[i–ii] blank; [iii] half-title ; [iv] list of previous works; [v] title-page; [vi] copyright and limitation; [vii] dedicatory verse; [viii] blank; [ix] contents; [x] blank; [13] prefatory note ; 14–78 text; [79–80] blank; [81] imprimerie: IMPRIMERIE VENDOME | MARCEL SERVANT | 338 Rue Saint-Honoré | Paris; [82] blank.

Binding
Plain dark blue boards, with paper label on spine.

Front panel: Blank.

Spine: White paper label. LAURENCE | DAKIN | THE | DREAM | OF | ABARIS | Obelisk | Press | Paris [blue]

Rear panel: Blank.

Publication
December 1933

Notes
First edition.

One hundred numbered and signed copies were issued simultaneously with a trade edition. Their collation is identical except on [vi], where the former carries a printed 'No.' a stamped number and the author's signature.

A copy in the author's collection, no. 18, is additionally inscribed by Dakin and dated 2 December 1933.

A–28 MY LIFE AND LOVES (4 vols.)

by FRANK HARRIS

(i) VOLUME ONE

Title page
MY LIFE AND LOVES | BY | FRANK HARRIS | PRIVATELY PRINTED

Collation
8vo. [x] 11–353 + [iii]. 18.5 × 13.3 cm. All edges trimmed.

Pagination
[i–iv] blank; [v] half-title ; [vi] blank; [vii] title-page ; [viii] copyright; [ix] foreword half-title; [x] blank; [11–24] foreword; 25–350 text; [351–353] afterword; [354] blank; [355] imprimerie: Lecram-Press | Paris; [356] blank.

Binding
Heavy paper wrappers.

Wrapper
Front panel: White flash running from bottom left to top right, triangulated corners in red. by FRANK HARRIS [red] | My [white] | Life | and [red] | Loves ['L' red, 'oves' white] | volume one [red] | MUST NOT BE imported into England or U. S. A. [white].
N.B: The 'i' of 'HARRIS', although a capital letter, is dotted.

Spine: White. FRANK | HARRIS | My | Life | and | Loves | VOLUME | ONE | PRIVATELY | PRINTED [red]

Rear panel: White. 50 frs. per vol. [red]

Publication
1934

Notes
[For notes to this title, see A–28(iv).]

(ii) VOLUME TWO

Title page
MY LIFE AND LOVES | BY | FRANK HARRIS | VOLUME TWO | PRIVATELY PRINTED

Collation
8vo. [x] 11–450 + [ii]. 18.3 × 13.3 cm. All edges trimmed.

Pagination
[i–iv] blank; [v] half-title; [vi] blank; [vii] title-page; [viii] copyright; [ix] foreword half-title; [x] blank; 11–23 foreword; 24–450 text; [451] imprimerie: Lecram-Press | Paris; [452] blank.

Binding
Heavy paper wrappers.

Wrapper
Same design as A–28(i).

Front panel: by FRANK HARRIS [red] | My [white] | Life | and [red] | Loves ['L' red, 'oves' white] | volume two [red] | MUST NOT BE imported into England or U. S. A. [white].
NB: The 'i' of 'HARRIS', although a capital letter, is dotted.

Spine: White. FRANK | HARRIS | My | Life | and | Loves | VOLUME | TWO | PRIVATELY | PRINTED [red]

Rear panel: As A–28(i).

Publication
1934

(iii) VOLUME THREE

Title page
MY LIFE AND LOVES | BY | FRANK HARRIS | VOLUME THREE | PRIVATELY PRINTED

Collation
8vo. [x] 11–265 + [iii]. 18.3 × 13.3 cm. All edges trimmed.

Pagination
[i–ii] blank; [iii] half-title; [iv] blank; [v] dedication; [vi] blank; [vii] title-page; [viii] copyright; [ix] foreword half-title; [x] Gower

quotation; [11–23] foreword; 24–265 text; [266] blank; [267] imprimerie: Lecram-Press | Paris [268] blank.

Binding
Heavy paper wrappers.

Wrapper
Same design as A–28(i).

Front panel: by FRANK HARRIS [red] | My [white] | Life | and [red] | Loves ['L' red, 'oves' white] | volume three [red] | MUST NOT BE imported into England or U. S. A. [white].
N.B: The 'i' of 'HARRIS', although a capital letter, is dotted.

Spine: White. FRANK | HARRIS | My | Life | and | Loves | VOLUME | THREE | PRIVATELY | PRINTED [red]

Rear panel: As A–28(i).

Publication
1934

(iv) VOLUME FOUR

Title page
MY LIFE AND LOVES | BY | FRANK HARRIS | VOLUME FOUR | PRIVATELY PRINTED

Collation
8vo. [x] 11–268 + [iv]. 18.3 × 13.3 cm. All edges trimmed.

Pagination
[i–iv] blank; [v] half-title; [vi] blank; [vii] title-page; [viii] copyright; [ix] second half-title; [x] blank; 11–268 text; [269] imprimerie: Lecram-Press | Paris; [270–272] blank.

Binding
Heavy paper wrappers.

Wrapper
Same design as A–28(i).

Front panel: by FRANK HARRIS [red] | My [white] | Life | and [red] | Loves ['L' red, 'oves' white] | volume four [red] | MUST NOT BE imported into England or U. S. A. [white].
N.B: The 'i' of 'HARRIS', although a capital letter, is dotted.

Spine: White. FRANK | HARRIS | My | Life | and | Loves | VOLUME | FOUR | PRIVATELY | PRINTED [red]

Rear panel: As A–28(i).

Publication
1934

Notes
Third edition.

My Life and Loves was first published privately by the author himself between 1922 and 1927, in Nice. A German edition of part of the book appeared in 1926 [S. Fischer, Berlin], and Kahane acquired the rights in 1931. Although unmarked, this edition can be identified as an Obelisk Press edition by a letter from Kahane to Frank Harris's widow Helen ('Nellie') Harris, dated 16 February 1935, in which Kahane states that Hachette refused to take copies of the book because it was 'Privately Printed'. This resulted in Kahane issuing another edition, bearing the Obelisk Press imprint, despite his first edition being 'very far from exhausted' [see A–28(b)].

Volume III is the only one to carry a dedication. It reads: *To Esar Levine | who has suffered imprisonment for his affection | to me and devotion to my welfare, I dedicate this | third volume of "My Life". It is the best I have | to give to the best and bravest of friends, and whatever | value it has, is due in great part to his help and | counsel. | Frank Harris. | Nice, 1926.*

Volume IV does not carry a foreword, and uses a different paper stock from p. 193 onwards.

(b) MY LIFE AND LOVES (4 vols.)

(i) VOLUME ONE

Title page
MY LIFE AND LOVES | BY | FRANK HARRIS | [logo] | THE OBELISK PRESS | 338 Rue Saint-Honoré | PARIS

Collation
8vo. [viii] 11–353 + [iii]. 19.4 × 14.2 cm. Edges untrimmed.

Pagination
[i–ii] blank; [iii] half-title; [iv] blank; [v] title-page; [vi] copyright; [vii]

foreword half-title ; [viii] blank; 11–24 foreword; 25–353 text; [354] blank; [355] imprimerie: Lecram-Press | Paris; [356] blank. [See notes.]

Binding
Heavy paper wrappers.

Wrapper
Same design as A–28(i).

Front panel: by FRANK HARRIS [red] | My [white] | Life | and [red] | Loves ['L' red, 'oves' white] | volume one [red] | MUST NOT BE imported into England or U. S. A. [white].
NB: The 'i' of 'HARRIS', although a capital letter, is dotted.

Spine: Not seen.

Rear panel: Not seen.

Publication
1935

Notes
The only copy located of this volume [BL] has been rebound, with the front wrapper bound in. Given the discrepancy in pagination between the preliminaries and the text, and the collation of the succeeding three volumes, it's likely that a front free endpaper was lost during the rebinding.

(ii) VOLUME TWO

Title page
MY LIFE AND LOVES | BY | FRANK HARRIS | VOLUME TWO | [logo] | THE OBELISK PRESS | 338, Rue Saint-Honoré | PARIS

Collation
8vo. [x] 11–450 + [ii]. 19.4 × 14.2 cm. Edges untrimmed.

Pagination
[i–iv] blank; [v] half-title; [vi] blank; [vii] title-page; [viii] copyright; [ix] foreword half-title; [x] blank; 11–23 foreword; 24–450 text; [451] imprimerie: Lecram-Press | Paris; [452] blank.

Binding
Heavy paper wrappers.

Wrapper
Same design as A–28(i).

Front panel: by FRANK HARRIS [red] | My [white] | Life | and [red] | Loves ['L' red, 'oves' white] | volume two [red] | MUST NOT BE imported into England or U. S. A. [white].
NB: The 'i' of 'HARRIS', although a capital letter, is dotted.

Spine: White. FRANK | HARRIS | My | Life | and | Loves | VOLUME | TWO | [logo] | OBELISK PRESS | 338 Rue St-Honoré | PARIS

Rear panel: As A–28(i).

Publication
1935

Notes
See A–28(b)(iv).

(iii) VOLUME THREE

Title page
MY LIFE AND LOVES | BY | FRANK HARRIS | VOLUME THREE | [logo] | THE OBELISK PRESS | 338, Rue Saint-Honoré | PARIS

Collation
8vo. [x] 11–265 + [iii]. 19.4 × 14.2 cm. Edges untrimmed.

Pagination
[i–ii] blank; [iii] half-title; [iv] blank; [v] dedication; [vi] blank; [vii] title-page; [viii] copyright; [ix] foreword half-title; [x] Gower quotation; [11–23] foreword; 24–265 text; [266] blank; [267] imprimerie: Lecram-Press | Paris [268] blank.

Binding
Heavy paper wrappers.

Wrapper
Same design as A–28(i).

Front panel: by FRANK HARRIS [red] | My [white] | Life | and [red] | Loves ['L' red, 'oves' white] | volume three [red] | MUST NOT BE imported into England or U. S. A. [white].
NB: The 'i' of 'HARRIS', although a capital letter, is dotted.

Spine: White. FRANK | HARRIS | My | Life | and | Loves | VOLUME | THREE | [logo] | OBELISK PRESS | 338 Rue St-Honoré | PARIS

Rear panel: As A–28(i).

Publication
1935

Notes
See A–28(b)(iv).

(iv) VOLUME FOUR

Title page
MY LIFE AND LOVES | BY | FRANK HARRIS | VOLUME FOUR | [logo] | THE OBELISK PRESS | 338, Rue Saint-Honoré | PARIS

Collation
8vo. [x] 11–268 + [iv]. 19.4 × 14.2 cm. Edges untrimmed.

Pagination
[i–iv] blank; [v] half-title; [vi] blank; [vii] title-page; [viii] copyright; [ix] second half-title; [x] blank; 11–268 text; [269] imprimerie: Lecram-Press | Paris; [270–272] blank.

Binding
Heavy paper wrappers.

Wrapper
Same design as A–28(i).

Front panel: by FRANK HARRIS [red] | My [white] | Life | and [red] | Loves ['L' red, 'oves' white] | volume four [red] | MUST NOT BE imported into England or U. S. A. [white].
NB: The 'i' of 'HARRIS', although a capital letter, is dotted.

Spine: White. FRANK | HARRIS | My | Life | and | Loves | VOLUME | FOUR | [logo] | OBELISK PRESS | 338 Rue St-Honoré | PARIS

Rear panel: As A–28(i).

Publication
1935

Notes
First Obelisk edition, second impression.

This second impression of the Obelisk edition, unlike the first, carries the Obelisk imprint and logo on both the title-page and the spine. Its edges are untrimmed, and it is slightly bigger than the first impression: the red triangles on the front panel do not extend to the edge of the wrapper, and are instead enclosed in a white border. The collation and pagination are identical.

(c) MY LIFE AND LOVES (4 vols.)
(i) VOLUME ONE

Title page
MY LIFE AND LOVES | BY | FRANK HARRIS | VOLUME I | AUTHO-RIZED UNEXPURGATED EDITION | [logo] | THE OBELISK PRESS | 16 PLACE VENDOME | PARIS

Collation
8vo. [x] 11–353 + [iii]. 19.3 × 14 cm. Top edge untrimmed, other edges rough trimmed.

Pagination
[i–iv] blank, [v] half-title; [vi] blank; [vii] title page; [viii] copyright; [ix] foreword half-title; [x] blank; [11–24] foreword; 25–350 text; [351–353] afterword; [354] blank; [355] imprimerie: GEORGES FRERE | TOUR-COING; [356] blank.

Binding
Heavy paper wrappers with fold-over flaps.

Wrapper
Front panel: White flash running from bottom left to top right, trian-gulated corners in red. by FRANK HARRIS [red] | My [white] | Life | and [red] | Loves ['L' red, 'oves' white] | volume one [red] | MUST NOT BE imported into England or U. S. A. [white].
NB: The 'i' of 'HARRIS', although a capital letter, is dotted.

Spine: White. FRANK | HARRIS | My | Life | and | Loves | VOLUME | ONE | [logo] | THE | OBELISK PRESS | 16 Place Vendôme | PARIS [red]

Rear panel: White. 60 frs. per vol. [red]

Front flap: Blank.

Rear flap: Blank.

Publication
1938

Notes
This edition carries the Place Vendôme address, which dates the publication of the book as no earlier than January 1938. The price on the rear panel of the wrapper is now Frs. 60, and the imprimerie on [355] cites a different printer. There is no white border on the front panels of the four volumes of this edition, the red triangles instead running to the edges of the books.

(ii) VOLUME TWO
Not seen.

(iii) VOLUME THREE

Title page
MY LIFE AND LOVES | BY | FRANK HARRIS | VOLUME THREE | [logo] | THE OBELISK PRESS | 16 PLACE VENDOME | PARIS

Collation
8vo. [x] 11–265 + [iii]. 19.3 × 14 cm. Top edge untrimmed, other edges untrimmed.

Pagination
[i–ii] blank; [iii] half-title ; [iv] blank; [v] title-page; [vi] copyright; [vii] foreword half-title; [viii] Gower quotation; [ix] dedication; [x] blank; [11–23] foreword; 24–265 text; [266] imprimerie: IMPRIMERIE | GEORGES FRERE | TOURCOING; [267–268] blank.

Binding
Heavy paper wrappers with fold-over flaps.

Wrapper
Front panel: White flash running from bottom left to top right, triangulated corners in red. by FRANK HARRIS [red] | My [white] | Life | and [red] | Loves ['L' red, 'oves' white] | volume three [red] | MUST NOT BE imported into England or U. S. A. [white].

NB: The 'i' of 'HARRIS', although a capital letter, is dotted.

Spine: White. FRANK | HARRIS | My | Life | and | Loves | VOLUME | THREE | [logo] | THE | OBELISK PRESS | 16 Place Vendôme | PARIS [red]

Rear panel: White. 60 frs. per vol. [red]

Front flap: Blank.

Rear flap: Blank.

Publication
1938

Notes
Unlike A–28(c)(i), the title page uses letters, not numbers, to denote the volume number. The 'authorized unexpurgated edition' notice is not present, and the imprimerie prints the word 'imprimerie'. [See note to A–28(c)(iv), below.]

(iv) VOLUME FOUR

Title page
MY LIFE AND LOVES | BY | FRANK HARRIS | VOLUME FOUR | [logo] | THE OBELISK PRESS | 16 PLACE VENDOME | PARIS

Collation
8vo. [x] 11–265 + [iii]. 19.3 × 14 cm. Top edge untrimmed, other edges untrimmed.

Pagination
[i–iv] blank; [v] half-title; [vi] blank; [vii] second half-title; [viii] blank; [ix] title-page; [x] blank; 11–268 text; [269] imprimerie: IMPRIMERIE | GEORGES FRERE | TOURCOING; [270–272] blank.

Binding
Heavy paper wrappers with fold-over flaps.

Wrapper
Front panel: White flash running from bottom left to top right, triangulated corners in red. by FRANK HARRIS [red] | My [white] | Life | and [red] | Loves ['L' red, 'oves' white] | volume four [red] | MUST NOT BE imported into England or U. S. A. [white].
NB: The 'i' of 'HARRIS', although a capital letter, is dotted.

Spine: White. FRANK | HARRIS | My | Life | and | Loves | VOLUME | Four | [logo] | THE | OBELISK PRESS | 16 Place Vendôme | PARIS [red]

Rear panel: White. 60 frs. per vol. [red]

Front flap: Blank.

Rear flap: Blank.

Publication
1938

Notes
Second Obelisk edition.

Apart from the second half-title, identical in format to A–28(c)(i), but with an imprimerie identical to A–28(c)(iii). The volume number is lettered on title page, not numbered.

Either the textual and collative differences between the volumes of this edition are the result of errors made by the printer, or the entry for this edition is a conflation of two different editions, neither of which has been seen in its entirety.

(d) MY LIFE AND LOVES (4 vols.)

(i) VOLUME ONE
Not seen.

(ii) VOLUME TWO
Not seen.

(iii) VOLUME THREE

Title page
MY LIFE AND LOVES | BY | FRANK HARRIS | VOLUME THREE | THE OBELISK PRESS | 16, PLACE VENDOME, PARIS

Collation
8vo. [x] 11–176. 18.3 × 14.3 cm. Edges untrimmed.

Pagination
[i–ii] blank; [iii] half-title; [iv] blank; [v] foreword half-title; [vi] Gower quotation; [vii] title-page; [viii] copyright; [ix] dedication; [x] blank; 11–18 foreword; 19–176 text; [176] imprimerie: Imp. CRÉTÉ, Corbeil, (S. -et- O.), | 3807 - 7 - 45. – C. O. L. 31 - 1631. | Dépôt légal, 30 trimestre, 1945.

Binding
Pale blue paper wrappers.

Front panel: MY LIFE | AND | LOVES [red, between horizontal lines [black]] | *BY FRANK HARRIS* | 3 [red] | THE OBELISK PRESS – PARIS [black]

Spine: Lettering running from bottom to top. *FRANK HARRIS* [black] MY LIFE AND LOVES 3 [red]

Rear panel: 120 Frs. per vol. [black] | MUST NOT BE BROUGHT INTO ENGLAND OR U. S. A. [red]

Publication
July 1945

Notes
The price on the rear panel of the Baxter copy has been cancelled. Reprinted above the cancelled price is: 150 Frs. per vol. [black]

(iv) VOLUME FOUR
Not seen.

Notes
Third Obelisk edition.

Published by Maurice Girodias in the immediate aftermath of the war.

Only one copy located [Baxter, one volume only].

(e) MY LIFE AND LOVES (4 vols.)

(i) VOLUME ONE

Title page
MY LIFE AND LOVES | BY | FRANK HARRIS | VOLUME I | AUTHORIZED UNEXPURGATED EDITION | THE OBELISK PRESS | 16, PLACE VENDOME | PARIS

Collation
8vo. [viii] 9–233 + [iii]. 19.3 × 14.4 cm. Top edge rough trimmed, others trimmed.

Pagination
[i–ii] blank; [iii] half-title ; [iv] blank; [v] title-page; [vi] copyright; [vii] foreword half-title; [viii] blank; 9–17 foreword; 18–231 text; [232–233] afterword; [234] blank; [235] imprimerie: Imp. CRÉTÉ, Corbeil, (S. -et-O.), l 3806 - 11 - 45. – C. O. L. 31 - 1631, l Dépôt légal, 4e trimestre, 1945.; [304] blank.

Binding
Pale blue wrappers.

Front panel: MY LIFE l AND l LOVES [red, between horizontal lines [black]] l *BY FRANK HARRIS* l 1 [red] l THE OBELISK PRESS – PARIS [black]

Spine: Text runs horizontally, bottom to top. *FRANK HARRIS* [black] MY LIFE AND LOVES 1 [red]

Rear panel: * 150 Frs. per vol. [black] l MUST NOT BE IMPORTED INTO ENGLAND OR U. S. A. [red]

Publication
November 1945

Notes
Copyright on [vi] states: Copyright by "Les Éditions du Chêne", l Paris 1945.

(ii) VOLUME TWO

Title page
MY LIFE AND LOVES l BY l FRANK HARRIS l VOLUME TWO l THE OBELISK PRESS l 16, PLACE VENDOME l PARIS

Collation
8vo. [viii] 9–302 + [ii]. 19.3 × 14.4 cm. Top edge rough trimmed, others trimmed.

Pagination

[i–ii] blank; [iii] half-title ; [iv] blank; [v] title-page; [vi] copyright; [vii] foreword half-title; [viii] blank; 9–17 foreword; 18–302 text; [303] imprimerie: Imp. CRÉTÉ, Corbeil, (S. -et- O.), l 3807 - 11 - 45. – C. O. L. 31 - 1631, l Dépôt légal, 4e trimestre, 1945.; [304] blank.

Binding
Pale blue paper wrappers.

Front panel: MY LIFE | AND | LOVES [red, between horizontal lines [black]] | BY *FRANK HARRIS* | 2 [red] | THE OBELISK PRESS – PARIS [black]

Spine: Text runs horizontally, bottom to top. *FRANK HARRIS* [black] MY LIFE AND LOVES 2 [red]

Rear panel: * 150 Frs. per vol. [black] | MUST NOT BE IMPORTED INTO ENGLAND OR U. S. A. [red]

Publication
November 1945

Notes
Copyright on [vi] states: COPYRIGHT BY LES ÉDITIONS DU CHÊNE, | 16, PLACE VENDOME, PARIS

(iii) VOLUME THREE

Title page
MY LIFE AND LOVES | BY | FRANK HARRIS | VOLUME THREE | THE OBELISK PRESS | 16, PLACE VENDOME | PARIS

Collation
8vo. [x] 11–176. 19.3 × 14.4 cm. Top edge rough trimmed, others trimmed.

Pagination
[i–ii] blank; [iii] half-title ; [iv] blank; [v] foreword half-title; [vi] Gower quotation; [vii] title-page; [viii] copyright; [ix] dedication; [x] blank; 11–18 foreword; 19–176 text; [176] imprimerie:Sociétéindustrielled'Imprimerie, Lavallois. – C. O. L. 31-0914 | Dépôt légal 4e trimestre 1945

Binding
Pale blue paper wrappers.

Front panel: MY LIFE | AND | LOVES [red, between horizontal lines [black]] | BY *FRANK HARRIS* | 3 [red] | THE OBELISK PRESS – PARIS [black]

Spine: Text runs horizontally, bottom to top. *FRANK HARRIS* [black] MY LIFE AND LOVES 3 [red]

Rear panel: * 150 Frs. per vol. [black] | MUST NOT BE IMPORTED INTO ENGLAND OR U. S. A. [red]

Publication
November 1945

Notes
Copyright on [viii] states: COPYRIGHT BY LES ÉDITIONS DU CHÊNE, 1945 | 16, place Vendôme, Paris

(iv) VOLUME FOUR

Title page
MY LIFE AND LOVES | BY | FRANK HARRIS | VOLUME FOUR | THE OBELISK PRESS | 16, PLACE VENDOME | PARIS

Collation
8vo. [viii] 9–178 + [ii]. 19.3 × 14.4 cm. Top edge rough trimmed, others trimmed.

Pagination
[i–ii] blank; [iii] half-title ; [iv] blank; [v] second half-title; [vi] blank;[vii] title-page; [viii] copyright; 9–178 text; [179] blank; [180] imprimerie: IMP. G. BLANCHONG ET Cie | 30, RUE DE POTEAU, PARIS | 31.1040 Dépôt légal, 4e Trimestre 1945

Binding
Pale blue paper wrappers.

Front panel: MY LIFE | AND | LOVES [red, between horizontal lines [black]] | BY *FRANK HARRIS* | 4 [red] | THE OBELISK PRESS – PARIS [black]

Spine: Text runs horizontally, bottom to top. *FRANK HARRIS* [black] MY LIFE AND LOVES 4 [red]

Rear panel: * 150 Frs. per vol. [black] | MUST NOT BE IMPORTED INTO ENGLAND OR U. S. A. [red]

Publication
November 1945

Notes
Third Obelisk edition, second impression.

[154]

This edition was published by Maurice Girodias shortly after the war, and at a number of different printers. As a result, although uniform in livery, there are variations in the preliminaries, imprimeries and copyright statements from volume to volume.

Copyright on [viii] states: PRINTED IN FRANCE | COPYRIGHT BY EDITIONS DU CHÊNE | 16, PLACE VENDÔME, PARIS

(f) MY LIFE AND LOVES (4 vols.)

(i) VOLUME ONE

Title page
MY LIFE AND LOVES | BY | FRANK HARRIS | VOLUME ONE | THE OBELISK PRESS BOOKS | LES ÉDITIONS DU CHÊNE | 4, RUE DE LA PAIX | PARIS

Collation
8vo. [viii] 9–233 + [iii]. 19.3 × 14.3 cm. Top edge rough trimmed, other edges untrimmed.

Pagination
[i–ii] blank; [iii] half-title; [iv] blank; [v] title-page; [vi] copyright; [vii] foreword half-title; [viii] blank; 9–17 foreword; 18–231 text; [232–233] afterword; [234] blank; [235] imprimerie: ACHEVÉ D'IMPRIMER | SUR LES PRESSES | DE L'IMPRIMERIE RÉGIONALE | 59, RUE RAYARD, TOULOUSE | LE VINGT AVRIL MIL NEUF | CENT QUARANTE HUIT. | No d'édition 257 No d'impression 50. 180 | Dépôt légal: 20 trimestre 1948; [236] blank.

Binding
Pale blue paper wrappers.

Front panel: MY LIFE | AND | LOVES [red, bordered top and bottom by two black lines] | BY FRANK HARRIS | I [red] | THE OBELISK PRESS BOOKS [black]

Spine: FRANK HARRIS [black] MY LIFE AND LOVES I [red] [lettering runs horizontally, bottom to top]

Rear panel: Fr. 200 per vol. [black] | MUST NOT BE IMPORTED INTO ENGLAND OR U. S. A. [red]

Publication
20 April 1948

Notes
Fourth Obelisk edition.

(ii) VOLUME TWO
Not seen.

(iii) VOLUME THREE
Not seen.

(iv) VOLUME FOUR
Not seen.

(g) MY LIFE AND LOVES (4 vols.)

(i) VOLUME ONE

Title page
As A–28(f).

Collation
8vo. [viii] 9–233 + [i]. 19.3 × 14.3 cm. Top edge rough trimmed, other edges untrimmed.

Pagination
[i–ii] blank; [iii] half-title; [iv] blank; [v] title-page; [vi] copyright; [vii] foreword half-title; [viii] blank; 9–17 foreword; 18–231 text; [232–233] afterword; [234] blank.

Binding
Pale blue paper wrappers.

Front panel: MY LIFE | AND | LOVES [red, bordered top and bottom by two black lines] | BY FRANK HARRIS | I [red] | THE OBELISK PRESS BOOKS [black]

Spine: FRANK HARRIS [black] MY LIFE AND LOVES I [red] [lettering runs horizontally, bottom to top]

Rear panel: Fr. 200 per vol. [black] | MUST NOT BE IMPORTED INTO ENGLAND OR U. S. A. [red]

Publication
Undated. [See notes to A–28(g)(iv).]

(ii) VOLUME TWO

Title page
MY LIFE AND LOVES | BY | FRANK HARRIS | VOLUME TWO | THE
OBELISK PRESS BOOKS | LES ÉDITIONS DU CHÊNE | 4, RUE DE
LA PAIX | PARIS

Collation
8vo. [viii] 9–302. 19.3 × 13.8 cm. Top and leading edge rough trimmed,
bottom edge untrimmed.

Pagination
[i–ii] blank; [iii] half-title; [iv] blank; [v] title-page; [vi] copyright; [vii]
foreword half-title; [viii] blank; 9–17 foreword; 18–302 text.

Binding
As A–28(c)(i).

Front panel: MY LIFE | AND | LOVES [red, bordered top and bottom
by two black lines] | BY FRANK HARRIS | 2 [red] | THE OBELISK
PRESS BOOKS [black]

Spine: FRANK HARRIS [black] MY LIFE AND LOVES 2 [red] [lettering
runs horizontally, bottom to top]

Rear panel: Fr. 200 per vol. [black] | MUST NOT BE IMPORTED INTO
ENGLAND OR U. S. A. [red]

Publication
Undated. [See notes to A–28(g)(iv).]

(iii) VOLUME THREE

Title page
MY LIFE AND LOVES | BY | FRANK HARRIS | VOLUME THREE |
THE OBELISK PRESS BOOKS | LES ÉDITIONS DU CHÊNE | 4, RUE
DE LA PAIX | PARIS

Collation
8vo. [x] 11–176 + [ii]. 19.3 × 13.8 cm. Top edge rough trimmed, leading
edge trimmed, bottom edge untrimmed.

Pagination
[i–ii] blank; [iii] half-title; [iv] Gower quotation; [v] title-page; [vi]
copyright; [vii] dedication; [viii] blank; [ix] foreword half-title; [x]
blank; 11–18 foreword; 19–176 text; [177–178] blank.

Binding
As A–28(c)(i).

Front panel: MY LIFE | AND | LOVES [red, bordered top and bottom by two black lines] | BY FRANK HARRIS | 3 [red] | THE OBELISK PRESS BOOKS [black]

Spine: FRANK HARRIS [black] MY LIFE AND LOVES 3 [red] [lettering runs horizontally, bottom to top]

Rear panel: Fr. 200 per vol. [black] | MUST NOT BE IMPORTED INTO ENGLAND OR U. S. A. [red]

Publication
Undated. [See notes to A–28(g)(iv).]

(iv) VOLUME FOUR

Title page
MY LIFE AND LOVES | BY | FRANK HARRIS | VOLUME FOUR | THE OBELISK PRESS BOOKS | LES ÉDITIONS DU CHÊNE | 4, RUE DE LA PAIX | PARIS

Collation
8vo. [viii] 9–178. 19.5 × 14.5 cm. Top edge rough trimmed, other edges untrimmed.

Pagination
[i–ii] blank; [iii] half-title; [iv] blank; [v] second half-title; [vi] blank; [vii] title-page; [vii] copyright; 9–178 text.

Binding
As A–28(c)(i). Wrappers slightly wider than text block.

Front panel: MY LIFE | AND | LOVES [red, bordered top and bottom by two black lines] | BY FRANK HARRIS | 4 [red] | THE OBELISK PRESS BOOKS [black]

Spine: FRANK HARRIS [black] MY LIFE AND LOVES 4 [red] [lettering runs horizontally, bottom to top]

Rear panel: Fr. 200 per vol. [black] | MUST NOT BE IMPORTED INTO ENGLAND OR U. S. A. [red]

Publication
Undated. [See notes.]

Notes
Fourth Obelisk edition, second impression.

Volume One of this edition is identical to A–28(f)(i), except that it carries no publication information.

(h) MY LIFE AND LOVES (4 vols.)

(i) VOLUME ONE

Title page
FRANK HARRIS | MY LIFE | AND LOVES | VOLUME ONE | THE OBELISK PRESS | PARIS

Collation
8vo. [viii] 9–228 + [iv] 18 × 13 cm. Edges trimmed.

Pagination
[i–ii] blank; [iii] half-title; [iv] blank; [v] title-page; [vi] copyright; [vii] foreword half-title; [viii] blank; [9–17] foreword; 18–226 text; [227–228] afterword; [229] blank; [230] imprimerie: IMPRIMÉ PAR | BRODARD ET TAUPIN | COULOMMIERS – PARIS | IMPRIMEUR No 9481 | 47669 - 3 - 1954; [231–232] blank.

Binding
Blue-grey paper wrappers.

Front panel: MY LIFE | AND | LOVES | BY | *FRANK HARRIS* [red]

Spine: FRANK | HARRIS [black | I [red] | MY | LIFE | AND | LOVES [black] | OBELISK | PRESS [red]

Rear panel: MUST NOT BE IMPORTED INTO ENGLAND OR U. S. A. [red] | 500 Frs. [black]

Publication
Early 1952.

Notes
The copyright notice on [vi] reads: DÉPOT LÉGAL: 1er TRI- | MESTRE 1952. No 4. | COPYRIGHT BY "ÉDITION | DU CHÊNE", 4, RUE | GALLIERA, PARIS | PRINTED IN FRANCE

(ii) VOLUME TWO

Title page
FRANK HARRIS | MY LIFE | AND LOVES | VOLUME TWO | THE OBELISK PRESS | PARIS

Collation
8vo. [viii] 9–228 + [iv]. 18 × 13 cm. Edges trimmed.

Pagination
[i–ii] blank; [iii] half-title; [iv] blank; [v] title-page; [vi] copyright; [vii] foreword half-title; [viii] blank; [9–17] foreword; 17–289 text; [290] blank; [291] imprimerie: IMPRIMÉ PAR | BRODARD ET TAUPIN | COULOMMIERS – PARIS | IMPRIMEUR No 9482 | 47670 - 3 - 1954; [292] blank.

Binding
Blue-grey paper wrappers.

Front panel: As Vol. I.

Spine: FRANK | HARRIS [black | 2 [red] | MY | LIFE | AND | LOVES [black] | OBELISK | PRESS [red]

Rear panel: As Vol. I.

Publication
Early 1952

Notes
The copyright notice on [vi] is as Vol. I.

(iii) VOLUME THREE

Title page
FRANK HARRIS | MY LIFE | AND LOVES | VOLUME THREE | THE OBELISK PRESS | PARIS

Collation
8vo. [x] 11–175 + [i]. 18 × 13 cm. Edges trimmed.

Pagination
[i–ii] blank; [iii] half-title ; [iv] Gower quotation; [v] title-page; [vi] copyright; [vii] dedication; [viii] blank; [ix] foreword half-title; [x] blank; 11–18 foreword; 19–175 text; [176] imprimerie: IMPRIMÉ PAR | BRODARD ET TAUPIN | COULOMMIERS – PARIS | IMPRIMEUR No 9483 | 47671 - 3 - 54

Binding
Blue-grey paper wrappers.

Front panel: As Vol. I.

Spine: FRANK | HARRIS [black | 3 [red] | MY | LIFE | AND | LOVES [black] | OBELISK | PRESS [red]

Rear panel: As Vol. I.

Publication
Early 1952

Notes
The copyright notice on [vi] is as Vol. I.

(iv) VOLUME FOUR

Title page
FRANK HARRIS | MY LIFE | AND LOVES | VOLUME FOUR | THE OBELISK PRESS | PARIS

Collation
8vo. [viii] 9–228 + [iv]. 18 × 13 cm. Edges trimmed.

Pagination
[i–ii] blank; [iii] half-title; [iv] blank; [v] title-page; [vi] copyright; [vii] foreword half-title; [viii] blank; 9–175 text; [176] imprimerie: IMPRI-MÉ PAR | BRODARD ET TAUPIN | COULOMMIERS – PARIS | IM-PRIMEUR No 9484 | 47672 - 3 - 1954

Binding
Blue-grey paper wrappers.

Front panel: As Vol. I.

Spine: FRANK | HARRIS [black | 4 [red] | MY | LIFE | AND | LOVES [black] | OBELISK | PRESS [red]

Rear panel: As Vol. I.

Publication
Early 1952

Notes
Fifth Obelisk edition.

The copyright notice on [vi] is as Vol. I.

(i) MY LIFE AND LOVES (4 vols.)

(i) VOLUME ONE

Title page
FRANK HARRIS | MY LIFE | AND LOVES | VOLUME ONE | THE
OBELISK PRESS | PARIS

Collation
8vo. [viii] 9–228 + [iv]. 18 × 13 cm. All edges trimmed.

Pagination
[i–ii] blank; [iii] half-title; [iv] blank; [v] title-page; [vi] copyright; [vii]
foreword half-title; [viii] blank; 9–17 foreword; 18–226 text; [227–228]
afterword; [229] blank; [230] imprimerie: IMPRIMÉ PAR | BRODARD
– TAUPIN | IMPRIMEUR – RELIEUR | COULOMMIERS – PARIS |
IMPRIMEUR No 50.176.04 | 55546 - 2 - 1960; [231–232] blank.

Binding
White paper wrappers.
Front panel: FRANK HARRIS [red] | MY LIFE AND LOVES [black] |
[star] [red] | [forward slash] [red] THE OBELISK PRESS [black]
Spine: FRANK | HARRIS [red] | MY LIFE | AND | LOVES [black] |
[circular device] [red] | THE OBELISK | PRESS [black]
Rear panel: Blank.

Publication
1960

Notes
The Bodleian copy has a price of 9.50 (francs) stamped on the rear panel.

(ii) VOLUME TWO

Title page
FRANK HARRIS | MY LIFE | AND LOVES | VOLUME TWO | THE
OBELISK PRESS | PARIS

Collation
8vo. [viii] 9–289 + [iii]. 18 × 13 cm. All edges trimmed.

Pagination
[i–ii] blank; [iii] half-title; [iv] blank; [v] title-page; [vi] copyright;

[vii] foreword half-title; [viii] blank; 9–16 foreword; 17–289 text; [290] blank; [291] imprimerie: IMPRIMÉ PAR | BRODARD – TAUPIN | IMPRIMEUR – RELIEUR | COULOMMIERS – PARIS | IMPRIMEUR No 50.177.04 | 55547 - 2 - 1960.; [292] blank.

Binding
White paper wrappers.

Front panel: FRANK HARRIS [red] | MY LIFE AND LOVES [black] | [two stars] [red] | [forward slash] [red] THE OBELISK PRESS [black]

Spine: FRANK | HARRIS [red] | MY LIFE | AND | LOVES [black] | [two circular devices] [red] | THE OBELISK | PRESS [black]

Rear panel: Blank.

Publication
1960

Notes
The Bodleian copy has a price of 9.50 (francs) stamped on the rear panel.

(iii) VOLUME THREE

Title page
FRANK HARRIS | MY LIFE | AND LOVES | VOLUME THREE | THE OBELISK PRESS | PARIS

Collation
8vo. [x] 11–175 + [i]. 18 × 13 cm. All edges trimmed.

Pagination
[i–ii] blank; [iii] half-title; [iv] Gower quotation; [v] title-page; [vi] copyright; [vii] dedication; [viii] blank; [ix] foreword half-title; [x] blank; 11–18 foreword; 19–175 text; [176] imprimerie: IMPRIMÉ PAR | BRODARD – TAUPIN | IMPRIMEUR – RELIEUR | COULOMMIERS – PARIS | IMPRIMEUR No 50.178.04 | 55548 - 2 - 1960.

Binding
White paper wrappers.

Front panel: FRANK HARRIS [red] | MY LIFE AND LOVES [black] | [three stars] [red] | [forward slash] [red] THE OBELISK PRESS [black]

Spine: FRANK | HARRIS [red] | MY LIFE | AND | LOVES [black] | [three circular devices] [red] | THE OBELISK | PRESS [black]

Rear panel: Blank.

Publication
1960

Notes
The Bodleian copy has a price of 9.50 (francs) stamped on the rear panel.

(iv) VOLUME FOUR

Title page
FRANK HARRIS | MY LIFE | AND LOVES | VOLUME FOUR | THE OBELISK PRESS | PARIS

Collation
8vo. [viii] 9–175 + [i]. 18 × 13 cm. All edges trimmed.

Pagination
[i–ii] blank; [iii] half-title; [iv] blank; [v] title-page; [vi] copyright; [vii] foreword half-title; [viii] blank; 9–175 text; [176] imprimerie: IMPRIMÉ PAR | BRODARD – TAUPIN | IMPRIMEUR – RELIEUR | COULOM-MIERS – PARIS | IMPRIMEUR No 50.179.04 | 55549 - 2 - 1960.

Binding
White paper wrappers.

Front panel: FRANK HARRIS [red] | MY LIFE AND LOVES [black] | [four stars] [red] | [forward slash] [red] THE OBELISK PRESS [black]

Spine: FRANK | HARRIS [red] | MY LIFE | AND | LOVES [black] | [four circular devices] [red] | THE OBELISK | PRESS [black]

Rear panel: Blank.

Publication
1960

Notes
Sixth Obelisk edition.

The Bodleian copy has a price of 9.50 (francs) stamped on the rear panel.

A–29 EASTER SUN

by PETER NEAGOE

Title page
EASTER SUN | BY | PETER NEAGOE | AUTHOR OF | *STORM* | [logo] |
THE OBELISK PRESS | 338, RUE SAINT-HONORÉ, | PARIS

Collation
8vo. [viii] 9–349 + [iii]. 19 × 14 cm. All edges trimmed.

Pagination
[i–ii] blank; [iii] half-title; [iv] list of previous work; [v] title-page; [vi]
copyright and publication: First published March 1934; [vii] second
half-title; [viii] blank; 9–349 text; [350] blank; [351] imprimerie: Lecram-
Press | Paris; [352] blank.

Binding
White heavy paper wrappers with fold-over flaps.

Front panel: Yellow sunset, with couple in foreground in silhou-
ette, man arms aloft, woman kneeling. EASTER SUN | by | PETER
NEAGOE | *author of* | STORM | RECOMMENDED BY THE BOOK OF
THE MONTH CLUB | THE OBELISK PRESS – PARIS [black]

Spine: Easter Sun | PETER | NEAGOE | author of | STORM | [logo] | THE
OBELISK PRESS | 338, Rue St-Honoré | PARIS [black]

Rear panel: [logo] [black]

Front flap: Blurb and price [50 frs.]

Rear flap: Eight titles, with blurbs, the first seven at Frs. 50 each, the
last at Frs. 60: 1. Storm; 2. The Lamb; 3. The Young and Evil; 4. Daffodil
(IN ITS NINTH IMPRESSION); 5. Amour French for Love (FIFTH
LARGE IMPRESSION); 6. The Well of Loneliness; 7. Sleeveless Errand;
8. Germany, Prepare for War!

Publication
April 1934

Notes
First edition.

Published by Hutchinson in England and by Coward-McCann in the
United States later the same year.

According to [iv], *Storm* was in its 3rd edition at time of going to print [see notes to A–16(b)].

The wrapper's illustration is signed MAURICE KAHANE. Always keen to cut costs, Kahane used his teenage son to design the wrappers of other Obelisk titles [see A–32].

Germany, Prepare for War! by Ewald Banse, advertised on the rear flap, was never published by the Obelisk Press, and the advertisement was removed from subsequent impressions of this title [see below].

(b) EASTER SUN

Title page
As A–29.

Collation
As A–29, except 18.5 × 14 cm.

Pagination
[i–ii] blank; [iii] half-title; [iv] listing of previous work; [v] title-page; [vi] copyright and publication: First published March, 1934 | Reprinted July, 1934; [vii] second half-title; [viii] blank; 9–349 text; [350] blank; [351] imprimerie: Lecram-Press | Paris; [352] blank.

Binding
As A–29.

Front panel: Yellow sunset, with couple in foreground in silhouette, man arms aloft, woman kneeling. EASTER SUN | by | PETER NEAGOE | *author of* | STORM | RECOMMENDED BY THE BOOK OF THE MONTH CLUB | THE OBELISK PRESS – PARIS (2nd impression) [black]

Spine: White. Easter Sun | PETER | NEAGOE | author of | STORM | 2nd Impression | [logo] | THE OBELISK PRESS | 338, Rue St-Honoré | PARIS [black]

Rear panel: As A–29.

Front flap: Blurb as A–29, with a puff from the Times Literary Supplement appended at bottom, price.

Rear flap: Ten titles, with blurbs: 1. Easter Sun; 2. Storm; 3. The Lamb; 4. The Young and Evil; 5. Daffodil (IN ITS NINTH IMPRESSION); 6. Amour French for Love (SEVENTH LARGE IMPRESSION); 7. Bright

Pink Youth; 8. The Well of Loneliness; 9. Sleeveless Errand; 10. Tropic of Cancer.

Publication
July 1934

Notes
First edition, second impression.

Prices on front and rear flaps are cancelled on the only copy seen [Baxter].

(c) EASTER SUN

Title page
As A–29.

Collation
8vo. [viii] 9–349 + [iii]. 19.2 × 14.3 cm. Edges untrimmed.

Pagination
As A–29(b).

Binding
As A–29.

Front panel: Yellow sunset, with couple in foreground in silhouette, man arms aloft, woman kneeling. EASTER SUN | by | PETER NEAGOE | *author of* | STORM | RECOMMENDED BY THE BOOK OF THE MONTH CLUB | THE OBELISK PRESS – PARIS (5th impression) [black]

Spine: White. Easter Sun | PETER | NEAGOE | author of | STORM | 5th Impression | [logo] | THE OBELISK PRESS | 338, Rue St-Honoré | PARIS [black]

Rear panel: As A–29.

Front flap: As A–29(b).

Rear flap: Twelve titles, with blurbs, at Frs. 50 each: 1. Uncharted Seas; 2. Black Spring; 3. The Rock Pool (2nd edition); 4. Bessie Cotter; 5. Star Against Star (2nd impression); 6. The Gentle Men; 7. Tropic of Cancer; 8. Boy; 9. Daffodil (In its **twelfth** impression); 10. The Well of Loneliness; 11. My Life and Loves; 12. Lady Chatterley's Lover.

Publication
No earlier than 1937 [see notes]

Notes
First edition, third impression ['Fifth impression'].

The inclusion of *Uncharted Seas* in the list of Obelisk Press titles on the rear flap puts the date of publication of this impression as no earlier than 1937. The book has not been reset, and the publication information on [vi] is the same as in A–29(b). Third or fourth impressions have not been located, and are presumed not to exist.

The copy in the author's collection has a new price label obscuring the original price on the front flap, and the prices on the rear flap have been cancelled.

A–30 POEMS FOR MUSIC
by NADEJDA DE BRAGANÇA

Title page
POEMS FOR MUSIC | *By* | NADEJDA DE BRAGANÇA | *Portrait by* | IACOVLEFF | PARIS | THE OBELISK PRESS | 338 Rue St-Honoré | 1934

Collation
Large 8vo. [viii] 11–54 + [iv]. 25.7 × 17 cm. Top edge trimmed, other edges untrimmed.

Pagination
[i–ii] blank; [iii] half-title; [iv] author's portrait; [v] title-page; [vi] limitation; [vii] dedication; [viii] copyright; 11–54 text; [55–56] blank; [57] imprimerie: LECRAM – SERVANT | 338, RUE ST-HONORÉ | PARIS; [58] blank.

Binding
Boards covered in off-white coarse-grained cloth. Paper label on spine: POEMS | FOR | MUSIC | NADEJDA | DE | BRAGANÇA | THE | OBELISK | PRESS.

White dustwrapper.

Wrapper
Front panel: Black border enclosing text. POEMS FOR MUSIC | *By* | NADEJDA DE BRAGANÇA | *Portrait by* | IACOVLEFF | PARIS | THE

OBELISK PRESS | 338 Rue St-Honoré | 1934 [black]
Spine: POEMS | FOR | MUSIC | NADEJDA | DE | BRAGANÇA | THE | OBELISK | PRESS | PARIS | 1934

Rear panel: Blank.

Front flap: Title, blurb and price [50 francs]

Rear flap: Blank.

Publication
July 1934

Notes
First edition.

Limitation on [vi] reads: OF THIS, THE ORIGINAL EDITION, 100 COPIES HAVE | BEEN PRINTED IN 12 POINT ELZEVIR ITALIC ON | MOULD-MADE JOHANNOT D'ANNONAY PAPER, | NUMBERED 1–100 AND SIGNED BY THE AUTHOR. | No. [stamped number]. Author's signature appears beneath. The wording of the limitation is confusing. It is unclear whether the 100 signed copies constitute the entire edition (in which case unnumbered, unsigned copies located are *hors de commerce*), or whether a trade edition, unnumbered and unsigned, accompanied its publication. Given the number of unnumbered, unsigned copies located, the latter seems more likely.

No. 25: Author's collection

No. 34: Brown University, Rhode Island

No. 35: Author's collection

No. 64: Yale University

Unnumbered: Baxter collection

Unnumbered and unsigned: Library of Congress

Unnumbered and unsigned: Bibliothèque Nationale de France (rebound)

Unnumbered and unsigned: Casson collection

Unnumbered and unsigned: Author's collection

A–31 BRIGHT PINK YOUTH
by CECIL BARR [JACK KAHANE]

Title page
BRIGHT PINK YOUTH | BY | CECIL BARR | AUTHOR OF | *DAFFODIL* | [logo] | THE OBELISK PRESS | 338 RUE SAINT-HONORÉ | PARIS

Collation
8vo. [x] 11–332 + [iv]. 18.7 × 14.3 cm. Edges trimmed.

Pagination
[i–ii] blank; [iii] half-title; [iv] list of previous works; [v] title-page; [vi] copyright and publication: First published August 1934; [vii] dedication; [viii] blank; [ix] second half-title; [x] blank; 11–332 text; [333] blank; [334] imprimerie: Lecram-Press | Paris; [335–336] blank.

Binding
Heavy paper wrappers with fold-over flaps.

Front panel: White. Illustration in pink and black, signed G. Goursat, of a topless woman smoking a cigarette in a long holder. BRIGHT PINK YOUTH [black] | by [pink] | CECIL | BARR [black] | author of [pink] | DAFFODIL [black] | 9th impression [pink]

Spine: BRIGHT PINK | YOUTH | CECIL BARR | author of | DAFFODIL | [logo] | THE OBELISK PRESS | 338, Rue St-Honoré | PARIS

Rear panel: [logo]

Front flap: Title, author, blurb, price [50 francs].

Rear flap: Ten titles, with blurbs, at Frs. 50 each: 1. Easter Sun; 2. Storm; 3. The Lamb; 4. The Young and Evil; 5. Daffodil (IN ITS NINTH IMPRESSION); 6. Amour French For Love (SEVENTH LARGE IMPRESSION); 7. Bright Pink Youth; 8. The Well of Loneliness; 9. Sleeveless Errand; 10. Tropic of Cancer.

Publication
August 1934

Notes
First edition.

Dedication on [vii] reads: To | LOUIS MELETTA | *who clothed Daffodil | in such enchanting French attire.* Meletta was the French translator of *Daffodil* [see A–8(g)].

The list of previous works on [iv] reads: 1. Suzy Falls Off ('Translated into half a dozen languages'); 2. Daffodil ('Ninth impression. A European best seller that still sells as well as ever. Shortly to appear in French in volume form, and on the French stage.'); 3. Amour French For Love (Seventh impression, with a puff from the *New York Herald Tribune*).

(b) BRIGHT PINK YOUTH

First edition, second impression ['9th impression']
Not seen. Copy at Northridge Library, California State University.

(c) BRIGHT PINK YOUTH

Second edition. 1955
Not seen. Copy at Indiana University Library.

A–32 TROPIC OF CANCER
by HENRY MILLER

Title page
TROPIC OF CANCER | BY | HENRY MILLER | PREFACE BY | *ANAÏS NIN* | [logo] | THE OBELISK PRESS | 338 RUE SAINT-HONORÉ | PARIS

Collation
8vo. [vi] 7–323 + [i]. 19 × 14 cm. All edges trimmed.

Pagination
[i–ii] blank; [iii] half-title; [iv] list of works in preparation, copyright, publication: September 1934; [v] title-page; [vi] Emerson quotation; 7–10 preface; 11–323 text; [324] imprimerie: Lecram-Press, | Paris.

Binding
Heavy paper wrappers with fold-over flaps.

Front panel: White, with blue-grey and black artwork depicting a crab holding an unconscious woman in its claws. TROPIC OF CANCER | by | HENRY MILLER [black] | NOT TO BE IMPORTED INTO GREAT BRITAIN OR U. S. A. [blue-grey]

Spine: White. TROPIC | OF | CANCER | HENRY | MILLER | [logo] | THE OBELISK PRESS | 338, RUE ST-HONORÉ | PARIS [black]

Rear panel: White. [logo] [black]

Front flap: Title, author, blurb, price [50 frs.]

Rear flap: Ten titles, with blurbs, at Frs. 50 each: 1. Easter Sun; 2. Storm; 3. The Lamb; 4. The Young and Evil; 5. Daffodil (ninth impression); 6. Amour French For Love (seventh large impression); 7. Bright Pink Youth; 8. The Well of Loneliness; 9. Sleeveless Errand; 10. Tropic of Cancer.

White wraparound band: *FOR SUBSCRIPTION.* | MUST NOT BE TAKEN INTO | GREAT BRITAIN OR U. S. A.

Publication
1 September 1934

Notes
First edition. 1000 copies.

The cover design is by Maurice Kahane (later Maurice Girodias), whom we must forgive since he was fourteen years old at the time.

(b) TROPIC OF CANCER

Title page
As A–32.

Collation
8vo. [vi] 7–323 + [i]. 19.4 × 14.4 cm. Edges untrimmed.

Pagination
[i–ii] blank; [iii] half-title; [iv] list of works in preparation, copyright, publication: First published September 1934 | Reprinted September 1935; [v] title-page; [vi] Emerson quotation; 7–10 preface; 11–323 text; [324] imprimerie: Lecram-Press, Paris.

Binding
Grey stiff paper covers in a detachable pale green wrapper of flimsy paper, with fold-over flaps.

Wrapper
Front panel: Faint reproduction of the crab design of A–32. TROPIC

OF CANCER | BY HENRY MILLER | SECOND PRINTING | A VERY REMARKABLE BOOK, WITH PASSAGES OF | WRITING IN IT AS GOOD AS ANY I HAVE SEEN | FOR A LONG TIME . . . . T. S. ELIOT | AT LAST AN UNPRINTABLE BOOK THAT IS FIT | TO READ . . . . EZRA POUND [black]

Spine: Not seen.

Rear panel: Puffs for the book from: 1. Cyril Connolly; 2. Herbert Read; 3. Aldous Huxley; 4. William Carlos Williams; 5. Blaise Cendrars; 6. Anaïs Nin; 7. Montgomery Belgion.

Front flap: Title, author, blurb and price [50 Frs.]

Rear flap: Eleven titles, with blurbs, at Frs. 50 each: 1. Star Against Star; 2. The Gentle Men; 3. Boy; 4. Daffodil (10th impression); 5. The Well of Loneliness; 6. The Young and Evil; 7. My Life and Loves; 8. Easter Sun; 9. Storm; 10. The Lamb; 11. Sleeveless Errand.

Publication
September 1935

Notes
First edition, second impression. 500 copies.

Mindful of his readers' problems with customs officials, Kahane issued this edition in a wrapper which relegates Maurice Kahane's crab design to a very faint background and which, when discarded, leaves plain grey wrappers and a less readily identifiable book. The result is that copies of this edition in the dustwrapper are extremely scarce.

(c) TROPIC OF CANCER

Title page
TROPIC OF CANCER | BY | HENRY MILLER | PREFACE BY | *ANAÏS NIN* | [logo] | THE OBELISK PRESS | 16, PLACE VENDÔME | PARIS | IMPRIMÉ EN HONGRIE

Collation
8vo. [vi] 7–318 + [ii]. 19.4 × 14.5 cm. Edges untrimmed.

Pagination
[i–ii] blank; [iii] half-title; [iv] list of previous works, copyright, publi-

[173]

cation date: First published September 1934 | Reprinted September 1935 | Reprinted March 1938; [v] title-page; [vi] Emerson quotation; 7–10 preface; 11–318 text; [319–20] blank.

Binding
Pale green heavy paper wrappers with fold-over flaps.
Front panel: TROPIC OF CANCER | BY HENRY MILLER | THIRD PRINTING | A VERY REMARKABLE BOOK, WITH PASSAGES OF | WRITING IN IT AS GOOD AS ANY I HAVE SEEN | FOR A LONG TIME . . . . T. S. ELIOT | AT LAST AN UNPRINTABLE BOOK THAT IS FIT | TO READ . . . . EZRA POUND [dark green]

Spine: TROPIC | OF | CANCER | HENRY | MILLER | THIRD | PRINTING | [logo] | OBELISK | PRESS | PARIS [dark green]

Rear panel: Puffs for the book from: 1. Cyril Connolly; 2. Herbert Read; 3. Aldous Huxley; 4. William Carlos Williams; 5. Blaise Cendrars; 6. Anaïs Nin; 7. Montgomery Belgion.

Front flap: Title, author, blurb and price [60 Frs.]

Rear flap: Twelve titles, with blurbs, at Frs. 60 each: 1. Half O'Clock in Mayfair; 2. Lady, Take Heed!; 3. Uncharted Seas; 4. Black Spring; 5. The Rock Pool (2nd edition); 6. Bessie Cotter; 7. Star Against Star (2nd impression); 8. Boy; 9. Daffodil (14th impression); 10. Sleeveless Errand; 11. Easter Sun (2nd large edition); 12. My Life and Loves

Publication
March 1938

Notes
Second edition. 500 copies.

The text for this edition is reset. All subsequent pre-war editions are typographically identical to this edition save for the printing desig-nation on the front panel of the wrapper and the copyright page [iv]. This edition dispenses with Maurice Kahane's cover design: the front panel of the wrapper, typographically similar to A–32(b), is plain. The publisher's blurb on the front flap is rewritten and the rear flap bears a different list of Obelisk titles to those appearing in A–32(b). Second imprimerie on [318]: IMPRIMÉ EN HONGRIE

(d) TROPIC OF CANCER

Title page
As A–32(c).

Collation
As A–32(c).

Pagination
[i–ii] blank; [iii] half-title; [iv] list of previous works, copyright, publi-
cation date: First published September 1934 | Reprinted September
1935 | Reprinted March 1938 | Reprinted June 1938; [v] title-page; [vi]
Emerson quotation; 7–10 preface; 11–318 text; [319–20] blank.

Binding
As A–32(c).

Wrapper
Front panel: TROPIC OF CANCER | BY HENRY MILLER | FOURTH
PRINTING | A VERY REMARKABLE BOOK, WITH PASSAGES OF |
WRITING IN IT AS GOOD AS ANY I HAVE SEEN | FOR A LONG
TIME . . . . T. S. ELIOT | AT LAST AN UNPRINTABLE BOOK
THAT IS FIT | TO READ . . . . EZRA POUND [dark green]

Spine: TROPIC | OF | CANCER | HENRY | MILLER | FOURTH |
PRINTING | [logo] | OBELISK | PRESS | PARIS [dark green]

Rear panel: As A–32(c).

Front flap: As A–32(c).

Rear flap: As A–32(c).

Publication
June 1938

Notes
Second edition, second impression. 500 copies.

Shifreen and Jackson notes a variant of this edition [Shifreen and
Jackson, A9f, p. 8]: cropped, with no wrappers, and bound in green
leather boards. The cropping has resulted in the Hungarian imprimatur being lost from the title-page [v] and from [318]. Why Shifreen
and Jackson believes this to be a variant, and not a cropped, rebound
copy of this edition, as described above, is beyond me.

(e) TROPIC OF CANCER

Title page
As A–32(c).

Collation
As A–32(c). Top edge rough trimmed, other edges trimmed.

Pagination
[i–ii] blank; [iii] half-title; [iv] list of previous works, copyright, pub-
lication date: First published September 1934 | Reprinted September
1935 | Reprinted March 1938 | Reprinted June 1938 | Reprinted January
1939; [v] title-page; [vi] Emerson quotation; 7–10 preface; 11–318 text;
[319–20] blank.

Binding
Pale green heavy paper wrappers with fold-over flaps.

Front panel: TROPIC OF CANCER | BY HENRY MILLER | FIFTH
PRINTING | A VERY REMARKABLE BOOK, WITH PASSAGES OF |
WRITING IN IT AS GOOD AS ANY I HAVE SEEN | FOR A LONG
TIME . . . . T. S. ELIOT | AT LAST AN UNPRINTABLE BOOK
THAT IS FIT | TO READ . . . . EZRA POUND [dark green]

Spine: TROPIC | OF | CANCER | HENRY | MILLER | FIFTH | PRINTING
| [logo] | OBELISK | PRESS | PARIS [dark green]

Rear panel: As A–32(c).

Front flap: As A–32(c).

Rear flap: As A–32(c).

Publication
January 1939

Notes
Second edition, third impression. 500 copies.

Preceded by a Czech translation, published in Prague in the winter of
1938 with the title *Obratnik Raka*, and with a drawing by Henri Matisse
on its front wrapper.
Second imprimerie on [318]: IMPRIMÉ EN HONGRIE

(f) TROPIC OF CANCER

Title page
TROPIC OF CANCER | BY | HENRY MILLER | PREFACE BY | *ANAÏS NIN* | [logo] | THE OBELISK PRESS | 16, PLACE VENDÔME | PARIS | IMPRIME EN HONGRIE

Collation
8vo. [viii] 7–318 + [iv]. 19.4 × 14.3 cm. Top edge rough trimmed, other edges trimmed.

Pagination
[i–iv] blank; [v] half-title; [vi] list of previous works, copyright, publication date: First published September 1934 | Reprinted September 1935 | Reprinted March 1938 | Reprinted June 1938 | Reprinted January 1939; [vii] title-page; [viii] Emerson quotation; 7–10 preface; 11–318 text; [319–22] blank.

Binding
Blue thin paper wrappers with no flaps.

Front panel: Blue, white boxes with black borders enclosing text. HENRY MILLER | TROPIC | OF | CANCER | THE OBELISK PRESS – PARIS [black on white]

Spine: Printed vertically, bottom to top. *HENRY MILLER* – TROPIC OF CANCER [black on blue]

Rear panel: Blank.

Publication
August 1945

Notes
Second edition, fourth impression. 10,000 copies.

Maurice Girodias rushed this first post-war edition onto the streets to take advantage of the hordes of American servicemen swarming through Paris in 1945. It was printed from the plates of A–32(e), with both the publication page [vi] and the title-page [vii] unamended. There is thus no mention of the 1945 publication date, and the Hungarian imprimatur of A–32(e) appears even though this edition was printed in France.

Between the publication of A–32(e) and this edition, two piracies had appeared on the market: the Book Lover's Club edition, printed in Shanghai, and the Medvsa edition (and its variants), printed in New York.

(g) TROPIC OF CANCER

Title page
TROPIC | OF | CANCER | BY | HENRY MILLER | PREFACE BY | ANAIS NIN | THE OBELISK PRESS BOOKS | LES ÉDITIONS DU CHÊNE | 4, RUE DE LA PAIX | PARIS

Collation
8vo. [vi] 7–366 + [ii]. 17.5 × 11.5 cm. Edges trimmed.

Pagination
[i–ii] blank; [iii] half-title; [iv] copyright; [v] title-page ; [vi] Emerson quotation; 7–10 preface; 11–366 text; [367] imprimerie: ACHEVE D'IMPRIMER LE 20 JUIN 1948 | SUR LES PRESSES DE LA S. F. E. I. R. | 26, RUE CLAVEL, 26 – PARIS-XIXe | No d'Edition: 268; [368] blank.

Binding
Red paper wrappers.

Front panel: Green sunburst. HENRY MILLER | TROPIC | OF | CANCER [white on green] | THE OBELISK PRESS [white on red]

Spine: HENRY | MILLER | TROPIC | OF | CANCER | THE | OBELISK | PRESS [white on red]

Rear panel: [publisher's device] [white on red] | * [black on red] FR. 400 | MUST NOT BE IMPORTED INTO ENGLAND OR U . S . A [white on red]

Publication
20 June 1948

Notes
Ninth edition.

Between A–32(f) and this edition two more non-Obelisk editions appeared on the market, both in 1947: a piracy carrying the imprint of the non-existent 'Lotus Press', and an illustrated edition with artwork by Timar. Both were published in Paris.

The publisher's device on the rear panel is not the Obelisk logo, but that of Editions du Chêne: an H inside a diamond.

(h) TROPIC OF CANCER

Publication
30 June 1949

Notes
Ninth edition, second impression.

Not seen. According to Shifreen and Jackson [A9bb], this issue is identical to A–32(g) except for the inclusion of the address of Les Editions du Chêne on the copyright page [iv].

(i) TROPIC OF CANCER

Publication
25 May 1950

Notes
Ninth edition, third impression.

Not seen. Shifreen and Jackson [A9cc]: [367] reads ACHEVÉ D'IMPRIMER LE 25 MAI 1950 | SUR LES PRESSES DE LA SOPAC | 26, RUE CLAVEL, 26. PARIS-XIXe | No d'édition: 268

(j) TROPIC OF CANCER

Title page
HENRY MILLER | TROPIC | OF | CANCER | PRÉFACE BY | ANAÏS NIN | THE OBELISK PRESS | LES ÉDITIONS DU CHÊNE | 28, RUE LA BOÉTIE | PARIS

Collation
8vo. [vi] 7–305 + [iii]. 17.5 × 11.5 cms. Edges trimmed.

Pagination
[i–ii] blank; [iii] half-title; [iv] blank; [v] title-page; [vi] Emerson quotation and copyright; [7–9] preface; [10] blank; 11–305 text; [306] blank; [307] imprimerie: IMPRIMÉ EN FRANCE | POUR LE COMPTE DE LA | SOCIÉTÉ NOUVELLE | DES ÉDITIONS DU CHÊNE | PAR BRODARD ET TAUPIN | COULOMMIERS-PARIS | DÉPÔT LÉGAL: 2e TRIM. 52 | EDITEUR: No 5 | IMPRIMEUR: No 8602 | 45105-4-1952; [308] blank.

[179]

Binding
As A–32(g).

Front panel: As A–32(g).

Spine: As A–32(g).

Rear panel: [publisher's device] [white on red] | * [black on red] FR. 600 | MUST NOT BE IMPORTED INTO ENGLAND OR U . S . A [white on red]

Publication
April 1952

Notes
Tenth edition.

Not seen. Shifreen and Jackson [A9dd].

(k) TROPIC OF CANCER

Title page
HENRY MILLER | TROPIC | OF | CANCER | PRÉFACE BY | ANAÏS NIN | THE OBELISK PRESS | LES ÉDITIONS DU CHÊNE | 4, RUE DE GALLIERA, PARIS

Collation
As A–32(j).

Pagination
As A–32(j), except [307] now reads: IMPRIMÉ EN FRANCE | POUR LE COMPTE DE LA | SOCIÉTÉ NOUVELLE | DES ÉDITIONS DU CHÊNE | PAR BRODARD ET TAUPIN | COULOMMIERS-PARIS | DÉPÔT LÉGAL: 3e trim. 53 | EDITEUR: No 5 | IMPRIMEUR: No 9231 | 46939 - 7 - 1953.

Binding
As A–32(g).

Front panel: As A–32(g).

Spine: As A–32(g).

Rear panel: As A–32(j).

Publication
July 1953

Notes
Tenth edition, second impression.

Not seen. Shifreen and Jackson [A9ee].

(l) TROPIC OF CANCER

Title page
TROPIC | OF | CANCER | BY | HENRY | MILLER | PRÉFACE BY | ANAÏS
NIN | THE OBELISK PRESS BOOKS | 4, RUE DE LA PAIX | PARIS

Collation
As A–32(j).

Pagination
As A–32(j).

Binding
As A–32(g).

Publication
1954.

Notes
Tenth edition, third impression.

Not seen. Shifreen and Jackson [A9gg] makes no mention of a change
to the printing information on [367]. Preceded by the first Keimeisha
edition [Tokyo, 1953].

(m) TROPIC OF CANCER

Title page
HENRY MILLER | TROPIC | OF | CANCER | PRÉFACE BY | ANAÏS
NIN | OBELISK PRESS | 4, RUE DE GALLIERA, PARIS

Collation
As A–32(j).

Pagination
As A–32(j), except [307] now reads: IMPRIMÉ EN FRANCE | PAR
BRODARD – TAUPIN | IMPRIMEUR – RELIEUR | COULOMMIERS
– PARIS | DÉPÔT LÉGAL: 2e TRIM. 56 | ÉDITEUR: No 31 | IMPRIMEUR:

No 1725 | 50745-5-1956

Binding
As A–32(g).

Front panel: As A–32(g).

Spine: As A–32(g).

Rear panel: As A–32(j).

Publication
Spring 1956

Notes
Tenth edition, fourth impression.

Between A–32(l) and this edition a second Keimeisha edition and a Japanese piracy appeared, both in early 1956.

Not in Shifreen and Jackson.

(n) TROPIC OF CANCER

Title page
HENRY MILLER | TROPIC | OF | CANCER | PRÉFACE BY | ANAÏS NIN | OBELISK PRESS | PARIS

Collation
As A–32(j)

Pagination
As A–32(j), except [307] now reads: IMPRIMÉ EN FRANCE | POUR BRODARD – TAUPIN | IMPRIMEUR – RELIEUR | COULOM-MIERS – PARIS | DÉPÔT LÉGAL: 3e TRIM. 57 | ÉDITEUR: No 35 | IMPRIMEUR: No 2337 | 52345-9-1957

Binding
As A–32(g).

Front panel: As A–32(g).

Spine: As A–32(g).

Rear panel: As A–32(j).

Publication
September 1957

Notes
Tenth edition, fifth impression.

Not seen. Shifreen and Jackson [A9jj].

(o) TROPIC OF CANCER

Title page
As A–32(n).

Collation
As A–32(j).

Pagination
As A–32(j), except [307] now reads: IMPRIMÉ EN FRANCE | POUR BR-
ODARD — TAUPIN | IMPRIMEUR – RELIEUR | COULOMMIERS –
PARIS | DÉPÔT LÉGAL: 2e TRIM. 58 | ÉDITEUR: No 38 | IMPRIMEUR:
No 2717 | 53351-5-1958

Binding
As A–32(g).

Front panel: As A–32(g).

Spine: As A–32(g).

Rear panel: As A–32(j).

Publication
September 1957

Notes
Tenth edition, sixth impression.

Not seen. Shifreen and Jackson [A9kk].

(p) TROPIC OF CANCER

Title page
As A–32(n).

Collation
As A–32(j).

Pagination
As A–32(j), except the copyright notice on [vi] now reads: *Tous droits*

réservés par les | ÉDITIONS DU CHÊNE, PARIS; and [307] now reads: ACHEVÉ | D'IMPRIMER | [printer's device] | SUR LES PRESSES D'AUBIN | LIGUGÉ (VIENNE) | LE 15 AVRIL | 1959 | D. L., 2-1959-Éditeur, No 38. — Imprimeur, No 2.034. | Imprimé en France.

Binding
As A–32(g).

Front panel: As A–32(g).

Spine: As A–32(g).

Rear panel: As A–32(j).

Publication
15 April 1959

Notes
Tenth edition, seventh impression.

Not seen. Shifreen and Jackson [A9ll].

(q) TROPIC OF CANCER

Title page
As A–32(n).

Collation
As A–32(j).

Pagination
As A–32(p), except [307] now reads: ACHEVÉ | D'IMPRIMER | LE 15 SEPTEMBRE 1959 | PAR L'IMPRIMERIE | NAUDEAU, REDON ET Cie | A POITIERS (VIENNE). | Procédé photo-offset | Dépot légal: 3e trimestre 1959. | Éditeur, no 38. – Imprimeur, no 342.

Binding
As A–32(g).

Front panel: As A–32(g).

Spine: As A–32(g).

Rear panel: As A–32(j).

Publication
15 September 1959

Notes
Tenth edition, eighth impression.

Not seen. Shifreen and Jackson [A9mm].

(r) TROPIC OF CANCER

Title page
As A–32(n).

Collation
8vo. [vi] 7–305 + [i]. 17.5 × 11.5 cms. Edges trimmed.

Pagination
[i–ii] blank; [iii] half-title; [iv] blank; [v] title-page; [vi] Emerson quotation and copyright; [7–9] preface; [10] blank; 11–305 text; [306] imprimerie: ACHEVÉ D'IMPRIMER | LE 20 OCTOBRE 1960 | PAR L'IMPRIMERIE | NAUDEAU, REDON ET Cie, | A POITIERS (VIENNE). | Procédé photo-offset | Dépôt légal: 4e trimestre 1960. | Imprimeur, no 467. | Imprimé en France.; [307–308] blank.

Binding
White paper wrappers.

Front panel: HENRY MILLER [red] | TROPIC | OF CANCER [black] | [forward slash] [red] | THE OBELISK PRESS [black]

Spine: HENRY | MILLER [red] | TROPIC | OF CANCER | THE OBELISK | PRESS [black]

Rear panel: *THE OBELISK PRESS* [black] | HENRY MILLER [red] | TROPIC OF CAPRICORN | BLACK SPRING | NEXUS [black] | FRANK HARRIS [red] | MY LIFE AND LOVES | (4 vol.) [black] | CECIL BARR [red] | BRIGHT PINK YOUTH | DAFFODIL [black] | SHEILA COUSINS [red] | TO BEG I AM ASHAMED [black]

Publication
20 October 1960

Notes
Sixteenth edition.

Shifreen and Jackson [A9mm].

Between A–32(p) and this edition two non-Obelisk editions were issued: a Taiwanese piracy, and a paperback edition published by

Keimeisha of Tokyo.

The copy examined [CUL] has a hand-printed price [9,50] at the bottom right of the rear panel.

(s) TROPIC OF CANCER

Title page
As A–32(n).

Collation
8vo. [vi] 7–305 + [iii]. 17.5 × 11.5 cms. Edges trimmed.

Pagination
[i–ii] blank; [iii] half-title; [iv] blank; [v] title-page; [vi] Emerson quotation and copyright; [7–9] preface; [10] blank; 11–305 text; [306] imprimerie: ACHEVÉ D'IMPRIMER | LE 5 MARS 1961 | PAR L'IMPRIMERIE | NAUDEAU, REDON ET Cie, | A POITIERS (VIENNE). | Procédé photo-offset | Dépôt légal: 1er trimestre 1961. | Imprimeur, no 524. | Imprimé en France.; [307–308] blank.

Binding
White paper wrappers.

Front panel: HENRY MILLER [red] | TROPIC | OF CANCER [black] | [forward slash] [red] | THE OBELISK PRESS [black]

Spine: HENRY | MILLER [red] | TROPIC | OF CANCER | THE OBELISK | PRESS [black]

Rear panel: Not seen.

Publication
5 March 1961

Notes
Sixteenth edition, second impression.

Not seen. Shifreen and Jackson [A9qq].

(t) TROPIC OF CANCER

Title page
As A–32(n).

Collation
As A–32(s).

Pagination
As A–32(s), except [306] now reads: ACHEVÉ D'IMPRIMER | LE 25 NOVEMBRE 1961 | PAR L'IMPRIMERIE | NAUDEAU, REDON ET Cie, | A POITIERS (VIENNE). | *Procédé photo-offset*

Binding
White gloss paper wrappers.

Front panel: HENRY MILLER [red] | TROPIC | OF CANCER [blue] | [forward slash] [red] | THE OBELISK PRESS [blue]

Spine: HENRY | MILLER [red] | TROPIC | OF CANCER | THE OBELISK | PRESS [blue]

Rear panel: Not seen

Publication
25 November 1961

Notes
Twenty-sixth edition.

Not seen. Shifreen and Jackson [A9qq].

(u) TROPIC OF CANCER

Title page
HENRY MILLER | TROPIC | OF | CANCER | PRÉFACE BY | ANAÏS NIN | OBELISK PRESS | [PARIS]

Collation
As A–32(s).

Pagination
As A–32(p), except [306] now reads: ACHEVÉ D'IMPRIMER | LE 30 NOVEMBRE 1962 | PAR L'IMPRIMERIE | NAUDEAU, REDON ET Cie, | A POITIERS (VIENNE). | Procédé photo-offset | D. L., – 1962. – | Imprimeur, no 744. | Imprimé en France.

Binding
As A–32(s).

Front panel: As A–32(s).
Spine: As A–32(s).

Rear panel: Not seen.

Publication
30 November 1962

Notes
Twenty-sixth edition, second impression.

Not seen. Shifreen and Jackson [A9uuu].

This was the last edition of *Tropic of Cancer* to carry the Obelisk Press imprint.

A–33 THE GENTLE MEN

by MARIKA NORDEN (MIRJAM VOGT)

Title page
THE GENTLE MEN | BY | MARIKA NORDEN | [logo] | THE OBELISK PRESS | 338 RUE SAINT-HONORÉ | PARIS.

Collation
8vo. [viii] 9–352 + [iv]. 19.3 × 14.3 cm. Edges untrimmed.

Pagination
[i–ii] blank; [iii] half-title; [iv] copyright and publication: First published May 1935; [v] title-page; [vi] blank; [vii] second half-title; [viii] blank; [9] quotation from *Zarathustra*; [10] section heading and quotation from Meleager; 11–352 text; [353] blank; [354] imprimerie: Lecram – Servant; [355–356] blank.

Binding
Gold heavy paper wrappers with fold-over flaps.

Wrapper
Front panel: Design in black of four women of ancient Egypt, black lines arcing from bottom left to top right. THE | GENTLE | MEN | MARIKA | NORDEN [black] | THE OBELISK PRESS _ PARIS [gold on black]

Spine: THE | GENTLE | MEN | MARIKA | NORDEN | [logo] | Obelisk Press | 338 Rue St-Honoré | PARIS [black]

Rear panel: Blank

Front flap: Title, author, blurb, price [50 Frs.]

Rear flap: Twelve titles, with blurbs: 1. The Gentle Men; 2. Star Against Star; 3. Daffodil (10th impression); 4. Amour French For Love (Seventh large impression); 5. Bright Pink Youth; 6. The Well of Loneliness; 7. Sleeveless Errand; 8. Tropic of Cancer; 9. Easter Sun; 10. Storm; 11. The Lamb; 12. The Young And Evil.

White wraparound band: CANNOT BE BOUGHT | in ENGLAND and U. S. A. | A | NORWEG- | IAN WOMAN | LAYS BARE HER | LOVE AFFAIRS WITH | FOUR ENGLISHMEN. THE | PASSION AND CONVICTION OF | THIS BOOK WILL STARTLE AND | STIR THE READER. HOW MANY, IN THEIR | HEARTS, WILL AGREE WITH HER ?

The rear of the band carries the Obelisk logo.

Publication
May 1935

Notes
First edition.

The copy in the author's collection has an Obelisk cancel sticker over the original price on the front flap, increasing the price to Frs. 60, and a further unprinted sticker over that with the handwritten figure '75', and carries pencilled notes on [i] guessing at the identities of the real-life counterparts of the characters in the novel.

The design of the wrapper has nothing whatsoever to do with the contents of the novel, and is lifted from the cover of an earlier book by Vogt called *Mens Sfinxen Våkner* (*When the Sphinx Awakens*) [1929], a travel book about Egypt.

The Gentle Men was published in Norwegian in 1937 with the title *Verdens Herrer* (*The World's Masters*).

(b) THE GENTLE MEN

Title page
As A–33.

Collation
As A–33.

Pagination
As A–33, except the publication information on [iv] now reads: First

published 1935 | Reprinted December 1935. The type on [10] has been reset, repositioning the section heading 'TONY' towards the centre of the page.

Binding
As A–33.

Wrapper
As A–33, except: Rear flap: Twelve titles, with blurbs, at Frs. 50 each: 1. Bessie Cotter; 2. Boy; 3. Star Against Star; 4. Tropic of Cancer; 5. The Well of Loneliness: 6. Daffodil (In its tenth impression); 7. The Young And Evil; 8. Storm; 9. Easter Sun; 10. The Lamb; 11. Sleeveless Errand; 12. My Life And Loves

Publication
December 1935

Notes
First edition, second impression.

(c) THE GENTLE MEN

Title page
As A–33, except the address now reads: 16, Place Vendôme.

Collation
8vo. [viii] 9–293 + [ii]. 18.1 × 13.5 cm. Edges trimmed.

Pagination
[i–ii] blank; [iii] half-title; [iv] copyright and publication: First published May 1935 | Reprinted January 1939; [v] title-page; [vi] quotation from *Zarathustra*; [vii] section heading and quotation from Meleager; [viii] blank; 9–293 text; [294] quotation from Agathias of Byzantium and imprimerie: (Imprimé en Belgique); [295–296] blank.

Binding
Blue paper wrappers.

Wrapper
Front panel: Text separated by white horizontal lines. THE | GENTLE | MEN | BY | *MARIKA NORDEN* | THE OBELISK PRESS – PARIS [black on blue]

Spine: THE | GENTLE | MEN | *BY* | *MARIKA* | *NORDEN* | THE | OBELISK | PRESS | PARIS [black on blue]

Rear panel: PRIX: 175 Fr. * [black on blue]

Publication
January 1939

Notes
Third edition. Second Obelisk edition.

Two copies located [NYPL (rebound); Casson].

[vi] carries a 'dedication' above the quotation: A LEGACY: | TO THE GENTLE MEN OF BRITAIN | FROM A BITER BITTEN

[vii] is reset once again, the quotation now just above the centre of the page, with the section heading towards the top left.

In the publication information on [iv], no mention is made of A–33b.

A–34 SONNETS AND LYRICS
by LAURENCE DAKIN

Title page
SONNETS AND LYRICS | BY | LAURENCE DAKIN | [logo] | PARIS | 1935

Collation
8vo. [x] 13–59 + [iii]. 18.5 × 13.5 cm. Top edge trimmed, others untrimmed.

Pagination
[i–ii] blank; [iii] half-title; [iv] list of previous works; [v] title-page; [vi] copyright; [vii] dedication; [viii] blank; [ix] contents; [x] blank; 13–59 text; [60] blank; [61] imprimerie: LECRAM-SERVANT | 338, Rue Saint-Honoré | Paris; [62] blank.

Binding
Plain red grain cloth.

Spine: White paper label. LAURENCE | DAKIN | SONNETS | AND | LYRICS | Obelisk | Press | Paris [brown]

Publication
June 1935

Notes
First edition.

Three copies located [BL; NYPL; author's collection]. The pagination given is taken from the NYPL copy. The BL copy, though similarly bound, lacks the front blank endpaper found in the other two copies located.

The list on [vi] includes: 'Shelley: The Man and Artist' (forthcoming). No copy of this book has been located, and it seems never to have been published.

A–35 STAR AGAINST STAR
by GAWEN BROWNRIGG

Title page
STAR AGAINST STAR | BY | GAWEN BROWNRIGG | [logo] | THE OBELISK PRESS | 338 RUE SAINT-HONORÉ | PARIS

Collation
8vo. [viii] 9–329 + [iii]. 18.5 × 13.5 cm. Top edge untrimmed, other edges trimmed.

Pagination
[i–ii] blank; [iii] half-title; [iv] copyright and publication: First published July 1935; [v] title-page; [vi] blank; [vii] second half-title; [viii] blank; 9–329 text; [330] blank; [331] imprimerie: LECRAM-SERVANT | 338 Rue Saint-Honoré | Paris; [332] blank.

Binding
Heavy paper wrappers with fold-over flaps.

Wrapper
Front panel: Dark blue, with two half-length female figures picked out in white.
star | against | star | by | gawen brownrigg [white, with a white star at each end of the title]

Spine: Dark blue.
star | against | star | by | gawen | brownrigg | [logo] | 338 rue St HONORÉ | PARIS [white]

Rear panel: White. [logo] [dark blue]

Front flap: Title, author, blurb and price [50 Frs.]

Rear flap: Twelve titles, with blurbs: 1. The Gentle Men; 2. Star Against Star; 3. Daffodil (tenth impression); 4. Amour French for Love (seventh large impression); 5. Bright Pink Youth; 6. The Well of Loneliness; 7. Sleeveless Errand; 8. Tropic of Cancer; 9. Easter Sun; 10. Storm; 11. The Lamb; 12. The Young and Evil.

Publication
July 1935

Notes
First edition.

The American edition was published by Macaulay in 1936.

(b) STAR AGAINST STAR

Title page
STAR AGAINST STAR | BY | GAWEN BROWNRIGG | *2nd Impression* | [logo] | THE OBELISK PRESS | 338 RUE SAINT-HONORÉ | PARIS

Collation
8vo. [viii] 9–329 + [iii]. 19 × 14 cm. Top edge untrimmed, other edges trimmed.

Pagination
[i–ii] blank; [iii] half-title; [iv] blank; [v] title-page; [vi] copyright and publication: First published July 1935 | Reprinted September 1936; [vii] second half-title; [viii] blank; 9–329 text; [330] blank; [331] imprimerie: LECRAM-SERVANT | 338 Rue Saint-Honoré | Paris; [332] blank.

Binding
Heavy paper wrappers with fold-over flaps.

Wrapper
Front panel: As A–35 [see notes].

Spine: As A–35.

Rear panel: As A–35.

Front flap: Title, author, blurb and price [50 Frs.].

Rear flap: Fourteen titles, with blurbs, at Frs. 50 each: 1. The Rock Pool; 2. Black Spring; 3. Bessie Cotter; 4. Star Against Star; 5. The Gentle

Men; 6. Tropic of Cancer; 7. Boy; 8. Daffodil (twelfth impression); 9. The Well of Loneliness; 10. My Life and Loves; 11. Storm; 12. The Lamb; 13. Sleeveless Errand; 14. Lady Chatterley's Lover.

Publication
September 1936

Notes
First edition, second impression.

The front flap has the words '2nd Impression' added to the foot of the blurb. The blurb itself is identical to that of A–35, but has been reset.

A–36 FOUR SCHOOLS
by ROBIN ANDERSON

Title page
FOUR SCHOOLS | BY | ROBIN ANDERSON | [logo] | THE OBELISK PRESS | 338 RUE SAINT-HONORÉ | PARIS

Collation
8vo. [x] 11–118 + [viii]. 18 × 13 cm. Edges trimmed.

Pagination
[i–ii] blank; [iii] title-page; [iv] copyright and publication: First published September 1935; [v] half-title; [vi] dedication; [vii] Blake quotation; [viii] blank; [ix] school/prison comparison; [x] quotation from an English hymn; 11–118 text; [119] blank; [120] place and date of authorship; [121–122] blank; [123] imprimerie: LECRAM-SERVANT | 338 Rue Saint-Honoré | PARIS; [124–128] blank.

Binding
Red heavy paper wrappers.

Front panel: FOUR SCHOOLS | by | ROBIN ANDERSON [black]

Spine: FOUR | SCHOOLS | by | ROBIN | ANDERSON | OBELISK | PRESS [black]

Rear panel: Blank.

Publication
September 1935

Notes
The book was priced at Frs. 20 or five shillings. B–4 cites the author as a translator of Georg Büchner: if he was, he was an unpublished one.

Dedication reads: TO ALL IN CAPTIVITY.

According to [120], the book was completed in London in January 1934.

A–37 BOY

by JAMES HANLEY

Title page
BOY | BY | JAMES HANLEY | (*Banned in England May 1935*) | [logo] | THE OBELISK PRESS | 338 RUE SAINT-HONORÉ | PARIS

Collation
8vo. [xii] 9–271 + [v]. 19.8 × 13.5 cm (wrappers wider at leading edge than text block). All edges untrimmed.

Pagination
[i–iv] blank; [v] half-title; [vi] blank; [vii] list of previous works; [viii] blank; [ix] title-page; [x] blank; [xi] dedication; [xii] disclaimer; 9–271 text; [272–276] blank.

Binding
Illustrated heavy paper covers with fold-over flaps.

Front panel: Illustration in red and black of a dancing girl performing for an audience of sailors. BANNED IN ENGLAND | MAY 1935 [black on red] | BOY [red on black] | THE OBELISK PRESS PARIS | JAMES HANLEY [red on black]

Spine: White. [line] [red] | BOY | * | JAMES | HANLEY [black] | [line] | [logo] [red] | THE OBELISK PRESS | 338 RUE ST-HONORÉ | PARIS [black]

Rear panel: White. [logo] [red]

Front flap: Five reviews, edition statement, price [60 francs]

Rear flap: Eleven titles, with blurbs, at Frs. 50 each: 1. Star Against Star; 2. The Gentle Men; 3. Tropic of Cancer; 4. Daffodil (tenth impression); 5. The Well of Loneliness; 6. The Young and Evil; 7. My Life and Loves; 8. Easter Sun; 9. Storm; 10. The Lamb; 11. Sleeveless Errand.

Publication
September 1935

Notes
Fourth edition.

Boy was first published by Boriswood in London in 1931 in both a limited, unexpurgated issue, and an ordinary issue in which on 52 pages the more contentious passages were replaced by asterisks or gaps in the text. A second impression appeared in December, with softened language replacing the asterisks and gaps to signify where some passages were missing altogether. An American edition was published by Knopf in 1932, for which the text was reset once again. A cheap edition with a lurid dustwrapper was published in England in 1934, and it was this edition which the police seized from a Manchester lending library. The librarian was prosecuted for obscene publication, and Boriswood and its directors with aiding and abetting. On legal advice all parties pleaded guilty, and were fined a total of £400. After the trial Kahane bought the sheets of the 1934 edition, composed a new title-page, and published the result as the first Obelisk edition. The edition statement on the front flap states (with dubious grammar): '*This is the only existing edition | of James Hanley's most famous | work suppressed in England.*'

The dedication is to Nancy Cunard, who, according to Kahane's son Eric, was at one time Kahane's lover.

Gibbs doubts the existence of this edition, having been unable to trace a copy. It is certainly rare: the BL, Armstrong and Gostock copies are the only three located.

(b) BOY

Title page
BOY | BY | JAMES HANLEY | (*Banned in England May 1935*) | [logo] | THE OBELISK PRESS | 16, PLACE VENDOME | PARIS

Collation
8vo. [xii] 9–271 + [v]. 19.8 × 13.5 cm (wrappers wider at leading edge than text block). Top edge trimmed, others rough trimmed.

Pagination
As A–37.

Binding
Cream heavy paper wrappers with fold-over flaps.

Front panel: Red horizontal lines. BOY | JAMES HANLEY | [logo] [black on white] | THE OBELISK PRESS [black on red]

Spine: Red horizontal lines separating text. BOY | JAMES | HANLEY | [logo] | OBELISK | PRESS | PARIS [black]

Rear panel: [logo] [red]

Front flap: As A–37.

Rear flap: Thirteen titles, with blurbs, at Frs. 60 each: 1. Half O'Clock in Mayfair; 2. Lady, Take Heed!; 3. Uncharted Seas; 4. The Rock Pool (2nd edition); 5. Bessie Cotter; 6. Boy; 7. Star Against Star (2nd impression); 8. Tropic of Cancer; 9. Black Spring; 10. My Live [sic] and Loves; 11. Easter Sun (2nd large edition); 12. Storm (4th edition); 13. Sleeveless Errand.

Publication
May 1938

Notes
Fourth edition, second impression.

The presence of *Half O'Clock in Mayfair* in the list of titles on the rear flap dates this impression as no earlier than the spring of 1938. Further, the absence of *To Beg I Am Ashamed* from the list, and that book's presence on the rear flap of A–53, suggest a publication date of no later than June.

The word 'as' is missing from the first line of the blurb for *Lady, Take Heed!* on the rear flap, a mistake repeated on the rear flaps of A–54, A–55 and A–57.

Not in Gibbs.

(c) BOY

Title page
JAMES HANLEY | BOY | THE OBELISK PRESS | 16, PLACE VENDÔME, PARIS

Collation
8vo. [viii] 9–173 + [iii]. 19.5 × 14.2 cm. Edges untrimmed.

Pagination
[i–ii] blank; [iii] half-title; [iv] blank; [v] title-page; [vi] copyright; [vii] disclaimer; [viii] dedication; 9–173 text; [174] blank; [175] imprimerie:

ACHEVÉ D'IMPRIMER | SUR LES PRESSES DE | L'IMPRIMERIE DE SCEAUX | – LE 15 AVRIL 1946 – | 21.589 – c. o. l. 31.3029 | DÉP. LÉG.: 1er TR. 1946 | No D'ÉDITION 251; [176] blank.

Binding
Blue-grey heavy paper wrappers.

Wrapper
Front panel: BOY [red, bordered top and bottom by two red horizontal lines enclosing two shorter, thicker black ones] | *BY JAMES HANLEY* | THE OBELISK PRESS – PARIS [black, imprint enclosed by two black horizontal lines]

Spine: BOY [red] | *BY* | *JAMES* | *HANLEY* | THE | OBELISK | PRESS | PARIS [black]

Rear panel: * [black] Frs. 175 [red]

Publication
15 April 1946

Notes
Fifth edition.

This book appears in Gibbs as item A6(h), wrongly listed as the presumed first Obelisk edition.

A–38 ALLER RETOUR NEW YORK

by HENRY MILLER

Title page
SIANA SERIES No 1 | Aller Retour New York | BY | Henry Miller | AUTHOR OF | *TROPIC OF CANCER* | [logo] | THE OBELISK PRESS | 338 RUE SAINT-HONORÉ | PARIS

Collation
8vo. [viii] 9–149 + [iii]. 20.7 × 13.6 cm. Edges trimmed.

Pagination
[i–ii] blank; [iii] half-title; [iv] copyright, limitation and publication: First published October 1935; [v] title-page; [vi] blank; [vii] second half-title, with additional explanatory heading; [viii] blank; 9–149 text; [150] blank; [151] imprimerie: LECRAM-SERVANT | 338 Rue Saint-Honoré | Paris; [152] blank.

Binding
Red heavy paper wrappers.

Wrapper
Front panel: Aller Retour New York | by | Henry Miller [black]
Spine: Printed horizontally, bottom to top: ALLER RETOUR NEW
YORK – HENRY MILLER [black]
Rear panel: [logo] [black]

Publication
October 1935 [see notes]

Notes
First edition.

Limitation on [iv] reads: *This, the original edition, printed on thin paper,* | *consists of 150 copies, numbered 1–150, and* | *signed by the author.* Miller retained several *hors de commerce* copies for distribution to his friends: these copies do not carry the printed number on [iv], and are affectionately inscribed rather than merely signed. The Leeds University copy, inscribed by Miller to Herbert Read, is dated '10/35' in Miller's hand, and is the earliest dated copy located. (Even so, it was later arriving in Read's hands than planned. Miller's inscription in Read's copy of *What Are You Going To Do About Alf?* [privately printed, Paris, 1935] reads: 'Dear Herbert Read, The "travel letter" follows in a day or two. Was held up for more lucrative jobs. Sincerely, Henry Miller'). Miller dated most of his copies of this title 11/11/35 [e.g. NYPL, Berg collection, two copies]. The Leeds copy suggests that, unusually for an Obelisk title, the printed publication date is accurate.

Kahane writes in his memoir: 'I had [*Aller Retour New York*] printed on Indian paper so that it could be posted by first-class mail.'[4]

According to the flyer issued by Obelisk to promote publication [see B–5] the book sold for Frs. 35 or $2.50.

The wrapper design is the same as that of A–36, published the previous month.

Number 1 of the Siana series. Siana – 'Anaïs' backwards, the name for the new venture having been suggested by Alfred Perlès – was set up at Louveciennes by Anaïs Nin in 1935. Although reliant on Nin's financing, control of the imprint was soon wrested from her by Perlès, Miller and Michael Fraenkel.

4 Kahane, *Memoirs*, p. 264.

A–39 BESSIE COTTER
by WALLACE SMITH

Title page
BESSIE COTTER | BY | WALLACE SMITH | *Author of* | THE CAPTAIN HATES THE SEA | [logo] | THE OBELISK PRESS| 338 RUE SAINT-HONORÉ | PARIS

Collation
8vo. [x] 11–363 + [v]. 19 × 14 cm. Edges untrimmed.

Pagination
[i–ii] blank; [iii] half-title; [iv] publication: First printed January 1936; [v] title-page; [vi] copyright; [vii] dedication; [viii] blank; [ix–x] contents; 11–363 text; [364–366] advertisements; [367] blank; [368] imprimerie: Lecram-Servant.

Binding
Heavy paper wrappers with fold-over flaps.

Wrapper
Front panel: Blue-black, illustration of street corner by night in yellow. BESSIE | COTTER | WALLACE | SMITH [yellow]

Spine: Yellow. BESSIE | COTTER | WALLACE | SMITH | [logo] | Obelisk Press | 338 Rue St-Honoré | PARIS [black]

Rear panel: Yellow. [logo] [black]

Front flap: Yellow. Title, blurb, price [50 Frs.]

Rear flap: Yellow. Twelve titles, with blurbs, at Frs. 50 each: 1. Star Against Star; 2. The Gentle Men; 3. Tropic of Cancer; 4. Boy; 5. Daffodil (10th impression); 6. The Well of Loneliness; 7. The Young and Evil; 8. My Life and Loves; 9. Easter Sun; 10. Storm; 11. The Lamb; 12. Sleeveless Errand.

Publication
January 1936

Notes
Third edition.

First published in the United States by Covici, Friede in 1934. The second edition was published in England in 1935 by Heinemann, who were then prosecuted in April of that year for publishing an obscene book. In his opening remarks for the prosecution the Attorney-General Sir Thomas Inskip declared: 'The book deals with what everybody will recognise as an unsavoury subject – gratification of sexual appetite'. Heinemann were convicted, and fined one hundred guineas.

The pages of advertisements are as follows:

[364]: "SOME OBELISK NOVELS: 50 Frs. EACH", followed by five titles, with blurbs: 1. Bessie Cotter; 2. Boy; 3. The Gentle Men (2nd impression); 4. Star Against Star; 5. Tropic of Cancer (2nd impression).

[365]: Eight titles, with blurbs: 1. Easter Sun; 2. Daffodil (10th impression); 3. The Young and Evil; 4. Storm; 5. The Lamb; 6. My Life and Loves; 7. Sleeveless Errand; 8. The Well of Loneliness.

[366]: "EDITIONS DE LUXE AND BELLES-LETTRES", followed by four titles, with blurbs and/or price details: 1. Haveth Childers Everywhere; 2. Pomes Penyeach; 3. Cléante and Bélise; 4. Poems for Music.

This is the only Obelisk title to carry pages of advertisements. They do not appear in the book's later impressions.

(b) BESSIE COTTER

Title page
As A–39, but with the Obelisk address changed to: 16 PLACE VENDOME.

Collation
8vo. [x] 11–259 + [i]. 19 × 14cm. Edges untrimmed.

Pagination
[i–ii] blank; [iii] half-title; [iv] publication: First printed January 1936 | Reprinted September 1938; [v] title-page (see above); [vi] copyright; [vii] dedication; [viii] blank; [ix–x] contents; 11–259; [260] imprimerie: Georges Frère | TOURCOING

Binding
Heavy paper wrappers with fold-over flaps.

Wrapper
Front panel: as A–37.

Spine: As A–37, except address now reads: 16, Place Vendome

Rear panel: As A–37.

Front flap: Title, author, blurb, price [60 Frs.] | THE OBELISK PRESS

Rear flap: Twelve titles, with blurbs, at Frs. 60 each: 1. Dark Refuge; 2. To Beg I Am Ashamed; 3. Half O'Clock In Mayfair; 4. Lady, Take Heed!; 5. The Rock Pool; 6. Boy; 7. Star Against Star (2nd impression); 8. Tropic of Cancer; 9. My Life and Loves; 10. Easter Sun (2nd large edition); 11. Storm (4th edition); 12. Sleeveless Errand.

Yellow wraparound band: **CANNOT BE BOUGHT IN ENGLAND OR U. S. A.** | BESSIE COTTER BIG-HEARTED, AMORAL HAS A PLACE OF HER OWN AMONGST THE GREAT HEROINES OF FICTION AND WILL LIVE AS LONG AS ANY OF THEM. 3RD IMPRESSION [blue-black]

Logo on spine [blue-black]

Rear blank.

The missing point in 'U S. A.' and the capricious use of commas are as printed.

Publication
September 1938

Notes
Fourth edition.

The wraparound band proclaims the third impression; the publication page calls it a first reprint (or second impression). The book was issued with entirely reset text, and is therefore the fourth edition (second Obelisk edition).

Kahane often exaggerated the number of impressions of a title in order to give an inflated view of the book's success. Although the wraparound band (3rd impression) disagrees with the publication page (2nd impression), it is likely that the band and the book started life together.

Unlike A–39, this edition does not carry pages of advertisements.

(c) BESSIE COTTER

Title page
WALLACE SMITH | BESSIE COTTER | THE OBELISK PRESS | 16, PLACE VENDOME, PARIS

Collation
8vo. [x] 11–227 + [i].

Pagination
[i–ii] blank; [iii] half-title; [iv] blank; [v] title-page; [vi] copyright; [vii] dedication; [viii] blank; [ix–x] contents; 11–227 text; [228] imprimerie: 31.0914 | SOCIÉTÉ INDUSTRIELLE | D'IMPRIMERIE | 10, rue Vallier, Levallois | Dépôt légal 20 trimestre 1946 | No d'Edition: 253

Binding
Green paper wrappers.

Front panel: BESSIE | COTTER [red, printed between three black lines and additionally enclosed by two red lines] | *BY WALLACE SMITH* [black] | THE OBELISK PRESS – PARIS [black, enclosed by two black lines]

Spine: BESSIE | COTTER [red] | *BY* | *WALLACE* | *SMITH* | THE | OBELISK | PRESS | PARIS

Rear panel: * [black] 175 FRS [red]

Publication
Spring 1946

Notes
Sixth edition.

Between A–39(b) and this edition, a French translation was published by Gallimard in 1939.

The markings on the rear panel may have been stamped on the book at a later date, but were present on both copies examined.

(d) BESSIE COTTER

Title page
WALLACE SMITH | BESSIE COTTER | THE OBELISK PRESS

Collation
Small 8vo. [x] 12–307 + [i]. 17.5 × 11.2 cm. All edges trimmed.

Pagination
[i–ii] blank; [iii] half-title; [iv] blank; [v] title-page; [vi] copyright; [vii] dedication; [viii] blank; [ix–x] contents; 11–307 text; [308] imprimerie: Brodard et Taupin.

Binding
Grey heavy paper wrappers.

Wrapper
Front panel: BESSIE | COTTER [red, enclosed in three ruled grey lines] | BY | WALLACE SMITH [black] | THE OBELISK PRESS – PARIS [red, enclosed in two ruled grey lines]
Spine: WALLACE | SMITH [black] | BESSIE | COTTER [red] | THE | OBELISK | PRESS [black]

Rear panel: [publisher's device] | Fr. 450 | MUST NOT BE IMPORTED IN TO ENGLAND OR U. S. A. [black]

Publication
February 1953

Notes
Seventh edition.
Published by Société Nouvelle des Editions du Chêne, using the Obelisk Press imprint.
The publisher's device on the rear panel is not the Obelisk logo, but that of Editions du Chêne: an H inside a diamond.

A–40 TRAGEDY IN BLUE
by [RICHARD] THOMA

Title page
TRAGEDY IN BLUE | BY | THOMA | (*Siana Series No. 2*) | [logo] | THE OBELISK PRESS | 338 RUE SAINT-HONORÉ | PARIS

Collation
Royal 8vo. [viii] 9–86 + [ii]. 26 × 16.3 cm. Top edge untrimmed, other edges rough trimmed.

Pagination
[i–ii] blank; [iii] half-title; [iv] blank; [v] title-page; [vi] copyright, limitation and publication: First published May, 1936; [vii] dedication; [viii] blank; 9–86 text; [87] blank; [88] imprimerie: LECRAM-SERVANT | 338 Rue Saint-Honoré | Paris

Binding
Blue card wrappers, with no fold-over flaps.

Wrapper
Front panel: TRAGEDY IN BLUE | THOMA | THE OBELISK PRESS
Spine: TRAGEDY | IN BLUE | THOMA | THE | OBELISK | PRESS
Rear panel: [logo]

Publication
May 1936

Notes
Number 2 of the Siana series [see A–38]. The author is Richard Thoma,
American poet, associate editor of *New Review*, and uncredited translator of *Forty-Seven Unpublished Letters from Marcel Proust to Walter Berry*,
published in Paris by the Black Sun Press in 1930.

No. 9: San Diego State University

No. 25: University of Alberta

No. 30: Author's collection

No. 38: Author's collection

No. 46: HRC (*ex libris* Stuart Gilbert)

No. 50: New Mexico State University

No. 51: Arizona State University

No. 52: Delaware State University

No. 55: Southern Illinois University

No. 57: UCLA

No. 83: Indiana State University

One hardbound *hors de commerce* copy, signed but unnumbered, has
been located [HRC].

A–41 THE ROCK POOL
by CYRIL CONNOLLY

Title page
THE ROCK POOL | BY | CYRIL CONNOLLY | *Ah dolor! ibat Hylas,
ibat Hamadryasin.* | [logo] | THE OBELISK PRESS | 338 RUE SAINT-
HONORÉ | PARIS

Collation
8vo. [xii] 13–248 + [iv]. 19.4 × 14.3 cm. Edges untrimmed.

Pagination
[i–ii] blank; [iii] half-title ; [iv] blank; [v] title-page; [vi] copyright and publication: First published May 1936; [vii xii] dedicatory letter; 13–248 text; [249] blank; [250] imprimerie: LECRAM-SERVANT | 338 Rue Saint-Honoré | Paris; [251–252] blank.

Binding
White heavy paper wrappers with fold-over flaps.

Wrapper
Front panel: Device in blue of incomplete figure-of-eight, the lower half encircling the author's name: The Rock Pool | by | Cyril Connolly [blue]

Spine: THE | ROCK | POOL | CYRIL | CONNOLLY | [logo] | Obelisk Press | 338 Rue St-Honoré | Paris [blue]

Rear panel: [logo] [blue]

Front flap: Title, author, blurb, price [50 Frs.]

Rear flap: Twelve titles, with blurbs, at Frs. 50 each: 1. Black Spring; 2. The Rock Pool; 3. Star Against Star; 4. The Gentle Men; 5. Tropic of Cancer; 6. Boy; 7. Daffodil (tenth impression); 8. The Well of Loneliness; 9. My Life and Loves; 10. Storm; 11. The Lamb; 12. Sleeveless Errand.

Wraparound band: Not seen [see notes].

Publication
May 1936

Notes
First edition.

Armstrong calls for a wraparound band for this book. This has not been seen.

Although *The Rock Pool* was published in the United States by Scribner's later in 1936, the first English edition did not appear until 1947, published by Hamish Hamilton and with a poignant postscript by Connolly, looking back across the war years to the time of the book's first publication, and his worry then that it was already a period piece:

> The fault of 'dating' of which the author complained has matured into what is almost a virtue, for nothing 'dates' us so much as an ignorance of

the horrors in store. And a tidal wave was to engulf the Rock Pool and wipe out all trace of it for seven years. Now, alas, of all those graceful originals from whom the principal characters were drawn hardly any survive. 'Toni' died a year or so after, of consumption, when barely twenty-one; 'Ruby' came also to a tragic end; and 'Sonia', being Jewish, perished in a Nazi extermination camp.

Speaking of himself, he goes on: 'Of the two young men from whose worst features the character of Naylor was so competently welded, one has lost all his arrogance and fire...'

The McFarlin Library, Tulsa, copy is inscribed by the author to Tom Driberg, and dated June 1936.

The Leeds University copy is inscribed to John and Penelope Betjeman, 'midsummer 1936'.

(b) THE ROCK POOL

Title page
As A–41, except there is no acute accent on the 'E' of 'HONORE'.

Collation
As A–41.

Pagination
As A–41, except publication on [vi] now reads: First published May 1936 | Reprinted January 1937

Binding
White heavy paper wrappers, with no fold-over flaps.

Wrapper
Front panel: As A–41.

Spine: THE | ROCK | POOL | CYRIL | CONNOLLY | 2nd | impression | [logo] | Obelisk Press | 338 Rue St-Honore | Paris

Rear panel: As A–41.

Publication
January 1937

Notes
First edition, second impression.

A–42 BLACK SPRING
by HENRY MILLER

Title page
BLACK SPRING | BY | HENRY MILLER | AUTHOR OF | *TROPIC OF CANCER* | [logo] | THE OBELISK PRESS | 338, RUE SAINT-HONORÉ. PARIS

Collation
8vo. [x] 11–267 + [iii]. 19.5 × 14.3 cm. Edges untrimmed.

Pagination
[i–ii] blank; [iii] half-title; [iv] list of previous and forthcoming works; [v] title-page; [vi] copyright and publication: First published June 1936; [vii] dedication; [viii] Miguel de Unamuno quotation; [ix] section heading and quotation; [x] blank; 11–267 text; [268] blank; [269] imprimerie: Lecram-Servant; [270] blank.

Binding
Tan heavy paper wrappers with fold-over flaps.

Wrapper
Front panel: Design in brown of a man chained to a machine. BLACK SPRING | HENRY MILLER | THE OBELISK PRESS – PARIS [brown]

Spine: BLACK | SPRING | HENRY | MILLER | [logo] | Obelisk Press | 338 Rue St-Honoré | PARIS [brown]

Rear panel: Seven quotations in praise of *Tropic of Cancer*. Price at bottom [50 Frs.] [brown]

Front flap: Title, author, blurb, price [50 Frs.]

Rear flap: Thirteen titles, with blurbs, at Frs. 50 each: 1. The Rock Pool; 2. Bessie Cotter; 3. Star Against Star; 4. The Gentle Men; 5. Tropic of Cancer; 6. Boy; 7. Daffodil (11th impression); 8. The Well of Loneliness: 9. My Life And Loves; 10. Storm; 11. The Lamb; 12. Sleeveless Errand; 13. Lady Chatterley's Lover.

Wraparound band: Not seen [see notes].

Publication
June 1936

Notes
First edition. 1000 copies.

Both Armstrong and Shifreen and Jackson call for a wraparound band for this title. This has not been seen.

Shifreen and Jackson calls for a clear wax paper jacket. This has not been seen and is probably a collector's later addition.

[iv] states that two further Miller volumes were in preparation at the time of publication. *Tropic of Capricorn* was later published by the Obelisk Press [see A–59]; *The World of Lawrence* was not published until 1980 [Henry Miller, *The World of Lawrence: A Passionate Appreciation*, Capra Press, Santa Barbara, 1980], and was the last of Miller's books to be published in his lifetime. [See also A–32.]

Miller had written much of *Black Spring* three years before its eventual publication. In a letter from William Bradley to Kahane dated 6 October 1933, Bradley quotes from a letter he had received from Miller: 'Will you please inform Kahane that I am doing my best to finish a second book for him, to be called "A Black Spring".'

Wrapper designed by Maurice Kahane (later Maurice Girodias).

Dedicated to Anaïs Nin.

(b) BLACK SPRING

Title page
BLACK SPRING | BY | HENRY MILLER | AUTHOR OF | *TROPIC OF CANCER* | [logo] | THE OBELISK PRESS | 16, PLACE VENDOME | PARIS

Collation
8vo. [x] 11–269 + [iii]. 19.5 × 14.5 cm. Bottom edge trimmed, others untrimmed.

Pagination
[i–ii] blank; [iii] half-title; [iv] list of previous works; [v] title-page; [vi] copyright and publication: First published June 1936 | Reprinted October 1938; [vii] dedication; [viii] Miguel de Unamuno quotation; [ix] section heading; [x] blank; 11–269 text; [270–272] blank.

Binding
Heavy paper wrappers with fold-over flaps.

Wrapper
Front panel: Black, with a grille of six vertical green lines behind the

title. BLACK | SPRING | HENRY MILLER [white] | SECOND EDITION | [logo] | THE OBELISK PRESS [green]

Spine: White, with green line running down the centre, broken by text. BLACK | SPRING | HENRY | MILLER | [logo] | OBELISK | PRESS | PARIS [black]

Rear panel: White. Seven blurbs for Tropic of Cancer, price [60 Frs.] [black].

Front flap: Title, author, blurb, price [60 Frs.]

Rear flap: Twelve titles, with blurbs, at Frs. 60 each: 1. To Beg I Am Ashamed; 2. Half O'Clock in Mayfair; 3. Lady, Take Heed!; 4. The Rock Pool (2nd edition); 5. Boy; 6. Star Against Star (2nd impression); 7. Tropic of Cancer; 8. Black Spring; 9. My Life and Loves; 10. Easter Sun (2nd large edition); 11. Storm (4th edition); 12. Sleeveless Errand.

Publication
October 1938

Notes
Second edition. 1000 copies.

Unusually for Obelisk titles, the printers [Ducros et COLAS, Paris.] are credited at the foot of the rear panel.

The blurbs for *Tropic of Cancer* on the rear panel are as they appear on the rear panel of the detachable wrapper on A–32(b).

(c) BLACK SPRING

Title page
As A–42, except the address now reads: 16, PLACE VENDOME, | PARIS

Collation
8vo. [x] 11–269 + [iii]. 19.7 × 14.3 cm. Bottom edge trimmed, others untrimmed.

Pagination
[i–ii] blank; [iii] half-title; [iv] list of previous and forthcoming works (*Max and the White Phagocytes* now appears in the list of previous works); [v] title-page [vi] copyright and publication: First published June 1936 | Reprinted October 1938; [vii] dedication; [viii] Miguel de

Unamuno quotation; [ix] section heading and quotation; [x] blank; 11–269 text; [270–272] blank.

Binding
Pale blue thin paper wrappers. No fold-over flaps.

Wrapper
Front panel: Three white boxes bordered in black enclosing the text: HENRY MILLER | BLACK | SPRING | THE OBELISK PRESS – PARIS [black]

Spine: Text running horizontally from bottom to top: *HENRY MILLER* – BLACK SPRING [black]

Rear panel: Blank.

Publication
1945

Notes
Second edition, third impression.

A Shanghai piracy of this title, photo-offset from A–42(b), appeared in 1939.

Photo-litho reprint of the second edition, with no correction made to the publication information on [vi]. Some copies examined have a price [175 00] stamped on the bottom right of the rear panel.

No imprimerie appears in the book, whose publication date Shifreen and Jackson identify from a letter written by Miller to Ben Abramson in August 1945.

(d) BLACK SPRING

Title page
BLACK SPRING | BY | HENRY MILLER | THE OBELISK PRESS | PARIS

Collation
[x] 11–259 + [i] 175 × 113 cm. Edges trimmed.

Pagination
[i–ii] blank; [iii] half-title; [iv] blank; [v] title-page; [vi] copyright; [vii] dedication; [viii] Miguel de Unamuno quotation; [ix] section

heading; [x] blank; 11–259 text; [259] imprimerie: Imprimé par Brodard et Taupin, Coulommiers – Paris. – 47708-5-54. | Imprimeur no 9602.; [260] blank.

Binding
White stiff paper wrappers.
Front panel: BLACK | SPRING | by | H. J. MILLER | OBELISK PRESS [black]
Spine: H. J. | MILLER | BLACK | SPRING | Obelisk | Press [black]
Rear panel: Must not be imported into England or U. S. A. | Prix: 525 Fr (b. c. + t. l.) [black]

Publication
May 1954

Notes
Fourth edition.

A Keimeisha edition, published in Tokyo, appeared early in 1954.

Miller's middle initial is wrongly given on the front wrapper and spine as J. (It's V., for Valentine.) Shifreen and Jackson states: '[Bibliographer of the Olympia Press] Patrick Kearney...noted that this edition was printed when the publishing house of Hachett [sic] had seized control of the Obelisk Press from owner Maurice Girodias. He adds that it was probably the confusion of the moment which led to the error in Miller's middle initial.' This does nothing to explain why Miller's initials – especially his middle one – were being used at all.

(e) BLACK SPRING

Title page
As A–42(d).

Collation
As A–42(d).

Pagination
[i–ii] blank; [iii] half-title; [iv] blank; [v] title-page; [vi] copyright; [vii] dedication; [viii] Miguel de Unamuno quotation; [ix] section heading; [x] blank; 11–259 text; [260] imprimerie: Imprimé en France par OFFSET NAUDEAU-REDON, à Poitiers. | D. L., 4e trimestre 1958. – Imprimeur, no 287.

Binding
White stiff paper wrappers.

Front panel: Background design of green scribble. BLACK SPRING |
by | HENRY MILLER | OBELISK PRESS [black]

Spine: HENRY | MILLER | BLACK | SPRING [black] | Obelisk | Press
[green]

Rear panel: Must not be imported into England or U. S. A. [green] |
Prix: 630 fr. (b. c. + t. l.) [black]

Publication
Late 1958

Notes
Fourth edition, second impression.

Two further impressions of the Keimeisha edition were published
in Tokyo in 1954 and 1956. This impression does not reset the text
used by A–42(d), but is marginally taller and produced by a different
printer.

(f) BLACK SPRING

Title page
As A–42(d).

Collation
As A–42(d).

Pagination
[i–ii] blank; [iii] half-title; [iv] blank; [v] title-page; [vi] copyright; [vii]
dedication; [viii] Miguel de Unamuno quotation; [ix] section heading; [x] blank; 11–259 text; [260] imprimerie: Imprimé en France par
OFFSET NAUDEAU-REDON, à Poitiers. | D. L., 4e trimestre 1960. –
Imprimeur, no 474.

Binding
As A–42(e).

Front panel: As A–42(e).

Spine: As A–42(e).

Rear panel: Not seen.

Publication
Winter 1960.

Notes
Fourth edition, third impression.

Not seen. Shifreen and Jackson [A12m].

A Taiwanese piracy appeared in 1959, and a fourth impression of the Keimeisha edition was published in 1960.

Shifreen and Jackson notes a variant wrapper for this impression [A12n], minus the green scribble on the front panel and with red and black lettering on the front panel and spine instead of green and black. The printing information on [260] is identical in both states.

A–43 LADY CHATTERLEY'S LOVER
by D. H. LAWRENCE

Title page
Impressionistic phoenix design in red, enclosing text.

LADY | CHATTERLEY'S LOVER | *by* | D. H. LAWRENCE | THE | OBELISK PRESS | *PARIS*

Collation
8vo. [vi] 1–360 + [iv]. 19.8 × 13 cm. Top edge rough trimmed, other edges untrimmed.

Pagination
[i–ii] blank; [iii] half-title; [iv] blank; [v] title-page; [vi] copyright; 1–360 text; [361] blank; [362] imprimerie: THIS EDITION IS COMPOSED IN | BASKERVILLE TYPE CUT BY THE | MONOTYPE CORPORA-TION, THE | PAPER IS MADE BY MOULIN-VIEUX, | PONTCHAR-RA-SUR-BREDDA, THE | PRINTING AND THE BINDING OF THIS | EIGHTH IMPRESSION ARE THE | WORK OF PROTAT BROTH-ERS, MACON; [363] blank.

Binding
Tan heavy paper wrappers with fold-over flaps.

Wrapper
Front panel: Impressionistic phoenix design in dark blue, enclosing text. LADY | CHATTERLEY'S LOVER | *by* | D. H. LAWRENCE | THE |

OBELISK PRESS | *PARIS* [black]

Spine: LADY | CHATTERLEY'S | LOVER | BY | D. H. LAWRENCE | [logo] | THE | OBELISK PRESS | PARIS [black]

Rear panel: Blank.

Front flap: Edition statement and price [Price: 50 francs]. Statement reads: UNEXPURGATED | AUTHORISED | COPYRIGHT | EDITION | OF | D. H. LAWRENCE'S | CLASSICAL NOVEL

Rear flap: Blank.

Publication
1936

Notes
Twenty-fifth edition, eighth impression.

First published in Florence in 1928 in an edition of 1000 copies – after which things became very complicated, very quickly. The publishing history of *Lady Chatterley's Lover* is almost impenetrably complex. The book was first published privately at Lawrence's expense, and quickly acquired a scandalous reputation which made it a target for forgers and pirates all over the world. Small editions were printed in a number of countries in a vain attempt to protect copyright, and censorious governments ensured that enough variant texts were printed world-wide to drive even the most conscientious bibliographer insane. By the time the Obelisk edition appeared, there had been six official editions: the Florence private edition (1000 copies); the cheap paper issue (Florence, 1928, 200 copies); the Popular edition (Edward Titus, 1929, Paris, 3000 copies); the first UK edition (expurgated, Secker, 1932, 3440 copies); the first American edition (expurgated, Knopf, 1932, 2000 copies); and the Odyssey edition (Paris, 1933). Odyssey was an imprint of the Albatross Press used by the parent company to distance itself from titles thought likely to alienate Albatross's more conservative readers, or to attract attention from the authorities. (Appropriately enough, Albatross also published *Ulysses* under the Odyssey imprint.) The Odyssey edition of *Lady Chatterley's Lover* had run through seven impressions when Kahane acquired the rights to publish the eighth. In addition to these legitimate editions, Roberts and Poplawski notes at least seven piracies between 1928 and 1936. Gertzman, with the confidence that befits a man whose bibliography of *just this book* runs to three hundred pages, states that when all legitimate editions, forgeries, piracies and variations in all three are taken into account, the Obelisk edition of *Lady Chatterley's Lover* checks in as the twenty-fifth edition, eighth impression. And if that's good enough for Mr Gertzman, it's good enough for me.

A–44 SONNETS AND OTHER VERSE
by HELBA BAKER RUSSELL

Title page
SONNETS AND OTHER VERSE | *By* | HELBA BAKER RUSSELL | THE OBELISK PRESS | PARIS

Collation
Large 8vo. [viii] 7–47 + [vii]. 25.7 × 16.5 cm. Top edge trimmed, others untrimmed.

Pagination
[i–iv] blank; [v] half-title; [vi] blank; [vii] title-page; [viii] copyright and limitation; 7–47 text; [48] blank; [49] imprimerie: LECRAM-SERVANT | 338 Rue Saint-Honoré | Paris; [50–54] blank. [47] is unpaginated.

Binding
Plain grey boards, white cloth at spine, in white dustwrapper.

Spine: White paper label. SONNETS | AND | OTHER | VERSE | HELBA | BAKER | RUSSELL | THE | OBELISK | PRESS [black]

Wrapper
Front panel: Black border enclosing text. SONNETS | AND | OTHER VERSE | *By* | HELBA BAKER RUSSELL | THE OBELISK PRESS | PARIS
Spine: SONNETS | AND | OTHER | VERSE | HELBA | BAKER | RUSSELL | THE | OBELISK | PRESS | PARIS

Rear panel: Blank.

Front flap: Price [25 francs]

Rear flap: Blank.

Publication
July 1936

Notes
First edition. 100 copies.

Four copies located [BL, no dustwrapper; three in author's collection, one without dustwrapper].

Limitation on [viii] reads: OF THIS, THE ORIGINAL EDITION, 100 COPIES I HAVE BEEN PRINTED IN 12-POINT ELZEVIR I ITALIC, ON DUTCH LAID PAPER, NUMBERED I 1–100 AND SIGNED BY THE AUTHOR. I NO. [stamped number] I [author's signature]

On the evidence of press reviews and advertisements, Armstrong gives the publication date of this title as no earlier than November 1936. However, a copy in the author's collection, no. 2, is additionally inscribed on [iii]: 'To adorable Beverly with fondest love and all possible good wishes for her unfailing "bonheur" – Devotedly – the author – "S. A." Paris – July '36'.

The BL copy is no. 8, and is additionally inscribed, almost certainly by the author, on [i]: 'To "[?]Sink" – with much love and every possible good wish for happiness – "Dolly" –'.

The book retailed at Frs. 25 a copy. Since there were only 100 copies to sell this was clearly not a money-making exercise, and the book was probably published at the author's expense.

A–45 A CHAUCER ABC

by GUILLAUME DE DEGUILLEVILLE

Title page
A CHAUCER A. B. C. I being a Hymn to the Holy Virgin I in an English version I by I GEOFFREY CHAUCER I from the French of I GUILLAUME DE DEGUILLEVILLE I Initial letters designed and illuminated I by I LUCIA JOYCE I Preface by I LOUIS GILLET I de l'Académie Française I [device] I THE OBELISK PRESS I 338, Rue Saint-Honoré I PARIS

Collation
4to. [x] 11–55 + [v]. 28.5 × 23 cm.

Pagination
[i–ii] blank; [iii] half-title; [iv] blank; [v] title-page; [vi] copyright and limitation; [vii–x] preface; 11–55 text; [56] blank; [57] imprimerie: THIS VOLUME IS DESIGNED BY JACK KAHANE I AND PRINTED BY LECRAM-SERVANT, MASTER- I PRINTER, 338 RUE SAINT-HONORÉ, PARIS.

Text is printed on rectos only.

Binding
Grey heavy paper wrappers. Blue chemise and slipcase, both edged in silver.

Front panel: A | CHAUCER | A. B. C. [blue]

Spine: Blank.

Rear panel: Blank.

The chemise has a silver spine, designed to face outwards when the book is cased, and a silver spine label: A | CHAUCER | A. B. C. [green]

Publication
October 1936

Notes
First edition thus. 300 copies.

The BL copy is date-stamped 10 October 1936, and advertisements and reviews only began to appear in the autumn. However, Joyce arranged for one copy of the book to be ready for presentation to Lucia on 26 July, her twenty-ninth birthday – just as Sylvia Beach had ensured that two copies of the first edition of *Ulysses* were ready in time for Joyce's birthday in 1922.

The alphabet features no J, U or W.

No. 11: HRC [*ex libris* Stuart Gilbert]

No. 33: McFarlin Library, University of Tulsa

No. 50: Bodleian Library

No. 60: British Library

No. 83: Author's collection [*ex libris* Stanislaus Joyce]

No. 128: University of Delaware

A-46 UNCHARTED SEAS

by ERIC WARD

Title page
UNCHARTED SEAS | BY | ERIC WARD | [logo] | THE OBELISK PRESS | 338 RUE SAINT-HONORÉ | PARIS

Collation
8vo. [viii] 13–272 + [iv]. 19.5 × 14.2 cm. Edges untrimmed.

Pagination
[i–ii] blank; [iii] half-title; [iv] blank; [v] title-page; [vi] copyright and publication: First published February 1937; [vii] Sand quotation; [viii] blank; 13–272 text; [273] blank; [274] imprimerie: LECRAM-SERVANT | 338 Rue Saint-Honoré | Paris; [275–276] blank.

Binding
White heavy paper wrappers with fold-over flaps.

Front panel: Monochrome drawing of two female figures. UNCHARTED SEAS | THE OBELISK PRESS [printed vertically] | BY | ERIC | WARD | .PARIS. [black]

Spine: UNCHARTED | SEAS | ERIC WARD | [logo] | Obelisk Press | 338 Rue Saint-Honoré | PARIS [black]

Rear panel. [logo] [black]

Front flap: Title, author, blurb and price [50 Frs.]

Rear flap: Twelve titles, with blurbs, at Frs. 50 each: 1. Black Spring; 2. The Rock Pool (2nd edition); 3. Bessie Cotter; 4. Star Against Star (2nd impression); 5. The Gentle Men; 6. Tropic of Cancer; 7. Boy; 8. Daffodil (twelfth impression); 9. The Well of Loneliness; 10. My Life and Loves; 11. The Lamb; 12. Lady Chatterley's Lover.

Publication
February 1937

Notes
First edition.

The Bodleian and BL copies of this title are rebound. The Armstrong copy has stamped figures on [276]: 8-37 862 50 00. The first denotes August 1937, the last is a price. A copy in the author's collection also has stamped figures on [276] – 11-38 60.00 – suggesting a price rise by November of the following year.

A–47 LADY, TAKE HEED!
by CECIL BARR (JACK KAHANE)

Title page
LADY, TAKE HEED! | BY | CECIL BARR | [logo] | THE OBELISK PRESS | PARIS

Collation
8vo. [x] 13–320 + [ii]. 19.5 × 14.5 cm. Edges untrimmed.

Pagination
[i–ii] blank; [iii] half-title; [iv] list of previous Barr works: 1. Daffodil (12th impression); 2. Amour French For Love (7th impression); 3. Bright Pink Youth (4th large impression); [v] title-page ; [vi] copyright and publication: First published June 1937; [vii] dedication; [viii] blank; [ix] second half-title; [x] blank; 13–320 text; [321] imprimerie: LECRAM-SERVANT | 338, Rue Saint-Honoré | Paris; [322] blank.

Binding
Light green heavy paper wrappers with fold-over flaps.

Wrapper
Front panel: Portrait of a chic woman perched on a stool, a nightclub scene faintly picked out behind her [light and dark green]. Lady, take heed! | by CECIL BARR | author of DAFFODIL | (12th printing) [dark green on light green] | THE OBELISK | PRESS [white on dark green]

Spine: LADY, | TAKE | HEED! | CECIL | BARR | [logo] | Obelisk Press| PARIS [dark green on light green]

Rear panel: [logo] [dark green on light green]

Front flap: Title, author, blurb, price [50 Frs.]

Rear flap: Twelve titles, with blurbs, at Frs. 50 each: 1. Uncharted Seas; 2. Black Spring; 3. The Rock Pool (2nd edition); 4. Bessie Cotter; 5. Star Against Star (2nd impression); 6. The Gentle Men; 7. Tropic of Cancer; 8. Boy; 9. Daffodil (twelfth impression); 10. The Well of Loneliness; 11. My Life and Loves; 12. Lady Chatterley's Lover.

Publication
June 1937

Notes
First edition.
Rare: only one copy in original binding located [Cornell].

(b) LADY, TAKE HEED!

Title page
LADY, TAKE HEED! | BY | CECIL BARR | [logo] | THE OBELISK PRESS | 16, PLACE VENDÔME | PARIS | IMPRIMÉ EN HONGRIE

Collation
[x] 11–288. 19.5 × 14.5 cm. Edges untrimmed.

Pagination
[i–ii] blank; [iii] half-title ; [iv] list of previous works: Daffodil (14th impression), Amour French For Love (7th impression), Bright Pink Youth (4th large impression); [v] title-page; [vi] copyright and publication: First published June 1937 | Reprinted March 1938 | SECOND PRINTING; [vii] dedication; [viii] blank; [ix] second half-title; [x] blank; 11–288 text.

Binding
Heavy paper wrappers with fold-over flaps.

Wrapper
Front panel: Illustration as A–47. Lady, take heed! | by CECIL BARR | author of DAFFODIL | (14th printing) [dark green on light green] | THE OBELISK | PRESS [white on dark green]

Spine: LADY, | TAKE | HEED! | CECIL | BARR | SECOND | PRINTING | [logo] | OBELISK | PRESS | PARIS [dark green on light green]

Rear panel. [logo] [dark green on light green]

Front flap: Title, author, blurb, price [60 Frs.]

Rear flap: Thirteen titles, with blurbs, at Frs. 60 each: 1. Half O'Clock in Mayfair; 2. Dark Refuge; 3. Uncharted Seas; 4. Black Spring; 5. The Rock Pool (2nd edition); 6. Bessie Cotter; 7. Star Against Star (2nd impression); 8. Tropic of Cancer; 9. Boy; 10. Daffodil (14th impression); 11. My Life And Loves; 12. Sleeveless Errand; 13. Easter Sun (2nd large edition).

Publication
March 1938

Notes
Second edition.
The publication page declares this to be a second printing, but the text has been entirely reset.

Only two copies located. In the Baxter copy (rebound) the price has been inked out on both front and rear flaps. The copy in the author's collection has had the flaps removed entirely, presumably to achieve the same end.

(c) LADY, TAKE HEED!

Title page
CECIL BARR | LADY, | TAKE HEED! | THE OBELISK PRESS | 16, PLACE VENDOME, PARIS

Collation
8vo. [iv] 5–200. 19.3 × 14 cm. Top edge untrimmed, others rough trimmed.

Pagination
[i] half-title; [ii] blank; [iii] title-page ; [iv] imprimerie: ACHEVE D'IMPRIMER | SUR LES PRESSES DE | L'ENTREPRISE DE | PRESSE ET D'IMPRIMERIE | 37, RUE DE LOUVRE | DEP. LEG.: 1er TR. 1946. | No DE L'EDITEUR 254; 5–200 text.

Binding
Green paper wrappers.

Wrapper
Front panel: Title printed between three white and two black lines. LADY, | TAKE HEED! [white] | *BY CECIL BARR* | THE OBELISK PRESS – PARIS [black]

Spine: LADY, | TAKE | HEED! [white] | *BY* | *CECIL* | *BARR* | THE | OBELISK | PRESS | PARIS [black]

Rear panel: *175 FRS [black]

Publication
Early 1946.

Notes
Third edition.

(d) LADY, TAKE HEED!

Title page
CECIL BARR|LADY,|TAKE HEED!|THE OBELISK PRESS|16, PLACE VENDOME, PARIS

Collation
[x] 7–245 + [vii]. 17.5 × 11.5 cm. Edges trimmed.

Pagination
[i–iv] blank; [v] half-title; [vi] blank ; [vii] title-page ; [viii] copyright; [ix–x] blank; 7–245 text; [246] blank; [247] imprimerie: ACHEVE D'IMPRIMER|LE 15 FEVRIER 1951 SUR|LES PRESSES DE LA SOPAC, | 26, RUE CLAVEL, PARIS-19e | No d'édition: 254 | Dépôt légal: 1er trimestre 1951; [248–252] blank.

Binding
Green stiff paper wrappers.

Front panel: Text printed between red lines. LADY, | TAKE HEED! [black]|*BY* | *CECIL BARR* | THE OBELISK PRESS – PARIS [red]
Spine: LADY, | TAKE | HEED! | *BY* | *CECIL* | *BARR* | THE | OBELISK | PRESS | PARIS [black]

Rear panel: 400 french francs [black]

Publication
15 February 1951

Notes
Fourth edition.

A piracy of this edition, probably from Japan, reproduces the text of this edition, including the copyright and imprimerie. It is bound in white stiff paper wrappers and measures 16.5 × 12.7 cm. The text on the front panel is printed in black and red, and is contained within green and yellow concentric boxes.

A–48 SCENARIO

by HENRY MILLER

Title page
SCENARIO | (A FILM WITH SOUND) | BY | HENRY MILLER | WITH
A FRONTISPIECE BY | ABRAHAM RATTNER | [logo] | PARIS | THE
OBELISK PRESS | 1937

Collation
4to. [viii] 9–40 + [iv]. 26 × 16.7 cm. Top edge untrimmed, others rough
trimmed.

Pagination
[i–ii] blank; [iii] half-title; [iv] list of previous works, and those
in preparation; [v] title-page; [vi] copyright and limitation; [vii]
acknowledgement of Anaïs Nin; [viii] blank; 9–40 text; [41] blank;
[42] imprimerie: LECRAM-SERVANT | 338 Rue Saint-Honoré | Paris;
[43–44] blank. Folded two-page illustration by Abe Rattner laid in
before [i].

Binding
Tan card covers with fold-over flaps. Unbound signatures laid in.

Wrapper
Front panel: SCENARIO | (A FILM WITH SOUND) | HENRY MILLER
| [logo] | THE OBELISK PRESS [red]

Spine: Blank.

Rear panel: Blank.

Front flap: Price [40 Frs.] [red]

Rear flap: Blank.

Shifreen and Jackson calls for a clear wax paper jacket. This has not
been seen and is probably a collector's later addition.

Publication
July 1937

Notes
First edition. 200 copies.

Limitation on [vi] reads: THIS THE ORIGINAL EDITION, PUB-
LISHED IN 1937, | IS LIMITED TO TWO HUNDRED COPIES
SIGNED | BY THE AUTHOR AND NUMBERED 1 TO 200. | No

[printed number]. Miller's signature appears below the number.
[vii] reads: *This scenario is directly inspired by a | phantasy called "The House of Incest", | written by Anaïs Nin.*

A–49 THROUGH THE ARK
by OLGA MARTIN

Title page
THROUGH THE ARK | BY | OLGA MARTIN | [logo] | THE OBELISK PRESS | 16, PLACE VENDOME | PARIS

Collation
Large 8vo. [viii] 9–198 + [ii]. 22 × 15.5 cm. Foredge untrimmed.

Pagination
[i–ii] blank; [iii] half-title; [iv] blank; [v] title-page; [vi] copyright; [vii] dedication; [viii] contents; 9–198 text; [199] imprimerie: JEL, 16, Rue Ernest Cresson, Paris-Bruxelles; [200] blank.

Binding
Green heavy paper wrappers, with fold-over flaps and wraparound band.

Wrapper
Front panel: THROUGH THE ARK | BY | OLGA MARTIN | [line drawing of giraffe grazing between fragments of facing walls] | THE OBELISK PRESS

Spine: THROUGH | THE ARK | by | Olga Martin | [logo] | THE | OBELISK PRESS | 16 PLACE VENDOME | PARIS

Rear wrapper: [logo]

Front flap: Title, author, blurb, price [30 FRANCS]

Rear flap: Six titles, with blurbs, at Frs. 50 each: 1. The Rock Pool; 2. Black Spring; 3. Tropic of Cancer; 4. Lady, Take Heed!; 5. The Black Book; 6. Star Against Star.

White wraparound band: **An extremely witty and amusing book** | [logo to left] "...gusto, a remarkable gift for epithet, | a painter's usual sense and a sudden | alarming laughter..." | V. S. PRITCHETT [black]

Publication
23 May 1938

Notes
First edition.

Precise publication date appears on a publisher's slip in the Baxter copy, probably in Kahane's hand. The same slip gives the UK price of the book: six shillings.

A–50 HALF O'CLOCK IN MAYFAIR

by PRINCESS PAUL TROUBETZKOY

Title page
HALF O'CLOCK|IN MAYFAIR|BY|PRINCESS PAUL TROUBETZKOY | AUTHOR OF | *STORM TARN, etc.* | [logo] | THE OBELISK PRESS | 16, PLACE VENDOME | PARIS

Collation
8vo. [viii] 9–266 + [ii]. 19.2 × 14.4 cm. Bottom edge trimmed, others untrimmed.

Pagination
[i–ii] blank; [iii] half-title; [iv] blank; [v] title-page; [vi] copyright; [vii] section heading; [viii] blank; 9–266 text; [267] blank; [268] imprimerie: Impr. JEL, 16, rue Ernest-Cresson | Paris-Bruxelles

Binding
White heavy paper wrappers with fold-over flaps.
Front panel: Brown horizontal stripes top and bottom, with brown double-rules running vertically between them and horizontally across the middle of the panel. HALF O'CLOCK | IN MAYFAIR | [logo] | Princess | Paul | Troubetzkoy [brown on white] | THE OBELISK PRESS . PARIS . [white on brown]

Spine: Half|O'Clock|In Mayfair|PRINCESS|PAUL|TROUBETZKOY | [logo] | THE | OBELISK PRESS | PARIS [brown]

Rear panel: [logo] [brown]

Front flap: Title, author, blurb and price [60 Frs.]

Rear flap: Thirteen titles, with blurbs, at Frs. 50 each: 1. Lady, Take Heed!; 2. Uncharted Seas; 3. Black Spring; 4. The Rock Pool (2nd edition); 5. Bessie Cotter; 6. Boy; 7. Star Against Star (2nd impression); 8. Tropic of Cancer: 9. My Life and Loves; 10. Easter Sun (2nd large edition); 11. Storm (4th edition); 12. Sleeveless Errand; 13. Daffodil (14th impression).

Publication
April 1938

Notes
First edition.

Two copies located [Armstrong collection; author's collection (rebound)].
No publication date appears in the book, but Armstrong notes that it was
reviewed in the *New York Herald Tribune* (Paris ed.) on 2 May 1938.

A–51 TO BEG I AM ASHAMED

by SHEILA COUSINS [RONALD MATTHEWS]

Title page
Sheila Cousins | TO BEG | I AM ASHAMED | [logo] | THE OBELISK
PRESS | 16, PLACE VENDOME | PARIS

Collation
8vo. [vi] 1–270 + [iv]. 18.9 × 14.2 cm. Edges untrimmed.

Pagination
[i–ii] blank; [iii] half-title; [iv] blank; [v] title-page; [vi] copyright and
publishers' note; 1–270 text; [271–274] blank.

Binding
Yellow heavy paper wrappers with fold-over flaps.
Front panel: To Beg | I am ashamed [red] | by | Sheila Cousins [black]
| The autobiography | of a London prostitute [red] | Only authorised
edition | Complete and unexpurgated [black] | [logo] [red] | THE
OBELISK PRESS [black]

Spine: TO BEG | I AM | ASHAMED | SHEILA | COUSINS [black] | [logo]
[red] | THE | OBELISK PRESS | PARIS [black]

Rear panel: [logo] [red]

Front flap: Title, blurb, price [60 Frs.]

Rear flap: Thirteen titles, with blurbs, at Frs. 60 each: 1. Half O'Clock
in Mayfair; 2. Dark Refuge; 3. Uncharted Seas; 4. Black Spring; 5. The
Rock Pool (2nd edition); 6. Bessie Cotter; 7. Star Against Star (2nd
impression); 8. Tropic of Cancer; 9. Boy; 10. Daffodil (14th impression); 11. My Life and Loves; 12. Sleeveless Errand; 13. Easter Sun (2nd
large edition).

Publication
June 1938

Notes
Second edition.

The publishers' note on [vi] states (in part): 'An attack against the book, in the London press, of unprecedented ferocity and vindictiveness caused its withdrawal before publication [by Routledge]. This, the Obelisk edition, published in May 1938, is therefore the first effective edition.' In fact, the Obelisk edition was not published until June 1938, as shown by the publication page of A–51(b) (see below). Despite being withdrawn before publication, a few copies of the projected Routledge edition have survived. These must therefore be designated the first edition, making the Obelisk edition the second.

No imprimerie. The words PRINTED IN FRANCE appear on [vi].

Book dealers keen to maximise their profits often claim this book was written by Graham Greene. It wasn't. Although Greene helped his friend by chipping in with a telling descriptive phrase here and there – phrases he would later quote approvingly when he contrived to review the book – *To Beg I Am Ashamed* is almost entirely the work of Ronald Matthews.

(b) TO BEG I AM ASHAMED

Title page
As A–51.

Collation
8vo. [vi] 1–270 + [iv]. Edges untrimmed.

Pagination
[i–ii] blank; [iii] half-title; [iv] publication: FIRST PUBLISHED JUNE 1938 I REPRINTED JUNE " I " JULY " I " JULY " I " JULY " I " AUGUST " I " AUGUST " I " AUGUST " ; [v] title-page ; [vi] copyright and publishers' note; 1–270 text; [271–273] blank; [274] imprimerie: IMPRIMERIE FRÈRE I TOURCOING

Binding
Yellow heavy paper wrappers with fold-over flaps.

Front panel: As A–51.

Spine: TO BEG | I AM | ASHAMED | SHEILA | COUSINS [black] | 8th | IMPRESSION [red] | [logo] [red] | THE | OBELISK PRESS | PARIS [black]

Rear panel: As A–51.

Front flap: As A–51.

Rear flap: As A–51.

Publication
August 1938

Notes
Second edition, second impression ['eighth impression'].

Although the publication page proclaims this to be the eighth impression of this title, no copies of impressions two to seven have been located. Kahane often inflated the number of impressions through which a title had passed, presumably in the hope that such a *mention fictive* would boost sales.

The publisher's note on [vi] is identical to that in A–51 except the heading now reads: PUBLISHERS' NOTE | (To first impression).
An American edition of this title was published by Vanguard, without controversy, in May 1938.

(c) TO BEG I AM ASHAMED

Title page
SHEILA COUSINS | TO BEG | I AM ASHAMED | THE OBELISK PRESS | 16, PLACE VENDÔME, PARIS

Collation
8vo. [vi] 7–171 + [v]. 19 × 14.2 cm. Bottom edge trimmed, others untrimmed.

Pagination
[i–ii] blank; [iii] half-title; [iv] publication: as A–51(b); [v] title-page; [vi] copyright and publishers' note as A–51(b); 7–171 text; [172] blank; [173] imprimerie: ACHEVÉ D'IMPRIMER | SUR LES PRESSES DE | L'IMPRIMERIE DE SCEAUX | – LE 30 MARS 1946 – | 21.574 – C. O. L. 31.3029 | DÉP. LÉG.: Ier TR. 1946. | No DE L'ÉDITEUR 250; [174–176] blank.

Binding
Yellow stiff paper wrappers.

Front panel: TO BEG | I AM ASHAMED | The autobiography | of a London prostitute [red, black lines separating text] | *BY* | *SHEILA COUSINS* [black] | THE OBELISK PRESS – PARIS [black, black lines enclosing text at top and bottom]

Spine: TO BEG | I AM | ASHAMED [red] | *BY* | *SHEILA* | *COUSINS* | THE | OBELISK | PRESS | [black line] | PARIS [black]

Rear panel: * [black] Frs. 175 [red]

Publication
30 March 1946

Notes
Fifth edition.

Preceded by the American edition [see note to A–51(b), above] and an Indian edition (pub. Kitabistan, Allahabad) of 1940.

(d) TO BEG I AM ASHAMED

Title page
SHEILA COUSINS | TO BEG | I AM ASHAMED | THE OBELISK PRESS | 16, PLACE VENDOME, PARIS

Collation
8vo. [vi] 7–267 + [v]. 17.8 × 11.5 cm. Edges trimmed.

Pagination
[i–ii] blank; [iii] half-title; [iv] publication: FIRST PUBLISHED JUNE 1938 | REPRINTED JUNE " | " JULY " | " JULY " | " JULY " | " AUGUST " | " AUGUST " | " AUGUST " ; [v] title-page; [vi] copyright and publishers' note; 7–267 text; [268] blank; [269] imprimerie: ACHEVE D'IMPRIMER | LE 15 FEVRIER 1951 SUR | LES PRESSES DE LA SOPAC, | 26, RUE CLAVEL, PARIS-19° | N° d'édition: 255 | Dépôt légal: 1er trimestre 1951; [270–272] blank.

Binding
Yellow card wrappers.

Front panel: TO BEG | I AM ASHAMED | The autobiography | of a London prostitute [black, red lines separating text] | *BY* | *SHEILA*

COUSINS [red] | THE OBELISK PRESS – PARIS [red lines enclosing text at top and bottom]

Spine: TO BEG | I AM | ASHAMED | *BY* | *SHEILA* | *COUSINS* | THE | OBELISK | PRESS | [black line] | PARIS [black]

Rear panel: 400 french francs [black]

Publication
15 February 1951

Notes
Sixth edition.

The publisher's note on [vi] is identical to that of A–51(b) except that in this edition the word 'obelisk' is not capitalised.

To Beg I Am Ashamed was re-published in England in 1953 by the Richards Press, without incident.

A–52 LIVES OF FAIR AND GALLANT LADIES
by SEIGNEUR DE BRANTÔME

Title page
LIVES | OF FAIR | AND GALLANT | LADIES | *by the* | SEIGNEUR DE BRANTÔME | THE ONLY COMPLETE TRANSLATION INTO | ENGLISH, WITH INTRODUCTION AND NOTES. | [logo] | THE OBELISK PRESS | 16, PLACE VENDOME | PARIS

Collation
Large 8vo. [xxviii] 1–415 + [xvi]. 22.8 × 15.5 cm. Top edge trimmed, others untrimmed.

Pagination
[i–ii] blank; [iii] half-title; [iv] limitation: THIS EDITION IS LIMITED | TO ONE THOUSAND COPIES | THIS IS NUMBER ; [v] title-page; [vi] blank; [vii–xiv] introduction (paginated v–xii); [xv–xxviii] contents (paginated xiii–xxvi); 1–415 text; [416–427] notes; [427] imprimerie: PRINTED AT TONBRIDGE BY TONBRIDGE PRINTERS LTD.; [428 432] blank.

Binding
Black cloth boards with silver paper labels at head and foot of spine, in a green-grey printed dustwrapper with fold-over flaps.

Spine of book: BRANTÔME | LIVES | OF FAIR | AND GALLANT | LADIES | THE | OBELISK | PRESS [black on silver]

Wrapper
Front panel: Classical pillared portico, enclosing text. THE | OBELISK CLASSICS [black] | BRANTÔME | LIVES | OF FAIR | AND GALLANT | LADIES [blue] | [logo] | THE OBELISK PRESS [black]

Spine: BRANTÔME | LIVES | OF FAIR | AND GALLANT | LADIES | THE | OBELISK | PRESS [blue]

Rear panel: [logo] [blue]

Front flap: Title, blurb and price [150 francs].

Rear flap: Blank.

Publication
1938

Notes
First Fortune Press edition, with Obelisk Press cancel title page.

Originally published in Paris in 1665 with the title *Vie des Dames Galantes*, the book was published in Alfred R. Allinson's English translation by Charles Carrington in Paris in 1901, and reprinted by the Fortune Press in London in 1934 [d'Arch Smith: 82]. Many books on the Fortune Press list were seized by police in August of that year, and *Lives of Fair and Gallant Ladies* was declared obscene by Westminster Police Court in March 1935. On 22 June 1938, Kahane acknowledged receipt from R. A. Caton of the Fortune Press of 45 copies of this title. The Obelisk edition is made up from sheets of the Fortune Press edition, with a new title-page, dustwrapper and spine labels (which probably cover the original Fortune Press typography).

Rare: one copy located [Armstrong collection]. The limitation on [iv] refers to the Fortune Press edition (see above), and gives no indication of the number of copies issued by the Obelisk Press.

See also A–53.

A-53 THE SATYRICON
by PETRONIUS

Title page
THE | SATYRICON | OF | PETRONIUS | THE ONLY COMPLETE
TRANSLATION INTO ENGLISH, WITH INTRODUCTION AND
NOTES. | *With Drawings By* | JEAN DE BOSSCHÈRE | [LOGO] | THE
OBELISK PRESS | 16, PLACE VENDOME | PARIS

Collation
8vo. [unpaginated ffep.] [lxii] 1–222 + [vi]. 19.5 × 13.5 cm. Top edge
trimmed, others untrimmed.

Pagination
[unpaginated ffep.]; [i–ii] blank; [iii] half-title ; [iv] limitation; [v]
title-page; [vi] blank; [vii–ix] contents; [x] blank; [xi–xvii] index; [xviii]
blank; [xix–xli] introduction; [xlii] blank; [xliii–lvii] synopsis; [lviii]
blank; [lix–lx] bibliography; [lxi] second half-title; [lxii] blank; 1–222
text; [223–228] blank.

Binding
Black cloth boards with silver paper labels at head and foot of spine.
Spine: PETRONIUS | THE | SATYRICON | THE | OBELISK | PRESS
[black on silver]

Wrapper
Not seen.

Publication
1938

Notes
First Fortune Press edition, with Obelisk Press cancel title page.

This translation, advertised as being by Oscar Wilde but probably the
work of Alfred R. Allinson, was first issued in Paris in 1902 by Charles
Carrington, and was reissued by the Fortune Press in 1933 [d'Arch
Smith: 428]. It was one of many Fortune Press titles seized by police
in 1934 [see also A–52] On 22 June 1938, Kahane acknowledged receipt
from R. A. Caton of the Fortune Press of 100 copies of this title. Like
A–52, the Obelisk edition is made up from sheets of the Fortune Press
edition, with a new title-page and spine labels (which probably cover
the original Fortune Press typography).

The dustwrapper for this title has not been seen but is presumed to exist, and to be in the same style as the wrapper for A–52.

Rare: one copy located [author's collection, no dustwrapper].

A–54 DARK REFUGE
by CHARLES BEADLE

Title page
DARK REFUGE | BY | CHARLES BEADLE | [logo] | THE OBELISK PRESS | 16, PLACE VENDOME | PARIS

Collation
8vo. [viii] 9–258 + [ii]. 19.5 × 14.5 cm. Bottom edge trimmed, others untrimmed.

Pagination
[i–ii] blank; [iii] half-title; [iv] publication: FIRST PUBLISHED JUNE 1938; [v] title-page; [vi] copyright; [vii] second half-title; [viii] blank; 9–258 text; [259] imprimerie: Imprimerie JEL | 24, Rue de Montessuy, Paris-Bruxelles; [260] blank.

Binding
Blue-grey heavy paper wrappers with fold-over flaps.

Wrapper
Front panel: Pink zigzag design down either side. DARK | REFUGE [maroon, white flashing] | BY | CHARLES BEADLE [maroon] | [logo] [pink] | THE OBELISK PRESS [maroon]

Spine: DARK | REFUGE | CHARLES | BEADLE [maroon] | [logo] [pink] | OBELISK | PRESS | PARIS [maroon]

Rear panel: White. [logo] | DUCROS ET COLAS, PARIS. [maroon]

Front flap: Title, author, blurb and price [60 francs].

Rear flap: Twelve titles, with blurbs, at Frs. 60 each: 1. To Beg I Am Ashamed; 2. Half O'Clock in Mayfair; 3. Lady, Take Heed! (14th impression); 4. The Rock Pool (2nd edition); 5. Boy; 6. Star Against Star (2nd impression); 7. Tropic of Cancer: 8. Black Spring; 9. My Live [sic] and Loves; 10. Easter Sun (2nd large edition); 11. Storm (4th edition); 12. Sleeveless Errand.

Publication
June 1938

Notes
First edition.

The word 'as' is missing from the first line of the blurb for *Lady, Take Heed!* on the rear flap [see also A–55, A–58].

A second impression of this title, referred to on the rear flap of A–63, has not been located and is presumed not to exist.

A–55 STARBORN
by ARION

Title page
STARBORN | BY | ARION | [logo] | THE OBELISK PRESS | 16, PLACE VENDOME | PARIS

Collation
8vo. [viii] 9–258 + [ii]. 19 × 14.2 cm. Bottom edge trimmed, others untrimmed.

Pagination
[i–ii] blank; [iii] half-title; [iv] publication: FIRST PUBLISHED JUNE 1938; [v] title-page; [vi] copyright; [vii] 'Part 1' heading, Milton quotation; [viii] blank; 9–258 text; [259] blank; [260] imprimerie: Impr. JEL, 24, rue de Montessuy | Paris-Bruxelles

Binding
Heavy paper wrappers with fold-over flaps.

Wrapper
Front panel: Pale green, text enclosed in white wavy border. STAR | BORN | BY | ARION | [logo] | THE OBELISK PRESS [dark green]

Spine: White. STAR | BORN | ARION | [logo] | OBELISK | PRESS | PARIS [pale green]

Rear panel: White. [logo] | DUCROS ET COLAS, PARIS. [pale green]

Front flap: Title, author, blurb, price [60 francs].

Rear flap: Twelve titles, with blurbs, at Frs. 60 each: 1. Dark Refuge; 2. To Beg I Am Ashamed; 3. Half O'Clock in Mayfair; 4. Lady, Take

Heed! (14th impression); 5. The Rock Pool (2nd edition); 6. Boy; 7. Star Against Star (2nd impression); 8. Tropic of Cancer; 9. My Live [sic] and Loves; 10. Easter Sun (2nd large edition); 11. Storm (4th edition); 12. Sleeveless Errand.

Publication
1938

Notes
First edition.

Armstrong notes that the book was not advertised until 1 August 1938. The publication date of June 1938 on [iv] is probably inaccurate.
The word 'as' is missing from the first line of the blurb for *Lady, Take Heed!* on the rear flap [see also A–54, A–58].

(b) STARBORN

Title page
As A–55.

Collation
8vo. [viii] 9–258 + [ii]. Only copy seen has been cropped [see notes].

Pagination
[i–ii] blank; [iii] half-title; [iv] publication: FIRST PUBLISHED JUNE 1938 | REPRINTED JANUARY 1939; [v] title-page; [vi] copyright; [vii] 'Part 1' heading, Milton quotation; [viii] blank; 9–258 text; [259] blank; [260] imprimerie: Imprimerie Groenighe | Courtrai

Binding
Heavy paper wrappers with no fold-over flaps [see notes].

Wrapper
Front panel: As A–55.

Spine: Not seen [see notes].

Rear panel: As A–55.

Front flap: Not seen [see notes].

Rear flap: Not seen [see notes].

Publication
1939

Notes
First edition, second impression.

One copy located [Ohio State University, cropped and rebound with the original wrappers bound in, but without front or rear flaps].

A–56 THE BLACK BOOK
by LAWRENCE DURRELL

Title page
THE BLACK BOOK | AN AGON | BY | LAWRENCE DURRELL | [logo] | THE OBELISK PRESS | 16, PLACE VENDÔME | PARIS

Collation
Large 8vo. [x] 11–260 + [iv]. 22 × 15.5 cm. Bottom edge trimmed, other edges rough-trimmed.

Pagination
[1–11] blank; [iii] half-title; [iv] publication: FIRST PUBLISHED JUNE 1938; [v] title-page; [vi] copyright; [vii] dedication; [viii] Tibetan quotation; [ix] section heading; [x] blank; 11–260 text; [261] place and date of completion; [262–264] blank.

Binding
Pale green heavy paper wrappers with fold-over flaps.

Wrapper
Front panel: Pale pink rectangle almost to margins. Large obelisk motif in white lines, within a white border. THE | BLACK | BOOK | BY | LAWRENCE | DURRELL | [logo] | THE OBELISK PRESS

Spine: THE | BLACK | BOOK | LAWRENCE | DURRELL [black] | [logo] [pink] | OBELISK | PRESS | PARIS [black]

Rear panel: [logo] [pink] | DUCROS ET COLAS, PARIS. [black]

Front flap: Title, author, blurb, price [75 francs].

Rear flap: Nine titles, with blurbs, the first three priced at Frs. 75 each volume, the following six at Frs. 60: 1. The Black Book; 2. Max and the White Phagocytes; 3. Chaotica; 4. The Rock Pool (2nd edition); 5. Boy; 6. Tropic of Cancer; 7. Black Spring; 8. Storm (4th edition); 9. Easter Sun (2nd large edition).

Publication
September 1938

Notes
First edition.

No. 1 in the Villa Seurat series, with what became the standard front panel design for the series.

Villa Seurat was established by Henry Miller and Lawrence and Nancy Durrell, in association with Kahane. The three agreed to find new work and cover all printing costs, while Kahane agreed to issue the books, with the Obelisk imprint, through his distribution system. Miller acted as editor of the series, and is credited as such on the rear flaps of all Villa Seurat titles. The printing costs for this title were met by Durrell's wife, Nancy.

The rear flap lists six Obelisk titles and three from Villa Seurat's prospective list, including *Chaotica* by Anais Nin. Henry Miller disliked the title, and in 1938 Nin wrote to Michael Fraenkel telling him that she had decided to change it. The book appeared the following year with the title *The Winter of Artifice* [see A–62].

In all copies examined pp. 115–118 have been printed in the wrong position on the signature, making it impossible to bind them in the correct order. Although paginated sequentially, the correct sequence of text runs as follows: 114, 117, 115, 116, 118.

A–57 MAX AND THE WHITE PHAGOCYTES
by HENRY MILLER

Title page
Max and the | White Phagocytes | by | Henry Miller | [logo] | THE OBELISK PRESS | 16, Place Vendôme | PARIS

Collation
Large 8vo. [xi] 12–324 + [iv]. 22 × 15.5 cm. Bottom edge trimmed, others untrimmed.

Pagination
[i–ii] blank; [iii] half-title; [iv] list of previous and forthcoming works, and publication: FIRST PUBLISHED SEPTEMBER 1938; [v] title-page; [vi] copyright; [vii] acknowledgements; [viii] dedication; [ix] contents; [x] blank; [xi] section heading; 12–324 text; [325–328] blank.

Binding
Heavy paper wrappers with fold-over flaps and gold wraparound band.

Wrapper
Front panel: Green. Villa Seurat series design [see A–56]. MAX I AND THE WHITE I PHAGOCYTES I BY I HENRY MILLER I [logo] I THE OBELISK PRESS

Spine: White. MAX I AND THE I WHITE I PHAGOCYTES I HENRY I MILLER [black] I [logo] [green] I OBELISK I PRESS I PARIS [black]

Rear panel: White. [logo] [green] I DUCROS ET COLAS, PARIS. [black]

Front flap: Title, author, blurb and price [75 francs].

Rear flap: As A–56.

Wraparound band: Cannot be Bought I in England and U. S. A. I The second volume of the Villa Seurat series, I Henry Miller has here written a book that I shows many facets of his unique genius. I "...Surely, the largest force lately risen on the I horizon of American letters." Paul Rosenfeld I in the Saturday Review of Literature.

Publication
October 1938 [see notes]

Notes
First edition. 1000 copies.

No. 2 in the Villa Seurat series. Ford states that Miller had this title printed in Bruges by St. Catherine's Press at a cost of Frs. 11,000, in an attempt to avoid the printing errors that plagued *The Black Book*. However, both books credit their printing to Ducros et Colas on their rear panels.

Shifreen and Jackson notes: 'Although September 1938 is listed on [iv] as the date of publication, a reviewer's copy of this title inspected had a tipped in notice from the publisher stating the date of publication was actually October 1938.'

(b) MAX AND THE WHITE PHAGOCYTES

Title page
As A–57.

Collation
Large 8vo. [xi] 12–324 + [iv]. 24.5 × 15.8 cm. Edges trimmed.

Pagination
[i–ii] blank; [iii] acknowledgments; [iv] dedication; [v] contents; [vi] blank; [vii] half-title; [viii] list of previous and forthcoming works, and publication: FIRST PUBLISHED SEPTEMBER 1938; [viii] title-page; [ix] copyright; [xi] section heading; 12–324 text; [325–328] blank.

Binding
Green thin paper wrappers.

Front panel: Three white boxes bordered in black, enclosing the text: HENRY MILLER I MAX I AND THE WHITE I PHAGOCYTES I THE OBELISK PRESS – PARIS

Spine: Text running vertically from bottom to top: *HENRY MILLER MAX AND THE WHITE PHAGOCYTES*

Rear panel: Blank.

Publication
1945

Notes
First edition, second impression. 1000 copies.

The text has not been reset, and the publication information on [viii] has not been updated. The acknowledgements, dedication and contents pages are now bound in before the title-page.

Shifreen and Jackson notes that all copies they examined carried a hand-stamped price of Frs. 200 on the rear panel of the wrapper, but a copy in the author's collection has not been so stamped, and other such copies are presumed to exist.

A–58 LOVE COUNTS TEN
by THEODOR ZAY

Title page
LOVE | COUNTS TEN | BY | THEODOR ZAY | [logo] | THE OBELISK
PRESS | 16, Place Vendôme. | PARIS

Collation
8vo. [vi] 7–238 + [ii]. 19.6 × 14.5 cm. Edges rough trimmed.

Pagination
[i–ii] blank; [iii] half-title; [iv] copyright and publication: FIRST
PUBLISHED DECEMBER 1938; [v] title-page; [vi] disclaimer; [7–11]
preface; [12] blank; 13–238 text; [239–240] blank.

Binding
Heavy paper wrappers with fold-over flaps.

Wrapper
Front panel: Blue.
love | counts ten | Theodor Zay [red] | A SENSATIONAL STORY | OF
THE NIGHT HAUNTS OF A GREAT CITY [white] | [logo] [black] |
THE OBELISK PRESS [white]

Spine: White, with red vertical stripe interrupted by text. LOVE |
COUNTS | TEN | THEODOR | ZAY | [logo] | OBELISK | PRESS | PARIS
[black]

Rear panel: White. DUCROS ET COLAS, PARIS. [black]

Front flap: Title, author, blurb and price [60 francs].

Rear flap: Twelve titles, with blurbs, at Frs. 60 each: 1. To Beg I Am
Ashamed; 2. Half O'Clock in Mayfair; 3. Lady, Take Heed! (14th impres-
sion); 4. The Rock Pool (2nd edition); 5. Boy; 6. Star Against Star (2nd
impression); 7. Tropic of Cancer; 8. Black Spring; 9. My Live [sic] and
Loves; 10. Easter Sun (2nd large edition); 11. Storm (4th edition); 12.
Sleeveless Errand

Publication
January 1939

Notes
First edition.

Although the publication date on [iv] is December 1938, Armstrong notes that the book was advertised in the Paris edition of the *New York Herald Tribune* on 9 January 1939. Since such advertisements were habitually used by Kahane to announce the actual rather than projected publication of Obelisk titles, this date is probably more reliable.

The word 'as' is missing from the first line of the blurb for *Lady, Take Heed!* on the rear flap [see also A–54, A–55].

A–59 PROMETHEUS THE FIRE GIVER

by LAWRENCE [LAURENCE] DAKIN

Title page
PROMETHEUS THE FIRE GIVER | A LYRICAL DRAMA IN THREE ACTS | BY | LAWRENCE DAKIN | [logo] | THE OBELISK PRESS | 16, PLACE VENDOME | PARIS

Collation
8vo. [iii–ix] 10–84 + [ii]. 23 × 17.8 cm. Top edge trimmed, others untrimmed.

Pagination
[iii–iv] blank; [v] title-page; [vi] dedication and copyright; [vii] half-title; [viii] list of previous works; [ix] dramatis personae; 10–84 text; [85] blank; [86] imprimerie: GEORGES FRERE | TOURCOING

Binding
Black cloth boards with paper label on spine.

Front panel: Blank.

Spine: White paper label with title printed horizontally, top to bottom: PROMETHEUS THE FIRE GIVER [tan]

Rear panel: Blank.

Publication
1939

Notes
First edition.

Dakin's forename is spelt with a 'W' on the title-page, the only place his name appears in the book. This is a misspelling. The correct spelling – Laurence – appears in A–14, A–27 and A–34.

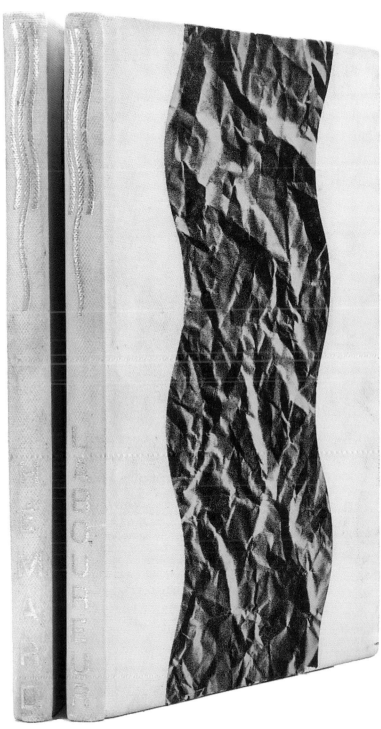

Marcel Valotaire, *Joseph Hémard*: A–2, pp. 81–82; *Laboureur*: A–5, pp.

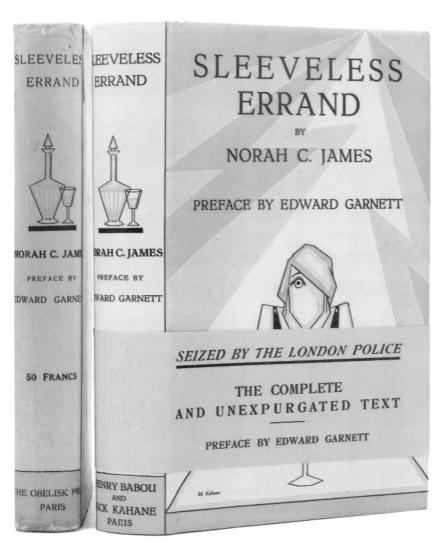

Norah C. James, *Sleeveless Errand*: A–1(b), A–1, pp. 79–81.

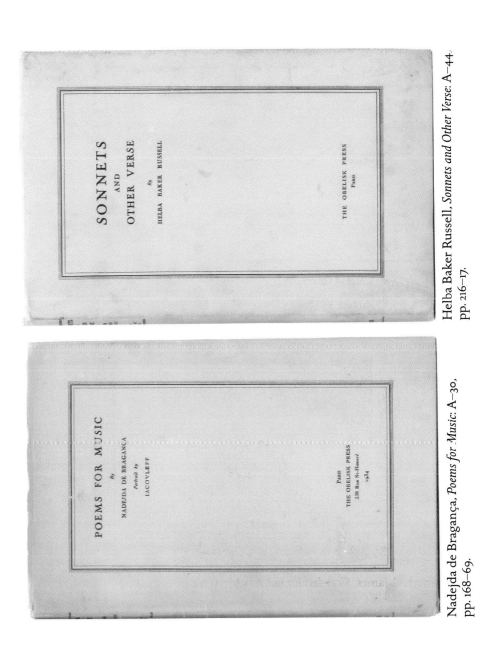

Helba Baker Russell, *Sonnets and Other Verse*: A–44.
pp. 216–17.

Nadejda de Bragança, *Poems for Music*: A–30,
pp. 168–69.

1. Philippe Hériat; 2. Raymonde Machard; 3. Richard Aldington;
4. Radclyffe Hall; 5. Frank Harris; 6. Princess Paul Troubetzkoy;
7. Charles Henri Ford; 8. Henry Miller; 9. Anaïs Nin; 10. Richard Thoma;
11 Lawrence Durrell; 12. Peter Neagoe; 13. Parker Tyler.

Philippe Hériat, *The Lamb*, The Lamb: A–15, A–15(c), pp. 114–17.

LYCIDAS

JOHN MILTON

JACK KAHANE
AT THE OBELISK PRESS
PARIS

John Milton, *Lycidas*: A–24, pp. 135–36.

Seigneur de Brantôme, *Lives of Fair and Gallant Ladies:* A–52, pp. 231–32; Petronius, *The Satyricon:* A–53, pp. 233–34.

Cecil Barr [Jack Kahane], *Daffodil*: A–8(c), pp. 97–98; *Amour French for Love*: A–18, pp. 124–27; *Lady, Take Heed!*: A–47, pp. 219–23; *Bright Pink Youth*: A–31, pp. 170–71.

Robin Anderson, *Four Schools*: A–36, pp. 194–95.

Henry Miller, *Aller Retour New York*: A–38, pp. 198–99.

Raymonde Machard, *Possession*: A–13, pp. 112–13.

Anne Bellinzini Ferrand, *Cléante and Bélise*: A–4, pp. 84–88.

Henry Miller, *Tropic of Cancer*: A–32, pp. 171–88; *Tropic of Capricorn*: A–60, pp. 243–56; *Black Spring*: A–42, pp. 208–14.

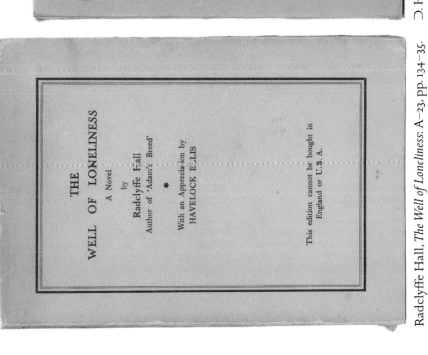

THE
WELL OF LONELINESS
A Novel
by
Radclyffe Hall
Author of 'Adam's Breed'

*

With an Appreciation by
HAVELOCK ELLIS

This edition cannot be bought in
England or U.S.A.

LADY
CHATTERLEY'S
LOVER
by
D. H. LAWRENCE

THE
OBELISK PRESS
PARIS

Radclyffe Hall, *The Well of Loneliness*: A–23, pp. 134–35.

D. H. Lawrence, *Lady Chatterley's Lover*: A–43. pp. 214–16.

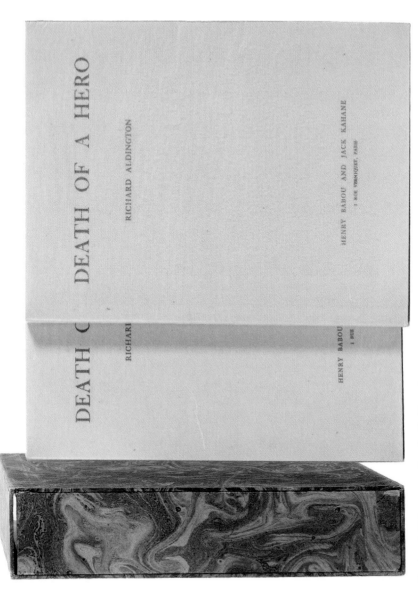

Richard Aldington, *Death of a Hero*: A–6, pp. 90–93.

James Hanley. *Boy*: A–37. A–37(b). pp. 195–97.

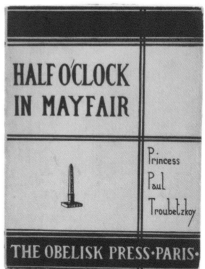

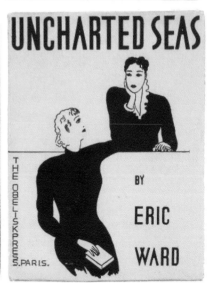

N. Reynolds Packard, *Mad About Women*: A–22, pp. 130–33; Princess Paul Troubetzkoy, *Half O'Clock in Mayfair*: A–50, pp. 226–27; Wallace Smith, *Bessie Cotter*: A–39, pp. 200–204; Eric Ward, *Uncharted Seas*: A–46, pp. 218–19.

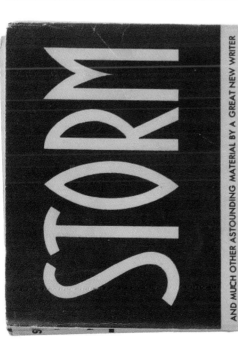

Peter Neagoe, *Easter Sun*: A–29, pp. 165–68.

Peter Neagoe, *Storm*: A–16, pp. 117–20.

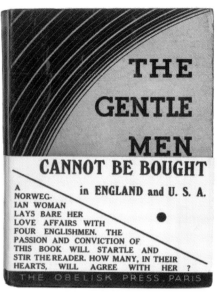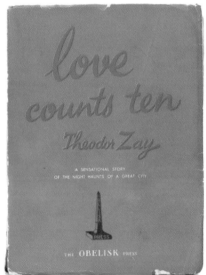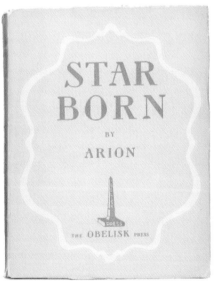

Gawen Brownrigg, *Star Against Star*: A–35, pp. 192–94; Marika Norden, *The Gentle Men*: A–33, pp. 188–91; Theodor Zay, *Love Counts Ten*: A–58, pp. 241–42; Arion, *Starborn*: A–55, pp. 235–37.

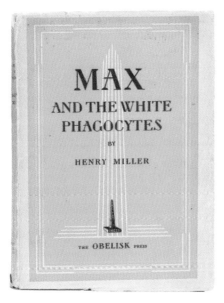

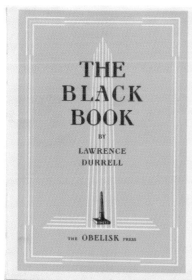

Henry Miller, *Max and the White Phagocytes*: A–57, pp. 238–40; Lawrence Durrell, *The Black Book*: A–56, pp. 237–38; Anaïs Nin, *The Winter of Artifice*: A–63, pp. 259–60.

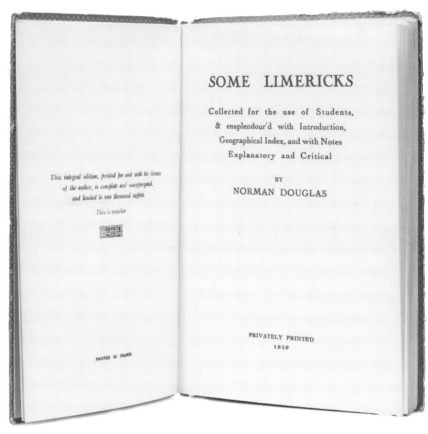

This integral edition, printed for and with the license of the author, is complete and unexpurgated, and limited to one thousand copies.

This is number

PRINTED IN FRANCE

SOME LIMERICKS

Collected for the use of Students,
& ensplendour'd with Introduction,
Geographical Index, and with Notes
Explanatory and Critical

BY

NORMAN DOUGLAS

PRIVATELY PRINTED
1939

Norman Douglas, *Some Limericks*: A–64, pp. 260–62.

Henry Miller, *Scenario: A–48,* pp. 224–25.

[Richard] Thoma, *Tragedy in Blue: A–40,* pp. 204–205.

Cecil Barr [Jack Kahane], *Suzy Falls Off*: C–8(b), pp. 297–98; Jack Kahane, *Laugh and Grow Rich*: C–2, pp. 282–86; *The Vain Serenade*: C–5, pp. 289–90; *The Gay Intrigue*: C–4, pp. 288–89; *The Pure in Heart*: C–6, pp. 290–93; *The Browsing Goat*: C–7, pp. 293–95; Cecil Barr [Jack Kahane], *It's Hard to Sin!*: C–9, pp. 299–300.

Frank Harris, *My Life and Loves*: A–28, pp. 140–64.

Charles Beadle, *Dark Refuge*: A–54. pp. 234–35.

Charles Ford and Parker Tyler, *The Young and Evil*: A–25, pp. 136–38.

Sheila Cousins [Ronald Matthews], *To Beg I am Ashamed*: A–51, pp. 227–31.

Cyril Connolly, *The Rock Pool*: A–41, pp. 205–27.

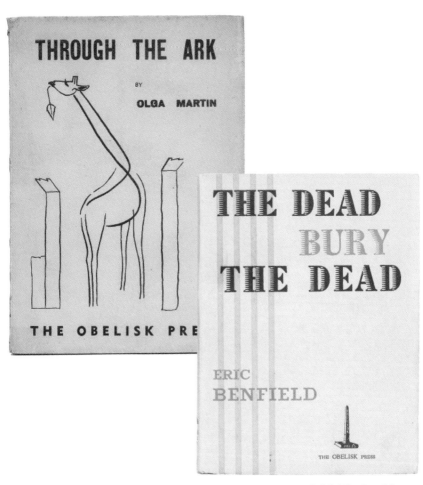

Olga Martin, *Through the Ark*: A–49, pp. 225–256; Eric Benfield, *The Dead Bury the Dead*: A–62, pp. 258–259.

Albert H. Whitin, *The Queen's Reverie*: A–20, pp. 128–29.

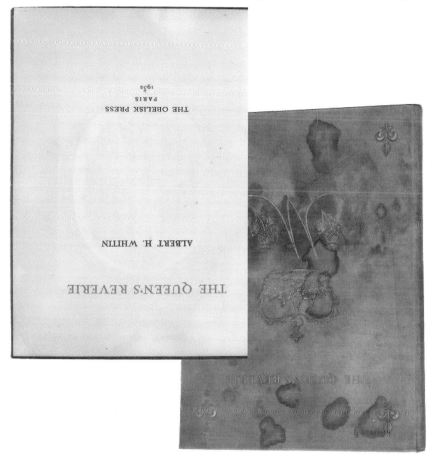

THE QUEEN'S REVERIE

ALBERT. H. WHITIN

THE OBELISK PRESS
PARIS
1933

Marjorie Firminger, *Jam To-day*: A–7, pp. 93–95.

Lawrence [Laurence] Dakin, *Prometheus the Fire Giver*: A–59, pp. 242–43; Harold Buckley, *Squadron 95*: A–21, pp. 129–30; Laurence Dakin, *The Dream of Abaris and Other Poems*: A–27, pp. 139–40.

James Joyce, *Haveth Childers Everywhere*: A–3, pp. 83–84.

James Joyce (illustrated by Lucia Joyce), *Pomes Penyeach*: A–17. pp. 121–23.

A CHAUCER A. B. C.

being a Hymn to the Holy Virgin
in an English version

by

GEOFFREY CHAUCER

from the French of

GUILLAUME DE DEGUILLEVILLE

Initial letters designed and illuminated

by

LUCIA JOYCE

Preface by

LOUIS GILLET

de l'Académie Française

THE OBELISK PRESS
338, Rue Saint-Honoré
PARIS

Guillaume de Deguilleville, trans. Geoffrey Chaucer (illustrated by Lucia Joyce), *A Chaucer A.B.C.*: A–45, pp. 217–18.

The completion date of the book is given on [84] as 8 March 1938.

Armstrong gives the price of the book as Frs. 50. The copy in the author's collection has a new price of 65 00 stamped on [86], and a flyer tipped in to the front free endpaper from the Librairie Joseph Gibert, Boulevard Saint-Michel, which confirms the new price .

Three copies located [BL; NYPL; author's collection].

A–60 TROPIC OF CAPRICORN
by HENRY MILLER

Title page
TROPIC | OF | CAPRICORN | BY | HENRY MILLER | [logo] | THE OBELISK PRESS | 16, PLACE VENDOME | PARIS

Collation
8vo. [x] 11–367 + [v]. 19.5 × 14 cm. All edges untrimmed.

Pagination
[i–ii] blank; [iii] half-title; [iv] list of works, and publication: FIRST PUBLISHED FEBRUARY 1939; [v] title-page; [vi] copyright; [vii] section heading; [viii] blank; [ix] dedication; [x] Peter Abelard quotation; 11 367 text; [368] blank; [369] imprimerie: IMPRIMERIE | GEORGES FRÈRE | TOURCOING; [370–372] blank. Yellow errata slip bound in at title-page.

Binding
Heavy paper wrappers with fold-over flaps.

Wrapper
Front panel: Red, with zodiacal sign and sun in white. TROPIC OF | CAPRICORN | BY HENRY MILLER | AUTHOR OF | TROPIC | OF | CANCER | the [logo] | OBELISK | press

Spine: White. TROPIC | OF | CAPRICORN | HENRY | MILLER | 60 FRS | [logo] | OBELISK PRESS | 16, Place Vendôme | PARIS

Rear panel: White. [logo]

Front flap: Title, author, blurb and price [60 francs].

Rear flap: Twelve titles, with blurbs, at Frs. 60 each: 1. To Beg I Am Ashamed; 2. Half O'Clock in Mayfair; 3. Lady, Take Heed! (*Daffodil* mentioned in the blurb as being in its 18th impression); 4. The Rock

Pool (2nd edition); 5. Boy; 6. Star Against Star (2nd impression); 7. Tropic of Cancer; 8. Black Spring; 9. My Life and Loves; 10. Easter Sun (2nd large edition); 11. Storm (4th edition); 12. Sleeveless Errand.

Publication
10 May 1939

Notes
First edition. 1000 copies.

Originally scheduled for publication in February but delayed for three months, as a result of which few copies were sold before the beginning of the war, the death of Kahane and the shutting down of the Obelisk Press. On these copies the original printed price on the spine and both flaps has not been inked out. The bulk of the first edition was sold only when Maurice Girodias reopened for business after the war. On these copies the price on the spine and flaps has been inked out: Shifreen and Jackson designates such copies first edition, second state. I've designated both states to be the first edition because they were all printed at the same time, from the same plates. The 'second state' copies were amended not by printers correcting textual errors, but by a publisher faced with a devalued franc, brandishing a rubber stamp.

The information on [vi] notwithstanding, Ford states that this title was printed in Bruges for Frs. 11,000.

Errata slip tipped in between [iv] and [v], though it does not record the misprint in l. 14 of [iv]: 'Vila' for 'Villa'.

[iv] records *Aller Retour New York* as being in its second impression, *Tropic of Cancer* in its fifth, and *Black Spring* in its second. A second impression of *Aller Retour New York* was never issued by the Obelisk Press.

Dedication on [ix] reads: TO HER

(b) TROPIC OF CAPRICORN

Title page
As A–60.

Collation
8vo. [iv] 11–365 + [i]. 19.2 × 14.5 cm. Top edge rough trimmed, others untrimmed.

Pagination
[i] title-page; [ii] copyright; [iii] dedication and section heading;
[iv] Peter Abelard quotation; 11–365 text; [365] imprimerie: 31. 0914 |
SOCIÉTÉ INDUSTRIELLE | D'IMPRIMERIE | 10, RUE VALLIER, 10
| LE VALLOIS-PERRET; [366] blank. Yellow errata slip bound in at
title-page.

Binding
Red wrappers. No fold-over flaps.

Wrapper
Front panel: HENRY MILLER | TROPIC | OF | CAPRICORN | THE
OBELISK PRESS – PARIS [black on white]

Spine: *HENRY MILLER* – TROPIC OF CAPRICORN [printed horizontally, bottom to top]

Rear panel: Blank.

Publication
August 1945

Notes
First edition, second impression. 10,000 copies.

Although the livery and preliminaries differ, and the book has been
reprinted on inferior paper, the text has not been reset, hence the
designation. Its large print run was designed to take advantage of the
huge numbers of Allied forces present in Paris immediately after the
war. The edition sold for Frs. 175 a copy.

Preceded by the second edition, a piracy, published in Shanghai in 1939.

(c) TROPIC OF CAPRICORN

Title page
As A–60(b).

Collation
As A–60(b).

Pagination
[i] title-page; [ii] copyright; [iii] dedication and section heading; [iv]
Peter Abelard quotation; 11–365 text; [365] imprimerie: SOCIÉTÉ
INDUSTRIELLE D'IMPRIMERIE; [366] blank. Yellow errata slip
bound in at title-page.

Binding
Brown wrappers. No fold-over flaps.

Wrapper
Front panel: As A–60(b).

Spine: Not seen.

Rear panel: Not seen.

Publication
1945

Notes
First edition, third impression.

The colour of the wrappers and the imprimerie are the only differences between this edition and A–60(b).

(d) TROPIC OF CAPRICORN

Title page
TROPIC | OF | CAPRICORN | BY | HENRY MILLER | THE OBELISK
PRESS BOOKS | LES ÉDITIONS DU CHÊNE | 4, RUE DE LA PAIX |
PARIS

Collation
8vo. [viii] 9–436 + [iv]. 17.5 × 11.5 cm. Edges trimmed.

Pagination
[i] half-title; [ii] blank; [iii] title-page; [iv] copyright; [v] section heading;
[vi] blank; [vii] dedication; [viii] Peter Abelard quotation; 9–436 text;
[437–438] blank; [439] imprimerie: ACHEVE D'IMPRIMER LE 3 JUIN
1948 | SUR LES PRESSES DE LA S. F. E. I. R. | 26, RUE CLAVEL, 26 –
PARIS-XIXe | N° d'Edition: 267; [440] blank.

Binding
Green paper wrappers.

Front panel: Red sunburst. HENRY MILLER | TROPIC | OF | CAPRI-
CORN [white on red] | THE OBELISK PRESS [white on green]

Spine: HENRY | MILLER | TROPIC | OF | CAPRICORN | THE | OBELISK
| PRESS [white on green]

Rear panel: [publisher's device] [white on green] | * [black on green]

FR. 400 | MUST NOT BE IMPORTED INTO ENGLAND OR U. S. A [white on green]

Publication
3 June 1948

Notes
Fourth edition.

Preceded by a 1948 American piracy.

The publisher's device on the rear panel is not the Obelisk logo, but that of Editions du Chêne: an H inside a diamond.

(e) TROPIC OF CAPRICORN

Title page
HENRY MILLER | TROPIC | OF | CAPRICORN | THE OBELISK PRESS, PARIS

Collation
8vo. [viii] 9–436 + [iv]. 17.5 × 11.5 cm. Edges trimmed.

Pagination
[i–ii] blank; [iii] title-page; [iv] copyright; [v] section heading; [vi] blank; [vii] dedication; [viii] Peter Abelard quotation; 9–436 text; [437] imprimerie: ACHEVE D'IMPRIMER LE 30 JUIN 1949 | SUR LES PRESSES DE LA S. F. E. I. R. | 26, RUE CLAVEL, 26 – PARIS-XIXe | No d'Edition: 267; [438–440] blank.

Binding
As A–60(d).

Front panel: As A–60(d).

Spine: As A–60(d).

Rear panel: Not seen.

Publication
30 June 1949

Notes
Fourth edition.

Not seen. Shifreen and Jackson [A21i].

(f) TROPIC OF CAPRICORN

Title page
As A–60(e).

Collation
As A–60(e).

Pagination
[i] half-title; [ii] blank; [iii] title-page; [iv] copyright; [v] section heading; [vi] blank; [vii] dedication; [viii] Peter Abelard quotation; 9–436 text; [437] imprimerie: ACHEVE D'IMPRIMER LE 25 MAI 1950 | SUR LES PRESSES DE LA SOPAC | 26, RUE CLAVEL, 26. – PARIS - XIXe | No d'édition: 268; [438–440] blank.

Binding
Green paper wrappers.

Front panel: As A–60(d).

Spine: As A–60(d).

Rear panel: [publisher's device] | FR. 500 | MUST NOT BE IMPORTED INTO ENGLAND OR U. S. A. [white on green]

Publication
25 May 1950

Notes
Fourth edition, second impression.

Shifreen and Jackson note a variant of this edition [A21j] with the imprimerie printed on [438].

(g) TROPIC OF CAPRICORN

Title page
As A–60(e).

Collation
8vo. [viii] 9–362 + [ii]. 17.5 × 11.5 cm. Edges trimmed.

Pagination
[i] half-title; [ii] blank; [iii] title-page ; [iv] copyright; [v] section heading; [vi] blank; [vii] dedication; [viii] Peter Abelard quotation; 9–362 text;

[363] blank; [364] imprimerie: Évreux – Imprimerie Hérissey | Dépôt légal: 2e trimestre 1952

Binding
Green paper wrappers.

Front panel: As A–60(d).

Spine: As A–60(d).

Rear panel: Not seen.

Publication
Spring 1952

Notes
Fifth edition.

Not seen. Shifreen and Jackson [A21k].

Shifreen and Jackson notes a variant of this edition [A21fff] in which the colophon is capitalised and printed on [363], with [364] blank.

(h) TROPIC OF CAPRICORN

Title page
As A–60(e).

Collation
As A–60(g).

Pagination
[i] half-title; [ii] blank; [iii] title-page; [iv] copyright and publisher details: *PUBLISHED BY SOCIÉTÉ NOUVELLE | DES ÉDITIONS DU CHÊNE | 28, rue la Boétie, Paris, France.*; [v] section heading; [vi] blank; [vii] dedication; [viii] Peter Abelard quotation; 9–362 text; [363] imprimerie: ACHEVÉ D'IMPRIMER | LE 30 NOVEMBRE 1954 | PAR L'IMPRIMERIE | NAUDEAU, REDON ET Cie, | A POITIERS (VI-ENNE). | DÉPOT LÉGAL: 4e TRIMESTRE 1954 | (16); [364] blank.

Binding
Dark green paper wrappers.

Front panel: As A–60(d).

Spine: As A–60(d).

Rear panel: [publisher's logo] | Fr. 600 | MUST NOT BE IMPORTED INTO ENGLAND OR U. S. A. [white]

Publication
30 November 1954

Notes
Fifth edition, second impression.

Not in Shifreen and Jackson.

Preceded by a 1953 Japanese edition [Keimeisha].

(i) TROPIC OF CAPRICORN

Title page
As A–60(e).

Collation
As A–60(g).

Pagination
[i] half-title; [ii] blank; [iii] title-page; [iv] copyright and publisher details: *PUBLISHED BY SOCIÉTÉ NOUVELLE | DES ÉDITIONS DU CHÊNE;* [v] section heading; [vi] blank; [vii] dedication; [viii] Peter Abelard quotation; 9–362 text; [363] imprimerie: ACHEVÉ D'IMPRIMER | LE 15 MAI 1956 | PAR L'IMPRIMERIE | NAUDEAU, REDON ET Cie, | A POITIERS (VIENNE). | *procédé photo-offset* | D. L., 2e trim. 1956. – No d'éditeur: 30 – No d'imprimeur: 91.; [364] blank.

Binding
Dark green paper wrappers.

Front panel: As A–60(d).

Spine: As A–60(d).

Rear panel: [publisher's logo] | Fr. 600 | MUST NOT BE IMPORTED INTO ENGLAND OR U. S. A. [white]

Publication
15 May 1956

Notes
Fifth edition, third impression.

Preceded by a 1955 Japanese piracy and a second Keimeisha edition of March 1956.

The address given for Editions du Chêne on [iv] is now 11, rue de Grenelle, Paris [cf. A–60(h)].

(j) TROPIC OF CAPRICORN

Title page
As A–60(e).

Collation
As A–60(g).

Pagination
[i] half-title; [ii] blank; [iii] title-page; [iv] copyright; [v] section heading; [vi] blank; [vii] dedication; [viii] Peter Abelard quotation; 9–362 text; [363] blank; [364] ACHEVÉ D'IMPRIMER | LE 5 MARS 1957 | PAR L'IMPRIMERIE | NAUDEAU; [364] blank.

Binding
White paper wrappers.

Front panel: HENRY MILLER [black] | TROPIC | OF CAPRICORN [red] | [forward slash] | THE OBELISK PRESS [black]

Spine: HENRY | MILLER [red] | TROPIC | OF | CAPRICORN | THE | OBELISK | PRESS [black]

Rear panel: Not seen.

Publication
5 March 1957

Notes
Fifth edition, fourth impression.

Not seen. Shifreen and Jackson [A210].

Although the wrappers have been changed for this edition the text has not been reset, hence the designation.

(k) TROPIC OF CAPRICORN

Title page
HENRY MILLER | TROPIC | OF | CAPRICORN | THE OBELISK PRESS, PARIS

Collation
As A–60(g).

Pagination
[i] half-title; [ii] blank; [iii] title-page; [iv] copyright; [v] section heading; [vi] blank; [vii] dedication; [viii] Peter Abelard quotation; 9–362 text; [363] imprimerie: ACHEVÉ D'IMPRIMER | LE 15 JUILLET 1957 | PAR L'IMPRIMERIE | NAUDEAU REDON ET Cie, | A POITIERS (VIENNE). | *procédé photo-offset* | D. L., 3e trim. 1957. | Éditeur, No 36 – Imprimeur, No 177. | *Imprimé en France.*; [364] blank.

Binding
Dark green paper wrappers.

Front panel: As A–60(d).

Spine: As A–60(d).

Rear panel: Not seen.

Publication
15 July 1957

Notes
Fifth edition, fifth impression.

Not seen. Shifreen and Jackson [A21p].

Although the wrappers have been changed for this edition the text has not been reset, hence the designation.

(I) TROPIC OF CAPRICORN

Title page
HENRY MILLER | TROPIC | OF | CAPRICORN | OBELISK PRESS, PARIS

Collation
As A–60(g).

Pagination
[i] half-title; [ii] blank; [iii] title-page; [iv] copyright; [v] section heading; [vi] blank; [vii] dedication; [viii] Peter Abelard quotation; 9–362 text; [363] imprimerie: ACHEVÉ D'IMPRIMER | LE 15 MARS 1958 | PAR L'IMPRIMERIE | NAUDEAU REDON ET Cie, | A POITIERS (VIENNE). | *procédé photo-offset.*; [364] blank.

Binding
Dark green paper wrappers.

Front panel: As A–60(d).

Spine: As A–60(d).

Rear panel: Not seen.

Publication
15 March 1958

Notes
Fifth edition, sixth impression.

Not seen. Shifreen and Jackson [A21q].

(m) TROPIC OF CAPRICORN

Title page
As A–60(l).

Collation
As A–60(g).

Pagination
[i] half-title; [ii] blank; [iii] title-page; [iv] copyright; [v] section heading; [vi] blank; [vii] dedication; [viii] Peter Abelard quotation; 9–362 text; [363] imprimerie: ACHEVÉ D'IMPRIMER | LE 20 AVRIL 1959 | PAR L'IMPRIMERIE | NAUDEAU REDON ET Cie, | A POITIERS (VIENNE). | *procédé photo-offset* | Dépôt légal : 2e trimestre 1959. | Imprimeur, no 303. | Imprimé en France; [364] blank.

Binding
Dark green paper wrappers.

Front panel: As A–60(d).

Spine: As A–60(d).

Rear panel: Not seen.

Publication
20 April 1959

Notes
Fifth edition, seventh impression.

Not seen. Shifreen and Jackson [A21r].

(n) TROPIC OF CAPRICORN

Title page
As A–60(l).

Collation
As A–60(g).

Pagination
[i] half-title; [ii] blank; [iii] title-page; [iv] copyright; [v] section heading; [vi] blank; [vii] dedication; [viii] Peter Abelard quotation; 9–362 text; [363] imprimerie: ACHEVÉ D'IMPRIMER | LE 20 AVRIL 1959 | PAR L'IMPRIMERIE | NAUDEAU REDON ET Cie, | A POITIERS (VIENNE). | *procédé photo-offset*; [364] blank.

Binding
Dark green paper wrappers.

Front panel: As A–60(d).

Spine: As A–60(d).

Rear panel: Not seen.

Publication
15 October 1959

Notes
Fifth edition, eighth impression.

Not seen. Shifreen and Jackson [A21s].

(o) TROPIC OF CAPRICORN

Title page
As A–60(l).

Collation
As A–60(g), but with an extra blank endpaper at each end (not included in the pagination).

Pagination
[i] half-title; [ii] blank; [iii] title-page; [iv] copyright; [v] section heading; [vi] blank; [vii] dedication; [viii] Peter Abelard quotation; 9–362 text; [363] imprimerie: ACHEVÉ D'IMPRIMER | LE 10 OCTOBRE 1960 | PAR L'IMPRIMERIE | NAUDEAU REDON ET Cie, | A POITIERS (VIENNE).

| *procédé photo-offset* | Dépôt légal : 4e trimestre 1960. | Imprimeur, no 468. | *Imprimé en France*; [364] blank.

Binding
White paper wrappers.

Front panel: As A–60(j).

Spine: As A–60(j).

Rear panel: Not seen.

Publication
10 October 1960

Notes
Fifth edition, eighth impression.

Not seen. Shifreen and Jackson [A21v]. Preceded by a Taiwanese piracy and a Keimeisha paperback edition.

(p) TROPIC OF CAPRICORN

Title page
HENRY MILLER | TROPIC | OF | CAPRICORN | OBELISK PRESS | [PARIS]

Collation
As A–60(g), but with an extra blank endpaper at each end (not included in the pagination).

Pagination
[i] half-title; [ii] blank; [iii] title-page; [iv] copyright; [v] section heading; [vi] blank; [vii] dedication; [viii] Peter Abelard quotation; 9–362 text; [363] imprimerie: ACHEVÉ D'IMPRIMER | LE 5 MARS 1961 | PAR L'IMPRIMERIE | NAUDEAU REDON ET Cie, | A POITIERS (VIENNE). | *procédé photo-offset* | Dépôt légal : 1er trimestre 1961. | Imprimeur, no 525.; [364] blank.

Binding
White paper wrappers.

Front panel: As A–60(j).

Spine: As A–60(j).

Rear panel: Not seen.

Publication
5 March 1961

Notes
Fifth edition, ninth impression.

Not seen. Shifreen and Jackson [A21w].

(q) TROPIC OF CAPRICORN

Title page
As A–60(o).

Collation
8vo. [x] 11–365 + [iii]. 17.5 × 11.5 cms. Edges trimmed.

Pagination
[i–ii] blank; [iii] half-title; [iv] blank; [v] title-page; [vi] copyright; [vii] section heading; [viii] blank; [ix] dedication; [x] Peter Abelard quotation; 11–365 text; [366] blank; [367] imprimerie: ACHEVÉ | D'IMPRIMER | [printer's device] | SUR LES | PRESSES D'AUBIN | LIGUGÉ (VIENNE) | LE 5 MARS | 1962 | D. L. 1-1962. – Imprimeur, no 2.710.; [368] blank.

Binding
White paper wrappers.

Front panel: As A–60(j).

Spine: As A–60(j).

Rear panel: Not seen.

Publication
5 March 1962

Notes
Eighth edition.

Not seen. Shifreen and Jackson [A21y], which also notes a variant of this edition [A21z] bound in glossy white wrappers printed in dark blue (instead of black) and red.

A–61 LA FABLE DE PHAËTON
by OVIDE

Title page
OVIDE | LA FABLE DE | PHAËTON | *Mise en vers français par* | *Thomas Corneille* | GRAVURES AU BURIN DE | ROGER VIEILLARD | JACK KAHANE, ÉDITEUR | THE OBELISK PRESS, 16, PLACE VENDÔME | PARIS

Collation
Folio. [viii] 5–38 + [vi]. Six illustrations laid in. 330 × 255 mm. Edges untrimmed.

Pagination
[1–iv] blank; [v] half-title; [vi] limitation; [vii] title-page; [viii] blank; 5–38 text; [39] imprimerie: Ce volume a été achevé d'imprimer | le 31 mai 1939. La version de la *Fable de Phaëton* a été relevée par | May Vieillard sur l'édition originale | des *Métamorphoses d'Ovide*, mises en | vers français par Thomas Corneille. | Les six gravures sur cuivre | de Roger Vieillard ont étés tirées à la | presse à bras par l'artiste lui-même, | et la typographie a été exécutée par | Ducros et Colas, maîtres imprimeurs | à Paris.; [40–44] blank. Illustrations laid in between: [viii] and [5]; [8] and [9]; [16] and [17]; [24] and [25]; [32] and [33]; [38] and [39].

Binding
Seven unbound signatures laid in to light brown paper wrappers, folded around card stiffeners.

Wrapper
Front panel: LA FABLE DE | PHAËTON | *SIX GRAVURES DE* | ROGER VIEILLARD [black]

Spine: Blank.

Rear panel: Blank.

Publication
31 May 1939

Notes
Limitation page reads: *Le tirage de ce volume* | *a été strictement limité* | *à cent exemplaires* | *sur vergé de Montval* | *fabriqué à la main,* | *numérotés de 1 à 100.* | EXEMPLAIRE | No [printed number]

Vieillard's signature appears in pencil beneath the number on the limitation page.

Placement of illustrations taken from NYPL copy, no. 80.

A–62 THE DEAD BURY THE DEAD

by ERIC BENFIELD

Title page
The Dead | bury The Dead | by | Eric Benfield | [logo] | THE OBELISK PRESS | 16, Place Vendôme | PARIS

Collation
8vo. [vi] 7–246 + [ii]. 19 × 13.5 cm. Edges untrimmed.

Pagination
[i–ii] blank; [iii] half-title; [iv] blank; [v] title-page; [vi] copyright; 7–246 text; [246] imprimerie: Printed in Belgium.; [247–248] blank.

Binding
White heavy paper wrappers with fold-over flaps.

Front panel: Four grey vertical lines running the length of the panel. THE DEAD [red] | BURY [grey] | THE DEAD [red] | ERIC | BENFIELD | [logo] | THE OBELISK PRESS [red]

Spine: THE | DEAD | BURY | THE | DEAD | Eric | Benfield | [logo] | OBELISK | PRESS | PARIS [red]

Rear panel: [logo] [grey]

Front flap: Title, author, blurb and price [50 FRANCS].

Rear flap: Thirteen titles, with blurbs, at Frs. 50 each: 1. Tropic of Capricorn; 2. To Beg I Am Ashamed; 3. Dark Refuge (2nd impression); 4. Lady, Take Heed!; 5. Tropic of Cancer (5th impression); 6. The Rock Pool (2nd edition); 7. Love Counts Ten; 8. The Gentle Men; 9. Bessie Cotter (3rd and only existing edition); 10. Boy; 11. Star Against Star (2nd impression); 12. Black Spring; 13. My Life and Loves.

Publication
July 1939

Notes
First edition.

The copy in the author's collection has the price on the front and rear flaps deleted but unreplaced. Another copy seen has the price inked out on both flaps, and a new price [*78 00] stamped at the foot of the rear endpaper.

On the title-page, the b in the word 'bury' has been printed in lower case.

A second impression of *Dark Refuge* [see A–54], referred to on the rear flap, has not been seen, and is presumed not to exist.

A–63 THE WINTER OF ARTIFICE
by ANAÏS NIN

Title page
The Winter of Artifice | by | Anaïs Nin | [logo] | THE OBELISK PRESS | 16, Place Vendôme | PARIS

Collation
Large 8vo. [viii] 9–289 + [iii]. 22 × 15.5 cm. Edges rough trimmed.

Pagination
[i–ii] blank; [iii] half-title; [iv] list of previous works, and publication: FIRST PUBLISHED JUNE 1939; [v] title-page; [vi] dedication and copyright; [vii] section heading; [viii] blank; 9–289 text; [289] imprimerie: *Imprimé en Belgique*; [290–292] blank.

Binding
Heavy paper wrappers with fold-over flaps.

Wrapper
Front panel: Blue. Villa Seurat series design [see A–55]. THE | WINTER | OF | ARTIFICE | BY | ANAÏS NIN | [logo] | THE OBELISK PRESS

Spine: White. THE | WINTER | OF | ARTIFICE | BY | ANAÏS NIN | [logo] | OBELISK | PRESS | PARIS

Rear panel: White. [logo] [blue] | DUCROS ET COLAS, PARIS. [black]

Front flap: Title, author, blurb and price [75 francs].

Rear flap: As A–55.

Publication
27 August 1939

[259]

Notes
First edition.

No. 3 in the Villa Seurat series, and the last Obelisk title to be published in Kahane's lifetime, 'printed one week before the outbreak of World War II and nine days before Kahane's death in Paris'.[5]

Completed in 1934 and accepted for publication in 1935, but only finally appearing when Lawrence and Nancy Durrell agreed to under-write the printing costs.

A–64 SOME LIMERICKS

by NORMAN DOUGLAS

Title page
SOME LIMERICKS | Collected for the use of Students, | & ensplendour'd with Introduction, | Geographical Index, and with Notes | Explanatory and Critical | BY | NORMAN DOUGLAS | PRIVATELY PRINTED | 1939

Collation
8vo. [iii–xiv] 15–116 + [ii]. 21.5 × 14 cm. Edges trimmed.

Pagination
[iii–iv] blank; [v] half-title; [vi] limitation; [vii] title-page; [viii] blank; [ix] dedication; [x] blank; [xi] contents; [xii] blank; [xiii] introduction half-title; [xiv] blank; [15–31] introduction; [32] blank; [33] text half-title; [34] blank; 35–107 text; [108] blank; [109] geographical index half-title; [110] blank; [111–116] index; [117] blank; [118] imprimerie: GEORGES FRERE | TOURCOING

Binding
Gold coarse-grain cloth boards. Flat spine. No lettering.

Wrapper
Not seen [see notes].

Publication
Late 1939 [see notes]

Notes
Fifth edition. 1000 copies.

5 Shari Benstock, *Women of the Left Bank* (Virago, 1987), p. 429.

Jack Kahane died in September 1939. This book, first published privately in Florence in 1928, seems to have been issued by Maurice Girodias, who worked at Obelisk after the company's move to new premises on the Place Vendôme in 1937. It carries no Obelisk insignia, and is identified as an Obelisk title by Cecil Woolf, who in his bibliography of Norman Douglas writes: 'This edition was issued by Les Editions du Chêne in their Obelisk Press series in Paris in 1939, at 130 francs. That another edition was contemplated by the same publishers is evident from the the following letter (dated January 8, 1947) which Douglas wrote to Mr. William King: "The (authorised) publisher in Paris sent me a draft contract for a new edition which struck me as so unreasonable that I have not answered him, especially as he has not paid a cent for the first, according to which we were to go halves and which, he tells me, is completely exhausted." Many writers who worked for Girodias's Olympia Press during the 1950s found his business practice largely unchanged.

Woolf calls for a light grey dustwrapper printed in blue. This has not been seen, but is present on the HRC copy, no. 433, inscribed by the author to Nancy Cunard.

The book is far rarer than its limitation would suggest, with only five copies located:

No. 232: Author's collection

No. 433: HRC

No. 810: Virginia Polytechnic Institute and State University

No. 864: University of Minnesota

No. 982: Princeton University

(b) SOME LIMERICKS

Title page
SOME LIMERICKS | Collected for the use of Students, | & ensplendourd'd with Introduction, | Geographical Index, and with Notes | Explanatory and Critical | BY | NORMAN DOUGLAS | BOSTON | NICHOLSON and WHITNEY | 1942

Collation
8vo. [xiv] 15–117 + [iii]. 20.8 × 14 cm. Edges trimmed.

Pagination
[i–iv] blank; [v] half-title; [vi] blank; [vii] title-page; [viii] copyright and
inprimerie: PRINTED IN THE U. S. A. ;[ix] dedication; [x] blank; [xi]
contents; [xii] blank; [xiii] introduction half-title; [xiv] blank; [15–31]
introduction; [32] blank; [33] text half-title; [34] blank; 35–107 text;
[108] blank; [109] geographical index half-title; [110] blank; [111–117] geographical index; [118] limitation; [119–120] blank.

Binding
Stiff paper wrappers [see notes].

Wrapper
Not seen [see notes].

Publication
1950 or 1951

Notes
?Fifth edition, second impression. ?1000 copies.

It is probable, but not proved, that this book is a pirate edition issued
by Maurice Girodias at the beginning of the 1950s. The letter from
Douglas to William King, quoted in the notes to A–64 above, shows
that it was Girodias's intention to reissue the book, and the text, as
Woolf notes, is a page-for-page reprint of the 1939 Obelisk edition,
faithfully reproducing all its misprints (and introducing a new one
on the reset title page ('ensplendourd'd')). Gershon Legman's *The Horn
Book* also inclines to this view.

Woolf calls for grey stiff paper wrappers and a buff paper wrapper,
printed with the word 'Poems' in black on the front panel and spine.
The wrapper has not been seen, and the stiff wrappers on the only
copy examined [author's collection] are badly sunned, but seem to
have begun life as light tan.

Given the provenance of the rest of the book the limitation page
cannot be relied on: the number of copies issued of this edition is
not known.

The following titles were issued much later by Maurice Girodias, using the Obelisk Press imprint. Although Obelisk itself died with Jack Kahane and the onset of war, Girodias occasionally revived the imprint's name in later years if he thought a book would sell better if issued by a publishing house with a scandalous reputation. Once Girodias's publishing house, the Olympia Press, had successfully established a scandalous reputation of its own, the practice was discontinued – except, oddly, for *Nexus* [see notes, A–68].

A–65 SEXUS (2 vols.)

by HENRY MILLER

(i) VOLUME ONE

Title page
HENRY MILLER | THE ROSY CRUCIFIXION | BOOK ONE | SEXUS | VOLUMES ONE TO THREE | THE OBELISK PRESS, PARIS

Collation
[x] 9–368 + [ii]. 19.5 × 14 cm. Edges trimmed.

Pagination
[i–iv] blank; [v] half-title; [vi] limitation and copyright; [vii] title-page; [viii] blank; [ix] section heading; [x] blank; 9–368 text; [369–370] blank.

Binding
Green cloth boards.

Front panel: Blank.

Spine: Box of dark green enclosing text in gilt. HENRY MILLER | THE | ROSY CRUCIFIXION | BOOK ONE | SEXUS | *VOLUMES I–III*

Rear panel: Blank.

(ii) VOLUME TWO

Title page
HENRY MILLER | THE ROSY CRUCIFIXION | BOOK ONE | SEXUS | VOLUMES FOUR AND FIVE | THE OBELISK PRESS, PARIS

Collation
[x] 9–326 + [iv]. 19.5 × 14 cm. Edges trimmed.

Pagination
[i–iv] blank; [v] half-title; [vi] limitation and copyright; [vii] title-page; [viii] blank; [ix] section heading; [x] blank; 9–326 text; [327] blank; [328] imprimerie: PRINTED IN FRANCE I BY S. F. E. I. R. I 26, RUE CLAVEL, A PARIS I Dépôt légal: 3ᵉ trimestre 1949 I N° d'édition: 383; [329–330] blank.

Binding
Green cloth boards.

Front panel: Blank.

Spine: Box of dark green enclosing text in gilt. HENRY MILLER I THE I ROSY CRUCIFIXION I BOOK ONE I SEXUS I *VOLUMES IV–V*

Rear panel: Blank.

Publication
10 August 1949

Notes
First edition. 3000 copies.

Book One of the trilogy known collectively as *The Rosy Crucifixion*. As the copyright page [vi] makes clear, the book was published by Girodias's company Les Editions du Chêne, but the prior association of Henry Miller with the Obelisk Press, and the scandalous reputation they both still enjoyed, was too good a business opportunity for Girodias to pass up, and it's the Obelisk imprint which appears on the title page. Unfortunately, the ploy worked too well: before the edition could sell out it was suppressed by the French authorities, and in December 1950 the Minister of the Interior forbade the publication of *Sexus* anywhere in France, in any language.

Book Two, *Plexus*, was published by Girodias in 1953 under his newly founded imprint, the Olympia Press, having been published in French the previous year under the title *La Crucifixion En Rose*, but for Book Three, *Nexus*, Girodias reverted to using the flag of convenience of the Obelisk Press [see A–68].

(b) SEXUS

Publication
1950

Notes
Second Obelisk edition.

Not seen. Cloth-bound, single-volume edition. Shifreen and Jackson (A76c). This edition was also issued in paper wrappers (not seen).

A–66 MEMOIRS OF FANNY HILL
by JOHN CLELAND

Title page
John Cleland | *MEMOIRS* | *of* | FANNY HILL | [device] | *THE OBELISK PRESS, PARIS* | 1950

Collation
12mo. [vi] 7–223 + [i]. 17.5 × 11.3 cm. Edges trimmed.

Pagination
[i–ii] blank; [iii] half-title; [iv] copyright and note to the text; [v] title-page; [vi] blank; 7–233 text; [234] imprimerie: ACHEVE D'IMPRIMER SUR | LES PRESSES DE LA SOPAC | 26, RUE CLAVEL. PARIS-19ᵉ | LE QUINZE FEVRIER MIL | NEUF CENT CINQUANTE | No d'Edition: 291 | Dépôt légal: 1er Tri. 1950

Binding
White card wrappers with red dustwrapper folded around card on three sides.

Wrapper
Front panel: White ornamented border enclosing text. *JOHN CLELAND* [dark red] | [ornament] [white] | MEMOIRS | *of* | *FANNY HILL* [dark red] | [ornament] [white] | THE OBELISK PRESS | PARIS [dark red]

Spine: [ornament] [white] | JOHN | CLELAND [dark red] | [floral ornament] [white] | MEMOIRS | OF *FANNY* | *HILL* [dark red] | [floral ornament] [white] | THE | OBELISK | PRESS [dark red] | [ornament] [white]

Rear panel: PRIX: 600 frs. [dark red]

Publication
15 February 1950

Notes
Issued by Maurice Girodias under the Obelisk imprint, in an attempt

to cash in on the notoriety of both book and publishing house. Originally published in two volumes in London in 1748–49.

A–67 THE MISFORTUNES OF VIRTUE
by MARQUIS DE SADE

Title page
MARQUIS DE SADE | THE | MISFORTUNES | OF | VIRTUE | TRANS-LATED BY | HARRIET SOHMERS | THE OBELISK PRESS, PARIS

Collation
8vo. [vi] 7–187 + [v]. 18 × 11.5 cm. Edges trimmed.

Pagination
[i–ii] blank; [iii] half-title; [iv] blank; [v] title-page; [vi] copyright; 7–187 text; [188] blank; [189] imprimerie: ACHEVÉ D'IMPRIMER | POUR | FASQUELLE ÉDITEURS | PAR L'IMPRIMERIE | BRODARD ET TAUPIN | LE 2 JUILLET 1953. | N° IMPRIMEUR 9172 | 46666-7-1953; [190–192] blank.

Binding
Paper wrappers.

Front panel: Mauve, with black and white stars enclosing text. *Marquis de Sade* [white] | THE | MISFORTUNES | OF VIRTUE [black] | *The Obelisk Press* [white]

Spine. White. *Marquis* | *de Sade* | THE | MISFORTUNES | OF VIRTUE | *The* | *Obelisk* | *Press* [black]

Rear panel: White. Blank.

Publication
2 July 1953

Notes
De Sade's *Justine*, published under the Editions du Chêne imprint by Maurice Girodias. I am grateful to Peter Mendes for pointing out that this version of the text was first published in Paris in 1930, in French, in an edition edited by Maurice Heine. The Obelisk edition is a translation of that text by the American writer Harriet Sohmers.

In the spring of 1953 Girodias had launched the Olympia Press, which over the next ten years would establish itself as the European market's leading supplier of 'dirty books'. Why Girodias chose to issue this title under the Obelisk imprint is unclear. Olympia had published an edition of this title, in a translation by Austryn Wainhouse, in May: it's possible that Girodias used two different imprints to gauge whether Obelisk's steamy reputation would shift more units. If so, the experiment clearly proved that it didn't: from this time on Girodias devoted his time to building the reputation of Olympia, and reverted to the Obelisk imprint only once more [see A–68].

Justine was first published in 1791.

A–68 NEXUS (Vol. I, all published)
by HENRY MILLER

Title page
NEXUS | (VOLUME I) | by | HENRY MILLER | THE OBELISK PRESS | PARIS

Collation
12mo. [viii] 7–378 + [iv]. 17.8 × 11.5 cm. Edges trimmed.

Pagination
[i–ii] blank; [iii] half-title; [iv] blank; [v] title-page; [vi] copyright, list of previous works; [vii] Russian quotation; [viii] blank; 7–378 text; [379] imprimerie: ACHEVÉ | D'IMPRIMER | [printer's device] | SUR LES | PRESSES D'AUBIN | LIGUGÉ (VIENNE) | LE 30 JUIN | 1960 | D. L., 3-1960. – Éditeur, no 49. – Imprimeur, no 2.304. | *Imprimé en France.*; [380–382] blank.

Binding
White paper wrappers.

Front panel: HENRY MILLER [red] | NEXUS [black] | [forward slash] [red] THE OBELISK PRESS [black]

Spine: HENRY | MILLER [red] | NEXUS | THE OBELISK | PRESS [black]

Rear panel: *THE OBELISK PRESS* [black] | HENRY MILLER [red] | TROPIC OF CANCER | TROPIC OF CAPRICORN | BLACK SPRING [black] | FRANK HARRIS [red] | MY LIFE AND LOVES | (4 vol.) [black] | CECIL BARR [red] | BRIGHT PINK YOUTH | DAFFODIL [black] | SHEILA COUSINS [red] | TO BEG I AM ASHAMED [black]

Publication
30 June 1960

Notes
Second edition. First edition in English.

The third volume of Miller's *Rosy Crucifixion* trilogy, for which Maurice Girodias reverted to the Obelisk imprint, having published the second part, *Plexus*, under his own imprint, the Olympia Press.

First published in French as *Nexus: La Crucifixion En Rose* by Buchet Chastel-Correa in Paris, one month before the Obelisk edition appeared.

B Items

Ephemera of
the Obelisk Press

B-1 FLYER: STORM

White flyer, printed on both sides on glossy white paper, reprinting the letter sent by the Chicago Customs Department to New Review Publications, notifying the publishers of the seizure of shipments of Peter Neagoe's *Storm* [New Review Publications, 1932] on the grounds of obscenity.

Recto: BANNED | IN AMERICA BY THE | U. S. CUSTOMS OFFICIALS! | Facsimilie [sic] of letter | The customs collector's | oftice [sic] | [four ruled lines] | [Collector's official seal, District no., address] | TREASURY DEPARTMENT | UNITED STATES CUSTOMS SERVICE | CHICAGO, ILL. | June 20, 1932. | The New Review and New Review Publications, | 42 Bis, Rue Du Plessis-Piquet | Fontenay-Aux Roses, France. (Seine) | Sirs: | In answer to your recent letter to this office | concerning copies of the book entitled "Storm", by Peter | Neagoe, you are informed that several shipments of the | above named book have been received at this port and have | been denied entry since the Bureau of Customs, Washington, | D. C. has held the same to be obscene within the provisions | of Section 305 of the Tariff Act of 1930. | In each case these shipments have been returned to | the foreign shipper. | Respectfully, | [signature] | Anthony Czarnecki | JCC/J Collector of Customs. | [four ruled lines] | "STORM" by PETER NEAGOE

Verso: The Obelisk logo appears in the bottom left and right hand corners of the page. WHAT THE CRITICS THINK | Clippings from the Press | [two ruled lines] | [six clippings from reviews] | [short single ruled line] | WHEN IT WAS LEARNED THAT STORM WAS BANNED BY THE U. S. CUSTOMS WE RECEIVED | LETTERS OF SYMPATHY IN SUPPORT OF PETER NEAGOE'S BOOK FROM WRITERS, EDUCATORS, | PROFESSIONALS, AND LIBERAL MINDED MEN AND WOMEN FROM ALL OVER THE WORLD. | [two ruled lines] | STORM IS BEING SOLD ALL OVER THE CONTI-NENT (14 FRANCS) | If you are not in touch with a book dealer write to NEW REVIEW PUBLICATIONS, 10, Rue | du Douanier | PARIS, 14e. | The first edition is out of print, and the rights have been acquired by The Obelisk Press for their well-known | 50FR. series. The new and greatly enlarged edition contains much astounding and hiterto unpublished material.

Publication
Summer 1932

Notes
On the only copy examined [Syracuse] the three lines of text on the verso giving the contact information for New Review Publications have been inked out.

B–2 FLYER: TROPIC OF CANCER

Pink flyer, printed in black on both sides, advertising the publication of *Tropic of Cancer* [see A–32]. 20 × 16 cm.

Recto: Reproduction of Maurice Kahane's crab illustration from the front panel of the book. TROPIC OF CANCER | BY | HENRY MILLER | THE OBELISK PRESS, 338, Rue Saint-Honoré – PARIS

Verso: Tropic of Cancer – by Henry Miller | 50 FRANCS | [English blurb with its French translation, side by side] | Ce volume ne doit pas être exposé en vitrine

Publication
September 1934

Notes
Kahane did little to draw attention to the publication of *Tropic of Cancer*, worried as he was about possible prosecution. This flyer was one of his few contributions to the book's promotion at the time of its first appearance; the rest he left to Miller, a tireless evangelist for his own work. In a letter to Anaïs Nin written in December 1934, Miller describes one of his many self-promotional tours of Paris, and mentions this item: 'I went to the other Montparnasse bookshop and I deposited a few circulars with them; they are considering whether they will order the book or not'.

B–3 THE OBELISK NOTES AND NEWS, No. 1

Single sheet of white paper, folded once to make a four-page pamphlet.

[1] carries an editorial, *Why a Paris Publisher?*, outlining the manifesto of the Obelisk Press: 'Any writer who has something grown-up to say but is restrained from saying it through fear and uncertainty should know that the Obelisk Press was created for him and, if his book is a good book, the Obelisk Press will publish it regardless of interests and informers'.

[2] carries a puff piece for Frank Harris, and for the Obelisk edition of *My Life and Loves*.

[3] carries blurbs for *The Gentle Men* and *Star Against Star*.

[4] carries advertisements for thirteen Obelisk trade titles, and five *Editions de luxe* (including *Haveth Childers Everywhere*, still not sold out although published five years previously).

Publication
Summer 1935

Notes
A note at the foot of [4] offers detailed prospectuses on application for the *Editions de luxe*. If these exist they have not been located.

B-4 PRINTED POSTCARD: FOUR SCHOOLS

Red postcard, printed in black, advertising *Four Schools*:

FOUR SCHOOLS
by Robin Anderson

A vivid, unique and convincing attack on educational methods, written by a young man whose impressions have not yet had time to grow stale. The author does not set out to analyse, to criticize or to construct. His bare narration of the facts is a crushing condemnation but with a strong underlying element of forceful and creative sugges- tion. This book voices with terseness, strength and clarity the feelings of an ever-increasing number of young captives and should inspire them to long desired action. Its author is responsible for a distin- guished translation of Georg Buchner, the early nineteenth century German revolutionary.
Price : 5/- net.
Obtainable through principal English book shops.
THE OBELISK PRESS, 338 RUE SAINT-HONORE, PARIS.

Publication
August 1935

Notes
One copy located [HRC]. Addressed in Kahane's hand to the literary agent William Bradley, it is postmarked 20 August 1935. The design

and typography are the same as those used both for *Four Schools* itself, and for *Aller Retour New York* [see A–36, A–38].

B–5 FLYER: ALLER RETOUR NEW YORK

Single sheet of white paper, 190 × 136 mm, inviting subscriptions for *Aller Retour New York*. Printed in black, on one side only:

THE SIANA SERIES | No. 1 | ALLER RETOUR NEW YORK | *by* | HENRY MILLER | A TRAVEL LETTER | by the author of | TROPIC OF CANCER | A hilarious view of the recovery | *1 vol. small octavo, 138 pages* | Frs. 35 or $2.50 post free | This, the original edition on India paper, is limited | to 150 copies, numbered and signed by the author. | THE OBELISK PRESS | 338 rue Saint-Honoré – PARIS | [perforations] | THE OBELISK PRESS | 338 Rue St-Honoré | PARIS 1er | *Please send me* .... *cop* .... *of "Aller Retour New | York", by Henry Miller, at 35 Francs or $2.50 (enclosed).* | *Name* .... | *Address* .... | ....

Publication
Autumn 1935 [see A–38]

Notes
Two examples in NYPL (Berg Collection). Not in Shifreen and Jackson.

B–6 THE OBELISK NOTES AND NEWS, No. 2

Single sheet of white paper, folded once to make a four-page pamphlet.

[1] carries an editorial, *Trumpet Solo*, in which Kahane congratulates himself for enabling Obelisk to thrive in adverse economic circumstances, and announces the imminent publication of *Bessie Cotter*.

[2] carries a puff piece for *Tropic of Cancer*.

[3] carries notes on four Obelisk writers and their books.

[4] carries advertisements for twelve Obelisk trade titles, and four *Editions de luxe*.

Publication
Winter 1935

Notes
A note at the foot of [4] offers detailed prospectuses on application

for the *Editions de luxe*. If these exist they have not been located.

B-7 OBELISK NOTES AND NEWS, No. 3

Single sheet of white paper, folded once to make a four-page pamphlet.

[1] carries an editorial, *The Legion of the Banned*, deploring the banning of Henry de Vere Stacpoole's *The Blue Lagoon* in Bournemouth, and championing the Obelisk list.

[2] carries puff pieces for *The Rock Pool* and *Black Spring*.

[3] carries notes on forthcoming Obelisk titles and current Obelisk bestsellers.

[4] carries advertisements for fifteen Obelisk trade titles, and four *Editions de luxe*.

Publication
Spring 1936

Notes
A note at the foot of [4] offers detailed prospectuses on application for the *Editions de luxe*. If these exist they have not been located.

A note at the foot of [3] suggests that more than 5000 copies of the Obelisk bulletin were sent out every three months. The three examples listed here [see also B–2 and B–5] are the only examples located.

B-8 PROSPECTUS: A CHAUCER A.B.C.

Single sheet of cream paper, 24.5 × 20 cm, printed on one side only.

THE OBELISK PRESS | 338, Rue Saint-Honoré – PARIS (1er) | Have the honour to announce, in view of the forthcoming | sexcentenary of the birth of Geoffrey CHAUCER, | the first publication commemorating this paramount event in the history | of English letters: | An | A. B. C. | being a Hymn to the Holy Virgin | in an English version by | C[lettrine by Lucia Joyce] HAUCER | from the French of | Guillaume De Deguilleville | (monk of Chaalis, XIIIth century) | with capital letters designed and illuminated in gold, silver and numerous | colours by | LUCIA JOYCE | Preface by | LOUIS GILLET | Member of the Academie Francaise, Curator of the Abbaye de Chaalis | This edition is limited to 300 numbered copies, hand-set in 18-point Elzevir, | printed on Arches mould-made vellum paper and boxed. | **Price, 100 francs for subscription,** | to be increased after publication. | The above C is a specimen of the initials in the size of the edition.

Publication
1936

Notes
One copy located [Sylvia Beach papers, Princeton].

B–9 REVIEW SLIP: OBELISK PRESS

Single sheet of white paper, printed on one side only:
[logo] | THE OBELISK PRESS | PUBLISHERS | 338 RUE SAINT-HONORÉ, – PARIS | TITLE .... | AUTHOR .... | TYPE .... | PRICE .... | DATE OF PUBLICATION .... | THE PUBLISHERS WILL BE MUCH OBLIGED FOR A COPY | OF THE ISSUE IN WHICH THE REVIEW APPEARS.

Notes
This item is laid in to the Baxter copy of *Through the Ark* [see A–49]. The original printed address has been typed out and replaced with the Place Vendôme address, dating the item to no later than January 1938.

B–10 LEAFLET: HENRY MILLER

Single sheet of white paper, folded once, producing an unpaginated four-page leaflet, 21 × 13.5 cm, printed in black, as follows:
[1] THE OBELISK PRESS | 16, PLACE VENDOME, PARIS | TÉL. OPÉRA 22. 76 - R. C. SEINE 696.777 [all printed to the right of the Obelisk logo] | HENRY MILLER | THE FOLLOWING ARE OPINIONS OF THIS WRITER'S WORK | EXTRACTED FROM THE IMMENSE PRESS | THAT HAS BEEN DEVOTED TO HIM [Four eulogies to Miller follow, from: 1. Paul Rosenfeld; 2. Desmond Hawkins; 3. Ralph Thompson; 4. Artur Lundkvist].

[2] Six eulogies: 1. Blaise Cendrars; 2. Raymond Queneau; 3. Wladimir Weidlé; 4. Montgomery Belgion; 5. George Orwell; 6. Edmond Wilson.

[3] Seven eulogies: 1. Aldous Huxley; 2. William Carlos Williams; 3. Dorothy Dudley; 4. Cyril Connolly; 5. Henry L. Mencken; 6. Charles Pearce; 7. Conrad Moricand.

[4] HENRY MILLER TITLES | **Already published:** | Tropic of Cancer | Aller Retour New York (limited edition) | Black Spring | Scenario (limited edition) | Max and the White Phagocytes (Villa Seurat Series, No. 2). | Money and how it gets that way (Booster Broadsides, No. 1). | Tropic of Capricorn, Vol. 1. (in the press). | **To be published shortly:** | Letters to Emil (Villa Seurat Series). | Hamlet (in collaboration with Michael Fraenkel). | The Sleeping Sleeper Asleep (Scenario). | The World of Lawrence. | **In preparation:** | Plasma and Magma (collected pieces). | Astrologic Effigies. | America, the air-conditioned nightmare. | The Rosy Crucifixion (Vol. 2. *Tropic of Capricorn*). | and | For 1942: | Draco and the Ecliptic. | FRERE - TOURCOING

Publication
Autumn 1938

Notes
This leaflet was laid in to the Christmas 1938, edition of *Delta*, the magazine produced by Miller, Lawrence Durrell, Alfred Perlès and their friends, and successor to *The Booster*.

Two copies in the author's collection; three copies in Houghton Library, Harvard (*ex libris* James Laughlin, Miller's first American publisher).

Not in Shifreen and Jackson.

C Items

The Plays, Novels, Short Fiction and Non-Fiction of Jack Kahane

C–1 TWO PLAYS

pub. SHERRATT AND HUGHES

Title page
TWO PLAYS | By | J. KAHANE | LONDON | SHERRATT AND HUGHES | Manchester: 34 Cross Street | 1912

Collation
8vo. [x] 11–118 + [ii]. 19 × 12.5 cm. Edges untrimmed.

Pagination
[i] half-title; [ii] copyright; [iii] title-page; [iv] blank; [v] dedication; [vi] blank; [vii] contents; [viii] blank; [ix] section heading; [x] blank; 11–118 text; [119–120] blank.

Binding
White stiff paper wrappers.

Front panel: Woodcut, white on black, of a Greek warrior with helmet, shield and sword. TWO PLAYS | BY J. KAHANE [black on white]

Spine: TWO PLAYS. J. KAHANE. [printed horizontally, bottom to top] | 1/- | net. [black on white]

Rear panel: Blank.

Publication
1912

Notes
First edition.

The two plays are *The Master* and *Black Magic*. In his preface to the first US edition of *Laugh and Grow Rich* [see C–2(b)], Kahane describes the plays as 'a grisly pair of tragedies, the milder of which ended in a murder; in the other, the people showed every sign of living unhappily ever after – much worse, of course, than an ordinary, reasonable murder'. *The Master*, a one-act play, received its only performance when it served as a curtain-raiser for H. M. Richardson's *The Awakening Woman* at the Gaiety Theatre, Manchester, on 28 November 1913. It was produced under the auspices of Esme Percy's company, and Percy himself played James Gillon. The theatre programme refers to the playwright as 'J. Cahane'. Kahane writes in his memoirs of the play also being staged in Dublin by Ben Iden Payne, as a curtain-raiser to a Shaw play. Kahane further maintains that a production of *Black*

Magic garnered him a mention in one of James Agate's books (Agate, like Kahane, was an alumnus of Manchester Grammar School). In his war memoir *Lines of Communication*, Agate describes Kahane as 'that very advanced young playwright of the violet sunsets and the purple passions – or the purple sunsets and the violent passions, I forget which'. [6]

The illustration on the front panel is the work of Ernest Marriott, a fellow member of the Swan Club in Manchester and a close friend of Kahane. Marriott's initials appear in the top left hand corner of the design.

The dedication reads: 'To Glad'.

Six copies located [Cornell; BL, rebound; Northwestern University; Indiana University; National Library of Wales; Syracuse, rebound].

C–2 LAUGH AND GROW RICH
pub. GRANT RICHARDS, LONDON

Title page
Laugh and Grow | Rich | *By* | Jack Kahane | [device] | London | Grant Richards Ltd. | mdccccxxiii

Collation
8vo. [x] 9–312 + [ii].19.4 × 12.5 cm. All edges trimmed.

Pagination
[i–ii] blank; [iii] half-title; [iv] blank; [v] title-page; [vi] imprimerie: PRINTED IN GREAT BRITAIN BY THE RIVERSIDE PRESS LIMITED | EDINBURGH; [vii] dedication; [viii] blank; [ix–x] contents; 9–312 text; [313–314] blank.

Binding
Blue cloth boards, lettered in black, in a pictorial dustwrapper [not seen].

Front panel: Laugh and | Grow Rich

Spine: Laugh | and | Grow | Rich | Jack | Kahane | Grant | Richards

Rear panel: Blank.

6 James Agate, *Lines of Communication* (Constable, 1917).

Wrapper
Not seen.

Publication
15 March 1923

Notes
First edition. 2040 copies.

Dedication on [vii] reads; 'à ma femme'.

Note at foot of text on [312] reads: LES FOND DES FORÊTS | *May – September 1922*

Laugh and Grow Rich was originally called *Mado VIII*, Mado being the French diminutive for Madeleine. Grant Richards, unhappy with the original title, pressed Kahane for alternatives; when he failed to better his first attempt, Richards came up with *Laugh and Grow Rich*, although Kahane was later to claim it as his own [see C–2(b)].

By late June, 1300 copies of *Laugh and Grow Rich* had been sold, and Richards was anticipating a second edition. The book continued to sell well through the summer. At the end of August, Richards sent Kahane a royalty cheque of £37 3s. 7d., and in the covering letter informed him that he had ordered a second edition of 1000 copies.[7]

(b) LAUGH AND GROW RICH
pub. GRANT RICHARDS, LONDON

Notes
Second edition. 1000 copies.

Not seen: whether or not the book's text is reset is unknown.

(c) LAUGH AND GROW RICH

Third edition.

Title page
Laugh and Grow | Rich | *By* | Jack Kahane | [device] | London | Grant Richards Ltd. | mdccccxxv

Collation
8vo. [x] 9–325 + [v]. 19.4 × 12.5 cm. Edges trimmed.

7 Grant Richards to Kahane, 30 August 1923, Grant Richards archive, BL.

Pagination
[i–ii] blank; [iii] half-title; [iv] blank; [v] title-page; [vi] publishing his-
tory: *First Published ... March 1923* | *Reprinted .... October 1923* | *Reprinted ....*
April 1925, and imprimerie: Printed in Great Britain | by The Riverside
Press Limited | Edinburgh; [vii] dedication; [viii] blank; [ix–x] con-
tents; 9–325 text; [326–330] blank.

Binding
Blue cloth boards, lettered in black.

Front panel: Laugh and | Grow Rich

Spine: Laugh | and | Grow | Rich | Jack | Kahane | Grant | Richards

Rear panel: Blank.

Wrapper
Not seen.

Publication
April 1925

Notes
The text in this edition has been reset, belying the reprint designation on [vi].

(d) LAUGH AND GROW RICH

pub. BRENTANO'S, NEW YORK

Title page
Laugh and Grow | Rich | *By* | Jack Kahane | [publisher's logo] | NEW
YORK | BRENTANO'S | Publishers

Collation
8vo. [xvi] 9–325 + [vii]. 19.8 × 14 cm. Top edge trimmed, others untrimmed.

Pagination
[i–iv] blank; [v] half-title; [vi] blank; [vii] title-page; [viii] copyright,
imprimerie: VAIL-BALLOU COMPANY | BINGHAMTON AND
NEW YORK; [ix] dedication; [x] blank; [xi–xiii] author's preface; [xiv]
blank; [xv–xvi] contents; 9–325 text; [326–332] blank.

Binding
Brown cloth boards, lettered in green, in an illustrated dustwrapper.
Front panel: LAUGH AND | GROW RICH | BY JACK KAHANE

Spine: LAUGH | AND | GROW | RICH | JACK | KAHANE | BREN-TANO'S

Rear panel: Blank.

Wrapper
Front panel: Colour design, signed 'HIGGINS' and continued on to the spine, depicting seven fashionably dressed young women on a pedestal labelling them Mado I, II, and so on, and in the foreground a man in evening dress courting a reluctant eighth. LAUGH AND | GROW RICH | By JACK KAHANE [black on mauve]
Spine: LAUGH AND | GROW RICH | JACK | KAHANE [black on mauve]

Rear panel: White. Title, author, blurb and publisher [see notes].

Front flap: Not seen.

Rear flap: Not seen.

Publication
August 1923

Notes
First US edition.

This edition carries a preface by Kahane, not carried by the first edition, in which he writes: 'Titles are always difficult things to find; they must combine so many different qualities. I eventually chose the present title, because, writing on a bed of sickness, after a war of great length and violence, I somehow felt that if one could manage to laugh just a little in spite of the apparent difficulty in the way of doing so, then all was not lost'. In fact, Kahane chose the present title because he was told to by his publisher, Grant Richards, who had decided that Kahane's original title – *Mado VIII* – would not shift many copies. Asked to come up with alternatives, Kahane offered (among others) *The Happy Fortune Hunters*, *At The Hotel Semlin*, and *Half Past Kissing Time* (which makes one suspect that he may have had a hand in the naming of Princess Paul Troubetzkoy's book, *Half O'Clock in Mayfair* [see A–50]). Unsurprisingly, none of Kahane's suggestions met with Richards' approval. When Kahane suggested *Tripes à la mode de Kahane*, Richards knew it was time to step in. He suggested *Laugh and Grow Rich*, and the matter was settled.

On 18 May 1923 Brentano made an agreement with Richards to publish the book in the United States, intially paying a royalty of ten per cent. By early 1925, 4155 copies of this edition had been sold.

Although the copyright on [viii] is dated [1923], no publication information is given. This omission was corrected in C–2(d) [see below]. One copy located [Cornell].

(d) LAUGH AND GROW RICH
pub. BRENTANO'S, NEW YORK

Title page
Laugh and Grow | Rich | *By* | Jack Kahane | [publisher's logo] | NEW YORK | BRENTANO'S | Publishers

Collation
8vo. [xvi] 9–325 + [vii]. 19.8 × 14 cm. Top edge trimmed, others untrimmed.

Pagination
[i–iv] blank; [v] half-title; [vi] blank; [vii] title-page; [viii] copyright, imprimerie: VAIL-BALLOU PRESS, INC. | BINGHAMTON AND NEW YORK; and publication: First printing, August, 1923 | Second printing, September, 1923; [ix] dedication; [x] blank; [xi–xiii] author's preface; [xiv] blank; [xv–xvi] contents; 9–325 text; [326–332] blank.

Binding
As C–2(c)

Wrapper
Front panel: As C–2(c)

Spine: As C–2(c)

Rear panel: As C–2(c)

Front flap: Blank.

Rear flap: Blank.

Publication
September 1923

Notes
First US edition, second impression.

One copy located in dustwrapper [SIU].

C–3 LOVE'S WILD GEESE
pub. GRANT RICHARDS, LONDON

Title page
Love's | Wild Geese | *By* | Jack Kahane | [publisher's device] | London | Grant Richards Ltd. | St Martin's Street | mdccccxxiv

Collation
8vo. [x] 9–307 + [iii]. 19.2 × 13 cm. Edges trimmed.

Pagination
[i–iv] blank; [v] half-title; [vi] list of previous works; [vii] title-page; [viii] imprimerie: PRINTED IN GREAT BRITAIN BY | THE DUNEDIN PRESS LIMITED, EDINBURGH; [ix] dedication; [x] blank; 9–307 text; [308–310] blank.

Binding
Red cloth boards, lettered in black.

Front panel: Love's | Wild Geese

Spine: Love's | Wild | Geese | Jack | Kahane | Grant | Richards

Rear panel: Blank.

Wrapper
Not seen.

Publication
15 April 1924

Notes
First edition. 2000 copies.

(b) LOVE'S WILD GEESE

Notes
First edition, second impression. 1900 copies.

Not seen.

A letter from Richards to Kahane dated 10 October 1924 states: 'of *Love's Wild Geese* we printed 2,000 to begin with and then 1,900.'[8] Whether these additional copies were a second impression or a second edition is unknown.

C–4 THE GAY INTRIGUE
pub. GRANT RICHARDS, LONDON

Title page
The | Gay Intrigue | *By* | Jack Kahane | [publisher's device] | London | Grant Richards Ltd. | St Martin's Street | mdccccxxv

Collation
8vo. [viii] 7–323 + [iii]. 19.5 × 12.5 cm. Bottom edge rough trimmed. Other edges trimmed.

Pagination
[i–ii] blank; [iii] half-title; [iv] list of previous works; [v] title-page; [vi] copyright; [vii] dedication; [viii] blank; [7–8] contents; 9–323 text; [324–326] blank.

Binding
Orange boards in pictorial wrappers, lettered in black.

Front panel: The Gay Intrigue | by | Jack Kahane

Spine: The | Gay | Intrigue | Jack | Kahane | Grant | Richards

Rear panel: Blank.

Wrapper
Front panel: Three female figures on an orange and black chessboard flooring, in front of an orange background. Two are modish young women in twenties' high fashion; they flank a disguised and elaborately dressed guest at a masked ball. THE GAY INTRIGUE | By JACK KAHANE [black]

Spine: White. THE | GAY | INTRIGUE | By | JACK | KAHANE | Author of | "LAUGH AND | GROW RICH" | 7/6 | net | GRANT | RICHARDS | [remainder of spine unseen] [blue]

Rear panel: White. Blank.

---

8 Grant Richards to Kahane, 10 October 1924, Grant Richards archive, BL.

Publication
29 January 1925

Notes
First edition. 3000 copies.

The dedicatee is Harold Brighouse, Kahane's friend from his Manchester days, and the author of *Hobson's Choice*.

The SIU copy of this title is inscribed on the day of publication by Kahane on the title-page: 'To Virginia | (Many happy returns of the day) | from Jack Kahane . | 29. I . 25 '. A copy of *Lycidas* [see A–24] is dedicated to Virginia Vernon.

Laid in to the Bodleian copy is a yellow flyer, printed on one side only, advertising Grant Richards' new novel *Every Wife*.

C–5 THE VAIN SERENADE
pub. CONSTABLE, LONDON

Title page
THE VAIN | SERENADE | BY | JACK KAHANE | LONDON | CONSTABLE & CO. LTD.

Collation
8vo. [x] 5–320 + [ii]. 19.5 × 12.6 cm. Lower edge rough trimmed, other edges trimmed.

Pagination
[i–iv] blank; [v] half-title; [vi] list of previous works; [vii] title-page; [viii] imprimerie: Printed in Great Britain at | *The Mayflower Press, Plymouth*. William Brendon & Son, Ltd.; and publication: *First published 1926*; [ix] dedication; [x] blank; 5–320 text; [321–322] blank.

Binding
Grey boards, bordered in black on front panel and spine, lettered in black.

Front panel: Two further black lines running vertically and enclosing text. THE [diamond device] VAIN | SERENADE | *By* JACK | KAHANE

Spine: Two further black lines running horizontally and enclosing text. THE VAIN | SERENADE | [diamond device] | JACK | KAHANE | CONSTABLE | [diamond device]

Rear panel: Blank.

The Bodleian copy is in a variant binding: blue boards, bordered in grey on front panel and spine, with text and devices also in grey.

Wrapper
Front panel: Coloured illustration of two young women, one standing and holding a palette and brushes, the other reclining on a chaise longue, smoking a cigarette in a holder. The | Vain Serenade | by | Jack | Kahane [red, bordered in white]

[Spine, rear panel and flaps not seen.]

Publication
February 1926

Notes
First edition.

Marcelle Kahane submitted designs for the book's dustwrapper. Jack suggested five guineas would be a fair price; Constable declined the offer.

The book is dedicated to Hinemoa and Vaughan Thomas. Thomas was 'a wartime friend. Thomas's charming wife was an excellent artist, and her two portraits of my wife and me were hung in the 1926 *Salon* and favourably noticed.'

The front panel of the dustwrapper on the SIU copy has survived [see above] but no complete wrapper has been located.

C-6 THE PURE IN HEART
pub. BRENTANO'S, LONDON

Title page
The Pure in Heart | By | JACK KAHANE | *"Tout importe et il importe de tout chanter."* | P. DRIEU LA ROCHELLE | [publisher's device] [red] | BRENTANO'S, LTD. | NEW YORK LONDON PARIS

Collation
8vo. [xii] 3–280 + [ii]. 18.8 × 12.7 cm. Edges trimmed.

Pagination
[i–ii] blank; [iii] half-title; [iv] list of previous works; [v] title-page; [vi] imprimerie: PRINTED IN GREAT BRITAIN BY FURNELL AND

SONS | PAULTON (SOMERSET) AND LONDON; and publication: *First published*, 1928; [vii] dedication; [viii] blank; [ix] contents; [x] blank; [xi] section heading; [xii] blank; 3–280 text; [281–282] blank.

Binding
Brown boards, stamped in gilt.

Front panel: The Pure in Heart | Jack Kahane

Spine: The Pure | in | Heart | [dot] | Jack | Kahane | BRENTANO'S

Rear panel: Blank.

Wrapper
Not seen.

Publication
1928

Notes
First edition.

When Kahane sent his agent the manuscript for this book it had the title *Trot Trot to Market*. Pinker hated it, and said so in a letter to Kahane dated 4 June 1926:

> Dear Kahane,
>
> I am in a real difficulty. 'Trot Trot' has disappointed me badly and I hardly know how to say so. Candidly the work will do both you and us harm if it appears as it is at present; and the trouble seems to me too deep for adjustment within the framework of what is already written.
>
> I suspect that you will smile when I say the tone of the book is too French for this market. But it is nevertheless true. The incidents are not too strong nor the language more definite than those of many novels published here; but there is a detachment about the whole presentment of the thing – a sort of indifference to the personalities of the characters – that is utterly foreign to the English novel and, so far as I can judge, characteristic of much French fiction.
>
> This in itself would not matter, were it not that this quality of French fiction is the quality most displeasing to the average English novel-reader. He – or rather she – insists (most of her insistencies have gone by the board but this remains) on a sympathetic character somewhere among the leading persons of a tale. Now in 'Trot Trot' there is no sympathetic character. Your personal contempt for them all is rather pleasing to me, partly because I share it, partly because I like French novels well enough to appreciate skilful adoption of a foreign mode by an English writer.

But I am a highbrow (so they say) and wholly untypical of the library subscriber's mentality (which, indeed, I rather hope to be the case). I do, however, know enough of that mentality to be able to guess with a fair degree of certainty how 'Trot Trot' will appeal to them. And it won't. At least that is my reluctant judgment.

Now we have not had much luck with <u>The Vain Serenade</u>. It is more than £100 off having earned its advance. 'TROT TROT' will come into being with no big success behind it, and I am sure it will crash even more disastrously.

I can't tell you how it distresses me to have to say all this. But I promised to be candid and must be so. I wish I could see you and hear what you yourself feel about the book so far as it has gone. Are you satisfied that it has depth as well as freshness of ornament? Do you <u>know</u> Orient and the Duke and Cheam? I can grasp Carrie. She is a character. But I have no vision of the rest.

[Ends, unsigned.] [9]

Kahane spent the next two years rewriting *The Pure in Heart*, working on translations, and writing short stories for weekly fiction magazines to make ends meet. He also wrote *Suzy Falls Off* with the intention of having it published pseudonymously. In the meantime, Pinker had secured for his client a three-book deal with Brentano's, and *The Pure in Heart* became their first Kahane publication.

The final title for the book was probably lifted from Joseph Kessel, whose *Princes of the Night* was published in an English translation by Kahane in 1928. Also in 1928, Kessel's novel *L' Equipage* [Gallimard, Paris, 1924] and his collection of stories *Les Coeurs Purs* [Gallimard, Paris, 1927] were published in one English-language volume by Gollancz under the title *The Pure In Heart*. The translator for the Gollancz edition is not named.

(b) THE PURE IN HEART

Publication
June 1930

Notes
?First edition, second impression.

Not seen, but recorded in the English Catalogue of Books, 1926–30.

9 J. R. Pinker to Kahane, 1 June 1926, Berg collection, NYPL.

'Cheaper edition' (3s. 6d.), with the same number of pages as C-6, suggesting no resetting of the text.

C-7 THE BROWSING GOAT
pub. BRENTANO'S, LONDON

Title page
THE | BROWSING GOAT | *A BUCOLIC* | by | JACK KAHANE | BRENTANO'S LTD. | NEW YORK LONDON PARIS

Collation
8vo. [viii] 7–288 + [ii]. 18.8 × 12.3 cm. Edges trimmed.

Pagination
[i–ii] blank; [iii] half-title; [iv] list of previous works; [v] title-page; [vi] imprimerie: *Printed in Great Britian by Ebenezer Baylis & Son, Ltd., The Trinity Press,* | *Worcester.;* [vii] dedication; [viii] blank; 7–288 text; [289–290] blank.

Binding
Brown boards, stamped in gilt, in a pictorial wrapper.
Front panel: THE | BROWSING GOAT | JACK KAHANE
Spine: THE | BROWSING | GOAT | JACK | KAHANE | BRENTANO'S
Rear panel: Blank.

Wrapper
Not seen, but probably as C–7(b).

Publication
June 1929

Notes
First edition. 2000 copies.

A version of this book was complete by November 1928, when Kahane wrote to his agent: 'I hope the M.S. of The Browsing Goat will not be too long at the typist's as I am very keen on having publication in January.'[10] In a letter to his agent dated 10 October 1930, Kahane wrote: 'I can pretty safely state that of The Browsing Goat [the publisher] made a first printing of two thousand copies, and before going to

10 Kahane to J. R. Pinker, 10 November 1928, Berg collection, NYPL.

press he ordered another 1500'. [11]

The Browsing Goat was written around the time that Kahane met Henri Babou, who would shortly become his partner in his first foray into the publishing business. The book is a half-hearted, lifeless bucolic set in and around a fictionalised version of Kahane's local inn in Rozoy-en-Multien, and shows every sign of having been written by an author with other things on his mind – and one keen to be free as soon as possible from a three-book contractual obligation to his publisher.

(b) THE BROWSING GOAT
pub. BRENTANO'S, LONDON

Title page
As C–7.

Collation
8vo. [viii] 7–288 + [ii]. 18.8 × 12.3 cm. Edges trimmed.

Pagination
[i–ii] blank; [iii] half-title; [iv] list of previous works; [v] title-page; [vi] publication: *First published – June,* 1929 | *Reprinted – – June,* 1929; [vii] dedication; [viii] blank; 7–288 text; [289–290] blank.

Binding
Blue boards, stamped in black, in a pictorial wrapper.

Front panel: THE | BROWSING GOAT | JACK KAHANE

Spine: THE | BROWSING | GOAT | JACK | KAHANE | BRENTANO

Rear panel: Blank.

Wrapper
Front panel: Coloured illustration, on a cream background, of the interior of a rural inn. THE | BROWSING | GOAT | BY JACK KAHANE

Spine: Cream. THE | BROWSING | GOAT | JACK | KAHANE | [illustration of the inn's sign [see notes]] | BRENTANO'S

Rear panel: White. Long puff for Kahane's The Pure In Heart [see C–6], publisher's name and address at foot, and imprimerie: Ducros et Colas, Paris

11 Kahane to Eric S. Pinker, Berg collection, NYPL.

Front flap: White. Blank, save for price in lower right-hand corner enclosed by a black diagonal line: 7/6 net

Rear flap: White. Blank.

Publication
June 1929

Notes
First edition, second impression. 1500 copies.

The first line of copy on the rear panel of the wrapper reads: *BY THE SAME AUTOR*. There is also a dropped full stop at the end of the blurb.

The wrapper is designed by Kahane's wife Marcelle, and bears her initials in the bottom right-hand corner.

The last page of text [288] gives the time and place of the book's completion: Le Fond Des Forêts, 1928/1929. Le Fond Des Forêts was the family home for most of the 1920s, in the village of Rozoy-en-Multien, forty miles from Paris. The village inn, Maurice Girodias later recalled, was called The Browsing Goat: 'But before you step in, just have a look above the door at the hanging signboard: It is my mother who painted that white goat in a flowery field.'[12]

The signboard's design is replicated on the spine of the book's wrapper.

(c) THE BROWSING GOAT

Publication
June 1930

Notes
?First edition, third impression

Not seen, but recorded in the English Catalogue of Books, 1926–30. 'Cheaper edition' (3s. 6d.), with the same number of pages as C–7, suggesting no resetting of the text.

12 Girodias, *Frog Prince*, p. 35.

C–8 SUZY FALLS OFF

pub. JOHN LONG, LONDON

Title page
SUZY FALLS OFF | By | CECIL BARR | [logo] | London | John Long, Ltd | 34, 35 & 36 Paternoster Row | [All Rights Reserved]

Collation
8vo. [x] 11–253 + [viii]. 19 × 12.5 cm. Edges trimmed.

Pagination
[i–ii] blank; [iii] half-title; [iv] blank; [v] title-page; [vi] dedication; [vii] contents; [viii] copyright and imprimerie: Northumberland Press Ltd., Thornton Street, Newcastle-on-Tyne; [ix] prologue; [x] blank; 11–253 text; [254–258] blank.

Binding
Red coarse-grain cloth boards, lettered in black.

Front panel: Blank.

Spine: SUZY | FALLS OFF | CECIL | BARR | John Long

Rear panel: Blank.

Wrapper
Unseen in its entirety, but the copy in the National Library of Scotland has a portion of the front panel pasted in, showing a young woman sitting at a dressing table, and a window giving on to a starry sky.

Publication
1928

Notes
First edition.

According to correspondence between Kahane and his literary agent J. R. Pinker [Berg collection, NYPL], Kahane had submitted the manuscript of *Suzy Falls Off* by the end of 1926. References to [Michael] Sadleir suggest that Kahane and Pinker were looking to place the book with Constable. Nothing came of this, or of Kahane's attempts to have the book issued with illustrations, presumably supplied as usual by his wife. In April 1927 Pinker was still struggling to place the book, and Kahane wrote to him suggesting that if all else failed he should try Edward Titus, of the Black Manikin Press in Paris. (It's unlikely that Titus, a publisher of high-brow literature in small, expensive editions, was aware of this idea, and it's even more unlikely that he would have thought it a good one.) By the autumn of that year the book had been placed with John Long and proofs were expected by the end of December, making it reasonable to suppose that publication followed in the early part of 1928.

(b) SUZY FALLS OFF
pub. ALBERT AND CHARLES BONI

Title page
SUZY FALLS OFF | *By* | CECIL BARR | [publishers' device] | NEW YORK | ALBERT AND CHARLES BONI | 1929

Collation
8vo. [xii] 11–285 + [v]. 19.3 × 13 cm. Edges trimmed. Top edge stained green.

Pagination
[i–ii] blank; [iii] half-title; [iv] blank; [v] title-page; [vi] copyright; [vii] dedication; [viii] blank; [ix] contents; [x] blank; [xi] prologue; [xii] blank; 12–285 text; [286–290] blank.

Binding
Orange boards.

Front panel: SUZY | FALLS OFF [black]

Spine: SUZY | FALLS | OFF | BARR [black, enclosed in black box] | ALBERT | & | CHARLES | BONI [orange on black square]

Rear panel: Blank.

Wrapper
[Second printing].

Front panel: White. Illustration of would-be lover of protesting woman being forced at gunpoint from her bed by her husband [yellow, red and black]. SUZY | FALLS OFF [red] | BY | CECIL BARR [yellow]

Spine: Red with white diamonds. SUZY | FALLS | OFF [red] | BARR [black, enclosed in yellow box] | ALBERT | & | CHARLES | BONI [white, enclosed in yellow box]

Rear panel: White. Title, author and blurb for the book: *Second Printing* [black, enclosed in yellow border]

Front flap: Title, price [$2.00] and seven titles from the publisher's list, with blurbs.

Rear flap: Puff for *Chéri*, by Colette.

Publication
1929

Notes
Second edition. First US edition.

First printing wrapper not seen.

In a letter of 9 November 1933 to the wife of William Bradley, Kahane notes that this edition 'was not a spectacular success.'[13]

(c) SUZY FALLS OFF

Notes
Third edition. First Obelisk edition [see A–9].

(d) SUSI RUTSCHT AUS
pub. AMONESTA-VERLAG

Title page
CECIL BARR | SUSI RUTSCHT AUS | ROMAN | [publisher's device] | AMONESTA-VERLAG | WIEN BERLIN LEIPZIG

Collation
16mo. [vi] 7–286 + [ii]. 16.5 × 10.5 cm. All edges trimmed, possibly cropped [see notes].

Pagination
[i] half-title; [ii] blank; [iii] title-page; [iv] copyright; [v] translator's credit; [vi] blank; 7–286 text; [287–288] list of chapter headings.

Binding
Paper pictorial wrappers.

Front panel: Colour illustration of a young woman standing on a

13 Bradley archive, HRC.

hillock, trying to pull her too-short skirt down to her knees. Cecil Barr: | Kart, M 3 [green] | Susi rütscht aus [white]

Spine: Not seen [see notes].

Rear panel: Critics' puffs for other Amonesta-Verlag books, bordered in red.

Publication
1931

Notes
Fourth edition. First German edition.

Although Kahane claims in his memoir that his books were translated into several languages, this is one of only two examples located [see also A 8(g)].

Two copies located [Austrian National Library [not seen] and Deutsche National Bibliothek [rebound with the original wrappers bound in, and probably cropped]].

C–9 IT'S HARD TO SIN!
by CECIL BARR [JACK KAHANE]

Title page
It's Hard to Sin! | By Cecil Barr | Author of "Daffodil" | [publisher's logo] | NEW YORK | GREENBURG : PUBLISHER

Collation
8vo. [viii] 1–248 + [ii]. 19.3 × 13.5 cm. Fore-edge rough trimmed, others trimmed, with top edge stained black.

Pagination
[i–ii] blank; [iii] blurb from front flap of wrapper; [iv] blank; [v] title-page; [vi] copyright; [vii] half-title; [viii] blank; 1–248 text; [249–250] blank.

Binding
Tan coarse-grained cloth boards in an illustrated wrapper, lettered in red.

Front panel: Smoke from a cigarette drifting through title. IT'S HARD TO | SIN!

Spine: IT'S | HARD | TO | SIN! | BARR | [publisher's logo] | GREEN-BURG

Rear panel: Blank

Wrapper
Front panel: Colour illustration, extending to spine, of a smoking woman in evening dress. IT'S HARD TO | SIN! [red, bordered in green] | *by* [red] | CECIL BARR [green]

Spine: IT'S | HARD | TO | SIN! [red, bordered in green] | CECIL BARR [green] | [publisher's logo] | GREENBURG [white]

Rear panel: White. Full-page advertisement for *Little Known Facts About Well Known People* by Dale Carnegie [black, boxed in black double lines]

Publication
1935

Notes
First edition.

The only Cecil Barr title not to be published by the Obelisk Press.

(b) ANY MAN'S WOMAN (IT'S HARD TO SIN!)

Title page
ANYBODIES | WOMAN | (It's Hard to Sin) | A Thrilling Romance | by | CECIL BARR | A UNIVERSAL ROMANCE BOOK | Published by Universal Publishing | and Distributing Corp. | New York, N. Y. | Manufactured in U. S. A.

Collation
8vo. [ii] 5–130. 19 × 14 cm. Edges trimmed.

Pagination
[i] title-page; [ii] copyright and dedication; 5–130 text.

Binding
Illustrated paper wrappers.

Front panel: Colour illustration of a blowsy, smoking redhead. THE INTIMATE STORY OF AN AVENGEFUL | WIFE WHO WANTED TO BE... [white] | ANY MAN'S WOMAN [yellow] | 35c | Formerly published | at $2.50 [white]

Spine: White. ANY MAN'S WOMAN [black, printed horizontally, top to bottom]

Rear panel: White. Title [red] and blurb [black, continuing on inside back cover]. Blue vertical line to left, broken by title.

Publication
1951

Notes
Second edition. First Canadian edition.

Shoddy reprint, almost opulent in its cheapness. The title page manages not only to misprint the original title (no exclamation mark) but also to misspell a wrong version of the new one. The front cover chips in with a word that doesn't exist, and despite the claim on the title page the book was published not in the United States, but in Winnipeg, Canada. A masterpiece of tat.

C–10 SHORT FICTION

(a) FACE VALUES

Publication
Pan: The Fiction Magazine, April 1924

Notes
Kahane sent the manuscript to his agent, Pinker, in February 1924, offering to write more stories around the central character if his agent thought there was a market for them. None has been located.

(b) THE COURSE OF TRUE LOVE

Publication
Woman, November 1924

Notes
Sent to Pinker on 25 April 1924. Kahane's subsequent correspondence shows that he had still not been paid for the story by January the following year.

(c) THE CLOCK: A STORY OF THE UNEXPECTED

Publication
Wheatsheaf: The Cooperative Wholesale Magazine, November 1925

Notes
Pinker had sold the story to *Wheatsheaf* by June 1925: in a letter of the 19th Kahane confesses: 'This is ths first time I have heard of this paper.'

(d) DEFEAT

Publication
Sunday Chronicle, 13 June 1926

Notes
This 200-word quip was first sent to the *London Mail*, which accepted it but then went out of business before it could be published.

(e) CONSTANCY

Publication
Passing Show, 28 August 1926

Notes
The publishers of *Passing Show* were Odhams', to whom Kahane had been introduced by Harold Brighouse. Kahane began sending short stories to them directly. *Constancy* is a humorous piece occupying familiar Kahane territory: the would-be romantic Englishman let loose in Paris, who is brought face to face with his own naivety, and who is frustrated by the delights of 'the modern Babylon' that always stay tantalisingly just out of reach. Having tried and failed to find an audience for his more serious writing, Kahane now resolved to write nothing but froth. At the time of *Constancy's* acceptance Kahane made his disillusionment clear in a letter to Pinker: 'These stories are in a new and trivial style for me at which I am working pretty hard, and I hope that once I have got going you will be able to place some in other papers. Evidently no living is to be made out of writing novels, and we have had singularly little success with the stories I have hitherto submitted to you. There may (I hope there will) be

something to be made out of the so-called humorous stories I am cultivating at present.'[14]

(f) IN THE KITCHEN: A STORY OF WASTED ENTERPRISE

Publication
Wheatsheaf: The Cooperative Wholesale Magazine, October 1926

Notes
Submitted to Pinker in April 1926 and published by *The Wheatsheaf* in October that year, having been rejected by *Passing Show.*

(g) FISHY

Publication
Wheatsheaf: The Cooperative Wholesale Magazine, April 1927

Notes
A joke spun out to the length of a saleable short story. Albert Rodd is a fishmonger. He falls in love with Angelina, a vegetarian. When she discovers his profession she breaks off the relationship: she can have nothing to do with someone who deals in dead animals. Lovestruck Albert pines for his lost love, and changes jobs in an attempt to win her back. When Albert tells Angelina that he is no longer a fishmonger but is now working for the Balkan Machine-Gun and Ammunition Supply Co. Ltd., she welcomes him back with open arms.

(h) THE AMULET

Publication
Hutchinson's Magazine, August 1927

Notes
A story much like Kahane himself: long and thin. After a period of conscientious application during which Kahane tried to write good stories carefully tailored to the magazine for which they were intended, financial necessity clearly got the better of him: stories seem to have been churned out as fast as he could type them, and any

14 Kahane to J. B. Pinker, 12 April 1926, Berg collection, NYPL.

magazine prepared to pay for them would do. This one was published by *Hutchinson's Magazine* in August 1927, although it had been sent to Pinker in November 1925. Kahane's financial situation and attitude to what he had come to see as hack work were made clear in a letter to his agent in January 1927: 'I suppose you had better accept Hutchinsons' miserly offer, especially as I can't for the life of me remember which it is for. If it is a "short" the pay is not too bad for the work involved; but if it is for a long story it looks like profiteering on the part of Hutchinsons'. However, pretty well anything is worth while from the point of view of publicity.'[15]

(i) TO SETTLE THE MATTER

Publication
Wheatsheaf: The Cooperative Wholesale Magazine, September 1927

Notes
More polished than usual, and with a suggestion that Kahane might have been reading some of Wodehouse's golfing stories at the time he wrote this one. With both *The Pure in Heart* and *Suzy Falls Off* about to be published, and with a contract with Brentano's in the United States being drawn up, it's probable that by this time Kahane was writing more out of desire than need, with a resulting upturn in quality.

(j) BARRING MIRACLES

Publication
Wheatsheaf: The Cooperative Wholesale Magazine, October 1928

Notes
Features the same principal characters as C–10(i). Apparently the last piece of short fiction Kahane published before devoting his time to publishing, and to producing the novels of 'Cecil Barr'.

15 Kahane to J. R. Pinker, 21 January 1927, Berg collection, NYPL.

C–11 MEMOIRS OF A BOOKLEGGER
pub. MICHAEL JOSEPH, LONDON

Title page
JACK KAHANE | [asterisk] | Memoirs of a | Booklegger | [publisher's logo] | MICHAEL JOSEPH LTD. | *26, Bloomsbury Street, London, W. C. 1*

Collation
8vo. [viii] 7–287 text + [iii]. 22.3 × 14.4 cm. Edges trimmed.

Pagination
[i–ii] blank yellow endpaper; [iii] half-title; [iv] blank; [v] title-page; [vi] imprimerie and publication: FIRST PUBLISHED IN 1939; [vii] dedication; [viii] blank; 7–278 text; [279–287] index; [288] blank; [289–290] blank yellow endpaper.

Binding
Blue cloth boards, stamped in silver, in a white wrapper.

Front panel: Blank.

Spine: JACK | KAHANE [boxed in silver] | Memoirs | of a | Booklegger [boxed in silver] | [publisher's logo] | MICHAEL | JOSEPH

Rear panel: Blank.

Wrapper
Front panel: Memoirs of | a Booklegger [red] | [photographic portrait of Kahane] | JACK KAHANE [initials in red, name in black]

Spine: Memoirs | of a | Booklegger [red] | [asterisk] | JACK | KAHANE [black] | [publisher's logo] | MICHAEL | JOSEPH

Rear panel: List of eleven new titles from the publisher's list.

Front flap: Lengthy blurb, continuing on to the rear flap. Price [12/6 net].

Rear flap: Continuation of blurb.

Publication
1939

Notes
First edition.

On 10 February 1939 *Memoirs of a Booklegger* was sent to Knopf for possible publication in the United States. The manuscript, at the time bearing the title *Paris, French for Freedom*, was rejected on 1 March. The reader's report commented: 'This is a perfectly readable performance, and I should think quite publishable except for the glut of auto-biographies of contemporary writers on the market.'[16]

16 C. Abbott, 15 February 1939, Knopf archive, NYPL.

D Items

Translations by Jack Kahane

D–1 PRINCES OF THE NIGHT

by JOSEPH KESSEL
pub. THE RICHARDS PRESS, LONDON

Title page
PRINCES OF | THE NIGHT | By | JOSEPH KESSEL | Translated by |
JACK KAHANE | [logo] | LONDON | THE RICHARDS PRESS LTD. |
PUBLISHERS

Collation
8vo. [x] 9–320 + [xxii]. 19.7 × 13 cm. Edges trimmed, top edge stained
green.

Pagination
[i–iv] blank; [v] half-title; [vi] blank; [vii] title-page; [viii] imprimerie:
PRINTED IN GREAT BRITAIN BY | M. P. ROBINSON & CO. LTD. AT
THE LIBRARY PRESS LOWESTOFT; [ix] section heading; [x] blank;
9–320 text; [321–339] publisher's advertisements, dated on [321] Autumn
1928 and [323–339] paginated 3–19; [340–342] blank.

Binding
Green boards, lettered in black.

Front panel: Princes of the Night

Spine: PRINCES | OF THE | NIGHT | JOSEPH | KESSEL

Rear panel: Blank.

Wrapper
Front panel: Blue, with pictorial central panel, bordered in dark blue,
depicting a solitary woman with dancing couples in the background.
Illustration is signed M. Leone. PRINCES OF THE NIGHT [dark blue]
| [illustration] | by JOSEPH KESSEL [dark blue] ['OF' printed above
'THE' in title]

Spine: White. PRINCES | OF THE | NIGHT | JOSEPH | KESSEL | Trans-
lated by | JACK KAHANE | [logo] | RICHARDS [blue]

Rear panel: White. Advertisement for five forthcoming Richards
Press titles [blue]

Front flap: Title, author blurb and price [7/6].

Rear flap: Blank.

Publication
1928

Notes
First English edition.

Precedence between this title and D–1(b) is not known.

(b) PRINCES OF THE NIGHT

pub. THE MACAULAY COMPANY, NEW YORK

Title page
PRINCES OF | THE NIGHT | BY | JOSEPH KESSEL | *Translated by* | JACK KAHANE | NEW YORK | THE MACAULAY COMPANY | PUBLISHERS

Collation
8vo. [viii] 7–288 + [ii]. 19.6 × 13.3 cm. Top edge trimmed, others untrimmed.

Pagination
[i–ii] blank; [iii] half-title; [iv] blank; [v] title-page; [vi] copyright; [vii] section heading; [viii] blank; 7–288 text; [289–290] blank.

Binding
Black boards.

Front panel: Russian cityscape on lower half, continuing on spine [lilac]. PRINCES | OF THE | NIGHT | BY | JOSEPH KESSEL [lilac]

Spine: PRINCES | OF THE | NIGHT [black, enclosed in lilac box] | BY | JOSEPH | KESSEL [lilac] | MACAULAY [black on lilac]

Rear panel: Blank.

Wrapper
Front panel: Illustration, continuing on spine, of four men in evening dress and four dressed as cossacks at head and foot, and a dancing girl with a samovar behind her at centre. PRINCES | OF/THE | NIGHT [black and red on white] | BY JOSEPH KESSEL [black on white]

Spine: PRINCES | OF THE | NIGHT | BY | JOSEPH | KESSEL | MACAULAY [black on white]

Rear panel: White. Three titles (including this one), with blurbs.

Front flap: Title, author, blurb and price [$2.00].

Rear flap: Puff for *The Laslett Affair*, by 'A Gentleman with a Duster'.

Publication
1928

Notes
First US edition.

Dropped 'l' from 'alcoholic' in l. 9 of the blurb on the wrapper's front flap.

D–2 THE VIRGIN MAN
by MARCEL PREVOST
pub. SHAYLOR

Title page
THE VIRGIN MAN | *By* | MARCEL PREVOST | *Translated by* | JACK KAHANE | ⌊publisher's logo⌋ | SHAYLOR | GOWER STREET | LONDON | W. C. | 1

Collation
8vo. [BL copy rebound, and possibly cropped] [??] 7–299 + [??]. 17.5 × 12 cm. Edges trimmed.

Pagination
[??]; [i] half-title; [ii] blank; [iii] title-page; [iv] imprimerie: *Made and printed in Great Britain by Ebenezer Baylis and Son, Limited | The Trinity Press, Worcester, for Harold Shaylor, Limited, London | and bound by G. and J. Kitcat, Limited, London*; and publication: *First published – September* 1930; [v] section heading; [vi] blank; 7–299 text; [300–302] blank; [??].

Binding
Not seen.

Wrapper
Not seen.

Publication
September 1930

Notes
Third edition. First edition in English.

First published in Paris as *L'Homme Vierge* [Les Editions de France, 1920].

[311]

Reprinted by the same publisher in 1929. An illustrated edition was published in Paris in 1930 as part of the series *Le Livre Moderne Illustré*.

(b) RESTLESS SANDS

pub. SEARS PUBLISHING COMPANY, NEW YORK

Title page
A NOVEL BY MARCEL PRÉVOST | RESTLESS | SANDS | Translated from the French by | JACK KAHANE | [publisher's device] | Sears Publishing Company, Inc. | New York

Collation
8vo. [xiii] 1–297 + [vii]. 19.5 × 13.5 cm. Top edge trimmed, leading edge untrimmed, bottom edge rough trimmed.

Pagination
[i–iv] blank; [v] half-title; [vi] blank; [vii] title-page; [viii] copyright; [ix] anonymous quotation; [x] blank; [xi] section heading; [xii] blank; 1–297 text; [298–304] blank.

Binding
Black cloth boards.

Front panel: Title and author in white rectangles, boxed in black. RESTLESS | SANDS [black on white] | [silhouette of woman in profile] [black and white] | MARCEL PREVOST [black on white]

Spine: RESTLESS | SANDS | PREVOST | SEARS [white on black]

Rear panel: Blank.

Wrapper
Not seen.

Publication
1931

Notes
First US edition, retitled.

[For details of Kahane's work as translator on Obelisk Press titles, see A–2, A–5, A–13, and A–15.]

Author Biographies

RICHARD ALDINGTON

Information about the Kahane and Babou edition of Richard Aldington's *Death of a Hero* is difficult to come by – which is strange, since everybody involved seems to have had reasons to be cheerful when the book first appeared. For Kahane, who in 1930 was still in partnership with Henri Babou, *Death of a Hero* was one of the first books he published that is of unassailable literary merit, and his pride in securing it for his fledgling company shows in the book's production values: two handsome volumes in two separate issues, the signed edition printed on Japon paper with a retail price of ten guineas, both issues protected by a glassine tissue wrapper and sheathed in a marbled chemise and slipcase. If this wasn't enough in itself to please Aldington he could also reflect on the fact that, while the book is not the full text (despite its claim to be unexpurgated) it was certainly a far more complete version than those which had appeared in Britain and the United States the year before. Yet everyone involved seems to have pretended that the edition never happened. An ex-soldier himself, Kahane the publisher always looked kindly on books which took war as their theme; further, his memoir takes obvious pride in the rare occasions he managed to recruit literary heavyweights such as Miller or Joyce to the Obelisk list. But here is a war novel by an established literary name, and neither Aldington nor his book rates a mention in *Memoirs of a Booklegger*. For his part Aldington is equally reticent: neither he nor his biographers seem ever to have felt the need to give anything more than a cursory bibliographical mention to the Paris edition of *Death of a Hero*, despite the fact that no more complete version of the text became available until the Consul edition appeared in England thirty-five years later in 1965 – the first truly unexpurgated edition.

Babou and Kahane's edition of *Death of a Hero* claims to be the full text, a claim lazily repeated by bibliographers, book dealers and auction houses whenever the book is discussed. It's not true. The book was first published simultaneously – and heavily cut – in 1929, by Chatto and Windus in England, and by Covici, Friede in the United States. The more extensive cuts made to the English edition show a publishing industry running scared after the prosecution of *Sleeveless Errand* and *The Well of Loneliness*; with *Death of a Hero* Chatto and Windus did the Home Secretary's work for him, voluntarily deleting not only all references to sex but also the caustic criticism of the prosecution of the war by England's ruling elite that was allowed to stand in the American version. Aldington was amazed that the book was considered unpublishable in full, but sanguine: 'I don't in the least blame [the publishers], they are only doing what I should do in their positions, i.e. trying to guard themselves against the working of a law which is vaguely worded and capriciously administered'.[1] For the American edition he wrote the following note:

> This novel in print differs in some particulars from the same work in manuscript. To my astonishment, my publishers informed me that certain words, phrases, sentences, and even passages, are at present illegal in the United States. I have recorded nothing which I have not observed in human life, said nothing I do not believe to be true; and I had not the slightest intention of appealing to anyone's salacious instincts. My theme was too seriously tragic for that. But I am bound to accept the advice of those who know the Law concerning the published word. I have therefore asked my publishers to delete everything they consider objectionable, and to substitute asterisks for every word deleted. I would rather have my book mutilated than say what I do not believe.
>
> En attendant mieux,
>
> R. A.
>
> P. S. I feel bound to add, in justice, that the expurgations required in the United States are much fewer and shorter that those demanded in England.[2]

At Aldington's insistence, neither the American nor the English editors used an arbitrary configuration of asterisks to denote cuts made to the text. Instead they replaced, say, a five-letter word with a run of five asterisks, a two-letter word with two, and so on.[3] This technique gives a determined reader with enough time on his hands a fighting chance of working out what has been excised from the book, which presumably was Aldington's intention. In the copy of the American edition inscribed to the writer John Cournos, now in the collection of the New York Public Library, Aldington has written in the expurgated words and phrases alongside the printed asterisks. Working from this copy, it is possible to test the 'unexpurgated' claims of all subsequent editions. The deletions, according to Aldington, were as follows:

i) p. 42: 'Come and see the fucking. Come and see the fucking.'

ii) p. 43: 'he had not the faintest idea how to postpone conception or that it might be well not to impregnate a virgin bride, indeed neither he nor Isobel had ever heard of such things: he did not know what was implied by "a normal sexual life"; he did not know that women can and should have orgasms: he did not know that to break a hymen violently and clumsily gives pain and so serious a shock that a woman may be for ever frigid with and repelled by the man who does it...'

iii) p. 64: 'Take care of your penis, and your life will take care of itself.'

iv) p. 97: 'Unconsciously he had thrown a leg on to her two legs as she lay on her back. Quite suddenly she opened her knees, and gave a sort of little moan.'

v) p. 119: 'Balls!'

vi) p. 127: 'Cold-hearted, cold-bollocked mingy sneaks!'

vii) p.127: 'Mingy, cold-hearted screwing!'

viii) p. 136: 'she who guides the slim eager ploughshare into the soft open welcoming furrow;'

ix) p. 243: 'Bloody old cunt.' (For some reason the noun in this phrase is not asterisked in the Covici, Friede edition, as the other deletions are. Instead, it is printed 'c ------'. The mind of a censor is a mysterious thing.)

x) p. 351: 'Balls!'

The Cournos copy reveals occasional discrepancies between Aldington's recollection of his text and the manuscript from which the typesetters worked. On p. 64 of the American edition, for example, Aldington's autograph annotation in the Cournos copy includes two uses of the phrase 'take care' where both the asterisk configuration and later, unexpurgated, editions of the book suggest the phrase should be 'look after.' Either Aldington's memory was faulty, or he was working from a different version of the manuscript to the one the printers used when he annotated Cournos' copy. (Or perhaps he was simply keener to restore the sense of the excised passages for his friend than to make the job of future bibliographers an easy one.)

All of the above deletions are made in the English edition, in many cases more extensively – in (ii), for example, the phrase 'he did not know that women have periods' is also excised. In addition, sideswipes at the hypocrisy and prudishness of British society and its media are removed (thereby proving Aldington's point) as well as all references to 'pupping' and 'intimate rubber goods', and the likening of Queen Victoria to a 'prehistoric beast'.

While the Babou and Kahane edition restores all the cuts made to the English and American editions, it is not the full text: as in the English edition, the word 'fuck' and its derivatives is softened to 'muck', 'mucker', 'mucking' etc. (Strangely, the word 'cunt' is printed in full.) All of which means that the first edition to print the whole text was the Consul edition, published in England in 1965 – thirty-six years after Aldington first handed the manuscript to his publisher.

How Babou and Kahane came to publish the book at all is unclear, but Kahane and Aldington had plenty of opportunity to run into each other, not least through their shared literary agency, James Pinker and Sons. *Death of a Hero* was Aldington's first novel. Until 1929 he'd been known primarily as a poet, one of the co-founders of the Imagist movement with Ezra Pound and Hilda Doolittle, the poet H. D., whom Aldington married in 1913. Imagists rejected the florid romanticism of their contemporaries, the Georgians, favouring instead a lean and literal verse whose articles of faith were promulgated in the movement's house journal, *The Egoist*, co-edited by Aldington from 1914 until 1917. But poets, even movement-leading ones, tend not to have agents, and Aldington didn't sign with Pinker's until 1930, by which time they had been representing Kahane for the best part of a decade. In 1930 Kahane was using Pinker's not only to represent him as an author but to recruit for him as a publisher – Eric Sutton's contract for the translation of *Cléante and Bélise*, for example, was negotiated through Pinker's – and his acquisition of the rights for *Death of a Hero* must have been made easier to secure by his prior association with Aldington's new representatives. Kahane and Aldington also had many mutual friends in Paris, among them Nancy Cunard, whose Hours Press published Aldington's *Last Straws* and *The Eaten Heart* in 1929 and 1930 respectively. (Aldington was Cunard's lover; so, according to Kahane's son Eric, was Kahane.[4]) In fact, most of Aldington's early career was centred around the literary magazines and private presses of the Left Bank: he would have known of Kahane's new venture, and must have been aware of the good it could do him.

The deal was good for both of them. Aldington had a near-unexpurgated version of his novel on the market, and Kahane had added to his company's list one of the finest acquisitions it would ever make, an anti-war novel to rank with *Goodbye to All That* and *All Quiet on the*

Western Front. *Death of a Hero* is a blistering tripartite rant against war, the complacency of an older generation, and the blithe indifference of pampered non-combatants. It's a novel gloriously disfigured by rage. (A friend and fellow soldier, the novelist Ralph Bates, wrote in a letter to Aldington: 'I wish I could hate like that'.[5]). Closely based on Aldington's own life, background and wartime experiences, *Death of a Hero* (the title is ironic) contains some of the most vivid and ghastly descriptions of life in the trenches to be found anywhere in literature, and its merciless attacks on incompetent generals, clueless Tories and sick-note Socialists alike ensured that the book was loved and detested by all the right people. The Establishment hated it (naturally enough, since the feeling was mutual) and although he was right-wing by nature, the book was the beginning of Aldington's lifelong antagonistic relationship with authority – more specifically, with authority wielded by idiots. The 'idiots' were further outraged in 1954, when Aldington's book *Lawrence of Arabia: A Biographical Inquiry* comprehensively stripped Lawrence of the myths surrounding him. (The title of the French edition was altogether more frank: *Lawrence l'Imposteur*.) His dismissal of Lawrence as an 'impudent mythomaniac' was not something either readers or publishers were prepared to countenance at the time, and Aldington, never a fashionable writer, fell out of favour still further. At the end of his life he enjoyed a brief and, given his politics, surprising flurry of popularity in the Soviet Union where, in a speech given to the Writers' Club in Moscow to celebrate his seventieth birthday in 1962, he was moved to say: 'Here, in the Soviet Union, for the first time in my life I have met with extraordinary warmth and attention. This is the happiest day of my life'.

Richard Aldington died later the same year.

By the same author

Poetry includes:
Images (1910–1915) (The Poetry Bookshop, 1915)
Images of War (Beaumont Press, 1919)
Hark the Herald (Hours Press, 1928)
The Eaten Heart (Hours Press, 1929)
The Poems of Richard Aldington (Doubleday, 1934)

Fiction includes:
The Colonel's Daughter (Chatto and Windus, 1929)
Women Must Work (Chatto and Windus, 1934)
Very Heaven (Heinemann, 1937)

Non-fiction includes:
D. H. Lawrence (Chatto and Windus, 1930)
W. Somerset Maugham (Doubleday, 1939)
Wellington (Heinemann, 1946)
Lawrence of Arabia (Collins, 1955)

Notes

1 Letter from Richard Aldington to Alec Craig, quoted in Alec Craig, *The Banned Books of England* (George Allen and Unwin, 1962), pp. 83–84.
2 Note to first American edition of *Death of a Hero* (Covici, Friede, 1929).
3 The American edition sticks to this policy throughout the text; the English edition makes an exception of large excisions, which are denoted by a single line of asterisks.
4 Eric Kahane in conversation with James Armstrong, 22 October 1996.
5 Quoted in Charles Doyle, *Richard Aldington: A Biography* (Southern Illinois University Press, 1989), p. 180.

ROBIN ANDERSON

Few of the unpleasant things that ever happened to Kahane are mentioned in his memoirs, and his days as a schoolboy at Manchester Grammar School are conspicuous by their absence. When Kahane was a schoolboy, corporal punishment was routinely used in British schools; later in life he came to believe that an education system in which morals were forged by fear was largely responsible for producing the sexually repressed adults who made up the farther reaches of Obelisk's clientele. It's unsurprising, then, that when a 21-year-old youth submitted a manuscript to Obelisk castigating the English public school system from which he had only just emerged, Kahane was inclined to give it a sympathetic hearing.

There can have been no reason for Kahane to publish *Four Schools* other than a desire to stand by Anderson in his suffering and righteous anger: it's hard to imagine Kahane thought there would be a readership for a book so uninterestingly written and on such an unpromising subject, and its extreme scarcity today suggests a tiny print run. It was published in late 1935, at the same time as Obelisk's edition of Henry Miller's *Aller Retour New York*; since the books share the same cover design and typeface it seems probable that the edition of *Four Schools* was run off simultaneously in a cash-saving deal with the printer. A second edition was never needed.

The schools that made the young Anderson so miserable either go unnamed in his book or are given pseudonyms. This was probably a precaution taken by Kahane at the time of publication in order to avoid possible legal action, but in 1966 Anderson published selections from a journal he had kept between 1932 and 1946. In it, the schools are named:[1] the first two Anderson attended were Westbourne House School in Folkestone and Copthorne Preparatory School in Crawley. But Anderson is no George Orwell, and *Four Schools* is no *Such, Such Were the Joys*. Descriptions of the uninspiring lessons at 'Cockthorn', taught by lifeless drudges in draughty Victorian classrooms, are so uninspiring and lifeless themselves that as you wade through them you begin to wish the staff had hit him harder. From 'Cockthorn' Anderson moves on to his public school, 'Knarlesborough' (Marlborough), which is vilified for its incessant use of the rod, as well as for teaching its charges nothing which could be usefully applied to the outside world. Finally, Anderson discusses a couple of terms spent at 'Byron College' (L'Ecole de Commerce at Neuchâtel in Switzerland), a school apparently populated by the mentally deficient, the idle, and the physically deformed, where boys would ignore lessons and instead spend their time 'masturbating under their desks into the inkpots',[2] a considerable feat of marksmanship if nothing else.

Kahane did his best for *Four Schools*, publishing fliers and taking out advertising space in the *Left Review*, a journal which could reasonably have been expected to warm to the book's theme. But unsurprisingly, *Four Schools* sank without trace immediately after publication.

For the next ten years Anderson seems to have disappeared as comprehensively as his book. His journal, *The Quiet Grave*, provides few clues as to what he was doing – but ends with the entry for 17 April 1946, the day he was received into the Roman Catholic Church at the Brompton Oratory, London, by a Father Dale-Roberts, with Anderson's godmother, Lady Holland, in attendance. The journal strains for a tone of high seriousness and contemplation; instead it reads like a commonplace book with ideas above its station. Its entries, spanning fourteen years, are mostly increasingly religious *pensées*, and are frustratingly short on details of Anderson's life. He was in Paris by 1932, met Eliot, Aldous Huxley and Stravinsky in 1935, and travelled around Scandinavia and Africa before the war. He registered for military service in 1940, but seems to have spent the war years in England: a fan of John Gielgud, he saw him play *Macbeth* in 1941, and *Richard II* at the Old Vic three years later. But as to how he was living and who he was spending his time with, the journal is silent.

As the list below shows, Anderson's religious conversion informed the rest of his life. It seems odd that a man who spent his youth angrily denouncing schools for their unbending dogmatism should end up finding peace in the arms of the Roman Catholic church.

By the same author

Non-fiction includes:
Rome Churches of English Interest (Vatican Polyglot Press,1960)
The Quiet Grave (St Albert's Press, 1966)
Between Two Wars: The Story of Pope Pius XI (Franciscan Herald Press, 1977)

Notes
  1 Robin Anderson, *The Quiet Grave* (St Albert's Press, 1966).
  2 Robin Anderson, *Four Schools* (Obelisk Press, 1935), p. 118.

ARION

Whoever Arion was, he wasn't a writer: *Starborn* is a deeply terrible book without even the saving grace of being so-bad-it's-good. A gay coming-of-age novel set in San Francisco in the 1910s, it's the story of James Macdonald, a sickly and effeminate boy who suffers endless – really, really endless – torment, both from his classmates at school and from his anguished, uncomprehending parents at home. Whenever he gets a spare moment he goes to his room and yearns. If the weather's fine, he goes to the park and yearns there. By the time puberty takes hold he's yearning pretty much full time: yearning at school for boys who either beat him up or ignore him, yearning at home for his parents' understanding, and yearning at the picture house for Lillian Gish (Judy Garland's career having not yet taken off). When he's fifteen James allies himself with two soulmates. Philip is five years older, irresistible, unattainable and selfish; Virgilio (yes, Virgilio) Cobelli is a middle-aged Italian poet partial to teenage boys, gnomic profundities and dancing in the nude at parties. Determined to woo James, Virgilio pulls out all the stops: 'You are a fragrant petal that pierces my nostril like a strong wine,' coos the poet. James' resistance crumbles, and the couple spend a deliriously happy summer together before Cobelli returns to Italy, leaving our hero with nothing but memories, regrets and a fistful of odes. After 258 pages, James feels strong enough to face the future alone. Which is more than could be said for me.

Presumably autobiographical, this story of relentless unhappiness endured by a small boy should elicit sympathy, but *Starborn* is a colossally disproportionate revenge on the world. That James is persecuted because of his sexuality is deplorable; that he's not beaten to a pulp by everyone he meets simply for being a posturing little creep is incomprehensible. 'Arion' mostly strives for a tone of high moral seriousness and operatic grandeur. Mostly, but not always. James' high school class is given a lesson of sex education by a man called Professor Biggerstaff, and the composer of the elegiac piano piece 'Starborn', an unhappy and repressed homosexual who eventually commits suicide, is called Eliot Bender. It's difficult for the reader to sympathise fully when all he can think of is Sid James and Kenneth Williams.

Arion's choice of pseudonym tells us nothing about him that can't be gleaned from his novel. In Greek mythology Arion was a poet and musician, a native of Lesbos who, having won a music contest in Sicily, is sailing back to Corinth with his winnings when the crew decide to rob him and throw him overboard. His last wish, to sing a song on deck before jumping into the ocean, is granted and, attracted by the beautiful sound he makes, enchanted dolphins gather around the ship and rescue him when he jumps into the sea. Reading *Starborn*, it comes as no surprise to find that its author identifies with a character who possesses great artistic gifts, who finds himself persecuted by a brutish rabble, and who with the help of understanding outsiders is finally avenged. The choice of pseudonym is as vain as the novel itself.

The identity of Arion is unknown. If it's assumed that *Starborn* tells its author's own story, then he was a native of San Francisco born in the early years of the twentieth century. He was gay, and unmissably so; he was of delicate health, probably tubercular; and he was a lover of the arts, a would-be practitioner of them, and a believer in their redemptive qualities. From this it's possible to believe he made his way to Paris, where both his nature and his aspirations would have passed unremarked, but there's no evidence to support the theory: Kahane makes no mention of *Starborn* in his memoir – hardly surprising given the novel's awfulness. About Arion's later years nothing is known, and since his book closes with its central character scarcely out of adolescence we can't even make a guess – although, on the evidence of *Starborn*, it's probably safe to assume that he didn't go on to win either the world heavyweight boxing championship, or the Nobel prize for literature.

AUTHOR BIOGRAPHIES

CECIL BARR

Pseudonym of Jack Kahane. See 'A Very British Pornographer', above.

CHARLES BEADLE

Of all the pulp writers published by Obelisk, the most accomplished was Charles Beadle. Most Obelisk novels set in the alcoholic, narcotic and sexual subcultures of the time manage, oddly, to be simultaneously daring and genteel: their authors peek at the *demi-monde* like children peeking over a fence, nervous visitors to an unfamiliar world. It was an attitude shared by most of the expatriates in Paris during the 1920s, and Charles Beadle hated them for it. He was much older – born around 1880 and a veteran of the Boer War – and had been a denizen of Montparnasse for many years before their arrival. He had known Modigliani, who died in 1920; he was an assiduous, evangelical user of opium and hashish; he was in for the long haul. He resented the presence of 'tourists' at the orgies and drug dens he frequented, and when he encountered them he seems to have done everything he could either to corrupt them completely or to scare them away. He was contemptuous of 'morals', dismissing them in one of his novels as mere superstitions of the majority, a majority he despised for lacking the intellectual rigour to disregard the taboos which tormented them.[1] His voice is the most convincingly decadent on the Obelisk list, and his decadence was ideological. There was the genuine whiff of sulphur about him.

Reliable biographical information about Charles Beadle is difficult to come by, but much of the first half of his life was spent in Africa as an adventurer and soldier. His first book, *The City of Shadows*, is set in Morocco and was published in 1911, but his writing didn't start to pay until 1918, when the fiction magazine *Adventure* accepted one of his African stories. Between 1918 and 1925 *Adventure* published 26 stories and serials by Beadle, and his work was equally popular with rival magazines. The stories, though clearly written in haste, are alive with a vivid, insider's sense of place – in Africa as in Paris, Beadle knew the world he wrote about intimately. In 1918, *Adventure* printed a potted biography of Beadle, supplied by the man himself. Although short on names and dates (and probably less than entirely reliable) it at least gives some idea of the sort of life he had led to that point, and a flavour of the man who lived it:

[322]

My native heath is somewhere in mid-Atlantic. I was born rolling and have been ever since. No moss. My infancy was spent around Siam and the farther East: early memories, fire-flies, mosquitoes and ayahs. Educated at boarding schools in England; hence no home life and consequent atrophy of the sentimentalities. Parental Government required me to become a consulting marine engineer; but a congenital dislike of work and a gaudy poster persuaded me to learn poker, to starve in Cape Town where I held down a waiter's job for four hours, and to join the British South African Police.

Too late for big rebellion but kindly chief got up a small one to console me; saw Boer War in B. S. A. P., Morley's Scouts (unpaid Looting Corps) (if any of the Scouts should read this should be glad to hear from them) and Stock Recovery Dept. After Peace held various jobs from three days to a week – in a news office, a bar, hawker, insurance agent – and peddled cheap jewelry for three months (and made money!); served in Transvaal Customs and became Asst. Compound Manager to the Witwatersrand Native Labour Association.

Then I raised a syndicate to support me for an exploring-trip on the headwaters of the Zambezi. Returned to London to promote a company; failed – of course. A head on a coin sent me to British East Africa and Uganda; native trading, running transport from Victoria Nyanza to the Kilo Mines, Congo; shooting and various ventures. England again, company promoting; and failed again.

Went to Dutch Borneo, rubber planting. Afterward returned to go to Morocco; penetrated into interior in disguise during rebellion; met Pretender Sultan, Mulai Hafid; instead of cutting my throat or crucifying me as predicted he gave me a palace and an escort and treated me as an Ambassador; eventually I failed and Hafid lost his throne. We both had a royal time, anyway.

Until I came to America last year I have lived in France.[2]

Beadle's stories disappear from the pulp magazines in 1925: it seems probable that it was then that he returned to Paris from the United States. *The Blue Rib* and *The Esquimeau of Montparnasse*, the novels in which he voiced his contempt for expatriate dilettantism, appeared towards the end of the decade, *The White Gambit* was published by a small Paris imprint in 1935, and in 1938 Jack Kahane published what seems to have been Beadle's last book to be published in his lifetime, *Dark Refuge*.

In earlier books Beadle denounces the Paris-based expatriates for a bohemianism he deemed so insipid as to scarcely merit the name; in *Dark Refuge* he spells out how it should be done properly, and does so without paying any heed to what was considered publishable at the time. Beadle's ticket to the dark side is opium, and in his world 'dark' has no negative connotations, but refers instead to the side of the self that sees too little light. Under the influence of opium – 'artificial paradise'[3] – characters engage in a sort of stream-of-dual-consciousness, with themselves and with each other, a discourse which builds through the book into a hallucinatory concertante of voices, all raised against the tyranny of convention. The language Beadle uses in *Dark Refuge* – 'cuntstruck', 'pussy', 'fuck' in all its derivatives – shows that by 1938 Kahane had lost all the timorousness which had characterised his negotiations with Henry Miller over *Tropic of Cancer*, and as for the sex and drug-taking scenes, if you removed them you'd be left with a pamphlet. It's a deliriously unbuttoned book, fetid and dank, written by someone embedded in its milieu. Obelisk's publicity material often promised books like this one; *Dark Refuge* is one of the few to deliver.

The date of Beadle's death is unknown. He would have been around sixty years old when *Dark Refuge* was published, and it seems to have been his last novel. A pseudonymous book about Modigliani, written in collaboration with Douglas Goldring, was published in London in 1941, and a single short story (which could have been written at any time) four years after that. He seems not to have survived the 1940s. I can find no picture of him, but there used to be one on the wall of Kahane's office in the Place Vendôme. After the death of Kahane, and as the Nazis pushed towards Paris, Maurice Girodias sat in his father's leather swivel chair, taking in the empty Obelisk office:

> Pinned to the gray burlap that covers the wall are the actors of the past, each one looking into the dim dusty room from his or her place in space and time. The mysterious eyes of Anaïs; a photo of Joyce, the sour-faced magister; Durrell's profile, chubby and pugnacious; the satanic face of Charles Beadle, the author of 'Dark Refuge' – who knows, perhaps one of the true prophets of the future?[4]

By the same author

Fiction:
The City of Shadows (Everett and Co., 1911)
A Whiteman's Burden (S. Swift and Co., 1912)
A Passionate Pigrimage (Heath, Cranton and Ouseley, 1915)
Witch-Doctors (Cape, 1922)
The Blue Rib (P. Allan and Co., 1927)
The Esquimeau of Montparnasse (John Hamilton, 1928, published in the United States as *Expatriates at Large* by Macaulay, 1930)

The White Gambit (Palais-Royal Press, 1933)

Short stories include:
'The Triumph of Tony', *The Windsor Magazine*, July 1912
'Uncle', *Pearson's Magazine*, October 1914
'The Cave', *Adventure*, 3 October 1918
'Red Infidel', *Adventure*, 18 May 1919
'The City of Baal', *Adventure*, 18 January 1921
'White Magic', *The Frontier*, March 1925
'The King of Many Voices', *Short Stories*, 10 November 1939
'The Baboon's Paw', *Short Stories*, 10 December 1945

Non-fiction:
Artist Quarter (Faber, 1941, written in collaboration with Douglas Goldring and
    published under the pseudonym 'Charles Douglas')

Notes
 1 Charles Beadle, *Expatriates at Large* (Macaulay, 1930), p. 222.
 2 'The Camp-Fire' column, *Action* magazine, 3 July 1918.
 3 Charles Beadle, *Dark Refuge* (Obelisk Press, 1938), p. 45.
 4 Girodias, *Frog Prince*, p. 349.

ERIC BENFIELD

Born in Worth Matravers on the Isle of Purbeck in Dorset, Eric
Benfield followed in his father's footsteps and became a quarryman,
mining Purbeck stone. He developed artistic aspirations at an early
age, and began to sculpt, at first confining himself to garden statuary
for the tourist trade, but soon producing nude figures whose leering
expressions and anatomical accuracy tried the patience of his fellow
villagers. According to Benfield's grandson Brian Bugler (who still lives
in Worth Matravers and works as a quarryman there) the village pub
became a popular meeting place for artists during the 1930s. Augustus
John and the actor Leslie Banks, among others, were regular visitors
to The Square and Compass, and mixing in such company encouraged Benfield in his preferred self-image: not artisan, but artist.

As well as sculpting, Benfield wanted to write. A limited education
meant that his family were constantly being asked to help with his
spelling, but *Purbeck Shop: A Stoneworker's Story of Stone* was completed
by 1930 (although not published until ten years later) and fiction soon
followed. In the early 1930s Benfield walked out on his wife and three
children and went to live with the writer Kathleen Wade in Basing,

near Basingstoke. He found himself uncomfortably adrift between the world he knew, which now shunned him, and the cosmopolitan and artistic world he'd been determined to join, but which he now saw regarded him as a rustic outsider. He managed to have two novels published: both are badly written and interesting only for the light they throw on Benfield's early life. More interesting is the direction taken by his sculpture, a newly politicised direction brought about by the company he was keeping.

On 21 June 1936 an Anti-Air War Memorial was unveiled on land owned by Sylvia Pankhurst in Woodford Green, Essex. The monument, carved by Benfield, consisted of a small stone bomb, its nose buried in the apex of a pyramid and the whole supported by a plinth, and was a protest against the latest method war had found to maximise its ability to kill: aerial bombardment. Being vandalised by fascists immediately after its unveiling was the making of Benfield's sculpture: restored, it was unveiled for a second time the following month, in front of an international array of dignitaries. It later became a rallying point for Quakers during the 1940s, and then for the peace movement which grew out of the Greenham Common campaign of the 1980s. This powerful, far-from-monumental monument still stands today on its little plinth on a verge in Woodford Green, squeezed by a row of houses on one side and the A104 arterial road on the other. It's protected by a rusting cage of railings, is almost completely hidden by bushes, and is the only monument anywhere to commemorate either its original cause, or its maker.[1]

Benfield continued to write through the 1930s, but he didn't improve. It's not known how he was put in touch with Kahane, but someone must have told him that *The Dead Bury the Dead* could only be published abroad. They could have added that that would be no bad thing. You'd think it would be impossible to write a boring book about the murder spree of a sex-crazed gravedigger, but Benfield found a way. You make your central character a murderer as lifeless as his victims, and then unfold the action exclusively through his eyes; you have the murderer live in a very small village and slaughter almost everyone he knows, and then have the case handled by policemen so stupid they shouldn't be allowed out on their own; you strip the book of any potentially diverting detail of period or place; and you then relate the whole thing in a prose style so tortured that it's almost impossible to find your way to the end of a sentence without a map and a torch. A nifty method of corpse disposal – shallow burial in a freshly dug grave in the morning, followed by comprehensive interment under the coffin of a dearly-departed in the afternoon – is the only mildly interesting thing about a book that is so badly written it scarcely counts as being written at all. Benfield could have provided Obelisk with a much better monument had he resorted to his first profession; as it is, *The Dead Bury The Dead* helped bring the Obelisk story to a turgid, lifeless end.

Benfield and Kathleen Wade stayed together for the rest of their lives. After the war Benfield, by now a Fellow of the Royal Society of Arts, taught therapeutic sculpture at Park Prewett psychiatric hospital in Basingstoke. He suffered a stroke in 1953, and committed suicide two years later. According to his grandson, Benfield's funeral was attended by no more than half a dozen people – among them Kathleen Wade, who promised to return all of Benfield's papers and unpublished manuscripts to his family. But Wade died of a stroke six weeks after Benfield's funeral and the papers were lost. This is unfortunate, as they apparently included a manuscript called *So We Set Up a Stone*, which presumably drew on Benfield's experiences with Sylvia Pankhurst and the anti-war movement during the 1930s. It was potentially a far more interesting document than the novels he left behind.

By the same author

Fiction:
Bachelor's Knap (Peter Davies, 1935)
Saul's Sons (Chatto and Windus, 1938)

Non-fiction:
Purbeck Shop (Cambridge University Press,1940)
Southern English (Eyre and Spottiswoode, 1942)
The Town of Maiden Castle (Robert Hale, 1947)
Dorset (Robert Hale, 1950)

Notes
1 I am grateful to Patrick Wright for talking to me about Eric Benfield's sculpture. Mr Wright's article on the subject, 'The Stone Bomb', was published in the *London Review of Books* in 2001, and can also be accessed at www.opendemocracy.net/arts/article_1131.jsp.

AUTHOR BIOGRAPHIES

NADEJDA DE BRAGANÇA

A descendant of the Portuguese royal family, Isabel Maria Teresa Micaela Rafaela Gabriela Nadejda (Nada) de Bragança was born in London in 1910. Her father was HRH Don Miguel, Duke de Viseu, and her mother was Anita Stuart, of the New York banking family. She lived in Germany during the war, the United States after it, and later settled in Europe. She married Wlodzimierz Dorozynski in 1930: the marriage produced one son and ended in divorce in 1932.

Maurice Girodias first met Nadejda de Bragança when he was introduced to her by his father in a dimly lit bar in Paris: 'My God, what a marvellous creature !... I learned that Nadejda wrote poetry, which was not at all surprising; that she was an authentic princess of royal blood, which went without saying; and that my dad was head over heels in love with her, which was the inevitable consequence of the foregoing data.' Monied, titled and beautiful, de Bragança appealed to Kahane three times over; that he would publish her poetry, good or bad, was a foregone conclusion. According to the biographical information on the dustwrapper of *Poems For Music* (published by Obelisk in the summer of 1934) de Bragança wrote the poems between the ages of 16 and 24 (her age when the book appeared). That much is clear from reading them: adolescent, hormonally overheated maunderings about love lost, love unreturned, love betrayed – any sort of love except the happy kind. Given de Bragança's youth, and her recently failed marriage, the subject matter of her poetry was perhaps inevitable, but its lifeless treatment ensured the book made no waves. It appeared in an edition of one hundred copies, and was never reprinted (although six of the poems were set to music by Alexandre Tansman, a Polish pianist and composer who was living in Paris at the time of the book's publication).

In the spring of 1937 Kahane threw a cocktail party to celebrate his long-sought freedom from his printer, Marcel Servant. Among the guests were Henry Miller, Alfred Perlès, Stuart Gilbert and his wife – and Nadejda de Bragança, suggesting that the affair between her and Kahane was either a long one, or had ended sufficiently amicably to enable the two to continue as friends. In 1942, de Bragança married her second husband, René Millet, but her life seems to have followed the lovelorn path pre-ordained by her poetry: on 13 June 1946, two weeks before her thirty-sixth birthday, she committed suicide in London by throwing herself out of a hotel window.

Notes
1 Girodias, *Frog Prince*, pp. 92–93.

HENRY BRIDGES

Probable pseudonym of Jack Kahane. See notes to A–11, and 'A Very British Pornographer', above.

GAWEN BROWNRIGG

Gawen Brownrigg's novel *Star Against Star*, published by Obelisk in 1935 and then by Macaulay in the United States the following year, conforms to the template of most lesbian novels of the period. It's set among the upper class, a world of money and privilege, a social stratum where loss of status is keenly felt; its gay characters are exotically named and histrionically unhappy; and its protagonists come to a sticky end, furnishing nervous publishers with the plea, should they ever need it, that they are responsible for a cautionary tale, not a salacious one. And also like most lesbian novels of the time, it's written by a man.

Gawen Egremont Brownrigg was born in Tokyo in 1911, where his father, Rear-Admiral Sir Douglas Brownrigg, was naval attaché to the British Embassy. (The Rear-Admiral wrote a book called *Indiscretions of the Naval Censor*, published in Britain by Cassell in 1920.) Educated at Wellington public school and Magdalen College, Oxford, Brownrigg worked in a London stockbroker's office for two years before becoming a literary editor at the publishing firm of Arthur Barker Ltd. In 1935 he left to become a full-time writer; his first book, *Star Against Star*, appeared later that year. Uninspired but competently written, it tells the story of Dorcas Castro (I know, I know...), who discovers her lesbianism while at a Swiss finishing school and then spends the rest of the book trying to reconcile her family, her social circle, and herself to the discovery. The book issues the usual heartfelt plea for tolerance and understanding and, also true to form, makes a secondary character the moral centre of the book, in this case a young and handsome widower called Forbes Michaelson, whose own illegitimacy enables him to understand Dorcas's feeling of exclusion. Through him the author editorialises to his heart's content: 'They'll tolerate cruelty, stupidity, bigotry, all their lives', rues

Michaelson/Brownrigg, 'but they'll remain the apostles of so-called normality.'[1] Sex does happen in the book, but it's either sex of the 'that night, they were as one' variety, or else sex described in a miasma of obliquely panting prose. Having been published without incident by Kahane in France, *Star Against Star* appeared uncut in the United States the following year, where its author came to the attention of the publishers Alfred A. Knopf.

Knopf published Brownrigg's only other novel, *Later Than You Think*, in 1938; having contracted him he was asked to complete an author's form, a document providing the company with details about their client which could then be used to field media inquiries. The document has survived. Asked to provide 'MISCELLANEOUS AUTOBIOGRAPHICAL DATA AT AUTHOR'S OWN DISCRETION', Brownrigg offers the following (I have retained his spelling):

> In spite of having lead a comfortable, not to say spoiled, existance, I am totally incapable of any sustained degree of happiness or content. This is nothing to do with being blasé, which I'm not. It's, rather, a morbid capacity for seeing the worst side of people in their relationship with myself, combined with an embarrassingly acute sense of the ridiculous. This has got me into trouble more than once.
>
> I know that I am much too concerned with other people's opinion of me – people who don't matter a damn in my life. I'm not at all fond of my fellow humans as a whole, though I know this to be due to jealousy as often as contempt.[2]

There is more, including denunciations of politics, the overly opinionated, and 'socially and financial[ly] unsuccessful parents trying to barter an attractive daughter's life at the expense of the child's emotions in order to satisfy themselves as to their own social adroitness and material perspicacity. It isn't a very original subject, but one which I happen to know a lot about.'[3] Quite how many books Brownrigg thought this would help his publisher to shift is unclear, but it's not surprising to discover that he was going through a divorce at the time he completed the form.

Brownrigg came from a high-born family and married into another: his wife was Baroness Lucia von Borosini. The couple met in Germany in 1930 and married the following year, when they were both barely twenty. In 1932 their only child was born, but the marriage was already in trouble and soon broke down completely: the couple divorced in 1936. In 1938 Brownrigg's second novel, *Later Than You Think*, was published in the United States by Knopf. It's an anaemic story about motor racing, occasionally enlivened by the appearance of the team manager, a lascivious homosexual with eyes for his driver (whose own eyes stay firmly on the road).

It's unlikely that Gawen Brownrigg ever saw the book in print, as by 1938 he was living in Nairobi. There, according to his widow (to whom I spoke more than sixty years later), he was 'writing a book on the effect of pills.'[4] He died of an overdose on 8 August 1938, aged 27, leaving everything – minus one dollar – to a girl in Nairobi of whom his family had never heard. The dollar he left to his son.[5]

By the same author
Later Than You Think (Knopf, 1938, published the same year in England as *Portrait in a Windscreen*, by Michael Joseph)

Notes
1 Gawen Brownrigg, *Star Against Star* (Obelisk Press, 1935), p. 152.
2 Gawen Brownrigg, unpublished 'author's form', p. 3, Alfred A. Knopf archive, HRC, Texas.
3 Brownrigg, author's form.
4 Telephone conversation with Mrs Lucia Batten, formerly Mrs Lucia Brownrigg.
5 As note 4.

HAROLD BUCKLEY

Harold Buckley was a war hero. Born in Westfield, Massachussetts in 1896, he attended Phillips Academy, Andover, before joining the American Ambulance Service in March 1917. While serving in France that summer, he joined the United States Air Service, and by March 1918 had been assigned to the 95th Pursuit Squadron, based at Toul. *Squadron 95* is his account of the last months of the war, during which he and his colleagues flew planes so unreliable that pilots were almost as likely to die from a mechanical failure as from enemy action. Engaging about life on the airbase, and unflinching about death, it's a well written and humbling account of the bravery of men who were barely into their twenties, and who were unlikely ever to leave them.

Americans sympathetic to the Allied cause had begun to take an active role in the war well before the United States' formal entry into the conflict in 1917. In April 1916 the Escadrille Américaine was founded. German diplomatic pressure caused the squadron to change its name to the Escadrille Lafayette, but could do nothing about its deployment of 38 American pilots, who between them downed 57 German planes before the squadron was subsumed into the 103rd Pursuit Squadron in February 1918, under the control of US forces. The 103rd was the first American squadron to see active service; the 94th and 95th were deployed soon after, in April. Harold Buckley, just turned 22, was attached to the 95th.

Stationed at Villeneuve, Buckley was stood down from the front to attend gunnery training at Arcachon, where the decrepit state of the training planes made flying almost as dangerous as the front line trenches. Once trained, Buckley was sent to Epiez, where on his first patrol he saw action at 17,000 feet. His descriptions of the squadron's aircraft are a stomach-churning reminder that in 1918 the aviation industry, like its pilots, was barely out of its infancy:

> [Our Nieuports (type 28)]...were fast, manoeuvrable and delicate to handle, though far from good in a dive. A tendency to catch fire upon starting we tried to overlook. The motor was a Gnome 'Monosoupape' [single valve] with no carburetor; raw gas was fed directly to the cylinders. When the motor was cold considerable gas accumulated while spinning the propellor before the motor caught hold... The horror of horrors to all of us was coming down in flames and we always had a worry about fire with these ships. Happily we did not know then that they were also structurally weak.[1]

The aeroplanes' machine guns would jam as often as they worked; gadgets designed to synchronise the firing of the pilot's machine gun with the rotation of the propellor would fail; failure to cut off the petrol flow when cutting the ignition on landing would turn the plane into a fireball; altitude sickness (the cockpits were open) would seriously undermine the pilot's ability to function; and parachutes were not standard issue until the war was practically over. There were so many different ways to die in a Nieuport that it's a miracle anyone survived at all.

Buckley's first patrol at Epiez was also his last: the squadron was moved to Toul, where it joined up with the 94th to form the nucleus of the First Pursuit Group. From here until the end of the war in November, Buckley's story is one of fierce dogfights and agonising death, dispassionately recounted in his book. Like Buckley, the reader learns to keep his distance, as characters turn into corpses with grim regularity. Despite the bloodshed, a ghoulish camaraderie grew between the opposing forces. Pilots would drop notes on enemy aerodromes, giving details of their lost planes and crewmen. This pooling of information allowed an accurate tally of 'downs' to be kept by both German and Allied forces, enabling kills to be ascribed with some confidence to individual pilots. Five kills or more, and a pilot became an ace. Few made it that far. Those who did carned the respect of pilots on both sides, but also became targets for those looking for kudos, or vengeance, or both.

In September 1918 the Argonne drive began, the 95th providing air cover for the advancing Allied troops. By this time Buckley and his colleagues were flying Spad XIIIs, a vast improvement on the Nieuports they replaced. They were less manoeuvrable, but they were also less likely to fall to pieces. Fatalities decreased, and the morning patrol was no longer referred to as the suicide club.

On 10 November, the call came through that the Armistice would be signed at eleven o'clock the following morning. Between April and November 1918, the squadron had about twenty men on active service at any given time. When casualties were taken, replacements would arrive. By the end of the war, nine men from the squadron had been killed in action, four wounded, four wounded and captured, and five captured. (Among the last was Lieutenant George Puryear, who was shot down behind enemy lines. The account of his escape to Switzerland from a German prisoner-of-war camp is told in his own words in the last fifty pages of *Squadron 95*.)

Buckley came through the war physically unscathed. He rarely refers to himself in the book; when he does, it's usually in the third person and in deprecating terms. By the armistice Buckley was an ace, having downed five aircraft during the summer, and was awarded the Distinguished Service Cross. His citation reads: 'For extraordinary heroism in action near Perles, France, 10 August 1918. Lt. Buckley was on a patrol protecting a French biplane observation machine when they were suddenly set upon by six enemy planes. Lt. Buckley attacked and destroyed the nearest and the remainder fled into their own territory. He then carried on with his mission until he had escorted the Allied plane safely to its own aerodrome.' His DSC Oak Leaf Cluster citation reads: 'For extraordinary heroism in action near Reville, France, 26–27 September 1918. Lt. Buckley dived through a violent and heavy anti-aircraft fire and set on fire an enemy balloon that was being lowered into its nest. The next day while leading a patrol, he met and sent down in flames an enemy plane while it was engaged in reglage work.'[2]

Squadron 95 was written between May and December 1932 while Buckley was staying at Leixlip Castle in County Kildare, Ireland. His permanent address at the time seems to have been Paris, a city he got to know during the war. According to his book, while on wartime leave Buckley made the rounds of the usual expatriate haunts: the Grande Bretagne bar, the Astra in rue Caumartin, the Crillon. All were still popular expatriate venues in the 1920s, when Kahane was often to be found in them. It's also possible that the two men got to know each other during the war, while Kahane was attached to the Fourth Army coordinating railway supply lines near Dunkirk: while there he often socialised with airmen attached to the Lafayette and other squadrons. But however the two men met, both Buckley and his book would have found a natural admirer in the old soldier Kahane, although it's likely Buckley had to pay for the publication of *Squadron 95* himself: the book is bound in the drab boards Kahane reserved for books published to please authors rather than readers. This may have been down to timing. At the beginning of 1933 money was tight for Kahane: Obelisk was still in its infancy, and the *de luxe* edition of Joyce's *Pomes Penyeach* which had appeared the previous year had badly dented the company's finances. But if Buckley did have to pay Kahane for the privilege of being published, he at least seems to have been able to afford a fairly large print run: the book is one of the more common Obelisk titles today.

After publication of *Squadron 95* Buckley found his way to Hollywood, where he spent the rest of the 1930s working as an advisor and screenwriter on 'B' movies, many of them with an aeronautical theme. His introduction to movies was probably provided by his friend Merian C. Cooper, a veteran of the 20th Air Squadron and, in 1933, the co-creator of *King Kong*. Buckley's writing or advisory credit is to be found on at least a dozen films, mostly studio 'quickies', churned out in the years leading up to the Second World War.

By the same author

Film credits:
West Point of the Air (1935, dir. Richard Rossen)
Road Gang aka *Injustice* (1936, dir. Louis King)
Public Enemy's Wife aka *G-Man's Wife* (1936, dir. Nick Grinde)

California Mail (1936, dir. Noel M. Smith)
Guns of the Pecos (1937, dir. Noel M. Smith)
That Man's Here Again (1937, dir. Louis King)
Idol of the Crowds (1937, dir. Arthur Lubin)
Carnival Queen (1937, dir. Nate Watt)
The Black Doll (1938, dir. Otis Garrett)
Air Devils (1938, dir. John Rawlins)
Sinners in Paradise (1938, dir. James Whale)
Nick Carter, Master Detective (1939, dir. Jacques Tourneur)

Notes
  1 Harold Buckley, *Squadron 95* (Obelisk Press, 1933), pp. 70–71.
  2 Cited at www.theaerodrome.com/aces/usa/buckley.php.

CYRIL CONNOLLY

Cyril Connolly was born in 1903, an exact contemporary of George Orwell's at prep school, and of both Orwell's and Anthony Powell's at Eton. He managed beautifully to pull off the trick of the age: combining apparent sloth with chronic over-achievement. A graduate of Balliol College, Oxford, by the age of 23 he was writing regularly, and brilliantly, for *The New Statesman*, but never allowed his burgeoning literary reputation to eclipse his standing as an epicurean, wit and ardent francophile. By the late 1920s Connolly had established himself as the coming man. Coming men don't stay critics forever, and it was universally accepted, not least by Connolly himself, that a triumphant first novel would shortly appear, to be followed by a succession of effortlessly elegant books that would assure their author of his place in the pantheon. All of which happened. Unfortunately for Connolly, it all happened to Evelyn Waugh.

No child, on being asked what he wants to be when he grows up, has ever answered: 'A critic.' Cyril Connolly was a superb critic, historically the least contented kind. Just as Kenneth Tynan spent most of his life wishing he was Laurence Olivier, so Connolly always longed to become a major literary force in his own right, not merely a fairground barker for the show. His failure to make the transition, and the personal unhappiness that failure bred, have obscured the enormous contribution Connolly made to the development of new writing in the mid-twentieth century. The role in which he found himself cast, that of facilitator rather than achiever in his own right, was a catastrophe only for Connolly himself.

Connolly wrote his first novel, *The Rock Pool*, in 1934. A comedy of manners set in the expatriate community of Trou-sur-mer (based on the French town of Cagnes), the book alludes in its title to the artists' colonies left stranded in the 1930s by the ebbing tide of expatriate bohemianism which by then was receding from Paris and its summer migratory destinations on the Mediterranean coast. Edgar Naylor, a nine-to-five pen-pusher with dreams of literary immortality, arrives in Trou determined to leave behind his life of humdrum suit-and-tie conformity in England, and to crack on with the writing of the masterwork he knows the world is waiting for, his biography of an obscure nineteenth-century banker-poet called Samuel Rogers. But his timing, like his inspiration, is lousy: he discovers that Trou-sur-mer's 1920s' heyday is over, and all the real artists have gone. Those that remain are the hangers-on: failed painters, failed lovers, failed lesbians, and assorted alcoholics. Undeterred, Naylor tries to assimilate himself into his new surroundings. But despite living a life of conscientious dissipation, despite conducting desultory affairs and picking up everybody else's drinks bills, he remains unpopular and unaccepted. He remains, in short, himself: 'He felt old and miserable, going through life trying to peddle a personality of which people would not even accept a free sample.'[1] After a humiliating fight with the last in a long line of deranged lovers – during which his precious manuscript is symbolically doused in blood and Pernod – Naylor withdraws to a bar. There the novel leaves him, drunkenly announcing plans for a future that will never come to an audience that isn't listening.

In 1935 *The Rock Pool* was offered to Faber. Fearful of prosecution, they turned it down. The convictions on charges of obscenity of *Boy* the previous year and of *Bessie Cotter* that April had made British publishers nervous of any manuscript likely to attract interest from the censor, and a book which featured women dancing together and unmarried people waking up together, however decorously described, was felt in the prevailing legal climate to be an invitation to the authorities to prosecute. An approach to a second British publisher (probably the Hogarth Press) also met with rejection, but a chance meeting with Jack Kahane in the middle of 1935 resulted in *The Rock Pool* – like *Boy* and *Bessie Cotter* before it – finding a home in Paris.

Connolly had already considered this option. Early in 1935 he had written to Sylvia Beach denouncing the timidity of the British publishing scene: 'I think that I must try and have it done in America, or else it will have to appear in an under the counter way, like the Obelisks.'[2] At about that time, Kahane had been asked if he would be interested in publishing a collection of letters from Henry James to Ralph Curtis. Seeing no likelihood of any profits coming from such a venture he declined, but agreed to see whether he could place them with someone else. Connolly had been suggested as a possible editor, and Kahane paid him a visit. The two hit it off immediately.

In 1944 Connolly famously wrote: 'Imprisoned in every fat man a thin one is wildly signalling to get out.'[3] (Less famously, Connolly stole this epigram from his friend George Orwell, who five years before had written in *Coming Up For Air*: 'I'm fat, but I'm thin inside. Has it ever struck you that there's a thin man inside every fat man, just as they say there's a statue inside every block of stone?'[4]) The rotund Connolly and the beanpole Kahane saw themselves in each other. Kahane remembered Connolly from that first meeting as 'a lovely talker, with a great appreciation of hospitality, and a robust interest in the finer facets of cooking',[5] attributes Kahane prized as much in himself as he did in others. For his part, Connolly found Kahane 'charming and faintly Mephistophelean', and admired him for 'waging a lonely guerrilla war against prudery'.[6] Connolly and Kahane quickly agreed that the Henry James project was a dead duck, and talk turned to their shared love of literature, women and all things French. The strong rapport between the two men would probably have led Connolly to look favourably on the Obelisk Press as a potential publisher of *The Rock Pool* even if others had been interested (which they weren't). Before Kahane left, Connolly mentioned his novel and the difficulties he was experiencing in placing it. Kahane asked to be sent the manuscript and – never one to miss an opportunity – wondered if in the meantime Connolly would consider reviewing Obelisk's latest publication. Connolly's review of Gawen Brownrigg's *Star Against Star* appeared in *New Statesman and Nation* in July 1935.

The Rock Pool had been turned down by two London publishers on the grounds that it was obscene, and was almost turned down by Kahane on the grounds that it wasn't. Acknowledging it to be 'as sweet a piece of writing as ever I have seen, the work of an exquisite, steeped in the classics, and in certain ways a model of impropriety',[7] Kahane nonetheless bemoaned its sexual tameness, noting wryly that it brought shame to his list.

It didn't bring shame, but it didn't bring sales either. The Obelisk edition of *The Rock Pool* appeared in June 1936; at about the same time Scribner's published an American edition which sold barely three hundred copies. Although the Obelisk edition limped in to a second impression the following year, the original print run had been so small, probably the usual run of one thousand copies, that this hardly constituted success. Neither Connolly's literary reputation nor Obelisk's scandalous one could shift *The Rock Pool*. The problem was the book itself.

The Rock Pool is a colourless, inert mess. Loosely based on the myth of Hylas, the Argonaut seduced by a water nymph who lures him into her pool, the book is arch but not funny, learned but not enlightening, affected but not affecting. Its characters are anaemically drawn and perfunctorily employed, and even the central character, Naylor, whose appearance and opinions are shared by the author, is little more than a cipher. The extended form of the novel defeats Connolly, a master of concision and epigrammatic wit: *The Rock Pool*, far more quotable than readable, just lies there, lifeless.

Connolly was too shrewd a critic not to know that *The Rock Pool* was a failure, but in the introductory letter that acts as a preface to the book he does what he can to divert attention away from the fact. A preface was much more familiar territory to Connolly than a novel, and in it he expertly takes to task the faint-hearted British publishers who had made *The Rock Pool*'s journey into print such an arduous one:

> I know there is a theory that a book, if it is any good, will always find a publisher, that talent cannot be stifled, that it even proves itself by thriving on disappointment, but I have never subscribed to it; we do not expect spring flowers to bloom in a black frost, and I think the chill wind that blows from English publishers, with their dark suits and dark umbrellas, and their habit of beginning every sentence with 'We are afraid', has nipped off more promising buds than it has stimulated.[8]

Beautifully put, but if the book been rejected on the grounds that it was no good rather than that it was potentially obscene Connolly would have had far less cause for complaint. Mindful of the book's shortcomings, Connolly launches a pre-emptive critical strike on those about to review it. On its awkward brevity: 'due to the subversity of Latin, I have been trained rather to condense than to amplify'; on the critic turning novelist: 'If one has criticised novels for several years one is supposed to have profited from them. Actually one finds one's mind irremediably silted up with every trick and cliché, every still-born phrase and facile and second-hand expression that one has deplored in others'; and, bailing out furiously: 'The fault I am most conscious of...', 'Any first book is always...', 'There is one more objection I should like to answer....'9

He needn't have worried: *The Rock Pool* was to be reviewed not by Connolly – who would have savaged it – but by Connolly's friends. A two-column review in *The Sunday Times* by Desmond MacCarthy rated it superior to Huxley and Waugh;10 Desmond Hawkins, Connolly's fellow reviewer on *The New Statesman*, raved about it in *The Criterion* – and even George Orwell, who in his writings at least was implacably opposed to the incestuousness of English reviewing, went easy on his friend. Although bracingly dismissive of the subject matter ('even to want to write about so-called artists who spend on sodomy what they have gained by sponging betrays a kind of spiritual inadequacy') he is generous in his praise of its treatment: 'during the past year I have only read about two new books that have interested me more, and I doubt if I have read even one that was more amusing.'11

The Rock Pool was first published in Britain in 1947, twelve years after its appearance in Paris. Connolly's foreword to this new edition is poignant and tellingly brief. Since the novel's first publication many of the people on whom the book's characters were based had died: of consumption, on active service, in Nazi death camps. But the foreword is not only a memorial to absent friends. It also reads as a threnody to *The Rock Pool* itself, and to Connolly's ambitions as a novelist, one who 'has long lost all his arrogance and fire.'12

Connolly never completed another novel. *The Rock Pool* was supposed to form part of a trilogy: *The English Malady* and *Humane Killer* were named but never written.13 Another unfinished novel, *Shade Those Laurels*, appeared in 1990, completed after Connolly's death by his friend Peter Levi, who would have proved a better friend by leaving well alone. A literary murder mystery set in an English country house, it's a highbrow take on the trashy thrillers to which Connolly was addicted all his life. Unsuccessful either as literature or pulp, it is worth mentioning here only to draw attention to the character of the publisher, Ginger Bartlett, who is an amalgam of all those who published Connolly during his lifetime: the memory of Kahane is evoked by descriptions of Bartlett's 'false teeth clicking briskly over the labials,'14 as well as his susceptibility to famous company: 'Mr.

Bartlett...seemed only to exist...when seeing off the Fitzgeralds at Grand Central or playing poker with the Bromfields a day out from Nantucket.'[15]

In January 1940 Connolly launched *Horizon*, a monthly literary magazine. With the onset of war many literary magazines were folding: *New Verse, Criterion* and *Twentieth-Century Verse* all went out of business. Connolly was repeatedly told that it was an act of madness to start up such a venture at such a time; Connolly countered that a time when civilisation is under threat from barbarism is exactly the right time to proclaim the values for which one is fighting. In his editorial comment for the first issue, Connolly wrote:

> The aim of *Horizon* is to give to writers a place to express themselves, and to readers the best writing we can obtain. Our standards are aesthetic, and our politics are in abeyance. This will not always be the case, because as events take shape the policy of artists and intellectuals will become clearer, the policy which leads them to economic security, to the atmosphere in which they can create, and to the audience by whom they will be appreciated. At the moment civilization is on the operating table and we sit in the waiting room.[16]

Until events took shape, then, Connolly intended to cast as wide a net as possible when looking for contributors to the magazine. The result was a vibrant mix of the established and the unknown, drawn from the fields of art, music, poetry and prose. Henry Miller was one of many who benefited from *Horizon's* eclectic recruitment policy: his Obelisk Press books were still unpublishable in Britain, but the reputation he enjoyed as their author brought him many commissions for new work, and three pieces by Miller appeared in *Horizon* in the early 1940s. Connolly's audacity paid off: contributors and readers alike wanted to do everything they could to ensure the survival of *Horizon*, partly out of self-interest but also as a political act. As a result the magazine not only survived, it prospered: *Horizon's* index of contributors over its ten-year existence is a comprehensive cast list of the most influential European artists and writers of the mid-twentieth century. The magazine stands as Connolly's finest achievement.

Shortly after *Horizon's* demise in 1950, Connolly became the lead reviewer for the *Sunday Times*, and over the next 24 years wrote long articles, short stories and parodies for a variety of newpapers and magazines. Among them was *The Downfall of Jonathan Edax*, a cautionary tale about a kleptomaniac bibliophile, published in the *Sunday Times* in 1961. Connolly later claimed that the central character was a composite of many people he'd known, Kahane among them, but it's difficult to discern the presence of any living person in the character of Edax save Connolly himself. Like Edax, Connolly was an obsessive collector of literary first editions; like Edax, he was less than scrupulous in his method of collecting, and would think nothing of slipping a second impression of a book on to the shelves of a non-collector friend to replace the first edition he'd just put in his briefcase; and, like Edax, Connolly would hurry to the deathbed of a distinguished author with flowers in one hand and a bag of unsigned books in the other. Connolly's primary collecting interest was the Moderns: his book *The Modern Movement: One Hundred Key Books from England, France and America 1880–1950* is still used as a template by collectors today. A letter from Connolly to the book-dealer John Heuston gives a flavour of his collection:

> There are several books of the 30's I am still looking for but I don't suppose you have any – *East Coker* (in the New English Weekly, a supplement), *A Clergyman's Daughter* and *Keep The Aspidistra Flying* (Orwell), *To The North* and *The Last September* (Bowen), *Panic Spring* (Norden)[Laurence Durrell], and *Being Geniuses Together* (McAlmon), *Maiden Voyage* (Denton Welch), *25 Poems* (Dylan Thomas), *92 Days* (Evelyn Waugh) and the last number (1939) of *New Verse* – also anything in English published in Paris.[17]

Cyril Connolly died in 1974.

By the same author

Fiction:
Shade Those Laurels (completed by Peter Levi) (Bellew, 1990)

Non-fiction:
Enemies of Promise (Routledge, 1938)
The Unquiet Grave (Horizon, 1944; revised edition: Hamish Hamilton, 1945)
The Condemned Playground (Routledge, 1945)
The Missing Diplomats (Queen Anne Press, 1952)
Ideas and Places (Weidenfeld and Nicolson, 1953)
Les Pavillons (Macmillan [US], 1962)
Previous Convictions (Hamish Hamilton, 1963)
The Modern Movement (André Deutsch/Hamish Hamilton, 1965)
The Evening Colonnade (Bruce and Watson, 1973)
A Romantic Friendship (Constable, 1975)
Journal and Memoir (Collins, 1983, ed. David Pryce-Jones)
Selected Works (2 vols.) (Picador, 2002, ed. Matthew Connolly)

AUTHOR BIOGRAPHIES

AUTHOR BIOGRAPHIES

Notes

1 Cyril Connolly, *The Rock Pool* (Obelisk Press, 1936), p. 137.
2 Letter, Cyril Connolly to Sylvia Beach, Box 190, Sylvia Beach papers, Special Collections, Princeton University Library.
3 Cyril Connolly as 'Palinurus', *The Unquiet Grave* (Horizon, 1944), p. 44.
4 George Orwell, *Coming Up For Air* (Gollancz, 1939), p. 29.
5 Kahane, *Memoirs*, p. 265.
6 Cyril Connolly, postscript to the Hamish Hamilton edition of *The Rock Pool* (1947).
7 Kahane, *Memoirs*, p. 265.
8 Introductory letter to *The Rock Pool*, p. 3 (though unpaginated).
9 Introductory letter to *The Rock Pool*, p. 3.
10 Desmond MacCarthy, *Sunday Times*, 23 August 1935.
11 George Orwell, *New English Weekly*, 23 July 1936.
12 Cyril Connolly, introduction to *The Rock Pool* (Hamish Hamilton, 1947), p. xii.
13 A nine-page fragment of *Humane Killer* was eventually published in the *London Magazine*, Volume 13, No. 3, in August/September 1973.
14 Cyril Connolly and Peter Levi, *Shade Those Laurels* (Bellew, 1990), p. 21.
15 Connolly and Levi, *Shade Those Laurels*, pp. 21–22.
16 Cyril Connolly, *Horizon*, Volume I, No. 1, January 1940, p. 5.
17 Undated letter from Cyril Connolly to John Heuston, author's collection.

SHEILA COUSINS

To Beg I Am Ashamed was not written by Graham Greene. As far as I'm aware that sentence has never appeared in the catalogues of auction houses or book-dealers, and they must have their reasons, but despite the intense speculation since its publication and immediate withdrawal, *To Beg I Am Ashamed* was not written by Graham Greene. Greene knew its author, he may even have provided a descriptive phrase or two, but he didn't write the book. As everyone has known for some time without really wanting to, *To Beg I Am Ashamed* was written by Ronald Matthews.

In 1957 Matthews' book *Mon Ami Graham Greene* was published, in French, in Belgium.[1] (German and Spanish editions also exist but not, it seems, an English one.) In the book Matthews writes of his first meeting with Greene, at a cocktail party in London in the summer of 1936. Matthews had come down from Oxford eleven years before, had tried and failed to become a poet, and although his first book had just been published and respectfully reviewed, he was in no position to give up his day job and was making ends meet as a newspaper sub-editor. At the time of their meeting Matthews' ailing career trajectory was mirrored almost exactly by Greene's, and the two found much to talk about. They were both around thirty years old and earning five hundred pounds a year, a sum which marked them neither as failures nor as successes, but which served instead to remind them that greater things had been expected of them. Both were converted Catholics; both had a passion for exotic travel; and both (a detail Matthews' book omits) were fascinated by prostitutes.

Both men were also creatures of habit. They began to meet every Saturday evening for what Matthews describes as 'pub crawls' in far-flung parts of London chosen at random, before returning to the West End for supper in as fine a restaurant as they could afford. These journeys into the suburbs, and into Greeneland, provided them with holidays from themselves and strengthened their sense of collusion with each other. Their relationship existed only in this self-made limbo: neither man ever visited the other at home, and after their first meeting they met in public only once, at a party to celebrate the launch of the magazine *Night and Day*, a magazine intended to be an English version of the *New Yorker* but which later collapsed when it was successfully sued by the parents of Shirley Temple after its film critic, Graham Greene, suggested in a review of *Wee Willie Winkie* that Miss Temple's screen persona had been deliberately designed to appeal to elderly perverts.

According to Matthews, at about this time he was approached by a prostitute in Piccadilly late one night while on his way home to his Holborn flat, and was struck by the demure dignity of the woman's dress, and also by her accent – the accent of a lady. In an unlikely inversion of the etchings gambit, Matthews asserts that he went to her flat in order to be shown a pile of papers: the prostitute was working on her autobiography. Matthews flicked through the pages and saw that, although the woman had a moving and surprising story to tell, she hadn't the skill to tell it herself, and he spent the next three months fashioning a book from the prostitute's faltering manuscript. If the prostitute ever existed her identity was never revealed, not even amid the glaring publicity the book attracted when it was published in 1938. A far more likely explanation is that the idea for the book was cooked up by Matthews, or by Matthews and Greene, during one of their 'pub crawls'. But the fact that the book got written was down to Matthews, and Matthews alone.

Graham Greene was occupied elsewhere at the time *To Beg I Am Ashamed* was being written. The court case arising out of his Shirley Temple review was approaching, and Greene decamped to Mexico, where he witnessed the anti-Catholic purges which prompted the writing of both *The Lawless Roads* and *The Power and the Glory*. The files of the publisher George Routledge, held at Reading University, show that in 1937 the manuscript of *To Beg* was submitted to its eventual publishers, Routledge, by Greene's literary agency Pearn, Pollinger and Higham, but that the author's contract was signed by Matthews. It was also Matthews who dealt with all pre-publication matters involving the book: in June he wrote to T. M. Wragg of Routledge, enclosing the blurb he'd written for the book's dustwrapper, and in January 1938 he changed many of the characters' names to avoid libel claims, this on the advice of Routledge's solicitors (although two of 'Sheila's' regulars in the book retain their original names: Graham and Matthew). The dustwrapper design is also discussed; Matthews is told of booksellers' nervousness, and their preference for as plain a wrapper as possible with no use of the word 'prostitute' anywhere. Matthews agreed, and also acted on the advice of Routledge's solicitors that pejorative references to Jews (and one to the French) should be removed from the manuscript before publication.

Yet despite the care taken by Routledge to avoid antagonising those who live to be antagonised, *To Beg I Am Ashamed* found trouble as soon as review copies were sent out. The outcry was partly caused by Routledge's decision to issue the book in a plain dustwrapper, as advised by their legal team, but to provide booksellers with a wraparound band which they could put on their copies if they so wished; since the band proclaimed the book to be 'The Authentic Biography of a London Prostitute', it did little to help Routledge's otherwise muted advertising strategy. But the book's undoing was the Public Morality Council, a body every bit as sinister and stupid as it sounds. Founded in 1899 and led for the first twenty-five years of its existence by the Bishop of London – a man who in 1934 declared during a House of Lords debate on contraceptives that he would like to make a bonfire of them and then dance around it[2] – the Public Morality Council sent the Home Office a copy of *To Beg I Am Ashamed*. The *Daily Mail* did the rest. One week after the Shirley Temple case was heard (and lost) in the High Court, the newspaper ran an editorial under the headline 'A Disgraceful Book – It Must Be Stopped', declaring that '[its] effect on the young and impressionable who may read it cannot fail to be debasing and demoralising.'[3] (The book, not the *Daily Mail*.) When Routledge's offices were visited by the police the publishers knew they were beaten, and rather than face a damaging and expensive court case, they withdrew the book. (The publication of the American edition the same year passed without incident.)

The simplest way to settle the attribution of *To Beg I Am Ashamed* is to read the book. (Its title comes from the Gospel of Luke: 'What shall I do, seeing that my lord taketh away the stewardship from me? I have not strength to dig; to beg I am ashamed.') Patrick Hamilton could depict torpid lives without producing a torpid book, and so could Graham Greene, but the skill is beyond Matthews, whose book limps leadenly along – enlivened by the occasional startlingly vivid character description. Greene's biographer Michael Shelden identifies these moments as possible evidence of Greene's marginal involvement in the writing of the book – and when it was republished in 1953 (uncut and without any legal repercussions) Greene's review for the *New Statesman* quoted approvingly some of the finer examples, which does suggest that some sort of in-joke was being played out.[4] But these momentarily enlivening passages aside, the book plods worthily along, too frightened of its material, and too frightened of what the public response might be, to engage with it meaningfully.

There is nothing that could be construed as obscene in the book: as with most books banned in England during the 1920s and 1930s, *To Beg I Am Ashamed* was proscribed not because of the treatment of its subject matter, but because of the subject matter itself. As such it was perfect for Kahane, bringing with it as it did a scandalous reputation but absolutely no chance of prosecution in France. The Obelisk edition appeared in June 1938, just three months after the book's denunciation in the *Daily Mail*, and a second impression (marked '8th impression') followed in August. According to Kahane: 'The book was a great success, and in consequence of the maladroit (but to me invaluable) publicity that the press attacks gave it, I got large orders for it from all over the world. This underlines the folly as well as the hypocrisy of such press campaigns... One publisher's poison is another publisher's meat.'[5]

By the same author

Fiction includes:
Red Sky At Night (Hollis and Carter, 1951)

Non-fiction includes:
English Messiahs (Methuen, 1936)
Sons of the Eagle (Methuen, 1937)
Mon Ami Graham Greene (Desclee de Brouwer, 1957)
Algeria: The Realities (Eyre and Spottiswoode, 1958)

Notes
1 Ronald Matthews, *Mon Ami Graham Greene* (Desclee de Brouwer, 1957).
2 Alec Craig, *The Banned Books of England* (George Allen and Unwin, 1962), pp. 96–97.
3 Editorial, *Daily Mail*, date? March 1938.
4 Michael Shelden, *Graham Greene: The Man Within* (Heinemann, 1994), pp. 253–54.
5 Kahane, *Memoirs*, p. 269.

LAURENCE DAKIN

With the exception of Kahane himself (under his various pseud-onyms) the most prolific Obelisk author was Laurence Dakin, four of whose books were published by the imprint between 1932 and 1939: three volumes of poetry, and *Prometheus the Fire Giver*, a verse drama. But the frequency with which Obelisk published Dakin had nothing to do with the quality of his work, and everything to do with his willingness to pay. All four of his books are bound in the standard, featureless blue binding Kahane reserved for those using Obelisk as a vanity publishing house, and in one case – *Prometheus* – the produc-tion values are so sloppy that the book's spine label and title page manage to misspell Dakin's first name, giving it as 'Lawrence'.

Information about Dakin is difficult to come by. Born in 1904, he was probably French Canadian: in later life his work was published by Canadian houses every bit as obscure as Obelisk, and he was an occasional contributor to poetry journals based in and around Montreal. Clearly he spent time in France during the 1930s, and an inscribed copy of *Prometheus the Fire Giver* tells us that he was in Monte Carlo in 1939. After that the trail goes cold until he begins to self-publish in Canada in the 1950s. A letter laid in to a copy of Dakin's *Lyrics and Epigrams* tells us that by 1969 he was living in Venice, that he had a son being educated in England, and that he planned to 'attend the IPA convention in Washington, after which I may get to Canada.'[1] Dakin's subject matter and style show that he was a classicist, and the quality of his work is probably best summed up by a contemporary review of one of his Obelisk collections, *Sonnets and Lyrics* (1935). In the *Times Literary Supplement*, Dakin is criticised for his 'tendency to lose the reality of an experience in the embellishment of it.'[2] The incessant ornamentation in Dakin's writing does nothing to disguise the poverty of its inspiration, and it's unsurprising that throughout his life he was rarely able to get his writing published, except at his own expense.

By the same author

Poetry includes:
The House of Orseoli (Falmouth Publishing House, 1952)
Lyrics and Epigrams (Evzone Books, 1969)

Plays include:
Ireneo (Falmouth Book House, 1936)
Pyramus and Thisbe (Falmouth Book House, 1939)
Marco Polo (Falmouth Publishing House, 1946)
Tancred, Prince of Salerno (J. M. Dent, 1948)

Biography:
Ernest Dowson: The Swan of Lee (Papyrus Books, 1972)
Translations include:
Lyrics and Epigrams (Evzone Books, 1969)

Contributor to:
The Dalhousie Review, Vols. 27 and 38

Notes
1 Typed letter from Laurence Dakin to a Professor Bennet, 29 January 1969, author's collection.
2 Unsigned review, *Times Literary Supplement*, 18 July 1935.

ROBERT DAVIS

Human Insights is one of the rarest Obelisk titles, and like Vivian E. Delbos' *For the Duration Or...?* seems to have been published by Kahane as a favour to a friend. The book is a collection of hokey essays and short stories, many of which were first published in the Paris edition of the *New York Herald*. Some are vaguely biblical parables, dour and turgid; most are whimsical, instantly forgettable fireside tales about slightly misbehaving husbands and their slightly disapproving wives, and nostalgic reminiscences about youth and times gone by.

Some of the detail in *Human Insights* appears to be autobiographical, and points to a childhood spent in Cape Cod with a father who conducted home missionary work in Michigan. It's likely that Davis and Kahane were friends: both were in Paris in the 1930s, but stronger evidence is provided by a piece in the book called 'The Man Who Knows His Job'. A bumptious paean to the virtues of hard work and knowing one's place, 'The Man Who Knows His Job' is interesting only for the trip the writer makes, with an unnamed friend, to the village of Arches: 'At Arches, a cleft between wounded hills, a one-storey factory sits at either end of the village, with some thirty peasant houses in between. Whenever a book is published in France the author hopes that he may allow himself the luxury of a few presentation copies upon Arches hand-made paper, not to be duplicated for its velvet texture.'

The Arches paper industry was established at the beginning of the seventeenth century, and a hundred years later was providing most of the paper used in France, including that used for documents and currency during the French Revolution. But by the twentieth century Arches paper had become a luxury item used only by well-to-do watercolourists – and by publishers of *de luxe* limited edition books, selling in small numbers at high prices. In 1929 Sylvia Beach issued 96 *verge d'Arches* copies of the snappily titled *Our Exagmination Round His Factification for Incamination of Work in Progress*, a collection of essays (one of them by Samuel Beckett, his first appearance in book form) discussing and promoting what would become James Joyce's *Finnegans Wake*, and by the time *Human Insights* was published in December 1932 Kahane had already published four *de luxe* editions himself: three (*Haveth Childers Everywhere*, *Cléante and Bélise*, and *Death of a Hero*) in partnership with Henri Babou, and *Pomes Penyeach* with Desmond Harmsworth. A trip to Arches seems a likely one for a fledgling publisher of *de luxe* editions to have made, and it does not seem overly fanciful to suppose that a real-life trip made by Davis and Kahane provided the material for the piece. That the two men were friends certainly seems a far likelier explanation for the publication of *Human Insights* than that anyone ever thought the book had genuine literary value.

The copy of *Human Insights* in the collection of the University of Iowa – one of only three copies located – has been signed 'with best regards' by the author, and bears the inked name 'Caroline Armitage Lee' on the front panel. The inscription was probably the last thing written by Davis ever to find its way into a book: his literary career seems to have begun and ended with this volume.

Note
1 Robert Davis, *Human Insights* (Obelisk Press, 1932), p. 27–28.

VIVIAN F. DELBOS

Unlike most independent imprints operating in Paris between the two world wars, Obelisk was run by a man who was not independently wealthy. Nancy Cunard, Harry Crosby, Edward Titus and Robert McAlmon could all afford to ignore such minor nuisances as profit and loss; for Jack Kahane it was vital that Obelisk made money. The result was a business that was unusual among its rivals for the businesslike way in which it was run. But this did not mean that Kahane was above impulsiveness or partisanship: occasionally he seems to have indulged himself by choosing a book for publication not because it was likely to make money but because it chimed comfortingly with his own sympathies. There can be no other explanation for his decision to publish Robin Anderson's *Four Schools*, for example: a facile rant, but one aimed squarely at a pet hate of Kahane's, the English education system. A war veteran, Kahane was also receptive to books which took the war as their subject. He published three. Of these, Richard Aldington's masterpiece *Death of a Hero* would have found a home on any publisher's list, but while Harold Buckley's *Squadron 95* was issued at the author's expense and so presented no financial risk to its publisher, it is Vivian F. Delbos' book *For the Duration Or...?* which seems to have caught Kahane on a good day. This is not to say that the book is bad – while no masterpiece, it's competently written and cumulatively effective – but its extreme scarcity today suggests what Kahane must have known then, that a slim memoir by an unknown soldier was never likely to shift many copies. Almost certainly Kahane published it as a favour to a friend. *For the Duration Or...?* takes its title from the undertaking given by volunteers who signed up to fight in 1914 that they would fight 'for three years or the duration of the war'. The book is a first-person memoir from the battlefields of the Somme and Passchendaele, told by a soldier called de Breuil who seems to have had a very similar war to Delbos himself.

Born in 1883 in Camberwell, Delbos was raised in Dartmouth, Devon, where his French father worked as a naval instructor. The family was firmly middle class: it had a live-in servant, a wide variety of interests, and was accustomed to achievement. The arts were an important part of family life, and Vivian's older brother Julius was a professor of music in Woldingham, Surrey.[1]

In August 1914 Delbos travelled to London to enlist in the Royal Fusiliers. His enlistment papers tell us that he was five feet seven and weighed only 136 pounds, with brown eyes, black hair, and a sallow complexion – although they're less helpful on how Delbos spent his pre-war years: to the question 'What is your Trade or Calling?' he simply wrote 'Independent'. On 29 August he was passed fit for service and became a private in the Royal Fusiliers; he was discharged four months later and appointed to a commission with the rank of lance-corporal. From there until the armistice, the war records of Delbos himself and de Breuil in *For the Duration Or...?* are so alike – at least, where Delbos' wartime movements can be verified – that it seems safe to assume that the whole book is autobiographical. Both Delbos and de Breuil enlist in London and are given commissions; both volunteer for machine gun sections; both are promoted to captain in 1916; both serve in the Intelligence Corps.[2] There is no evidence to suggest that Delbos saw a friend killed while digging a trench, or that he was given leave in November 1915 to attend his father's funeral, or that he was subjected to a gas attack at the Somme during the battle for Delville Wood, except that all of these these things happen to de Breuil in Delbos' book. Similarly, the accounts of work for Heavy Artillery Intelligence, identifying targets at Passchendaele for infantry attack, of being in Amiens during its bombardment, and of accompanying John Singer Sargent on tours of the front, where he makes endless sketches, are either very well imagined by Delbos the writer, or had been lived by Delbos the soldier.

Exactly when the paths of Delbos and Kahane crossed is unknown, but both enlisted for the Royal Fusiliers in August 1914, and both spoke fluent French, a skill which may have resulted in their being given similar postings. Kahane's memoirs don't mention Delbos (they miss out a lot regarding his war years) but a shared war and enduring friendship seem the likeliest reasons for the appearance of *For the Duration Or...?* on the Obelisk list – one of the rarest of all Obelisk titles.

How Delbos spent the rest of his life, and how and when it ended, is unknown: a travel memoir, *Visages du Maroc* (1937), and a flimsy commonplace book called *Bachelor's Jottings* (1938) are the last footprints he left.

By the same author

Non-fiction:
Visages du Maroc (Fernand Sorlot, 1937)
Bachelor's Jottings (Arthur H. Stockwell, 1938)

Notes
1. Census records, The National Archives, Kew, ref. RG13/2069.
2. War service records of Vivian Francesco Delbos, The National Archives, Kew.

G. SHEILA DONISTHORPE

Gladys Sheila Donisthorpe was a playwright – a fact gleaned partly from her memoir, but mostly from reading her novels.[1] Born in 1898, she was raised in South London and spent three years studying piano at the Royal Academy of Music, before deciding she would prefer a literary career to a musical one. She got her start when Gordon Selfridge hired her to write advertising copy for his London department store, and she supplemented her income for the next three years writing short stories for women's magazines – the legacy of which is unhappily borne by her first novel, *You*, a treacly love story inspired by Donisthorpe's adolescent romance with Freddy Grisewood (who later became the voice of BBC radio for more than fifty years). Three more novels followed – but only two of them are mentioned in Donisthorpe's memoir.

The third, *Loveliest of Friends!*, was published by Old Royalty Book Publishers in London in 1931. It appeared the following year in Paris as part of Kahane's shortlived Boulevard Library series, in a deal brokered by the Paris-based literary agent William Bradley. *Loveliest of Friends!* is a terrible book, but Donisthorpe's reticence about it is probably explained not by its lack of quality but by its subject matter.

It's a novel about lesbians. This is not to say that it's a gay novel, in the way that, say, *The Well of Loneliness* or *The Young and Evil* are gay novels, books whose universes are created and described by authors whose perspective is determined by their sexuality. Donisthorpe's impulse to write her book on the subject probably came from youthful experimentation; it may have been inspired by the experiences of friends. But whatever the reason, Donisthorpe's sexual orientation can be discounted. She wasn't gay, and it shows.

Loveliest of Friends! barely features any real lesbians at all. Instead the book is populated by lots of brisk and sensible women called Audrey or Marjorie, women who pride themselves on their broadmindedness and their ability to look life squarely in the eye. They go to the theatre a lot, squeeze women's hands, and gaze longingly at each other over candlelit supper tables. Then they decide they don't like lesbianism after all and catch the next train back to their husbands in Guildford. It's hilariously serious and achingly awful, and since everything else Donisthorpe wrote seems to have been drawn from life it's probably safe to assume that *Loveliest of Friends!* describes a phase in her personal development she chose not to revisit in her memoirs. (Donisthorpe married in 1916 when she was eighteen years old, and the relationship, though childless, seems to have been a long and happy one.) As a snapshot of 1930s-style lipstick lesbianism, *Loveliest of Friends!* is mildly interesting; as a novel it's catastrophic.

Despite overtures from Jonathan Cape, Donisthorpe mercifully abandoned fiction in the early 1930s. She became a playwright, and her book *Show Business*, published in 1943, is a diverting if conceited look at British theatre of the 1930s and the wartime West End. Her plays were quite successful, despite her belief that 'the recipe of playmaking...may well be compared with the making of a pudding', and her acknowledgement that plots were 'something in which I can summon little interest'.[2] Her first play to be produced, *Children, To Bless You!*, opened at the Ambassadors theatre in 1936 and ran for five months. The following year *Guests of Lancaster Gate* was also a success, and although a farce called *Mermaid's Gout* deserved to flop on the basis of its title if nothing else, a 1941 play based on Donisthorpe's experience of wartime evacuation, *Other People's Houses*, also enjoyed a long and successful run. Her last West End appearance was *Fruit of the Tree*, produced in 1958.

By the same author

Plays include:
Children, To Bless You! (French, 1936)
Other People's Houses (Fortune Press, 1942)
Fruit of the Tree (French, 1958)

Fiction includes:
You (Hurst and Blackett, 1927)
Sets Your Star (Hutchinson, 1933)

Non-fiction:
Show Business (Fortune Press, 1943)

Notes
1 Sheila Donisthorpe, *Show Business* (Fortune Press, 1943).
2 Donisthorpe, *Show Business*, pp. 23 and 55.

NORMAN DOUGLAS

Some time ago a girlfriend who was not much interested in books wandered into my library for the first time. She knew the moment required an appreciative response, and it's to her credit that she did her best to appear interested and impressed. I should have left it at that. Instead, when she asked me to show her something in the room that was particularly special to me, I put in front of her a pamphlet entitled *Report on the Pumice Stone Industry of the Lipari Islands*. She looked at me, I looked at her, and a few days later we called the whole thing off.

If only I'd explained. *Report on the Pumice Stone Industry of the Lipari Islands* was the first title to be issued by Nancy Cunard's Paris-based Hours Press, which between 1928 and 1931 published hand-printed limited editions of books by Samuel Beckett, Richard Aldington, Robert Graves and Ezra Pound, among others. Cunard first met the novelist and travel writer Norman Douglas in 1923; he became a close friend, and a mentor to her for the rest of her life. Born in 1868 but as un-Victorian as it's possible to be, Douglas was an aesthete, polymath and omnisexual hedonist who started out as a naturalist before joining the diplomatic service in 1894. He was later thrown out for sexual misconduct. Somewhat optimistically, Douglas married in 1898: the union produced two children and a divorce, but also produced Norman Douglas, the writer. While married he and his wife collaborated on a collection of short stories which were published in 1901 under the title *Unprofessional Tales*, and although the book sold few copies it set Douglas on his future course. In 1916 he fled England while awaiting trial on charges of indecency with a teenage boy. Unable to return, he spent the rest of his life in seedily glamorous exile, mostly in Florence, Naples or Capri – the setting for his most famous and enduring book, *South Wind*.

Douglas had written his pumice stone report in 1895 while he was still employed by the Foreign Office, and when he heard about Cunard's intention to become a publisher he sent her his only copy so that she could practise her typesetting. (All Hours Press books were hand-set on a 200-year-old Belgian Mathieu hand-press Cunard had bought from William Bird, proprietor of the recently defunct Three Mountains Press.) The pamphlet was a typographical nightmare, which is why Douglas sent it. Cunard knew she was being tested. She slaved over the setting of the text, determined to demonstrate to Douglas (and probably to herself) not only that she was serious about her new enterprise, but also that she was capable of pulling it off. Her edition of Douglas's report ran to just eighty perfectly printed copies; Douglas was delighted, and proudly distributed most of them to friends and collectors of his work. All of which explains how a dreary little pamphlet about pumice stone became item A–1 in the illustrious output of the Hours Press, as well as a touching token of love between friends.

The following year, the Hours Press published a more substantial work by Douglas: *One Day*, a ruminative account of a traveller's wanderings in Athens. It was a productive time for Douglas. Just as his work was helping to launch one press, he was busy in Italy preparing the book which, eleven years later, would bring down the curtain on another.

Norman Douglas was a brilliant and learned man of wide, and in some cases illegal, interests. He liked his art high and his sex low, and his book, *Some Limericks*, is a riotous mixture of both. Published privately in Florence in 1928, the collection is a small one, comprising only 68 examples, but all the old favourites are there: limericks featuring adventurous souls from Devizes, Buckingham, St Paul's, Madras, and, of course, Nantucket. The limericks themselves are prime examples of the genre and of quite outstanding filthiness, but what makes the book laugh-out-loud funny are Douglas's mock-scholarly introduction and his textual annotations. Studious footnotes inform the reader precisely *why* the young man from Newcastle tied up a shit in a parcel and sent it to Spain, while extensive bibliographical cross-referencing is used to solve the mystery of precisely what happened to the offspring of the man from Peru and his parrot. At the time of its writing *Some Limericks* was unpublishable by any reputable company, so Douglas did it himself. He also printed his name on the title page, making *Some Limericks* the first book of its kind to be publicly acknowledged by its author.

Throughout its ten-year existence the Obelisk Press traded on its reputation as a purveyor of smut, but it wasn't until the publication of *Some Limericks* in 1939 – the last book secured for the company during Jack Kahane's lifetime – that the Obelisk list at last included a book that was, by anybody's definition, obscene. Blasphemy, incest, paedophilia, bestiality, Douglas's collection had it all; in fact, the book was so incendiary that it was thought prudent to issue the Obelisk edition stripped of any of the company's usual identifying insignia. Quite *who* issued it is unclear. Kahane died in September 1939: it seems likely that the deal for the book was concluded during his lifetime, but that the book was seen into the bookshops by Maurice Kahane. Douglas's bibliographer Cecil Woolf mentions Girodias's company Les Editions du Chêne in connection with this title, and Girodias was almost certainly responsible for the 'Nicholson and Whitney' piracy of the early 1950s. As proprietor of the Olympia Press, Girodias published *Count Palmiro Vicarion's Book of Limericks* in 1955. Vicarion was the pseudonym of Christopher Logue, and the Olympia book is an expanded version of Douglas's collection, complete with an equally facetious (but nowhere near as funny) introduction in which the debt to *Some Limericks* is cryptically acknowledged, as the 'Count' recalls 'those warm evenings, so long ago but so well-remembered, when that great fellow Douglas and I would swap limericks and trouble the Mediterranean air with our laughter... (Even then I could not resist polishing a little, rerhyming a bit or even borrowing a good idea and casting it into new forms).' In one guise or another, Douglas's *Some Limericks* outlived the Obelisk Press by many years.

Norman Douglas died in Capri in 1952.

By the same author

Fiction includes:
Unprofessional Tales (T. Fisher Unwin, 1901)
South Wind (Martin Secker, 1917)
They Went (Chapman and Hall, 1920)
In the Beginning (privately printed, Florence, 1927)

Non-fiction includes:
Report on the Pumice Stone Industry in the Lipari Islands (HMSO, 1895; Hours Press, 1928)
Siren Land (J. M. Dent, 1911)
Fountains in the Sand (Martin Secker, 1912)
Old Calabria (Martin Secker, 1915)
One Day (Hours Press, 1929)

Notes
1 (Pseud. Christopher Logue), *Count Palmiro Vicarion's Book of Limericks* (Olympia Press, 1962), p. 2 of Foreword.

LAWRENCE DURRELL

Although the two didn't meet until two years later, Lawrence Durrell was first introduced to Henry Miller in the summer of 1935. That year a friend, Barclay Hudson, visited the 23-year-old Durrell in Corfu, and arrived with a copy of *Tropic of Cancer* in his luggage. Durrell was awestruck, and wrote its author a fan letter: '[*Tropic of Cancer*] strikes me as being the only man-size piece of work which this century can really boast of. It's a howling triumph from the word go; and not only is it a literary and artistic smack on the bell for everyone, but it really gets down on paper the blood and bowels of our time. I have never read anything like it.'[1] Miller couldn't have agreed more, and wrote back: 'You're the first Britisher who's written me an intelligent letter about the book. For that matter, you're the first anybody who's hit the nail on the head.'[2] The exchange was the beginning of a lifelong friendship, annotated by a correspondence which spanned nearly half a century and ran to more than a million words.

Tropic of Cancer had been in print for a year by the time Durrell discovered it, and it had brought Miller 'a steady stream of letters and visitors and invitations and what not – which is beginning to bore the shit out of me, though at first it seemed wonderful.'[3] Recognising a kindred spirit, Miller was prepared to make an exception for

[356]

Durrell, and not only encouraged his letters but also urged Durrell to send examples of his own writing 'so that I can return some of the audacious compliments you pay me.'⁴ Durrell stalled: his only novel so far, *Pied Piper of Lovers*, was competent but dully conventional, and in no way representative of the writer he wanted to become. He fobbed Miller off by sending him examples of his poetry ('Think they are splendid,' wrote Miller, 'though the fact is I know nothing about verse'⁵) until, in 1937, he finished *The Black Book*, a book which demonstrated that at the time of its writing the writer Durrell most wished to become was Henry Miller himself.

Tropic of Cancer is what *The Black Book* wants to be when it grows up. Brashly iconoclastic and noisily, pointlessly brilliant, *The Black Book* is an attack on what Durrell saw as the torpid conformism of modern-day life and culture, an epidemic of stultification he christened 'the English Death.' In *Tropic of Cancer* Miller is also scathingly dismissive of social and literary conservatism, and his tone is just as apocalyptic. But Miller was Durrell's senior by twenty years: what reads in Miller as the caustic and ripened raillery of a man enraged by a world which has kicked him all his life comes across in Durrell's book as the shrill hysteria of a child who won't stop screaming unless you give him a sweet. To his credit the difference wasn't lost on Durrell, and in a preface for Maurice Girodias's Olympia edition of *The Black Book*, published in 1959, he acknowledges that the novel was a stage on his journey to authorial maturity rather than an arrival in itself. He also makes a persuasive case for the necessity of writing it: 'With all its imperfections lying heavy on its head, I can't help being attached to it because in the writing of it I first heard the sound of my own voice, lame and halting perhaps, but nevertheless my very own. This is an experience no artist ever forgets – the birth-cry of a newly born baby of letters, the genuine article.'⁶

But the midwife, Miller, was enraptured. Durrell had sent Miller his only copy of the manuscript, disingenuously advising him to 'pitch it in the Seine' if it failed to meet with his approval.⁷ Instead, Miller responded to the book in his characteristically understated way: '*The Black Book* came and I have opened it and I read goggle eyed, with terror, admiration and amazement. I am still reading it – slowing up because I want to savour each morsel, each line, each word. You are *the* master of the English language... You have written things in this book which nobody has dared to write. It's brutal, obsessive, cruel, devastating, appalling. I'm bewildered still. So this is no criticism – and did you want criticism? No, this is a salute to the master!'[8] Miller undertook to do all he could to find a publisher for Durrell, who at the time was only one book in to a three-book contract with Faber, but knew that *The Black Book* would be unpublishable in Britain in unexpurgated form. He wondered: would Miller's Paris publisher be interested?

Miller despised Kahane. He despised him for his vacillation and parsimony while he waited for him to publish *Tropic of Cancer*; he despised him as the author of *Daffodil* and *Suzy Falls Off*; he despised him for being '[a] really impossible fellow, stupid as they make 'em, and yet "sharp", I suppose, in a business way'.[9] But Miller mostly despised Kahane because he was beholden to him, forced by necessity into a business relationship with a man who, under any other circumstances, he would have crossed continents to avoid. As with *Tropic of Cancer*, no other publisher would dream of handling *The Black Book*. But the thought of negotiating with Kahane all over again, and of bolstering his reputation by delivering to him a writer of ability and promise, was more than Miller could bear. Durrell came to see that he would have to cajole Miller into overcoming his prejudices in the interests of art (and of Durrell). He was unable to bring enough pressure to bear on Miller from Corfu, and so in 1937, after two years of letter-writing, Durrell and his wife Nancy travelled to Paris to meet Miller in person for the first time.

Miller and Durrell got on as famously in person as they had by post. Alfred Perlès witnessed their first meeting at Miller's studio in the Villa Seurat, and remembered Durrell being

> fresh from Corfu, with the Ionian tan still on his face and hands. Of him, I first perceived the laughter, which kept reverberating through the high-ceilinged studio: an almost continuous laughter, loud and persistent: from the guts. He and Henry were gay. They were having a party that must have been going on for the better part of the day, and which was to go on, intermittently, for over a year. The place was littered with bottles and glasses, books, remnants of food and manuscript pages, the smoke of their cigarettes spiralling up to the ceiling, curling along the ceiling, like clouds of incense.[10]

One of the highlights of this year-long party was the group's brief but colourful administration of a magazine called *The Booster*. At the time of Durrell's arrival in Paris Perlès was working part-time as a subscription collector for the American Golf and Country Club at

Ozoir-la-Ferrière. The club secretary asked Perlès if he and his writer friends would be interested in taking over the running of the club magazine. Yes, said Perlès, they would. The September 1937 issue of *The Booster* notified the club's membership of a few changes to the magazine's editorial board. Durrell, Miller and William Saroyan were made Literary Editors. The Society Editor was Anaïs Nin, with the Oriental Department taken care of by Tcheou Nien-Sien. In an exciting departure for a golf club magazine, Michael Fraenkel was put in charge of the Department of Metaphysics and Metempsychosis, while Butter News was entrusted to Walter Lowenfels. This eclectic editorial board produced an invigorating mix of literary experimentalism, pornographic poems, and golf news. *The Booster* was a Dadaist battle cry issued, in true Dada style, to the golfers of France. It was an experiment which, understandably, has never been repeated and which after four issues got everyone involved with it fired (although the same group resurfaced three months later with a new and similarly short-lived magazine, *Delta*).

But although Durrell was having the time of his life, the publication of *The Black Book* was no nearer. By now its author realised that although his friend's appreciation of his work was effusive and sincere, Miller's preference for self-promotion above any other kind made him an unreliable champion of other people's work. The project would need to be refocused in order to secure his help. At the time Anaïs Nin was also looking for a publisher for her new book, *Winter of Artifice*, while Miller's *Max and the White Phagocytes* was almost finished. Durrell floated the idea of publishing all three books as the first in a series which would look to bring work by new writers to a discerning and adventurous readership. The list would be headed by Miller, whose reputation would attract other writers to the stable (subject to Miller's approval of them). This rebranding did the trick: the upgrading of Miller's role from helpful friend to founder of a literary movement helped him see what a very good idea it would be to get *The Black Book* published, and he started to work on Kahane by plying him with drinks at his 'office', the Castiglione bar. From Kahane's standpoint there were myriad reasons *not* to publish the expected slow sales, the prohibitive exchange rate, the absence of tourists in Paris, and the increasingly threatening international situation were four of them – but a deal was eventually thrashed out. The books would be published by Obelisk with Kahane taking 20 per cent of the income from sales, but they would have their own collective identity, with a slightly different design, a slightly higher retail price, and a name of their own: the Villa Seurat series. Secondly, while they would be issued through Obelisk's established chain of distribution, printing costs for *The Black Book* and *Winter of Artifice* would be borne by the authors. (The bill was probably picked up by Durrell's wife, although Maurice Girodias later asserted that Durrell and Nin each paid for the other's book, so that neither would feel they were involved in anything that might be construed as vanity publishing.)

The fine print of the deal notwithstanding, everybody was happy – although Durrell had good reason to complain when *The Black Book* finally appeared, strewn with misprints and with pages misbound (the result of a combination of a greenhorn editor – Miller himself – and printers who couldn't read English). But as Miller had found when the first copies of *Tropic of Cancer* were delivered to him encased in Maurice Kahane's luridly inappropriate jacket design, the mere fact of his book's existence was enough for Durrell. He had threatened to give up writing altogether if no publisher could be found for *The Black Book*; his subsequent career, and not the book itself, is the reason to be most grateful that one was.

By the same author

Fiction includes:
Pied Piper of Lovers (Cassell, 1935)
Panic Spring (as 'Charles Norden') (Faber and Faber, 1937)
Justine (Faber and Faber, 1957)
Balthazar (Faber and Faber, 1958)
Mountolive (Faber and Faber, 1958)
Clea (Faber and Faber, 1960)

Poetry includes:
Quaint Fragment (Cecil Press, 1931)
Bromo Bombasts (Caduceus Press, 1933)
Transition (Caduceus Press, 1934)
A Private Country (Faber and Faber, 1943)
Collected Poems: 1931–1974 (Faber and Faber, 1980)

Non-fiction includes:
Prospero's Cell (Faber and Faber, 1945)
Bitter Lemons (Faber and Faber, 1957)
Spirit of Place (Faber and Faber, 1969)
The Greek Islands (Faber and Faber, 1978)

Notes

1 Ian S. MacNiven, ed., *The Durrell–Miller Letters, 1935–80* (Faber and Faber, 1989), p. 2.
2 MacNiven, ed., *The Durrell–Miller Letters*, p. 3.
3 MacNiven, ed., *The Durrell–Miller Letters*, p. 5.
4 MacNiven, ed., *The Durrell–Miller Letters*, p.5.
5 MacNiven, ed., *The Durrell–Miller Letters*, p. 14.
6 Lawrence Durrell, preface to *The Black Book* (Olympia Press, 1959), p. 7.
7 MacNiven, ed., *The Durrell–Miller Letters*, p. 25.
8 MacNiven, ed., *The Durrell–Miller Letters*, p. 55.
9 MacNiven, ed., *The Durrell–Miller Letters*, p. 70.
10 Alfred Perlès, *My Friend Lawrence Durrell* (Scorpion Press, 1961), p. 10.

ANNE BELLINZANI FERRAND

In *Cléante et Bélise*, Bélise has been in love with the much older Cléante since childhood. A little later in life, her advantage of youthfulness cancelled out by her physical plainness, Bélise cultivates her intellectual attainments in an attempt to arouse Cléante's interest. On discovering him to be in love with another woman she tries to become a nun but is thwarted by her father, who marries her off to a man of his own choosing. Cléante's wife dies, Bélise resumes her wooing, and the two begin an affair. When Cléante is sent to Italy as the king's ambassador, absence fails to make the heart grow fonder: he writes only occasionally and without feeling, she begins an affair with another man, and physical love is identified as the destroyer of the pure *galanterie* that had bound the two so closely together.

When the first edition of *Histoire Nouvelles des Amours de la Jeune Bélise et de Cléante divisée en Trois Parties* appeared in 1689, its author was identified only as 'Mr. D.' This was no more than a nod in the direction of anonymity: Bellinzani, whose maiden name was also spelt 'Belisani' and who was a well-known figure in Parisian society, ensured she would be quickly identified as the novel's author by making its heroine her namesake. Since the book draws heavily on its author's own life, and since its subject is adulterous love and ensuing heartbreak, Bellinzani seems to have decided that if she couldn't be happy she would settle for notoriety and defiance, hoping to find in them if not contentment, at least an absence of actual misery.

Born in 1658, Anne Bellinzani was the wife of Michel Ferrand, president of the first chamber of requests in the Paris parliament. Cléante's real-life counterpart was the Baron de Breteuil and, like Cléante,

Breteuil was betrayed by Bellinzani when she took a lover in his absence. She obtained a separation from her husband in 1686, but lost custody of her three children and was confined to a convent. Already pregnant, she gave birth seven months later to a child whom Ferrand refused to recognise, and was then sent by Ferrand to an abbey near Chartres where she spent the next four years, during which time she wrote *Cléante et Bélise*. After her exile Bellinzani returned to Paris where, although barred from court, she presided over her own *salon*. In 1715 she was taken to court by her 'illegitimate' daughter who was seeking recognition as one of Ferrand's heirs. The case wasn't settled until 1738, when the court found in the daughter's favour. Bellinzani died in 1740 at the age of 83.

It seems likely that Kahane conceived the idea of publishing *Cléante and Bélise* after reading *Nous Deux*, an erotic novel written, like much of *Cléante and Bélise*, in epistolary form. *Nous Deux* is widely believed to have been written by Marcel Valotaire, illustrated by Jean Dulac, and published privately by Valotaire in Paris in 1929. This was the year Kahane was translating Valotaire's work on Babou's series *Les Artistes du Livre*, and it's reasonable to suppose that he would have known about, and read, *Nous Deux*. It would have been a forceful (and graphic) reminder that Valotaire's interests were not confined to minor French illustrators, and may have been an incentive to Kahane to cast his own net a little wider too. The text and illustrations of *Nous Deux* are much more sexually frank than anything in *Cléante and Bélise*, but by toning down both words and pictures – and by retreating into the comparative safety of 'literature' – Kahane aimed to produce a book whose contents would be sufficiently rarefied to cultivate a reputation for himself as a serious publisher, sufficiently *risqué* to ensure healthy sales, and sufficiently demure to avoid police attention. In this Kahane was 'moderately successful: one of the engravings had a little too much Gallic freedom for English and American custom agents, who could not appreciate the delicious wittiness of it. But we got most of our money back.'[1]

Notes
1 Kahane, *Memoirs*, p. 222.

MARJORIE FIRMINGER

Marjorie Firminger first met Wyndham Lewis in the middle of 1929. That March she'd gone to Berlin to be at the bedside of a friend who was having an abortion, and while she'd been away the actor and painter Elliott Seabrooke had been using her upper maisonette at 19 Glebe Place, Chelsea, as a makeshift studio. Seabrooke and Lewis had recently met, and when Firminger returned to London Seabrooke was keen to introduce his old friend to his new one.

Marjorie Firminger was born in Streatham, South London, in 1899. Her father died when she was seven, after which her relationship with her mother, a grief-stricken, emotionally stunted woman who rarely praised her daughter, was always difficult. A bright girl, Marjorie was educated first by a governess, and later at Cheltenham Ladies' College, eventually returning to the capital a socially confident, vivacious young woman, lacking money but with style in abundance, someone perfectly at home among the flappers and floozies of 1920s' smart-set London.

Now thirty years old, five years earlier she'd made a promising start as an actress when she'd been cast by Kenneth Barnes as the girl-about-town Penelope Foxglove in his play *The Letter of the Law*. In September 1924 the play opened at the Grand Theatre, Putney Bridge, to enthusiastic reviews, many of which gave Marjorie's cameo appearance an honourable mention: 'as a flighty and unprincipled pleasure-seeker [she] contributed valuable support,'[1] noted one critic; 'the epitome of Miss Mayfair 1924,'[2] gushed another. But the 28 performances of *The Letter of the Law* turned out to be the high point of Marjorie's acting career. Worse, her marriage to a 'wild young gunner'[3] called Julian Firminger failed, and by 1929 she was scratching a living writing fashion notes for women's weekly magazines. She had a lover, but more for practical reasons than romantic ones: the rent on her home in Glebe Place, Chelsea, was £180 per annum, and was being paid in part by Sir Edward Morphy. He would visit Marjorie every Wednesday evening – Wednesday being the day his wife visited *her* lover – but rarely at any other time. When she got back home from what must have been a grim trip to Berlin, she was unlikely to have been in any mood to entertain an over-achieving, intellectual alpha-male of the magnitude of Wyndham Lewis.

If Marjorie was intimidated in advance, the personal appearance of Lewis, nearly twenty years her senior and an 'arch highbrow',[4] would have done nothing to put her at ease. He arrived at her flat on the appointed evening, Seabrooke in tow, wearing a crumpled dark suit and a large black hat with a floppy brim which remained on his head all evening. He chose a hard chair, slouched forward with his elbows on his knees, and looked up at her from under the brim of his hat. Marjorie, underconfident, flustered and fearing a catastrophic evening, did what she'd always done in such situations ever since she was a child, and blushed bright scarlet. She needn't have worried. To her relief, Lewis didn't ask for her opinion of Vorticism, or the London School, or what she thought of his books, and he didn't mention those subjects himself. Instead, he set about filleting Marjorie of all the gossip she had about London's smart set, the 'bright young things' whose exploits were outraging their elders and delighting the daily scandal sheets in roughly equal measure. Marjorie was delighted to be able to oblige him: gossip – or 'chit', as she called it – was a subject which, as an ex-actress and part-time fashion correspondent, came easily to her. Remembering the pinnacle of her acting career she eased herself back into the role of Penelope Foxglove, and told Lewis scurrilous stories about her friends, their intrigues and rivalries, and about the lesbians that formed part of the set – the 'chaps'. Lewis was especially gratified to hear stories about people he knew well, people such as Sidney Schiff and Richard Wyndham, who had strayed sufficiently far into Marjorie's social orbit to enable her to be indiscreet about them. But there was one titbit she decided not to mention. That summer she had begun work on a novel, set in the same world and featuring the same people that she and Lewis were spending the evening dissecting. She felt she would only make herself look ridiculous by telling Lewis about her project: she had yet to get very far with it, she was an unpublished amateur, and he was Wyndham Lewis. For now at least she kept her secret to herself.

The evening was a big success: Lewis was thrilled to hear all the gossip, and Marjorie was thrilled Lewis had found her interesting. They stayed in touch, at first through their mutual friend Seabrooke, later independently of him. Marjorie's gloom started to lift, and her self-esteem rose. She began to believe in herself as a writer, was heartened that the lightweight subject matter of her book had interested a heavyweight such as Lewis, and began to apply herself more seriously to getting the novel written.

One day later that summer Lewis arrived unannounced at Glebe Place to invite Marjorie to dinner at his flat, alone. Marjorie (who was thirty years old and should have known better) was becoming starstruck. She was flattered that she had been singled out 'by the artist who had been outstanding before World War I as a founder of the Vorticist movement in painting (I was a bit hazy as to what that was)... [but] above all by the author of *Tarr*, which I had now read, and which was fast becoming my Bible.'[5] (By this time she'd also fought her way through Lewis's *Time and Western Man*, resolving to read every philosopher Lewis mentioned in the book so that she would have a fighting chance of understanding it the next time she read it.) The elation she felt at having an established artist wanting to spend time with her was making her oblivious to the imbalance of power between them.

That first evening alone together, in the room Lewis rented in Bayswater at 53 Ossington Street, followed a pattern similar to that of their previous meetings, and was a similar success. Just as before, he kept his hat on; just as before, she blushed bright red. This time a convenient alibi was provided by the room's gas fire, which Lewis kept on at full blast even in the height of summer. But even if he'd noticed her blushing, Marjorie tried to persuade herself that it didn't matter, 'because surely Lewis did not see me primarily as a woman any more than I saw him primarily as a man. He was the Genuine Artist with whom I could laugh and even be of small use to by giving him gossip.'[6] The subject of conversation for the evening was Berlin. Lewis had been there the previous year, and was flirtatiously keen to hear Marjorie's impressions of the transvestite clubs and lesbian bars (which she'd been to) and the bondage brothels (which she hadn't). Marjorie, unable to blush any deeper than she had already, held her own, and when the conversation turned back to London she put the seal on her sophistication by confiding to Lewis about her lover Sir Edward Morphy and the contribution he made to her rent. Lewis, equally sophisticated, was appalled that Morphy wasn't paying all of it. Had Marjorie been more inclined to be wary of Lewis she would have been put on her guard when he leaned in and advised her, slowly and deliberately: 'People. Are. There. To. Be. Used.' That evening Lewis was particularly taken with a phrase Marjorie used to denote a sexual conquest – 'got him in the bed' – and intoned it to himself several times. He made Marjorie promise to bring one of her lesbian friends along with her next time, and peremptorily bundled her into a taxi in the Bayswater Road, announcing that he had to get back to the provinces.

[365]

'Getting back to the provinces' was the euphemism Lewis used for going to bed. He had a 'house' of sorts, but it consisted of a number of rooms scattered all over London. In the summer of 1929, the room in which he and Marjorie gossiped was Lewis's study, and his library was in a house a few doors along. His studio was somewhere else entirely, and his bedroom was in Notting Hill – 'the provinces'. This unusually elastic domestic arrangement was perfect for a man with as many enemies and creditors as Lewis, enabling him as it did to be simultaneously at home, and out. Marjorie, whose fear of appearing to pry enabled Lewis to get away with telling her almost nothing about himself, never cottoned on to the arrangement, and always wondered why such a distinguished artist, who could command sixty or seventy pounds for a single drawing, was apparently living in one room.

The relationship between the two seemed to Marjorie to deepen with the lengthening of the year. Happy, she worked steadily on her novel, *Jam To-day*, and introduced many of the characters' real-life counterparts to Lewis. Among them were Michael Bruce, who appears in the novel as Lord Jerry Poon; and the model for the book's principal lesbian character, Bracken Dilitor, who in real life went by the altogether more sensible name of Heather Pilkington. (It was Pilkington whom Firminger paraded before Lewis in response to his request to meet one of her lesbian friends.) Pilkington was 'mannishly suited and with cropped hair, [and] she was often to be seen in Chelsea driving her huge car, her dalmatian alongside, probably en route for the house of her beloved, the wife of a theatrical manager.'[7] The beloved in question was Wyn Henderson, a friend of Nancy Cunard, and a collaborator with Cunard on the Hours Press in Paris. She appears in *Jam To-day* as Mrs Wikk, who is 'over six feet and colossally fat', and who 'rapes her way about a bit and got a sausage millionaire to buy her a bookshop'.[8] The new friend she had found in Lewis had clearly given her the confidence not to mind losing a few old ones.

At Christmas Marjorie, now very much the self-assured novelist-to-be, wrote to Lewis: 'I've just finished writing, as a letter, the Heather episode and I think it's the funniest I've written. I read it aloud to Alick [Schepeler] last night to see what it sounded like, and she took it quite seriously and said that I should make enemies if I publish it. Heather now calls me a cad.'[9]

In January 1930, she finally summoned up the courage to ask Lewis to 'flick over' the typescript of *Jam To-day*, but she received no reply from him and for weeks he disappeared from view, her letters unacknowledged. He resurfaced in March. Marjorie had been disconcerted by his absence, but he'd never vouchsafed her any information about his private life and she was too meek to ask. She was happy to forget the whole thing when he invited her to Ossington Street just as before. This time he asked her not about her friends, but her book. By now *Jam To-day* had been submitted to publishers in London, Duckworth and Wishart among them, but had been turned down for fear there would be 'an awful row among the lesbians',[10] with the possibility of libel actions to follow. Marjorie wondered aloud to Lewis whether she was being let down lightly, whether privately the publishers thought the book had no literary merit:

> 'But they wouldn't know if it had,' Lewis said firmly.
>
> It was then that I saw him as God. Of course 'They' – the agents and publishers – wouldn't know. Unlike Lewis, they weren't the All Knowing All Seeing Eye – the only Eye I must approach, if I wanted a true verdict on the chances of being published. So I asked him if he could possibly spare time to flick over the typescript... I told him I had mentioned him by name in the novel, quoting from his book *Paleface*. Any reference to himself aroused his interest, and this certainly seemed to. I also told him that I had made one of my characters say something that I had been told he himself had said. This really roused him. 'What was that?', he asked. Well, I had been told that when a woman had once asked him for some money for the two children he was supposed to have had by her, all he had replied was 'Really? Were there two?' This seemed to strike him as funny, just as it had struck me, and we both had one of our unselfconscious bursts of laughter. He must certainly have a look at my novel, he said.[11]

Marjorie returned home that night 'feeling giddy with happiness'[12] and sent the book to Lewis the next day.

On her next visit to Ossington Street Marjorie found her typescript strewn all over the floor. Choosing to see this as an indication that Lewis had been reading it, she was further heartened when he asked to be allowed to send it to his new American publisher, Donald Friede. Americans were less prudish and less litigious, Lewis advised – they might even want the manuscript gingered up a little. The search for a publisher in Britain having come to nothing, Marjorie was only too happy to agree, and returned home 'feeling happier than ever, and determined to get down to my next novel, which I was going to call *That Cad Jane* and preface with a quotation from *Time and Western Man*'.[13]

By now the secret of Marjorie Firminger's novel was out. Copies had been submitted to publishers, and publishers had slipped the word to their friends. As a result, the bright young things were now aware of *Jam To-day*'s existence, and of the fact that many of them played leading roles in it. Wyn Henderson had been complimentary about the book at first, declaring that Marjorie might be what they'd all been looking for, the female Casanova. But she hadn't read the whole novel before delivering her verdict, and the character based on her, a colossally fat dyke being bankrolled by a sausage millionaire, doesn't appear in the first two hundred pages; by the time Henderson finished the book her admiration for it had, not surprisingly, cooled. Nancy Cunard, who on rather flimsy evidence also believed herself to be lampooned in the novel, was similarly outraged. Heather Pilkington had more reason than anyone to be upset, since apart from a change of name she appears almost completely undisguised, and her attempt, probably sexually motivated, to persuade Marjorie to share a flat with her is recounted in the novel verbatim. Pilkington was hurt, and said so, but Marjorie was dismissive of the hostile reaction of her social circle. She'd been sufficiently swayed by Lewis's dictum – 'friends are there to be used' – not to be troubled by the fact that she had made her own unhappy. It was an attitude that later was to leave her short of supporters when she needed them most.

By now Firminger had known Lewis for almost a year and still knew practically nothing about him. Her long, effusive and frequent letters were answered, if they were answered at all, with brief, uninformative notes. When they were together it was always the same: she would talk, and he would listen. She was happy to regard his uncommunicativeness as part of the true artist's brooding mystique. He was happy to let her.

When Wyndham Lewis's *The Apes of God* was published on 3 June Marjorie was frantic to get hold of a copy, but the 600-page, three-pound breezeblock of a book cost three guineas, more than she could afford. She wrote to Lewis asking to borrow a copy, but received no reply, so 'eventually I pawned something and bought...copy no. 697 (signed)'.[14] *The Apes of God* is a vast, sprawling satire in which Lewis takes aim at everyone he ever met whom he regarded as dull, talentless, unattractive, or all three. One of Lewis's lifelong grievances was the tyranny that money, or the lack of it, imposes on the genuine artist, and the injustice of wealthy but untalented imposters – the

'Apes' – buying up all the best studio spaces in London and Paris, space that would be far better used by the poor but gifted artist. Lewis gives the subject its most caustic outing in *The Apes of God*. The Sitwells are filleted, the Bloomsbury Group fares no better and, further down the literary food chain, every high-born, inbred no-hoper who ever put down his monocle and picked up a pen is kicked to within an inch of his life . The book is massive, but its targets are tiny: the result is an occasionally dazzling, mostly dull, ultimately pointless 250,000-word exercise in score-settling.

Marjorie loved it – at least, she loved the chapters she managed to get through. She didn't read it all (few have) but the scabrous portrait of their mutual friend and gossip-subject Sydney Schiff – a generous patron of Lewis whose reward was to be insulted and ridiculed in print – delighted her, confirming her in her belief that she was not just a friend to Lewis the man, but also a muse to Lewis the artist.

In July she became his patron, too. Lewis arrived unexpectedly at Glebe Place one day, explained that the book had made him unpopular with a number of people, and that he needed to get up a manifesto to defend himself. He wondered if he could borrow five pounds 'to get a bit of typing done':

> 'Of course, of *course*,' I said, hastening to write the cheque. 'Pay Wyndham Lewis £5. Marjorie Firminger.' I had never enjoyed writing a cheque before.
>
> When I gave it to him he looked at it carefully for quite a time, which made me fear I had made some slip. But no. The thing was, would it be convenient for him to have cash instead? 'Of course of *course*,' I said again, though not now as I had none, and the bank would be shut – or just about. 'Never mind,' he said. He'd look in to collect it in a few days. About the same time if that was convenient?[15]

Lewis's pamphlet *Satire and Fiction* appeared later that year, although it's unlikely that any of Marjorie's five pounds was spent on its production.

The campaign to find a publisher for *Jam To-day* received another setback when after a long delay (probably caused by Lewis's neglecting to send off the manuscript when he said he would) Covici rejected the book. At Lewis's suggestion Marjorie had gingered up the text before submitting it, but in so doing had crystallised the problem facing any prospective publisher: Covici wrote to her saying that 'with the details it could not be sold and without them it would not sell'.[16] But before the disappointment could cast her too low, Marjorie received a rare lucky break: a friend, Audrey Lucas, offered to introduce her to Moma Clarke. Clarke was a writer of dress notes for *The Times* and was also the wife of the Paris-based printer and publisher Herbert Clarke, which made her a potentially useful contact for Marjorie on two fronts. On hearing about her forthcoming trip to Paris to meet the Clarkes, Lewis suggested she drop in on Edward Titus of the Black Manikin Press during her visit. Marjorie left England in an optimistic mood: 'It was a still hot morning of exceptional beauty, and when the boat sailed out of Newhaven Harbour I felt nearly faint with excitement. I have seldom had any but bad premonitions, but as I crossed the calm glittering sea I felt sure something extraordinary was going to come of this visit. Knowing Lewis seemed to make this inevitable.'[17]

It didn't start well. Titus was out when she went to visit him at his shop in the rue Delambre: 'Just as well I thought as I looked at the books in his shop window: surely I could not hope to be included in a list like that?'[18] Tea with the Clarkes was much more productive. Herbert Clarke had just turned down the opportunity of publishing a cheap edition of *Lady Chatterley's Lover* because his wife had found the language in it offensive; now he was having to sit and watch while Titus's edition flew off the shelves. The experience had made him determined to publish the next 'hot' book that came his way, regardless of his wife's objections. Marjorie gave him *Jam To-Day*, promised to spice it up still further if he'd like – and a deal was done:

> I did not wholly believe I was to be published till the following morning. Then, as I sat in the Tuileries, my last apprehensions faded away with the last curves of the pale autumn mist and I was filled with an unearthly joy. Not only of having got something I wanted, but of having got rid of something too; from henceforth I needn't strive to play any one particular part in life – not even Penelope Foxglove ['Miss Mayfair 1924'] to please Lewis. My characters would take over instead. I myself would be no-one and everyone. I would be *all* the characters I could create. And how they came crowding in on me as I sat on and on, dreaming.[19]

While in Paris Marjorie met another author about to be published by Clarke: a 'tall, flamboyant-looking man'[20] called Jack Kahane. Sheepish about the lowly literary status of his book *Daffodil*, Kahane explained to Marjorie that his novel-writing was just a sideline, that as a publisher he was about to issue a book by James Joyce with his business partner, Henri Babou. Attracted as he always was by the combination of risqué material and a female author, he made Marjorie promise to keep in touch. When she returned home it was with a fuller address book, a three-book contract, and a commitment from Herbert Clarke to publish *Jam To-day* in December.

Marjorie's stay in London was brief, and most of the rest of the year was spent in Paris, but while she was home Lewis took the oppor tunity to grill her for news of his Paris enemies, real and imagined. By now Marjorie, as enthralled as ever by Lewis's stature as an artist, was wearying of the unchanging nature of their relationship: she had hoped that after an acquaintance of more than a year she would have become something more to him than a noticeboard. She was clearly attracted to Lewis, not just as an artist but as a man, and her infatu-ation was enough to make her swallow her disappointment at the little time they spent together and the infrequency of his letters. She preferred always to see him as the preoccupied creator, as a loner subject to moods, an explanation far more palatable to her than indif-ference. Once safely back in Paris she composed her most forthright letter yet, written from behind a barricade of piled-up saucers on her table at the Café Flore: 'I have enjoyed seeing you very much, annoying though I have found it to be limited so much to time. About an hour of me seems enough for you! Why? Does my giggle annoy you? Really, I only do it when I am nervous, and I have felt rather nervous during the short times I have seen you... I've wanted to get all I could said in it – and all the time I've been aware it was hopeless to try to.'[21]

Having said her piece, her other letters to Lewis written in the autumn of 1930 revert to type: flattering, full of the gossip he liked, and flirtatious. Her excitement at the prospect of soon becoming a published writer is obvious and touching, and seems to have given her the confidence to believe that she was now approaching Lewis, if not on an equal footing, at least as one author to another.

When not writing Lewis long and chatty letters Marjorie worked on two books: *That Cad Jane*, already begun in London, and a new novel to which she'd given the provisional title *After Thirty*. Marjorie envisaged *After Thirty* as an outspoken novel, confrontational and 'frank', a racier and more bitingly satirical version of *Jam To-day*. Lewis irked her by insisting on referring to it as her 'filthy book'. She had shown sections of it to Samuel Putnam at New Review Publications in Paris, and had been encouraged by the response. Jack Kahane, too, was hovering, careful always to stress how little money he had, but always on the lookout for anything he and his new partner might publish.

On 25 November 1930 Marjorie sent an advance copy of *Jam To-day* to Lewis in London, taking care to cut the pages herself 'in case you'd like to flick them over and see how it's printed'.[22] A delay at the bindery set back publication until the middle of December, and Marjorie spent the time at the Hotel Nacional in Madrid working over the chapters of *That Cad Jane* she was planning to submit to Kahane. She held out little hope that her association with him would bear fruit. She found him irritating both socially and professionally ('he hinted [the book] might be a bit too strong – he is still on the naughty-naughty track'[23]) and was anyway tied to a three-book deal with Herbert Clarke. But seeing problems ahead for her newly 'frank' style of literary expression she made the decision to cultivate everyone who might be useful to her in the future. Even Edward Titus, whose shop window had so intimidated Marjorie when she'd first arrived in Paris, was not ruled out as a possible future publisher if Clarke and Kahane found her new material too hot to handle.

By Christmas Marjorie was back in Paris, and had heard from London that trouble was brewing:

> I hear from Elliott [Seabrooke] that Heather is going to sue me if the Jam book comes out in England. He met her at a party Nancy Cunard took him to lately. Certain people are being very nasty – I hear. I am looking forward to finding out particulars when I get back. The book is only just out here, and there has been no publicity yet: it is better to wait 'til after Christmas. I was interviewed by the Tatler a few days ago and hope something comes of it... I have seen noone but Kahane. He's given me a note to Sylvia Beach, saying she must sell my book. He suggested my meeting him there that afternoon, when he was meeting Joyce – but I'd had enough of him for one day.[24]

By early January 1931 Marjorie was back in London. Her delight at finally being published was matched by Herbert Clarke's glee when a crate en route to England containing copies of *Jam To-day* was seized by Customs. This enabled Clarke to attach a label to copies being sold in France proudly declaring that the book had been BANNED IN ENGLAND. Lewis teased Marjorie that her 'dirty books' would soon be flooding Europe. She took exception, as she always did when Lewis failed to take her work seriously, but was more than mollified when he suddenly offered to draw her portrait. Marjorie was thrilled, not least because before leaving Paris in January Herbert Clarke, aware of her friendship with Lewis, had asked whether it might be possible to elicit a portrait from him that could be put on the cover of her next book. She'd not felt she had the right to ask, but now that he'd offered of his own volition she was determined to hold him to his word, and when Lewis failed to follow up his offer with an appointment for a sitting she wrote him gentle reminders, trying to tempt him with promises of 'chit'.

Marjorie had arranged to visit Clarke in Paris to show him *After Thirty*, and had hoped to arrive with a Lewis drawing under her arm; when she got there she had to explain that Lewis had not yet kept his promise. This would have mattered more if the meeting had gone well, but Clarke rejected *After Thirty*, and was baffled by Samuel Putnam's apparent interest in it. Things were no better in London. Despite at least one affair during her stay in Paris the previous winter, Marjorie's relationship with Sir Edward Morphy had been staggering on. Now it fell: Morphy's wife had been scandalised by *Jam To-day*, and was worried that sooner or later she and her husband would turn up in print. Sir Edward shared his wife's outrage and concern, and put an end to the affair in a letter in which he told Marjorie: 'I leave you to get on with your vomit.'[25] Single again, the rent became a problem. Marjorie moved all her things into the upstairs rooms at Glebe Place and sublet the lower floor.

One morning in the spring of 1931 Lewis arrived at Glebe Place unannounced. He was always welcome whether he was expected or not, but this time he'd chosen badly. Marjorie was in agony from 'an unusually painful dose of the curse, an indication, possibly, of the big operation [for the removal of a fibroid] I was to have within a year.'[26] To make matters worse, Lewis had arrived with a large portfolio under his arm, with the intention of making good on his promise to draw Marjorie's portrait. Rather than tell Lewis the truth, that she was in terrible pain, Marjorie extemporised some excuse about being in the wrong clothes. Seeing his chance, Lewis conveniently inferred indifference, packed up his things and left. Marjorie was mortified, and wrote Lewis a note the next day, urging him to come back soon.

But having sent the letter Marjorie felt depressed that she was courting contact so abjectly. In a rare moment of lucidity she saw her relationship with Lewis for what it was rather than what she would have liked it to be. Her letters to him had always been long and chatty, full of gossip and personal confidences; his replies were infrequent, uncommunicative and short. During the two years they had known each other Marjorie had kept Lewis fully informed about everything that was going on in her life. During those same two years, unbeknown to Marjorie, Lewis had provided financial and legal assistance to an illegitimate son who'd been involved in a burglary; he'd visited Berlin where, in an epiphany that was to have catastrophic repercussions for his reputation, he'd been seduced by the proselytising of Goering and Goebbels before a crowd of twenty thousand people; and he'd got married. Marjorie's disillusionment with Lewis's treatment of her coincided with a more general disillusionment at the life she'd been living. Both were crystallised in a letter she sent him:

> You probably won't want to see me again for some time, as I don't think you like me as a human being – I have been, to you, just a giggling confused source of chit! But I like you as a person very much indeed, and think of you a great deal, and should be delighted as ever if you turned up. You probably realise this, but it's just possible that you don't, so I write it. I think we should meet, but it may be years hence.
>
> Unless I have a good bit of news about myself or you, I won't write again. I'm not likely to hear so much chit now, as I'm not interested in it, and don't see many of the people I used to. They are no use to me – I shall not again, I think, be gossip column news! If I am heard, which eventually I shall be, I shan't need them.

For the first and only time in her correspondence with Lewis, she signed off the letter 'with love'.[27]

Some much-needed good news arrived from Paris when Herbert Clarke wrote to her to say that *Jam To-day* was selling well, and that he'd taken orders from as far afield as Chicago, Singapore and Cape Town. But the letter was the last she was to receive from him. Clarke died suddenly, and the Vendôme Press was bought, contracts and all, by the man who had bored her so comprehensively during her time in Paris, Jack Kahane. Some small compensation had been provided by the French paper *Aux Ecoutes*, which had compared Kahane's novel *Daffodil* unfavourably to *Jam To-day*, calling Marjorie's book 'beaucoup plus drôle, plus vigoreux et plus vrai'.[28] Marjorie had by now laid aside *That Cad Jane* and had started work on another novel, provisionally entitled *Love at Last*. On taking charge at the Vendôme Press, Kahane had 'lost no time in writing to me to say that he hoped that *Love at Last* wouldn't be long in arriving. He had changed the name of the VENDOME press to the OBELISK, and wrote on bright yellow paper with a phallic looking obelisk rearing up at the top. His letter depressed me'.[29] Also depressing was the news from America: Samuel

Putnam wrote to say that although everyone there had liked *After Thirty*, all had agreed it was unpublishable. By then Marjorie was convinced that 'the sort of life I was living wasn't the one I really wanted. And as *After Thirty* seemed part of it, part of something I had finished with, I asked for the manuscript to be sent back, and within a year I had burnt it. I was very unhappy during the summer of 1931. All the excitement of being published had gone.[30]

Marjorie suffered one last relapse before freeing herself for good from her infatuation with Wyndham Lewis. She'd spent the autumn finishing *Love at Last*, not because she'd wanted to, but because it was the only way to extricate herself from her three-book contract with Kahane. Once the manuscript was delivered she could move on and start to write the serious novels she felt she had in her, unhampered by a publisher's expectation of smut. In November, his interest having been revived as a result of being ignored, Wyndham Lewis got in touch again. He hadn't forgotten his promise to draw her portrait, and he wanted to make good on it. An appointment was made; uncharacteristically, he kept it. Before getting down to work they caught up on Marjorie's news. She proudly showed Lewis a card she'd received from Kahane telling her that the publishers Hachette were interested in taking up *Jam To-day*, which Vendôme was also about to issue in a cheap edition. Lewis, seeing a copy of the *Times Literary Supplement* on the divan, asked if there was anything in it, an enquiry Marjorie chose to see as an encouraging sign: 'I felt happier than ever, as it seemed to imply that I would know what was of interest. At last I was being treated as friend, and a friend who could help.[31]

Lewis sat Marjorie in a high-backed chair, took out various tools from his portfolio, and began to draw in silence. Suddenly, after completing no more than a few exploratory squiggles, he jumped up, announcing that he must go around the corner immediately to see someone who had promised to buy one of his paintings. He would, however, be back almost at once: 'On that you can absolutely rely.[32] Marjorie waited all evening; only at midnight did she finally admit to herself that he wasn't coming back. She took off the clothes in which she'd been posing, got into bed, and cried herself to sleep.

The next morning Marjorie was still in bed, wrapped only in a cardigan and fortifying herself with toast, coffee and the morning paper, when there was a knock at the front door. Assuming the caller to be a tradesman and that her cleaning lady would deal with it, she stayed where she was. A few minutes later there was a knock at her bedroom door. Unasked, Lewis strode in as if he'd only been away a few minutes, sat down and began to unpack his portfolio preparatory to starting work:

> The pleasure of seeing him sitting there was so great that it was some time before I realised that I wasn't going to do as he wanted. To get out of bed, undress and then dress in front of him... no, I just couldn't. I could never undress in front of anyone who had written about the human body as he had... I remember drawing my cardigan tighter across my chest and wondering how, without making a fool of myself or hurting his feelings, I could explain that I would rather not be drawn by him at all than get up and pose here and now as he was expecting.
>
> With his uncanny sense of the unspoken word he must have got what I was thinking, as gradually I became aware that he was telling me so, and blaming me for it. Blaming me for not giving him the opportunity to pay back what he had borrowed. Making out that I, like other people, would go round saying that he owed me money. Like them, I would run him down without cause. In the nightmare moments that followed I remember him wagging a finger at me and saying 'It's in places like this that I have been consistently run down', and my denying it, hotly and truthfully.
>
> I was just about to tell him that I'd never connected the £5 with the drawing when I became aware that he was coming up to the divan and very politely and courteously holding out his hand in farewell. As far as I remember I eventually held out mine too. What I know is that I have never, in all my life, controlled myself so successfully as I did at that moment.[33]

Marjorie had seen the £5 as a gift to a friend who needed it, and a gift she'd been glad to give. And she'd seen Lewis's drawing as a gift *from* a friend. Knowing as she now did that Lewis saw the portrait as a way of settling a debt killed her desire for it – and for him. The relationship in which she'd invested so much and from which she'd received so little was over.

Some time later Marjorie wrote several letters to Lewis. It wasn't her intention to revive their relationship; she'd wanted merely to tell him clearly and calmly what she had been unable to trust herself to say without bursting into tears the last time they'd met. When in later life Marjorie contacted the curator of the Wyndham Lewis archive at Cornell University wishing to reread the letters she sent him, she found that none of them had ever been deposited there. Feeling wronged and slighted by their absence she wrote a memoir called *No Quarter*, which is now in the archive at Cornell in place of the missing letters, and which is the main source of this story.

Elliott Seabrooke, whose first introduction had been so disastrous, made amends with his second. At Seabrooke's insistence Marjorie met Francis Hemming, a civil servant; to her surprise and happiness they fell in love. Hemming was alarmed by Marjorie's menstrual agonies and bullied her into seeing a specialist, who diagnosed a large fibroid; athough the ensuing operation left her sterile it freed her from pain. (The fibroid may have been caused by an illegal abortion some years before: in *No Quarter* Firminger writes of 'deciding not to have a child' with her first husband, Julian Firminger. This is ambiguous, and probably intentionally so.) She had written to Lewis informing him of her impending operation, hoping to receive good wishes in return, but had heard nothing. After the operation she wrote again, this time to tell him about Francis. She remembered writing: ' "I have met a man I like immensely. His name is Francis Hemming."... I remember so well my shame at not feeling able to write what I really wanted to – "I have met a man I love." Somehow I just couldn't manage to write the words "I love" to Lewis.' [34]

Marjorie Firminger's last letter to Wyndham Lewis (the presence of which in the Cornell archive lends weight to the theory that its predecessors were deliberately withheld) is dated 31 May 1931. In it she wrote:

> Dear Lewis,
> I am now living with Francis Hemming, and we are going to marry when the divorce is through. I have given up my telephone number and he has had his transferred here (Just in case you feel like an enemy chat!).

Given what happened a few months later, it's unlikely they ever spoke again.

Wyndham Lewis is often described as having suffered from persecution mania. More accurately, Lewis had a mania for persecution – persecution of others, followed by reciprocal attacks from them about which he could complain. His self-esteem seems to have been index-linked to the number of people who disliked him at any given time, and some of his novels seem to have been written with the express intention of provoking people he knew in order to ensure that he remained what he most liked to be: the reviled outsider, talked about everywhere, welcome nowhere. The reason Lewis spent so much time complaining to his few trusted friends that people were out to get him was because they were – he made sure they were. His pathological desire to be unpopular may have been behind his long flirtation with the trappings, if not ultimately the core philosophy, of National Socialism. (Only in 1939 did he finally concede that he'd been wrong about Hitler.) As old enemies shunned him and lapsed into wounded but dignified silence, new ones had to be found in order to keep the fires of animosity well-stoked. He would take on titans if titans could be found, but if none presented themselves the weak and defenceless would do. No target was too small or too fragile to make Lewis think twice about giving it both barrels. It made him a dangerous friend.

Wyndham Lewis's view of his relationship with Marjorie Firminger was markedly different to hers, as Marjorie was to discover when Lewis published a novel called *Snooty Baronet* in 1932. Typically shapeless and typically spiteful, the plot treads characteristic Lewis territory, charting the destructive journey of a writer-genius-hero through a supporting cast of incompetents, poseurs, has-beens and neverweres whose presence he is forced to endure but whose existence he deplores. Among them is an occasional lover and would-be writer, a character given the name of Valerie Ritter, whose 'expressions were quite unprintable, except in de luxe editions privately printed in Paris or Milan.'[35] Lewis is merciless:

> I rang up old Valerie at once. She was there of course. She was always there! Of late her one or two earlier boyfriends fought shy of the old girl (because she's got into hot water with a group of 'Gossip-Stars' – gilded young girl-bachelors and middle-aged monocled martinets, one especially named Venetia – on account of literary indiscretions. She just sat there near her bed-telephone all day long, hoping against hope that she'd get a call... You dreaded to think how long she had sat there.[36]

Val is asked for a date the following evening:

> 'Tomorrow!' A short sharp pause. 'I think that will be all right. Let me see.' A much shorter pause – she was afraid I was about to suggest a more distant evening! 'If you don't mind holding on just a moment Snoots – just hold on will you and I will look at my engagement-book – I'm sure it will be all right though!'
> I was positive it would be too: I picked my teeth and tapped my foot, while she pretended to look in her book.[37]

The description of Val's appearance is sadistically unflattering: eyes too close together, forehead too narrow, hair too thin, the suspicion of a double chin. 'Her face has a swarthy massaged flush. (If you look too close, it is full of pits; under the make-up is a field of gaping pores – her nose is worst in this respect: some day it will disintegrate for all practical purposes)'.[38] Worst of all, according to Lewis, is her incessant giggle, which is supposed to be coquettish but only succeeds in being infuriating. Supper has to be endured ('made out of threepennyworth of dogbones and yesterday's vegetable scraps'[39]) and so has her mindless conversation: 'daring' chatter punctuated by giggles and a forest of meaningless Christian names, 'all those bright nebulous mononominal patrons, of Gossip-column-class – on to the hem of whose garment she had clung like grim death – but who had shaken her off, of one accord, and by common consent, about a year since, when she had pooped in their faces'.[40] Val, 'this unimportant hanger-on of the big Chelsea "Party"', has torpedoed her own social life by committing it to print, has 'thrown away the few poor little trumps she had somehow or other trumped-up'.[41] With neither income nor strength of character to fall back on, Val resorts to an air of bluff bonhomie in an attempt to disguise her loneliness. Pausing only to note her halitosis Snoots gets her into bed. In the morning he throws up in her chamberpot on his way out.

When *Snooty Baronet* was published Marjorie Firminger was devastated. Being variously described in its pages as a 'bawdy hermit-crab'[42] and a 'giggling fantoche'[43] was bad enough, but that she'd been so viciously drawn by someone to whom she'd been so kind and tolerant, and whose affection and approval she'd courted so intently, affected her for the rest of her life. She needed the support of friends, but the publication of *Jam To-day* had ensured that friends, as Lewis had so cruelly and publicly noted, had become thin on the ground. So traumatised was she by *Snooty Baronet* that her husband took it from her and removed it from the house. She later claimed never to have looked at it again.[44]

I wish I could tell you *Jam To-Day* is a good book. I wish I could tell you it's average. But although Lewis is needlessly brutal in *Snooty Baronet* in his dissection of Firminger's appearance, mannerisms and character, he can't honestly be described as anything but accurate in his assessment of her abilities as a writer. He cites Val/Marjorie's inability to distinguish between her tongue and her pen, and this is the fundamental problem of *Jam To-day*: it is not so much a book as an arbitrary collection of mildly salacious prattle, pointlessly transcribed. Characters are interchangeable because characterisation is non-existent, and even mildly arresting dialogue is so infrequent that when it does turn up the reader assumes it must have been something that Firminger overheard rather than invented. *Jam To-day* is an 80,000-word gossip column – something no newspaper ever thought was a good idea.

Marjorie Firminger wasn't a writer, and she made the mistake of gossiping about her friends in print, a mistake which left her defenceless when the tables were turned. She was starstruck, credulous and desperate to be liked. None of these is an attractive quality, but none of them is a crime, and Firminger did nothing to deserve the literary kneecapping Lewis gave her in *Snooty Baronet*, the humiliation of which clouded the rest of her life.

Jam To-day was the only book Marjorie Firminger ever published, and it has never been reissued. After the appearance of *Snooty Baronet* she briefly toyed with a revenge novel in which Wyndham Lewis would appear thinly disguised, but realised early on that the project was futile, and abandoned it. *That Cad Jane* was never finished, and she recalled the early chapters of *Love at Last* from Jack Kahane (to whom she'd sent them for approval) and burned them, bringing an end to her literary career at the age of 33.

The rest of her life was a struggle. She married Francis Hemming in 1933 but they were later divorced. During the war she lived in a flat in Tavistock Place ('Overrun with mice, but it does'[45]) and served as an Air Raid Warden at Fitzroy Square. She worked in a department store, selling hats. She moved to Millbank, and in her old age to a flat in the Barbican. She never lost her enthusiasm for writing long gossipy letters, but her enthusiasm for life seemed to go into a slow decline. She harked back constantly to the twenties, devoured the books of biographers and social historians of the period, and scoured them for references to people she had known, as well as for references to herself. As an ex-actress, ex-writer, and ex-socialite, she'd had in her youth a glimpse of fame without ever getting to taste it herself. As a result, she seems to have found the rest of her life small and disappointing.

Despite his betrayal, Marjorie Firminger never completely rid herself of her infatuation with Wyndham Lewis, and for the rest of her life her common sense struggled to overcome a strong streak of emotional masochism. Lewis himself died in 1957, but his ability to upset and humiliate Marjorie outlived him. In an article by Kenneth Marshall which appeared in the *London Magazine* in 1976, Marjorie was publicly identified for the first time as the model for, in her words, the 'pretentious, absurd'[46] Valerie Ritter in *Snooty Baronet*. By then she was 77 but she was every bit as upset by this public revelation as she'd been when Lewis's novel had first appeared 34 years earlier. In a letter to a friend following publication of Marshall's article she talks of her shock, and of how 'Lewis' novel had hurt me, though I blame myself for behaving as I did with him'.[47] (Adding insult to injury, Marshall gets the name of her only novel wrong, calling it *No Jam To-day*.) Although by now she'd come to see *Jam To-day* as little more than a relic from a painful time in her life ('I can't even bear to look at it now'[48]) it must have been hurtful to be reminded of how comprehensively everyone else had forgotten it too.

Shortly after the article in the *London Magazine* appeared, Marjorie Firminger died in London.

By the same author

Fiction:
After Thirty (unpublished, destroyed)
That Cad Jane (unfinished, destroyed)
Love at Last (unfinished, destroyed)

Non-fiction:
No Quarter (unpublished, typescript in the Wyndham Lewis Collection, Cornell University)

Notes
1 Marjorie Firminger archive, Theatre Museum, London.
2 Cited but not sourced in Paul O'Keeffe, *Wyndham Lewis: Portrait of a Genius* (Cape, 2000).
3 Marjorie Firminger, *No Quarter* (unpublished manuscript, no date, Division of Rare and Manuscript Collections, Cornell University). Firminger – née Hiscox but later Mrs Marjorie Hemming – died on 23 June 1976. The manuscript of *No Quarter* was found in a sealed envelope in her home at 62 Defoe House, Barbican, London, after her death. Another, condensed draft at Cornell bears the address 54 Millbank, SW1. In it, Firminger talks of writing the memoir 'well over thirty years later', which would date its composition to the mid- to late 1960s. In accordance with instructions in her will, it was deposited at Cornell University Library, where it now forms part of the University's Wyndham Lewis archive.
4 Firminger, *No Quarter*.

5 Firminger, *No Quarter.*

6 Firminger, *No Quarter.*

7 Firminger, *No Quarter.*

8 Marjorie Firminger, *Jam To-Day* (Vendôme Press, 1931), p. 218.

9 Firminger, *No Quarter.*

10 Firminger, *No Quarter.*

11 Firminger, *No Quarter.*

12 Firminger, *No Quarter.*

13 Firminger, *No Quarter.*

14 Firminger, *No Quarter.*

15 Firminger, *No Quarter.*

16 Firminger, *No Quarter.*

17 Firminger, *No Quarter.*

18 Firminger, *No Quarter.*

19 Firminger, *No Quarter.*

20 Firminger, *No Quarter.*

21 Firminger, *No Quarter.*

22 Letter from Marjorie Firminger to Wyndham Lewis, 25 November 1930, Cornell University.

23 Firminger, *No Quarter.*

24 Letter from Marjorie Firminger to Wyndham Lewis, 21 December 1930, Cornell University.

25 Firminger, *No Quarter.*

26 Firminger, *No Quarter.*

27 Firminger, *No Quarter.*

28 Firminger, *No Quarter.*

29 Firminger, *No Quarter.*

30 Firminger, *No Quarter.*

31 Firminger, *No Quarter.*

32 Firminger, *No Quarter.*

33 Firminger, *No Quarter.*

34 Firminger, *No Quarter.*

35 Wyndham Lewis, *Snooty Baronet* (Black Sparrow Press, 1984), p. 23.

36 Lewis, *Snooty Baronet*, pp. 23–24.

37 Lewis, *Snooty Baronet*, p. 25.

38 Lewis, *Snooty Baronet*, p. 28.

39 Lewis, *Snooty Baronet*, p. 29.

40 Lewis, *Snooty Baronet*, pp. 41–42.

41 Lewis, *Snooty Baronet*, p. 39.

42 Lewis, *Snooty Baronet*, p. 42.

43 Lewis, *Snooty Baronet*, p. 47.

44 Firminger, *No Quarter.*

45 Letter from Marjorie Firminger to Francis and Sylvia Beaufort-Palmer, 21 February 1943, Cornell University.

46 Firminger, *No Quarter*.
47 Firminger, *No Quarter*.
48 Firminger, *No Quarter*.

CHARLES HENRI FORD

Charles Henri Ford was born in Hazlehurst, Mississippi, in 1908. His middle name was originally spelt with a 'y' but he changed it in later life, having wearied of being regularly asked if he was related to the automobile tycoon. His father owned hotels, and Charles' childhood was spent on the road. He never settled for long in any one school and was frequently expelled, but he managed to stay in one of them long enough to edit a journal called *The Brass Monkey*. At the age of twenty he borrowed a hundred dollars and founded a poetry magazine, *Blues*. In search of material for an expatriate edition of the magazine he wrote to Gertrude Stein in Paris; she responded favourably, and the two began a correspondence. Stein loved flattery, Ford was happy to oblige her, and by the time Ford arrived in Paris in 1931 all doors were open to him. He quickly established himself in the expatriate community: as well as meeting for the first time contributors to *Blues* such as Kay Boyle, Richard Thoma and Harry Crosby, he struck up friendships with Natalie Barney, Paul Bowles and René Crevel. He moved in with Djuna Barnes, and typed up part of the manuscript of her novel *Nightwood*. In 1933, the same year that *The Young and Evil* was published by the Obelisk Press, Stein's *The Autobiography of Alice B. Toklas* appeared. In it, Stein showed that Ford's cultivation of her had not been in vain:

> Of all the little magazines which as Gertrude Stein loves to quote, have died to make verse free, perhaps the youngest and freshest was the Blues. Its editor Charles Henri Ford has come to Paris and he is young and fresh as his Blues and also honest which also is a pleasure. Gertrude Stein thinks that he and Robert Coates alone among the young men have an individual sense of words.[1]

Before arriving in Paris, Ford had spent most of 1930 in New York with Parker Tyler, a poet, a contributor to *Blues* and eventually its co-editor. Parker introduced Ford to New York's underground gay scene, and the drag balls of Harlem and the speakeasies of Greenwich Village would provide the backdrop for their collaboration the following year on *The Young and Evil*.

[383]

Underground pornography aside, gay literature was a genre that barely existed in 1932; what few examples there were were either cryptic to the point of invisibility or relentlessly self-loathing. But Ford was perfectly well adjusted to himself and saw no reason for either secrecy or shame. He saw no reason for proselytising, either, and the refreshing result is that *The Young and Evil* is not a plea for understanding, or a cry for help, or a call to arms. For all its modernist trappings the novel is a conventional one, building through a series of more or less unconnected scenes a picture of homosexual life in New York at the beginning of the 1930s: lovers' fights and reconciliations, open assignations with poets and drag queens, secret assignations with married men, cruisings, beatings, arrests, and wild Harlem parties where gay men of all races come together to celebrate rather that hide their status as outsiders. The fuel of the book is Prohibition hooch, its drive the drive of youth well lived. That the youths concerned are almost exclusively male and wearing mascara had the result of depriving New York of this sight of itself until 1975, the year *The Young and Evil* eventually appeared in print in an American edition.

By January 1932 Ford and Tyler's novel was finished, bearing the title *Jump Back*. *Jump Back* was knocked back by Liveright, by Cape and by Gollancz, but Gertrude Stein was evangelically enthusiastic. She sent the manuscript to her agent William Bradley, who shared her enthusiasm, and on 5 August Bradley sent the manuscript, which by now bore the title *The Young and Evil*, to Jack Kahane.

The manuscripts for *The Young and Evil* and *Tropic of Cancer*, which Bradley sent Kahane in October 1932, put the fledgling publisher on the spot. Unlike the proprietors of the rarefied expatriate imprints of the 1920s, Kahane had resolved to run the Obelisk Press as a proper business. Proper businesses must turn a profit, and in order for a publishing house to turn a profit it must sell books. Kahane the businessman knew that in this context a good book was one that sold, but Kahane the lover of literature was determined to use the finances generated by his business to give a home to books of great literary merit that would almost certainly sell slowly, and that were unpublishable anywhere else. Well, here were two. Reluctant to risk a prosecution that would destroy the company almost before it had begun, but reluctant also to pass up the chance of bringing literary respectablility to his imprint, which until then had published pulp and little else, Kahane did what he always did in such circumstances: he entered into protracted and complex contractual negotiations which were primarily designed to give him time to think.

The Young and Evil was uncuttable, and both its cast and its milieu were unacceptable to the mainstream readership of the 1930s. The fact that the book's characters occasionally use words such as 'fuck' and 'cocksucker' – and the fact that, when they acknowledge their existence at all, they refer to women by the generic term 'cunt' – was the least of Kahane's problems. The characters wear make-up and women's clothes, they have sex with strangers, they sleep three to a bed – and they're *happy*. Kahane could not even pretend that *The Young and Evil* was a cautionary tale. The book's tone is exuberant and assured; no one dies, no one is punished, no one repents. The complete absence of editorial moralising is *The Young and Evil's* most revolutionary attribute, and gave Kahane his biggest headache.

His best hope of avoiding prosecution lay in the opacity of the book's style. *The Young and Evil* is ostentatiously modernist. Textual experimentation and stylistic tropes borrowed none too subtly from Stein and Djuna Barnes obscure the more visceral action of the book: maiden aunts and masturbators alike would be confounded. Kahane suggested to Bradley an expensive limited edition, signed by the authors, that would sell slowly to a small, rarefied elite and pass under the radar of the authorities. Ford (who conducted the negotiations on both his and Tyler's behalf) agreed to this, but insisted Kahane either issue a trade edition 'of one or two thousand copies' as well, or give Ford the right to arrange for such an edition to be published elsewhere.[2]This was a naïve bluff – there was nowhere else for Ford to go – but somehow it resulted in Kahane publishing both a limited and a trade edition, even though the existence of the latter rendered the former pointless. Kahane also asked for translation rights and an option on future books. Ford refused.[3] Although he was to produce two more novels during the 1930s, they were never published, and he was beginning to realise that his future lay in poetry rather than prose. He anticipated no need of protection from censorship in the future, and since there was no other reason to commit himself to an obscure publishing house in Paris, he declined to do so. The relationship between Ford and Kahane would be strictly a one-book stand.

By 15 November 1932 the contracts were signed, and by the end of the following February Ford had corrected the proofs. By March,

Kahane was worrying again. Keen both to make a pre-emptive bid to establish the book's artistic credentials as a defence against prosecution, and to push sales, Kahane wrote to Bradley: 'I want to prepare a prospectus for Ford's book which should consist of about 200 or 300 words [of] descriptive matter, as full of selling points as possible. Do you think you could get any intelligent friend of the author, such as Djuna Barnes, to do this? I don't feel myself frightfully competent to write about it in as convincing a manner as should be done.'[4] Barnes provides a puff on the book's front flap; the unsigned blurb is probably her work, too.

The Obelisk Press edition of *The Young and Evil* was published in August 1933. There were fifty copies of the limited edition, signed by the authors and priced at Frs. 200. Estimates of the size of the trade edition range from one thousand, Obelisk's usual print run, to 2500. The book suffered the usual casualties in transit: five hundred copies were destroyed by British customs, and shipments to the United States were intercepted and turned back.[5] (The book is one of the scarcer Obelisk titles today, suggesting that the print run was probably at the lower end of the various estimates.) By February 1934, six months after publication, *The Young and Evil* had sold 79 copies of the trade edition, and two of the limited edition; the next six months saw sales drop to 53.[6] Kahane had succeeded in avoiding the attention of the French authorities; unfortunately, the reading public were equally oblivious.

In 1932, Djuna Barnes had introduced Ford to the Russian artist Pavel Tchelitchev. By 1934 they were a couple, and the relationship was to last until Tchelitchev's death in 1957. (Tchelitchev's illustrations for *The Young and Evil* were used in a 1988 edition of the novel.) Ford's first collection of poetry was published in 1936, and in 1940 he and Tyler founded another magazine, *View*. Reflecting Ford's new and abiding passion, *View* was a forum for surrealist painters and writers, and ran until 1947. During the 1950s Ford largely dropped from view, but after the death of Tchelitchev he resurfaced as a painter and photographer, published two more collections of poetry in the late 1960s and, as a result of his association with Andy Warhol's Factory, made two films. Ford met the nineteen-year-old Indra Tamang in Katmandu in 1972. The two were to remain together for the next thirty years until Ford's death in Manhattan in 2002 at the age of 94.

Charles Henri Ford turned his hand to many art forms, and never established a reputation at the forefront of any of them; if he is remembered at all now it is as a facilitator for others rather than as a creator in his own right. But this is to short-change him, since with *The Young and Evil* Ford and Tyler can lay strong claim to having created a new literary genre: a gay literature, stripped of moralising and miserabilism, that proved to be more than thirty years ahead of its time.

By the same author

Fiction:
Life of a Child (unpublished)
Confessions of a Freak (unpublished)
Verse includes:
A Pamphlet of Sonnets (Caravel Press, Majorca, 1936)
The Garden of Disorder (Europa Press, 1938)
Overturned Lake (Little Man Press, 1941)
Poems for Painters (View Editions, 1945)
The Half-Thoughts, The Distances of Pain (QVS Press, 1947)
Sleep in a Nest of Flames (New Directions, 1949)
Silver Flower Coo (Kulchur Press, 1968)
Flag of Ecstasy (Black Sparrow Press, 1972)
7 Poems (Bardo Matrix, Katmandu, 1974)
Om Krishna 1 (Cherry Valley Editions, 1979)
Out of the Labyrinth (City Lights, 1991)

Non-fiction includes:
I Will Be What I Am (unpublished memoir, Beinecke Library, Yale University)

As editor:
Blues (San Antonio and New York, 1929–30)
View (New York, 1940–47)
The Mirror of Baudelaire (New Directions, 1942)
A Night with Jupiter (View Editions, 1945)

Notes
1 Gertrude Stein, *The Autobiography of Alice B. Toklas* (Penguin, 1987), p. 260.
2 Letter from William Bradley to Kahane, 1 October 1932, HRC.
3 Letter from Bradley to Kahane, 1 October 1932.
4 Letter from Kahane to William Bradley, 20 March 1933, HRC.
5 Hugh Ford, *Published in Paris* (Garstone Press, 1975), pp. 357–59.
6 Accounts submitted by Kahane to William Bradley, 20 February 1934, HRC.

RADCLYFFE HALL

The long, depressing history of literary censorship in Britain reached its nadir with the prosecution of Radclyffe Hall's *The Well of Loneliness*, a plea for tolerance and understanding which found precious little of either when it was published in 1928. A sexless and unrelievedly gloomy story of unhappy lesbians, the theme of *The Well of Loneliness* was enough to condemn it: newspaper editors, politicians and the judiciary combined to do whatever was necessary, however immoral, to ensure that moral values were upheld. The book's suppression ushered in an era of self-censorship among British publishers which lasted thirty years, benefiting no one – except a few British publishers based abroad.

But for all its troubled history, and for all the good intentions of its pleading, *The Well of Loneliness* is as difficult to like as its author. Marguerite Radclyffe Hall was born in Bournemouth in 1880, the daughter of parents who separated almost as soon as she was born: the result was a lonely and loveless childhood. The inheritance of her paternal grandfather's fortune at the age of 21 gave Hall the means to free herself from her unhappy past; instead, she used it to launch herself into a determinedly unhappy future. Now financially as well as dispositionally independent, Hall spent her twenties travelling through Europe, embarking on relationships with a succession of women who would eventually leave her in order to get married. In 1908 she began an affair with the already married Mabel Batten; when Batten died in 1915 she transferred her affections to Batten's cousin, Una, Lady Troubridge. The two were a couple for the rest of Hall's life. Insulated from public disapproval both by money and by the enlightened company they kept, John (as Hall was now known) and Una divided their time between London and Paris, where they were frequent visitors to the lesbian *salon* of the fabulously wealthy and evangelically lesbian Natalie Barney: there John found both comforting kinship and fortifying encouragement for her literary aspirations. Through the 1920s she published a number of unexceptional and unexceptionable novels, before using a thinly disguised version of her own life as the subject matter for *The Well of Loneliness*.

Wealth doesn't preclude unhappiness, but it doesn't preclude stupidity, either, and *The Well of Loneliness* is riddled with that infuriating brand of ignorance which only privilege can confer. The book's remit is honourable and, given the time in which it was written, brave: to explain to a general readership the nature of lesbianism in a frank but unsensational way, in order to foster understanding and acceptance. But Hall's unwavering concentration on the suffering of her central character, a character as mummified by privilege as Radclyffe Hall herself, turns what should have been a noble entreaty into an almost unreadable 500-page whine. Hall spends most of the the book deploring not the persecution of her kind but the persecution of herself, her honourable intentions suffocated by unshakeable self-obsession. The plight of lesbians on a rather less exalted rung of the social ladder, lesbians unable to buy their way to acceptance, and forced by circumstance to lead unhappy, closed lives with never a *salon* in sight, goes completely unremarked. And the book's style doesn't help: the narrative is radical, but the manner of its telling never rises above sentimental moralising, a stolid Victorianism dipped in pink. As with so many other persecuted books of the twenties and thirties, when *The Well of Loneliness* found itself under attack, lovers of literary freedom found themselves being asked to rally behind a less than inspirational flag.

Having been turned down by Cassell, Heinemann and Martin Secker, *The Well of Loneliness* was eventually published by Jonathan Cape on 24 July 1928. The critical response was mostly favourable, praising the book's seriousness and lack of prurience; the few bad reviews the book received were written by critics who made the point that moral courage had to be twinned with literary merit before a book could be described as a good one. Sales were brisk, and Cape made plans for a second and third edition. But on 17 August, Jonathan Cape received a letter from James Douglas, editor of the *Sunday Express*, notifying him that an editorial would be appearing in that weekend's edition calling for the book's suppression. In it, Douglas declared:

> This novel forces upon our Society a disagreeable task which it has hitherto shirked, the task of cleaning itself from the leprosy of these lepers and making the air clean and wholesome once more...
>
> The book is a seductive and insidious piece of special pleading designed to display perverted decadence as a martyrdom inflicted upon these outcasts by a cruel society. It flings a veil of sentiment over their depravity. It even suggests that their self-made debasement is unavoidable because they cannot save themselves.
>
> This terrible doctrine may commend itself to certain schools of pseudo-scientific thought, but it cannot be reconciled with the Christian religion

or with the Christian doctrine of free-will. Therefore, it must be fought to the bitter end by the Christian Churches. This is the radical difference between paganism and Christianity.

If Christianity does not destroy this doctrine, then this doctrine will destroy it, together with the civilisation it has built on the ruins of paganism. These moral derelicts are not cursed from their birth. Their downfall is caused by their own act and their own will. They are damned because they choose to be damned, not because they are doomed from the beginning.

We must protect our children against their specious fallacies and sophistries. Therefore, we must banish their propaganda from our bookshops and libraries. I would rather give a healthy boy or a healthy girl a phial of prussic acid than this novel. Poison kills the body, but moral poison kills the soul.

... I appeal to the Home Secretary to set the law in motion. He should instruct the Director of Public Prosecutions to consider whether *The Well of Loneliness* is fit for circulation, and, if not, to take action to prevent its being further circulated.

Finally, let me warn our novelists and our men of letters that literature as well as morality is in peril. Fiction of this type is an injury to good literature. It makes the profession of literature fall into disrepute. Literature has not yet recovered from the harm done to it by the Oscar Wilde scandal. It should keep its house in order.[1]

It's difficult to imagine either the Church of England or the Express group of newspapers mouthing such moronic bigotries today, of course, but in 1928 the editorial was enough to panic Jonathan Cape into a bad decision: he sent a copy of the book to the Home Secretary, and invited him to pass it to the Director of Public Prosecutions if he thought there was a case to answer. The Home Secretary of the day was Sir William Joynson-Hicks, a Grundyite of legendary toxicity: President of the National Church League, President of the Zenana Bible Mission, and a fervent opponent of the Revised Prayer Book, even the Bishop of Durham called him a 'dour fanatic' who proceeded against one cause after another with 'dervish-like fervour'.[2] Unsurprisingly, 'Jix' did not take to *The Well of Loneliness*, and told Cape so.

Rather than go to the expense of a trial that would probably result in conviction, Cape wrote to *The Times*:

Sir,
We have today received a request from the Home Secretary asking us to discontinue publication of Miss Radclyffe Hall's novel 'The Well of Loneliness'. We have already expressed our readiness to fall in with the

wishes of the Home Office in this matter, and we have therefore stopped publication.

I have the honour to be your obedient servant,

Jonathan Cape[3]

Obedient he may have been, but he was a businessman too. Demand for the book had been stimulated by the scandal surrounding it. Cape had moulds of the book's type made, and his business partner Wren Howard spirited them to Paris, where John Holroyd-Reece of the Pegasus Press issued four different impressions of *The Well of Loneliness* in the space of five months. Demand for the book continued to grow in Britain, and when copies of the various Pegasus editions began to arrive in the UK, Joynson-Hicks found himself in a difficult position. Since the book had been not banned but voluntarily withdrawn by the publisher, there was no immediate legal action that could be taken against its importation. Jix stalled by signing warrants instructing Customs to seize any copies discovered in transit until a decision could be made as to whether or not they were obscene – a decision entrusted to a man Jix presumed would share his opinion of *The Well of Loneliness*, the Chairman of Customs and Excise, Sir Francis Floud. But Sir Francis proved himself one of the few sane voices of the whole saga. In a report to the Chancellor of the Exchequer, Winston Churchill, Floud expressed his strong opinion that *The Well of Loneliness* was *not* obscene, and should neither be prosecuted nor denied entry from abroad.[4]

Realising that he was going to receive no support from Customs, Joynson-Hicks decided to go it alone. Two consignments of copies of the book intercepted by Customs, which had been destined for Jonathan Cape's offices and a bookseller in Great Russell Street, were ordered to be released and sent on to their intended destinations – but only after warrants authorising their seizure on arrival had been issued. The books were duly seized, summonses were issued by Sir Chartres Biron, the Chief Magistrate of Bow Street court and close friend and co-conspirator of Joynson-Hicks, and the hearing was set for 9 November 1928. There the case would be heard by ... Sir Chartres Biron.

The trial was a travesty. The defence counsel, Harold Rubinstein, lined up an army of high-profile witnesses, all prepared to testify that *The Well of Loneliness* was not obscene. Biron refused to admit their evidence. It became clear very quickly that it wasn't the treatment of the book's thematic material that was on trial, but the thematic material itself. Biron – and Jix – believed that the subject matter of *The Well of Loneliness* rendered the book obscene no matter how decorously it was treated; they believed, in short, that lesbianism should be unmentionable in print, by law. Since Jix had discussed the charges beforehand with Biron, and since Biron was conducting the trial, the outcome was a foregone conclusion: on 16 November 1928 *The Well of Loneliness* was banned not only in Britain, but throughout the British Empire.[5]

Jack Kahane did not secure the rights to *The Well of Loneliness* until 1933. Peter Neagoe, second only to 'Cecil Barr' as Obelisk's best-selling author, had just relocated to the United States, and had severed his association with Obelisk. Kahane's acquisition of the rights to Hall's book provided some compensation, but by then Pegasus had already done a pretty thorough job of saturating the market. Although *The Well of Loneliness* was a prestigious and natural addition to the Obelisk list it was only a modest commercial success for Kahane, and a second impression was never needed.

Radclyffe Hall died of cancer in 1943, and is buried in Highgate cemetery.

By the same author

Fiction includes:
The Unlit Lamp (Cassell, 1924)
A Saturday Life (Arrowsmith, 1925)
Adam's Breed (Cape, 1929)
The Master of the House (Cape, 1932)
The Sixth Beatitude (Heinemann,1936)

Poetry includes:
Twixt Earth and Stars (John and Edward Bumpus, 1906)
A Sheaf of Verses (John and Edward Bumpus, 1908)
Poems of the Past and Present (Chapman and Hall, 1910)
The Forgotten Island (Chapman and Hall, 1915)
Rhymes and Rhythms (Maggiore, Milan, 1948)

Notes
1 James Douglas, 'A Book That Must Be Suppressed', *Sunday Express*, 19 August 1928.
2. Quoted in C. H. Rolph, *Books in the Dock* (Deutsch, 1969), and Alan Travis, *Bound and Gagged* (Profile Books, 2000).

3. Letter from Jonathan Cape to the *Daily Express*, published in the edition of 21 August 1928.

4 Home Office case files, HO 144/22547, The National Archives, Kew. The document in which Floud expressed this opinion was only released into the public domain in 1998, as a result of pressure orchestrated by Radclyffe Hall's biographer, Diana Souhami. It was suppressed at the time of its writing because those determined to see *The Well of Loneliness* declared obscene realised that no jury would convict if the opinion of Customs and Excise was known. Why the document was withheld until 1998 – and why the Home Office wanted to withhold it until 2007 before pressure was brought to bear – is harder to explain.

5 For a full account of the trial, see Travis, *Bound and Gagged*, pp. 45–73.

JAMES HANLEY

By the age of seventeen, James Hanley was already a war veteran of four years' standing. Born in Dublin on 3 September 1901, he'd moved to Liverpool with his family when he was eight years old, and at twelve left school to follow his father into the merchant navy. He made his first voyage in 1914, and was at sea when war was declared. For the next three years he worked on commandeered merchant ships carrying troops to the Dardanelles, before jumping ship at New Brunswick, lying about his age, and enlisting in the Black Watch Battalion of the Canadian Expeditionary Force. In August 1918 he was gassed during action near Arras. After convalescing in hospital, the nineteen-year-old Hanley settled once again in Liverpool, and for the first time in his life did something to be expected of a boy of his age: he sat in his room and wondered what to do with his life.

Although his parents were poor and his father was at sea for months at a time, Hanley's home life was secure and happy: curiosity was encouraged, books were all over the house, and the family went to plays and concerts whenever money allowed. Hanley's formal education had been truncated by circumstance but his appetite for information was huge: during the day he worked as a railway porter, but at night he gorged himself on culture, mostly literature and music. He took up the piano, read widely, started to write, and had the occasional article published in a local newspaper.

He spent the years immediately following the war completing his own education, studying alone in his room. The time did much to forge his private and guarded character, a character which would later be described, wrongly, as reclusive. At the railway station his interests set him apart from his workmates, and although in the evenings the committed socialist would occasionally attend a political meeting, more often Hanley's studies would take precedence over the social life people of his age and class were expected to lead. He was reading Molière and Calderon, Ibsen and Hauptmann. He worshipped Strindberg. While reading lists like these were doing a good job of fattening up the writer-to-be, they didn't give Hanley much to talk about in the saloon bar, or on Platform Four. Not that Hanley missed the social life: 'I was now so used to being alone that the thought of any possible friendship now or in the near future gave me uncomfortable feelings. I wasn't lonely now, having all these riches at my hands. I could be independent of everybody.'[1]

Hanley had by now educated himself out of his class, but felt at ease nowhere else. At work one day he overheard a commuter discussing the country's classical percussionists. Summoning up his courage Hanley butted in, and ventured the opinion that the Dutch timpanist currently employed by the Hallé Orchestra in Manchester was the finest he'd ever heard. A friendship was born, and the commuter, a surgeon and keen amateur musician and musicologist, invited the railway porter to visit him at his home, where Hanley's musical education advanced quickly under the commuter's tutelage. More importantly, his future options were crystallised. Hanley had been harbouring vague ambitions to become a pianist, but on hearing his new friend's beautiful playing, he realised that his ex-seaman's hands would never be able to earn him a living on the concert platform, and that his love of music would always remain an amateur passion. Instead, he resolved to become a full-time writer.

As far as his parents were concerned Hanley had already been a full-time writer for some years, and so far had nothing to show for it. Their support for their son now began to manifest itself in gentle words of caution, and reminders of the importance of earning a living. Hanley's father urged a return to the sea, and by the time his first novel, *Drift*, had collected seventeen rejection slips, Hanley was on the verge of taking the advice. But then the eighteenth publisher said yes. *Drift* was published in February 1930 by Eric Partridge at the Scholartis Press (who a year earlier had published Norah James' *Sleeveless Errand*). Five hundred copies were printed, Hanley was paid five pounds, the reviews were favourable, the tiny edition sold out – but a second impression didn't. Critical success combined with commercial failure was to prove the leitmotif of Hanley's career.

Shortly after the publication of *Drift* Hanley moved to London, where *The German Prisoner*, a war story with an introduction by Richard Aldington, was published privately in March 1930. In August he began work on *Boy*, finished it the same month, and in October visited North Wales, where he fell in love with the country and with one of its citizens, Dorothy Thomas. The couple lived in Wales for most of the next thirty years.

Boy had been sent to Bodley Head, with whom Hanley had signed a contract, but in February 1931 they rejected the book. During his time in London Hanley had briefly stayed at the home of C. J. Greenwood, proprietor of the publishing firm Boriswood. Greenwood offered to negotiate with Bodley Head on Hanley's behalf to extricate him from his contract on condition that, if successful, Hanley would allow Boriswood to publish *Boy*. Hanley was delighted, negotiations were successful, and the Boriswood edition of *Boy* appeared in September 1931.

Boy is the story of thirteen-year-old Arthur Fearon. His ambition to become a chemist is aborted when he's withdrawn from school by his parents and forced to start earning a wage. His home life is brutal – his father beats him regularly, his bovine mother doing nothing to intervene – and his first day at work in Liverpool docks is just as hellish: he spends it chipping salt from the insides of hot and claustrophobic boilers, and is subjected to a humiliating initiation by the older boys of the gang. Unhappy and desperate both at home and at work, Arthur runs away to sea; when he's discovered hiding in the ship's coal bunker he's made to work his passage. The terrified Arthur can do little to hide that he is a boy in a man's world, and he's verbally ridiculed, physically assaulted, and sexually abused. When the ship ties up in Alexandria, Arthur asserts his manliness by accompanying some of the crew to a brothel. The result is a fleeting happiness – the first he's known. But on the voyage home Arthur becomes delirious and unable to work: he's contracted syphilis. The captain quietly smothers him, and wires home to Liverpool that Arthur Fearon has been lost at sea.

The public reaction to *Boy*, and Hanley's reaction to that reaction, were defining moments in Hanley's life and career. Because of its thematic material *Boy* was attacked as obscene, an allegation that wasn't true. But because the attacks on *Boy* threatened freedom of speech the book's defenders made extravagant claims about its literary value which weren't true either. Everyone, on both sides of the question, talked too much; the exception was Hanley himself who, mortified, didn't say a word. As a result Hanley is now remembered, if at all, for a promising but overheated book, riddled with flaws, written at the beginning of a career which produced many novels, plays and short stories far more accomplished than *Boy*, but which are now forgotten.

Things began well. On 3 September 1931 Boriswood published *Boy* in both a limited and a trade edition. Hanley dedicated the novel to Nancy Cunard, who had presented him with a typewriter when he had been unable to afford one, and who at the time was, like Kahane, the proprietor of an English-language press in Paris: her Hours Press published work by Beckett, Pound, Aldington, Graves and Laura Riding during its three years' existence. The limited edition of *Boy* ran to 145 copies, numbered and signed by Hanley, with an additional 15 copies for presentation. It contained the full text and sold for 42 shillings. The trade edition sold for 7s 6d and was heavily cut, with asterisks and large gaps appearing on more than fifty pages to denote deleted passages. Leaving aside the ridiculous proposition that shock-ability is somehow dependent on income, everybody was happy: the limited edition served Art, the trade edition, Mammon. In December a second impression of the trade edition was issued in which the gaps and asterisks were replaced by acceptable words and phrasing. A third impression followed in January 1932, and in April the first American edition was issued by Knopf, textually different again from its predecessors, and a second impression followed a month later. By February 1932, then, four different versions of *Boy* had been issued in a total of six impressions, and readers on both sides of the Atlantic had had ample opportunity to make up their minds about the book. No one had expressed outrage. Then in 1934, more than three years after *Boy*'s first appearance, a bad business decision collided with a taxi driver from Bury. There were many casualties.

In May 1934 Boriswood published a cheap edition of *Boy*, and decided to play up the 'scandalous' nature of the book in a drive for sales. The edition used the expurgated text, but the dustwrapper was deliberately sensational: it carried a near-naked dancing girl from the novel's brothel scene, and a blurb from Hugh Walpole. Walpole was the son of a bishop, and a light novelist whose work was old-fashioned even when it was new. He'd been lampooned by Somerset Maugham in *Cakes and Ale* but the experience hadn't taught him to keep his mouth shut, and on reading *Boy* Walpole declared it to be '[a] novel so unpleasant and ugly, both in narration and in incident, that I wonder the printers didn't go on strike while printing it'. Boriswood thought Walpole's outrage would be good for sales and put the quote on the wrapper of the book.[2]

The sales drive worked well, and the edition sold fifteen hundred copies in its first six months. It worked *too* well. In November 1934 police removed the book from the Bury branch of the National Libraries following a complaint from a taxi driver and his wife, neither of whom had taken the trouble to read the book but who had seen the salacious cover, read Walpole's blurb, and then decided to share their outrage. Mr and Mrs Grundy made a formal complaint at their local police station, and in January 1935 the book was withdrawn from sale and prosecution proceedings began.

By the time of *Boy's* prosecution Hanley's relationship with Boriswood had soured. Boriswood had published two more of Hanley's books since *Boy*, but sales had been poor, and the firm had cut the weekly allowance it had been paying Hanley as an advance against future royalties. At the time Hanley was having to run two households: his own in London, and the house in Wales to which his wife was necessarily confined while going through a difficult pregnancy. Hanley never forgave his publishers for kicking him at a time when both his wife and his career were ailing, and by May 1934, after protracted and rancorous negotiations, he'd managed to free himself from his contract with the 'swines and bastards',[3] and had signed to Chatto and Windus.

Hanley saw no reason to revise his opinion of Boriswood when the case against *Boy* came to court. The novel had been widely available for more than three years before a single complaint was made, and when the complaint did come it was made against a heavily edited version of the text from which all potentially contentious material had already been removed. The book appeared to be going to court not because of its contents, but because of its dustwrapper. (At the time of *Boy's* prosecution in Britain the novel was on open sale in the United States, and the Knopf edition was never subjected to any legal scrutiny.) The case against the book was weak, and Boriswood's directors thought that testimony from the distinguished names who had already publicly supported the book – Richard Aldington, E. M. Forster, and T. E. Lawrence among others – would weaken it still further. Boriswood's legal advisors took a different view. Mindful of the recent successful prosecutions of *Sleeveless Errand* and *The Well of Loneliness*, they advised the publisher and George Franks, the National Libraries' director, to admit their guilt and cut their losses: fighting the case, they claimed, would lead not only to conviction but imprisonment. The lawyers didn't believe that calling on big-name supporters would help: 'our own impression is that evidence of this sort is not of very great assistance, as every person (not least the persons on the jury) think they are just as well able to form a judgement as the people who are put into the box.'[4] Their clinching argument, given *Boy*'s subject matter, was that Lancastrian juries of the 1930s were not renowned for their enlightened views on homosexuality, and such a jury would probably feel 'that it is its duty to vindicate at least the honour of Lancashire.'[5] Boriswood decided to go down without a fight. On 20 March 1935 the directors pleaded guilty to the crime of uttering and publishing an obscene libel, and were fined £50 each. The company itself was fined £250.

Hanley was disgusted by Boriswood's capitulation, and mortified by its consequences. The reputation he'd enjoyed among the few people who had read him was now obliterated by the opinion of him fed to people who read only newspapers. The court had decreed that Hanley was nothing but a smut-peddler, the Press had reported the fact, and his mother and sister – both devout Catholics – now had to live with the shame. After the trial Hanley, never gregarious, withdrew from public view almost completely. He surrounded himself with family and a few close friends, among them the novelist John Cowper Powys, and retreated to deepest Wales. He buried himself in work, refused all requests for interviews, and never allowed *Boy* to be republished in his lifetime.

In the absence of any word from Hanley himself, many spoke on his behalf. In June 1935 E. M. Forster, addressing the Congrès International des Ecrivains in Paris on the subject of 'Liberty in England', condemned the prosecution of *Boy* and ridiculed the law which allowed it.[6] William Faulkner – a fellow outsider whose work, like Hanley's, did not fall easily into any recognised school – praised Hanley's uncluttered style: 'Just language like a good clean cyclone.'[7]

Aldington compared him to D. H. Lawrence, and T. E. Lawrence called *Boy* 'remarkable', and praised its author's 'sanity and general wholesomeness.'[8]

Those who praised Hanley as a stylist and as a writer of promise found themselves in less need of hyperbole than those who praised the achievement of *Boy* without qualification. Like most of Hanley's early work *Boy* is a tale of the sea; comparisons with Joseph Conrad were inevitable, and Henry Green (among others) made them. But Hanley would have none of it, rightly believing that his treatment of the sea, both as a setting and as a character in its own right, was antithetical to Conrad's. For Conrad's characters the sea is a liberating influence; for Hanley's, it's a prison. An unflinching documentarist, Hanley wrote about the daily life of a ship's crew in all its miserable, uncomfortable, dangerous detail. He didn't romanticise his charac-ters, and saw no equivalence between his own work and Conrad's, who he said saw all English sailors with Hamlet on their jerseys.

But while *Boy* has a strong sense of place – especially of workplace, like the novels of his fellow working-class writers Robert Tressell and Walter Greenwood – its characterisation is sketchy and its timeframe fatally compressed. Not surprisingly in a book written in a little over a week, *Boy*'s structure wobbles badly. The dates don't work, Arthur Fearon's age varies from page to page, and so many cataclysmic events befall him in so short a space of time that by the time he's dying of syphilis it's only the calibre of the prose, vivid and evocative, which prevents the book from tipping over into unintentional hilarity. Hanley knew all this. In later life he sent a correspondent a list of fourteen of his books that he would include in a collected edition: *Boy* wasn't one of them.

Hanley remained silent on the subject of *Boy* for eighteen years. Then in 1953, probably to dispel persistent rumours that the story was closely based on Hanley's own experiences as a boy at sea, he published a piece called *Oddfish* in a collection called *Don Quixote Drowned*. In *Oddfish* Hanley describes how once while on watch he had overheard an officer on the ship's bridge talking about the killing of a boy at sea:

> I wrote about this, it took me ten days. Now I realize it should have taken much longer than that. So shapeless and crude and overburdened with feelings. And in any case it struck some Northerners as something less tham normal and some critics as rather odd. I have, however, never been

able to believe that a searchlight on a scab was anything less than normal, and anything one might call odd. The Mandarins had the best defence, they just giggled.[9]

Having spoken once, Hanley never mentioned *Boy* or its prosecution again.

Boy was tailor-made for Jack Kahane. Like *Sleeveless Errand*, *The Well of Loneliness* and, later, *Bessie Cotter*, the book arrived in Paris on a wave of scandalous publicity caused by its prosecution. People were talking about it in England, which meant that tourists would come looking for it in France. They'd find it, too: Kahane used the unexpurgated text for the Obelisk edition, and the lurid wrapper design that had caused all the trouble in England, and by the autumn of 1935 the bare-breasted dancing girl was installed in bookshop windows all over Paris. She is almost certainly the reason the Obelisk edition is so rare today. It was not only foreign travellers who had been alerted to the existence of the book by the court case: customs officers were looking for it too. As late as 1954 *Boy* remained one of nine Obelisk titles on a Customs list of 'books which are to be seized as indecent or obscene',[10] and with a wrapper featuring a naked woman on a vivid red and black background it couldn't have been that hard for customs officers to spot. (The second Obelisk edition was dressed more demurely when it appeared in 1938.)

Had the collaboration between Hanley and Kahane begun in happier circumstances it might have been more fruitful. The quality of Hanley's writing combined with his background and wartime experience were all likely to have found in Kahane both a sympathetic friend and a useful associate. But the deal struck for the Obelisk edition of *Boy* was made not by Hanley but by Boriswood, who were far keener to offset their fines and legal fees than to do the right thing by their author. The mean-spirited and short-sighted contract they signed with Kahane ensured that the 10 per cent royalty on sales of the Obelisk edition of *Boy* went direct to themselves: Hanley received nothing at all from the French edition of his book. The deal poisoned Hanley's relationship with Boriswood beyond salvage, and ensured that Hanley and Kahane remained strangers. Kahane makes only a fleeting reference to *Boy* in *Memoirs of a Booklegger*, describing Hanley as 'a fine, rugged writer'.[11] The book seems to have sold slowly in Paris. Certainly anyone judging the book by its cover would have been badly disappointed: although the dancing girl makes a fleeting appearance towards the end of the book, *Boy*'s sexual content mostly consists of a series of violent and less than titillating homosexual assaults. Word of mouth among the one-handed readership would not have been good. In 1946 Maurice Girodias published a third Obelisk edition, designed like all immediately post-war Obelisks to sell to the huge numbers of Allied troops passing through Paris on their way home. But *Boy* never recovered from the attack made on its dustwrapper by a taxi driver from Bury. Today it is comprehensively out of print.

While the controversy surrounding *Boy* raged, Hanley had been getting on with writing the first of a number of books that should have cemented his reputation. *Time* magazine named *The Furys* its Book of the Year for 1936, and in the same year Hanley was commissioned by *The Spectator* to visit the depressed areas of South Wales; his study of the region's mining communities, *Grey Children*, appeared in 1937. The First World War novel *Hollow Sea* (1938) received great critical acclaim but sold poorly, a pattern which by now had firmly established itself. At the outbreak of the Second World War the Hanleys moved to London, and lived through the blitz: *No Directions* (1943) is Hanley's account of the experience. The book is fragmentary, visionary, and possesses all the technical assurance that had been lacking in *Boy*; an admiring Henry Miller wrote an introduction for the Uniform Edition, published in 1946.

By the end of the war the Hanleys had settled in the village of Llanfechian, near Welshpool, where they lived for the next twenty years. During the war Hanley had written plays for the BBC, propagandist pieces designed to boost the war effort. He continued to write novels during the 1950s, but his readership showed no sign of expanding and in time he turned his attention to drama. Writer's block was never a problem for Hanley, who wrote 79 plays for BBC radio, and in 1962 his play *Say Nothing* was produced by Joan Littlewood's theatre workshop at the Theatre Royal, Stratford East, where it was favourably compared (by Kenneth Tynan, among others) to Beckett and Pinter. Hanley rewrote it as a novel, and BBC Television transmitted it in its original form in 1964, the first of nine of Hanley's plays to be broadcast during the next five years.

During the 1970s Hanley turned his attention back to books. In 1972 he published *Another World*: it was his first novel for a decade, and three more were to follow in the next six years. His last book, *Lost*, appeared in 1979. Dorothy, Hanley's partner for almost half a century, died suddenly in 1980, and after her death he wrote nothing else.

James Hanley died in 1985, and is buried in Llanfechian church-yard.

By the same author

Fiction includes:
Drift (Eric Partridge, 1930)
The German Prisoner (privately printed, 1930)
A Passion Before Death (privately printed, 1930)
The Last Voyage (William Jackson, 1931)
Men in Darkness (John Lane, 1931)
Ebb and Flood (John Lane, 1932)
Captain Bottell (Boriswood, 1933)
Resurrexit Dominus (privately printed, 1934)
Quartermaster Clausen (Arlan, 1934)
The Furys (Chatto and Windus, 1935)
Stoker Bush (Chatto and Windus, 1935)
Hollow Sea (John Lane, 1938)
People Are Curious (John Lane, 1938)
The Ocean (Faber and Faber, 1941)
No Directions (Nicholson and Watson, 1943)
At Bay (Grayson Books, 1935)
The Closed Harbour (Macdonald, 1952)
The Welsh Sonata (Derek Verschoyle, 1954)
Say Nothing (Macdonald, 1962)
Another World (Deutsch, 1972)
Dream Journey (Deutsch, 1976)

Non-fiction includes:
Broken Water (Chatto and Windus, 1937)
Grey Children (Methuen, 1937)
Between the Tides (Methuen, 1939)
Don Quixote Drowned (Macdonald, 1953)

Plays include:
Plays One (Kaye and Ward, 1968)

Bibliography:
James Hanley: A Bibliography (William Hoffer [Vancouver], 1980)

Notes
1 James Hanley, *Broken Water* (Chatto and Windus, 1937), p. 259.

AUTHOR BIOGRAPHIES

2 Quoted in Linea Gibbs, *James Hanley: A Bibliography* (William Hoffer, 1980), p. 26.
3 Letter from James Hanley to Alan Steele, 8 July 1933, papers of Alan Steele, CUL.
4 Letter from Field Roscoe and Co. to Boriswood Ltd, 11 February 1935, Boriswood archive, HRC.
5 Letter from Field Roscoe to Boriswood, 11 February 1935.
6 This address was published in E. M. Forster, *Abinger Harvest* (Edward Arnold and Co., 1936).
7 Quoted in Frank G. Harrington, *James Hanley: A Bold and Unique Solitary* (Typographeum, 1989), p. 10.
8 Letter from T. E. Lawrence to James Hanley, 2 July 1931, *The Collected Letters of T. E. Lawrence* (Cape, 1938), p. 729.
9 James Hanley, *Don Quixote Drowned* (Macdonald, 1953), p. 53.
10 The National Archives, Kew, file no. CUST 49/4357.
11 Kahane, *Memoirs*, p. 257.

FRANK HARRIS

Like most chronic over-achievers, Frank Harris's sense of under-achievement was acute. Born James Thomas Harris in Galway, Ireland, in 1856, he was at various times in his life a cowboy, lawyer, novelist, biographer, newspaper editor, politician, playwright, and builder of Brooklyn Bridge. Barely five and a half feet tall, barrel-chested, with a booming voice that brooked no argument and the luxuriant moustaches of a pantomime villain, Harris was a polyglot classicist, a political fixer and sexual adventurer, a friend of Wilde and Shaw and Maupassant, and a man who, through the various offices he held, met Ruskin, Rhodes, General Gordon, Parnell, Kitchener, Marx and the Prince of Wales – all of whom feature in Harris's sprawling and preposterous four-volume memoir, *My Life and Loves*, first published at the author's expense in the 1920s, and then in 1934 by the Obelisk Press. The book – the only thing for which Harris is now remembered – is a turgid one-thousand-page exercise in autohagiography, occasionally enlivened by unlikely bouts of sex with women who get younger and younger the older Harris gets. A deranged monument to egotism, and by the standards of the 1920s shockingly explicit, *My Life and Loves* destroyed Harris's reputation, crippled him financially and, for all the other accomplishments of his life, reduced him in the eyes of literary history to a bumptious loudmouth, a man who was little more than vanity wrapped in skin.

[403]

Kahane and Harris first met in Manchester in 1912. Then 25 years old, Kahane had recently been elected to the committee of the city's Playgoers' Club following a speech in which he had suggested that meetings would be far more interesting if they were addressed by theatre professionals rather than by 'stage-struck members drivelling commonplaces'.[1] True to his word, during his year in office the club played host to John Galsworthy, Hilaire Belloc, the theatre designer Gordon Craig (who that year designed Stanislavsky's production of *Hamlet* at the Moscow Arts Theatre) – and Frank Harris. At the time Harris was 56 years old, and the embodiment of everything the young and aspiring members of Manchester's artistic community hoped to achieve. When he was fifteen Harris had sailed for America, where he worked as a shoeshine boy and construction worker in New York before travelling west to work as a cattle-driver. He enrolled at Kansas University as James Frank Harris (dropping his father's name, Thomas), and was admitted to the Bar in Douglas County in June 1875. The rest of the decade was spent studying and travelling in Europe. Once back in England he established himself as a social commentator and critic before becoming the editor of the *London Evening News* in 1884. Two years later he became editor of the *Fortnightly Review*, where he remained for eight years, and it was during this time that society's estimation of Frank Harris began to edge towards his own.

Non-aligned but with a broadly liberal perspective, the *Fortnightly Review* was founded in 1865 by Anthony Trollope, and served as both literary journal and a forum where issues of the day such as womens' rights and labour and education reform could be discussed in articles signed by their authors – a radical innovation at the time, and one which sharpened debate by attracting the leading writers of the day. Harris, a progressive with more opinions than he knew what to do with, was now in his element helping shape the national debate, and in his eight years as the *Review's* editor came to know almost every leading literary and political figure in the country. In 1889 he was adopted as Conservative candidate for South Hackney – a bizarre career move given his support for nationalisation, Parnell, Irish nationalism, and women's rights – but resigned, never having been elected, two years later. In 1895 Harris was one of the few people to stand by his friend Oscar Wilde following his conviction for gross indecency, and the following year he again outraged conservative opinion, this time on South Africa, by denouncing the Jameson Raid,

the disastrous attempt to provoke the British expatriate workforce to
rise up against Paul Kruger's Boers.

In the mid-1890s Harris began to write fiction. A volume of short
stories, *Elder Conklin*, appeared in 1895; *Mr and Mrs Daventry*, a play based
on an idea of Oscar Wilde's, in 1900; and *The Bomb*, a novel broadly
sympathetic to anarchism, in 1905. He was still editing journals
and magazines to earn a living but now became more and more
outspoken, in print as well as in person. In an article published in the
English Review in 1911 he argued for greater freedom to discuss sexual
matters in both literature and life, a position which, much to his satisfaction, caused an outcry in the national press. In the outspoken and
controversial Frank Harris, then, the Manchester Playgoers' Society
had secured themselves a star attraction.

The subject of Harris's lecture at the Midland Hotel was Shakespeare – one of the few writers Harris was prepared to acknowledge
as greater than himself. Three years earlier he had published *The
Man Shakespeare*, a biography in which he argued that Shakespeare's
personality was discernible from his plays because of his habit of
ascribing personal attributes to his characters; Harris also argued
that Mary Fitton, a maid of honour to Elizabeth I, was the mysterious
Dark Lady of the sonnets. The book, while entertaining, was highly
speculative (Harris preferred the word 'intuitive'), and (along with
the rest of the academic community) C. H. Herford, then Professor of
English at Manchester University, had given it a scathing review when
it was published, calling it 'a disgrace to British scholarship'. Rather
unwisely he now decided to attend Harris's lecture at the Midland.
In his memoir *Set Down in Malice*, Kahane's friend Gerald Cumberland
remembers Harris spotting Herford in the audience, and zeroing in:

> Each sentence he spoke appeared to be the last word in bitterness; but
> each succeeding sentence leaped above and beyond its predecessor, until
> at length the speaker had lashed himself into a state of feeling to express
> which words were useless. He stopped magnificently, and the room rang
> with applause... they applauded him with enthusiasm, and they did so
> because they had been deeply stirred by eloquence that can only be
> described as superb and by anger that was lava hot in its sincerity. Briefly,
> the lecture was an overwhelming success.[2]

After the lecture Cumberland and Kahane took Harris for supper
in the French restaurant attached to the hotel, where for six hours
Harris talked while his hosts listened. The experience led Cumber-

land to hope that one day Harris might 'be induced to print all the indiscreet things he says over coffee and liqueurs'.[3] In 1923, with the publication of *My Life and Loves*, he did.

By then, Harris's fortunes had changed. In 1914 he'd been briefly jailed for contempt following a typically grandstanding court appearance during a libel hearing, and in 1915 he'd published *England or Germany?*, in which he argued against the United States entering the war on the grounds that the injustices ingrained in the English political and social system were not worth defending with American blood. The book was a spectacular misjudgement: what would have been seen in peacetime as a characteristic piece of loudmouthed mischief-making was in wartime regarded as little short of treason. Denounced by the British press, Harris spent the rest of the war in the United States, acquired the New York magazine *Pearson's*, and became a naturalised citizen there in 1921. The same year he moved to Tannersville in upstate New York to begin work on *My Life and Loves*.

It's hard to imagine how a book which features almost every major figure of the late nineteenth century, and which throws in regular and graphic bouts of sex into the bargain, could turn out to be deadly dull. It is much easier to imagine once you've read *My Life and Loves*, a book with a cast of thousands, but only one character. If Harris were more likeable this would be less of a problem, but one thousand pages spent in the company of a solipsistic boor, however talented and well-connected, is hard to take. Harris knew everyone, but more importantly for Harris, everyone knew him. On almost every page, ominously long paragraphs begin with lines like 'I was lunching one day about 1889 with the Princess of Monaco at Claridge's...', and the reader hunkers down, reaches for his thermos flask, and waits for the point to arrive. (It rarely does.) Harris's opinions on *everything* litter each page, until it becomes automatic to dismiss whatever he says merely because he is the one saying it, while his prejudices, such as the 'abnormal' nature of homosexuality – only male homosexuality, of course – and the hypervirility of the otherwise subhuman negro race, mark Harris out as one of literature's more myopic visionaries.

If *My Life and Loves* had been merely turgid, self-absorbed and barking mad it would have caused its author far less trouble, but while its incessant self-regard and reheating of old personal battles gave Harris's many detractors plenty of ammunition with which to attack him, it was the book's sexual episodes that generated most uproar. When *My Life and Loves* was published Harris was 66 years old. He'd long been a supporter of greater sexual openness but no one had ever heard him argue in favour of pornography, and *My Life and Loves* was (and is) pornographic: what Harris presumably intended to be seen as an unflinching appraisal of his own sexual history was instead dismissed as what Sinclair Lewis called the 'senile and lip-wetting giggle of an old man about his far-distant filthiness'.[4] Even this was kind, since many of the sexual episodes were clearly invented, among them Volume Four's weekly orgies at Harris's San Remo villa populated by hordes of beautiful and willing adolescent girls apparently unencumbered by parents wondering where their children are spending the weekend. (In 1954 Maurice Girodias published a fifth volume of *My Life and Loves*. Worked up into book form by Alexander Trocchi from notes left by Harris, it cuts almost all of Harris's usual name-dropping and banquets and balls, so making room for avowedly pornographic (and avowedly fictional) odysseys through India and the Far East, prominent amongst which is a lubricious account of a night spent playing nude leapfrog with teenage girls, all related in a pitch-perfect imitation of Harris's style. Riotous and raunchy but stripped of all po-faced self-importance, it's a far more satisfying book – in every way – than any of the instalments Harris wrote himself.[5])

Kahane mentions Harris's visit to Manchester in his memoirs; he doesn't mention that he later published *My Life and Loves*. Mainstream publishers in England, France and the United States shared his trepidation: Harris had the first volume printed in Berlin and then began distributing it himself through a network of friends and associates willing to turn smuggler for the purpose. As usual, news of the latest book to affront public decency reached readers and the Customs authorities at about the same time, and the usual battle was joined. Hundreds of copies were seized and destroyed, many others were mysteriously 'lost' in transit. The financial cost to Harris was huge, and was ratcheted still higher when the publication of the later volumes resulted in police raids and legal action. The prosecution was eventually withdrawn, but by then the damage was done. Harris's money was gone, his fear of arrest if he left France made rejoining the lucrative lecture circuit impossible, and his reputation was ruined. He sat in Nice, watched the girls go by, and grew old.

By 1929 the storm had largely blown itself out, and although Harris was still short of money and plagued by bronchitis and stomach ulcers, he had resumed some of the duties of a society host. That year the novelist Julian MacLaren-Ross, then eighteen years old, was invited to a lunch given by Harris at his home in the hills overlooking Nice, where he was introduced to a familiar-sounding figure:

> [a man], whom Harris said, with his gusty whistling laugh, was 'a fellow-Scotchman' though he spoke English in a manner scarcely compatible with a countryman of Burns: I soon discovered he was a Hungarian named Kalnay who had written a book about Jews under the pseudonym Jim McKay.
> 'McKay's not merely a writer,' Harris told me. 'He's something much more important,' he drew a deep breath and hissed with extraordinary venom: 'A *publisher!*'[6]

Whether 'Kalnay' was Kahane cannot now be known for sure. What *is* certain is that five years later in 1934, three years after the death of Frank Harris at the age of 75, the Obelisk edition of *My Life and Loves* was published in Paris. It became, with *Daffodil*, Obelisk's biggest ever moneyspinner, and was still being reprinted by Maurice Girodias under the Obelisk imprint more than a quarter of a century later.

Frank Harris died in Nice in 1931, at the age of 75.

By the same author

Fiction includes:
Elder Conklin and Other Stories (Heinemann, 1895)
Montes the Matador and Other Stories (Grant Richards, 1900)
The Bomb (John Long, 1908)

Non-fiction includes:
The Man Shakespeare (Frank Palmer, 1909)
The Women of Shakespeare (Methuen, 1911)
Contemporary Portraits (Methuen, 1915)
England or Germany? (Wilmarth Press, 1915)
Oscar Wilde (privately published, 1916)
On the Trail (John Lane, 1930)
Bernard Shaw (Gollancz, 1931)

Play:
Mr and Mrs Daventry (Richards Press, 1956)

Notes
1 Kahane, *Memoirs*, p. 29.
2 Gerald Cumberland, *Set Down in Malice* (Grant Richards, 1919), p. 34.
3 Cumberland, *Set Down in Malice*, p. 39.

4 Quoted in 'The Great Egoist', an unsigned review of the 1963 Grove Press edition of *My Life and Loves*, *Time* magazine, 8 November 1963.
5 Frank Harris [Alexander Trocchi], *My Life and Loves: Fifth Volume* (Olympia Press, No. 10 in the Atlantic Library series, 1954).
6 Julian MacLaren-Ross, 'A Visit to the Villa Edouard Sept', *London Magazine*, June 1955.

PHILIPPE HÉRIAT

In what must have been a very lean year, Philippe Hériat's first novel, *L'Innocent*, won the Prix Théophraste Renaudot, one of France's major literary prizes. The novel was published in 1931 and is an inert story of young love, only briefly enlivened by a scene set at a 1920s' Wimbledon tennis championship and then by a hint of sibling incest towards the end. It was offered to Kahane by Hériat's agent William Bradley in December the same year, by which time it had sold well in French, and carried with it a sufficiently scandalous reputation to convince Kahane that its success could be repeated in an English-language edition. He spent the first three months of 1932 translating the book himself, and published *The Lamb* in hardback in July. A paperback version followed in August.

Perhaps the jurors on the committee of the Prix Théophraste Renaudot were overly impressed by Hériat's many other careers. Born Raymond Gérard Payelle in Paris in 1898, Hériat enlisted in the French army in 1916, and after the armistice studied film alongside René Clair. He worked both as an assistant director and as an actor, making his debut in *Le Carnaval der Vérités* in 1920 and appearing in more than twenty films in the next ten years, notably as Antonio Salicetti in Abel Gance's 1927 masterpiece, *Napoleon*. As for *L'Innocent*, it's bad enough to kill off most writing careers at birth, but nevertheless Hériat went on to enjoy a career as novelist, playwright and screenwriter that spanned the next forty years. His 1939 novel *Les Enfants Gâtés* won the Prix Goncourt, and five years later *Famille Boussardel* won the Grand Prix du Roman de l'Académie Française.

Hériat died in 1971.

By the same author

Fiction includes:
La Main Tendue (Denoël et Steele, 1933)
L'Araignée du Matin (Denoël et Steele, 1933)

Les Enfants Gâtés (Gallimard, 1939)
Famille Boussardel (Gallimard, 1944)
Les Grilles d'Or (Gallimard, 1957)

Plays include:
Les Noces de Devil (France Illustration, 1953)

GEORGE HOUGHTON

Born in England in 1905, George Houghton was a writer and cartoonist who in the 1920s was working in Nice as a caricaturist, circulation manager and general dogsbody on a newspaper called *Continental Life*. (The elderly Frank Harris, by then all but bankrupt and scratching a living working for the rival *Riviera Season*, was a regular and noisy visitor to the office.) *Continental Life* catered to the transient population of the Riviera: expatriate artists, writers and hangers-on who every year decamped from Paris to winter in the south. Houghton began his career by writing about the 'smart set', at first from the outside, later as part of it. His 1936 book *The Adventures of a Gadabout* is a typical account of the period, all pipes and flannels and slicked-back hair, and coastal drives in open-topped cars. Houghton produced many such books through a long life, fast-selling and instantly forgettable, from which he made money out of fun.

Houghton married in Nice in 1926 and first moved to Paris the following year to supervise the launch of the Paris edition of *Continental Life*. It failed after only two months, and so Houghton returned to Nice to work on the pleasingly named *Nice Times*. His reputation as a caricaturist had grown, and gained him access to heavyweight interviewees. One such was George Bernard Shaw, who was so delighted with Houghton's drawing of him that he responded with a self-caricature, giving greater emphasis to his spindly legs than Houghton had thought tactful to include in his own.

But the two-month stay in Paris had given the Houghtons a taste for the capital, and soon after relocating there for good he was working for as many publications as he could fit into the day – chief among them the continental edition of the *Daily Mail*. The *Mail* was Kahane's main publicity outlet for Obelisk's books, and it's probable that the two men met as a result of the business Kahane regularly conducted with the paper. However the meeting came about, it had happened by the winter of 1931: Houghton's book of caricatures, *Here's Looking at You*, was published by Obelisk in February 1932.

Here's Looking at You is one of the imprint's oddities. The folio of fifteen full-page caricatures was supposed to be the first of a series, but sales were evidently so poor that the second instalment never materialised. (The book is extremely rare: I can locate only two copies, both in institutional libraries.) Its failure to sell is unsurprising: with the exception of Sisley Huddleston none of the subjects of the caricatures is known today, and a cursory and uninformative foreword makes little attempt to contextualise them. According to Houghton's widow a lavish party was held to celebrate the book's publication, but it generated no business, and *Here's Looking at You* disappeared without trace.

Houghton learned from the failure of *Here's Looking at You*, and in future took care to ensure that his artwork was always accompanied by text; *The Adventures of a Gadabout*, published four years later, heeded the lesson and was a great success. And as well as continuing to work as a journalist, Houghton found other ways to make money (sports cartoonist, illustrator, commercial artist), always combining the necessity of earning a living with the necessity of having fun.

During the war Houghton served as a Squadron Leader in the Royal Air Force in the Western Desert, and later wrote about his experiences in *They Flew Through Sand*, and in 1952 he managed to set himself up for the rest of his life by publishing *Confessions of a Golf Addict*, a flimsy self-illustrated stocking-filler which to everybody's surprise sold in vast numbers. Its phenomenal success led Houghton to write more than forty *Golf Addict* titles, as well as serving a fifteen-year term as associate editor of *Golf World* and becoming president of the Golf Addicts' Society from the mid-1960s onwards. But British readers of a certain age will, without knowing it, remember Houghton most fondly for his work as a commercial artist in the 1970s: he designed the animated polar bear for the Fox's Glacier Mint campaign.

George Houghton died in Bridport, Devon, in 1993.

By the same author
Non-fiction includes (among many others):
The Adventures of a Gadabout (Selwyn and Blount, 1936)
They Flew Through Sand (Jarrolds, 1943)
Between the Red Lines (Newnes, 1949)
Portrait of a Golf Addict (Country Life, 1960)
Golf Addict Among the Scots (Country Life, 1967)
Golf Addict In Gaucho Land (Pelham, 1970)

NORAH JAMES

Norah Cordner James was born into a wealthy family in Hampstead, London, in 1896. Her father was a heavy-handed disciplinarian whose behaviour ensured that most of his daughter's childhood memories were unhappy ones, and as she grew the antagonism between the two intensified. He was irritated by her atheism, and enraged by her espousal of women's suffrage; when Norah attended the funeral procession of suffragette Emily Davison, killed in 1913 when she threw herself under the King's horse on Derby day, the estrangement of father and daughter became irrevocable.[1]

In 1915 James entered the Slade School of Art, but left after six weeks to help the war effort and to pursue her political interests. As well as her involvement in the suffragette movement she joined pro-Sinn Fein organisations, and after a six-week stint as a Land Girl became a Trades Union organiser at the Pensions Issue Office. By 1921 she was on the Executive Committee of the Save the Miners' Children Fund under chairman George Lansbury, and was addressing rallies in Trafalgar Square. She dropped the paternal half of her surname – Cordner – and became plain Norah James. In 1926 she moved from her post at the Trades Union Congress to work as a publicity manager for Jonathan Cape, and in 1928 sat in the public gallery during the trial of Radclyffe Hall's *The Well of Loneliness* (which Cape had published) at Bow Street Magistrates' Court.

James had started writing in the mid-1920s, turning out articles and short stories to pass the time while convalescing from an operation. She managed to sell some of her work to women's magazines, and started to take her new interest more seriously. In 1927 she began her first novel, *Sleeveless Errand*. Written shortly after James had been jilted by her lover, the book's central character Paula Cranford is... a woman who has just been jilted by her lover. In a Lyon's teashop she meets a man whose wife has been having an affair, and the couple spend the next 24 hours together, Paula trying to persuade Bill to return to his wife, Bill trying to persuade Paula not to kill herself. Their relationship is played out over the background hum of 'the Crowd', a decadent gaggle of alcoholics, prostitutes, homosexuals and blithely promiscuous couples in whose company Paula has spent too much time, and whom she now blames for her unhappiness. *Sleeveless Errand* is a deeply terrible book, maudlin, melodramatic, and fatally upstaged by its obvious and unabsorbed influences, in particular

Hemingway's *The Sun Also Rises*. More interesting than the novel itself, and certainly more important, is the story of how the book's persecution in Britain kickstarted Jack Kahane's publishing career (see 'A Very British Pornographer', above, pp. 63–67).

Norah James may not have been the world's greatest writer, but she was evidently a decent human being: when the contract with Kahane was signed for the French edition of *Sleeveless Errand*, James stipulated that half of all monies due to her should be sent to her English publisher Eric Partridge to compensate him for the loss he had sustained as a result of the court case. She also promised to place her next novel with his company, Scholartis. (*Hail! All Hail!* was published by Scholartis late in 1929.) James left Cape to work as a literary talent scout for her American publisher William Morrow (for whom she recruited James Hilton, author of *Goodbye, Mr Chips* and *Lost Horizon*) and later for Covici, Friede. She continued to be politically active, and represented the Authors' Society on the National Book Council. But mostly, she wrote.

The catalogue of the British Library lists more than 70 books by Norah James. None is in print. Most of her books were novels, but she also wrote cookery and children's books, some of them co-written with Barbara Beauchamp, James' partner for the second half of her life and the dedicatee of her autobiography *I Lived in a Democracy* (1939). James' last books, mostly hospital romances, were published in the early 1970s.

At some point Norah James renounced the atheism that had so enraged her father. Her literary executor is the Priory Church of St Bartholemew the Great, West Smithfield, in London: 'Miss James, a former nurse, is remembered by one of our churchwardens as an elderly member of this congregation in the 1960s and 1970s. We do have 24 of her books here at the church, and I believe that it was intended that we should receive the royalties from their sale, but no one can remember seeing any money.'[2]

Norah James died in London on 19 November 1979.

By the same author
Fiction includes:
Hail! All Hail! (Scholartis, 1929)
Hospital (Duckworth, 1932)
Jealousy (Duckworth, 1933)
The Lion Beat the Unicorn (Duckworth, 1935)

The Hunted Heart (Cassell, 1941)
Enduring Adventure (Cassell, 1944)
Pay the Piper (Macdonald, 1950)
Mercy In Your Hands (Hutchinson, 1956)
Small Hotel (Hurst and Blackett, 1965)
Ward of Darkness (Hurst and Blackett, 1971)
If Only (Hurst and Blackett, 1972)

Non-fiction includes:
I Lived in a Democracy (Longmans, 1939)
Greenfingers and the Gourmet (Nicholson and Watson, 1949)
Cooking in Cider (Kingswood, 1952)

Notes
1 Norah James, *I Lived in a Democracy* (Longmans, 1939), p. 40. Most of the information given in this entry comes from this source.
2 Letter from Robin Goodgame, Lay Assistant, The Priory Church of St Bartholemew the Great, to James Armstrong, 4 March 1994.

JAMES JOYCE AND LUCIA JOYCE

Every literary expatriate in Paris was infatuated with James Joyce; Jack Kahane's infatuation with him almost cost him his livelihood. In 1929 he had gone into business with the publisher Henri Babou, and had bought for the company the rights to *Sleeveless Errand*. Over the next year the book had sold and sold well, but since then Kahane's duties as the 'most somnolent of sleeping partners'[1] had been confined to translating Babou's *Les Artistes du Livre* series into English for the American market. But he was keen to make his mark on the business, and had begun to make frequent visits to Shakespeare and Company, Sylvia Beach's expatriate bookshop on the rue de l'Odéon. The quiet and rather prim publisher of *Ulysses* enjoyed the attentions of the mildly flirtatious Kahane in spite of herself, and for his part Kahane never ceased to be amazed that his 'excellent friend',[2] with no prior experience, had managed to pull off the publishing coup of the century.

Beach valued Kahane for his 'good humour', but was mistaken in crediting him with 'a scorn of pretences', since his interest in James Joyce was far more commercial than literary.[3] As a cultural activist in pre-war Manchester Kahane had fetishised everything that was new; as an older man in France, had found that his love for the modern did not extend to a capital M. He was awed by Joyce's reputation, but baffled by his work:

James Joyce is perhaps the only original genius of letters since the war [but] even his inspiration is small and poor. But for his astonishing technical resources he would have written himself out in the *Portrait of the Artist as a Young Man*. In *Ulysses* he harps on the same theme using another instrument, and *Finnegans Wake*, I declare now, even if once I published a section of it with touching reverence and incomparable luxury, is perhaps a happy hunting-ground for the philologists, but from the point of view of literature, creative literature, is no more and no less than literary buncombe, a world for adepts at jigsaw puzzles ...[4]

The section of *Finnegans Wake* to which Kahane refers was wrested from Joyce, via Beach, in 1930:

Mr. Kahane used to drive up in his convertible Voisin, a sort of glass-enclosed station wagon, for a chat with his colleague at Shakespeare and Company. He would ask, 'How's God?' (meaning Joyce). He admired me 'no end' for my discovery of such an 'obscene' book, as he termed it, as *Ulysses*, and never relinquished the hope of persuading me one day to let the Obelisk Press take it over. Meanwhile, he was obliged to be content with an extract from Joyce's new work, entitled *Haveth Childers Everywhere*, which Kahane thought lacking in sex interest.[5]

The deal for *Haveth Childers Everywhere* was sealed at an awkward audience with 'God', at which a tongue-tied Kahane sat before a near sightless Joyce, listening meekly to the chatter of the master's assembled acolytes while Nora bustled about with tea and cake. One of those present was Stuart Gilbert, who later became friends with Kahane. He remembered Joyce emerging from the room in which the negotiations had been conducted and telling him that the deal was done, and that he was now twenty-five thousand francs richer: 'Good business – for him!' noted Gilbert later.[6] It was even better business than Gilbert knew: Joyce, notoriously slippery on the subject of money, clearly thought better of alerting creditors to the true magnitude of his windfall. In fact, Kahane had just handed Joyce a cheque for *fifty* thousand francs for the right to publish a 5000-word extract from *Work in Progress*.

In a near-fatal blow to his business, Kahane had allowed hero-worship to cloud his commercial judgment. Henri Babou was at first delighted that Kahane had landed such a big name for the company's list, but his enthusiasm waned when it was explained to him what Kahane had actually bought: *Haveth Childers Everywhere*, into which, in the course of describing Humphrey Earwicker's building of Dublin, Joyce hurls a welter of puns on the names of streets, parks and buildings of more than thirty cities around the world, as well as plays on the names of sixty Dublin mayors, a list of which Joyce had had compiled for the purpose from the city's postal directory of 1904.

Kahane tried to read *Haveth Childers Everywhere*, but couldn't get through it. He was unable to explain to his partner's satisfaction why he couldn't read a book written in his own language, why he had bought such a book in the first place, why he had paid such a price, or why he expected it to sell. Worse, production costs on the book, which was to be issued in a *de luxe* edition, brought the company's pre-publication outlay to nearly one hundred thousand francs: with only five hundred copies to sell, a high retail price was inevitable. Subscribers didn't need this extra disincentive to buy, but they got it anyway when it was announced that copies of *Haveth Childers Every-where*, signed by Joyce, would cost Frs. 850, or $40, and unsigned ones Frs. 500, or $20. Unsurprisingly, orders were catastrophically low as the publication date neared. But at the last moment Kahane managed to avert disaster by the simple expedient of entering into a deal with a publisher who was as starstruck as he was. Elbridge Adams ran the Fountain Press in New York, and was a fervent admirer of Joyce. Too fervent: over lunch at the Scribe Hotel in the Boulevard des Capucines, Kahane managed to strike a deal which saw Adams buy half of the edition of *Haveth Childers Everywhere* for distribution in New York – a deal which saw Kahane save his bacon, and Adams lose his shirt. (The Fountain Press was later forced to remainder most of its copies.) But although Kahane managed to save his business he never managed to find a market for the book, and was still advertising copies for sale as late as 1936.

By the time the prospect of a second collaboration with Joyce arose, Kahane had learned from his previous mistakes. By 1932 he was free of Babou and running his own business, an altogether cannier operator than the one who, two years previously, had handed Joyce a small fortune for the rights to an unsaleable book. But even in his earlier callow and starstruck incarnation, Kahane would surely have spotted the extremely limited commercial possibilities of the proposition Joyce brought to him in 1932.

Joyce's daughter, Lucia, had a long history of mental instability. Throughout her childhood the Joyce family had been on the move almost constantly, and Lucia had moved with them from home to home, school to school, country to country, her head full of half-learned languages and her heart grieving for yet another clutch of lost friends. By the time Lucia reached her teens the Joyce family had more or less settled in Paris (although their address continued to change regularly). Now a new problem confronted her: freed from the burden of having a nomadic exile for a father, she now had to acclimatise to the fact that the world was hailing him as a genius. Both Joyce's children struggled to emerge from his shadow; for Lucia the struggle proved catastrophic. Early enthusiasm for the piano and for singing came to nothing, and many years of intensive training as a dancer were aborted when Lucia declared (possibly as a result of her mother's active discouragement of her aspirations) that she lacked the stamina for the profession. Joyce's friends had long recommended he seek professional care for his daughter, but Joyce kept her close, and encouraged her to fill the void left by her abandonment of dance by returning to one of her old enthusiasms, drawing.

In 1929, Lucia had started work on a series of illuminated letters: Joyce christened them 'lettrines.' His failing eyesight clouded further by a father's love, Joyce convinced himself that the lettrines had artistic as well as therapeutic value, and scenting the possibility of a career for Lucia at last, he touted her work to artists, illustrators and designers. He found no takers: only when he offered them attached to his own work did anybody show even a passing interest. At the end of 1931 the Oxford University Press was preparing to publish *The Joyce Book*, settings by thirteen different composers of the poems Sylvia Beach had first published in 1927 under the title *Pomes Penyeach*. *The Joyce Book* was edited by the composer Herbert Hughes (a close friend of Kahane's) and he had commissioned contributions from, among others, John Ireland, Arthur Bliss, Arnold Bax and George Antheil. When Joyce sent Lucia's lettrines to Hughes for inclusion in the book's accompanying text Hughes quickly returned them, explaining that the type had already been set. (It's unlikely that this was true, since *The Joyce Book* wasn't published until 1933). Joyce next tried Caresse Crosby, who got as far as making plans for a *de luxe* edition of the poems, in a facsimile of Joyce's handwriting, and with the first letter of each poem illuminated by Lucia. But the plans came to nothing when she failed to arouse any interest in the project among her collaborators in America.

As so often in his publishing career, Kahane found himself the last resort of an author unable to place his work with anyone else. He was not about to turn Joyce down – he remained as starstruck as ever –

but he now knew better than to allow his idolatry to jeopardise his business. It was agreed between Kahane and Joyce that a mutual friend, Desmond Harmsworth, be recruited as co-publisher, and Kahane further stipulated that Joyce should underwrite the production costs of the enterprise and recruit subscribers for the edition, which would consist of just 25 *de luxe* copies. The book would be printed on Japan *macre* paper; the lettrines would be reproduced using the *pochoir* stencil method (one of the few useful legacies of Kahane's association with Babou); and it would retail at Frs. 1000 or £12.

Unpublished letters from James and Lucia Joyce to Desmond Harmsworth make very clear where the impetus for the *Pomes Penyeach* project lay.[7] In the first half of 1932 Lucia's behaviour had become increasingly erratic, and her brother Giorgio had her admitted to a psychiatric institution at l'Hay-les-Roses. When Joyce travelled to Zurich in July to consult his eye surgeon he took Lucia out of the hospital and placed her in the care of a nurse at the home of his friends Eugene and Maria Jolas at nearby Feldkirch. From there Lucia wrote to Desmond Harmsworth. She had received a letter from Mr Kahane, who wanted to know what kind of a binding she would like for *Pomes Penyeach*. She had told him that she would have nothing to do with the decision, and that he should consult either her father or Stuart Gilbert about it. But she declared herself glad that the book was coming out later that month, and hoped that it would be a success.

This attitude of passive well-wisher to her own book contrasts strongly with her father's tireless promotion of Lucia's work on the project. As early as six months before publication Joyce had been telephoning Harmsworth in London to suggest the names of possible subscribers (among them Lady Ottoline Morrell, Sydney Schiff and Brian Guinness) and when the book was issued in September Joyce again contacted Harmsworth with sales ideas. Playing down his own involvement in the project he refers instead to 'the book of lettrines', and asks Harmsworth to telephone three people, Harriet Weaver, Ralph Pinker (from Joyce's literary agency), and the novelist and poet James Stephens, and invite them to look at the book with a view to buying a copy. Joyce was particularly keen that Stephens should see *Pomes Penyeach*, as he had an idea for another book on which he hoped he could persuade Stephens to collaborate with Lucia. Even before a copy of *Pomes Penyeach* had been sold, Joyce was planning another project for his oblivious daughter.

In his memoir Kahane describes *Pomes Penyeach* as 'a curiosity rather than a real book, and although it was pretty to look at, I was never really proud of it.'[8] Since what little circulation of the edition there was was supervised by Joyce himself, the rarefied company the 25 copies have kept down the years reinforces the impression that they are more *objets d'art* than books. Customs officers at Dover certainly thought so: in October, the silk casing resulted in ten copies on their way to Harmsworth being impounded until a luxury tax amounting to a third of their retail value was paid.

Despite Joyce's best efforts the 25 copies sold slowly: a prospectus issued by Harmsworth in the autumn of 1932 notes that five copies remained unsubscribed, and Kahane was still advertising the book for sale in Paris as late as 1936. According to Lucia Joyce's biographer, Carol Locb Schloss, Joyce sent copies to T. S. Eliot, to Frank Morley at Faber, and to Hubert Foss at the Oxford University Press, as well as buying two copies himself and arranging for them to be deposited at the British Library and the Bibliothèque Nationale.[9] He also sent Kahane a thousand francs to send on to Lucia as an ego-boosting 'royalty'. Harriet Weaver and Robert McAlmon subscribed, and probables included Nancy Cunard, Wyndham Lewis and George Antheil. Payment from these luminaries was slow in arriving, but this time the non-existent cash flow was Joyce's problem, not Kahane's.

When the Obelisk/Harmsworth edition of *Pomes Penyeach* was first published its limited print run and its price – more than 25 times that of the average hardback – made it all but unobtainable, and little has changed since 1932. Most copies have still never been on open sale, and now reside in institutional libraries, bequeathed to them either by Joyce himself or by their first owners. (A census of the book is provided in the notes to item A–17 of the bibliography.)

By the time *A Chaucer ABC* was published four years later in October 1936, its only therapeutic benefit was to Joyce's anguished conscience. In 1932, when *Pomes Penyeach* was being prepared for publication, Lucia had been working on a complete alphabet of lettrines. Joyce had searched for a suitable text for the lettrines to illuminate, and had eventually settled on the suggestion of his friend, the art critic Louis Gillet: Chaucer's translation of Guillaume de Deguilleville's *Hymn to the Holy Virgin*, each stanza of which begins with a different letter of the alphabet. When favourable notices of Lucia's work on *Pomes Penyeach* began to appear (admittedly in publications such as Eugene Jolas's *transition*, which were heavily reliant on their association with Joyce and so unlikely to publish anything *unfavour-able*) Joyce was keen to exploit the publicity. John Holroyd-Reece, controller of the company that published D. H. Lawrence in Paris under the Albatross Press imprint, offered to show Lucia's lettrines to the London publishers Burns and Oates. Joyce agreed, and gave him Lucia's artwork to take to London. There it was promptly lost, and remained lost until September 1934.

Joyce found a little work for Lucia in the interim. Carolus Verhulst at the Servire Press in The Hague was either sincerely interested in Lucia's work, or canny enough to realise that an expression of such interest might get the signature of Joyce *père* on a publishing contract. Whatever his motives, *The Mime of Mick, Nick and the Maggies*, Chapter Nine of *Finnegans Wake*, was published by Servire late in 1933, with artwork and an illuminated first letter by Lucia. But the loss of the lettrines in London had induced another relapse in their creator; although the curative benefit of Lucia's artwork was always dubious, the corrosive effect of its interruption was clear.

The lettrines finally resurfaced late in 1934 – too late to capitalise on the minor flurry of interest caused by the publication of *Pomes Penyeach* two years earlier. No other publisher presenting himself, Joyce settled, once again, for Kahane, and underwrote the edition himself. It was published in October 1936 in an edition of three hundred copies, with one copy prepared in time for presentation to Lucia on 26 July, her twenty-ninth birthday, so that, as Joyce wrote to Harriet Weaver, 'she may see something to persuade her that her whole past has not been a failure.'[10]

Lucia was plagued by mental illness for the rest of her life. She died in Northampton, England, in 1982.

By the same author

Fiction includes:
Dubliners (Grant Richards, 1914)
A Portrait of the Artist as a Young Man (Huebsch, 1916)
Ulysses (Shakespeare and Company, 1922)
Finnegans Wake (Faber, 1939)

Poetry includes:
Chamber Music (Elkin Mathews, 1907)

Pomes Penyeach (Shakespeare and Company, 1927)
Collected Poems (Black Sun Press, 1936)

Play:
Exiles (Grant Richards, 1918)

Notes
1 Kahane, *Memoirs*, p. 217.
2 Kahane, *Memoirs*, p. 217.
3 Sylvia Beach, *Shakespeare and Company* (Faber and Faber, 1960), p. 140.
4 Kahane, *Memoirs*, p. 32.
5 Beach, *Shakespeare and Company*, p. 140.
6 Stuart Gilbert, *Reflections on James Joyce* (University of Texas Press, 1993), p. 22.
7 Unpublished letters from James and Lucia Joyce to Desmond Harms-worth, kindly shown me by Harmsworth's daughter Margaret. The inevitable objections from the Joyce estate make direct quotation impossible.
8 Kahane, *Memoirs*, p. 244.
9 Carol Loeb Schloss, *Lucia Joyce: To Dance in the Wake* (Bloomsbury, 2004), p. 241.
10 Letter from James Joyce to Harriet Weaver, 9 June 1936, published in *The Letters of James Joyce, Volume III*, ed. Richard Ellmann (Viking Press, 1966).

D. H. LAWRENCE

O the stale old dogs who pretend to guard
the morals of the masses,
how smelly they make the great back-yard,
wetting after everyone that passes.

When Martin Secker published the first edition of D. H. Lawrence's *Pansies* in 1929 the book was fourteen poems shorter than its author had intended. One of the casualties was 'The Young and their Moral Guardians', the first stanza of which is quoted above; other poems deleted by the jittery publisher included 'The Little Wowser' ('There is a little wowser / JohnThomas by name, / and for every bloomin', mortal thing / that little blighter's to blame'); 'The Jeune Fille' ('Oh the innocent girl / in her maiden teens / knows perfectly well / what everything means'); and 'My Naughty Book – ':

They say I wrote a naughty book
With perfectly awful things in it,
putting in all the impossible words
like balls and fuck and shit.[1]

[421]

The 'naughty book' was *Lady Chatterley's Lover*. Its private publication in Florence in 1928, combined with the appearance in Paris of *Ulysses* in 1922 and *Tropic of Cancer* in 1934, marked the beginning of the end for literary censorship – although it would take another thirty years before the 'stale old dogs' finally allowed the publication of *Chatterley* and *Cancer* in their authors' home countries.

Lady Chatterley was a long way from being Lawrence's first confrontation with those he called the 'censor-morons'. In 1915 *The Rainbow* was declared obscene and half of its first printing was destroyed; the following year the manuscript of *Women In Love* prompted Methuen to cancel their contract with Lawrence, who then had to wait four years before the book was published in a private, subscribers' edition (which itself was pursued by the New York Society for the Suppression of Vice). Lawrence's paintings, too, suffered from the attentions of 'the grey ones': in 1929 a London gallery showing Lawrence's work was raided by police who, unsure of quite what they'd been sent to seize, erred on the side of caution and took away half the exhibition. But while in England Lawrence was beseiged by those in high office still determined to defend the moral standards of the nineteenth century – 'the century of mealy-mouthed liars, the century of purity and the dirty litle secret' – he found respite from them on the continent.

Harry Crosby of the Black Sun Press was the first of the independent publishers of Paris to offer Lawrence's work a home. A character straight from the pages of F. Scott Fitzgerald – complete with tragic ending – Crosby was from a fabulously wealthy Boston family, and a volunteer ambulance driver in the Great War. In 1917 his vehicle was hit by a shell, killing everyone in it, but leaving Crosby miraculously unscathed. Unhinged by the experience and unable to settle back in Boston, he had arrived in Paris in 1922 with bottomless pockets, a Croix de Guerre, and a nascent death wish. He went on to develop a full-blown pagan devotion to the sun, and when he read Lawrence's *The Plumed Serpent*, a novel set in Mexico and steeped in pagan rites, ritual sacrifice and sun worship, he came to believe – wrongly – that in Lawrence he had found a kindred spirit, that they shared a devotion to the sun's power both to give and to reclaim life. Even before he'd finished reading the novel Crosby wrote to Lawrence. He lavished praise on the book, and asked if Lawrence had anything the Black Sun Press might have the honour of publishing, promising to pay in gold pieces, 'the eagle and the sun'. Lawrence sent them the full manuscript of his short story 'Sun', which had been published before in London in an expurgated edition. Harry agreed to publish the story in full and, true to his word, made arrangements to have the gold coins which would serve as Lawrence's fee smuggled from the United States into France. They duly arrived in the boots of a painter called, happily enough, Bill Sykes, and were forwarded to Lawrence, who was in Italy, in a hollowed-out book. Lawrence was thrilled both with the money and with the manner of payment, and a mutually useful if slightly uneasy partnership was born.[2]

But Lawrence turned away from 'the Sun' when he found himself in need of a French publisher for *Lady Chatterley's Lover*. Written between 1926 and 1928, the book was unpublishable in English-speaking countries and had been privately published in Florence, in a limited edition of one thousand signed copies, in July 1928. Copies were smuggled into England (by Richard Aldington, among others) and as the book's scandalous reputation grew so did Lawrence's need to secure its copyright against the many pirate editions which began to appear. Black Sun, whose books appeared in expensively produced and very limited editions, was unsuited to the purpose; what was needed was a publisher who had both the means to produce a large, cheap edition, and the courage to publish the book in unexpurgated form. Lawrence's first approach was to Sylvia Beach. Six years after her publication of *Ulysses*, Beach no longer saw herself as a publisher, had no wish to become known as a purveyor of erotica, and while liking Lawrence personally she was not an admirer of his writing. She turned him down. Kahane, on the other hand, *was* an admirer of Lawrence, both as a writer and as 'a man who was fighting a colossal battle for free expression'.[3] It became one of Kahane's greatest professional regrets that at the time Lawrence was looking for help he was in no position to provide any.

In 1929 Kahane was still in partnership with Henri Babou. The enterprise was bleeding money, and most of it was Kahane's. When Lawrence telephoned to offer the publication rights to *Lady Chatterley's Lover* Kahane was, at first, thrilled:

> Here was a huge step in the direction I was planning. And then I thought rapidly. This was in a special sense one of the most important books of the day, and it would not be I who would be responsible for it, but a man [Babou] over whom I had no practical control, and whose reliability I questioned. I dared not risk it. I told Lawrence I was afraid to take it on

for his own sake. He could not understand me, and it was difficult for me to tell him over the telephone that I was not in command of the business, but only financially interested in it, and that it seemed to my mind to be heading towards insolvency. Lawrence thought I was afraid because of the contents of the book, and I could hear his disappointment even over a very bad line.[4]

As Henry Miller's two-year wait for *Tropic of Cancer* to be published showed, Kahane was not above pleading hardship in order to conceal his jitters about content. But in Lawrence's case Kahane really *was* short of both cash and a firm business footing, and it agonised him to see Edward Titus at Black Manikin become the beneficiary of his own misfortune. Titus published the Paris Popular edition in a print run of three thousand copies, sold it quickly, issued a second printing in September 1929, and a third shortly after that. As a precautionary measure, the Popular edition did not bear the usual Black Manikin imprint, but it did carry a new introduction by Lawrence, 'My Skirmish with Jolly Roger', in which he denounces pirates and puritans alike.

The publication of the Titus edition of *Lady Chatterley's Lover* did little to stop the stream of piracies, but it did convince other continental companies that the book could be published profitably and without attracting unwelcome legal attention. In 1933 the Paris-based firm Odyssey, an offshoot of the Albatross Press, published the book, and three years and seven impressions later Kahane, by now free of Babou and financially secure, finally managed to add *Lady Chatterley's Lover* to the Obelisk list when he acquired the rights to impression number eight. The print run is unknown, but *Chatterley* is one of the most common Obelisk titles today, suggesting that Kahane, anticipating large sales, issued many more copies than the usual thousand.

D. H. Lawrence died of tuberculosis in Vence, France, in 1930. Thirty years later the full text of *Lady Chatterley's Lover* was finally passed fit for publication in England when a jury found in favour of Penguin Books on 2 November 1959 – just in time for the sixties.

Paris editions of the work of D. H. Lawrence

Sun (Black Sun Press, 1928)
The Escaped Cock (Black Sun Press, 1929)
Lady Chatterley's Lover (Edward Titus, 1930)
Chariots of the Sun (introduction) (Black Sun Press, 1931)
Lady Chatterley's Lover (Albatross, 1933)

Notes

1 These poems, dropped by Martin Secker from the first edition of *Pansies*, first appeared in the second edition, published later in 1929, in London, in a private edition of 500 copies. Although all the poems Lawrence originally wished to include in the collection are present for the first time in this edition, it is not entirely unexpurgated: the last line of the first stanza of 'My Naughty Book – ', quoted above, is printed 'like b— and f— and sh—'.

2 Geoffrey Woolf, *Black Sun* (Random House, 1976), pp. 200–202.

3 Kahane, *Memoirs*, p. 225.

4 Kahane, *Memoirs*, pp. 225–26.

RAYMONDE MACHARD

The first chapter of *Possession* describes, in gruesome detail, an emergency Caesarian operation performed on a woman about to die of eclampsia – an opening scene which must have been disconcerting to readers of the Boulevard Library of Lighter Modern Fiction series, under whose banner Jack Kahane published the book in 1932. From Chapter 2 onwards the body count decreases significantly, but so does interest, as a dour and melodramatic love story plods lumpenly along.

Kahane had inherited the book from Herbert Clarke: 'it had been written by a friend of his, and I had no alternative but to publish it. I tried to polish it up, but I was not proud of it.'[1] Inexplicably, the book had been a bestseller when it was first published, in French, in 1927, and by 1930 it had run to three impressions and sold more than a quarter of a million copies. But the success wasn't repeated in English: *Possession* has never been reprinted, and has now become one of the rarest books Kahane ever published. Its author was Raymonde Machard. Born in Paris in 1889, Machard's first novel, *Tu Enfanteras*, was published in 1919. It was the first of six: the last, *Les Françaises*, appeared in 1945. A feminist, she launched *Le Journal de la Femme* in 1932, but as an author, Machard never replicated the 1927 success of *La Possession*, and after the war she embarked on a new career.

Given the predilection for gore she demonstrated in the opening pages of *Possession*, it's perhaps unsurprising that by the 1950s Raymonde Machard was running the Théâtre du Grand-Guignol in Pigalle, then as now one of the seedier *quartiers* of Paris. Founded in 1897, the Grand-Guignol's eclectic repertoire of eroticism, comedy and, above all, blood-curdling violence kept theatregoers enthralled, titillated and revolted for more than sixty years. During its heyday, doctors employed full-time by the theatre would treat scores of audience members who had either fainted or vomited on seeing the maimings and decapitations with which the evening's entertainment invariably culminated, and which were staged with as much blood-soaked realism as possible. But by the 1950s the theatre's popularity had waned: it struggled to compete with the increasingly sophisticated special effects of cinema – and with its audience's recent experience of war, and wartime atrocity. After 1945, French audiences began to find the depiction of extreme violence less and less entertaining, and Machard was unable to revive the theatre's fortunes. The Grand-Guignol closed for good in 1962.

By the same author

Tu Enfanteras (Flammarion, 1919)
Les Deux Baisers (Flammarion, 1930)
L'Oeuvre de Chair (Flammarion, 1937)
Les Femmes Cachées (Flammarion, 1938)
Les Françaises (Flammarion, 1945)
La Seduction (Baudinière, 1951)

Note
1 Kahane, *Memoirs*, p. 232.

OLGA MARTIN

Dr F. R. Walters, Medical Officer of Health for a large part of Surrey, had three daughters, of whom Olga was the youngest. Those who knew her when she was growing up remembered her for her

> complex, fey, and self-analytical nature... an original and entertaining girl with a love of fantasy, some skill as an artist, a painstakingly ornamental and stylised way of writing, and a habit of speech which owed much to the emerging popularity of A. A. Milne and the Christopher Robin syndrome. She was slender and rather tall, with regular features, a lean and well-modelled head, and a hair-style which in those days was known as an Eton crop. She fluttered her eyelids as she talked. Some of her contemporaries recall her as an undeveloped version of Virginia Woolf – to whom, in her twenties, she bore a striking resemblance which, in all likelihood, she would have been at some pains to cultivate.[1]

Sadly, Olga's resemblance to Virginia Woolf was not confined to her physical appearance: her febrile mental state set in early, fermented by an unhappy childhood. Neglected by a father she adored but who was always working, and ignored by a mother who paid others to do her parenting for her, it was to no one's surprise that she grew into a woman of low self-esteem, a woman whose incessant craving for approval made her difficult to be with and difficult to like.

In the company of the brilliant the merely bright are stupid, and it was Olga's misfortune to be surrounded by intellectual over-achievers all her life. She read anthropology at Newnham College, Cambridge, where a girl called Peggy Martin was a fellow undergraduate. Peggy's brother was Kingsley Martin: when Olga met him in 1922, he was a 25-year-old graduate of Magdalene College, Cambridge, a war veteran and a socialist. As editor of *New Statesman and Nation* between 1931 and 1960, Kingsley Martin would spend his life at the heart of British left-wing politics, through the rise and fall of Hitler, the creation of the welfare state, and into the Cold War. By the time the couple married in 1926 Kingsley's path was already clear. Olga's was not.

Now immersed in a world of high-profile, high-achieving career-ists, Olga Martin felt her own lack of direction all the more acutely. The diary she kept around this time is full of bold but callow declara-tions of intent such as 'Let This Page Mark The Beginning Of A More Objective Life', and Christmas-cracker phrasemaking: 'Drama, sculp-ture, passion, music – vessels whence rises the divine fire, the incense of eternity', is just one of many examples.[2] Fear of failure rendered her inert – 'I want to write ; but in order to write well, I must think penetratingly and serenely'.[3] After her marriage she whiled away long and lonely stretches of time designing the occasional book jacket, and communing with her diary.

In 1927, after three years spent lecturing on politics at the London School of Economics, Kingsley took a job as leader writer on the *Manchester Guardian*. The move to Manchester was disastrous for Olga, who knew no one in the city and rarely saw her husband, who was by now immersed in a booming career. According to C. H. Rolph, it was at this time that Olga 'began to develop a kind of poetic solitude from which she never emerged'.[4] It was a tendency in herself of which she had long been aware – 'At school I worked hard at everything and behaved mostly correctly because I was terrified of being reproved, but remained solitary and without genuine social feeling'[5] – but it now became corrosive to her mental state. Her marriage began to disintegrate: Kingsley found his wife's unpredictability when in company a problem better avoided than confronted, and began to keep a distance between Olga and his increasingly illustrious friends. It was an exile Olga felt acutely. (He also preferred not to discuss his wife in his writings. In two volumes of autobiography, Kingsley deals with the subject of Olga in three sentences: 'I never fell in love, in any serious way, until I was twenty-six, and I was still sexually inexperienced when I made a foolish marriage two years later. She was an *artiste manquée* and I an ambitious extrovert. We spent a baffling seven years together, never unkind to each other, but never at one, and, not believing in amateur psychoanalysis, I do not propose to write more about our relationship.'[6])

The marriage dwindled to a halt in 1934, when the couple formally separated. (They divorced in 1940.) Motivated by an enduring affection tinged by guilt, Kingsley did what he could to keep Olga busy, and commissioned some book reviews from her for the magazine. His efforts helped improve her mental state, and in September 1934 Olga wrote in her diary: 'Necessary to consider future since suicide idea abandoned.'[7] The future she decided upon was a literary one.

Diary entries from as early as 1929 show that Olga had toyed with the idea of becoming a writer for years, but she seems to have toyed with it the way a small boy toys with the idea of becoming a racing driver or an astronaut. She was educated beyond both her intelligence and her inspiration; she watched her husband turn out heavyweight books which were read and discussed widely; and, before Kingsley thought better of it, she had spent time rubbing shoulders with the literary heavyweights among whom her husband moved. She came to feel that she was *required* to produce something, that it was expected of her, and spent years discussing with her diary what that something might be: 'What do I want to do?... What is there to write about?'[8] She started poems and short stories which were never completed; a projected autobiography came to nothing. Eventually material began to coalesce – congeal might be a better word – into what would become Olga Martin's only book: *Through the Ark*, published by the Obelisk Press in 1938.

The ark is a recurring image in Olga Martin's diaries, its meaning as changeable as Martin herself. Sometimes it represents sanctuary for her, a self-contained place away from the destabilising influence of others; at other times the image is inverted and the ark is full of people of achievement and status, people who have sailed away over the horizon leaving Martin alone on the shore. By 1933 she had decided to write a novel, and without ever having made a decision as to what the ark truly meant to her she decided to make it the central image of the book. Provisionally entitled *Into the Ark*, the novel, she told her diary, would be mildly satirical of those writers and thinkers she had come to know through her husband, portraying them as figures not only adrift from mainland opinion but floating further and further away from it in an insular vessel of their own making. It was also to be 'an attempt to make my present view of life three-dimensional', a book through which Martin would try 'to make head or tail of the familiar'.[9] Published as *Through the Ark* five years later, the novel 'likens the world [Martin] knew to the Ark in which Noah had cared for the world's animals; but the part of Noah is played by "Longinus", who is a giraffe and can therefore see further than anyone else. The giraffe is probably Maynard Keynes, whose range of vision amazed [Olga] and who, she thought, looked like a giraffe. And the rest of the animals almost certainly include a number of other people she had met through Kingsley. They can hardly have been gratified. Among them, to judge from her written notes, are Kingsley, the Webbs, Professor Andrade, Bertrand Russell, R. H. Tawney, and members of her family'.[10] The fact that C. H. Rolph, a man who knew Olga Martin well, had to consult her notes in order to hazard a guess as to the identities of those being satirised bears witness to the scale of the book's failure. As confused and unfocused as its author, *Through the Ark* is unreadably opaque, and must surely have been published as a favour to a friend – Kahane certainly had contacts at *New Statesman and Nation*, among them Cyril Connolly, who had reviewed Gawen Brownrigg's novel *Star Against Star* for the magazine when it was published by Obelisk in 1935, and whose own book *The Rock Pool* Kahane published the following year.

The rest of Olga Martin's life was spent in tragic mental decline. During the war a close friend called Charles Skepper was betrayed to the Gestapo while working for the French Resistance, and was never seen again: Olga's grief 'was thought to have added greatly to the stresses that finally unhinged her mind'.[11] After the war she developed a full-blown persecution mania, a condition intensified rather than ameliorated by a stay in Bodmin mental hospital in 1952. Kingsley remained loyal, and from a discreet distance did what he could to help her. A note written to him by a Harley Street consultant that year suggests that he was paying her mounting medical bills; it also paints a clear and saddening picture of Olga's condition:

> Dear Martin,
> Just a line to let you know that Mrs. Martin is leaving us to go to her Sister on Saturday.
>
> Although the fundamental delusional ideas persist and always will, she has otherwise quite recovered. She is quiet, in good spirits, and the burns on her leg have almost fully recovered ..."[12]

By 1955 Olga Martin was living in Guildford as a recluse, curtains permanently drawn and no visitors admitted, her only company the twenty-odd cats who lived with her, turning her house into a stinking health hazard. She was often seen in the high street talking to herself, and always carried two bags, one filled with clothes, the other with coal and cat food. On 17 December 1964 she was knocked down by a car and killed, 'still holding her two carrier bags.'[13]

Notes

1 C. H. Rolph, *Kingsley: The Life, Letters and Diaries of Kingsley Martin* (Gollancz, 1973), p. 109. C. H. Rolph was the pseudonym of Cecil Rolph Hewitt. Between 1921 and 1946 Hewitt was a member of the City of London police force, rising to the rank of Chief Inspector, before becoming a journalist. He was on the editorial board of *New Statesman and Nation* for more than twenty years while it was under Kingsley Martin's editorship, and wrote books and articles arguing for penal reform and the abolition of the death penalty. Rolph also wrote *Books in the Dock* (Deutsch, 1969), an account of the way in which Britain used its obscenity laws to suppress uncomfortable works of literature during the first half of the twentieth century – an invaluable source of information during the writing of this book.

2 Both quotations taken from Olga Martin's diary, handwritten and unpaginated, volume 6/2, papers of Olga Martin, housed in the Kingsley Martin archive, Special Collections Library, University of Sussex.

3 Olga Martin, diary, volume 6/2.

4 Rolph, *Kingsley*, p. 116.

5 Olga Martin, diary, volume 6/5.

6 Kingsley Martin, *Editor* (Penguin, 1969), pp. 15–16.

7 Olga Martin, diary, volume 6/5.

8 Olga Martin, diary, volume 6/5.

9 Olga Martin, diary, volume 6/5.

10 Rolph, *Kingsley*, pp. 115–16.

11 Rolph, *Kingsley*, p. 128.

12 Letter from W. Lindesay Neustatter, of Harley Street, to Kingsley Martin, 29 May 1952, file 6/9, Kingsley Martin archive, Sussex University.

13 Rolph, *Kingsley*, p. 130.

HENRY MILLER

I was twenty years old when I first read *Tropic of Cancer*, Miller's Whitmanesque song of the self, an autohagiography in which the city of Paris is more character then setting. It's a Paris teeming with artists and writers, pimps and whores, highbrows and lowlifes, a Paris seen mostly at night, illuminated by the flare of a match reflecting off the waters of the Seine. It's a Paris populated by a confederacy of outsiders making good on their promises to themselves, a Paris of seedy brothels and seedier hotels, of empty bellies and full hearts, of cafés seething with self-declared geniuses. It's a place where self-expression is at long last possible, and the fact that nobody is listening does nothing to extinguish the joy of the song. The Paris of *Tropic of Cancer* is a twenty-year-old's dream – and as such bears witness to the rejuvenating effect the city had on Miller, who was forty when he wrote it.

The first half of Henry Miller's life was the detonator for the second: it also provided its subject matter. He was born in Manhattan in 1891 and raised in Brooklyn, New York. The son of a tailor, he got out of the family business as early as he could and trudged his way through a blizzard of dead-end jobs. A talented pianist who at one time harboured ambitions as a soloist, Miller married his piano teacher, Beatrice Wickens, in 1917, and their daughter, Barbara, was born two years later. The marriage was stormy from the first. But although some relationships thrive on a little friction, hardly any are strengthened by the husband fucking his mother-in-law: Henry and Beatrice divorced in 1924.[1]

Miller married again the same year; his new wife was June Mansfield, whom he'd met at Wilson's Dance Hall near Broadway, where she'd been selling dances for a dime. Despite their poverty and lack of prospects, this marriage looked a much better bet than Miller's first. Unlike Beatrice, June encouraged Henry in his ambition to become a writer; also unlike Beatrice, June shared her husband's uninhibited and unpossessive attitude to sex. June combined these two qualities when touting his writing around the speakeasies of New York. Signing them 'June Mansfield' to make them more saleable, she would offer for sale Henry's impressionistic prose poems – 'mezzo-tints', he called them – and would often throw herself in as part (the main part) of the deal. Tormented by jealousy, Miller would wait up all night for her: sometimes she would come home, sometime she wouldn't.

In April 1928, with money provided by one of June's 'literature-lovers', the couple sailed for Europe. Henry was in a bad way: his abandonment of his daughter, June's sexual adventurism (which by now included women as well as men), and a painful awareness of how little he'd achieved in his first 37 years had all conspired to send him into a depressive freefall. The European tour, beginning and ending in Paris, did little to smooth relations between the couple, and in the entire nine months (it was supposed to be a year, but the money ran out) Miller wrote practically nothing. But his time in Europe wasn't wasted: it showed him that a fresh start was possible. Whitman and Dreiser excepted, most of his literary heroes were Europeans: Rabelais, Nietzsche, Dostoyevsky, Lawrence, Hamsun and Joyce. Miller had a strong mystical streak, and the idea of settling on the continent that had spawned his idols appealed to a sense of literary atavism in him. The European way of life – incomparably freer, especially in Paris – also exerted a powerful pull. But Henry was not only attracted to Europe, he was repulsed by New York: his home town had become a sensory mnemonic of everything he wanted to forget, a mirror held up to his failures. Henry and June returned to the United States in January 1929, but Henry, travelling alone this time, returned to Paris on 4 March 1930. What happened to him there over the next two years, a near-hallucinogenic spiritual release occasioned by his love for a city that was feeding his soul even while it was starving his body, was to provide the subject matter for his first published book: *Tropic of Cancer*.

When Henry Miller returned to Paris he moved in with Alfred Perlès, an Austrian émigré ekeing out a living as a proofreader and writer of occasional pieces for the *Chicago Tribune*, an English-language newspaper, published in Paris, which drew its readership from the large expatriate community living there. The two men had met during Miller's first visit to Paris in 1928, and the friendship between them was to become one of the defining relationships of Miller's Paris years. In 1930 Perlès was living in a single room in the Hôtel Centrale, a flea-bitten flophouse on the Rue du Maine; Miller had to be spirited in and out at odd hours of the day and night so as not to alert the concierge to his presence. The two men quickly became close friends and literary allies: both were destitute foreigners with literary ambitions who had chosen a life of self-imposed exile, and hope, over one of conformism and artistic sterility. They found a natural ally in Michael Fraenkel, an American Jew of Russian extraction, an intellectual who bore a striking resemblance to Trotsky and who'd lived in Paris since 1926. Fraenkel was a relentless talker, and a talker with only one topic: the 'spiritual death' that he maintained was the First World War's legacy to its survivors. Miller and Perlès were far more interested in the fact that Fraenkel had money. Destitute and always hungry, they were thrilled to have stumbled upon someone who was willing to pay for their supper just so long as he was allowed to talk, and so at Fraenkel's home in Villa Seurat, and in cafés and bistros around Montparnasse, Miller and Perlès would listen, challenge, theorise, counter-theorise – but most of all they would eat. At first Fraenkel was more tolerated than liked, and he was always more voluble than talented, but Miller respected unwavering commitment wherever he found it, and soon Fraenkel became one of the leading players in Miller's early life in Paris.

In the winter of 1930 Miller spent two months sharing the studio flat of Richard Osborn, another expatriate American who fitted the favoured profile: single, literary and moneyed. Other friends were Wambly Bald, who wrote a gossipy column for the *Tribune* which Miller would occasionally ghost-write in exchange for a few francs, and the Hungarian photographer Brassaï, who inducted the American into the underside of his adoptive city. All were later to find themselves populating the pages of *Tropic of Cancer*, and as Miller's Parisian support system grew, so did his happiness and self-belief: 'The main thing is to eat. Trust to Providence for the rest!'[2]

Slowly, Miller's writing began to sell. In the summer of 1931 Samuel Putnam bought for his magazine, *New Review*, an article Miller had written about Luis Buñuel's *L'Age d'Or*, and in a later issue published Miller's 'Mademoiselle Claude', a short profile of a prostitute Miller knew called Germaine Daugeard.[3] In both style and subject matter 'Mademoiselle Claude' is the earliest of Miller's writing that hints at the later, mature style: unflinching, joyous, unmindful of social or literary norms, and exulting in life – any life – lived fully. During his early days in Paris Miller had spent most of his time working on a book called *Crazy Cock*, a masochistic and lifeless exercise chronicling his wife's lesbian affair with Jean Kronski. But by August 1931 he'd outgrown his obsession with the past: he laid *Crazy Cock* aside and began work on what would become *Tropic of Cancer*.

Miller was spellbinding company. With his thick features and rimless glasses, dressed in a shabby suit with his wide-brimmed hat pulled down over one eye, he looked like an under-employed private detective. A prodigious talker with a bottomless supply of topics, opinions and philosophies, all delivered in a rasping Brooklyn accent much in evidence whether he was speaking English or French, Miller liked nothing better than to take his seat in a café, have someone fill his glass, and let rip. Miller in full oratorical flight was mesmerising; when he discovered that he could get himself fed simply by shooting his mouth off, he drew up a roster of people he could call on once a week for a meal. He would talk for his supper, and soon the demand for his conversation was so great that he started to pick and choose: bad cooks or bores were quietly dropped, to be replaced by others equally eager to be dazzled, but with better culinary skills.

Miller couldn't understand why everyone wanted to hear him talk but nobody wanted to read his work. Perlès and Fraenkel could. They advised Miller to start again, to abandon literary convention and simply write as he spoke. Miller took their advice: he sat down in front of his typewriter, and talked to it. The dam burst.

On 14 October 1932, a package arrived at Kahane's office in the Rue St-Honoré from the office of the Paris-based literary agent William Bradley. The cover note read:

> Dear Mr. Kahane,
> We are sending you herewith, as requested, the typescript of MADO VIII (French translation of LAUGH AND GROW RICH). May we ask you to return to us the enclosed receipt invested with your signature for our discharge, as Lt.-Colonel Laforgue has in his hands our own receipt, delivered to him in exchange for said typescript?
> We are also sending you ILEANA THE POSSESSED (revised version by P. Neagoe), and TROPIC OF CANCER (anonymous), as promised this morning by Mr. Bradley.
> Very faithfully yours,
> W. A. BRADLEY
>
> p.p. Secretary[4]

Kahane took the manuscript of *Tropic of Cancer* home with him and read it in one sitting:

> I had read the most terrible, the most sordid, the most magnificent manuscript that had ever fallen into my hands; nothing I had yet received

was comparable to it for the splendour of its writing, the fathomless depth of its depair, the savour of its portraiture, the boisterousness of its humour. Walking into the house I was exalted by the triumphant sensation of all explorers who have at last fallen upon the object of their years of search. I had in my hands a work of genius and it had been offered to me for publication.[5]

It was a shrewd move on William Bradley's part not to disclose Miller's name before Kahane read the manuscript. *Cancer* is the work of a fully fledged talent; Kahane would have been tempted to believe that behind the 'Anonymous' lurked a well-known author, someone whose reputation a defiant publisher could brandish in response to the inevitable attacks from prudes, philistines, and Customs authorities; knowing that the author of *Tropic of Cancer* was an unpublished nobody would only make Kahane faint-hearted at the prospect of the fight ahead. The first thing to do was to make sure Kahane fell in love with the book. The strategy worked. Having read it, Kahane was desperate to publish *Tropic of Cancer*; that it turned out to have been written by an unknown author was a problem to be overcome, but not a reason to walk away. And the quality of the writing aside, there were other reasons to press ahead with publication. The book would establish Kahane's literary credentials; it would attract other new and daring writers to the Obelisk Press; and crucially, if he could just work out how to bring the sex in the book to the attention of his readers without alerting the authorities, it would sell. This last was a serious and apparently insoluble problem.

By 1932, the year in which *Tropic of Cancer* was submitted to Kahane, the Obelisk list had carried nothing that could be described – in France, at least – as anything more than risqué. The books Kahane had published so far which had got into trouble in Britain, books such as *Sleeveless Errand* and *The Well of Loneliness*, had done so not because they posed any real challenge to the moral standards the law sought to defend, but because the judicial authorities thought they should be seen to be doing something in response to a tendency among writers to be marginally more frank. If these books were subsequently published in France, Kahane reasoned, the British authorities would be unlikely to apply pressure, since having prosecuted the book in the United Kingdom they had already been seen to act. Britain had been cleansed. In the wake of successful prosecutions, Customs officers now had the power to seize and destroy copies of any banned book they found in the luggage of British travellers making their way home from Europe, and the nation was safe once more for wives and servants. But Kahane was worried that if the trickle of saucy books became a flood, or if the 'filth' became filthier, the Home Office *would* feel obliged to act, and would apply pressure to the French authorities to stem the tide. Publishing *Tropic of Cancer* would raise the stakes significantly.

When Norah C. James's *Sleeveless Errand* had been published by Scholartis Press in London in 1929, the entire edition had been seized, prosecuted, found guilty of obscenity, and burned; within a month of the trial, Kahane and his then business partner, Henri Babou, had rushed their own edition into the bookstores of Paris. In London the prosecution had argued that *Sleeveless Errand* contained 'conversations by persons entirely devoid of decency and morality... Blasphemy is freely indulged in by all the characters, and filthy language and indecent situations appear to be the keynote.'[6] The 'filthy language' complained of is as follows: 'bloody hell', 'whores', 'for Christ's sake', 'bitch', 'homos', 'like Hell', 'balls' and 'buggery', most of which appear no more than a couple of times in a book more than two hundred pages long.

Here is an extract from the opening of *Tropic of Cancer*:

O Tania, where now is that warm cunt of yours, those fat, heavy garters, those soft, bulging thighs? There is a bone in my prick six inches long. I will ream out every wrinkle in your cunt, Tania, big with seed. I will send you home to your Sylvester with an ache in your belly and your womb turned inside out. Your Sylvester! Yes, he knows how to build a fire, but I know how to inflame a cunt. I shoot hot bolts into you, Tania, I make your ovaries incandescent. Your Sylvester is a little jealous now? He feels something, does he?He feels the remnants of my big prick. I have set the shores a little wider. I have ironed out the wrinkles. After me you can take on stallions, bulls, rams, drakes, St. Bernards. You can stuff toads, bats, lizards up your rectum. You can shit arpeggios if you like, or string a zither across your navel. I am fucking you, Tania, so that you'll stay fucked. And if you are afraid of being fucked publicly I will fuck you privately. I will tear off a few hairs from your cunt and paste them on Boris' chin. I will bite into your clitoris and spit out two franc pieces ...[7]

Kahane needed some time to think. He took two years.

In addition to Kahane's worries about the likely reaction of Customs authorities around the world to *Tropic of Cancer*, there was also disquiet from within his own firm. Kahane's printer, Marcel Servant, thought prosecution was certain if they published, and that in any case the book wasn't worth the risk because it wouldn't make any money, that the high franc and the dearth of tourists in Paris would kill it at birth. Servant's unshakeable preference for saleability over art was a constant source of frustration for Kahane. He shared his associate's liking for a profit, but Servant was interested in printing *only* what would sell and sell quickly: Kahane's 'Cecil Barr' novels were always welcome, but when it came to literature Servant always insisted on payment in advance. Kahane was determined to add *Tropic of Cancer* to his list, however, and a meeting with Bradley and Miller was held at Bradley's office to discuss a contract.

The negotiations were never going to be easy. Although his working relationship with Bradley was perfectly friendly, Kahane was not enamoured of literary agents as a breed, and in his memoirs he deplored 'the invention of that monstrous parasite'.[8] This was Kahane the publisher talking; Kahane the author had had nothing but praise for Eric Pinker's efforts on his behalf when he was a struggling writer in the 1920s. Now that any intervention from an agent cost him rather than made him money, Kahane had grown to resent them. But in both the negotiations for *Tropic of Cancer* and in the ensuing contact between Kahane and Miller, Bradley more than earned his keep, acting as a buffer between two mutually dependent but completely unsympathetic characters.

From their first meeting and for the next seven years, Miller veered wildly between a deep gratitude to Kahane for taking the risk of publishing him, and an unconcealed hatred of everything he did, everything he wrote, and everything he was. Miller was overjoyed to be told by Kahane at their first meeting in October 1932 that he wanted to publish *Tropic of Cancer*; the bad news was that Kahane was offering a 10 per cent royalty on all sales, and no advance. This was cheap of Kahane, who seems to have forgotten very quickly how he used to rail against the parsimony of publishers offering him only 'meagre' advances, and it was a body blow to Miller, who'd spent the last four years living on practically nothing and who'd been hoping to eat a little more regularly as a result of the acceptance of his book. Bradley's bloodless assurance that the offer was reasonable left Miller no choice but to accept, but he regarded the absence of any money upfront as mean-spirited of Kahane, and Miller despised mean-spiritedness in any form. The take-it-or-leave-it offer ensured that the relationship between the two men was tense from the beginning, and as the subsequent delay between acceptance and publication lengthened, so Kahane's offence became, in Miller's eyes, more and more egregious.

Kahane antagonised Miller still further when at the same meeting he asked if Miller would write a treatise – a *plaquette* – on D. H. Lawrence, before the publication of *Tropic of Cancer*. Lawrence's influence on Miller's writing was clear, and Kahane reasoned that if he could first publish a work by Miller which established his critical and intellectual credentials, then *Tropic of Cancer*, being the work of a known and serious writer, would be more difficult to attack when it eventually appeared. It was a ploy that had worked in the past both for Joyce and for Lawrence himself, but Miller was infuriated; while it was true that *Tropic of Cancer* clearly showed Lawrence's influence on Miller, Miller had no wish to advertise the fact. In *Tropic of Cancer* Miller had taken his reading of Lawrence – and Céline, and Joyce, and Rabelais – and refracted it through the prism of himself, had synthesised his reading into a world view and literary style uniquely his own. To write a eulogy to Lawrence, Miller reasoned, would make him look like a disciple, a follower rather than a pioneer. Later, in a letter to Bradley, he complained about Kahane's treatment of him: 'It was humiliating to me to sit in your office and be requested to write a little brochure about this man or that man in order to introduce myself. I don't want any introduction. I wanted simply to stand up and let go – be knocked over for it or lauded for it. But not apologize, not *explain* myself. I can't tell you how ignominious that seemed to me.' [9]

His masochistic relationship with June notwithstanding, Miller hated to be beholden to anyone, and to be beholden to a man like Kahane was torture for him. An English writer of trashy fiction turned tightwad publisher, Kahane was the personification of just about everything Miller loathed, and it's both heartbreaking and hilarious to imagine him, keen to know more about the man who would decide his future, settling down to read *Daffodil*, or *Suzy Falls Off*. But however infuriated he became, Miller never lost sight of the fact that Kahane was his only hope. (And the only hope of his friends, too: when Lawrence Durrell was looking for a publisher for *The Black Book* in 1937, Miller wrote a letter which recommended and damned Kahane at the same time: 'It seems to me, at the moment, that Kahane would be the only man to do it... No commercial, legitimate publisher can possibly bring it out... (He writes too you know, under the name of Cecil Barr – vile vile crap, the vilest of the vile – and he admits it, but with that English insouciance that makes my blood creep).'[10])

There was nothing to be done. On 11 November 1932 Miller signed a contract with Kahane giving Obelisk a year's option on *Tropic of Cancer*, and Miller also agreed, reluctantly, to give the *plaquette* idea some thought. To everybody's surprise, when Miller reread Lawrence his reluctance quickly turned to enthusiasm, and the writing of the treatise turned from a tedious chore into an evangelical imperative. Miller's renewed reverence for Lawrence found a sympathetic ally in Miller's lover Anaïs Nin, whose own study of Lawrence had just been published by Edward Titus at the Black Manikin Press. Their correspondence on the subject stoked Miller's fervour, and while he waited for Kahane to do something he devoted his time to two projects: trimming *Cancer*, and expanding the *plaquette*. The result was that when it was finally published *Cancer* was only a third of the length of the manuscript Miller had originally submitted to Bradley, and the Lawrence project, originally envisaged by Kahane as a 50-page brochure, was now, Miller reckoned, likely to run to a thousand pages.

The *plaquette* idea had been scuppered not by Miller's aversion but by his zeal, and it was now clear that if Kahane was going to publish Miller at all, he would have to start with *Tropic of Cancer*. But Kahane's option on the book was running out, and on 29 September 1933, he wrote to William Bradley asking for a six-month extension. Bradley put the proposal to his client. Miller wrote back: 'Regarding Kahane's request for an extension of the time limit in connection with *Tropic of Cancer* – why yes, what else can I do? So long as it is six months and not six years!'[11]

It was neither. Just under a year later, Anaïs Nin stripped Kahane of any further excuse for delay when she offered to loan him money to cover *Cancer*'s printing costs. (She herself had borrowed the money from a lover, the psychoanalyst Otto Rank.) Forced into making a decision, Kahane made the right one. On 1 September 1934 *Tropic of Cancer* was published, and the one thousand poorly made paperbacks set about establishing Henry Miller's literary reputation.

The first edition of *Tropic of Cancer* is a beautiful thing, but not to look at. A shabbily made, paper-bound octavo, the front wrapper carries an illustration of a giant crab holding in its pincers a prone and suffering woman: a trite, adolescent image illustrating nothing so much as a comprehensive misunderstanding of the book. That the image is adolescent is unsurprising: it was the creation of the publisher's fifteen-year-old son, Maurice. That it came to adorn the front cover of *Tropic of Cancer* is also unsurprising: the Obelisk Press was small and new, a publishing house yet to find its financial feet. Kahane was keen to save money wherever he could, and he saw no point in employing a professional artist to illustrate his publications when there were members of his immediate family who could draw. So his son was 'commissioned', the book went to print, and on 1 September 1934 Kahane carried the first copies off the press to Miller's apartment at 18 Villa Seurat, in the 14th *arrondissement*. Predictably, Miller was horrified by the illustration, but the relief and exhilaration of seeing *Tropic of Cancer* in print after so long a wait and so many setbacks swamped all Miller's misgivings about the design of its wrapper; the book was published – it *existed*. It had been a long time coming, and it was enough.

In the first three trading years of the Obelisk Press, Kahane had taken few risks. Nearly all the books he'd published had cleverly taken advantage of the gap between British and French perceptions of respectability; what was disgusting in London was merely saucy in Paris, and Kahane quietly made money from the difference. But *Tropic of Cancer* was different, and called for careful handling. In 1929, when Kahane was still in partnership with Henri Babou, D. H. Lawrence had offered the firm the French rights to *Lady Chatterley's Lover*, the first edition of which had been published in Florence the previous year. Kahane had declined the book, citing lack of funds; actually, he had feared that his new and still fragile business would be closed down if he took the risk. He'd then had to watch as Lawrence's second choice, Edward Titus at the Black Manikin Press, enjoyed a lucrative success with the first French edition of *Chatterley*, quickly selling out the first print run of three thousand. A second print run, also of three thousand, was issued the same year, and that too sold out. By December 1930 Titus was able to send Lawrence's widow Frieda a statement showing that the Lawrence estate's share of the profits from both printings had risen to Frs. 90,000. A third printing, this time of five thousand copies, appeared shortly after.

Kahane was determined to emulate that success with *Tropic of Cancer* – but he was also determined to stay in business. Lawrence, he reasoned, had been difficult for the authorities to attack because at the time of the Paris publication of *Lady Chatterley's Lover* his reputation both as an artist and as an intellectual was unassailable. (This hadn't prevented Lawrence being persecuted by the British authorities, but it had provided his French publisher with a robust insurance policy.) His attempt to persuade Miller to produce a pre-emptive work of criticism in order to beef up his intellectual bona fides had come to nothing, but Kahane still thought the idea had legs. He had taken note of Miller's flair for self-publicity – he thought him 'the most useful collaborator a book publisher ever had'[12] – and decided to exploit it.

Kahane published *Tropic of Cancer* to as resounding a silence as he could orchestrate. This wasn't difficult to do: wholesalers and booksellers 'handled it with the utmost caution as if it had been a lump of gelignite.'[13] None of the usual newspapers and literary magazines was sent a copy for review, and no advertising space was taken in the literary press. Silence descended, and Kahane waited for Miller to go to work. The plan was to allow Miller to promote his book himself by firing off letters to anyone he could think of – the great and the good, people he knew, people he didn't know but admired, people he couldn't stand but who might be useful – looking to garner praise and publicity for the book from any and every conceivable source. Thanks to his friendship with the well-connected Anaïs Nin, Henry was now moving in influential circles, and Kahane was sure that Miller's friends would spread the word about the book far quicker and far more favourably, and to far more useful names, than would happen through the usual publicity outlets. By adopting this plan of inaction Kahane calculated that *Tropic of Cancer* would become a *succès d'éstime* as well as a *succès de scandale*, and that by the time the authorities began to consider whether they should take action against it they would be faced with an intimidating array of potential witnesses for the defence. Kahane's best hope of avoiding prosecution, he calculated, lay in the French regard for the intellectual.

For his part, when it came to writing letters Miller had never needed any encouragement. The first copies of the book were delivered by Kahane on 1 September 1934, and Henry immediately put one in the mail to Michael Fraenkel, then in China. The accompanying note was infused with relief and elation: 'These are good times for me. I move with the changing climate. I move with the sun and light. With the birds. With the wild flowers. Dear Fraenkel, I don't know what to say. I am so happy'.[14]

By November, Miller had exhausted his Paris network and was casting his net wider. He wrote to William Bradley asking for the addresses of Blaise Cendrars, Richard Aldington – and Ezra Pound, by then living in Rapallo, Italy. Miller knew neither Pound nor his work, and wrote to him solely on the strength of his reputation, but it paid spectacular dividends. Pound loved *Tropic of Cancer*, and wrote effusively to Miller to say so. When Miller's letter had arrived in Rapallo Pound had a visitor called James Laughlin staying with him; Laughlin was also impressed, and when in the 1940s he founded his publishing house New Directions in the United States he became Miller's American publisher (though not of the still unpublishable *Tropics*). To cap it all, Pound had also forwarded his copy of the book to T. S. Eliot at Faber in London, who was to write to Miller the following year declaring *Tropic of Cancer* a vastly superior book to *Lady Chatterley's Lover*.

As Christmas approached, Miller was doing a far better job of shifting his book than Kahane, and on 10 December he met with his publisher to discuss the situation. While keeping his softly-softly strategy to himself, Kahane did point out in mitigation of poor sales that unfavourable exchange rates were scaring tourists away from Paris, and buyers away from books: *Tropic of Cancer* cost Frs. 50, a whopping $2.50. He showed Henry the Obelisk accounts ledger, which told the pitiful story of the preceding ten days' business: just nine books sold. The good news was that six of them were *Tropic of Cancer*, and Henry left the meeting trying to take comfort from the fact that he was currently responsible for two thirds of all Obelisk sales.

Miller's publicity drive was having more success, though: by the end of the year, anybody who was anybody knew all about *Tropic of Cancer*, and nobody else knew it existed. But things were soon to change: word was starting to filter through to a differently discriminating readership that when it came to sex, Miller's book delivered. Copies began to leave the few bookshops that stocked them, and Eve Adams, an expatriate friend of Miller's, was doing a brisk trade selling copies on the street outside Le Dôme and La Coupole. While glad of the sales, Miller wasn't keen to cultivate the acquaintance of his new one-handed readership: 'Much *réclame* in Montparnasse. Have to keep away from Dome and other places because I am constantly being introduced to jackasses who read the book and whom I don't care to know.'[15] Gradually, the one thousand copies of the first edition started to sell – and then to disappear. The early Obelisk Press books were not built to last, and *Tropic of Cancer* was no exception: poorly made, with the text block carelessly glued into flimsy paper wrappers. Many copies were simply read to death, passed from reader to reader until they fell to pieces; others were seized from returning travellers by Customs and Excise, and destroyed. The lurid design on the front of the book made it easy for the authorities to spot; seeing this, travellers determined to get their copies home took to ripping the covers off the book before beginning their return journey. Thus mutilated, copies were less likely to attract attention. A few such copies have survived and occasionally appear on the rare book market, rebound and so worth only a fraction of the price of a complete copy.) Many copies disappeared because there was a difference between what a businessman was willing to read while abroad and what he was happy to have his wife find in his luggage when he got home; copies were bought, read, guiltily enjoyed, and sheepishly disposed of. By the spring of 1935, *Tropic of Cancer*'s reputation was secure, both in the *salon* and on the street. Its scarcity only added to its allure.

That September Kahane issued a second edition of 500 copies. Mindful of his readers' problems with Customs officials, this edition came with a dustwrapper which, when discarded, left plain grey wrappers and a far less readily identifiable book. The dustwrapper itself relegated Maurice's crab design to a faint background, and quoted Henry's new-found admirers. Ezra Pound, whose fan letter from Rapallo had claimed that in *Tropic of Cancer* Miller had out-Ulyssesed Joyce, allowed Kahane to quote him: 'At last an unprintable book that is fit to read'. Eliot wouldn't allow his favourite comparison with Lawrence to be used, but Kahane was more than happy with 'A very remarkable book, with passages of writing in it as good as any I have seen for a long time', and plastered the puff across the front cover alongside Pound's. With praise from Aldous Huxley, Cyril Connolly and William Carlos Williams also festooned across the wrapper, Kahane now felt confident enough to trumpet his author himself, and wrote the effusive blurb that appears on the front flap.

By now influential praise was flooding in from every quarter. Although the book was legally unobtainable in England, both Herbert

Read and George Orwell had raved about it in *New English Weekly*, and Blaise Cendrars had arrived on Miller's doorstep one evening, taken him to the Restaurant des Fleurs, and during the course of a gargantuan meal had announced to everyone in the room that they were in the presence of the natural successor to Rabelais. And word came via Kahane of an unlikely admirer:

> I had sent a copy to a dear friend, Countess Edith Gautier-Vignal, the sister of the Baroness de Marwicz, that charming and gifted English-woman living in Paris, to whom I am devoted. I received in return, to my delight, an enthusiastic letter. A wonderful book, and she had lent her copy of it to Somerset Maugham, her friend and neighbour, and he was no less enthusiastic.[16]

The eulogies piling up on his desk gave Miller an idea – Kahane's idea, if only he had known it. In November 1935 he wrote to Lawrence Durrell:

> I am going to make a reprint, at my own expense, of all the important letters and reviews... I will send this brochure out to every fucking magazine, revue, and newspaper in the world of any consequence... It's a colossal job and is going to cost me a pretty penny – and for the moment I don't even know where the dough is going to come from – but I'll do it nevertheless. I am thoroughly disgusted with the general inertia. *Action at any cost!* that's my motto... I won't have the book die in its second printing![17]

It didn't. A third edition of five hundred copies was published in March 1938, and the publicity brochure eventually appeared in December. By then Miller had published six more books, and the four-page flier laid in to the Christmas issue of *Delta* ('Special Peace and Dismemberment Number with Jitterbug-Shag Requiem', ed. Henry Miller), carried praise from Cendrars, Queneau, Huxley, Orwell, Cyril Connolly and many others, not only for *Tropic of Cancer*, but of Miller as a consolidated literary force.

A total of 22 editions of *Tropic of Cancer* were eventually published by the Obelisk Press imprint, the last in 1961. In the same year, the book appeared legally for the first time in the United States, 27 years after it was first published in Paris. The first print run of thirty thousand copies sold out before publication day; by the end of the year more than a million copies had been sold.

AUTHOR BIOGRAPHIES

By the same author

Non-Obelisk fiction includes:
Plexus (Correa, 1952)
Quiet Days in Clichy (Olympia Press, 1952)

Non-fiction includes:
What Are You Going To Do About Alf? (privately printed, 1935)
Money and How It Gets That Way (Booster, 1938)
Hamlet (Carrefour, 1939)
The Cosmological Eye (New Directions, 1939)
The World of Sex (Chicago [publisher?], 1940)
The Colossus of Maroussi (Colt, 1941)
The Air-Conditioned Nightmare (New Directions, 1945)
Reunion in Barcelona (Scorpion Press, 1959)
The World of Lawrence (Capra, 1979)
The Durrell–Miller Letters: 1935–80 (New Directions, 1988)

Notes

1 Jay Martin, *Always Merry and Bright* (Sheldon Press, 1979), pp. 49–50.
2 Henry Miller, *Tropic of Cancer* (Obelisk Press, 1934), p. 195.
3 Henry Miller, 'Mademoiselle Claude', *New Review*, Aug.–Sept.–Oct. 1931.
4 Letter from WIlliam Bradley to Jack Kahane, 13 October 1932, HRC.
5 Kahane, *Memoirs*, p. 260.
6 Trial transcript. The prosecution of the publishers of *Sleeveless Errand* took place at Bow Street Magistrates' Court, London, on 3 March 1929.
7 *Tropic of Cancer*, pp. 15–16.
8 Kahane, *Memoirs*, p. 32.
9 Letter, Henry Miller to WIlliam Bradley, May 1933, HRC.
10 Ian S. McNiven, ed., *The Durrell–Miller Letters, 1935–1980* (Faber and Faber, 1988), p. 56.
11 Letter, Henry Miller to William Bradley, 4 October 1933, HRC.
12 Kahane, *Memoirs*, p. 263.
13 Kahane, *Memoirs*, p. 262.
14 Kathryn Winslow, *Henry Miller: Full of Life* (Putnam, 1986), p. 26.
15 Letter, Henry Miller to Anaïs Nin, 11 December 1934, in Guther Stuhlmann (ed.), *A Literate Passion: Letters of Anaïs Nin and Henry Miller 1932–1953* (W. H. Allen and Co., 1988), p. 248.
16 Kahane, *Memoirs*, pp. 263–64.
17 McNiven, ed., *The Durrell–Miller Letters*, pp. 6 7.

AUTHOR BIOGRAPHIES

JOHN MILTON

According to Harold Brighouse, Jack Kahane held Milton's *Lycidas* to be the finest poem in the English language.[1] It was first published in 1638 in a book of elegies commemorating the death of Edward King, a contemporary of Milton's at Cambridge who drowned in a shipwreck off the Welsh coast in August 1637. In 1933 Kahane had the poem printed privately, using the Obelisk imprint, in an edition running to just 25 copies. Each copy bears a unique printed dedication; the paper used is handmade Montval; the sheets are sewn, not glued, into the binding; and the volume was issued in a marbled chemise, the title of the poem stamped in gilt on the spine. These weren't the usual production values assigned to a book from the Obelisk Press; no other bears the words 'PRINTED UNDER THE DIRECTION OF JACK KAHANE' in the colophon. A meditation on death, sumptuously printed and bound, never offered for sale but instead presented only to a very few close friends, the Obelisk *Lycidas* seems to have been not so much a book as a *memento mori* distributed by a man preoccupied by death.

This was certainly the opinion of Harold Brighouse, one of *Lycidas*'s dedicatees: '[T]houghts of death, if hardly an obsession, were characteristic... [Kahane] had been near to death three times before his fatal illness, and besides shell damage on the Western Front he was critically ill. His father, a Rumanian Jew by origin, committed suicide... There was death in the family.'[2]

In 1933 Kahane seems to have been preoccupied by death – whether as a result of his tuberculosis, his war injuries, thoughts of suicide, or a combination of all three is impossible to say. He continued to live the expensive life of the man about town – 'Recklessness of living is venial in a man convinced that he has not long to live', noted Brighouse[3] – and was typically blithe on a presentation card he tucked into Caresse Crosby's copy of *Lycidas*: 'Please accept this little edition of one of the finest pieces of English, done to please myself'.[4] Which self was most pleased? The mortally ill Kahane would have been drawn by the poem's tender ruminations on premature death; the Kahane who aspired to be Balzac but had to settle for being Cecil Barr would have responded to Milton's fear, expressed in the poem, of dying before fulfilling one's promise; Kahane the spendthrift philanderer would have been comforted by Milton's faith in redemption.

The individual dedication in each copy of *Lycidas* builds a checklist of those whom Kahane regarded as the important people in his life, at a time when he seems to have thought he was about to leave it. As well as Brighouse and Crosby, copies of *Lycidas* were dedicated to Sylvia Beach; to Michel Bogouslavski, head of the foreign books department at Hachette and the man who brokered Kahane's split from his partner/printer Marcel Servant in 1937; to Virginia Vernon, writer and wife of Broadway director Frank Vernon; and to Auriol Lee, a theatre actress and director, who appeared in Alfred Hitchcock's 1941 thriller *Suspicion*. Kahane's connection to Vernon and Lee is unknown, as is the whereabouts of the other nineteen copies. Kahane's wife Marcelle must be one of the missing dedicatees; other likely recipients include Kahane's younger brother Fred, Stuart Gilbert, Nancy Cunard... but until the missing copies surface, best not '[let] our frail thoughts dally with false surmise'.[5]

Notes
  1 Harold Brighouse, *What I have Had* (Harrap, 1953), p. 43.
  2 Brighouse, *What I have Had*, p. 43.
  3 Brighouse, *What I have Had*, p. 43.
  4 Copy in the Dartmouth College Library collection.
  5 John Milton, *Lycidas* (Obelisk Press, 1933), p. 8.

PETER NEAGOE

Peter Neagoe (pronounced Nay-ah-gway) was born in a small village in the Carpathian mountains of Romania, in 1881. After studying fine art in Bucharest and New York he settled in Paris in 1926, gave up painting for writing, and over the next forty years published novels and short stories, most of them chronicling Romanian peasant life remembered from his childhood. Although briefly famous in the 1930s following a censorship row, for most of his life Neagoe was more respected than read. Obelisk published two of his books, *Storm* (1932) and *Easter Sun* (1934), and Kahane regarded Neagoe as the perfect Obelisk writer: the acclaim Neagoe's early work enjoyed brought kudos to its publisher, and subsequent skirmishes with censorious Customs officials brought publicity, which in turn boosted sales. And the two men had more in common than a contract: while their own work is now forgotten, both spent the 1930s bringing to public attention the work of writers whose reputations *have* endured.

Neagoe was born into a remote rural community in Transylvania, but his stock was solidly middle class. His father was a notary who set aside time to work free of charge on behalf of the village's illiterate peasants when they found themselves involved in disputes over the land they worked. At the age of eight Neagoe began providing a similar service to the village's young men and women, helping them compose their love letters and reading aloud the replies, an experience he later credited with providing him with both the material for his literary career, and the ability to use it.[1]

In 1898 Neagoe enrolled at the Bucharest Academy of Fine Arts, and after a brief period at the Polytechnic University in Munich moved to New York to study at the National Academy in 1901. Before arriving in America Neagoe had made money writing occasional pieces of journalism; anxious not to lose this source of income he learned English as quickly as he could. For the next 25 years he lived and worked in New York, struggling to balance his vocational need to read, write and paint with the necessity of making a living. In 1911 he married Anna Frankel, a fellow art student, and the couple divided their time between Manhattan and a small farm in the Berkshire hills in upstate New York. In the United States and later in France, Neagoe always found somewhere to live for at least part of the year that reminded him of his childhood surroundings.

By 1926 Anna was earning enough as an artist to keep them both – more than enough if they traded in their dollars for French francs. The couple relocated to the rue de Dounier in the fourteenth *arrondissement* of Paris, where Neagoe stopped painting and took up writing full time. For Neagoe, 45 years old and domestically settled, Paris was an inspiration rather than a distraction. He worked hard, producing scores of short stories, almost all of them folk tales set among the rural Romanian peasantry of his childhood. He had his first success in 1928 when one of these stories, 'Kaleidoscope', was accepted for publication by *transition*, the expatriate literary magazine edited by the writer and critic Eugene Jolas and the novelist Elliot Paul.

Not yet a year old, *transition* was militantly high-brow, the in-house journal of Modernism, home to those Neagoe was later to describe as the 'literary extremists' of Paris.[2] Its main distribution outlet was Sylvia Beach's expatriate bookshop Shakespeare and Company, on the rue de l'Odéon. The magazine was an unlikely host for Neagoe's slight and simple piece: 'Kaleidoscope' is a collage of half-remembered sights and sounds, those of a sleepy child at a peasant dance, now recalled in adulthood by the writer the child became. Although competently done it's hardly revolutionary either in subject matter or in style, but for some reason it caused a sensation when it arrived at the offices of *transition*, and Jolas wrote to Neagoe immediately to arrange a meeting. The two men quickly became friends, and *Kaleidoscope* was published in the March 1928 issue of *transition*, where it sat between a sample chapter of André Breton's surrealist novel *Nadja* and the latest instalment of Joyce's *Work in Progress*, later to become *Finnegans Wake*. Neagoe became a regular contributor to the magazine, which in time led to his work being picked up by literary periodicals all over the continent.

Neagoe's reputation began to grow, but it was a reputation cultivated mostly by his friends: he was not so much absorbed into the Paris literary community as adopted by it. Squat, thickly featured and powerfully built, Neagoe's rural (if not peasant) background was unmistakable. He looked more like an artisan than an artist, and there is a whiff of inverse snobbery about the way he was championed by the *avant garde*, a feeling of the noble savage being paraded and patronised by the cosmopolitans of Paris. Neagoe's writing is only occasionally exceptional, most often when writing fondly about people remembered from his childhood. But his stories and novels rarely engage emotionally, and the lack of human inflection gives them the dessicated feeling of parable. Also, Neagoe could only write well about his Romanian roots: his work set in the United States is uniformly hopeless. But his friends remained oblivious to his shortcomings, and since his friends were mostly drawn from the heavyweight ranks of the Modernist movement most newspaper reviewers of Neagoe's work contrived to overlook them too.

This pattern was established with the publication of Neagoe's first book. By 1932 Neagoe had become a partner with Jolas in New Review Publications, the publisher of *transition*. In that year the imprint issued *Storm*, a collection of Neagoe's short stories. The book is a representative selection of Neagoe's work, clearly illustrating both its strengths and its weaknesses. Neagoe's friends saw only the strengths. Reluctant to criticise him for his lack of complexity, instead they praised him for his simplicity. Adjectives such as 'childlike' and 'rustic' were used to describe his work; 'banal' and 'agricultural' might have been nearer the truth. English wasn't Neagoe's first language (in fact it was his fourth) and his syntax is occasionally clunky; this was presented as linguistic experimentalism akin to Conrad. The worst offender was Jolas himself, who in his introduction to the first edition of *Storm* wrote:

> I know few modern writers in the English language in whose work there is such a complete balance between a sincere telluric sense and its expression. Your work has the quality of rich, brown loam, one feels in it a paradoxically pure sensuality, the paganism of man who loves the primal elements of life; one who senses strongly your sympathy with the chthonian forces dominating man. The men and women you evoke accept the body with a simple feeling of eros.[3]

It was left to those less intimately involved with Neagoe to speak more truthfully. There was much in *Storm* to commend, and Henry Miller wasn't slow to do it. Still unpublished in 1932, he was a close follower of literary fashion, had read the short story 'Storm' before its appearance in the collection that bore its name, and had written to Neagoe to congratulate him, saying that it was 'exceptionally well done. A certain almost incredible power in the use of English is what astonished me particularly... I think you accomplished something quite extraordinary.'[4] Compliments from Henry Miller always carried a lot of weight, since he was always prepared to be equally forthcoming about work he *didn't* like – as Neagoe found out when the book was published: 'I must say that "Storm" appears to me a very poor book', wrote Miller. 'With the exception of Storm itself there seems to be no excuse for printing these stories. They impress me as being amateurish, still-born, often trashy. They do not represent your real capabilities. They expose you in your larval state, and that's a pity because I certainly believe that you have left all this sort of writing far behind. It would have been better to destroy them.'

He nails Eugene Jolas in the same letter:

> I think he makes an ass of himself praising the piss out of a work which in a few years you will want to forget. What is he going to say when you write a really swell book? He's almost exhausted his vocabulary here. It was as though he was more interested in showing us what a fine writer he is than to convince us that he had genuinely appraised the book.
>
> I suppose my words will wound your pride a bit, and if they do, so much the better. What's the sense of kidding each other? I'm as harsh with myself – why should I spare you?[5]

(In fact, Neagoe *was* spared Miller's final verdict on his writing: in 1936, Neagoe's anticipated masterpiece having failed to materialise, Miller wrote to Lawrence Durrell dismissing Neagoe's work as 'feeble shit', adding the entirely unsubstantiated allegation that 'he doesn't even write his own books (*entre nous*).'[6])

The New Review edition of *Storm* was published in February 1932, but while favourably reviewed its commercial success wasn't assured until the summer. Although the book is written in an earthy tone that befits its rustic setting, only an idiot could have found *Storm* obscene; fortunately for Neagoe, such an idiot was working in the Chicago Customs Office when a shipment of the book arrived there in June. The consignment was returned to the shipper. New Review Publications was informed that *Storm* had been declared obscene under Section 305 of the Tariff Act of 1930, and that as a result of the ruling copies would not be allowed into the United States.[7] Neagoe was mystified: 'It seems to me that if the authorities devoted more time and attention to their Al Capones and a little less to the effort to reduce the intelligence of the well known average reader to that of a six-year-old girl, things might be a little fairer in that fair but windy city.'[8] Friends and fellow writers wrote to commiserate, Malcolm Cowley and Richard Aldington among them, but they needn't have worried: the row that followed its American ban raised the profile of the book, and in July Neagoe's agent, William Bradley, sent a copy to Kahane. Two days later, a contract for an expanded popular edition of *Storm*, to be published by the Obelisk Press, was signed by Neagoe and delivered by his wife to Kahane's office.[9]

Neagoe's haste to cash in on the book's sudden notoriety was a good career move, but it cost him the friendship of Eugene Jolas. The decision to change publishers was taken by Neagoe unilaterally: he wanted it to happen, and Samuel Putnam at NRP duly signed away the rights.[10] This must have been galling enough for Jolas, who was responsible for launching Neagoe's career, but what came next was worse. As well as adding another five stories to the collection (and dropping one, 'Dreams'), Kahane launched the Obelisk edition by trading on the book's scandalous reputation. The Jolas introduction was dropped, a flyer was issued ahead of publication reproducing the banning letter from Chicago Customs, and the book's blurb proudly announced that it had been 'Banned in America'. Jolas was disgusted by what he saw as Neagoe's prostitution of his work. He returned the Obelisk edition that Neagoe had sent him, and broke off their friendship:

Dear Peter,
Maria and I feel that we prefer not to own a copy of the last edition of

Storm, and we are therefore returning it.

Since my name which you eagerly sought in order to launch the book – it is the only introduction I have ever written and I hope I've learned my lesson – apparently compromised your chances for success with the 'vulgar reader' whom Mr. Kahane told me he hoped to reach, the gesture of presenting me with a second copy seemed meaningless.

I take it for a compliment that with your publisher's avowed invitation to the sensation-seeking public he should have felt that both my name and that of Transition were out of place. This proves to me that I have attained much more than I dreamed something of my aims concerning Transition. It is easy to understand, too, the inclusion of such a name as Waverly Root. I cannot but believe, however, that men like Dr. Brill and Richard Aldington will resent the use of their names as recommendation for a 'banned-in-America-book' which exploits this fact in order to appeal to the pornographic snobs. Although I may add that your book is better than that.

I hope that in view of the circumstances of the second edition, you will be good enough to destroy the few pages containing my introduction before circulating any further volume of the first edition. I regret exceedingly to have been connected with the matter at all.

I am very sorry that things should have taken this turn, for you were one of the few writers in this town infested with literary politicians whom I had hoped to keep as a friend.

Very sincerely yours,
Eugene Jolas (sgd)[11]

For his part, Kahane saw no reason to apologise for looking to make a profit. In *Memoirs of a Booklegger* he claims to have first encountered Neagoe's work in the *New Review*, and to have been impressed by it. But, then as now, collections of short stories are notoriously difficult to sell, and it's unlikely that Kahane would have taken the chance of publishing Neagoe without the attendant controversy in the United States which suddenly made him saleable. (Stuart Gilbert was sure that 'if the U. S. Customs had not excluded [*Storm*], [Kahane] would have esteemed it dull.'[12]) Certainly Kahane was confident that he could present Neagoe's work more advantageously than NRP had done: in his memoirs he denounces the NRP edition of *Storm* for having 'more misprints to a page, and evil printing generally, than one usually comes across even in the productions of the hole-in-corner printers who will tackle work of such doubtful economic advantage.'[13] And although Kahane's appeal to the 'pornographic snobs' cost Neagoe a friend, it did much to advance the careers of both men:

Much indignation was aroused in the United States that the book should ever have been banned, and the Neagoes and their large circle of friends in America were careful to see that the indignation did not die down. The first duty of American tourists of a literary turn of mind, when in France, was to buy *Storm*, and thanks to my unremitting efforts to ensure that the book should be prominent in every appropriate shop window, the appropriate tourist could not miss it. Royalty statements were not unsatisfactory, and Neagoe, if not yet the Obelisk Press, began to be talked about.[14]

Storm's high profile during the summer of 1932 made its author's other project for that year much easier to complete. The previous September Neagoe had been asked by Samuel Putnam, the publisher of *New Review*, to edit an anthology of contemporary work by American expatriate writers; now that his clash with the American censors had turned him into the year's literary *cause célèbre*, Neagoe found himself far better placed to ask favours of people he didn't know. First he ransacked his own address book: as well as Putnam himself, Neagoe quickly recruited a presumably pacified Jolas, as well as James Farrell, Robert Sage and Gertrude Stein. Enthusiastic about the project, these friends duly contacted friends of their own: Neagoe's approach to Kay Boyle, for example, resulted not just in her own recruitment but also the participation of Ernest Walsh, Emanuel Carnevali and Laurence Vail. Word of the anthology quickly spread, and soon Neagoe was receiving submissions and suggestions from strangers. One such was Alfred Perlès, who urged him to consider the work of his friend Henry Miller. An essay of Miller's was included in the anthology, which eventually appeared under the title *Americans Abroad*: 'Mademoiselle Claude', Miller's first appearance in book form, pre-dates the publication of *Tropic of Cancer* by two years.

The Paris grapevine ensured that Neagoe was not short of submissions from new and unknown writers, and as well as Miller two other Obelisk authors of the future, Richard Thoma and Charles Henri Ford, had pieces accepted for the book. Securing the participation of those further up the literary food chain, however, proved more difficult. William Faulkner and T. S. Eliot were approached: both declined. Laura Riding also declined, but eventually allowed her letter of refusal to be printed in the anthology and to stand as her contribution. Ezra Pound at first declined by insisting on payment, then relented and allowed Neagoe to include the twentieth Canto (although he huffily refused to provide a biographical note, instead referring readers to the

British edition of *Who's Who* 'as his name has been removed from the American one'[15]). But Neagoe's biggest catch was Ernest Hemingway, who after much chasing allowed Neagoe to republish his long short story, *Big Two-Hearted River*. Written in Paris in 1924 and first published in the expanded, second edition of *In Our Time* the following year, *Big Two-Hearted River* tells the story of Nick Adams, now grown up and suffering from shell-shock, returning to an old fishing haunt of his youth in search of the peaceful certainties of the past. Spare, mysteriously evocative and finally shattering, the story is quintessential early Hemingway, and its inclusion in Neagoe's anthology clinched not only literary gravitas for the book, but commercial clout as well.

Americans Abroad was published by the Servire Press in Holland in December 1932. The work of 52 writers is represented in it, representing a broad range of the established and the aspiring, the Modern, the mainstream, and the downright weird. The book provides an insight into the influence of post-war Europe on the American intellect, and gives the lie to the widely held view that the Paris expatriate movement was extinguished by the Wall Street Crash: the Depression ended the party, certainly, but those who had come to Paris to work stayed on. *Americans Abroad*, never reprinted and today a valuable book in its own right, serves as a monument to them all, both as individual writers and as members of a loose-knit but homogeneous movement.

Americans Abroad was favourably reviewed – in many cases, it must be said, by people who had contributed to it – and was widely discussed on both sides of the Atlantic. This, combined with the furore caused by the banning of *Storm* and the public support expressed for its author by a host of famous literary names, meant that by the beginning of 1933 Neagoe's stock in the United States was sky-high, and in May he and his wife returned there after seven years away. The following year the pressure that the American Civil Liberties Union had been applying since the imposition of the *Storm* ban bore fruit: the ban was lifted, and in 1935 Coward McCann published *Winning a Wife* in the United States, a collection of stories featuring all but two of those contained in the Obelisk edition of *Storm*, and eight more besides, with an introduction by Edward O'Brien. (The book's publication was made possible by Kahane acceding to Neagoe's request for a renegotiation of their contract which enabled Neagoe to sign with American and British publishers in return for Kahane receiving a small slice of the profits.)

The early 1930s proved the high point of Neagoe's literary career. Although disappointed by its lack of any content likely to be objectionable to the censors, Kahane exercised his option on Neagoe's next book and published *Easter Sun* in April 1934, one month after the American edition had appeared. (He later declined the third and final book covered by the contract, *There Is My Heart*.[16]) Originally entitled *Ileanna the Possessed* after the novel's central character, *Easter Sun* tells the story of a beautiful Romanian peasant girl suspected of demonic possession by her jealous neighbours. Stronger on local colour than either narrative or characterisation, it's a simple story, simply told. Crucially, it contained nothing censorable, and without the attendant publicity of a *succès de scandale* Neagoe's book was left floundering badly in the market. The reviews were generally good – the *New York Times* went so far as to call the book 'a Rumanian *Good Earth*' (it isn't) – but the word 'primitive', intended as a compliment, turns up in the notices a little too often for comfort. Appearing 'primitive' seems to have been what Neagoe was afraid of, and in an attempt to avoid the charge he employs a kind of faux-literary piss-elegance throughout the book, using 'visage' whenever 'face' would do, 'yet' for 'still', and 'whence' wheresoever he may. The book strains for effect, and the critics, possibly mindful of how lavishly they had praised *Storm* at the time of its censorship troubles, strained to like it. The reading public were unmoved.

Now back in the United States, Neagoe moved away from his usual thematic material and tried to write in the American idiom, with disastrous results. In 1937 Coward McCann released him from his contract and Neagoe, fluent in five languages, spent the war years working for the US Office of War Information. He continued to produce books after the war, including a novel based on the life of his friend and countryman Constantin Brancusi, but never replicated the commercial and critical success his early work enjoyed. He died in New York in 1960.

By the same author

Fiction includes:
Storm (New Review Publications, 1932)
Winning a Wife (Coward McCann, 1935)
There Is My Heart (Coward McCann, 1936)
A Time To Keep (Coward McCann, 1949)

No Time For Tears (Kamin, 1958)
The Saint of Montparnasse (Chilton, 1965)
A Selection of Stories (Syracuse University, 1969)

Non-fiction includes:
What is Surrealism? (New Review Publications, 1932)
As editor:
Americans Abroad (Servire Press, 1932)

Notes

1 *Biographie de M. Peter Neagoe* (unsigned typescript in French, no date), Peter Neagoe archives, Syracuse University).
2 Transcript of speech, *Trends in Modern Literature*, Peter Neagoe archives, Syracuse University.
3 Eugene Jolas, introduction to *Storm* (New Review Publications, 1932), p. 10.
4 Letter from Henry Miller to Peter Neagoe, 21 May 1932, Peter Neagoe archives, Syracuse University.
5 Letter from Henry Miller to Peter Neagoe, 26 July 1932, Peter Neagoe archives, Syracuse University.
6 Ian S. McNiven, ed., *The Durrell–Miller Letters, 1935–80* (Faber and Faber, 1989), p. 13.
7 Letter from Chicago Customs Department to New Review Publications, 20 June 1932, reprinted on a publicity flyer for the Obelisk edition of *Storm* [see bibliography, B–1].
8 Note in Peter Neagoe archives, Syracuse University.
9 Letters from William Bradley to Jack Kahane, 28 and 30 July 1932, William Bradley archives, HRC.
10 Letter from Jack Kahane to William Bradley, August 1932, William Bradley archives, HRC.
11 Letter from Eugene Jolas to Peter Neagoe, 28 November 1932, Peter Neagoe archives, Syracuse University.
12 Stuart Gilbert, *Reflections on James Joyce* (University of Texas, 1993), pp. 54–55.
13 Kahane, *Memoirs*, p. 240.
14 Kahane, *Memoirs*, pp. 242–43.
15 Peter Neagoe, ed., *Americans Abroad* (Servire Press, 1932), p. 315.
16 Letter from Jack Kahane to William Bradley, 20 February 1936, Bradley archives, HRC.

ANAÏS NIN

Anaïs Nin's *The Winter of Artifice* was almost certainly the last Obelisk book to be published in Kahane's lifetime: it appeared nine days before his death, and just a week before the outbreak of World War

II. The book had been completed as early as 1934, but although Kahane accepted it for publication in 1935 it didn't go to print until four years later – and only then after Nancy Durrell had agreed to underwrite the whole Villa Seurat series, under whose banner Nin's book was to appear.[1] According to Maurice Girodias, the Miller camp saw the long delay as further evidence of Kahane's 'phlegmatic indolence',[2] but the decision not to publish made good business sense. Miller's *Tropic of Cancer* had taken a long time to pay off its debts, and *The Winter of Artifice*, more opaque and far less sexually explicit than its predecessor, stood no chance of selling in a Paris which the rapidly deteriorating international situation had rendered devoid of tourists. Even finding a printer was difficult. Kahane had managed to wrest Obelisk away from what he had always seen as the undue influence of his former printer, Marcel Servant, but with businesses closing down all over Paris in anticipation of the war, the search for a new printer took Girodias (who by now was working for his father) as far afield as Belgium and Hungary: 'we had to wait weeks for the delivery to reach us, since [the books] were transported on slow-moving barges along the waterways of Europe.'[3] As far as the prospects for *The Winter of Artifice* were concerned, the effort was scarcely worth it.

Nin was born in France in 1903 to a Cuban mother and a Spanish concert pianist father, whose desertion of the family when Anaïs was ten years old led to her keeping a diary which would eventually run to more than a quarter of a million pages, and which in adult life would become the engine room powering almost everything else she wrote. Her first book, *D. H. Lawrence: An Unprofessional Study*, was published by Edward Titus in 1930, and her first novel, *House of Incest*, followed in 1936.

Winter of Artifice (originally to be called *Chaotica*, and advertised as such in some Obelisk books, but changed at Miller's suggestion) is a condensation of what were originally conceived as three discrete novels, in which Nin anatomises her relationship with Henry Miller and his wife June, her relationship with her absent father, and her reliance on psychoanalysis and the interpretation of dreams to help her to understand her waking self. The first section, 'Djuna' (after Djuna Barnes, whose *Nightwood* heavily influenced the novelette's style), is the story of the Henry–June–Anaïs triangle. It has never been reprinted, the story having been far better told elsewhere, not only by Miller but also by Nin herself, in her novel *House of Incest*, and also in her diary, later published as a book in its own right. The second section, 'Lilith', also mines the diary to dissect Nin's adult response to the father who abandoned her as a child. In the final section, 'The Voice', 'Djuna' surrenders herself to the analyst's couch, only to find the analyst as lost behind his mask as she is behind hers.

Knowing Nin's life and work as well as we do now, *The Winter of Artifice* has some limited retrospective interest, but at the time of its publication Nin was an unknown writer with no readership. On top of that, her subject matter was impenetrably personal, and the book is delivered in a falteringly executed stream-of-consciousness style which, for this reader at least, made the turning of the next page an act of supreme sacrifice. Since Nin at this point was literarily as well as romantically enslaved to Miller, it's impossible to read her early work without wishing you were reading her idol. As Maurice Girodias noted: 'Between her dedication to the genius of a man she admired, and her own need for self-expression as a writer, she was still torn by a conflict for which there seemed to be no solution.' [4]

Girodias was under no illusion about the saleability of *The Winter of Artifice* (which, even before war intervened, had become the final book in the Villa Seurat series, Nancy Durrell's seed money having been exhausted by the first three titles). 'Sending out the review copies of Anaïs Nin's *Winter of Artifice*, after those of *Max and the White Phagocytes* and *The Black Book*, gave me the satisfaction of having accomplished a truly useless labour', he later wrote. 'This mad rush for the publication of a first book [sic] that no one would read appeared more and more like the perfect metaphor for the malefic absurdity of our time.' [5] Nin published her own edition of the book in New York in 1942. To her it must have felt like the first edition: the outbreak of war and the death of Kahane had rendered Obelisk's *The Winter of Artifice* – the last true Obelisk book – still-born.

By the same author

Non-fiction includes:
D. H. Lawrence: An Unprofessional Study (Edward Titus, 1932)
The Diary of Anaïs Nin (Harcourt Brace, 1967–1980)

Fiction includes:
House of Incest (Siana Editions, 1936)
Under a Glass Bell (privately printed, 1944)
Children of the Albatross (Dutton, 1947)
The Four-Chambered Heart (Duell, Sloan and Pearce, 1950)

Notes

1 Jay Martin, *Always Merry and Bright* (Shelden Press, 1979), p. 330. Girodias's version of events is different: '[Lawrence Durrell] had enough money put aside to finance the printing of his own book [*The Black Book*], and he knew that Anaïs herself could do the same for her own; but paying to have your own book published was too much like an admission of defeat, and so Larry, the diplomat, suggested that he pay for Anaïs's book, and she would do the same for his' (Girodias, *Frog Prince*, p. 239).
2 Girodias, *Frog Prince*, p. 231.
3 Girodias, *Frog Prince*, p. 254.
4 Girodias, *Frog Prince*, p. 233.
5 Girodias, *Frog Prince*, p. 296.

MARIKA NORDEN

'I'm born to write. There is no other justification for my life, and nothing but my writing is of real consequence.'[1] Judging from her novel, Marika Norden was born to wealth, privilege, and exalted social status, but she was not born to write, and the quotation, which is taken from Norden's *The Gentle Men* and which manages in just a few words to show both limitless self-regard and non-existent self-knowledge, sets the tone for the whole book. Published by Obelisk in 1935, *The Gentle Men* comprises four letters to four different ex-lovers: a married man in his fifties, better at declaring his commitment than showing it; an ageing aesthete whose head briefly turns towards Norden's self-proclaimed beauty and intensity before turning back once more to books and bachelordom; a bright young thing, much too married, much too young and much too bright to hang around for long; and a married Irishman, a political exile who is briefly mesmerised by Norden's surface, only to flee from the dog beneath the skin. Norden, who is herself married, fires a tirade at each lover in turn, and blames each for her unhappiness. The objective is clearly revenge, but the outcome is self-incrimination: *The Gentle Men* is the story of four very lucky escapes, told by a self-absorbed non-writer.

Norden's real name was Mirjam Vogt. She published a travel book in 1929, in her native Norway and under her real name, and occasional pieces of non-fiction through the 1930s. *The Gentle Men* seems to have been her only work published in English, and nothing bearing either of her names appeared later than 1944.

By the same author (as Marika Norden or Mirjam Vogt)
Mens Sfinxen Våkner (*When the Sphinx Awakes*) (Gyldendal, 1929)
Sjelelegen (Lapidarskrift, 1937)
Verdens Herrer (*The World's Masters*, Norwegian translation of *The Gentle Men*)
    (Lapidarskrift, 1937)
Kjærlighet ånd Kleopatras nål (Lapidarskrift, 1938)
Ibsenkvinnen (Lapidarskrift, 1941)

Notes
1   Marika Norden, *The Gentle Men* (Obelisk Press, 1935), p. 113.

N. REYNOLDS PACKARD

Nathaniel Reynolds Packard, author of *Mad About Women*, was many
things during a long and noisy life. First and foremost he was a newspaperman: 'newspaperman' would have been his preferred description, and to call him a journalist would in any case be stretching
a point. Burly, red-haired, loud-mouthed, and with a byline famous
more for entertainment value than accuracy, Packard lived both his
life and his job as if he'd been created by Ben Hecht. In both his fiction
and his non-fiction (his journalism was mostly the former) Packard
was always the leading man, a sexed-up Hildy Johnson living his own
private version of *The Front Page*: monitoring tickertape, wiring 'exclu-
sives' across the world from his bureau in Buenos Aires or Paris or
Rome, beating deadlines and rivals by seconds. The scoop filed, he'd
unwind in an all-night bar with a drink, a fight, a woman, or a combination of all three. He never went quite so far as to depict himself
chewing on a cheap cigar while wearing a green eyeshade, but this
was only because he chose, in more than one book, to depict himself
chewing on a cheap cigar while wearing a velour hat punctured by
two bullet-holes. His boorish bragging and relentless self-regard
don't take long to prompt speculation in the reader as to just how
tiny his penis was; unfortunately, his complete and unembarrassable
ease in his own skin leads him in his last book, to tell us. Even from
this distance, N. Reynolds Packard is infuriating and ridiculous. Spare
a thought for those who knew him.

    Born in Atlantic City, New Jersey, in 1903, Reynolds Packard
attended Bucknell University for two years. He left in 1924, and after a
short stint as a lifeguard went to Argentina, where he found a job in
Buenos Aires with the United Press news agency. What little money

he made was quickly spent on drink and whores. Later, in his novel *Mad About Women*, a character compares the fleshpots of Buenos Aires and Paris, and finds Paris wanting:

> 'That's what I like about Baires,' commented Rip. 'There's genuine vice here. In Paris, it's artificial, tawdry and theatrical. They exploit a make-believe badness. The so-called underworld of Paris caters to tourists, not to degenerates, not to the real exponents of vice. I like vice. Vice is an art if extended far enough to influence one's conception of life.'[1]

Posted to Bolivia in the late 1920s to cover the industrial unrest that followed the Depression, Packard was fired by the boss he had cuckolded, and made for Paris: 'My only ambition is to become a literary vagabond, with no possessions but a suitcase and typewriter.'[2] He spent his first six months in Paris on the breadline, having failed to find work with the English-language newspapers there. After weeks of fleeing hotels and restaurants with his bills unpaid, Packard moved in to a cheap hotel on the Boulevard St-Michel with his girlfriend, whose income from whoring supported them both, and he began to write.

Packard's years in Paris produced two books, and the material for a third. The first was a volume of verse, *The Serpentining Boardwalk*, seven poems recounting seven adolescent affairs Packard had conducted back in Atlantic City. Combining Packard's twin preoccupations, sex and self-importance, the collection is hilariously inept. It kicks off with 'Noxia, the Nymphomaniac', the tender story of a young man losing his virginity to a woman he has to queue up to screw. Apparently under the impression that poetry is just prose with wider margins, Packard wades in undaunted:

> Walking home
> Along the boardwalk
> I passed a group of friends.
> 'I am a man at last,'
> I told them,
> Explaining
> Why and wherefore.
> 'She was the bastard
> Who gave me
> Gonorrhea,'
> Spoke up one of them.
> 'She was the dirty bitch
> Who contaminated Alexandrius

With syphilis,'
Chimed in another.
'Christ,
What shall I do?'[3]

He has a surprising, not to say alarming, way with simile: 'Her lips, / Like two succulent worms, / Closed on mine'; 'Her stomach / Swelled out before me / With the tautness / Of a dying blowfish'; and my personal favourite: 'A dollar / Was the price / Of Perlinas, the Prostitute, / Whose fat breasts / Protruded / Like two one-eyed tom-cats / From beneath a Spanish shawl.'[4]

The collection comes to a lifeless end in more ways than one with the poem 'Cadavia, the Corpse', during which, while working as an assistant in his uncle's mortuary, our hero buries himself a little too literally in his work.

The Serpentining Boardwalk was published in a limited edition by a vanity publishing house in Paris in 1932. Attempting to play up the book's scandalous subject matter in a bid to boost sales, the publisher's blurb on the dustwrapper spoke truer than it intended when it screamed: 'This book is beyond the bounds of all aesthetic considerations.'

In the summer of 1930, and by now working once more for the United Press, Packard was standing at the bar of the Café Select in Montparnasse when he was introduced to Eleanor Cryan, a recent graduate of the Columbia School of Journalism. UP did not allow women to work in its American offices but their rules were less primitive in Europe, and Eleanor had come to Paris in search of a job. In his memoir *Rome Was My Beat* (1975), Packard is in his customary lyrical form as he recalls the first night he and his future wife spent together:

> We drank more straight cognac and still more as we became more and more friendly.
> When I woke up it was morning. We were both in bed. Naked.
> 'I can't remember whether we screwed or not,' I said, kissing her on the cheek and pulling her towards me. She didn't resist. I kissed her on the mouth and she responded. 'Let's make sure,' I said and pushed myself into her.
> 'Kerhist that was good,' I said.
> She didn't answer but breathed heavily.[5]

Reader, she married him – although the marriage took place purely for practical reasons. Neither Pack (as Packard liked to be known) nor Pibe (Pack's pet-name for Eleanor, Argentine slang for 'kid') believed in marriage as an institution, but travelling around Europe the unmarried couple often had trouble in persuading hotel managements to give them a room together. In order to ease their travelling arrangements the couple were married at the Vienna Rathaus – at the second attempt. According to Packard, the first had to be abandoned when drunken friends, ridiculing the free-lovers' descent into conformity, brought the ceremony to a halt.

Between their meeting and their marriage the couple spent time apart. Eleanor embarked on what was to become a distinguished career in Paris, and Packard gave up his job with United Press and went to Juan-les-Pins 'to write a philosophical novel'.[6] This passing reference, in *Rome Was My Beat*, is as near as Packard ever came to mentioning *Mad About Women* in print; his subsequent books' blurbs, and his obituaries, are silent on the subject. In the light of his later literary career the silence is hardly surprising: his novel *The Kansas City Milkman* (1950) re-uses *Mad About Women*'s plot and characters so blatantly that had his publishers known of the first book's existence they would probably have taken back their advance. *Mad About Women* is the story of a cub reporter, fresh off the boat from New York. Looking for work, women and adventure in Paris, he is introduced to all three when he lands a job with the Amalgamated Press Syndicate and is taken under the wing of a hard-nosed hack. Tediously detailed explanations of the working practices of a news agency are interspersed with fights in restaurants and visits to brothels. When the reporter falls in love with a woman already living with another man he suffers predictable agonies before the three reach an understanding, engendering a lifelong commitment to free love.

This is also the plot of *The Kansas City Milkman*. ('And remember, you are writing so it can be understood by the Kansas City milkman. If the Kansas City milkman can't understand it, the dispatch is badly written'.[7]) This time the story is told not from the point of view of the cub reporter but from that of the hack. The sexual content is diluted, 1930s' France being far more permissive than 1950s' America, but in every other respect *Mad About Women* and *The Kansas City Milkman* are the same book. The cast list is unchanged, the hat with two bulletholes retains centre stage, and Packard doesn't even bother to give the lovers different pet-names: they continue to refer to each other, with appropriate agelessness, as Peter Pan and Wendy.

Mad About Women at least has the advantage of having some sex in it. *The Kansas City Milkman*, published under the constraints of the prudery of 1950s' America, has to resort repeatedly to the literary fadeout, and in trying to keep up the page count Packard inserts so much detail about the way a newsroom operates that at times you could be forgiven for thinking you were reading a manual. This newsman's mania for detail is put to more interesting use in *Mad About Women*: the addresses of brothels are given – the one that existed at 32, Rue Blondel comes in for particular praise – and there is corroboration of an interesting Paris phenomenon which is also described in Cecil Barr's *Lady, Take Heed!*: the housewives' knocking-shop, 'the little-known apartment in the Faubourg Saint-Martin, where psychopathic married women, wearing black masks and no clothes, lay about on sofas in two dimly-lit rooms.'[8] But the lifelessness of both *Mad About Women* and *The Kansas City Milkman* suggests that if Packard had any flair for fiction at all, he saved it for his journalism.

The newly married Packards travelled to Tahiti, writing South Seas features together for the Hearst news agency, and spent a year in China working for the United Press. The posting was cut short when, in a moment of passion, Reynolds bit off the nipple of a Mongolian woman in Peking.[9] Because of the Packards' habit of using the UP wires for private communication while on separate postings, word got out, and Eleanor had to rush to Peking to smooth things over both with the woman's relatives and with United Press, who feared that the incident was about to escalate into a diplomatic catastrophe. Eleanor, emphatically the couple's dominant force, somehow managed to defuse the crisis, and the couple were hastily reassigned to Egypt.

When Ethiopia was invaded by fascist Italy, Packard was posted to Eritrea as the UP correspondent. Eleanor's accreditation took longer to secure, but when it came she took full advantage. Readers were captivated by the idea of a woman in a war zone; her copy was being picked up more often than her husband's, and it was often syndicated worldwide. She was beginning to make a name for herself not just as a journalist but, with Margaret Bourke-White, Josephine Herbst and Martha Gellhorn, as a pioneer of women's rights in journalism, using her talent and her courage to demonstrate that front-line reportage was woman's work too. Her husband was by now having to rein in professional as well as sexual jealousy.

Between 1934 and 1942 the Packards covered Italian affairs almost exclusively. In 1939 Reynolds became the UP bureau chief in Rome: a prestigious job, but deskbound. It was Eleanor who was now leading the gung-ho lifestyle Reynolds boasted of in his books. In 1939 the Packards watched from the press gallery as Italian tanks trundled past a victorious Franco at the Nationalist victory parade in Madrid, and when Italy declared war on the United States and closed down the UP bureau they stayed on in Italy as internees, eventually returning home in the spring of 1942. The following year the couple published *Balcony Empire*, a joint account of their time in Italy. Its measured tone, more broadsheet than tabloid, suggests that Eleanor's was the guiding editorial hand. Reynolds' more idiosyncratic version of events would come later.

With the Rome bureau closed, Packard returned to the frontline lifestyle he preferred. He covered Hitler's invasion of Czechoslovakia, the movements of Allied Forces through North Africa, and the US campaigns in the Mediterranean, making sure that everywhere he went truth was a casualty of war. 'If you've got a good story,' he once said, 'the important thing is to get it out fast. You can worry about details later. And if you have to send a correction that will probably make another good story. What I want to do is to let my readers participate in my experiences in collecting news, whether it's real or phony.'[10] Packard, always the star of his own stories, was not about to yield the spotlight to a puny little thing like World War II, and for the rest of the conflict he filed copy confidently predicting the outcome of battles that were still under way, and sending dramatic stop-press updates when he turned out to be wrong.

In 1946 Packard was sent to China to cover the civil war. He was a risky choice for such a crucial posting, and the risk didn't exactly pay off. UP stood by their man when, a month or so into the job, he exclusively revealed that the Russians had evacuated the entire population of the city of Dairen, more than a million people, even though no such evacuation had taken place. They also stood by him when he filed a story revealing the existence of a Russian atomic bomb factory on Lake Baikal, a story which was true in every particular except the bit about the existence of a Russian atomic bomb factory on Lake Baikal. But when Packard filed a story announcing that he'd discovered a human-headed spider living in the suburbs of Peiping, and his evidence turned out to be flimsy, UP fired him. According to a report in *Time* magazine, a farewell party was quickly arranged by Packard's ecstatic colleagues: 'Their guest of honor had made their lives miserable with his peculiar scoops. The peculiarity of his scoops lay in the fact that so many of them were phony. His imminent departure made him very popular.'[11]

In 1948 Packard became Rome correspondent for the *New York Daily News*, and he and Eleanor made the Italian capital their home for the rest of their lives. Peacetime reporting was less arduous; Packard still filed features and the occasional political story, but he felt the need to diversify. He wrote *The Kansas City Milkman*, he appeared in small roles in Italian films – *È Più Facile che un Cammello* (1950), *Altri Tempi* (1951) – but mostly he and Pibe had sex. Lots of sex, with each other and with anyone else they could recruit. The couple's goldfish-bowl philosophy seemed to provide Packard with both his reason for living and the subject matter for his books, and although Reynolds was the more evangelical of the pair the arrangement seemed to suit Eleanor equally well. Her husband was a pot-bellied loudmouth with a ginger beard; God knows a change of scenery must have been welcome from time to time.

The Packards lived in Rome, as quietly as they knew how, until Eleanor's death in 1972. Three years later Packard published *Rome Was My Beat*. Where *Balcony Empire* is sober and historically responsible, *Rome Was My Beat* is a souped-up, I-was-there take on the Packards' reporting of life in Mussolini's Italy, with regular infusions of improbable and exuberantly described sex to keep up the interest levels. Now that his wife was safely (or, as we are about to see, not so safely) dead, Packard felt able to include a catalogue of the couple's sexual adventures which had punctuated their time in wartime Italy, but which were unlikely to have been acceptable to Chatto and Windus, the publishers of *Balcony Empire*. The result is that *Rome Was My Beat*, with its dedication reading 'To My Wife's Lovers, with appreciation and friendship', is a deeply weird hybrid. Part military history, part *Penthouse*, it's as if some mix-up at the office resulted in a porn star becoming the UP's man in fascist Italy. Whole chunks of *Balcony Empire* are transcribed verbatim into the new book, which Packard then breaks up with anecdotes of varying degrees of credibility. He claims, for example, to have been having dinner in Rome with the fascist convert Ezra Pound when the news broke of the Japanese attack on Pearl Harbor. (He also claims that he and Eleanor had known Pound 'in Paris in the old days of Hemingway, Elliot Paul and Gertrude Stein.'[12] They hadn't: Pound had left Paris years before either of them had arrived.) But most of the tall tales are of sex: covert sex with housekeepers, anal sex with whores, threesome sex with his wife, Randolph Churchill's impotence, gay sex with an ageing queen ... Pathé News was never like this.

The second half of the book covers Packard's post-war life in Rome. Ingrid Bergman and Roberto Rossellini fall in love, and Packard screws a society hostess in front of her guests. A new Italian government is installed, and Packard gets a blow job from an ancient, toothless hooker. The Pope dies and a new one is elected, and Packard has a threesome with an American translator and Brownie, her fox terrier. (Later, the terrier has to be put down when its owner falls for a less adventurous diplomat. 'You must destroy it,' barks the diplomat, 'I won't have a mongrel dog around that nuzzles anuses and testicles.'[13] Which seems fair enough.) Finally, just when it seems impossible for the editor of *Rome Was My Beat* to prove himself any more incompetent, Packard is allowed to describe his wife's decline, and death.

In 1972, after being mugged and badly beaten outside their local bar, Eleanor, now in her sixties, becomes bedridden. Her condition quickly worsens and she's admitted to hospital, but dies shortly after. Packard is taken to the chapel of rest and given a few minutes alone with his wife:

> 'Darling, darling,' I whispered, 'I love you even in death.' ...
> I let my hand slip beneath the shroud and found her breasts. I pulled down the white cloth and kissed one after the other of them, sucking each erect nipple. I opened my fly and began masturbating. My rod stood up as stiff as in rigor mortis. I pulled off the shroud, with my unoccupied hand, letting my incubus mouth meander downwards, licking her navel and muffing the frigid gash like a wound between her legs.
> 'Darling, darling Pibe, you arouse me even in death,' I muttered. 'I'm coming. I'm coming, I tell you. Really coming. It's wonderful jerking off and lapping you at the same time. I'm no necrophile. You are still alive to me. What edible pussy! What hair pie! What a gourmet dish!'[14]

Touching. Illegal, obviously, but touching.

Having exhausted every possible sexual permutation, Packard has no choice but to bring *Rome Was My Beat* to a close. Summing up, he describes the Italian people as 'the most exasperating, elbowing, loudmouthed, ill-mannered, melodramatic, and irresponsible people in the world.'[15] Reynolds Packard lived happily among them, perfectly assimilated, for 35 years. The self-styled 'Marco Polo of sex' died, leaving no next of kin, in 1976.

AUTHOR BIOGRAPHIES

By the same author

Fiction:

The Kansas City Milkman (Dutton, 1950), also published as *Low-Down* (Bantam, 1951), and *Dateline: Paris* (Berkley, 1959)
Word of Fear (Edizioni Nazionali, 1965)

Verse:

The Serpentining Boardwalk (Books From Paris, 1932, published in an edition of 285 copies)
Non-fiction:
Balcony Empire (with Eleanor Packard) (Chatto and Windus, 1943)
Rome Was My Beat (Lyle Stuart, 1975)

Notes

1 N. Reynolds Packard, *Mad About Women* (Obelisk Press, 1933), p. 132.
2 Obituary, *The Washington Post*, 17 October 1976.
3 N. Reynolds Packard, *The Serpentining Boardwalk* (Books From Paris, 1932), pp. 5–6.
4 Packard, *Serpentining Boardwalk*, pp. 15, 20, 22.
5 N. Reynolds Packard, *Rome Was My Beat* (Lyle Stuart, 1975), p. 55.
6 Packard, *Rome Was My Beat*, p. 57.
7 N. Reynolds Packard, *The Kansas City Milkman* (E. P. Dutton, 1950), quotation from the book, printed on the front flap of the dustwrapper.
8 Packard, *Mad About Women*, p. 279.
9 Yes, I thought you'd look this one up, and I only wish there was more detail to give you. The incident is referred to, in a footnote only, in Nancy Caldwell Sorel's *The Women Who Wrote the War* (Arcade, 1999), a book about female war correspondents, Eleanor Packard among them. The incident is recounted by an elderly man who was an associate of Eleanor's during the war, and I can only assume that the interviewer was either the least inquisitive researcher in history, or just too stunned to ask any supplementary questions.
10 Obituary, *Washington Post*.
11 *Time*, 21 April 1947.
12 Packard, *Rome Was My Beat*, p. 67.
13 Packard, *Rome Was My Beat*, p. 328.
14 Packard, *Rome Was My Beat*, p. 337.
15 Packard, *Rome Was My Beat*, p. 299.

HELBA BAKER RUSSELL

Obelisk published Helba Baker Russell's *Sonnets and Other Verse* in 1936. The edition comprised one hundred copies and was almost certainly paid for by its author, who never published another book. Some of the poems in *Sonnets* had first appeared more than fifteen years previously in American light fiction magazines such as *Top Notch*, *Life* and *Ainslee's*, which were published monthly and provided their readers with a regular diet of romantic novelettes and light-hearted cautionary tales. These story magazines, which thrived on both sides of the Atlantic in the first quarter of the twentieth century, gave their contributors a place to learn their trade, to fail in comparative anonymity, and to earn some money. Kahane was a regular contributor to the British-based titles, and in the United States *Ainslee's* boasted of having published the early work of Jack London, Arthur Conan Doyle and Stephen Crane, as well as one of the masters of light short fiction, O. Henry. Very occasionally, one of Helba Baker's poems was used to fill out the bottoms of pages left unused by the end of a story – a fact which had more to do with their size than with their quality. Baker had ten or so poems published in these magazines between 1917 and 1920, in issues in which her fellow contributors included Edna St Vincent Millay (who as well as providing poems also wrote short stories under the pseudonym Nancy Boyd), and Hugh Lofting, creator of Dr Doolittle. New York theatre notes were provided by Dorothy Parker.

As well as Baker, at least two of her fellow contributors crossed the Atlantic to Paris in the ensuing years: William van Wyck, whose *On the Terrasse* was published by Edward Titus in 1930, and the novelist Solita Solano, who for many years was the partner of the *New Yorker's* Paris correspondent, Janet Flanner ('Genet'). But Paris wasn't the making of the now-married Helba Baker Russell. Her clunky sonnets, antiquated remembrances of love lost in a variety of exotic locations, would scarcely pass muster at Hallmark; they were published in Paris, presented to friends, and then, like their author, forgotten.

WALLACE SMITH

Bessie Cotter is the story of a prostitute in Chicago in the early 1900s. The novel was first published by Covici, Friede in the United States in 1934, and then in England by Heinemann in January 1935. For the four months following its publication the English edition sold well and without incident, but in April, by which time six thousand copies had already been sold, the government had one of its regular moral cramps and prosecuted the book for obscenity.[1]

Even by the standards of the day this was surprising. *Bessie Cotter* is hardly literature, but it's competently written, devoid of any lurid detail, and probably only got into trouble because of its uncensorious tone. The central character is in the job by choice, a woman who has decided she would prefer to earn a lot in a bedroom rather than a little in a factory. The book is set almost entirely in a 'parlour house', a type of saloon bar familiar to anyone who's ever seen a Hollywood Western, but with rooms attached. The tone is Western, too: all rye whiskey, petticoats and badly tuned pianos. But the fact that no one is made to suffer for their sins seems to have needled the authorities into taking action against the book. At the trial Heinemann pleaded guilty: they were fined £100, and the edition was withdrawn.

The London trial wasn't the first time Wallace Smith's work had been prosecuted for obscenity. Born in Chicago in 1888, Smith was a talented artist who as a young man led an adventurous outdoor life, riding with Pancho Villa's horsemen during the Mexican Revolution, sometimes as a journalist, but often just for fun. By the early 1920s he was working alongside the writers Ben Hecht and Maxwell Bodenheim at the *Chicago Daily News*, where he was prized not only for his journalism but also for his cartoons and artwork. In 1922 he provided the illustrations for Ben Hecht's decadent novel *Fantazius Mallare*: his macabre and atmospheric drawings owe much to Aubrey Beardsley. (They are also stylistically similar to the work of 'Alastair' (Hans Henning von Voight), whose work featured in many of the books published by Harry Crosby's Black Sun Press in Paris at about the same time.) Smith's artwork complemented Hecht's crazed novel perfectly, but the combination was too much for the US government: both Hecht and Smith were prosecuted for obscenity, found guilty, and fined $1,000 each – costs offset by the book's publisher running off another 2000 copies for under-the-counter sale in the wake of its conviction. (Kahane's business plan for Obelisk was a long way from being the first of its kind.)

Another writer employed at the *Chicago Daily News* during the early 1920s was its literary editor, Harry Hansen, who in his book *Midwest Portraits* devotes a chapter to Smith:

Externally there are half a dozen Wallace Smiths. There is Wallace Smith in khaki, riding over the Mexican foothills, strong, robust, radiating health and energy. There is Wallace Smith of the editorial room, quick, nervous, chafing at confinement within four walls. There is Wallace Smith as you meet him on the Avenue – a jaunty air, a springy step, clear-eyed, well-groomed, a marigold in the buttonhole of a double-breasted serge coat; swinging a cane. And the Wallace Smith of the room in which he works, bending over an improvised desk, drawing with an old pen and a withered ruler, applying himself to the task, hour after hour ...[2]

Hansen's *Midwest Portraits* was published in 1923, at a time when Smith was capitalising on the publicity the *Fantazius* trial had brought him by providing illustrations for a number of books, among them new novels by Bodenheim (*Blackguard*) and Hecht (*The Florentine Dagger*). He was also keen to enjoy literary success in his own right: his first book, *The Little Tigress: Tales Out of the Dusk of Mexico*, appeared in 1923, and *On the Trail in Yellowstone* in 1924, both illustrated by Smith himself. In 1927 he went to Hollywood, where his Latin American experiences got him hired as a consultant on the Douglas Fairbanks vehicle *The Gaucho*. Work as a scriptwriter followed, and in the early 1930s Smith also produced two novels. The first, *The Captain Hates the Sea*, was published in 1933, and filmed by Lewis Milestone the following year: a sort of floating *Grand Hotel*, it starred John Gilbert in his last role. The second novel was *Bessie Cotter*.

After Heinemann's prosecution in Britain it was only a matter of time before *Bessie Cotter* found its way to Paris. In *Memoirs of a Booklegger* Kahane professes himself shocked that Heinemann had risked publishing the book in the first place, but then concedes that the novel is innocuous enough: 'There was no real harm in the book for adults; it was a humorous and sentimental description of one of those houses that are not supposed to exist in England, and in its way and within its limits a little masterpiece.'[3] 'Masterpiece' is pushing it, but it has a keen sense of place, and since the place in question is a brothel it had no trouble finding a readership. With the scandalous story of its British ban acting as a free and self-fuelling publicity machine, *Bessie Cotter* proved one of Obelisk's most enduring and profitable titles, and was still being reprinted by Maurice Girodias as late as the 1950s.

Smith's last novel, *The Happy Alienist*, appeared in 1936, and coincided with its stage incarnation: *May Wine*, adapted from the novel by Smith and Erich von Stroheim, and with music by Sigmund Romberg. The show ran for six months on Broadway at the St James theatre.

Wallace Smith died of a heart attack in Hollywood in 1937, at the age of 48.

By the same author

Fiction:
The Little Tigress (Putnam's, 1923)
Tiger's Mate (Putnam's, 1928)
The Captain Hates the Sea (Covici-McGee, 1933)
The Happy Alienist (Smith and Haas, 1936)

Non-fiction includes:
On the Trail in Yellowstone (Putnam's, 1924)
Oregon Sketches (Putnam's, 1925)
Are You Decent? (Putnam's, 1927)
Work as illustrator includes:
Fantazius Mallare (Covici-McGee, 1922)
The Shining Pyramid (Covici-McGee, 1923)
Blackguard (Covici-McGee, 1923)
The Florentine Dagger (Boni and Liveright, 1923)
Screenwriting credits include:
Two Arabian Knights (dir. Lewis Milestone, 1927)
The Dove (dir. Roland West, 1927)
Bordertown (dir. Archie Mayo, 1935)
The Gay Desperado (dir. Rouben Mamoulian, 1936)
Her Husband Lies (dir. Edward Ludwig, 1937)

Notes
1 Alec Craig, *The Banned Books of England* (George Allen and Unwin, 1962), p. 94.
2. Harry Hansen, *Midwest Portraits* (Harcourt Brace, 1923), p. 290.
3 Kahane, *Memoirs*, pp. 264–65.

RICHARD THOMA

More earnest than able, more literary ideologue than creative artist, Richard Thoma produced a tiny body of work which is today much sought after by collectors, and no one else. An American, born in Lausanne, Switzerland in 1902, his first published work appeared in New York in 1927, when the mildly erotic anthology *Americana Esoterica* included his play *Elagabalus*. (Fellow contributors included Djuna Barnes and Robert McAlmon.) In Paris Thoma put down roots in the gay community: Jean Cocteau was a mentor to him, and through his association with the artist and illustrator Hans Henning von Voight ('Alastair') he came to know Harry and Caresse Crosby at the Black Sun Press. Thoma's relationship with Caresse soured in 1930 when Black Sun published *Forty-Seven Unpublished Letters from Marcel Proust to Walter Berry* without acknowledging Thoma's work on the translation, but by then his devotion to Harry was fixed.

Rich, handsome and glamorous, the Gatsby-like Harry Crosby had died the previous year in a suicide pact with his lover Josephine Bigelow. From their first meeting Thoma had been starstruck, infatuated even, by the wild and charismatic Crosby, whose horrific wartime experiences as an ambulance driver had left him permanently and self-destructively deranged. But Thoma's assessment of Crosby's life and suicide made the mistake, common among literary hero-worshippers, of taking his idol's mental instability to be evidence of tortured artistic genius, a naïve misconception which Thoma made the mistake of committing to print.

By 1930 Thoma was an occasional contributor to the many small literary magazines then springing up on both sides of the Atlantic, and that winter Edward Titus's Paris-based *This Quarter* accepted for its December issue a Thoma short story called 'Death Like Sun', based very obviously on the suicides of Crosby and Bigelow. It's an abject, fawning piece of work, and the simplicity of its style leaves Thoma's lack of imagination, intellect and technical skill all hideously exposed. After the embarrassing publication of 'Death Like Sun', and for the rest of his spasmodic career, Thoma retreated into an impenetrable opacity of style designed more for the protection of the author than the enlightenment of his readers.

Ever since the publication of *Ulysses* in 1922 the competing literary movements of Paris had been trying to decide amongst themselves in which direction Joyce's signpost was pointing. The result was a deluge of unreadable work which proved nothing so much as the fact that Joyce was inimitable. It also produced, around the turn of the decade, a paper storm of mission statements and manifestos. Easier to write than novels, manifestos were wildly popular with the less gifted or less focused *littérateurs* of Montparnasse. Under the editorship of Eugene Jolas (a genuine literary and intellectual heavyweight) *transition* had established itself as the most important literary magazine of its day, the house journal of Modernism with James Joyce as its standard-bearer. In its manifesto *The Revolution of the Word* the editorial board of *transition* had declared itself for the primacy of form over content: 'The writer expresses, he does not communicate. The plain reader be damned.'[1] In an advertising push masquerading as an intellectual counterstrike, Samuel Putnam, erstwhile associate editor of *This Quarter*, publicised the launch of his forthcoming magazine *New Review* with *Direction*, a placard distributed around the cafés of the Latin Quarter in which he denounced the foot-soldiers of Modernism – 'The past decade has been one of pretenders, corpse-raisers, and cheap miracle-men'[2] – and reasserted the importance of established literary values such as narrative and characterisation. The arbitrariness governing people's affiliations at this time was demonstrated by Putnam's co-signatories to *Direction*. One was Harold Salemson, the editor of *Tambour*, who, confusingly, had also signed the *transition* manifesto. The other was Richard Thoma himself. He was a contributor to the June edition of *transition* that year, and just as he was signing a document affirming his belief in the importance of lucidity, he was busy developing a personal style deliberately designed to obfuscate.

The blinkered self-importance of these phoney wars was not lost on the more perceptive commentators of the time. Between 1929 and 1933 an expatriate journalist called Wambly Bald wrote a weekly column on life in Montparnasse for the Paris edition of the *Chicago Tribune*. Every week in *La Vie de Bohème*, Bald provided a wry, occasionally critical but essentially supportive bulletin on the latest Left Bank gossip for his readers, most of whom were denizens of the Montparnasse cafés themselves. His reporting of the *transition/New Review* spat made it clear that he saw the posturing and jockeying for position for what it was:

> Ezra Pound has been engaged as associate editor of *The New Review*, the Montparnasse monthly whose first number will appear on January 1, 1931. Shoulder to shoulder, Samuel Putnam, its editor and publisher, and the Voice from Rapallo, will march toward an 'honesty' in literature... Putnam contends that the so-called moderns are fumblers in the fascinating but obscure and exhausted realm of the subconscious. He will fight for a 'concise and incisive intelligence'. And he got Ezra Pound to help him. This is serious.[3]

But the joke was lost on Thoma, who in the absence of a publishing deal became more literary activist than author. He wrote a gnomic introduction for Solon R. Barber's *Cross-Country* [Servire Press, 1931]; he wrote to the *Tribune* angrily defending the work of his friend Charles Henri

Ford when *The Young and Evil* was poorly reviewed by Waverley Root; he translated much of the work in Putnam's 1931 anthology *The European Caravan*, and worked alongside Samuel Beckett to render into English the copy for *This Quarter's* Surrealist issue. But, occasional magazine articles aside, his own work was ignored by publishers, and surfaced only very occasionally in self-published editions with tiny print runs. They have never been reprinted and are all but unfindable today.

How *Tragedy in Blue* came to be published by Obelisk in 1936 is baffling – as is the silence on the subject of everyone who was there at the time. A wilfully obscure and rarefied account of the post-Joan of Arc life of Gilles de Rais, French soldier, nobleman, serial pederast and child-murderer, *Tragedy in Blue* is almost unreadable, found no readership at the time of its publication, and has never been reprinted. Why Kahane countenanced its inclusion in Miller's Siana series is a mystery (Thoma goes unmentioned in *Memoirs of a Booklegger*), as is Miller's relationship with Thoma. In a letter written in 1979 Miller recalls having known Thoma, but only vaguely. This is odd: not only did Thoma live in Villa Seurat for a while as a very near neighbour of Miller during the early 1930s, but when Miller returned to the United States in the early 1940s he stayed briefly at Thoma's house in Beverly Glen.[4] Furthermore, the two men were regular if infrequent correspondents during the 1950s.[5] By that time Thoma's literary career was over (though he was still writing) and he was working, without satisfaction, as a company accountant. The tenor of Miller's letters to Thoma suggests someone who wishes to be generally supportive but who doesn't want to get involved. Thoma, clearly keen to use his now-famous friend to help revive his own career, sent Miller a copy of *Tragedy in Blue* to remind him of his work. Miller replied with the formulaic enthusiasm he reserved for time-wasters (only writers Miller regarded as talented ever received criticism from him): 'Your book came. I devoured it in one reading – and was literally [sic] knocked out! It's an amazing "performance" you give. I can't get over it.'[6] In 1956 Thoma submitted a manuscript to Maurice Girodias, presumably for publication by Olympia, but Girodias rejected it. Throughout the correspondence Miller says the right things: 'Follow your instincts – your poet's instincts!'; 'Do continue on your own true path – a glorious one. Don't weaken.'[7] Miller's side of the correspondence paints Thoma as a supplicant at the end of his tether, being simultaneously encouraged and rebuffed.

AUTHOR BIOGRAPHIES

When *Americana Esoterica* was published in 1927, the play *Elagabalus* was listed as the work of Louis Richard Thoma; by the time *This Quarter* published 'Death Like Sun' in 1930 he'd slimmed down to Richard Thoma; six years later the title page of *Tragedy in Blue* declared its author to be, simply, Thoma. After that, he disappeared completely. Thoma died, comprehensively unrediscovered, in 1972.

By the same author

Poetry includes:
Green Chaos (Fontenay-aux-Roses, 1931)
The Promised Land (Nine rue Vavin, 1935)

Notes
1 Proclamation printed in *transition*, no. 16–17, pub. Eugene Jolas, June 1929.
2 The writing and distribution of the placard *Direction* is described by Samuel Putnam in his book *Paris Was Our Mistress* (Viking, 1947), pp. 226–29. The quotation is cited in Wambly Bald's newspaper column *La Vie de Bohème*, published in the 4 November 1930 edition of the Paris *Chicago Tribune*. Excitingly – from a collector's point of view – no copy of *Direction* is known to have survived.
3 Wambly Bald, *La Vie de Bohème*, published in the Paris *Chicago Tribune*, 4 November 1930. Bald's entertaining and flavoursome columns are collected in *On the Left Bank 1929–1933*, edited by Benjamin Franklin V. (Ohio University Press, 1987).
4 Jay Martin, *Always Merry and Bright* (Shelden Press, 1979), p. 397.
5 Letters from Henry Miller to Richard Thoma, various dates between 1948 and 1957, kindly shown me by the bookseller Thomas Goldwasser of San Francisco.
6 Letter from Henry Miller to Richard Thoma, 20 December 1950.
7 Letter from Henry Miller to Richard Thoma, 12 March 1951.

PRINCESS PAUL TROUBETZKOY

According to the dustwrapper of her first novel, Princess Paul Troubetzkoy was born in Westmorland, in England's Lake District. By the early 1930s she was best known for the 'rather frivolous, rather sophisticated articles and short stories she writes for the newspapers.'[1] These two facts provide the background for two of her novels. One, *Storm Tarn* (1933), is an ably written but terminally bleak family drama set in the Cumbrian fells – a sort of *Wuthering Heights* but without the laughs; the second, *Half O'Clock in Mayfair*, was published by Obelisk in 1938. Kahane had been introduced to its author in the Castiglione bar. Troubetzkoy's book 'was the record in novel form of a famous scandal, involving a murder or at least some form of homicide or suicide, that had shaken London a year or so before... [It] was quite brilliantly written, and was the first book I published under the new régime'.[2] 'Brilliantly written' is pushing it, but *Half O'Clock in Mayfair* is certainly a highly competent dissection of London's atrophied high society of the late 1930s, ten years on from the zenith of the Bright Young Things. No longer bright or young, yesterday's debutantes rush around London from party to party in an increasingly desperate search for a husband, usually finding nothing but short-lived oblivion in drugs and drink. Troubetzkoy can write, and she understands her characters in all their sad vacuity; Marjorie Firminger's *Jam To-day*, set in the same milieu and published by Kahane in 1931, suffers badly by comparison.

Opinions differ as to who Princess Paul Troubetzkoy was, and how she should be addressed. Armstrong gives her given first name as Marie.[3] The British Library catalogue refers to her as Mariya Trubetskaya, but seems to have confused her with HIH The Grand Duchess Marie Georgievna, author of the children's book *Katoufs* (1925). Armstrong may have repeated this mistake. In *Published in Paris*, Hugh Ford lists the author as Amélie Rives Troubetzkoy,[4] but Amélie Rives Troubetzkoy was a nineteenth-century American poet – who in any case was married to a Prince Troubetzkoy whose first name was Pierre, not Paul. ('Prince' was a Russian honorary title founded by Peter the Great; there have been many Prince Troubetzkoys.) The Copac library catalogue, a database of the holdings of all major university and national libraries in Britain and Ireland, lists Princess Troubetzkoy's Christian name as Maire.[5] The Hulton archive has a photograph of the author taken around 1940 at her home in Park Lane, the caption of which describes her as American:[6] if she was, it was by marriage. A possible candidate for her husband is a sculptor called Prince Paul Troubetzkoy who lived between 1866 and 1938. He would have been much older than his wife, but his American mother would explain the Hulton archive's attribution of American nationality to Maire.

But whoever her husband was, Princess Paul Troubetzkoy herself was almost certainly the one referred to in a death notice placed in the *New York Times* on 4 April 1999: 'SHURTLEFF – Mary (née Princess

Troubetzkoy). On April 3. Panihida, Sunday April 4, Church of the Transfiguration, 35 Sickletown Road, Pearl River, NY at 6PM. Funeral service at same church on Monday 10AM, followed by burial in St. Nicholas Russian Orthodox Cemetery in Norwich, CT.

By the same author

Fiction:
Storm Tarn (Grayson and Grayson, 1933)
Gallows' Seed (Grayson and Grayson, 1934)
Exodus A. D. (Hutchinson, 1934)
Jonlys the Witch (Methuen, 1935)
Spider Spinning (R. Hale and Co., 1936)
Basque Moon (R. Hale and Co., 1937)
The Clock Strikes (Rich and Cowan, 1943)

Notes
1 Dustwrapper notes, *Storm Tarn* (Grayson and Grayson, 1933).
2 Kahane, *Memoirs*, pp. 267–68. The 'new régime' Kahane mentions refers to his recent split from his printer and business partner Marcel Servant, and Obelisk's move to new premises in the Place Vendôme.
3 James Armstrong, 'The Obelisk Press Imprint, 1931–50', item 51, *The Book Collector*, Vol. 51, No. 1, Spring 2002.
4 Hugh Ford, *Published in Paris* (Garnstone Press, 1975), p. 451.
5 www.copac.ac.uk.
6. Pic. ref. 96b12/huch/3721/17.

PARKER TYLER

Parker Tyler was born in New Orleans in 1904, and raised in Chicago. He was briefly an actor in Cleveland before arriving in New York in 1926, where he flitted from one artistic discipline to another with a restlessness characteristic of the autodidact he was. It was Tyler's activity as a poet that led to his introduction to Charles Henri Ford in the late 1920s, via Ford's magazine *Blues*. Their association would be lifelong.

After collaborating with Ford on *The Young and Evil* Tyler's interest turned to cinema, and by the 1940s he had become a film critic. He promoted the burgeoning underground cinema of the time, and in 1946 published *The Hollywood Hallucination*. The book was one of the first to try to apply rigorously intellectual standards of criticism to mainstream Hollywood films, standards previously applied only to 'highbrow' art forms such as art, music, and literature. This would have been fine if Parker Tyler had possessed either rigour or intellect; his lack of either resulted in a body of work which for sheer migraine-inducing unreadability remains impressive even today. His posturing was all too much for Gore Vidal, who would sit down with a volume of Tyler's 'pretentious guff'[1] whenever he needed a laugh. In 1968 Vidal went public with his scorn, mercilessly ridiculing Tyler in *Myra Breckenridge* simply by quoting him verbatim and then having a deranged transsexual agree with him:

> as Parker Tyler puts it with his usual wisdom: 'The [Betty] Hutton comedienne is a persuasive hieroglyph that symbolizes something deeply ingrained in modern morality: the commoner man's subconscious impulse, when a girl evades or refuses a kiss, to knock her out, take it, and have done.'
>   Never was Tyler more on the mark than when he analyzed Hutton's 'epileptico-mimetic pantomime', in which he saw straight through the strenuous clowning to the hard fact that American women are eager for men to rape them and vice versa; and that in every American there is a Boston Strangler longing to break a neck during orgasm. Ours is a violent race.[2]

Myra Breckenridge prompted an appropriately perverse resurgence of interest in Tyler's film criticism, and books of his which had been out of print since their first appearance in the 1940s began to be reissued. (Vidal later told Charles Henri Ford that he had done for Tyler what Edward Albee had done for Virginia Woolf.) In a hilariously inept preface to the first British edition of *Magic and Myth of the Movies*, published in 1971, Tyler tries to dismiss Vidal's characterisation of him as a pseudo-intellectual buffoon, but succeeds only in demonstrating that Vidal had him bang to rights. The charge being undeniable, Tyler chooses instead to defend himself against accusations that haven't been laid, charges which reflect rather well on him, such as 'supersubtlety'. He is especially ridiculous when defending his right to be ambiguous in his writing: Vidal's charge in *Myra Breckenridge* is not that Tyler's writing has two or more meanings, but that it doesn't even have *one*.

(It should be noted that Gore Vidal wasn't overly impressed with the man he called 'Charles Ennui Ford', either, which is unsurprising given that when they first met Ford's opening remark to Vidal was: 'You can't be a good novelist, you have such lovely legs.'[3])

In 1945 Tyler met and fell in love with the experimental filmmaker Charles Boultenhouse. The couple remained leading (or at least noisy and ever-present) figures in New York's avant-garde arts scene for the next 29 years. Tyler never lost his cultural restlessness: as well as continuing to write about both mainstream and underground cinema for a variety of magazines he became a contributing editor to *ArtNews*, and spent nearly ten years researching and writing a biography of Ford's partner, the artist Pavel Tchelitchev.

Parker Tyler died in 1974.

By the same author

Verse includes:
Three Examples of Love Poetry (Parnassus Press, 1936)
The Metaphor in the Jungle (James A. Decker, 1940)
Yesterday's Children (Harper Bros., 1944)
The Granite Butterfly (Bern Porter, 1945)
The Will of Eros (Black Sparrow Press, 1972)

Film writing includes:
The Hollywood Hallucination (Creative Age, 1944)
Magic and Myth of the Movies (Henry Holt, 1947)
A Little Boy Lost: Marcel Proust and Charles Chaplin (Prospero Pamphlets, 1947)
Chaplin: Last of the Clowns (Vanguard Press, 1948)
Classics of the Foreign Film (Citadel Press, 1962)
Underground Film (Grove Press, 1969)
Sex Psyche Etcetera in the Film (Horizon Press, 1969)
Screening the Sexes (Holt, Rinehart and Winston, 1972)
The Shadow of an Airplane Climbs the Empire State Building (Doubleday, 1972)
A Pictorial History of Sex in Films (Citadel Press, 1974)

Writing on art includes:
Marca-Relli (Georges Fall, 1960)
Florine Stettheimer (Farrar, Straus, 1963)
The Divine Comedy of Pavel Tchelitchew (Fleet, 1967)
Renoir (Doubleday, 1968)
Van Gogh (Doubleday, 1968)

Notes
1 Interview with Gore Vidal, conducted by J. A. Lee for *Gay Community News*, April 1992. The portion of the interview from which this quotation is taken did not appear in the published article, but can be read at www.torriblezone.com/gore.html.
2 Gore Vidal, *Myra Breckenridge* (Bantam, 1968), p. 53.
3 Lee, interview with Vidal.

AUTHOR BIOGRAPHIES

MARCEL VALOTAIRE

In 1928 Kahane met a short and dapper man called Henri Babou at a lunch party in Paris. Babou was a French publisher of *éditions de luxe*, and had just launched a series celebrating French book illustrators: the books looked expensive but were cheap to produce, and the series was heavily subscribed. Kahane later noted: 'At that time there was an extraordinary vogue for *éditions de luxe* of all kinds and almost irrespective of quality. One only had to "limit" an edition in order to be able to sell it at many times its value, always supposing it had value, but anyway to sell it.'[1] At the time of his first encounter with Babou, Kahane's career as a novelist was not so much ailing as terminally ill and, desperately short of money, he wasn't blind to the business opportunity presented to him by the meeting. Shortly afterwards the two men met again, this time at Kahane's home, where they discussed the possibility of Babou publishing an edition of *Song of Solomon* with illustrations by Kahane's wife, Marcelle. Although nothing came of the project the meeting wasn't wasted. Kahane saw no reason why the success enjoyed by Babou's *Les Artistes du Livre* series in France couldn't be repeated with English-language versions of the books translated by Kahane and supplied, via Brentano's, to the American market. Babou thought it was a good idea, so did Brentano's, but neither was willing to pay for it, so Kahane 'proposed to Monsieur Babou that I should invest some money in his elegant and prosperous business. He showed a proper reluctance but, to cut a long and painful story moderately short, he conveyed to me in a letter of dazzling eloquence that he would feel flattered to acquire my collaboration, accompanied by the sum of three hundred thousand francs.'[2] The 'collaboration' Kahane acquired proved expensive and short-lived. Babou remained in complete control, and Kahane found himself 'the most somnolent of business partners'.[3] Given no other duties in the business, he began work on the translations.

The French version of the *Artistes du Livre* series eventually ran to 24 volumes, published between 1928 and 1933. The series was edited by Marcel Valotaire, who also wrote four of the books – including two, *Joseph Hémard* and *Laboureur*, which appeared in 1929 and which became numbers one and two (of two) in the projected English-language series translated by Kahane. The translations can do nothing to enliven the lumpen text, knocked out by Valotaire as filler for books whose main attractions were their illustrations and the fact that they would look nice on their purchaser's coffee table. The project was so far from being a labour of love for either Valotaire or Kahane that it's unsurprising they found other things to discuss when the work brought them together.

As the uninspired prose of *Joseph Hémard* and *Laboureur* suggests, Valotaire seems to have had other things on his mind in 1929. One of them was almost certainly an erotic novel called *Nous Deux*, which erotica scholars believe to have been written by Valotaire under the pseudonym 'Nelly et Jean': it was published privately in 1929 with explicit illustrations provided by Jean Dulac. An altogether livelier offering than anything mustered by the *Artistes du Livre* series, *Nous Deux* is epistolary in form – a form much loved by antique pornographers, conferring as it does a sort of pre-packed intimacy on its material. Valotaire's partiality to the genre (and to its titillating possibilities) was not lost on Kahane, who quickly tired of translating biographies of minor French illustrators and came to the conclusion that, like Valotaire, it might profit him to cast his own net a little wider. Although Dulac provided the illustrations for both books, the text and illustrations of *Nous Deux* are much more explicit than anything in Kahane's 1930 production *Cléante and Bélise* [see A–4]. But by toning down both words and pictures, and by retreating into the comparative safety of 'literature', Kahane, with Valotaire's example to encourage him, seems to have set the future course of his business. With *Cléante and Bélise*, Kahane aimed to produce a book whose contents would be sufficiently rarefied to cultivate a reputation for himself as a serious publisher, sufficiently risqué to ensure healthy sales, and yet sufficiently demure to avoid police attention. In this Kahane was 'moderately successful: one of the engravings had a little too much Gallic freedom for English and American custom agents, who could not appreciate the delicious wittiness of it. But we got most of our money back.'[4]

By the same author

Fiction:
?*Nous Deux* (privately published, Paris, 1929)

Non-fiction includes:
Carlègle (Henri Babou, 1928)
Charles Martin (Henri Babou, 1928)
La Typographie (Henri Babou, 1930)
L'Imprimerie et les Métiers Graphiques (Arts et Métiers Graphiques, 1947)

Notes

1 Kahane, *Memoirs*, p. 216.
2 Kahane, *Memoirs*, p. 217.
3 Kahane, *Memoirs*, p. 217.
4 Kahane, *Memoirs*, p. 222.

ROGER VIEILLARD

The *livre d'artiste* is a French art form bringing together an author and an artist as equal collaborators on the creation not just of a book, but of an object which is a work of art in its own right. Production values are high and the book's illustrations are original, their printing usually supervised by the artist himself. The text and its accompanying artwork are usually presented *en feuilles*, unsewn signatures housed in a chemise or an ornate presentation slipcase enabling each component of the book to be separated from the rest. The print run is small and the finished item expensive, both to produce and to buy. The *livre d'artiste* was not the natural territory of the Obelisk Press.

Kahane published *La Fable de Phaëton* in May 1939. Neither *Cléante and Bélise* nor *Pomes Penyeach*, Kahane's only other *éditons de luxe*, had made their publisher any money, and *La Fable de Phaëton*, issued in an edition of just one hundred copies, would be no different. But in 1939, with war looming and Kahane's health deteriorating, the addition of something beautiful to the Obelisk list must have seemed infinitely more important to the publisher than his company's spiralling debts.

Kahane had met Vieillard through Vieillard's wife, Anita de Caro, an American artist who had been commissioned by Kahane to provide artwork for Obelisk (it was never used). Born in Mans in 1907, Vieillard moved with his family to Paris in 1911. He studied political science at university, worked as an economist from 1931 onwards, and as well as having a highly developed artistic life he also found time to play tennis for France. In 1934 he met the British graphic artist S. W. Hayter, who seven years earlier had formed the experimental workshop Atelier 17 in Paris. Hayter encouraged Vieillard's development into one of the pre-eminent engravers of the period, although Vieillard's day job meant that he could only come to the Atelier in the evenings. The idea for *La Fable de Phaëton* was hit on jointly by an artist keen for publicity and a publisher hungry for kudos; the text was a Corneille translation of Ovid, adapted by Vieillard's sister May. The six engravings were made in the winter of 1938–39, and Vieillard supervised every aspect of the book's production. The finished item was exhibited at an Atelier 17 *vernissage* in the rue de Beaune in April 1939, and went on sale the following month.

ERIC WARD

In *Uncharted Seas* a fabulously wealthy woman called Diana is made fleetingly happy and then terminally miserable by her lovers, both male and female. First up is a mannish lesbian in New York: Dexter seduces Diana, and having seduced her loses interest and leaves. When Diana's husband is transferred to Paris the family move with him, enabling Diana to forget all about Dexter by mooching about the Luxembourg Gardens and eventually falling into the arms of Fran. Fran sports a monocle and a cough. She makes Diana happy by taking her to concerts and staring half-smiling into open fires, and then makes her unhappy by dying of diphtheria. Broken by grief, Diana does what we all do in such situations, and embarks on a film career to help her forget. En route to location filming in Egypt she has an affair with the ship's captain, and this time resolves to behave more like a man: she loves him, leaves him... and is still miserable. Back in Paris there is just time for an unsuccessful suicide attempt before the family relocate to New York once more. There Diana falls in love with a woman called Jane, and the couple are deliriously happy until Jane brings their relationship to an abrupt end by marrying a man called Jim. But Diana is unbowed. Her pain has brought her self-knowledge and an inner peace. She looks to the future with a steady gaze and a slightly quivering lower lip.

According to the book's blurb, Eric Ward was a California newspaperman and poet. He certainly wasn't a novelist, and *Uncharted Seas* is interesting only because its treatment of its subject matter is so typical of its time. The open depiction of lesbianism and bisexuality, even in semi-underground literature like that published by the Obelisk Press and its rivals, was so new in the 1930s that authors seem to have been hypnotised by their own daring, with the result that all other aspects of novel-writing – narrative and characterisation, for example – are ignored. In *Uncharted Seas* lesbians is all the characters are, colliding rather than interacting, and lurching from one set-piece to another. Consciously or not, Ward also obeys the two golden rules of the period when writing about 'inverts': they must be unhappy, and they must be rich. The editorial reason for the unhappiness is understandable enough: cautionary tales are easier to defend against charges of salaciousness. But why the wealth? The assumption that homosexuality is decadent, and that decadence is the preserve of the rich, runs through most of the gay literature of the period, and gives rise to the suspicion that most of it was written by sympathetic but uninformed heterosexuals.

Having published *Uncharted Seas* is nothing to boast about, and Kahane doesn't: the novel goes unmentioned in *Memoirs of a Booklegger*, and no details of the circumstances of the book's publication survive. The year 1937 was a terrible one for the Obelisk Press. Kahane must have hoped that *Uncharted Seas'* whiff of sexual corruption would result in healthy sales. Its single printing and its scarcity today suggest otherwise.

ALBERT H. WHITIN

Albert Henry Whitin was born into a family of Massachusetts industrialists. In 1815 a Colonel Paul Whitin had opened the Whitin and Fletchers Cotton Mill, and had stocked it with machinery forged by his own ironworks, the Paul Whitin Manufacturing Company. Eventually the wealth and influence of the family grew so large that the area in which they lived and worked, a suburb of Northbridge, was renamed Whitinsville. Most of Colonel Whitin's sons and grandsons went into the family business as managers, engineers and salesmen; Albert, who never married and was uninterested in commerce, spent most of his life abroad.

The Whitin family was descended from Nathaniel Whiting, a miller from Middlesex, England, who made the voyage to New England in 1638. The bequests Albert Whitin would later make in his will reflect his attachment to his family's European roots, and to his adopted home: legatees include the National Portrait Gallery in London and the Trinity Hospital in Salisbury. He also endowed an Albert H. Whitin Traveling Fellowship at the Museum of Fine Arts in Boston, still bestowed today.

Whitin's only book is *The Queen's Reverie*. Published by Obelisk in December 1932, almost certainly at Whitin's expense, *The Queen's Reverie* is a dismal commemoration – in verse, God help us – of the life and death of Mary, Queen of Scots. When it was published Whitin sent a copy of the book to the Lyon King of Arms, the official responsible for organising state ceremonial in Scotland, who had helped him with his research while the book was being written. The book is now in the collection of the National Library of Scotland. Laid in is the Pooterish thank-you letter Whitin wrote to the official to whom the book was sent, a letter showing he was a far better critic than writer. His book is awful, bless him, and his politely self-effacing remarks about his own work can be taken as gospel:

> My dear Sir,
> In token of appreciation of your gracious and helpful response to my wish for information of the correct design of the crown of Mary Queen of Scots, I venture to ask your kind acceptance of a copy of the book which the crown so fittingly adorns.
> Its contents can hardly be thought <u>verse</u>, but rather a brief rhythmic narration of the Queen's character and her earlier life in France, mostly such a tragic contrast to her long and fateful years in English captivity.
> I regret the inverted wording 'Palace House of Holyrood', a metrical exigency which might in a more ambitious case be called Poetical License.
> I dare say the '<u>Stewart page</u>' may be thought pedantic yet why?? when the 'House of Stewart' was the armorial appellation of that monarchical line – The book has a certain value in the engravings, all but one of which are rare and accurately of the Queen's period – entirely of the XVI century –
> I will not inflict further references to my ephemeral rhymes,
> My thanks for your <u>crowning</u> assistance, I am my dear Sir,
> > Yours very truly,
> > > Albert H. Whitin
> > > to the Lyon King of Arms.[1]

Albert H. Whitin died in the Hotel Continentale in Paris on 6 March 1935.

Notes
1 Letter laid in to Albert H. Whitin, *The Queen's Reverie* (Obelisk Press, 1932), National Library of Scotland.

THEODORE ZAY

Love Counts Ten is the story of Ernest von Sternheim, a beautiful and successful *über*-gigolo catering to the demands of both sexes in the

Weimar Berlin of the 1920s. Having fallen in love, and beginning to feel the pace at the age of 27, he decides to retire, but has to think again when the New York stock market crashes, costing him most of his fortune. When the Swedish krone follows the dollar down the drain he's left penniless. Unable any longer to satisfy his clients, and unable to turn his hand to anything else, Ernest has nowhere to go but down. Consumption takes his sweetheart, a suicide attempt takes his sight, and the reader last sees him, old and broken, selling matches on a street corner in Paris.

The first half of *Love Counts Ten* is briskly efficient pulp, fast-moving and mildly erotic, culminating in a storm at sea so vividly written it deserves to be in a much better book. From there the wheels fall off spectacularly. The plot demands that the heroine leaves the scene for a while, so she's given a convenient bout of tuberculosis and packed off to a clinic in Switzerland. Suicides and near-suicides cut down the supporting cast, and the two leads are eventually married by Ernest's long-lost uncle, who is discovered living in a monastery under the name of Father Hyacinth, which had the unfortunate effect on this reader of evoking a wedding conducted by a smurf. The whole crumbling mess hurtles towards a conclusion like a writer hurtling towards a deadline, and when everyone's dead or as-good-as, it doesn't so much finish as stop.

Whoever wrote *Love Counts Ten* it wasn't, as the book's blurb alleges, a Hungarian nobleman called Theodor Zay. No paper archives bear any trace of him, and the name reduces computer search engines, usually the most loquacious of sources, to a stunned and defeated hush.

(Given both the subject of the novel and the home address of the Obelisk Press the name 'Theo d'Orsay' seemed worth a Google, and it turns out that an artist of that name appeared in a film called *Rural Erections* in 2001. *Rural Erections* is not a documentary about farm buildings, as you might have thought, but a gay pornographic film featuring men having sex in the country. The website priape.com ('Canada's Favourite Gay Store') informed me that *Rural Erections* includes 'Older Men' among its themes, but even so it seems unlikely that Theo d'Orsay is our man: surely not even the more *outré* element of the gay community wants to see a man the wrong side of ninety *in flagrante* with fellow *Rural Erections* cast members Buddy Masturs, Randy Dick and Helden Lednutz. The Theo d'Orsay theory had clearly come to nothing.)

The book's demotic suggests that 'Zay' was American – terms such as 'dough', 'lousy' and 'stow it' appear throughout the book – and the storm scene, convincingly detailed, suggests a nautical background. After that, the trail goes cold. The author wrote no other book under the Zay pseudonym, neither Zay nor *Love Counts Ten* is mentioned in Kahane's memoirs, and the book itself – printed in Belgium and littered with misprints – was never reprinted or republished.

Picture Credits

The publishers are grateful to the following for permission to reproduce copyright material: photograph of Richard Aldington © Yale Collection of American Literature, Beinecke Rare Book and Manuscript Library, Yale University; photographs of Henry Miller and Lawrence Durrell © The Anaïs Nin Trust; photograph of Anaïs Nin © Carl Van Vechten, courtesy of Anaïs Nin Trust; photographs of Radclyffe Hall and Frank Harris © Bettmann/Corbis; photograph of Philippe Hériat © Lipnitzki/Roger Viollet/Getty Images; photograph of Princess Paul Troubetskoy © Hulton Archive/Getty Images. The publishers would be pleased to be informed of any errors or omissions for correction in future editions. Photographs of Obelisk book jackets by Matt Pia.

Works Consulted

Agate, James, *Lines of Communication: Being the Letters of a Temporary Officer in the Army Service Corps* (Constable, 1917)

Aldington, Richard, *Death of a Hero* (Chatto and Windus, 1929)

— *Death of a Hero* (Covici, Friede, 1929)

— *Death of a Hero* (Consul Books, 1965)

Armstrong, James, 'The Obelisk Press Imprint, 1931–1950', *The Book Collector*, Vol. 51, No. 1, Spring 2002

— '"An Account of Literary Indiscretions": Wyndham Lewis and the Publication of Marjorie Firminger's *Jam To-day*', *The Library*, Series VII, Volume I, September 2000

— ' "Banned in America by the U. S. Customs Officials!": The Publication of Peter Neagoe's *Storm* (1932)', *Bibliographical Society of America*, 93/1, 1999

Bair, Deidre, *Anaïs Nin* (Bloomsbury, 1995)

Bald, Wambly, *On the Left Bank 1929–1933* (Ohio University Press, 1987)

Brighouse, Harold, *What I Have Had* (Harrap, 1953)

— *Three Lancashire Plays* (Samuel French, 1920)

Burgess, Anthony, Introduction to *Boy* (Deutsch, 1990)

Brome, Vincent, *Frank Harris* (Thomas Yoseloff, 1960)

Caldwell Sorel, Nancy, *The Women Who Wrote the War* (Arcade Publishing, 1999)

Campbell, Lee G., *A Descriptive Catalogue of the Dr. James F. O'Roark Collection of the Works of Henry Miller* (Joseph the Provider, n. d.)

Chisholm, Anne, *Nancy Cunard* (Sidgwick and Jackson, 1979)

Connolly, Cyril [as Palinarus], *The Unquiet Grave* (Hamish Hamilton, 1945)

Craig, Alec, *The Banned Books of England and Other Countries* (George Allen and Unwin, 1962)

Cumberland, Gerald, *Set Down in Malice* (Grant Richards, 1919)

Cunard, Nancy, *These Were The Hours* (SIU Press, 1969)

Doyle, Charles, *Richard Aldington* (SIU Press, 1989)

Durrell, Lawrence, *The Black Book* (Olympia Press, 1959)

Falls, Cyril, *War Books: A Critical Guide* (Peter Davies, 1930)

Fordham, John, *James Hanley: Modernism and the Working Class* (University of Wales Press, 2002)

Gilbert, Stuart, *Reflections On James Joyce* (University of Texas Press, 1993)

Girodias, Maurice, *The Frog Prince* (Crown, augmented edition, 1980)

Hacker, P. M. S., ed., *Gravure and Grace* (Ashmolean Museum, 1993)

Hanley, James, *Broken Water* (Chatto and Windus, 1937)

— *Don Quixote Drowned* (Macdonald, 1953)

Hansen, Harry, *Midwest Portraits* (Harcourt Brace, 1923)

Houghton, George, *The Adventures of a Gadabout* (Selwyn and Blount, 1936)

James, Norah C., *I Lived in a Democracy* (Longmans, Green and Co., 1939)

Jensen, Katharine A., *Writing Love: Letters, Women, and the Novel in France, 1605–1776* (Southern Illinois University Press, 1995)

Kahane, Jack, *Memoirs of a Booklegger* (Michael Joseph, 1939)

Lawrence, D. H., *Pansies* (privately printed, London, 1929)

Legman, Gershon, *The Horn Book* (Cape, 1970)

— *The Limerick* (Jupiter Books, 1974)

Lewis, Jeremy, *Cyril Connolly: A Life* (Cape, 1997)

Lewis, Wyndham, *Snooty Baronet* (Black Sparrow Press, 1984)

Loeb Schloss, Carol, *Lucia Joyce: To Dance in the Wake* (Bloomsbury, 2004)

MacLaren-Ross, Julian, 'A Visit to the Villa Edouard Sept', *London Magazine*, June 1955

MacNiven, Ian S., ed., *The Durrell–Miller Letters, 1935–80* (Faber, 1989)

Martin, Jay, *Always Merry and Bright* (Sheldon Press, 1979)

Martin, Kingsley, *Editor* (Penguin, 1969)

Matthews, Ronald, *Mon Ami Graham Greene* (Desclee de Brouwer, 1957)

Neagoe, Peter, ed., *Americans Abroad* (Servire Press, 1932)

O'Keeffe, Paul, *Some Sort of Genius: A Life of Wyndham Lewis* (Cape, 2000)

Orwell, Sonia, and Ian Angus, eds., *The Collected Essays, Journalism and Letters of George Orwell* (4 vols., Penguin, 1984)

Packard, N. Reynolds, *Rome Was My Beat* (Lyle Stuart, 1975)

Partridge, Eric, *The First Three Years: An Account and a Bibliography of the Scholartis Press* (Scholartis Press, 1930)

Perlès, Alfred, *My Friend Lawrence Durrell* (Scorpion Press, 1961)

—— *My Friend Henry Miller* (Neville Spearman, 1955)

WORKS CONSULTED

Porter, Peter, ed., *The Reader's Companion to the Twentieth Century Novel* (Fourth Estate, 1994)

Pryce-Jones, David, *Cyril Connolly: Journal and Memoir* (Collins, 1983)

Pullar, Philippa, *Frank Harris* (Penguin, 2001)

Putnam, Samuel, *Paris Was Our Mistress* (Southern Illinois University Press, 1970)

Rhodes, Anthony, *The Poet as Superman* (Weidenfeld and Nicolson, 1959)

Richards, Grant, *Grant Richards Ltd. Archive*, BL, MIC B. 53/ 233-374

Rolph, C. H., *Books in the Dock* (Deutsch, 1969)

— *Kingsley: The Life, Letters and Diaries of Kingsley Martin* (Gollancz, 1973)

Salisbury Local History Group, *Caring: A Short History of Salisbury City Almshouse and Other Charities from 14th to 20th Centuries* (Salisbury, 2000)

Shelden, Michael, *Friends of Promise: Cyril Connolly and the World of Horizon* (Hamish Hamilton, 1989)

— *Graham Greene: The Man Within* (Heinemann, 1994)

Souhami, Diana, *The Trials of Radclyffe Hall* (Virago, 1999)

— *Wild Girls* (Weidenfeld and Nicolson, 2004)

Vicarion, Count Palmiro, *Count Palmiro Vicarion's Book of Limericks* (Olympia, 1962)

Vidal, Gore, *Myra Breckinridge* (Bantam, 1968)

Winslow, Kathryn, *Henry Miller: Full of Life* (Putnam, 1986)

Woolf, Cecil, *A Bibliography of Norman Douglas* (Rupert Hart-Davis, 1954)

Woolf, Geoffrey, *Black Sun* (Random House, 1976)

Wyke, Terry, and Nigel Rudyard, *Manchester Theatres* (Manchester, Bibliography of North West England, 1994)

— *A Biographical Register of Old Mancunians 1888–1951* (H. Rawson & Co., 1965)

WEBSITES

theaerodrome.com [medal citations for Harold Buckley]

jca-online.com   [interview with Charles Henri Ford]

torriblezone.com [interview with Gore Vidal]

jameshanley.mcmail.com [ed. Chris Gostock]

diacritica.com [monograph on Gabriele d'Annunzio]

Index of Obelisk Authors